WHO OWNS
THE CROWN LANDS
OF HAWAI'I?

WHO OWNS
THE CROWN LANDS
OF HAWAI'I?

Jon M. Van Dyke

University of Hawai'i Press   •   Honolulu

13 12 11 10 09 08   6 5 4 3

Library of Congress Cataloging-in-Publication Data

Van Dyke, Jon M.

    Who owns the Crown lands of Hawai'i? / Jon M. Van Dyke.

       p. cm.

    Includes bibliographical references and index.

    ISBN 978-0-8248-3210-0 (hardcover : alk. paper) —
ISBN 978-0-8248-3211-7 (pbk. : alk. paper)

      1. Crown lands—Law and legislation—Hawaii.

2. Land tenure—Law and legislation—Hawaii.

3. Public lands—Hawaii. 4. Hawaiians—Claims.

I. Title.

    KFH451.V36 2008

    346.96904'32—dc22

                         2007031670

Designed by Paul Herr

Printed by The Maple-Vail Book Manufacturing Group

Contents

Contents

Maps follow page 68

Foreword

THIS IMPORTANT BOOK is designed to sort out a complex body of legal history and thereby to give us guidance about how to evaluate and act upon these historical events. It should prove to be a valuable resource for everyone interested in addressing and resolving the claims of the Native Hawaiian People, which continue to haunt and divide our community.

This book was initiated and inspired by Richard Dwayne Nakila Steele (1934–2006), who was a student of Hawaiian history and culture throughout his life. He saw the Crown Lands as the key to the sad history of loss of lands and resources and destruction of culture and historical continuity suffered by Hawai'i's native people. He understood that the Hawaiians did not see their 'Āina as something capable of private ownership, and that it was a living part of their communities that would bring forth food and sustenance if cared for properly (Malama 'Āina). But as Kamehameha III (Kauikeaouli) faced the devastating health problems that brought death and disease to vast numbers of Hawaiians, as he considered the pressures being brought on his isolated islands by the imperialist powers from faraway who were circling the Pacific and claiming islands as their own, and as he observed the tactics of westerners who had come to Hawai'i seeking economic advancement, he decided it was necessary to embark on a Mahele (division) of the lands. His goal in this effort was to protect the lands from being transferred into foreign hands, and he believed that if the lands were in private hands their private ownership would be protected even if a foreign power engaged in a regime change and claimed sovereignty over the islands. He thus distributed the lands to the Ali'i, keeping about one-fourth of the 'Āina—about one million acres—for himself.

The sad irony of this effort was that these lands picked by Kamehameha III for himself, which were among the most special lands in the islands, evolved to be considered as public lands and were merged into the Public Lands Trust after the Kingdom was illegally overthrown in 1893. As Dwayne Steele himself put it in an essay he wrote in 1992: "It is ironic that the thing Kamehameha III feared most, perhaps the single most important reason that the Land Division of 1848 took place when it did, i.e., the possible loss of his personal lands to a foreign government, had come to pass. A foreign country had annexed his kingdom and had confiscated his lands."

Dwayne was moved and troubled by this evolution of the King's Lands, and he wanted to see the preparation of a thorough legal analysis of the developments producing these changes so all could understand the sequence of events and their current legal significance. Through the efforts of Robert Ferrigno and others, Dwayne was connected with Professor Jon Van Dyke, who agreed to undertake this challenging assignment. With the help of funding that Dwayne had provided, Professor Van Dyke chose two of the top law students—Rhoda Kealoha-Spencer and Kapua Sproat—to assist in undertaking some of the original research and writing for this project. A first draft was prepared that addressed the central events and themes. When reviewers examined this effort, they said it was good but that it could be more thorough and suggested additional sources that should be examined. Working with other talented law students, Professor Van Dyke continued to examine additional sources, rewriting the various historical chapters and adding new chapters addressing specific issues and examining recent decisions and statutes. In all, this project has taken more than ten years, but the version that has emerged is detailed and careful in its analysis, and it provides important material for everyone struggling to find an equitable and just solution to these issues.

This book begins with the concepts that Hawaiians used in their communities before contact with westerners and then explains how the collision between Hawaiian and Western values led to disruption and a restructuring of governance and governing law. The book focuses on certain key legal events, such as the decision by the Hawai'i Supreme Court in 1864, the statute passed by the Hawai'i Legislature in 1865, the overthrow and annexation in the 1890s, the effort by Queen Lili'uokalani to reclaim the Crown Lands in the U.S. Claims Court in 1910, the Hawaiian Homes Commission Act, and recent litigation involving land. Certainly the Hawaiians were the losers in this protracted process, and they now inhabit their own islands with almost nothing in the way of land and resources.

But the Hawaiian culture and the links of Hawaiians to their heritage have somehow survived the efforts to suppress them, and we have seen a strong Hawaiian Renaissance during the past thirty-five years. The language is being brought back, the navigational traditions are being relearned and relived, the hula and chants are seen and heard once again, Kaho'olawe has been cleared and is being restored for use by Hawaiian communities, and the momentum to reestablish a Native Hawaiian government now seems irresistible. Once this government is reestablished, negotiations will begin to return lands and resources to Hawai'i's native people in order to compensate them for the takings and subjugation that occurred.

This process will be a difficult one, because it is hard to meld the legal concepts employed by Hawaiian communities before Western contact with the very different Western legal values that were brought to the Islands. During my time as chief justice, the Hawai'i Supreme Court addressed a number of specific issues requiring us to attempt this task, and we issued a number of opinions that offered approaches to address this challenge, including *In re Application of Ashford,* 50 Hawai'i 314, 440 P.2d 76 (1968); *McBryde Sugar Co. v. Robinson,* 54 Hawai'i 174, 504 P.2d 1330 (1973), *affirmed on rehearing,* 55 Hawai'i 260, 517 P.2d 26 (1973); *County of Hawaii v. Sotomura,* 55 Hawai'i 176, 517 P.2d 57 (1973); *State v. Zimring,* 58 Hawai'i 106, 566 P.2d 725 (1977); *Robinson v. Ariyoshi,* 65 Hawai'i 641, 568 P.2d 287 (1982); and *Kalipi v. Hawaiian Trust Co., Ltd.,* 66 Hawai'i, 656 P.2d 745 (1982).

But the challenge of bringing coherence to the law that governs Hawai'i remains unfinished, largely because the claims of the Native Hawaiian People remain unresolved. This book should move this process forward, because it explains with clarity and detail what has happened to the Crown Lands and why the Native Hawaiians still have a strong claim to all of these lands.

William S. Richardson
Chief Justice
Hawai'i Supreme Court
(1966–82)

Acknowledgments

MANY PEOPLE have offered important resources and support during the process of preparing this book, but the primary impetus was provided by Richard Dwayne Nakila Steele (1934–2006), who offered both moral and financial support during the beginning of the project. His vision about the nature of the problem and the importance of trying to unravel this history encouraged the author to continue searching for sources and to try to find the right way to present complicated historical events. Among those who joined Dwayne Steele in providing guidance and support during the early years of this project were Robert Ferrigno, Ron Poepoe, and Oswald Stender.

In the first year of the research and writing for this project, two very talented law students played a central role in the effort to locate and master the documents and data found in this volume, and they also helped enormously in providing perspective on Hawaiian values and on the dynamics of the historical episodes described in this book.

Rhoda A. N. Kealoha-Spencer graduated from the Kamehameha Schools in 1977, earned her B.A. from the University of Redlands in California in 1981, and earned her J.D. from the William S. Richardson School of Law, University of Hawai'i at Mānoa in 1997. After law school, she served as law clerk for various judges in the Criminal Division of the First Circuit Court in Honolulu, and she is presently working as a law clerk for the Domestic Division of the Family Court for the First Judicial Circuit. She has always been interested in Hawaiian culture, history, and practices.

D. Kapua'ala Sproat was born and raised on Kaua'i and is a member of the Akana and Sproat 'Ohana of Kalihiwai Kaua'i and Kohala Hawai'i. Kapua graduated from Kamehameha Schools in 1991, earned her B.A. from Mills College in California, and received her J.D. from the University of Hawai'i's William S. Richardson School of Law in 1998. She has worked at Earthjustice (a public interest environmental law firm) in Honolulu since 1998. Committed to protecting and restoring Hawai'i's natural and cultural resources, Kapua litigates state and federal cases in the area of Native Hawaiian rights and environmental protection. Kapua is now visiting assistant professor at the William S. Richardson School of Law.

In the later stages of this project, a myriad of talented law students helped with sources, research materials, and analysis. Sat Khalsa Freedman, Katie Lambert, and Kanale Sadowski played central roles in tracking down sources and reviewing drafts; Della Au Bellotti, Karl Espaldan, Steven Howard, Justine Hura, Le'a Kanehe, Sechyi Laiu, Anne Lee, Cameron Nekota, Byron Shibata, Heather Stanton, Sarah Sutherland, and Bennett Wisniewski also helped with research on parts of the project. Among the law students who helped me to understand the nature of Hawai'i's history, some even before this book project began, were Keoni Agard, Dale Bennett, Karen Napua Brown, Dayna Dias, Joe Kamelamela, Quentin Kawananakoa, Poka Laenui (Hayden Burgess), Shaunda A. K. Liu, Kaipo Prejean, and Donna Richards. Among the many scholars and colleagues who have provided important insights into the events described in this book are James Anaya, Carlos Andrade, Dan Boylan, Jon J. Chinen, Carl Christensen, Tom Coffman, David Forman, David Getches, Douglas Ing, Mel and Randy Kalahiki, Mahealani Kamaau, Lilikala Kame'eleihiwa, Neil Levy, Melody Kapilialoha MacKenzie, Davianna Pomaika'i McGregor, Alan Murakami, Jonathan Kay Kamakawiwo'ole Osorio, Robert H. Stauffer, and William Tam.

Professor Carlos Andrade of the University of Hawai'i's Center for Hawaiian Studies prepared the maps of the Crown Lands that are used in this book and provided support and encouragement throughout.

Some of the material in chapters 23 and 24 was adapted from pleadings filed in litigation on behalf of the Office of Hawaiian Affairs in documents prepared jointly by Sherry P. Broder, Melody K. MacKenzie, and Jon M. Van Dyke. An earlier version of some of the material in chapter 19 appeared in Jon M. Van Dyke, "Reconciliation between Korea and Japan," 5 *Chinese Journal of International Law*, 215–39 (2006). Much of the material in chapter 15 also appears in Jon M. Van Dyke, "Population, Voting, and Citizenship in the Kingdom of Hawai'i," 28 *University of Hawai'i Law Review* 81–103 (2006).

Support for this research has been provided by the deans at the William S. Richardson School of Law—Dean Emeritus Lawrence Foster, Dean Aviam Soifer, Associate Dean Carol Mon Lee, and Assistant Dean Laurie Tochiki—and by the school's secretarial staff, especially Helen Shikina. Great appreciation goes to Lee S. Motteler, the copy editor for the book, to William H. Hamilton, director of the University of Hawai'i Press, and to Ann M. Ludeman, managing editor of the Press, who provided excellent guidance in bringing this book to press.

I would like to extend my particular gratitude to my wife Sherry P. Broder (an attorney who has been vigorous in fighting for Hawaiian rights and a loving and supportive partner during the long efforts to craft the chapters in this volume), to my wonderful children Jesse, Eric, and Michelle (who have grown up into adults during the years that this book has been researched and written), and to my encouraging and inspiring parents, Stuart and Eleonora Van Dyke.

Jon M. Van Dyke

1

Introduction

The history of Hawai'i is a history of lands moving from the Native Hawaiian People into the hands of others.[1] During the nineteenth century, Hawai'i was transformed from an isolated Polynesian culture into a multiethnic military outpost of the United States. Prior to this time, Native Hawaiians had "lived in a highly organized, self-sufficient, subsistent social system based on communal land tenure with a sophisticated language, culture, and religion."[2] This self-sustaining economy was based on agriculture, fishing, and a rich artistic life in which they created substantial temples, rugged voyaging canoes, carved images, colorful feathered capes, tools for fishing and hunting, surfboards, weapons of war, and moving and joyful dances.[3] The westerners who came to the Islands during the nineteenth century brought their technology, their religions, their ideas about property and government, and their diseases.[4] They imported contract workers from East Asia and elsewhere, many of whom remained to change the Islands' demography

---

1. The term "Native Hawaiian" is used in this book to refer to all persons descended from the Polynesians who lived in the Hawaiian Islands when Captain James Cook arrived in 1778. Native Hawaiians frequently use other terms to refer to themselves, such as "ka po'e Hawai'i," "Kanaka Maoli," "Kanaka," "Hawai'i Maoli," or simply "Hawaiian." The first federal statute establishing a program for Native Hawaiians, the Hawaiian Home Commission Act, 1920, ch. 42, sec. 201(a)(7), 42 Stat. 108 (1921), defines "native Hawaiian" as a person with 50 percent or more Hawaiian blood, but all federal statutes enacted since 1970 define "Native Hawaiian" as a person with any Hawaiian ancestry. *See, e.g.*, Joint Resolution to Acknowledge the 100th Anniversary of the January 17, 1893 Overthrow of the Kingdom of Hawaii, Sec. 2, S.J. Res. 19, 103d Cong., 1st Sess., Pub. L. 103-150, 107 Stat. 1510 (1993), hereafter cited as "Apology Resolution" ("As used in this Joint Resolution, the term 'Native Hawaiian' means any individual who is a descendent of the aboriginal people who, prior to 1778, occupied and exercised sovereignty in the area that now constitutes the State of Hawaii."); Hawaiian Homelands Homeownership Act of 2000, Pub. L. No. 106-568, 114 Stat. 2868 (2000), sec. 801(a). For discussion of the status of Native Hawaiians under U.S. law, *see* Jon M. Van Dyke, "The Political Status of the Native Hawaiian People," 17 *Yale Law & Policy Review* 95 (1998), and *Rice v. Cayetano,* 528 U.S. 495 (2000).

2. "Apology Resolution," *supra* note 1.

3. *See, e.g.,* Joseph Feher, *Hawaii: A Pictorial History,* 36–132 (1969).

4. *See generally* Lilikala Kame'eleihiwa, *Native Land and Foreign Desires: Pehea La E Pono Ai?* 67–93 (1992); David E. Stannard, *Before the Horror,* 50, 55–58, 69–78 (1989), describing the introduction of diseases into Hawai'i; Melody K. MacKenzie, "Historical Background," in *Native Hawaiian Rights Handbook,* 3–6 (Melody K. MacKenzie, ed., 1991), describing the introduction of Western ideas regarding land and government); O. A. Bushnell, *The Gifts of Civilization: Germs and Genocide in Hawai'i* (1993), describing the diseases.

permanently.[5] These changes occurred during a period when cultures were clashing and power was changing throughout the region.

During the nineteenth century, the Western imperialist powers engaged in an "orgy of national enslavement,"[6] seeking territory in the Pacific to add to their empires. The Hawaiian Monarchs tried earnestly—but ultimately unsuccessfully—to protect their people, their culture, and their land in the face of these challenges and changes. In failing to fend off Western domination, the Hawaiian Kingdom was not alone, and every other Pacific Island community also succumbed to foreign rule in one form or another during this period.[7]

In 1840, Great Britain gained control over Aotearoa (New Zealand) through a treaty signed with the Maori chiefs in which the British promised to respect Maori control of their lands and resources.[8] Despite the treaty language, however, the British proceeded systematically during the following decades to loot the lands and resources of the Maori people.[9] In 1874, under pressure from British officials and a threat of invasion by Tonga, the King and chiefs of Fiji transferred sovereignty over most of the current territory of Fiji to Britain's Queen Victoria.[10] Britain established protectorates over Kiribati (Gilbert Islands) and Tuvalu (Ellice Islands) in 1892 and effectively annexed them in 1916 by an Order of the Council.[11] Great Britain declared the southern Solomon Islands as protectorates in 1893, adding adjacent islands between 1898 and 1900 and gaining several northern islands later from Germany in exchange for withdrawing from Western Samoa.[12] Tonga tried to maintain its independence, but in 1900 it also succumbed to becoming a protectorate of Great Britain, "whereby Britain handled foreign affairs and some internal powers, but the Tongan royalty and nobility provided . . . the most centralized government in the region."[13]

In the early 1840s, France and Britain both took an interest in Tahiti and its adjacent islands, "and the two countries almost reached the brink of war" over these

5. *See infra* chapter 15.

6. *Tom Coffman, Nation Within: The Story of America's Annexation of the Nation of Hawai'i*, 63 (1998).

7. *See generally* Ron Crocombe, *The South Pacific,* 412, 415–16 (2001).

8. In the Treaty of Waitangi, signed February 6, 1840, and proclaimed on May 21, 1840, the principal Maori chiefs accepted the formal sovereignty of Queen Victoria but insisted on language that would protect their land and resources. *See New Zealand Encyclopedia,* 640–43 (Lynn Richardson, ed., 5th ed., 2000); *Concise Encyclopedia of Australia and New Zealand,* 1059 (1995).

9. *See generally* Ann Parsonson, "The Fate of Maori Land Rights in Early Colonial New Zealand: The Limits of the Treaty of Waitangi and the Doctrine of Aboriginal Title," in *Law, History, Colonialism: The Reach of Empire,* 173–86 (Diane Kirby and Catherine Coleborne, eds., 2001), explaining that the recognition of aboriginal land rights in the Treaty of Waitangi and common law did not protect Maori property rights after the British assumed sovereignty.

10. Crocombe, *supra* note 7, at 416; D. P. O'Connell, "Mid-Ocean Archipelagos in International Law," *British Yearbook of International Law,* 1, 48 (1971), citing 66 *British and Foreign State Papers* 953.

11. Neil M. Levy, *Micronesia Handbook,* 14 (6th ed., 2003); *Pacific Islands Yearbook,* 360 (Norman Douglas and Ngaire Douglas, eds., 17th ed., 1994). Tabuaeran (Fanning Island) and Teraina (Washington Island) had been acquired by Britain in 1888 and 1889, respectively, and were incorporated into the Gilbert and Ellice Islands Colony. *Pacific Islands Yearbook, id.,* at 360–61.

12. *Pacific Islands Yearbook, supra* note 11, at 605–06.

13. Crocombe, *supra* note 7, at 417.

islands.[14] France gained the upper hand over Britain but then spent three years "to crush the native resistence" of the Tahitians, fighting under Queen Pomare IV,[15] who fought with whatever weapons they had, losing only after "heavy fighting and reinforcement from France."[16] France claimed the Marquesas in 1842 and again faced a local rebellion, emerging victorious only after decades of fighting and disease decimated the native population.[17] France claimed New Caledonia in 1853,[18] and used it as a penal colony for French criminals between 1863 and 1897.[19] In 1886, Britain and France established a Joint Naval Commission to maintain order in Vanuatu (which they called the New Hebrides) and then converted these islands into a formal condominium in 1906 "while German interests were trying to gain a foothold."[20]

Germany was also interested in the economic benefits that might be obtained from a presence in the Pacific. In 1884, Germany annexed part of New Guinea and some of its adjacent islands, and for the next fifteen years these islands were governed by a German trading company.[21] Germany competed with Spain for the Caroline Islands in Micronesia, and finally the Pope mediated their dispute, awarding most of the islands to Spain in 1885 but allowing Germany to retain fishing and trading rights and to annex the Marshall Islands.[22]

The islands of Samoa were sought by Britain, Germany, and the United States. In 1899, Britain agreed to withdraw its interests in return for German concessions in Tonga, the Solomon Islands, and West Africa. Samoa was then divided between Germany, which had an established presence in the islands of Western Samoa (now officially just "Samoa"), and the United States, which acquired the smaller eastern islands and called them American Samoa.[23]

---

14. *Pacific Islands Yearbook, supra* note 11, at 233; Jane Samson, *Imperial Benevolence: Making British Authority in the Pacific Islands,* 45–46 (1998).

15. *Pacific Islands Yearbook, supra* note 11, at 233.

16. Nic MacLellan and Jean Chesneaux, *After Muraroa: France in the South Pacific,* 46 (1998).

17. *Id.* at 46, 54.

18. *Id.* at 46.

19. *Id.* at 44.

20. *Pacific Islands Yearbook, supra* note 11, at 708.

21. *Id.* at 530.

22. Levy, *supra* note 11, at 15; *Pacific Islands Yearbook, supra* note 11, at 149; *Close Up Foundation, Micronesia: A Guide through the Centuries* 26 (2000). In 1899, after their defeat in the Spanish-American War, Spain sold the Caroline Islands and the Mariana Islands (except Guam) to Germany. These islands were later governed by Japan between World War I and II and then by the United States until they became "freely associated states" in the 1970s and 1980s.

23. Convention between the United States of America, Germany, and Great Britain to Adjust Amicably the Question between the Three Governments in Respect to the Samoan Group of Islands, December 2, 1899, 31 Stat. 1878, reprinted in *American Samoa Code Annotated,* sec. 5 (1973). John W. Hart, et al., *History of Samoa,* 87 (1971); Malama Meleisea, *The Making of Modern Samoa,* 41–42 (1987). The Kingdom of Hawai'i for a brief period tried to block European domination of the Pacific Islands by forming a Polynesian League and to this end entered into an agreement in February 1887 with the Samoan king Malietoa to form a political federation between Hawai'i and Samoa. Charles Callan Tansill, *Diplomatic Relations between the United States and Hawaii 1885–1889,* 25–29 (Fordham University Historical Series No. 1, 1940). This agreement was short lived and came to an end after the Bayonet Constitution was imposed upon King Kalākaua in July 1887. *See infra* chapter 14.

The Hawaiian Islands were viewed by many as the real prize in the Pacific and were a focus of attention by the Western powers.[24] In 1794, Captain George Vancouver claimed the Islands for Great Britain.[25] Russia built structures in Honolulu and on Kaua'i in 1815–16 and briefly hoisted its flag over the Islands.[26] In July 1839, the French captain Cyrille Laplace threatened war if Kamehameha III did not relax the laws restricting activities of the French Catholic missionaries.[27] In 1842, after the French took the Marquesas and established a protectorate over Tahiti, "[t]here was considerable discussion of the possibility that France might occupy Hawaii."[28] In February 1843, responding to disputes over property claims made by British residents in the Islands, Lord George Paulet, commander of the British frigate *Carysfort*, issued an ultimatum backed by the warship's guns, which led King Kamehameha III (Kauikeaouli) to cede sovereignty of his Kingdom (under protest) to Great Britain.[29] The Mō'ī (King) was in despair during this episode (he "declared himself a dead man")[30] and considered ceding the Kingdom to France or the United States in order to prevent it from coming under the control of the British.[31] Five months later, British Rear Admiral Richard Thomas arrived from Chile on his frigate *Dublin*, and, based on his understanding of British foreign policy, took down the British flag and restored the sovereignty of the Kingdom of Hawai'i, addressing the property disputes with an agreement that the King was forced to sign.[32] This disturbing episode "bulked large in the collective memory of the people,"[33] and the Mō'ī feared other foreign attempts to take over Hawai'i. He became convinced that he had to take steps to ensure that his people would retain control over their lands even if they were later forced to transfer sovereignty to one of the great powers. These military incursions continued periodically, with boatloads of French sailors under the command of the French naval commander for the Pacific, Rear Admiral Legoarant de Tromelin, landing in Honolulu in August 1849, apparently to retaliate for perceived slights against

---

24. *See generally* Linda S. Parker, *Native American Estate: The Struggle over Indian and Hawaiian Lands,* 87–104 (1989), summarizing the efforts of the Western powers to assert power over the Hawaiian Islands in the first half of the nineteenth century.

25. Lucien Young, *The Boston at Hawaii,* 226 (1898); 1 Ralph S. Kuykendall, *The Hawaiian Kingdom 1778–1854: Foundation and Transformation,* 21 (1938, 7th printing, 1989); Marion Kelly, "Changes in Land Tenure in Hawaii, 1778–1850," 69–70 (Master's Thesis, 1956, University of Hawai'i Library).

26. Young, *supra* note 25, at 226; 1 Kuykendall, *supra* note 25, at 55–60.

27. 1 Kuykendall, *supra* note 25, at 165–66.

28. Kelly, *supra* note 25, at 122.

29. *See infra* chapter 3, text accompanying notes 89–92. This episode is described in 1 Kuykendall, *supra* note 25, at 206–26, and in Walter F. Judd, *Hawaii Joins the World,* 127–51 (1999).

30. 1 Kuykendall, *supra* note 25, at 215, quoting from a letter written by Dr. Gerrit P. Judd to the Commissioners in Europe, February 27, 1843.

31. *Id.* at 215–16.

32. *Id.* at 219–20.

33. *Id.* at 206. *See also id.* at 291, quoting from a letter written by R. L. Wyllie to Dr. Judd on November 19, 1849, explaining that if the Kingdom were overthrown, "it is only private property that is respected, and therefore it would be wise to put every native family throughout the Islands, in possession of a good piece of land, in fee simple, as soon as possible."

Queen Emma

French merchants and Catholic missionaries. They proceeded to occupy the Hono-lulu Fort for five days and largely destroy it, to free prisoners, to seize the royal yacht, to ransack Governor Mataio Kekūanaōʻa's house, and to cause more than $100,000 damage, "or about a year's revenue for the kingdom."[34]

To try to keep the lands in Native Hawaiian hands—and also to respond to Western advisors who argued that a system of private property would promote economic stability and development—the Mōʻī agreed in 1846–48 to supervise the "Mahele" (division), which transformed Hawaiʻi's land system from collective to private ownership, modeled after Western concepts.[35] Although the original goal was to divide the lands into equal shares, with one-third going each to the Mōʻī, the

---

34. Gavan Daws, *Shoal of Time: A History of the Hawaiian Islands*, 133–34 (1968, reprinted 1974); *see also* Sylvester K. Stevens, *American Expansion in Hawaii 1842–1898*, 50 (1945, reissued 1968); W. D. Alexander, *A Brief History of the Hawaiian People*, 268 (1899, reprinted 2001).

35. *See infra* chapter 4.

Waipi'o Valley, sketched by William Ellis, 1824

Ali'i (chiefs), and the maka'āinana (commoners),[36] the latter actually received only a small amount through the Kuleana Act of 1850.[37]

The lands of the Mō'ī were then further divided into two categories: (1) the Government Lands and (2) what we now call the Crown Lands, which were then thought of simply as the King's Lands. The Mō'ī managed these latter lands personally, transferring some, acquiring others, mortgaging some, and raising revenues from them.[38] He also understood his responsibility as the Ali'i Nui to care for the people of the Kingdom, and he recognized the gathering and other traditional rights of the maka'āinana. Because the new Western-based land system was foreign to the Native Hawaiians, it is difficult to apply modern legal concepts to describe how they conceptualized "ownership" during this period. Another reason why modern notions of personal ownership are not easy to apply is that the Mō'ī had no personal or private life. He was Mō'ī—always—and could never escape that role and responsibility.

When Kamehameha III died in 1854, his will left these King's or Crown Lands

36. MacKenzie, *supra* note 4, at 7, explaining the plan developed by Justice William Lee, described in 4 *Privy Council Records,* 296–306 (1847).

37. Act of August 6, 1850 (Kuleana Act of 1850), 2 Revised Laws of Hawaii, 1925, at 2,141–42 (Appendix); MacKenzie, *supra* note 4, at 8, explaining that the maka'āinana received only 28,600 acres, less than 1 percent of the total land; *see generally* Jon J. Chinen, *They Cried for Help* (2002), analyzing the reasons why the maka'āinana received such a small amount of the land. *See infra* chapter 4.

38. *See infra* chapter 4.

Kamehameha III
(Kauikeaouli)

to his hānai (adopted) son and heir Alexander Liholiho, who became Kamehameha IV. Liholiho managed these lands in the same manner as had his predecessor, exercising complete dominion over them.[39] He transferred them at will to others and had his wife Queen Emma waive her "dower" rights when lands were sold. But this Mōʻī did not view these lands as private or personal in the Western sense, because his paramount duty was to care for the people, and the revenues generated by the lands were used for the common good. The role of the Mōʻī was changing rapidly during these years, as was Hawaiian culture and its traditional hierarchical relationships. Western legal concepts were merging with Native Hawaiian customs, creating confusion.

In 1863, at the young age of 29, Alexander Liholiho died unexpectedly of chronic asthma and grief over the recent death of his four-year-old son. The throne went to his older brother Lot Kapuāiwa, who became Kamehameha V. Because Liholiho had not prepared a will, the status of his lands became a major matter of con-

---

39. *See infra* chapter 6.

Alexander Liholiho
(Kamehameha IV)

troversy, and his heirs (his wife, Queen Emma, and his father, Mataio Kekūanaō'a) asserted that they—rather than the new Mō'ī—should inherit the lands.[40]

The Hawai'i Supreme Court ruled in 1864[41] that the lands should go to the new Monarch rather than to the heirs, but the Court also recognized the "dower" right of Queen Emma, a ruling that has seemed legally inconsistent to many. The Legislature then passed a statute in 1865 declaring that the Crown Lands could not be sold or transferred by the Mō'ī,[42] thus making it clear that these lands were no longer the private property of the Monarch in any real sense.[43] During the next three decades, the legal status of these lands remained controversial.

In January 1893, the Kingdom was overthrown by Western businessmen (primarily Americans), with the support of U.S. military forces and the U.S. diplomatic official posted in Honolulu.[44] These westerners and their supporters established a Pro-

---

40. *See infra* chapter 8.

41. *Estate of His Majesty Kamehameha IV*, 2 Hawaii 715 (1864); *see infra* chapter 8.

42. An Act to Relieve the Royal Domain from Encumbrances and to Render the Same Inalienable, 1 Haw. Sess. Laws 69 (1851–70); *see infra* chapter 9.

43. *See infra* chapters 9–13.

44. *See infra* chapter 16.

visional Government in 1893 and later the "Republic of Hawaii," which lasted from 1894 to 1898.[45] The Republic confiscated the Crown Lands, merged them administratively with the Government Lands, and established homestead programs through which some acreage was transferred into private hands.[46] In 1898, when Hawai'i was annexed to the United States, the Republic "ceded" the remaining Crown and Government Lands to the United States, and they became a Public Land Trust managed by the United States but maintained separately from the government's other public lands because they were held in trust for the people of Hawai'i.[47] In 1959, the United States transferred about 1.4 million acres of these lands in trust to the new State of Hawai'i but retained the remaining 373,720 acres.[48]

The fear that drove Kamehameha III to transform the lands in Hawai'i from a collective resource into private property during the Mahele—that is, the fear that the lands would be taken, along with sovereignty, by a foreign power—thus became a reality despite his best efforts to prevent that from occurring. From 1864 to 1893, the Crown Lands supported the Hawaiian Monarchs and enabled them to fulfill their roles as Ali'i Nui to govern the Kingdom and the Native Hawaiian People. But after 1893, the Native Hawaiian People were deprived of their links to these lands and their sovereign independence. Looking back upon these historical episodes, it becomes clear that the Native Hawaiians have been deprived of their lands without compensation or their consent,[49] and that these lands must be returned to them.

Under the Republic of Hawaii and during the territorial and statehood periods, the Kingdom's Government Lands and Crown Lands were joined together and managed simply as the Ceded Lands or the Public Lands Trust. It is necessary, however, to examine the Crown Lands separately and to recognize that they were created for a different purpose than the Government Lands and now have a different status. The Government Lands were designed to be "public lands" in the usual sense of that term, to provide for the general needs of the population. As the demographics of Hawai'i's population have changed and as new governmental structures have emerged, the flexible use of the Government Lands to support the general population has made some logical sense.

But the Crown Lands are different. They were originally part of the personal domain of Kamehameha III and evolved into a resource designed to support the Hawaiian Monarchs, who embodied the Native Hawaiian culture and spirit. The

---

45. *See infra* chapter 17.

46. *See infra* chapter 18.

47. Joint Resolution to Provide for Annexing the Hawaiian Islands to the United States, S.J. Res. 55, 55th Cong., 2nd Sess., ch. 55, 30 Stat. 750 (1898); An Act to Provide a Government for the Territory of Hawaii, ch. 339, sec. 73, 31 Stat. 141 (1900). *See infra* chapter 19.

48. Admission Act of 1959, Pub. L. No. 86-3, 73 Stat. 4 (1959).

49. *See, e.g.,* "Apology Resolution", *supra* note 1, stating in its opening sections that "the Republic of Hawaii also ceded 1,800,000 acres of crown, government and public lands of the Kingdom of Hawaii, *without the consent of or compensation to the Native Hawaiian people* of Hawaii or their sovereign government" (emphasis added).

Monarchs understood that these 'Āina (lands) were a collective resource and should be used to support the common Hawaiians.

These Crown Lands should once again be managed by and for the Native Hawaiian People. The logic of this result comes into clear focus by comparing the Crown Lands to the "Ali'i trusts."[50] The Ali'i trusts, such as the Kamehameha Schools, were created from lands assigned to high-ranking Ali'i at the Mahele, who recognized in their wills their responsibility to all Native Hawaiians by creating the trusts designed to serve them. But the Crown Lands, which were assigned at the Mahele to the Ali'i Nui (the Mō'ī), have been denied their special status as Native Hawaiian lands and have been treated simply as a part of the Public Lands of Hawai'i. The Native Hawaiian People have been denied any role in managing these lands and have received only a modest share of their revenues. The current status of the Crown Lands, as simply part of the Public Land Trust, ignores the significance of these lands to Native Hawaiians and their strong claim to them.

This book describes and analyzes the history and legal status of the Crown Lands in detail. The purpose of reexamining each of the historical events that transformed the Crown Lands is to help the current residents of Hawai'i understand that these lands are unique and should not be carelessly lumped together with other lands. Kauikeaouli (Kamehameha III) selected these 'Āina because they had special cultural and spiritual significance and beauty—and indeed, many exemplify the magic and splendor of Hawai'i.

As the new sovereign Native Hawaiian Nation emerges, the Native Hawaiian People must decide the fate of these lands. The Crown Lands may provide an appropriate core for the land base that the Nation will need. Difficult choices lie ahead, but these choices can best be made with a full understanding of how the Crown Lands passed from Native Hawaiian control despite the best efforts of the Hawaiian Monarchs to fulfill their obligations as Ali'i Nui and to prevent the Lands from passing into foreign hands.

---

50. *See infra* chapters 25–26.

2

Land Tenure on the Eve of Western Contact

Before continuous contact with westerners began in 1778, the dominant system of land tenure was an intricate and interdependent arrangement based on agricultural needs and hierarchical structure.[1] Individuals lived in reciprocity with the ʻĀina (land), which they believed would sustain them if properly respected and cared for. ʻĀina was not a commodity and could not be owned or traded. Instead, it belonged to the Akua (gods and goddesses),[2] and the Aliʻi[3] (the chiefs and chiefesses who were the human embodiment of the Akua) were responsible for assisting ka poʻe Hawaiʻi (the people of Hawaiʻi) in the proper management of the ʻĀina.[4]

This system of joint responsibility and accountability maintained balance through an adherence to traditional principles. Precontact Hawaiians honored the natural life forces, which took many forms.[5] All natural life forces exerted an energy beyond human origin or control.[6] The islands were believed to be the offspring of Papa (the earth mother) and Wākea (the sky father).[7] Some versions of this legend say that the first offspring of Wākea and Hoʻohokukalani, named Hāloa-naka (long

---

1. *See, e.g.,* Davianna Pomaikaʻi McGregor, "An Introduction to the Hoaʻāina and Their Rights," 30 *Hawaiian Journal of History* 1, 3–7 (1996), explaining the five distinct eras of the precontact period; Patrick Kirch, *Feathered Gods and Fishhooks: An Introduction to Hawaiian Archeology and Prehistory,* 216 (1985), explaining that the Hawaiian planter's "system of agriculture—along with an intricate web of social, religious, and political relationships—tied him to the land, to his chiefs, and to his gods."

2. In Mary Kawena Pukui and Samuel H. Elbert, *Hawaiian Dictionary,* 15 (1986), "akua" is defined as "God, goddess, spirit, ghost, devil, image, idol, corpse; divine, supernatural, godly."

3. "Chief, chiefess, officer, ruler, monarch, peer, headman, noble, aristocrat . . .". *Id.* at 20.

4. "It is important to emphasize that the concept of fee-simple ownership of land was unknown to Hawaiians. The high chiefs did not own the land—they merely managed the land and other resources." 1 *Native Hawaiians Study Commission, Report on the Culture, Needs and Concerns of Native Hawaiians,* 253 (Report issued pursuant to Pub. L. 96-565, Title III, 1983).

5. "The Hawaiian people are a part of nature and nature is a part of them." Davianna Pomaikaʻi McGregor, "The Cultural and Political History of Hawaiian Native People," in *Our History, Our Way: An Ethnic Studies Anthology,* 336 (Gregory Yee Mark, Davianna Pomaikaʻi McGregor, and Linda A. Revilla, eds., 1996).

6. *See generally* David Malo, *Hawaiian Antiquities,* 81–87 (National B. Emerson, trans., 1898, republished by Bishop Museum, 1951).

7. *Id.* at 3; King David Kalākaua, *The Legends and Myths of Hawaii,* 38 (1983).

trembling stalk), was born prematurely and died, but a Kalo (taro) plant grew from the spot where he was buried. The second child of this union was named Hāloa (in honor of his older brother) and "is the progenitor of all the peoples of the earth."[8] Thus, it is believed that Kalo is the older brother of all Native Hawaiians and must be cared for (and in turn will reciprocate with similar care).[9]

This moʻolelo (history) illustrates the concept and practice of Malama ʻĀina, or caring for the land, which is the basis of the Hawaiian system of land tenure.[10] Hawaiians nurtured and respected the ʻĀina as an older sibling, which in turn provided protection, sustenance, and security.[11] The ʻĀina was not a commodity to be owned or traded, because such actions would disgrace and debase one's family and oneself. The Hawaiians were said to have had an "organic relationship" with the ʻĀina, and the ʻĀina was part of the ʻohana (extended family) that connected individuals with each other.[12]

At some point, probably after the migrations that occurred around A.D. 1300, a chiefly class of Aliʻi emerged, and these Aliʻi exercised control and guidance over the ʻĀina and the makaʻāinana[13] (the common people, tillers of the soil, or tenant class).[14] But the Aliʻi and even the Aliʻi Nui (or Mōʻī, the great chief),[15] "in old Hawaiian thinking and practice, did not exercise personal dominion, but channeled dominion. In other words, he was a trustee."[16] David Malo, the Native Hawaiian historian who wrote in the mid-nineteenth century, explained that

> The king was appointed (*hoonoho ia mai;* set up would be a more literal translation) that he might help the oppressed who appealed to him, that he might succor those in the right and punish severely those in the wrong. *The king was over all the people; he was the supreme executive, so long, however, as he did right.*[17]

If an Aliʻi did not treat others in a manner that was pono (just, respectful, righteous), the Aliʻi could be "rejected and even killed."[18] Malo described the preparation and training of a young chief destined to become king in the following language:

---

8. Malo, *supra* note 6, at 244; E. S. Craighill Handy and Elizabeth Green Handy, *Native Planters in Old Hawaii,* 80–81 (1972).

9. "Food was a child to be cared for, and it required great care." Malo, *supra* note 6, at 206.

10. Lilikala Kameʻeleihiwa, *Native Land and Foreign Desires: Pehea La E Pono Ai?* 24–25 (1992).

11. *See generally* Kalākaua, *supra* note 7, at 33–55.

12. Handy and Handy, *supra* note 8, at 42–43.

13. "Commoner, populace, people in general; citizen, subject." Pukui and Elbert, *supra* note 2, at 224.

14. McGregor, "Hoaʻāina," *supra* note 1, at 4–5.

15. The term "Mōʻī" comes from "mō," meaning a gourd, and "ī," which means "'to speak,' hence 'a gourd to contain words,' meaning that the important decisions of the government are contained within him." *Kepelino's Traditions of Hawaii,* 142 (Martha W. Beckwith, ed., Bernice P. Bishop Museum Bulletin 95, 1932).

16. Handy and Handy, *supra* note 8, at 63.

17. Malo, *supra* note 6, at 53 (parenthetical translation in 1951 edition; emphasis added).

18. Handy and Handy, *supra* note 8, at 63. *See also* McGregor, "Hoaʻāina," *supra* note 1, at 7 ("Although the chiefs and their *konohiki* had full appropriation rights over the land and the people, in the main this was a system of mutual obligation and benefit between the chiefs and the people"); *Kalipi v. Hawaiian Trust Co., Ltd.,* 66 Hawaii 1, 6-7, 656 P.2d 745, 749 (1982) ("The well-being of ruler and ruled was thus intertwined and thus the use of undeveloped lands by commoners for subsistence and culture was to the benefit of all").

The young man had first to be subject to another chief, that he might be disciplined and have experience of poverty, hunger, want and hardship, and by reflecting on these things learn to care for the people with gentleness and patience, with a feeling of sympathy for the common people, and at the same time to pay due respect to the ceremonies of religion and the worship of the gods, to live temperately, not violating virgins (aole lima koko kohe), conducting the government kindly to all.[19]

The Aliʻi provided guidance over the land through a tiered system of control. Although these configurations changed over time, each separate kingdom in the archipelago was divided into smaller land units. Mokupuni (islands) were typically divided into pie-shaped land areas running along the ridges of the mountains or banks of streams down to the ocean.[20] These larger Moku were subdivided into many different Ahupuaʻa, or land units,[21] and were managed by Konohiki (land agents).[22] Each self-sufficient Ahupuaʻa varied in size and was further subdivided into individual farming parcels cultivated by the makaʻāinana.[23]

The ʻohana of makaʻāinana were generally able to maintain a long-term relationship with a specific parcel of land, even though the governing Aliʻi might change as a result of death or conquest.[24] They were not forever tied to the land if they wanted to leave: "These tenants were not serfs; they had the right to abandon the land and move into the territory of another overlord if they were unfairly treated by their *konohiki* or *aliʻi*." [25]

The essential nature of precontact society was collective and cooperative through the ʻohana structure. At least during certain periods, however, complex cultural and religious beliefs divided communities along class lines, distinguishing the Aliʻi from the makaʻāinana and the kauwā (outcasts).[26] By the late eighteenth cen-

---

19. Malo, *supra* note 6, at 53–54. Of course, not every high chief maintained these high standards. Kamakau wrote that some chiefs were oppressive and tyrannical, although also noting that "[i]t is said that on Oahu and Kauai the chiefs did not oppress the common people." Samuel M. Kamakau, *Ruling Chiefs of Hawaiʻi*, 230 (1961, revised ed. 1992); *see generally id.* at 229–35.

20. John H. Wise, "The History of Land Ownership in Hawaiʻi," in *Ancient Hawaiian Civilization,* 79 (lectures delivered at the Kamehameha Schools in the 1930s, Frank Midkiff, ed., revised ed. 1933).

21. *A Dictionary of Hawaiian Legal Land-Terms,* 4 (Paul F. Nahoa Lucas, ed. 1995).

22. *Id.* at 57.

23. Makaʻāinana cultivated sections of ʻĀina for their own subsistence (referred to as Ili, Lele, and Kuleana), as well as working parcels for the Aliʻi. For further explanation of farming / housing subdivisions, *see id.* at 4, 40, 61, 66; *see also* C. J. Lyons, "Land Matters in Hawaii, Nos. 2-3," *The Islander,* July 9, 1875, at 111, and July 16, 1875, at 118–19.

24. "[T]he tenants who faithfully cultivated the acreage allotted to them were usually secure in their occupancy. It was wholly to the advantage of the *aliʻi* landlord and his *konohiki* (land supervisor) to maintain this permanent bond between planter families and their land." Handy and Handy, *supra* note 8, at 41. "In the old days, though the common people were not land owners, and though they might be dispossessed at any time, as a matter of fact it was not customary to remove the people from their homes and fields when the island was redivided by a new chief." Wise, *supra* note 20, at 82.

25. Handy and Handy, *supra* note 8, at 41.

26. This word is also spelled "kaua" in Pukui and Elbert, *supra* note 2, who define it at 134 as "Outcast,

tury, these distinctions had become sharply defined, and strict kapu (taboos, rules forbidding certain conduct) regulated the amount and type of interactions permitted among the groups.[27] David Malo said that "In my opinion, the establishment of the tabu system is not of very ancient date, but comparatively modern in origin."[28]

The maka'āinana actively practiced Malama 'Āina, nurturing the resource base to produce the physical and spiritual products necessary for survival through fishing, farming, and managing other resources such as forests and wildlife. Maka'āinana did not hold title to the 'Āina they occupied in a fee simple sense but utilized the land in consultation with a Konohiki or some other agent of the Mō'ī.[29] The maka'āinana owed certain obligations to the Ali'i, but most of the crops they produced could be kept and consumed by the local 'ohana. Samuel M. Kamakau, the prolific Native Hawaiian historian of the mid-nineteenth century, explained this complex relationship as follows:

> True the Chiefs had the right to the fruits of the land and the property of the people. . . . But it was they [the Chiefs] who were the wanderers; the people born of the soil remained according to the old saying, "It is the top stone that rolls down; the stone at the bottom stays where it is" *(O ko luna pohaku no ke ka'a ilalo, 'a'ole i hiki i ko lalo pohaku ke ka'a).* Some chiefs laid claim to certain land sections in old days, but it is not clear that the residents born on the land held no rights therein. At any rate there are families who have lived on the same land from very ancient times. *In that way the land belonged to the common people.*[30]

For these reasons, the relationship between the Ali'i and maka'āinana was one of interdependence and cooperation.[31] Just as the maka'āinana depended on the Ali'i

---

pariah, slave, untouchable, menial, a caste which lived apart and was drawn on for human sacrifices." Marion Kelly has explained this category of people as follows:

> The persons referred to as *kauwā* comprised a relatively small group of social outcasts. In some areas *kauwā* were segregated in localities beyond the boundaries of which they were forbidden to pass. In other areas they were tattooed and allowed to roam the countryside at will. Nothing is known of their social life other than that *kauwā* were at times marked by the *kahuna* for human sacrifice by hanging a gourd around their necks, especially when law breakers or prisoners were not available for the purpose. . . . These people did not function within the society as slaves, *i.e.,* owned by other human beings, but rather were social outcasts whose descendants continued to live within a limited area of Hawaiian society. They were in no manner employed as slave labor by other Hawaiians.

Marion Kelly, "Changes in Land Tenure in Hawaii, 1778–1850," 48–49 (1956) (Master's Thesis, 1956, University of Hawai'i Library). *See also* Malo, *supra* note 6, at 68–72; Kalākaua, *supra* note 7, at 52; *Kepelino's Traditions of Hawaii, supra* note 15, at 142–47.

27. *See generally* Malo, *supra* note 6, at 55–58.

28. *Id.* at 56.

29. See Kamakau, *supra* note 19, at 229.

30. *Id.* at 376 (emphasis added). Malo gave a rather grim description of the life of the maka'āinana, stating that their condition "was that of subjection to the chiefs, compelled to do their heavy tasks, burdened and oppressed, some even to death." Malo, *supra* note 6, at 60. "It was the *ma-ka-aina-na* also who did all the work on the land; yet all they produced from the soil belonged to the chiefs; and the power to expel a man from the land and rob him of his possessions lay with the chief." *Id.* at 61.

31. Malo, *supra* note 6, at 60–62.

for permission to occupy and cultivate land, the Aliʻi relied upon the skill and labor of the makaʻāinana for sustenance, because they provided for the basic needs of the Aliʻi, including food, housing, clothing, and other items.[32] One writer, describing the important cooperative behavior that characterized the use of water, which was essential for taro production, said that a "spirit of mutual dependence and helpfulness prevailed, alike among the high and the low, with respect to the use of the water."[33] David Malo's conclusion was that "[t]he best course for the king would have been to submit to the will of the people."[34]

The Aliʻi were obliged to manage the Hawaiian social hierarchy in accordance with the wishes of the Akua (gods). Under the careful guidance of spiritual and political advisors, the Aliʻi directed the rituals and the flow of mana (spiritual power) to maintain a system that was pono (proper and just). Because the Akua were sacred, the makaʻāinana were not permitted to interact with the Aliʻi on the same basis as they interacted with each other.[35] Strict kapu separated the high-ranking Aliʻi from the makaʻāinana,[36] and most communication between the classes took place through the lower-ranking Aliʻi (Kaukau Aliʻi[37] or Konohiki).[38]

These lower-ranking Aliʻi took care of the day-to-day management of the ʻĀina, relaying the concerns of the makaʻāinana and bringing hoʻokupu (gifts) in the form of products to the Aliʻi Nui and Mōʻī. The higher ranking Aliʻi were responsible in turn for caring for the Akua and maintaining a state of pono. A portion of the hoʻokupu given to these Aliʻi was used to maintain favor with the Akua in religious ceremonies. If a disaster occurred, such an event was blamed on the Aliʻi, who were seen as unsuccessful in their duties to maintain favor with the Akua, and the Aliʻi then faced the possibility of replacement or abandonment.[39]

Because the Hawaiian population was large and widely distributed among the various islands, and because each person could claim a link to Papa and Wākea, genealogy became a distinguishing factor. Exactly how one traced lineage to the parents of the Hawaiian Islands became paramount. A complex process for evaluating rank evolved, and within the Aliʻi, class distinctions were drawn depending on the rank of an individual's parents and their relationship to each other.[40]

The most desirable mating was the Piʻo pairing between siblings, and an off-

32. *Id.* at 61.
33. Antonio Perry, "Hawaiian Water Rights," in *Hawaiian Almanac and Annual,* 90 (Thomas G. Thrum, compiler and publisher, 1912).
34. Malo, *supra* note 6, at 62.
35. Kameʻeleihiwa, *supra* note 10, at 26.
36. The kapu of the Aliʻi differed by rank. The kapu observed for the child of a Nīʻaupiʻo union (between a half brother and half sister or uncle and niece), which required inferior chiefs and others to sit in their presence, was different from that of a Piʻo mating (between siblings), which required all others "to fall to the ground in an attitude of worship." Malo, *supra* note 6, at 54–55.
37. "If the father was a high chief, and the mother of low rank, but a chiefess, the child would be called a kau-kau aliʻi." *Id.* at 55.
38. Kameʻeleihiwa, *supra* note 10, at 37.
39. *Id.* at 26.
40. Malo, *supra* note 6, at 52–56.

Kamehameha I, sketched by
Louis Choris, published in 1822

spring produced by such a union was viewed as a divine Akua.[41] Also of very high rank were Nī'aupi'o—the offspring of half-siblings or matings between an uncle and a niece.[42]

Merely having one parent of Ali'i descent did not automatically confer chiefly status upon a child, because only certain offspring were recognized (and those who were the products of secret affairs tended not to be treated as Ali'i).[43]

The right to rule, although established at birth, could be enhanced or degraded by an Ali'i's behavior.[44] Ali'i were respected only as long as they were able to maintain favor with the Akua. If an Ali'i appeared to be losing favor, either the maka'āinana would rise up or another Ali'i would challenge the current leader in war.[45] Ali'i were not automatically assured a position as a matter of birthright. Although high rank provided the opportunity to rule, Ali'i had to establish their ability to do so and attain approval from the Akua, maka'āinana, and other Ali'i in order to remain in power.[46]

Many different ways of establishing one's rule emerged in the separate king-

41. *Id.* at 54; Kalākaua, *supra* note 7, at 53.
42. Malo, *supra* note 6, at 54-55.
43. *Id.* at 56.
44. Kame'eleihiwa, *supra* note 10, at 26, 31.
45. *Id.* at 38–39; Malo, *supra* note 6, at 190; *see generally* Kamakau, *supra* note 19, at 13–14, 35.
46. Kame'eleihiwa, *supra* note 10, at 46–48.

doms that evolved in each of the islands. But relatively common—at least during the eighteenth century—was the right of Kālaiʻāina, or redistribution of the ʻĀina by each new Mōʻī, a practice that was central to the hierarchical structure and had profound social and political significance.

When a Mōʻī was instated, either through inheritance or victory in war, all land would revert to the new leader, who would consummate his rule through his Kālaiʻāina, whereby he would name loyal Aliʻi to manage each Mokupuni, Moku, and Ahupuaʻa within the kingdom. The Kālaiʻāina was the first political action taken by the new Mōʻī, and it determined who would have control of the ʻĀina, which was the "essence of sovereignty."[47] Usually a Mōʻī would appoint allies as managers in the Kālaiʻāina, thereby rewarding them for their support and ensuring that control of the land was in the hands of individuals who could be trusted.[48]

Even when the Islands were unified into a single Kingdom by Kamehameha I, the traditional practice of Kālaiʻāina persisted, with some modification.[49] Although Kamehameha awarded some lands to his supporters after each Mokupuni was conquered, when all of the islands were under his control, he initiated a final Kālaiʻāina. In this division, Kamehameha awarded Keʻeaumoku, Kamanawa, Kameʻeiamoku, and Keaweaheulu significant holdings on each of the islands.[50] These four Aliʻi Nui from Kona were indispensable organizers of Kamehameha's war effort, and, in the tradition of Kālaiʻāina, they were duly rewarded.

Kamehameha made two significant exceptions from the usual practice in making these grants. Usually, "[t]he largest districts were not generally assigned to the highest chiefs, lest they might thus be enabled to rebel against the government,"[51] but Kamehameha's substantial grants to his four Kona "uncles" departed from that practice. Second, Kamehameha included in those awards the right of hereditary succession, thus allowing his four favored Aliʻi Nui the ability to maintain control of their ʻĀina in perpetuity and pass it on to their heirs.[52]

Some scholars attribute these diversions from tradition to the cultural politics that Kamehameha was faced with. In light of the vast expanse of his Kingdom and the subsequent challenge of overseeing all of the islands, Kamehameha may have made

---

47. *Id.* at 56.

48. Before ʻUmialiloa, a great Aliʻi of Hawaiʻi Island, died, for instance, he instructed that his kingdom should be divided between his two sons, Keliʻiokaloaaʻumi and Keawenuiaʻumi. Keliʻiokaloaaʻumi was thus given the kingdom of Kona, while his brother became the ruler of the Hilo District. After a period of years, Keawenuiaʻumi became renowned for his generosity and skill as a leader. Unlike his brother, Keliʻiokaloaaʻumi did not observe the advice of his father and began to oppress his makaʻāinana by seizing their belongings and requesting that they perform tedious tasks. Finally, some of the Aliʻi and makaʻāinana appealed to Keawenuiaʻumi and his Aliʻi and offered them the kingdom of Kona. Upon defeating Keliʻiokaloaaʻumi's armies in battle, Keawenuiaʻumi rightfully claimed his brother's domain and distributed the ʻĀina amongst his children and grandchildren while denying the heirs of Keliʻiokaloaaʻumi a right to the Kona kingdom. *See* Kamakau, *Ruling Chiefs, supra* note 19, at 34–36.

49. Kameʻeleihiwa, *supra* note 10, at 51–52.

50. *Id.* at 52.

51. Malo, *supra* note 6, at 194.

52. Kameʻeleihiwa, *supra* note 10, at 52, 58.

Sketch of Kaua'i by John Webber, 1784

considerable grants to the four Ali'i Nui as a means of securing loyalty and perhaps to thwart the demands for land by foreigners.[53]

Kamehameha's example also presents a helpful approach on how to view the Hawaiian system of land tenure. Although some of the same principles were observed within the different kingdoms, Mō'ī were progressive in the sense that they crafted solutions to problems based on their own political, religious, and life experiences. Despite any variations that occurred, Ali'i throughout Hawai'i, in the time of Kamehameha and before, respected the 'Āina and acknowledged their Kuleana (rights and responsibilities), as Ali'i, in caring for it. The 'Āina could not be owned, or even really possessed, in the way westerners view private property. Instead, the Ali'i and maka'āinana cultivated a relationship with the 'Āina based on different values. Control of the 'Āina was vital for political and social success, but this power was secured through care and attention as opposed to mere seizure. Although Ali'i could gain territory by capturing it, they would not be able to retain control unless they succeeded in fulfilling their responsibilities to the 'Āina and maka'āinana. Although individual leaders rose and fell from power, the respect for and careful management of the 'Āina sustained the traditional system of land tenure.

53. *Id.* at 60, 62.

3

Before the Mahele

The foreigners who came to Hawai'i brought with them a host of bacteria, viruses, and diseases. The isolation of the Islands and the limited contact between the natives and pathogens common elsewhere drastically increased the impact of foreign illnesses on the Native Hawaiians and ravaged the population, culture, and society of ka po'e Hawai'i. The communal lifestyle and cultural practices of the Hawaiians, as well as their inexperience with infectious diseases, compounded the spread and effect of sickness, and the scarcity of doctors and medicine aggravated the rate of death.[1]

Chronic, insidious diseases swept through the Native Hawaiian population from their first contact with Western visitors, and epidemics overwhelmed them throughout the 1800s in unrelenting waves.[2] The early visits by European ships to the Islands introduced a host of venereal diseases to Hawai'i, including gonorrhea and syphilis, and also brought sicknesses such as tuberculosis, leprosy, and scabies that thoroughly devastated the islanders.[3] The venereal diseases (sometimes referred to as the "Curse of Cook")[4] and other foreign viral maladies served to weaken the already susceptible native immune system and may have been a significant factor in the declining birthrate among Native Hawaiians during this period.[5]

The first major epidemic in Hawai'i was "the severe pestilence of 1804 when so many chiefs and commoners perished."[6] The Hawaiians called the disease ma'i 'ōku'u, or "the squatting sickness," suggesting that the epidemic may have been typhoid fever, some kind of dysentery, or Asiatic cholera.[7] It was so virulent that

---

1. William Fremont Blackman, *The Making of Hawaii: A Study in Social Evolution*, 220–21 (1906, reprinted 1977). *See also* "Introduction," *Must We Wait in Despair: The 1867 Report of the 'Ahahui La'au Lapa'au of Wailuku, Maui on Native Hawaiian Health*, iii (Malcom Naea Chun, trans./ed., First Peoples' Productions, 1994).

2. O. A. Bushnell, *The Gifts of Civilization: Germs and Genocide in Hawai'i*, 276–77 (1993).

3. *Id.* at 230–34, 277.

4. *Id.* at 230.

5. *Id.* at 190, 293–95; Samuel M. Kamakau, *Ruling Chiefs of Hawaii*, 237 (1961, revised ed. 1992), noting "a large mortality among children and a decline in the birthrate."

6. Kamakau, *supra* note 5, at 236–37.

7. Bushnell, *supra* note 2, at 281–82; *see also* Sally Engle Merry, *Colonizing Hawaii: The Cultural Power of Law*, 44 (2000), characterizing this disease as cholera.

"[o]ne might go for food and water and die so suddenly that those at home did not know what had happened." [8] This "pestilence" raged "from Hawaii to Kauai" and a "vast number of people died." [9] Some commentators have estimated that as many as 150,000, or "half the population," may have died. [10] Other instances of mass gastro-intestinal infection also occurred, apparently caused by the excrement of foreigners, infected with harmful microbes, which inevitably polluted water sources and caused "epidemic and almost unending" bouts of diarrhea, hepatitis, dysentery, and enteric fevers. [11]

Hawaiians lacked the immunities of their Western visitors and succumbed even to the common cold and flu; 1826 saw an epidemic of "coughs, congested lungs, and sore throat," [12] "coughs and bronchitis," [13] and an influenza epidemic. [14] "From 1818 to 1825, Marin [a Spaniard who served as a doctor to the royal family] made numerous notations in his diary of the epidemics of colds and flu among Hawaiians," and reported that "many people had died." [15] There was "a severe epidemic of colds, dull headache, sore throat, and dizziness" in 1844. [16] In 1845, "a foreign-introduced influenza epidemic raged throughout Hawai'i wiping out Hawaiians like the flames of candles in a wind." [17] And in 1857, "many died" of "an epidemic of colds, dull headache, sore throat, and deafness." [18] Diseases usually considered childhood rites of passage also decimated the population. A breakout of measles in 1848 "spread and carried away about a third of the population." [19] Between 1838 and 1839, mumps afflicted the islanders. [20]

As trade and visits by whalers increased, more serious diseases started arriving from Europe and Asia. [21] Despite efforts by some captains to avoid coming into port if a crewmember or passenger had smallpox, in March or April of 1853, a ship with

---

8. Kamakau, *supra* note 5, at 189.

9. David Malo, *Hawaiian Antiquities,* 246 (National T. B. Emerson, trans., 1898, republished by Bishop Museum, 1951).

10. *See, e.g.,* W. D. Alexander, *A Brief History of the Hawaiian People,* 153 (1899, reprinted 2001): "After Kamehameha had made vast preparations for the invasion of Kauai, and had collected an overwhelming force, a pestilence broke out among his troops, which spread through the island and carried off half the population." It is difficult to evaluate such statements today, because scholars disagree on the population of the Islands when Captain Cook arrived in 1778. *See infra* note 28.

11. Bushnell, *supra* note 2, at 191.

12. Kamakau, *supra* note 5, at 236.

13. *Id.* at 274.

14. Walter F. Judd, *Hawaii Joins the World,* 66 (1999).

15. Marion Kelly, "Changes in Land Tenure in Hawaii, 1778–1850," 96 (Master's Thesis, 1956, University of Hawai'i Library), citing extracts from the *Journal of Don Francisco de Paula Marin* (Robert C. Wyllie trans., Captain Cook Collection, Archives of Hawaii).

16. Kamakau, *supra* note 5, at 236–37.

17. Davianna McGregor-Alegado, "Voices of Today Echo Voices of the Past," in *Malama: Hawaiian Land and Water,* special issue of 29 *Bamboo Ridge: The Hawaiian Writers Quarterly,* 44, 47 (Dana Naone Hall, ed., 1985).

18. Kamakau, *supra* note 5, at 236–37.

19. *Id.*

20. *Id.* at 345.

21. Bushnell, *supra* note 2, at 210.

an infected sailor landed in Honolulu, and an epidemic began in May causing wide-spread sickness and sadness.[22] When "small pox came, . . . dead bodies lay stacked like kindling wood, red as singed hogs."[23] Some 6,500 cases were reported during the 1853 smallpox epidemic, leading to 2,500 reported deaths,[24] but some felt that the real death toll "was probably as high as five or six thousand."[25] Another "small pox epidemic ravaged Honolulu in 1881," causing 780 cases of illness and 282 deaths.[26] And in 1899, the bubonic plague finally reached the Islands, as rats spread the virus among the populace of Oʻahu, Maui, and Hawaiʻi.[27]

This drastic decline in population, combined with the inundation of foreign culture and individuals, pushed the Kingdom into a state of disorder and confusion.[28] The precontact system of land tenure and social organization was strained as individuals died off or left their rural communities for the expanding urban areas. The foreign demands for goods, especially ʻiliahi (sandalwood), added to the burden on the makaʻāinana, who were sent mauka (into the mountains) to gather wood for the Aliʻi and neglected the loʻi ʻai (taro patches) and other resources.[29] This new focus on producing items for a monetary economy disrupted the balance that had existed in precontact society. As communities fell apart, the few makaʻāinana remaining in the taro fields lacked the time and resources to meet the changing demands of the Aliʻi.[30]

The desperation caused by sickness and economic dislocation was exacerbated by the collapse of the traditional religion and the new visions introduced by Christian missionaries. The Hawaiians relied on their spiritual heritage and depended upon Akua for guidance and protection.[31] These religious beliefs were challenged, however, by foreigners who did not respect the kapu but nonetheless failed to suffer

22. *Id.*

23. Kamakau, *supra* note 5, at 416.

24. Alexander referred to 1853 as "one of the darkest in the history of this nation" and reported that between 2,500 and 3,000 persons died during the smallpox epidemic. Alexander, *supra* note 10, at 275–76.

25. Gavan Daws, *Shoal of Time: A History of the Hawaiian Islands,* 140 (1968, reprinted 1974); *see also* 1 Ralph S. Kuykendall, *The Hawaiian Kingdom 1778–1854: Foundation and Transformation,* 412 (1938, 7th printing 1989); George S. Kanahele, *Emma: Hawaiʻi's Remarkable Queen,* 48 (1999).

26. Kanahele, *supra* note 25, at 333, 337.

27. Bushnell, *supra* note 2, at 281.

28. The rate of depopulation was swift as well as massive. Historians debate the number of Hawaiians who populated the Islands at the time of Captain Cook's landing in 1778. Although the traditional figure used has been 300,000 (Office of Hawaiian Affairs, *Native Hawaiian Data Book,* 4, tbl. 1.1. [Mark Eshima, ed. 1998]) or 400,000 (King David Kalākaua, *The Legends and Myths of Hawaii,* 23, 64 [1990]), David Stannard has argued that the number was 800,000 or more (David Stannard, *Before the Horror,* 30–58 [1989]) and estimated a decline of 80 percent in the first fifty years of Western contact. *Id.* at 51, fig. 5. King Kalākaua wrote in 1887 that "Within a century [the natives] have dwindled from four hundred thousand healthy and happy children of nature, without care and without want, to a little more than a tenth of that number of landless, hopeless victims to the greed and vices of civilization." Kalākaua, *supra,* at 64. According to Professor Kameʻeleihiwa, "Hawaiians suffered a depopulation rate of at least 83 percent in the first forty-five years of contact." Lilikala Kameʻeleihiwa, *Native Land and Foreign Desires: Pehea La E Pono Ai?* 141 (1992).

29. Kameʻeleihiwa, *supra* note 29, at 140.

30. *Id.*

31. *Id.* at 26; Kamakau, *supra* note 5, at 201–02.

punishment from the wrath of Akua, and their traditional activities and practices were similarly challenged by the many new games, animals, and inebriating beverages brought by foreign visitors.[32] Also of importance were the views of the two leading female Ali'i, Ka'ahumanu and Keopuolani, who "detested it [the kapu system] as oppressive to their sex and themselves,"[33] as well as the ongoing struggle among chiefs for power.[34] As faith faded, numerous kapu were abolished following the death of Kamehameha on May 8, 1819, and finally Kamehameha II (Liholiho) ended the restrictive kapu system in an "extraordinary event"[35] in October 1819 "by partaking of food from vessels from which women were feasting, and the same day decreed the destruction of every temple and idol in the kingdom."[36] With the termination of a set of beliefs central to the organization of Hawaiian society, the order and stability of the traditional culture was dramatically weakened.[37] But the ending of the kapu allowed women to play a more active role in providing for the needs of the household, because they had previously been "restricted from planting and cultivating the land, fishing, or cooking food."[38] Once the women could assist with these tasks, the men could engage in "productive labor outside the context of the 'ohana as wage laborers."[39]

On March 30, 1820, only months after the abandonment of the kapu, a party of Calvinists from the American Board of Commissioners for Foreign Missions sailed into the heart of this spiritual vacuum.[40] After Liholiho granted the missionaries permission to stay for a year, some members of the original group remained on the island of Hawai'i while others set out for O'ahu and Kaua'i.[41] Although their recep-

---

32. Kame'eleihiwa, *supra* note 28, at 67; Blackman, *supra* note 1, at 73.

33. Blackman, *supra* note 1, at 73.

34. "By abolishing the traditional chiefly religion under which rivals could claim rank, prestige, and position, the Kamehameha chiefs consolidated political power under their control." Davianna Pomaika'i McGregor, "An Introduction to the Hoa'āina and Their Rights," 30 *Hawaiian Journal of History* 1, 8–9 (1996). After the abolition of the kapu in October 1819, "the traditional ritual chiefs organized a rebellion against the central government," led by the Ali'i Nui Kekuaokalani. Ka'ahumanu, Liholiho, and the Council of Chiefs were able to suppress the rebellion "and consolidated the monarchy as a centralized secular government." Davianna Pomaika'i McGregor, "The Cultural and Political History of Hawaiian Native People," in *Our History, Our Way: An Ethnic Studies Anthology*, 333, 343 (Gregory Yee Mark, Davianna Pomaika'i McGregor, and Linda A. Revilla, eds., 1996); Judd, *supra* note 14, at 19.

35. Kamakau, *supra* note 5, at 224.

36 Kalākaua, *supra* note 28, at 27; *see also id.* at 32–33; Kamakau, *supra* note 5, at 219–28; Malo, *supra* note 9, at 29; Kame'eleihiwa, *supra* note 28, at 74–79, 1 Kuykendall, *supra* note 25, at 68–70.

37. For a description of the complex role played by the kapu system and the nature and causes of its termination, *see* Marshall Sahlins, *Historical Metaphors and Mythical Realities: Structure in the Early History of the Sandwich Islands Kingdom,* 43–66 (1981).

38. McGregor, "Cultural and Political History," *supra* note 34, at 343. Kamakau reported that on Kaua'i, O'ahu, and Molokai, the common rule was that "[a]ll the work outside the house was performed by the men, such as tilling the ground, fishing, cooking in the *imu,* and furnishing whatever the women needed in the house," but that "on Maui and Hawaii the women worked outside as hard as the men, often cooking, tilling the ground, and performing the duties in the house as well." Kamakau, *supra* note 5, at 238–39.

39. McGregor, "Cultural and Political History," *supra* note 34, at 343.

40. 1 Kuykendall, *supra* note 25, at 100–02; Kamakau, *supra* note 5, at 246.

41. Kamakau, *supra* note 5, at 247.

tion was mixed among the Ali'i, it did not take long for the Protestant missionaries to secure their place in the Islands.[42]

The missionaries opened schools almost immediately and began teaching the English language, reading, and writing.[43] They adapted the Roman alphabet to the Hawaiian language and arranged for the translation of the Bible into Hawaiian.[44] New opportunities for learning attracted many Hawaiians, who were interested in what the newcomers had to offer.[45]

Although Keopuolani was the first of the Ali'i to convert in 1823,[46] it was Ka'ahumanu who gave Christianity its legitimacy.[47] The Hawaiians' acceptance of the new religion expanded as missionaries claimed that the rampant spread of disease and death resulted from their failure to believe in Jesus Christ.[48] When the number of converts began to increase, the influence of the missionaries spread from the religious to the political sector, and individual missionaries became instructors and advisors to the Ali'i.

The death of King Kamehameha II (Liholiho) and his Queen Kamāmalu of measles in London in 1824 while visiting the British royal family[49] further solidified the role of the missionaries in Hawaiian society. Before his departure for England (on November 27, 1823), Liholiho had named his younger brother Kauikeaouli to be Mō'ī in his absence.[50] Because Kauikeaouli was only nine at the time, Ka'ahumanu, as Kuhina Nui, assumed control of the kingdom, sharing power with the respected and powerful high chief Kalanimoku.[51] When Kauikeaouli was later confirmed as Mō'ī (as Kamehameha III) in 1825, when he was 11, Ka'ahumanu's influence increased. Members of Protestant missions, especially Ka'ahumanu's advisor Hiram Bingham, also gained authority.[52] Although not all of the Ali'i embraced Christianity, those who did convert maintained political control.[53]

Ka'ahumanu died on June 5, 1832, and the eighteen-year-old Kauikeaouli then had the opportunity to rule on his own.[54] The problems that plagued the reigns of his

---

42. "[T]he first party of Christian missionaries . . . were well received. They found a people without a religion, and their work was easy." Kalākaua, *supra* note 28, at 29.

43. Kamakau, *supra* note 5, at 248.

44. *Id.* at 248–49; Lawrence H. Fuchs, *Hawai'i Pono: A Social History,* 12 (1961).

45. "They [Ali'i and maka'āinana] were delighted with the *palapala* [writing] because it allowed them to extend their great intellectual and poetic traditions." Kame'eleihiwa, *supra* note 28, at 142.

46. *Id.* at 143–45; Kamakau, *supra* note 5, at 254.

47. *See* Kamakau, *supra* note 5, at 306–08.

48. Kame'eleihiwa, *supra* note 28, at 142–43.

49. Judd, *supra* note 14, at 37.

50. Kamakau, *supra* note 5, at 265.

51. *Id.* Although Liholiho died in London on July 13, 1824, the bodies of the royal party did not return to the Islands until May 4, 1825. Shortly thereafter, a council of Ali'i Nui met and confirmed Kauikeaouli as Mō'ī. *Id.* at 257–58.

52. Kame'eleihiwa, *supra* note 28, at 154.

53. *See generally* 1 Kuykendall, *supra* note 25, at 122–27, describing the influence of the Protestant missionaries on "several of the leading chiefs."

54. *Id.* at 133–34.

Kamehameha III
(Kauikeaouli)

predecessors persisted, however—particularly the dramatic population loss.[55] With death consuming his people at a voracious rate, with foreigners demanding material goods and land, and with the missionaries pressuring the Hawaiians to conform to their Christian standards, the new Mō'ī worked to secure his Kingdom for his people and to improve their conditions.

Kauikeaouli embraced his cultural traditions, resulting in rebukes from the missionaries and other advisors.[56] Because of the problems plaguing his nation, the Mō'ī could not wholeheartedly embrace a system that was not working for his people. Kauikeaouli thus reinstituted cultural pastimes, such as games, hula, and drinking of 'awa, and encouraged the maka'āinana to celebrate precontact traditions that had been forbidden by the missionaries.[57] The Mō'ī attempted to reinstate traditional policies (such as the Kālai'āina—redistributing the lands when a new Mō'ī came into power), much to the opposition of Christian Ali'i.[58]

---

55. *See supra* text at notes 1–27.

56. Kame'eleihiwa, *supra* note 28, at 157–58; *see also* Kamakau, *supra* note 5, at 334–35.

57. Kame'eleihiwa, *supra* note 28, at 157–58; 1 Kuykendall, *supra* note 25, at 134.

58. Kame'eleihiwa, *supra* note 28, at 159.

Kauikeaouli also sought to provide the young Ali'i with schooling in formal Western thought, in order to increase their ability to deal with the complex issues of Hawaiian and Western society. On August 18, 1837,[59] and again in June 1839,[60] he asked the American Missionary Society for a teacher to educate the Ali'i children. Just after the second request, newly arrived missionary teacher Amos Starr Cooke and his wife Juliette Montague Cooke established a school for the children of royal lineage.[61] At first they operated out of their home,[62] but within a year they moved into a newly constructed school building complete with boarding facilities.[63] The Royal School was in operation from June 1839 to 1850, educating sixteen Ali'i children[64] in Western practices and religion in order to "qualify them for their future stations and duties in life."[65]

Perhaps the most important contribution of Kauikeaouli was his enactment of a series of laws designed to codify and protect the rights of the Hawaiian People, especially the maka'āinana (commoners). With foreigners demanding land, both in lease and fee, and the Ali'i increasingly in debt, the maka'āinana were exploited for their labor[66] and were disenfranchised from the 'Āina.[67] As the number of foreigners arriving in the Islands increased, the pressure on the Mō'ī to grant landownership to protect the capital investments of immigrants likewise multiplied.[68]

The council of Ali'i that met on June 6, 1825, to confirm the young Kauikeaouli as Mō'ī also accepted the proposal of the high chief Kalanimoku that 'Āina should not revert to the new king according to the tradition of the Kālai'āina[69] but should continue to be held by the chiefs as before and could be passed on to their heirs under the principle of hereditary succession.[70] After the period of regency ended in 1832 and

---

59. Mary Atherton Richards, "Foreword," in *The Hawaiian Chiefs' Children's School 1839–1850*, xiii (1970); *see* discussion of the Royal School *infra* in chapter 28, text at notes 35–41.

60. "Family School for the Children of the Chiefs," *The Polynesian*, July 4, 1840.

61. Richards, *supra* note 59, at xiii.

62. "Family School for the Children of the Chiefs," *The Polynesian*, July 4, 1840. The Rev. William Richards had previously been instructing the Ali'i in "political economy and jurisprudence and all matters connected with the government." *Id.* Richards, *supra* note 59, at xiii. Later, he became an advisor of Kauikeaouli.

63. "Family School for the Children of the Chiefs," *The Polynesian*, July 4, 1840.

64. *Id.* The sixteen students educated at the Royal School were (1) Moses Kekuaiwa, (2) Lot Kamehameha, (3) Alexander Liholiho, (4) Victoria Kamamalau, (5) William Charles Lunalilo, (6) Bernice Pauahi, (7) Abigail Maheha, (8) Jane Loeau, (9) Elizabeth Keka'aniau, (10) Emma Rooke, (11) Peter Young Kaeo, (12) James Kaliokaani, (13) David Kalākaua, (14) Lydia Maheha (Lili'uokalani), (15) Polly Paaaina, and (16) John Pitt Kinau. Kamakau said these pupils were "like a happy family" and that they "were bright and delighted their teachers." Kamakau, *supra* note 5, at 405.

65. "Family School for the Children of the Chiefs," *The Polynesian*, July 4, 1840.

66. Maka'āinana owed obligations of service to the Konohiki and Mō'ī. *See In the Matter of the Estate of His Majesty Kamehameha IV*, 2 Hawai'i 715, 718–19 (1864).

67. Kame'eleihiwa, *supra* note 28, at 140.

68. W. Hutchins, *The Hawaiian System of Water Rights*, 22 (1946), explaining that "foreigners were aided in some cases by diplomatic agents of the governments to which they owned allegiance."

69. *See supra* chapter 2, text accompanying notes 47–53.

70. 1 Kuykendall, *supra* note 25, at 119, citing *Voyage of H.M.S. Blonde to the Sandwich Islands in the Years 1824–1825*, 152–53 (1826)). Hereditary succession is the passing of property to an individual's heirs at death. *Black's Law Dictionary*, 1,445 (7th ed., 1999).

Kauikeaouli became Mō'ī in his own right, he promulgated the Declaration of Rights of 1839, followed by the Constitution of 1840 (which included an amended version of the Declaration) to protect the interests of all inhabitants of the Kingdom.[71]

These documents made "startling changes in the authority of the chiefs and the Moi"[72] and were designed to ensure, for the first time, security for the maka'āinana independent of their Ali'i. They prohibited the oppression of the maka'āinana and provided that all Ali'i or government agents who violated the Constitution would be removed from their positions.[73] In its 1839 language, the Declaration of Rights said that it is not "proper to enact laws for the protections of rulers only" or "to enact laws to enrich the chiefs only, without regard to the enriching of their subjects also."[74] The Declaration also recognized property rights, stating that "Protection is hereby secured to the persons of all the people, together with their lands, their building lots and all their property while they conform to the laws of the kingdom, and nothing whatever shall be taken from any individual, except by express protection of the laws."[75] Prince Kūhiō later called the 1839 Declaration "the Hawaiian Magna Charta" and explained that it was significant that it had not been "wrung from an unwilling sovereign by force of arms," but rather was the free surrender of power "by a wise and generous ruler, impressed and influenced by the logic of events, by the needs of his people, and by the principles of the new civilization that was dawning on his land."[76]

The 1840 Constitution went still further in its preface, explaining that although all the land had belonged to Kamehameha I, "it was not his own private property. *It belonged to the chiefs and people in common,* of whom Kamehameha I was the head, and had management of the landed property."[77] This early legal document thus recognized the trust relationship that existed between the Ali'i and the maka'āinana regarding the land, and the rights of the common people to a share of the 'Āina. By explaining that the Mō'ī did not own the land "as private property," this Constitution acknowledged "that the common people had some form of ownership in the land, aside from an interest in the products of the soil."[78] As the Hawai'i Supreme Court

---

71. Ralph S. Kuykendall, "Constitutions of the Hawaiian Kingdom: A Brief History and Analysis," 21 *Papers of the Hawaiian Historical Society* 8 (1940). W. H. Richards played a significant role in drafting the 1839 Declaration of Rights and the 1840 Constitution. Merry, *supra* note 7, at 78, citing "Biographical Note by Meiric K. Dutton," in *William L. Lee: His Address at the Opening of the First Term of the Superior Court* (Honolulu: Loomis House Press, 1953).

72. Jonathan Kay Kamakawiwo'ole Osorio, *Dismembering Lāhui: A History of the Hawaiian Nation to 1887,* 25 (2002).

73. Kuykendall, *Constitutions, supra* note 71, at 10.

74. 1 Kuykendall, *supra* note 25, at 160, quoting from text in 2 *Hawaiian Spectator,* 347–48 (July 1839).

75. *Id.* at 160 and 271–72; Blackman, *supra* note 1, at 107.

76. Prince J. K. Kalanianaole, "The Story of the Hawaiians," 21 *Mid-Pacific Magazine* 117, 124 (February 1921).

77. 1840 Constitution, para. 14 (emphasis added). The Constitutions of the Hawaiian Kingdom are available at <http:www.hawaii-nation.org/constitution-1852.html> and at <http:www.pixi.com/kingdom>.

78. Jon J. Chinen, *The Great Mahele: Hawaii's Land Division of 1848,* 8 (1958).

later explained, the 1840 Constitution "acknowledged that the people of Hawaii are the original owners of all Hawaiian land."[79]

The 1840 Constitution marked the establishment of a constitutional monarchy in the Kingdom, with power shared between the Mō'ī and the people through their elected representatives.[80] This Constitution created a "house of representatives, chosen by the people, as part of the national legislature," which served as a second branch of the legislature, supplementing the council of chiefs or house of nobles, and which "for the first time gave the common people a share in the government—actual political power."[81] The 1840 Constitution also created a six-person Supreme Court, consisting of the Mōʻī, the Kuhina Nui, and four others appointed by "the representative body."[82]

Samuel Kamakau, who was himself elected to the Legislature from Maui in 1842,[83] praised the new constitutional structure, saying that it was a unique historical example of a ruler agreeing to share power without "war and bloodshed."[84] But he also noted that "because of the affection existing between the commoners and the chiefs the people did not take advantage of the benefits conferred upon them by the constitution." In fact, he explained, "the people who most benefited from it were the foreigners."[85] "To the foreigners the establishment of a constitutional form of government was very gratifying. Perhaps they foresaw the passing to them of the land under the constitution and its laws."[86] Reflecting, no doubt, his own experience in the Legislature, Kamakau explained sadly that "The stranger [foreigner] has no more skill with the axe than the wornout hewers of Hawaii, but not ten Hawaiians combined have the skill and wit to equal that of the stranger in the legislature."[87]

Despite Kauikeaouli's efforts to address the issue of proper land use and management, foreigners continued to demand possession in lease or fee. Beginning in 1836, representatives of overseas nations (primarily Great Britain, France, and the United States) began expressing their concern over their subjects' inability to own property, sometimes supported by warships.[88]

Following visits from the French and Americans (when Kauikeaouli articulated his opposition to foreign ownership of land), Lord George Paulet sailed the British Warship *Carysfort* to Honolulu on February 10, 1843.[89] After investigating com-

79. *State v. Zimring*, 58 Hawai'i 106, 111, 566 P.2d 725, 729 (1977).
80. *See* 1 Kuykendall, *supra* note 25, at 167–69; Kamakau, *supra* note 5, at 366–78; McGregor, "Hoa'āina," *supra* note 34, at 9.
81. 1 Kuykendall, *supra* note 25, at 167.
82. *Id.* at 167–68.
83. Kamakau, *supra* note 5, at 397.
84. *Id.* at 371.
85. *Id.* at 370.
86. *Id.* at 377.
87. *Id.*
88. 1 Kuykendall, *supra* note 25, at 144–52.
89. *Id.* at 213; Kamakau, *supra* note 5, at 359–65; *see infra* chapter 1, text at notes 29–33.

plaints made by British Counsel Richard Charlton, Paulet made several demands (including the payment of more than $100,000 for debts) under the threat of force.[90] Because of this intimidation, Kauikeaouli ceded his Kingdom to the British military on February 25, but it was restored to him on July 31, 1843, by British Rear Admiral Richard Thomas, commander in chief of the British squadron in the Pacific,[91] who negotiated a settlement of the financial disputes and made it clear that claiming sovereignty over the Islands was not within Paulet's authority or orders.[92] This episode was clearly traumatic for the Kingdom and for the Mō'ī. Having temporarily lost control of the government largely because of disputes over land, Kauikeaouli set to work to find a method of protecting his own interests, as well as those of his people.

With his people and Kingdom on the brink of extinction, relying on the wisdom of missionaries and other foreign advisors,[93] Kauikeaouli made yet another attempt to protect the Kingdom's sovereignty and Hawaiian control of the 'Āina by changing the system of land tenure. The Legislature created the Board of Commissioners to Quiet Land Titles to address and resolve all land claims as a separate section of a long organic act designed to organize executive branch departments, which was promulgated by the Mō'ī on December 10, 1845, to take effect on February 7, 1846.[94]

The foreigners eagerly promoted the transition to a system of private ownership because they wanted to obtain secure land titles for themselves and also because such a system was the one with which they were familiar and one that, in their view, promoted hard work and economic prosperity.[95] Initially, the Ali'i were skeptical of redefining property interests and were wary about how the lands should be divided.[96] The maka'āinana were likewise suspicious about the increased number of foreign advisors and the ability of foreigners to obtain land.[97] They anticipated difficulties with the process and continually petitioned Kauikeaouli, cautioning him not to proceed with the changes in land tenure as planned. More than 1,600 residents of Lahaina articulated their hesitancy to compete with foreigners and urged that more time was

---

90. Kamakau, *supra* note 5, at 359–65; 1 Kuykendall, *supra* note 25, at 213–16; Judd, *supra* note 14, at 132.

91. Merze Tate, "Great Britain and the Sovereignty of Hawaii," 31 *Pacific Historical Review,* 327, 329 (1962); 1 Kuykendall, *supra* note 25, at 216–21.

92. Judd, *supra* note 14, at 144–46.

93. Kauikeaouli explained why he was relying on foreign advisors in a letter written to Samuel M. Kamakau in August 1845, saying that he needed advisors who could "understand the laws of the great countries who are working with us," and that he wanted also to give positions to "the commoners and to the chiefs as they are able to do the work connected with the office." Kamakau, *supra* note 5, at 401.

94. 1 Kuykendall, *supra* note 25, at 280; Lorrin Thurston, *Fundamental Laws of Hawaii,* 137 (1904).

95. 1 Kuykendall, *supra* note 25, at 290. At least a few Hawaiians also supported this view. *See id.,* quoting a letter written by David Malo to W. Richards on June 2, 1846, where Malo says: "I believe it best that at this time, the people should own lands as they do in foreign lands; they [the people in foreign lands] work all the harder knowing they own the land, and very likely it is the reason why they love their country, and why they do not go to other places and perhaps that is the reason why they are great farmers."

96. 4 *Privy Council Records,* 250–72 (May 17, 1847–August 26, 1848).

97. A Kona Petition (300 signatures): "Would Not Sell Public Lands to Foreigners," Hawai'i State Archives (June 12, 1845).

needed before a change of this scale could be implemented.[98] Kamakau wrote that the changes in land tenure were possible only because the traditional chiefs had passed away.[99] In any event, the Privy Council and the Mōʻī decided that change was necessary, and the Land Commission proceeded with the Mahele process.[100]

98. A Lahaina Petition (1,600 signatures), Hawaiʻi State Archives (August 1845); *see also* A Lanaʻi Petition (300 signatures), Hawaiʻi State Archives (April 1845). *See generally* Kameʻeleihiwa, *supra* note 28, at 193.

99. Kamakau, *supra* note 5, at 404–05: "There was no powerful chief to stand back of the people and put together again the parts that were broken to pieces. It is a wonder that the land survives at all as a so-called independent kingdom when the rock that forms its anchor is shattered by the storm." *See also id.* at 370, stating that the 1840 Constitution whereby the Mōʻī and Aliʻi shared power with the makaʻāinana could be promulgated "because the old chiefs were dead."

100. 1 Kuykendall, *supra* note 25, at 287–88.

4

The Mahele

In 1840, Kauikeaouli (Kamehameha III) proclaimed the Kingdom's first Constitution, and in the years that followed he promulgated a series of laws designed to maintain Native Hawaiian control of the ʻĀina. His efforts were undercut, however, by the increasing debts of the Aliʻi to the recently arrived westerners, which presented a continuing threat to this control. Requests by local foreigners for land in lease or fee and offers by foreign nations to accept acreage in lieu of debts created anxiety among both the Aliʻi and the makaʻāinana. Resident missionaries and merchants filed complaints with their foreign consuls and home governments regarding their inability to gain title to land, and military vessels from Europe and the United States came to the Islands to investigate these claims.[1]

As Britain, France, and the United States competed for territories in the Pacific to expand their military and economic interests, Hawaiʻi, with its harbors and choice location in the North Pacific, was desired by all three nations.[2] After being forced to cede his Kingdom to Lord George Paulet of Britain for five months in 1843,[3] and realizing that Great Britain had annexed Aotearoa (New Zealand) in 1840[4] and that France had taken Tahiti and the Marquesas militarily in 1842,[5] Kauikeaouli focused in earnest on the need to assuage the demands for land from westerners living in the Kingdom and those patrolling the Pacific with their warships, while also protecting the interests of his people. "The king was deeply concerned over the hostile activities of the foreigners in the Islands. He did not want his lands to be considered public domain and subject to confiscation by a foreign power in the event of a conquest."[6]

---

1. "In August, 1844, Wyllie, as British pro-counsel, courteously informed the Hawaiian government that several British subjects had made complaints, alleging interference with lands long held by them." 1 Ralph S. Kuykendall, *The Hawaiian Kingdom 1778–1854: Foundation and Transformation*, 278 (1938, 7th printing 1989).

2. *Id.* at 196; *see supra* chapter 1, text accompanying notes 7–34.

3. *See supra* chapter 1, text accompanying notes 29–33, and chapter 3, text accompanying notes 89–92.

4. 1 Kuykendall, *supra* note 1, at 187.

5. *Id.* at 210.

6. Jon J. Chinen, *The Great Mahele: Hawaii's Land Division of 1848*, 25 (1958). *See also* Sally Engle Merry, *Colonizing Hawaii: The Cultural Power of Law*, 93 (2000): "The king hoped by this land allocation to protect his lands from confiscation in the event of foreign conquest."

Kamehameha III
(Kauikeaouli)

The Mōʻī was also alarmed about the health problems affecting the Hawaiians. With large numbers of his people dying from introduced diseases, the question of who would assume control of the ʻĀina had to be addressed.[7] Many land areas were effectively abandoned during this period because of the epidemics and because many of the surviving Hawaiians left the rural lands for the towns to participate in the trading society that developed around the visits of the whaling ships.[8] Kauikeaouli faced challenges and problems everywhere he turned, and the foreigners who had his ear were giving self-interested advice regarding these unresolvable issues.

Kauikeaouli (Kamehameha III)

Kauikeaouli was the longest reigning Mōʻī, serving first from 1825 to 1832 under a regency and then on his own from 1832 when he turned eighteen until his death in 1853 at the age of thirty-nine. "[K]nown to the Hawaiians as Kamehameha the Good,"[9] his life spanned the period of greatest turmoil and transition among Hawaiians. He was born in the Kona District of the Island of Hawaiʻi in 1814, the son of

---

7. 1 Kuykendall, *supra* note 1, at 386; *see supra* chapter 3, text accompanying notes 2–30.

8. Davianna Pomaikaʻi McGregor, "The Cultural and Political History of Hawaiian Native People," in *Our History, Our Way: An Ethnic Studies Anthology,* 345–46 (Gregory Yee Mark, Davianna Pomaikaʻi McGregor, and Linda A. Revilla, eds., 1996) (hereafter cited as McGregor, "Cultural and Political History").

9. Prince J. K. Kalanianaole, "The Story of the Hawaiians," 21 *Mid-Pacific Magazine* 117, 123 (February 1921).

Kamehameha I and Keopuolani and the younger brother of 'Iolani Liholiho, who became Kamehameha II.[10] His mother was a leader in the movement that enabled the overthrow of the kapu system in 1819 and was the first Ali'i to convert to Christianity in 1823. Kauikeaouli learned English and the teachings of Christianity along with his mother from the missionaries who arrived in 1820.

When he was twenty, in 1834, he married his sister Nahi'ena'ena, who was one year his junior. This marriage was terminated, as a formal matter, after seven months because of pressure from the missionaries, and she died in late 1836, shortly after the death of her infant son.[11] Kauikeaouli then married Hakaleleponi Kalama, a Kaukau Ali'i, who served as his queen for seventeen years and bore him two children, both of whom died in infancy.[12] In 1834, Kauikeaouli had taken as a hānai (adopted) son Alexander Liholiho, the son of Mataio Kekūanaō'a and Kauikeaouli's half sister Kīna'u, who became his heir and was named Kamehameha IV at Kauikeaouli's death. When Kauikeaouli's regency ended in 1832, the Council of Chiefs named Kīna'u to be Kuhina Nui, but Kauikeaouli had difficulties with his half sister and terminated her position the following year, restoring it in 1835 under pressure from the other chiefs. Although he was Christian, Kauikeaouli tried to revive the Hawaiian culture through reintroduction of the hula, traditional games, and the drinking of 'awa,[13] and he went through episodes of alcohol abuse and sexual dalliances.[14]

In 1845, he moved his capitol and the court back to Honolulu from Lahaina, Maui, where he had moved seven years earlier because of his grief over the death of his sister and her son.[15] He oversaw vast changes and promulgated two constitutions, in 1840 and 1852, which transformed the Kingdom into a constitutional monarchy, as described below. Kamakau wrote that Kauikeaouli had been "so beloved by the whole people" and said that "[p]erhaps no king born to the throne ever made a better ruler," emphasizing that "[h]e made all men free and equal" by ensuring that no laws enforced any class distinctions and that "[t]he tabus of the chiefs were all done away."[16] "But his greatest achievement was the change in the form of government to a constitutional monarchy and to a kingdom based upon law."[17]

The Creation and Role of the Land Commission

On October 29, 1845, the Legislature enacted and Kauikeaouli approved the first of a series of acts to "Organize the Executive Ministry," which are traditionally referred

---

10. Samuel M. Kamakau, *Ruling Chiefs of Hawaii,* 260 (1961, revised ed. 1992).

11. Lilikala Kame'eleihiwa, *Native Land and Foreign Desires: Pehea La E Pono Ai?* 165 (1992); *see also* Jean Iwata Cachola, *Kamehameha III: Kauikeaouli,* 31–34 (1995).

12. Kame'eleihiwa, *supra* note 11, at 166.

13. *Id.* at 157–58.

14. *Id.* at 167 and 366 n. 120; *see also Id.* at 289: "Considering that the weighty responsibility for the nation's welfare sat upon his shoulders alone, one would be surprised if he did not drink."

15. Kamakau, *supra* note 10, at 342.

16. *Id.* at 419–20.

17. *Id.* at 427.

John Ricord

to as the Organic Acts.[18] This October 1845 enactment created a five-department executive branch—the Departments of the Interior, Foreign Relations, Finance, Public Instruction, and the Attorney General—each directed by a Minister.[19] These five Ministers, along with the KiaʻĀina (Governors) of the four main Mokupuni (islands) and other individuals appointed by the Mōʻī, also became members of the Privy Council.[20] This statute marked an important step in the evolution of the constitutional monarchy, which slowly emerged during the remainder of the century. During this process, the role of the Mōʻī changed from that of an all-powerful warrior-chieftain serving as the human embodiment of and trustee for the Akua to that of a political and cultural leader guiding the government and working closely with other elected and appointed officials.

On December 10, 1845, in response to a proposal put forward by his Minister of Interior Dr. Gerrit P. Judd, Kauikeaouli created the Board of Commissioners to Quiet Land Titles, which is usually referred to as the Land Commission.[21] The Mōʻī

---

18. 1 Kuykendall, *supra* note 1, at 262–63.

19. *Id.*

20. The provision establishing the Privy Council in the first Organic Act formalized the council of Aliʻi that had been advising the Mōʻī. *Id.* at 263.

21. "Commission to Quiet Land Titles; Awards, Patents, Etc: An Act to Organize the Executive Depart-

appointed five commissioners to this body, and they had the awesome responsibility to determine the scope and outcome of all land claims.[22]

The first five members appointed in 1846 to the Land Commission were Attorney General John Ricord, James Young Kanehoa (son of John Young—known as 'Olohana—the English sailor captured by Kamehameha I who later became governor of Maui, Moloka'i, and Lana'i),[23] Ioane Papa 'Ī'ī (son of a high chief and a long-time legislator and judge and the only person to serve continuously during the life of the Commission), Zorobabel (sometimes spelled Zorobalea) Ka'auwai (a lesser chief from Maui, an entrepreneur who later became a legislator and judge),[24] and William Richards (who had come from Massachusetts to Hawai'i in 1823).[25] Two were Native Hawaiian, two were foreigners, and one was half-Hawaiian and half of foreign blood. Ricord resigned as Attorney General and left Hawai'i in 1847.[26] He was replaced by Joseph Henry Smith, who had arrived from England in 1845. Later in 1847, Judge William Little Lee (who was born in New York and arrived in Hawai'i in 1846 and served as president of the Commission from 1847 until its dissolution in 1855) and Nueku

---

ment of the Hawaiian Islands," Apr. 27, 1846, L. 1846 at 107, pt. I, ch. VII (April 27, 1846), art. IV (passed separately on December 10, 1845), also printed in 2 *Revised Laws of Hawai'i,* 2120 (1925); 1 Kuykendall, *supra* note 1, at 278–79. Although the second Organic Act was not formally enacted until April 27, 1846, the section establishing the Land Commission was issued on December 10, 1845, and became effective on February 7, 1846, earlier than the act as a whole. *Id.* at 263.

22. "An Act to Organize the Executive Department of the Hawaiian Islands," Article IV § 1, in 2 *Revised Laws of Hawai'i,* 2120 (1925), also printed in *The Fundamental Law of Hawaii,* 137 (Lorrin A. Thurston, ed., 1904):

> His Majesty shall appoint through the minister of the interior, and upon the consultation with the privy council, five commissioners, one of whom shall be the attorney general of this kingdom, *to be a board for the investigation and final ascertainment or rejection of all claims of private individuals, whether natives or foreigners, to any landed property acquired anterior to the passage of this Act; the awards of which board, unless appealed from as hereinafter allowed, shall be binding upon the minister of the interior and the applicant.* (Emphasis added.)

23. *See* 1 Kuykendall, *supra* note 1, at 24–25.

24. Professor Osorio has reported that Ka'auwai "nearly succeeded in purchasing the island of Kaho'olawe from the Mō'ī and the Land Commission in 1849." Jonathan Kay Kamakawiwo'ole Osorio, *Dismembering Lāhui: A History of the Hawaiian Nation to 1887,* 76 (2002).

25. Chinen, *The Great Mahele, supra* note 6, at 9; Jon J. Chinen, *They Cried for Help,* 27–28 (2002).

26. John Ricord arrived in Hawai'i on February 27, 1844, when he was thirty-one, after studying law in Buffalo, New York, and traveling extensively across the United States. He was the first trained lawyer to arrive in the Islands. Eleven days after he came ashore, Kauikeaouli appointed him to be his legal advisor, and he later became the Kingdom's first Attorney General on April 13, 1846. He resigned in May 1847, apparently because his actions to bring order to the government had made enemies. He then spent the next fourteen years traveling around the world, dying in Paris in 1861 at the age of 48 from an illness he had contracted in Liberia. Charleen Aina, "John Ricord: Hawaii's First Attorney General," *Hawaii Bar Journal,* October 1999, 104–05. Kamakau referred to Ricord as "this deeply-loved man." Kamakau, *supra,* note 10, at 407. Kuykendall wrote that Ricord had "some fine qualities, such as absolute loyalty to his trust, unwearying industry in the conduct of his office, and a sort of grim delight in wrestling with hard problems," but also noted that his "general attitude was not conciliatory and he must therefore bear some part of the responsibility for the rancorous turmoil and ill feeling that existed in Honolulu during these years." 1 Kuykendall, *supra* note 1, at 245. Daws reported that Ricord's "temper matched [Dr. Gerrit] Judd's" and that "to complicate matters Ricord became hopelessly infatuated with Judd's fifteen-year-old daughter Elizabeth and was desperately hurt when she turned down his proposal of marriage." Gavan Daws, *Shoal of Time: A History of the Hawaiian Islands,* 144 (1968, reprinted 1974), citing E. Judd, *Journal* (Hawaii Mission Children's Society, January 6, 1850).

Namauʻu (brother of Mataio Kekūanaōʻa and a member of the House of Nobles and the Privy Council) replaced Richards and Kanehoa. When Namauʻu died in 1848, he was replaced by the legislator, judge, and historian Samuel M. Kamakau. In 1850, Joseph Kekaulahao (who later became a legislator and judge) replaced Kaʻauwai and George M. Robertson (who later wrote the key 1864 decision on the nature of the Crown Lands described below in Chapter 8) replaced Kamakau.[27]

In their first meeting on February 11, 1846, the members analyzed the existing land tenure system and elected William Richards as their president.[28] The Commission then published a notice in the February 14, 1846, edition of *The Polynesian*, informing the general public that it would hold weekly meetings to review claims for fee simple land patents and term leases.[29]

On August 20, 1846, the Commissioners adopted seven principles to govern the processing of claims.[30] These guidelines were based on the civil code, the oral testimony of Aliʻi and other witnesses, and the customs and traditions of the community, and they were designed to provide the people with an understanding of how land disputes would be resolved.[31] To fulfill its objective of interpreting and protecting individual interests, the Commission analyzed the history and fundamental concepts of land tenure in Hawaiʻi and identified three classes of people with interests in the ʻĀina: the Mōʻī, the Aliʻi, and the makaʻāinana.[32] The principles then explained how claims would be reviewed.

The first five principles provided the methods of evaluation that would be used to determine the validity of claims.[33] The sixth principle outlined the amount that would have to be paid to the government in order to extinguish the interest of the Mōʻī in the land.[34] The last of the seven principles stated that all claims must be filed and proved within two years—but the deadline for proving the claims was later extended.[35] Individuals interested in obtaining a lease or land patent were thus

---

27. Chinen, *They Cried, supra* note 25, at 28–32, 172; 1 Kuykendall, *supra* note 1, at 264, 280 n. 37.

28. "Principles Adopted by the Board of Commissioners to Quiet Land Titles in Their Adjudication of Claims Presented to Them," Oct. 26, 1846, L. 1847, at 81, in 2 *Revised Laws of Hawaiʻi*, 2131 (1925); also printed in *The Fundamental Law of Hawaii*, 140 (Lorrin A. Thurston, ed., 1904).

29. Chinen, *They Cried, supra* note 25, at 33; 2 *Revised Laws of Hawaiʻi*, 2132 (1925).

30. 2 *Revised Laws of Hawaiʻi*, 2124 (1925).

31. *Id.* at 2124–30.

32. *Id.* at 2126.

33. *Id.* at 2135. *See* text of principles 2–4 *infra* in text at note 84. The requirements for establishing a claim varied depending on whether the ʻĀina was obtained before or after June 7, 1839, and on who had granted permission for possession (i.e., whether the Mōʻī, an Aliʻi, or a Konohiki had given oral permission or had issued a written lease, etc.). *Id.*

34. *Id.* at 2136. Although the Land Commission established the commutation fee, the Mōʻī could accept a reduced amount. Although the payment of the commutation fee terminated the undivided interest that the Mōʻī had held in that particular parcel, the rights of the makaʻāinana were not addressed. Thus, the land was still subject to the rights of the native tenants occupying the ʻĀina. *Id.*

35. Because many Hawaiians (especially Konohiki) failed to prove their claims, the original deadline of February 1850 was extended by subsequent legislation in 1854, 1860, and 1892. Eventually, the Konohiki or their heirs had until January 1, 1895, to file their claims. *See* statutes listed *infra* in note 123. The makaʻāinana were barred, however, from submitting evidence to prove any claims for Kuleanas after 1854. "Limitation of

required to file a written request with the Land Commission establishing the nature of their claim. If the Commission issued an award, roughly one-third of the unimproved value of the parcel had to be paid to the government (in cash or by relinquishing one-third of the land) in order to extinguish the interest of the Mō'ī.[36] The Minister of the Interior would not issue a Royal Patent imparting title until this commutation fee was paid.[37]

Despite its ambitious responsibilities, the Land Commission adjudicated only a handful of claims during the first years of its existence.[38] Because the Commission did not have the power to allocate the undivided interests of the Mō'ī, Ali'i, and maka'āinana, its actions focused on claims for leases. The Privy Council and its advisors were in bitter disagreement on how those interests should be partitioned—or if a separation should even be attempted—and discussions on the advisability and methods of dividing the lands continued for two years before the actual division began. The maka'āinana submitted numerous petitions to Kauikeaouli, urging him not to rely on foreign advisors or to allow foreign ownership of the 'Āina.[39]

William Little Lee

Perhaps because of his legal background, Judge William Little Lee played a dominant role in the activities of the Commission. He was born in New York in 1821 and grew up in New England. He received legal training at Harvard under U.S. Supreme Court Justice Joseph Story and Professor Simon Greenleaf,[40] was admitted to practice law in New York State, and had practiced law for only one year in Troy, New York, before arriving in Hawai'i as a young man on October 12, 1846, along with his

---

Time for Proving Claims: An Act Relating to the Board of Commissioners to Quiet Land Titles, May 26, 1853," in 2 *Revised Laws of Hawai'i*, 2145 (1925). In the end, the process of filing and proving claims and then receiving a perfected fee simple title differed for three different groups: the Ali'i, the foreigners, and the maka'āinana (or hoa'āina, as those who filed claims were called). The Ali'i filed and proved their claims in a personal meeting with the King. By paying the commutation fee, they were able to eliminate the King's and the Government's interest and to receive a perfected title (which was still subject to the rights of native tenants). Foreigners had to prove their claims by obtaining a survey and collecting testimony verifying their ownership of the land parcel. Upon proving their claim, they could perfect title by paying the required commutation. Hoa'āina were held to the same standards as the foreigners, but because they had no money to pay the commutation fee, and because they had too little land to pay their commutation in land, the Kuleana Act of 1850 (discussed below in the text accompanying notes 104–45) waived their commutation requirement. The land received by hoa'āina was not subject to the rights of anyone because the rights of the Ali'i, the Mō'ī, and the Government had been separated out earlier.

36. Because of delays between the filing and adjudication of claims by the Land Commission, the commutation fee was based on the date the claim was filed as opposed to the date it was settled.

37. On October 26, 1848, the Legislature adopted the seven principles that had been drafted by the Commission on August 20, 1846, as rules to guide the partition of the 'Āina. "Ratification of Principles," 2 *Revised Laws of Hawai'i*, 2137 (1925).

38. Chinen, *Great Mahele, supra* note 6, at 12.

39. *See supra* chapter 3, text at note 98. For a flavor of the interaction between the Mō'ī and the Ali'i during this period, *see State v. Midkiff,* 49 Hawai'i 456, 421 P.2d 550 (1966).

40. Merry, *supra* note 6, at 3, citing Meiric K. Dutton, "Biographical Note," in *William L. Lee: His Address at the Opening of the First Term of the Superior Court* (Honolulu: Loomis House Press, 1953).

William Little Lee

best friend Charles Reed Bishop.[41] He was the second lawyer to come to the Islands (after John Ricord), and within two months of his arrival, he was appointed to be a trial and appellate judge in the recently created judicial system.[42] The following year he was appointed to the Land Commission to replace the ailing William Richards, and he served as President of the Commission from August 25, 1847, until the Commission terminated in 1855.[43] Lee was thus both a member of the Commission and a member of the court that "was responsible for any appeals from the decisions of the Land Commission."[44]

Along with John Ricord, Lee played a key role in drafting the organic acts that established the executive branch departments and the courts.[45] In September 1847, he

---

41. Chinen, *They Cried, supra* note 25, at 29; Kameʻeleihiwa, *supra* note 11, at 298, citing Rev. S. C. Damon, *Tribute to the Memory of Hon. William L. Lee, Late Chief Justice of the Hawaiian Kingdom,* 15 (Honolulu: H. M. Whitney Press, 1857). Apparently they were on their way to the Oregon Territory in search of a more healthful climate, but Lee was persuaded to stay by Kauikeaouli (Kamehameha III), who appointed him to become a judge. Merry, *supra* note 6, at 3.

42. 1 Kuykendall, *supra* note 1, at 244.

43. Chinen, *They Cried, supra* note 25, at 27–29, citing *Land Commission Minutes, Transactions,* vol. 1, 3/4/1846–5/3/1855, and 105.

44. Robert H. Stauffer, *Kahana: How the Land Was Lost,* 11 (2004).

45. A. Grove Day, *History Makers of Hawaii,* 84 (1984).

was appointed Chief Justice of the newly created Superior Court of Law and Equity, which was nominally below the Supreme Court but took over much of its work;[46] it was above the four circuit courts.[47] During the next several years, he worked on the drafting of a criminal code for the Kingdom (based primarily on the Massachusetts and Louisiana codes),[48] which was completed in 1850, and a civil code, which took several more years to complete.[49] He also served in the Legislature, where he "introduced a bewildering array of rules and procedures in the first week of the 1851 session."[50] He served as the Speaker of the House of Representatives from April 1851 to April 1852[51] and was one of the three drafters of the Constitution of 1852.[52] On December 6, 1852, he was appointed Chief Justice of the Supreme Court, a position he held until his death on May 28, 1857.[53] "[I]n a few short years this trained lawyer dramatically reshaped the legal landscape of the kingdom."[54] At the time of his death, he was said "to control almost every important action of the government."[55]

As explained below,[56] Lee made the key proposals in 1847 that persuaded the Ali'i to accept the idea of dividing up the land, which recognized that the Mō'ī should be able "to retain his private lands as his individual property"[57] but that have also been characterized as causing "the death of local culture."[58] He defended the distribution of property by proclaiming that it would "emancipat[e]" the natives "from a state of hereditary servitude, to that of a free and independent right in the soil they cultivate,"[59] but his actions were not always designed to enable the average Hawaiian to obtain an adequate amount of land to achieve economic independence. Kamakau denounced Lee for requiring the natives "to lick ti leaves like the dogs and gnaw bones thrown at the feet of strangers, while the strangers became their lords, and the

---

46. Merry, *supra* note 6, at 92. The Supreme Court, with the Mō'ī and designated Ali'i as its judges, was still utilizing the Hawaiian language at this time and applying Hawaiian customary law, but its role became "merely nominal." *Id.*, citing Dutton, *supra* note 40; *see also id.* at 103.

47. Chinen, *They Cried, supra* note 25, at 25. Merry, *supra* note 6, at 3 and 92, reports that Lee was "elected" to be chief justice of this court.

48. Merry, *supra* note 6, at 99.

49. 1 Kuykendall, *supra* note 1, at 264; Lani Ma'a Lapilio, "The 19th Century Hawaiian Judicial System," *Hawaii Bar Journal,* October 1999, 86, 88.

50. Osorio, *supra* note 24, at 75.

51. Chinen, *They Cried, supra* note 25, at 30, citing *Journal of the House of Representatives* (1851–53) Series 221-7.

52. 1 Kuykendall, *supra* note 1, at 266–67. The other drafters were Dr. Gerritt Judd and Judge John 'Ī'ī, but "the main work was done by Lee." Merry, *supra* note 6, at 102.

53. Chinen, *They Cried, supra* note 25, at 30.

54. Merry, *supra* note 6, at 93.

55. Merze Tate, *Hawaii: Reciprocity or Annexation,* 10 (1968), citing "David L. Gregg to U.S. Secretary of State William L. Marcy," March 9, 1857, No. 207, USDS, *Dispatches, Hawaii,* VIII.

56. *See infra* text at notes 79–84.

57. 1 Kuykendall, *supra* note 1, at 286; Kame'eleihiwa, *supra* note 11, at 215.

58. Stauffer, *supra* note 44, at 63.

59. Chinen, *They Cried, supra* note 25, at 73, quoting a December 14, 1847, letter from Lee to Kamehameha III, *Supreme Court Letters of C. J. Lee, 1847–1854,* Series 240, Box 1; *see also* Kame'eleihiwa, *supra* note 11, at 215, quoting from *Privy Council Records,* vol. 4A:286, December 18, 1847, Hawai'i State Archives, and characterizing Lee's predictions about the impact of the Mahele on the maka'āinana as "delirious and erroneous."

hands and voices of strangers were raised over those of the native race." [60] Chinen has reported that Lee gave the makaʻāinana "harmful advice," [61] helped his friends obtain land awards,[62] "made no effort to assist the *hoaʻāina* in distress," [63] and "when Lee learned that these poor *hoaʻāina* were unable to pay the expenses to perfect their claims, Lee purchased their claims." [64]

In 1849–50, Lee played a major role in promoting the enactment of legislation allowing foreigners to own land.[65] He became a major landowner during this period, and in 1849, when he was both Chief Justice of the Superior Court and President of the Land Commission, he persuaded Kauikeaouli to sell him the Līhuʻe Plantation on Kauaʻi, containing thousands of acres of choice lands, for $9,350, which Lee (along with his friend Charles Reed Bishop) used to grow sugar.[66] Lee also purchased (again with his friend Bishop) 27 acres in Mānoa, Oʻahu, near Punahou School from Mataio Kekūanaōʻa for $2,000.[67] Lee wrote the Act for the Government of Masters and Servants in 1850, which regulated the contract labor system in Hawaiʻi during the next half century and essentially kept the immigrant workers in a slavelike condition until their contractual terms were fulfilled.[68] He also helped draft the Kuleana Act of 1850,[69] which granted some gathering and use rights to the makaʻāinana but excluded the important right of pasturage, causing substantial hardship to them.[70] Later, he was buying claims to Kuleana at the same time that he was serving on the Land Commission and the Court adjudicating such claims.[71] In 1850, Lee became the first president of the Royal Hawaiian Agricultural Society, which evolved into the Hawaiian Sugar Planters' Association.[72] He had diplomatic responsibilities as well, working to defuse a tense situation with France in 1849 [73] and negotiating a reciproc-

---

60. Kamakau, *supra* note 10, at 399. Kamakau does not mention Lee by name, but Merry says he "was probably referring to Lee" in this discussion. Merry, *supra* note 6, at 5.

61. Chinen, *They Cried, supra* note 25, at 104–05.

62. *Id.* at 103–04; *see also* Kameʻeleihiwa, *supra* note 11, at 299.

63. Chinen, *They Cried, supra* note 25, at 130. The term "hoaʻāina" has the literal meaning of "friends of the land" and came to refer to those makaʻāinana who had applied for Kuleana lands. *See* Osorio, *supra* note 24, at 53.

64. Chinen, *They Cried, supra* note 25, at 130.

65. *Id.* at 68–69; *see infra* text at notes 150–55.

66. Chinen, *They Cried, supra* note 25, at 138; *see also* Kameʻeleihiwa, *supra* note 11, at 299, stating that "As soon as foreigners were allowed to own Land in 1850, Lee entered into a partnership with [Charles Reed] Bishop, and together they began Lihuʻe sugar plantation on Kauaʻi," citing "W. L. Lee to J. Turrill: December 29, 1850," Hawaiian Historical Society, 1957:35.

67. Kameʻeleihiwa, *supra* note 11, at 299.

68. 1 Kuykendall, *supra* note 1, at 330; *see also* Merry, *supra* note 6, at 97.

69. 1 Kuykendall, *supra* note 1, at 291; *see infra* text at notes 104–45.

70. Chinen, *They Cried, supra* note 25, at 69–70.

71. *Id.* at 130–31. Another example of an apparent conflict of interest, by modern standards, occurred when Land Commissioner Zorobabel Kaʻauwai served as agent to assist the high Aliʻi Keohokalole in presenting her land claim in Kahana Valley, Oʻahu, to the Land Commission. Stauffer, *supra* note 44, at 61: "The fact that Kaauwai was a member of the Land Commission undoubtedly increased his marketability as an agent preparing claims before it."

72. Chinen, *They Cried, supra* note 25, at 30; 1 Kuykendall, *supra* note 1, at 327–28; Merry, *supra* note 6, at 3.

73. 1 Kuykendall, *supra* note 1, at 393–94.

ity treaty (which never went into effect) after serving as Envoy Extraordinary and Minister Plenipotentiary to the United States in 1855–56.[74]

The Actual Division

Although the Ali'i agreed that the three classes of individuals entitled to awards were the Mō'ī in his role as head of the government, the Ali'i, and the maka'āinana, they were concerned about the amount of 'Āina they would be required to relinquish.[75] They agreed that they should turn over a portion of their holdings to the Mō'ī but objected to the Government's claiming an additional one-third commutation fee on the remainder.[76] In an effort to expedite the division, it was suggested that the "King's Foreign Officers" present their suggestions to the Privy Council.[77]

On December 14, 1847, Minister of the Interior Gerrit P. Judd presented his opinion on the claims of the Mō'ī (and other Ali'i) and a plan for partitioning the 'Āina.[78] Judge William Little Lee responded with some amendments to Judd's opinion, seeking to ease the resistance of the Ali'i to ceding a portion of their holdings to the Mō'ī and to the Government.[79] Judge Lee's understanding of and ability to interpret the law persuaded the Privy Council to accept his opinion, and on December 18, 1847, the Council adopted Lee's proposed resolutions and created a committee to assist in the division of lands between the Mō'ī and the Ali'i.[80]

Lee's opinion was based on the Constitution of 1840 and the Principles adopted by the Land Commission on August 20, 1846, and emphasized the distinction between the Mō'ī and the Government.[81] Although "[u]ntil a few years earlier the King *was* the State, and there could be no distinction between king's property and public property,"[82] Lee proposed that Kauikeaouli retain his own 'Āina, subject to claims of resident tenants, and divide the remainder in thirds between the Government, the Ali'i, and the maka'āinana.[83] First, Kauikeaouli should select the parcels he

---

74. Chinen, *They Cried, supra* note 25, at 30; Tate, *supra* note 55, at 30–36.

75. 3A *Privy Council Records,* Series 421, at 47–56.

76. *Id.*

77. *Id.*

78. *Id.*

79. *Id.*

80. The members appointed to the Committee by Kauikeaouli were Keoni Ana, Pi'ikoi, Gerrit Judd, and Mataio Kekūanaō'a. *Id.* (December 18, 1847).

81. *Id.*

82. Thomas Marshall Spaulding, *The Crown Lands of Hawaii,* 6 (University of Hawai'i Occasional Papers No. 1, October 10, 1923).

83. 3A *Privy Council Records,* Series 421, at 47–56. The key language explaining the difference between the Mō'ī and the Government stated that

> The King and the Government were one and the same in most things, but not in every thing. From the Constitution it seemed clear that in property the King and the Government were two separate and distinct persons. . . . In [my] opinion it would be agreeable to the Constitution and principles of the Land Commission for the King to retain his private lands as his individual property, and then for one third of the remaining lands to go to the Govt.—one third to the Chiefs, and one third to the Tenants.

would retain. After his ʻĀina was set aside, the Aliʻi would identify the portions that they wished to keep. Finally, the division between the Aliʻi and makaʻāinana could take place at the discretion of either party, with confirmation of the Privy Council. Principles 2, 3, and 4 explicitly addressed the rights of the makaʻāinana:

> 2. One third of the remaining lands of the Kingdom shall be set aside, as the property of the Hawaiian Government subject to the direction and control of His Majesty, as pointed out by the Constitution and Laws, one-third to the chiefs and Konohikis in proportion to their possessions, to have and to hold, to them, their heirs and successors forever, *and the remaining third to the Tenants, the actual possessors and cultivators of the soil, to have and to hold to them, their heirs and successors forever.*

> 3. The division between the Chiefs or the Konohikis and their Tenants, prescribed by Rule 2, shall take place, whenever any chief, Konohiki or Tenant shall desire such division, subject only to confirmation by the King in Privy Council.

> 4. *The Tenants of His Majesty's private lands, shall be entitled to a fee simple title to one-third of the lands possessed and cultivated by them;* which shall be set off to the said Tenants in fee simple, whenever His Majesty or any of said Tenants shall desire such division.[84]

After Kauikeaouli identified the ʻĀina he wished to reserve, a period of quit-claiming took place from January 27 to March 7, 1848, in order to sever the undivided interests of the Aliʻi and the Mōʻī in the remaining ʻĀina. In what is now known as the *Buke Mahele,* or *Mahele Book,* between 245 and 251 Aliʻi relinquished their interest to Kauikeaouli's chosen ʻĀina, and he did the same with respect to the parcels they wanted to retain.[85] In the pages on the left side of the *Buke Mahele,* the Aliʻi quitclaimed a portion of their ʻĀina to Kauikeaouli, stating that they had no further

---

Lee thus perceived the lands that would be claimed by Kauikeaouli as "his individual property," just as the Aliʻi lands would also become the individual property of the chiefs.

84. *Id.* (emphasis added).

85. The exact number of Aliʻi is disputed. Kameʻeleihiwa has used the number 251 (Kameʻeleihiwa, *supra* note 11, at 227), and that number is also found in Russ Apple and P. Apple, "The Great Mahele," *Honolulu Star-Bulletin,* June 16, 1978, at A-19, col. 6, and in Stauffer, *supra* note 44, at 22. In a lecture on September 26, 1996, Professor Kameʻeleihiwa said that she reached this 251 figure by counting and recounting each entry in the *Mahele Book.* Stauffer has written that "[t]wo hundred forty-five high Hawaiian (or part-Hawaiian) *aliʻi* and six high foreign-born, naturalized *aliʻi* then came forward." Stauffer, *supra* note 44, at 63. Kuykendall, Kelly, Levy, MacKenzie, McGregor, and Merry have stated that 245 Aliʻi participated in the division. 1 Kuykendall, *supra* note 1, at 287; Marion Kelly, "Land Tenure in Hawaiʻi," 7:2 *Amerasia Journal* 65(Asian American Studies Center, University of California at Los Angeles, Fall-Winter 1980); Neil M. Levy, "Native Hawaiian Land Rights," 63 *California Law Review* 848, 855 (1975); Melody K. MacKenzie, "Historical Background," in *Native Hawaiian Rights Handbook,* 7 (Melody Kapilialoha MacKenzie, ed., 1991); Davianna Pomakaʻi McGregor, "An Introduction to the Hoaʻaina and Their Rights," 30 *Hawaiian Journal of History,* 1, 9 (1996); Merry, *supra* note 6, at 93. Chinen wrote that "More than two hundred and forty of the highest ranking chiefs and *konohikis* in the kingdom joined Kamehameha III in this momentous task." Chinen, *Great Mahele, supra* note 6, at 16.

interest in the parcels they listed.[86] On the facing (or right-hand) pages, Kauikeaouli quitclaimed his interest in the parcels that the Ali'i would retain.

On March 8, 1848, the day after the quitclaim divisions were complete, Kauikeaouli held title to nearly 2.5 million acres, or 60 percent of the land in the Kingdom.[87] But almost immediately, after identifying the parcels that he wanted to retain, Kauikeaouli ceded about 1.5 million acres to the Government for the benefit of the people of his Kingdom, and these lands became known as the Government Lands.[88] In ratifying this action on June 7, 1848, the Legislature thanked the Mō'ī for his generosity and acknowledged Kauikeaouli's effort "to surrender and forever make over to his Chiefs and People, the greater portion of his Royal Domain."[89] These Government Lands, like all 'Āina in the Kingdom, remained subject to any claims of the maka'āinana.[90] As of the middle of 1848, the lands (4,126,000 acres) were divided as follows:

The Mō'ī's lands	984,000 acres (23.8%)
Government Lands	1,523,000 acres (37%)
Lands granted to the Ali'i	1,619,000 acres (39.2%) [91]

Allocation of 'Āina

Despite Kauikeaouli's intention to secure a land base for his people, the Mahele of 1848 resulted in Ali'i giving up substantial portions of the 'Āina they had previously exercised authority over. The underlying idea was that the Ali'i were to give up roughly 50 percent of their holdings, but the amount actually relinquished varied, depending on where the 'Āina was situated and the Ali'i's relationship with the

---

86. In the quitclaims signed by the Ali'i, the last statement reads "Aohe oia kuleana maloko," meaning "I have no further interest therein."

87. Melody K. MacKenzie, *supra* note 85, at 7.

88. *Id.*; Jon J. Chinen, *Original Land Titles in Hawaii,* 15 (1971).

89. "Act Relating to the Lands of His Majesty the King and of the Government," June 7, 1848, L. 1848 at 22, in 2 *Revised Laws of Hawai'i,* 2152 (1925). The first section states, "Whereas, It hath pleased His Most Gracious Majesty Kamehameha III., the King, after reserving certain lands to himself as his own private property, to surrender and forever make over unto his Chiefs and People, the greater portion of his Royal Domain . . .". *Id.* This act is also discussed *infra* in chapter 5, text at notes 7–9; chapter 6, note 12; chapter 8, text at note 28; and chapter 21, text at note 24.

90. *Id.* at 2156.

91. McGregor, "Cultural and Political History," *supra* note 8, at 351. These same figures appear in Jean Hobbs, *Hawaii: A Pageant of the Soil,* 52 (1935), citing "Hawaiian Land Systems and Transactions Thereunder," Senate Comm. on Foreign Relations, Senate Document No. 72, 56th Cong., 1st Sess. (1899) and William Fremont Blackman, *The Making of Hawaii: A Study in Social Evolution,* 159 (1906, reprinted 1977), as the distribution of lands as of 1855, except that the Government Lands had become 1,495,000 acres and 28,600 acres had been distributed to the maka'āinana in Kuleana Awards. *See also* 1 Kuykendall, *supra* note 1, at 294; U.S. Dept. of the Interior and U.S. Dept. of Justice, *From Mauka to Makai: The River of Justice Must Flow Freely,* 52 (Report on the Reconciliation Process between the Federal Government and Native Hawaiians, October 23, 2000), available at < http://www.doi.gov/nativehawaiians/pdf/1023fin.pdf > (site visited May 24, 2004), both using similar figures.

Mōʻī.[92] Some Aliʻi gave up as much as 73 percent of their pre-Mahele holdings, while others gave up only 40 percent.[93]

Kauikeaouli selected for himself a total of 144 ʻIli and Ahupuaʻa from the islands of Hawaiʻi, Maui, Molokaʻi, Oʻahu, and Kauaʻi.[94] Of the parcels he retained, many were "personal ʻĀina" that belonged to his immediate family (father, brother, etc.) before the division.[95] The Mōʻī received more ʻĀina than any other Aliʻi in the Mahele, but he nonetheless turned over 82 percent of his holdings (790 of the 934 ʻĀina he held before the Mahele) in order to provide sufficient ʻĀina for the other Aliʻi, the Government, and the makaʻāinana.[96] These distributions were consistent with his goal of protecting the lands of the Native Hawaiians from foreigners.

After the Mahele, Kauikeaouli managed the ʻĀina he had selected for himself as his private and personal property. He sold and mortgaged those lands through an agent, and his wife Queen Kalama signed all deeds of conveyance in order to extinguish her dower rights.[97] But he also used the revenues from these lands to assist the Government and the Hawaiian People where appropriate. Following his death, a significant portion of the King's land was auctioned off to satisfy his $31,000 personal debt.[98] Alexander Liholiho (Kamehameha IV) did not receive any ʻĀina in the Mahele, because it was understood that he was to inherit Kauikeaouli's portion.[99]

Of the more than 240 Aliʻi who participated in the Mahele, nine were Aliʻi Nui who received substantial ʻĀina.[100] The remaining two dozen Kaukau Aliʻi and the

---

92. Because the ʻĀina distributed at the time of the Mahele was not surveyed but was instead selected by name (with natural boundaries based on community knowledge), awards are generally examined by the number of ʻĀina selected as opposed to a figure based on acreage.

93. Kameʻeleihiwa, *supra* note 11, at 243.

94. *Id.* at 233. The *Buke Mahele* listed 144 ʻĀina as lands selected by Kauikeaouli, but the June 7, 1848, Legislative Act confirming Kauikeaouli's grant of Government Lands listed only 138 ʻĀina as Crown Lands (see appendix 2, *infra*). For a comparison, *see* the *Buke Mahele* at the Hawaiʻi State Archives and the "Act Relating to the Lands of His Majesty the King and of the Government," June 7, 1848, in 2 *Revised Laws of Hawaiʻi*, 1925, 2152–76.

95. Kameʻeleihiwa, *supra* note 11, at 233.

96. *Id.* at 229, 233.

97. In 1846, a law of dower was instituted granting widows a life estate (possessory interest for her lifetime) in one-third of the real property her husband had ever owned (unless she signed a release when the property was conveyed). "Second Act of Kamehameha III," Ch. IV, sec. IV, *Session Laws of 1846*, at 59. The fact that Queen Kalama signed all conveyances of Kauikeaouli's real property illustrates that the royal couple treated these lands as if they were the personal and private property of the Mōʻī.

98. Although Kauikeaouli's probate file contains various lists of debts, expenditures, and dispersals from the estate of His Late Majesty, it does not contain a comprehensive list of the lands auctioned off to pay the debt. Judge Lorrin Andrews granted an order on March 10, 1855, empowering the executors to sell, lease, or mortgage as much land as necessary to settle Kauikeaouli's debts, and the debts were paid and probate closed. The list of receipts includes a sale of land at Peleula for $200 and another sale of land in Hawaiʻi in 1853 for $255.60, indicating that large portions had to be sold to cover the $31,000 debt. "Will of His Majesty Kamehameha III," First Circuit Probate No. 2410, *Petition to Probate Judge Andrews from Executors of Kamehameha III's Estate* (March 9, 1855).

99. Kameʻeleihiwa, *supra* note 11, at 246.

100. *Id.* at 307: ·

Mikahela Kekauʻonohi	77 ʻĀina
William Lunalilo	65 ʻĀina
Ane Keohokalole	50 ʻĀina

more than 200 Konohiki received varying amounts, depending on their relationship with the Mō'ī and the location of the 'Āina.[101]

The *Buke Mahele* represented the quitclaim agreements between the Ali'i and the Mō'ī. These agreements did not confer legal title but merely extinguished the rights of each party in the lands of the other. The Ali'i were still required to file their claims with the Land Commission, identify and establish the nature of their title, and pay the commutation fee of one-third of the unimproved value of the land at the date of the award in order to receive Royal Patents for their parcels.[102] After releasing through these quitclaims about half of the 'Āina they controlled, the Ali'i were thus required to turn over an additional third (via their commutation fee) to the Minister of the Interior, to be added to the Government Lands. In the end, most of the Ali'i wound up retaining about one-third of the 'Āina they had controlled before the Mahele.[103]

The Kuleana Act of 1850

In the early discussions regarding the nature of the division, the general notion that the maka'āinana should receive one-third or at least one-fourth of the lands seemed to always to be an element of the package deal that was being developed.[104] The original Principles adopted by the Land Commission on August 20, 1846, and ratified by the Legislature on October 26, 1846, spoke of the idea that "the King allow to the landlord one third, to the tenant one third and retain one third himself." [105] In the key discussions in December 1847, Judge William L. Lee proposed that Kauikeaouli retain his own 'Āina, subject to claims of resident tenants, and divide the remainder in thirds between the Government, the Ali'i, and the maka'āinana.[106] In a letter written in November 1849, R. C. Wyllie wrote to Dr. Judd stating that "by the principle adopted by the Land Commission, the poor natives are entitled to one-third." [107] An

Victoria Kamamalu	48 'Āina
Leleiohoku	36 'Āina
Lota Kapuaiwa	17 'Āina
Ruta Ke'elikolani	12 'Āina
Laura Konia	11 'Āina
Mosese Kekuaiwa	9 'Āina

101. *Id.* at 227. For a comprehensive examination of the awards of the *Buke Mahele, see id.* at 201–318.

102. 2 *Revised Laws of Hawai'i,* 2124 (1925).

103. For example, an Ali'i holding twelve 'Āina before the Mahele would have relinquished about six to Kauikeaouli through the quitclaim process. For the remaining six, the Ali'i would then have had to pay a commutation fee of two 'Āina (or the cash equivalent thereof), retaining only four.

104. *See* discussion of the "Principles Adopted by the Commission and the Legislature," *supra* text at notes 30–37 and 78–85.

105. "Principles Adopted by the Board of Commissioners to Quiet Land Titles in Their Adjudication of Claims Presented to Them," Act of October 26, 1846, *Revised Laws of Hawai'i,* 2124, 2126 (1925).

106. 12 *Privy Council Records* (December 14, 1847), 272, 274 (May 17, 1847–August 26, 1848).

107. 1 Kuykendall, *supra* note 1, at 291, quoting from a letter written by Wyllie to Judd, November 19, 1849, in *Report of Secretary of War,* 1855, appendix, 7–8.

1877 opinion of the Hawai‘i Supreme Court also summarized the decisions made during the early phase of the Mahele as establishing "that the King should allow the landlord (2d class) one-third; the tenants (3d class) one-third; and retain himself (1st class) one third." [108] When he was President of the Republic of Hawaii, Sanford Ballard Dole confirmed that the "terms of division of the lands of the kingdom were arranged, after much deliberation" in 1848 to the effect that "To the king a third, to the chiefs a third, and to the people a third." [109] And the Hawai‘i Supreme Court later summarized the governing principles adopted by the Mō‘ī and the Privy Council by saying that after the King retained his private lands as individual property, "of the remaining lands, one-third was to be set aside for the Government, one-third to the chiefs and konohiki, and one-third for the tenants." [110] But the "poor natives" never received anything near the one-third or one-fourth they were promised,[111] and they were the clear losers in the division.[112]

After the Ali‘i had received their Mahele awards, many maka‘āinana were unable to maintain legal possession of the lands that they and their families had traditionally occupied. The Ali‘i were selling off the lands they had been awarded, by choice or by force in order to pay debts, and many of the individuals who replaced the Konohiki were unwilling to permit the maka‘āinana to remain on the ‘Āina. Because the Ali‘i were responsible for managing the ‘Āina for the benefit of the native tenants, their loss of title effectively disenfranchised the maka‘āinana, leaving them homeless and unable to live self-sufficiently.[113] The maka‘āinana were confused and did not know

---

108. *Harris v. Carter,* 6 Hawai‘i 195, 1877 WL 7591, at *2 (1877). It was clear to all concerned that the maka‘āinana had to receive some land, because that would be the only way to eliminate, or at least reduce, their claims to use the lands in their Ahupua‘a. In an 1851 decision, for instance, the Hawai‘i Supreme Court ruled that the Mō‘ī could not convey a title to land greater than the title he held, and that if he purported to convey land without reserving the claims of native tenants, the grantee nonetheless could not dispossess the native tenants. *Kekiekie v. Dennis,* 1 Hawai‘i 69 (1851); see Chinen, *Original Land Titles, supra* note 88, at 16 n. 7.

109. Sanford B. Dole, "Hawaiian Public Lands," in *Government for the Territory of Hawaii,* House Comm. on Territories, Rpt. No. 305, 56th Cong., 1st Sess., Appendix I, at 105 (1900).

110. *State v. Zimring,* 58 Hawai‘i 106, 112, 566 P.2d 725, 730 (1977), citing *Privy Council Records,* vol. 2, 250–308.

111. Kuykendall has written that it is "wholly erroneous" to think that it was ever intended that the maka‘āinana would receive one-third of the land (1 Kuykendall, *supra* note 1, at 282), but he never fully explains the disconnect between the language used in the "Principles" and related early statements and the outcome of the division which left the maka‘āinana with less than 1 percent of the land. Stauffer has written that "the conventional wisdom is that this early statement of principles granting a third of the lands to the people was little more than propaganda to convince the *Maka‘āinana* to go along," asserting also that the value of the lands awarded to the maka‘āinana was roughly similar to that awarded to the Mō‘ī and to the Ali‘i. Stauffer, *supra* note 44, at 12, 226.

112. "Even pro-Western historians now concede that the Mahele's long-term effects were disastrous for the Hawaiian people." Jocelyn Linnekin, *Sacred Queens and Women of Consequences,* 7 (1990).

113. The Legislature passed a joint resolution on November 7, 1846, empowering the Minister of the Interior to confer allodial title to maka‘āinana upon receipt of a written petition and a determination regarding the terms of sale: "Rights of Hoa‘āinas and Konohikis; Sales to Same: Joint Resolution on the Subject of Rights in Land and the Leasing, Purchasing, and Dividing of the Same," 2 *Revised Laws of Hawai‘i,* 2193–95 (1847). But because of the Minister's inability to sever the undivided interests of the Hawaiian claimant (similar to the dilemma faced by the Land Commission before the Mahele of 1848), little was actually accomplished by this 1846 resolution. Levy, *supra* note 85, at 855 n. 46. The rights of the maka‘āinana therefore remained contingent on those of their respective Ali‘i.

what they needed to do to obtain their land. Many were unaware that they needed to do anything, because they had always had access to whatever lands they needed. Many preferred continuing with the old system, whereby they had access to all the lands of the Ahupua'a, for pasturing, fishing, and gathering, in exchange for providing some labor to the Konohiki.[114] On October 19, 1849, the Privy Council met to discuss the shortcomings of the Mahele and the problems faced by the maka'āinana,[115] and two months later the Council adopted four resolutions designed to secure title for maka'āinana to any 'Āina they had "occup[ied] and improve[d]."[116]

In accordance with the statute formally called the "Enactment of Further Principles," which is usually called the Kuleana Act of 1850, maka'āinana were encouraged to file claims with the Land Commission for 'Āina, but only for the acreage that they were currently cultivating, plus an additional quarter of an acre for a house lot.[117] The process of application was burdensome, and although no commutation fee was required, a claim could be filed only after the claimant arranged and paid for a survey, and after two witnesses had validated the petition.[118] Before confirming the bill on August 6, 1850, the Legislature also provided the maka'āinana with rights of access, gathering, and resource use in other areas of the Ahupua'a.[119]

For numerous reasons, fewer Kuleana Awards were granted than expected.[120] The factors frequently mentioned for the low number of land awards include the unfamiliarity of the maka'āinana with the concept of private property,[121] the failure to educate them about the changes and the steps they needed to take to claim property,[122] the difficulty in filing and proving claims (which required a survey for a fee that many did not have), the short period of time allowed to file and prove

---

114. 1 Kuykendall, *supra* note 1, at 289.

115. *Id.* at 290–91.

116. "An Act Confirming Certain Resolutions of the King and Privy Council, Passed on the 21st Day of December, A. D. 1849, Granting to the Common People Allodial Titles for Their Own Lands and House Lots, and Certain Other Privileges (The Kuleana Act), Enactment of Further Principles," August 6, 1850, L. 1850, at 202, in 2 *Revised Laws of Hawai'i*, 2141–42 (1925), reprinted in Chinen, *They Cried, supra* note 25, at 182–84.

117. 2 *Revised Laws of Hawai'i*, 2141–42. The requirement that land be "really cultivated" in Section 6 of the Kuleana Act limited the amount of farmland an individual could apply for, because cropland that was normally cultivated but currently in rotation and without a crop did not meet the standard. *See infra* note 127.

118. Unlike house lots located elsewhere in the Islands, a commutation fee of one-fourth the unimproved value of the parcel at the date of the award was required to be paid by the maka'āinana for house lots in Honolulu, Lahaina, and Hilo. *Id.* at 2141. The commutation fee for other parcels (either farmland or house lots not located in Honolulu, Lahaina, and Hilo) was waived for the maka'āinana and instead applied against the Konohiki of the Ahupua'a or 'Ili to which the 'Āina belonged. Chinen, *Great Mahele, supra* note 6, at 30.

119. 2 *Revised Laws of Hawai'i*, 2142 (1925).

120. Compare the accommodations given to the Ali'i to perfect their claims, described *infra* in note 123, with the strict rules applied to the maka'āinana.

121. *See, e.g.,* Kame'eleihiwa, *supra* note 11, at 297–98, explaining that Hawaiians "could not fully comprehend a system wherein profit—that is the denial of one's surplus for another's use—was more important than unstinting generosity"; 1 Kuykendall, *supra* note 1, at 293 n. 97a, noting criticism of the commissioners for not going "in the field to investigate who were in fact the *occupiers of kuleanas*, not claimants. . . . This mistaken policy resulted in many natives not submitting claims, because of lack of knowledge as to how to proceed."

122. Chinen, *They Cried, supra* note 25, at 74.

claims,[123] which was particularly burdensome on the natives living in the country,[124] the inconsistencies and expense of surveyors, fraud, conflicts of interest,[125] favoritism, delays in processing claims, and the interference of some Ali'i who sought to discourage such claims.[126] The erratic nature of the surveying has been commented upon by numerous authors. Writing in 1875, C. J. Lyons (a surveyor himself) wrote that the Kingdom did not contain "a single thoroughly competent land surveyor on the ground," that the Land Commission established no uniform rules and did not require that a single surveyor be utilized for each district to promote uniformity, and therefore that "we have every possible method of measurement adopted, every conceivable scale employed, meridians pointing everywhere; no making of corners; in

---

123. The initial time for proving claims was extended, but in 1853, in "An Act Relating to the Board of Commissioners to Quiet Land Titles," May 26, 1853, L. 1853, at 26, in 2 *Revised Laws of Hawai'i*, 2145 (1925), the Legislature barred all claims by maka'ainana for Kuleanas not filed by May 1, 1854.

Many Ali'i were also late in filing their claims, but "several acts were subsequently passed, one as late as 1892, for the relief of such konohikis, enabling them or their heirs to obtain titles for the lands assigned to them in the Mahele Book." 1 Kuykendall, *supra* note 1, at 288. *See, e.g.,* "An Act for the Relief of Certain Konohikis," August 10, 1854, Laws, 1854, at 25, in 2 *Revised Laws of Hawai'i*, 2147 (1925), granting an extension until November 1854; "An Act for the Relief of Certain Konohikis, Whose Names Appear in the Division of Lands from Kamehameha III," August 24, 1860, Laws, 1860, at 127, *in* 2 *Revised Laws of Hawai'i*, 2148 (1925), granting an extension until June 30, 1862; "An Act Authorizing the Minister of Interior to Issue Royal Patents (Grants) for Certain Lands Named in the Mahele of 1848, Which May Have Reverted to the Government Under the Act of August 24th, 1860, and Not Disposed of by the Government in the Meantime," December 16, 1892, Laws, 1892, at 68, in 2 *Revised Laws of Hawai'i*, 2151, granting an extension until January 1, 1895; Chinen, *Original Land Titles, supra* note 88, at 24 and 37, discussing the act of Aug. 28, 1860, which granted Konohiki until June 30, 1862, to present their claims for land awards by paying commutation, which allowed another 60 Royal Patent Grants to be issued. *See also* Chinen, *They Cried, supra* note 25, at 41 and 65, explaining also that some Ali'i failed to pay the required commutation fee—usually one-third of the value of the lands—and that a law had to be enacted in 1909—*Laws of Hawai'i*, 1909, Ch. 90, sec. 1—to enforce such payments.

124. Kamakau wrote that "This law would have been better had the time for registering titles been extended for twenty years. Very few of the people living in the country were educated and knew how to apply for their titles." Kamakau, *supra* note 10, at 407; *see also* Chinen, *They Cried, supra* note 25, at 80.

125. Chinen has reported, for instance, that "[t]here was definitely a conflict of interest on the part of [William L.] Lee," who had "secretly purchased some [Kuleana] claims, without informing the other members of the Land Commission. . . . As Chief Justice of the Supreme Court and President of the Land Commission, he knew or should have known that it was improper for him to purchase claims of the *hoa'āina*. He was supposed to be neutral at all times, and not to have personal interest in the cases." Chinen, *They Cried, supra* note 25, at 130–31. Commissioner Joseph Kekaulahao "also purchased land from a claimant." *Id.* at 131.

126. Kamakau, who was himself a member of the Land Commission between 1848 and 1850, discussed this problem several times; *see, e.g.,* Kamakau, *supra* note 10, at 403: "some commoners . . . lost their land through ignorance, favoritism, or interference by chiefs and land agents"); *id.* at 407: "Others wanted to remain on the lands under their chiefs, and when the trading days came, and the chiefs leased their lands to the foreigners [and these people were obliged to leave them], they learned their mistake and were left to wander in tears on the highway"; *id.* at 410: "The trouble was that some neglected to take out the papers of appeal, others refused to do so and continued to live under their landlord *(konohiki),* and some just let their land go and are regretting their stupidity today"); *see also* John H. Wise, "The History of Land Ownership in Hawaii," in *Ancient Hawaiian Civilizations,* 88 (Lectures delivered at the Kamehameha Schools in the 1930s, Frank Midkiff, ed., rev. ed., 1965): "In some cases, they were intimidated by the local konohikis who discouraged them from putting in claims. In other cases, they were unwilling to seem to be taking land away from their alii"; Osorio, *supra* note 24, at 55, explaining that the Mahele had converted Ali'i and maka'ainana into "competitors rather than . . . caretakers of the 'Āina"; McGregor, "Cultural and Political History," *supra* note 8, at 352: "Many of the Maka'ainana were intimidated by the chiefs not to make land claims against them"; Kame'eleihiwa, *supra* note 11, at 297–98; Chinen, *They Cried, supra* note 25, at 72–127, 141–44.

short, everything left to the sweet will of the man who was hired at from two to three dollars per kuleana to do the measurement."[127]

A total of 14,195 claims were filed and about 8,421 awards were approved to about 29 percent of the 29,220 adult Native Hawaiian males living in the Islands at the time of the Mahele,[128] averaging 3 acres each.[129] Only about 3 percent of the claimants received awards of more than 10 acres of land.[130] Thus, out of the 1,523,000 acres given to the Government by Kauikeaouli for his people, only 28,658 acres, or less than 1 percent of Hawai'i's land area, was awarded to the maka'āinana.[131] Commissioner James Blount later wrote that the Mahele had left "the people . . . with an insignificant interest in lands" and that "[t]he story of this division is discreditable to King, chiefs, and white residents."[132] "All of the land granted to the maka'āinana could have fit into the island of Kaho'olawe, which has 28,800 acres."[133] Prince Kūhiō later compared the 28,658 acres distributed to all the maka'āinana to the 41,000 acres that went to thirty-three missionary families.[134]

The small size of the Kuleana Awards—averaging 2.57 acres each[135]—may have been even more significant in preventing the maka'āinana from maintaining an independent subsistence life than the small number of awards given to them. An area of 3 acres is not "sufficiently large to adequately provide a decent livelihood,"[136]

127. C. J. Lyons, "Land Matters in Hawaii, No. 7," *The Islander,* August 13, 1875, at 151. *See also* C. J. Lyons, "Land Matters in Hawaii, No. 6," *The Islander,* August 6, 1875, at 143, explaining that some surveyors included only the land actually under cultivation, but others included fallow lands or upland regions, and noting that many of the surveyors did not understand the Hawaiian language or customs and used crude and inadequate instruments; Wise, *supra* note 126, at 88–89 (same); *see generally* Chinen, *They Cried, supra* note 25, at 114–27, providing details on surveying practices; C. J. Lyons, "Land Matters in Hawaii, No. 5," *The Islander,* July 30, 1875, at 135, explaining that "the poor natives" had a hard time collecting the fees needed for surveying and Land Commission approval.

128. Kame'eleihiwa, *supra* note 11, at 295, citing Marion Kelly, "Results of the Great Mahele of 1848 and the Kuleana Act of 1850," unpublished manuscript. No explanation is available for the petitions that were denied, since the Land Commission did not keep minutes of its meetings. Quite a few petitions were withdrawn, frequently because of encouragement or coercion from the Ali'i. *Id.* at 296; Chinen, *They Cried, supra* note 25, at 75 ("many *konohiki* were able to persuade their tenants not to file their claims, or if filed, to withdraw such claims"); *id.* at 85–96, giving examples.

129. Kame'eleihiwa, *supra* note 11, at 297; Linnekin, *Sacred Queens, supra* note 112, at 204, reporting also that the median award was 1.54 acres.

130. Linnekin, *Sacred Queens, supra* note 112, at 204.

131. Kame'eleihiwa, *supra* note 11, at 295. The Kuleana Awards were not distributed equally around the Islands. Citing the 1896 *Thrum's (Hawaiian) Annual,* Chinen has reported the following distribution: Hawai'i, 9,412.87 acres; Maui, 7,379.74 acres; O'ahu, 7,311.17 acres; Moloka'i, 2,288.87 acres; Kaua'i, 1,824.17 acres; Lana'i, 441.97 acres. Chinen, *They Cried, supra* note 25, at 141–42. These same figures appear in a report by Surveyor-General W. D. Alexander in "Report of Commissioner to the Hawaiian Islands," in 27 *Executive Documents of the House of Representatives for the Second Session of the Fifty-Third Congress, 1893–94,* 640 (1895), originally in Executive Document No. 47, 53rd Cong., 2d Sess. (1893) (hereafter cited as "Blount Report"). The low number on Kaua'i and the absence of any awards on Ni'ihau are surprising.

132. Letter from Commissioner James Blount to U.S. Secretary of State W. C. Gresham, July 17, 1893, in "Blount Report," *supra* note 131, at 106.

133. McGregor, "Cultural and Political History," *supra* note 8, at 351.

134. Kalaniana'ole, *supra* note 9, at 130.

135. Dole, "Hawaiian Public Lands," *supra* note 109, at 105.

136. Chinen, *They Cried, supra* note 25, at 32.

and "in many cases," the "poor people" abandoned "their newly acquired property as utterly insufficient for their needs."[137] The leader in limiting the Kuleana Awards to modest acreage apparently was George M. Robertson, who was appointed to the Land Commission in 1850 and who later wrote the key 1864 Hawai'i Supreme Court opinion defining the status of the Crown Lands.[138] In the September 1850 hearings over the maka'āinana claims for land in Kahana Valley, O'ahu, Robertson denied the claims for "most of the uncultivated *kula* (dry-land agricultural lots)."[139] In July 1851, he wrote to fellow commissioner J. H. Smith (who also served as secretary to the Commission) that he thought the Kuleanas being awarded were too large.[140] When Commissioner Kamakau, who had rejoined the House of Representatives in 1851, presented a petition to the House later that year complaining that "the land awarded the people were too small," Commissioner Robertson, who also had been elected to the House in 1851, succeeded in having the matter tabled.[141]

Section 7 of the 1850 Kuleana Act offered some rights to the Kuleana claimants, allowing them "to take firewood, house timber, aho cord, thatch, or ti leaf" from adjacent lands in their Ahupua'a and guaranteeing them the "right to drinking water, and running water, and the right of way."[142] This provision was added at the urging of the Mō'ī, who was concerned that a "little bit of land even with allodial title, if they [the people] be cut off from all other privileges would be of very little value."[143] These rights were not insignificant, but this listing excluded important rights that had previously belonged to the maka'āinana, such as pasturage, fishing in adjacent coastal areas, and the tending of lo'i (wetland taro patches) in unoccupied lands.[144] The act originally required the maka'āinana to obtain permission from their Konohiki before exercising these rights, but that requirement was eliminated in 1851.[145]

---

137. Lyons, "No. 6," *supra* note 127, at 143; *see* Stauffer, *supra* note 44, at 32, explaining that an award of 2 or 3 acres would have been "an adequate size in a wet-land area but inadequate to support a family on dry land" and at 21, explaining that the thirty-four awards in Kahana Valley on O'ahu "averaged nine taro *lo'i* (gardens) of about two-tenths of an acre each . . . capable of feeding about thirty people per award, suggesting a more than adequate award to each household."

138. *In the Matter of the Estate of His Majesty Kamehameha IV*, 2 Hawai'i 715 (1864).

139. Stauffer, *supra* note 44, at 33.

140. Chinen, *They Cried*, *supra* note 25, at 32 and 126, quoting from a letter written July 23, 1851, in which Robertson told Smith, "I would advise you not to issue the awards without giving due notice, as many of the *kuleanas* appear to me to be too large. If they are not contested by the *konohikis* all [will] be right, but they may be disputed." *Interior Dept. Land Letters (Incoming)* (1851–1852, Box 8, Archives of Hawai'i).

141. *Id.* at 32, quoting from *Journal of the House of Representatives 1851–1853*, Series 221–7).

142. Kuleana Act, *supra* note 116, § 7, *in* 2 Revised Laws of Hawai'i, 2,142 (1925); this language is now found in Section 7-1 of the *Hawai'i Revised Statutes.*

143. *Kalipi v. Hawaiian Trust Co., Ltd.*, 66 Hawai'i 1, 7, 656 P.2d 745, 749 (1982), citing *Privy Council Minutes*, July 13, 1850.

144. Chinen, *They Cried*, *supra* note 25, at 70; Osorio, *supra* note 24, at 54; *see also id.* at 78, reporting that "in 1852 over a hundred subjects in Ko'olauloa, O'ahu, petitioned the legislature complaining that the konohiki were charging up to $10 (up from $1.50 the year before) for the people to use the kula for grazing"; *Oni v. Meek*, 2 Hawai'i 87 (1858) (grazing); *Haalelea v. Montgomery*, 2 Hawai'i 62 (1858) (fishing).

145. McGregor, "Hoa'āina," *supra* note 85, at 11. In 1858, the Hawai'i Supreme Court ruled that the rights of native tenants, both under ancient custom and prior legislation, were abrogated and superseded by the listing in Section 7 of the Kuleana Act. *Oni v. Meek*, 2 Hawai'i 87 (1858). But in recent years, a more flexible and

The Maka'āinana Retained a Beneficial Interest in the 'Āina

Because the distribution of lands and rights in the Mahele clearly shortchanged the maka'āinana ("a one-third interest of the common people had been recognized, but ignored in the division"),[146] they always believed that their claims continued and would be addressed in the future. This belief logically flowed from the trust relationship that had historically existed between Ali'i and maka'āinana in relation to 'Āina. As Prince Kūhiō later explained, "The common people, being left out in the division after being recognized as owners of a third interest in the kingdom, believing that new methods had to be adopted to place them in possession, assumed that these lands were being held in trust by the crown for their benefit."[147] This view, in part, supported the action of Congress to establish the Hawaiian Home Lands Program,[148] and it continues today to support the view that the emerging Native Hawaiian Nation is entitled to the Crown Lands.[149]

Allowing Foreigners to Own Land

The other monumental change that occurred during this period was the adoption of the Alien Land Ownership Act of July 10, 1850 (enacted before the Kuleana Act of August 6, 1850) granting foreigners the right to own land.[150] This issue had been one of great concern to both natives and foreigners. During the 1840s, Dr. Geritt P. Judd had strenuously opposed allowing foreigners to have the unrestricted right to obtain land, but while he was away on a one-year trip to Europe with the future Kings

---

dynamic approach toward recognizing customary rights has emerged, as exemplified by Article XII, Section 7 of the Hawai'i Constitution, added in 1978, which reads as follows: "The State reaffirms and shall protect all rights, customarily and traditionally exercised for subsistence, cultural and religious purposes and possessed by ahupua'a tenants who are descendants of native Hawaiians who inhabited the Hawaiian Islands prior to 1778, subject to the right of the State to regulate such rights." The committee report explained that this provision was designed "to remove the limit on what could be gathered to the five listed items—firewood, house-timber, aho cord, thatch, and ki leaf." McGregor, "Hoa'āina," *supra* note 85, at 12, citing 1 *Proceedings of the Constitutional Convention of Hawaii of 1978*, 638–40 and 2 *Id.* at 433–37. In *Kalipi v. Hawaiian Trust Co., Ltd.,* 66 Hawai'i 1, 10, 656 P.2d 745, 751 (1982), the Court distinguished Oni by explaining that the grazing of horses involved in that case had not been a traditional and customary right, because precontact Hawai'i had no herd animals, and said that Section 1-1 of the *Hawai'i Revised Statutes* (which refers to "Hawaiian usage" as a source of law in Hawai'i) protected Native Hawaiian customs and rights not specifically enumerated in the Kuleana Act "for so long as no actual harm is done thereby." *See generally* Paul Lucas, "Gathering Rights," in *Native Hawaiian Rights Handbook,* 223–28 (Melody Kapilialoha MacKenzie, ed., 1991). In *Pele Defense Fund v. Paty,* 73 Hawai'i 578, 620, 837 P.2d 1246, 1272 (1992), the Court ruled that Native Hawaiians rights "may extend beyond the ahupua'a in which a native Hawaiian resides where such rights have been customarily and traditionally exercised in this manner." In *Public Access Shoreline Hawaii v. Hawaii County Planning Commission,* 79 Hawai'i 246, 253, 903 P.2d 1313, 1320 (1995), the Court confirmed that all government agencies have an obligation to protect the customary and traditional rights of Native Hawaiians.

146. Kalaniana'ole, *supra* note 9, at 129.

147. *Id.* at 126.

148. *See infra* chapter 22.

149. *See infra* chapter 29.

150. "An Act to Abolish the Disabilities of Aliens," July 10, 1850, 2 *Revised Laws of Hawai'i,* 2233–34 (1925); 1 Kuykendall, *supra* note 1, at 294–98; Chinen, *Great Mahele, supra* note 6, at 12; Chinen, *They Cried, supra* note 25, at 129–30, 135–40; *see generally* Kame'eleihiwa, *supra* note 11, at 298–301.

Kamehameha IV and V in 1849–50, Judge William L. Lee persuaded the Privy Council and the Legislature to enact the law granting such rights to foreigners.[151] These settlers then directly competed with the makaʻāinana for ʻĀina, and their greater familiarity with allodial title and their access to capital gave them a significant advantage. Kamakau criticized the decision to allow foreigners to buy land in the following vivid language:

> It would have been better moreover if, when the law made the sale of government lands available, these could have been sold so reasonably, to the descendants of Kamehameha alone, that his toil and blood might not have been spent in vain. His children do not get the milk; his adopted children have grasped the nipples and sucked the breasts dry.[152]

Section 4 of the 1850 Kuleana Act mandated that segments of the Government Land on each Mokupuni be available for Native Hawaiians who did not file, or did not otherwise qualify, for Kuleana Awards to purchase lots in fee simple (from 1 to 50 acres), "at a minimum price of fifty cents per acre."[153] By May 1, 1850, the Government had sold about 2,700 parcels of government land on all of the islands of land under this program.[154] Most of the individual purchasers were Hawaiians, but foreigners acquired almost two-thirds of the total land area.[155]

A Contemporary Look at the Lands Awarded in the Mahele

Despite the attempts of the Privy Council and Land Commission to fulfill Kauikeaouli's objective of ensuring Native Hawaiian control over the lands of Hawaiʻi, both the Mahele in 1848 and the Kuleana Act of 1850 failed to accomplish this goal. Not only was a mere fraction of the ʻĀina intended for the makaʻāinana actually awarded to them, but also many of the lands that were distributed to both Aliʻi and makaʻāinana did not remain in the hands of Native Hawaiians for long.

What is the significance of this history for our present understanding of the legal status of the Crown Lands? Although many hoped that the institution of private

---

151. *See generally* Chinen, *They Cried, supra* note 25, at 68–69; Kameʻeleihiwa, *supra* note 11, at 299; 1 Kuykendall, *supra* note 1, at 298, expressing the view that "[a]lthough Dr. Judd in 1848 had earlier opposed the policy embodied in this act, there are grounds for believing that in 1849 and 1850 he would have been willing to yield the point if a suitable *quid pro quo,* such as a guarantee of Hawaiian independence, could have been obtained from the United States." As explained above, *supra* text at note 66, Judge Lee, then both Chief Justice and President of the Land Commission, had in 1849 persuaded Kauikeaouli to sell him the Lihuʻe Plantation on Kauaʻi, containing thousands of acres of choice lands, for $9,350, which Lee used to grow sugar. Chinen, *They Cried, supra* note 25, at 138.

152. Kamakau, *supra* note 10, at 407.

153. The Kuleana Act, *supra* note 116, § 4 *in* 2 *Revised Laws of Hawaiʻi,* 2142 (1925). *See generally* Chinen, *They Cried, supra* note 25, at 132–34.

154. Kelly, *supra* note 85, at 67. Section 4 of the 1850 Kuleana Act, *supra* note 116, and Part I, Chapter 7, Art. II, Secs. I–IX of "Disposition of Government Lands: An Act to Organize the Executive Departments of the Hawaiian Islands," 2 *Revised Laws of Hawaiʻi,* 2190–91 (1925).

155. Kelly, *supra* note 85, at 67.

property would facilitate the maintenance of a self-sufficient society while safeguarding the 'Āina of the Native Hawaiians from foreign possession, did the division actually provide protection for the people? Did it provide stability for commerce? Did it protect the Kingdom's sovereignty from foreign encroachment?

Kauikeaouli selected the Crown Lands in accordance with William Little Lee's opinion (which had been accepted by the Privy Council) that the Constitution and Principles adopted by the Land Commission confirmed that the Mō'ī should "retain his private lands as his individual property."[156] The instrument describing the lands he had chosen says that "I hereby retain (or reserve) *for myself and for my heirs and successors forever,* my lands inscribed at pages 178, 182, 184, 186, 190, 194, 200, 204, 206, 210, 212, 214, 216, 218, 220, 222, of this book, *these lands are set apart for me and for my heirs and successors forever, as my own property exclusively.*"[157] The Legislature likewise acknowledged that the lands retained by the Mō'ī were his personal property, noting that he "reserv[ed] certain lands to himself as his own private property."[158] Writing in 1875, C. J. Lyons confirmed that "[t]he Crown Lands were set aside for the private emolument of the king."[159]

Kauikeaouli took direct control of these lands by leasing, selling, and mortgaging various parcels through his land agent. His belief that he controlled these lands is confirmed in his will, which bequeathed the Crown Lands and all other remaining properties to his adopted son Alexander Liholiho.[160] Although the Mō'ī also named Liholiho to be his successor to the throne, he did so in a separate provision of his will.[161] This mandate, when combined with the fact that alternate heirs were provided for the throne but not for the lands, appears to establish Kauikeaouli's intent to retain these lands for his heirs and devisees.

Despite Kauikeaouli's actions and beliefs (which appear to have been supported by the Legislature and Attorney General at that time), within a few years the Supreme Court of Hawai'i ruled that the Crown Lands were not the private property of the Mō'ī and could not be conveyed by will to a designated heir; instead, they belonged to the Crown and must be passed on to the succeeding monarch.[162] Shortly after this 1864 decision, the Legislature passed an act making the Crown Lands inalienable and restricting the Mō'ī to the use—rather than full ownership—of these lands.[163] But did

---

156. 3A *Privy Council Records,* Series 421, at 47–56. *See supra* note 83 and accompanying text.

157. This instrument, written in Hawaiian, was signed and sealed on March 8, 1848, and was translated in the language given in the text in the case of *In the Matter of the Estate of His Majesty Kamehameha IV,* 2 Hawai'i 715, 723 (1864) (emphasis added).

158. "Act Relating to the Lands of His Majesty the King and of the Government," June 7, 1848, 2 *Revised Laws of Hawai'i,* 2152 (1925).

159. C. J. Lyons, "Land Matters in Hawaii, No. 8," *The Islander,* August 20, 1875, at 159, adding by way of contrast that "The Government Lands were for the benefit of the whole—for the parties as a whole, that divided the land."

160. "Will of His Majesty Kamehameha III," sec. 5, First Circuit Probate No. 2410 (1855).

161. *Id.* at sec. 1.

162. *In the Matter of the Estate of His Majesty Kamehameha IV,* 2 Hawai'i 715 (1864). *See infra* chapter 8 for a discussion of this case.

Kauikeaouli intend that the Crown Lands be treated in the same fashion as the lands he ceded to the Government? Or did he consider them to be his private property, while acknowledging the interests of the maka'āinana already residing on them?

When the 'Āina that Kauikeaouli reserved for himself are compared to the 'Āina awarded to the nine other Ali'i Nui in the *Buke Mahele*,[164] only Kauikeaouli's came to be viewed as lands that were not private property. The Government, both at the time of the Mahele and subsequently, respected all other Ali'i awards as creating a private fee simple title in the awardee. In fact, the ten Land Commission Awards to six of the Ali'i Nui in the Mahele were later consolidated through their wills into the Estate of Princess Bernice Pauahi Bishop, who decreed in her will that these 'Āina should be used to support the Kamehameha Schools.[165]

Ke Ali'i Bernice Pauahi Bishop was the daughter of Laura Konia and Abner Pākī and therefore received some property from both of her parents.[166] As is explained in more detail in chapter 25, Ke Ali'i Pauahi received the bulk of her 'Āina from her cousin Ruth Ke'elikolani,[167] who was also an Ali'i Nui and had retained twelve 'Āina in the Mahele.[168] Ruth had inherited 'Āina from her first husband Lelei'ohoku, her father Mataio Kekūanaō'a, her uncle Namau'u, her half brothers Moses Kekuaiwa and Lot Kapuāiwa, and her half sister Victoria Kamāmalu.[169] Ruth left these lands to Pauahi, who bequeathed them to the charitable trust created in her will. William Charles Lunalilo also set aside the 'Āina remaining from his Mahele award in trust for the care of elderly Hawaiians.[170]

If each of these awards was regarded as the personal private property of the respective Ali'i and apportioned according to the owner's wishes, why was Kauikeaouli's award treated differently? Should the Crown Lands have descended to Alexander Liholiho's heirs, rather than to his older brother Lot who succeeded him to become Kamehameha V? Was it appropriate for the Government to take possession of the Crown Lands in 1864–65 via the Supreme Court and the Legislature? If so, should the Government have taken control of the 'Āina of the other nine Ali'i Nui as well? What about the lands of the two dozen Kaukau Ali'i and of the more than 200 Konohiki?

The Crown Lands—originally 984,000 acres—are now seen by many as the core of the land base for the forthcoming Native Hawaiian Nation. Should the lands of the other Ali'i now held by private trusts also be part of this land base?

---

163. "An Act to Relieve the Royal Domain from Encumbrances, and to Render the Same Inalienable," January 3, 1865, 1 *Session Laws of Hawai'i*, 69 (1851–70). *See infra* chapter 9 for a discussion of this enactment.

164. For a listing of the nine other Ali'i Nui, see Kame'eleihiwa, *supra* note 11, at 228 n. 99.

165. *See infra* chapter 25 for a discussion of the Kamehameha Schools.

166. Kamehameha Schools Bernice Pauahi Bishop Estate, *The Land of KSBE* (1983).

167. *Id.*

168. Kame'eleihiwa, *supra* note 11, at 246.

169. *Id.* at 310. Ke Ali'i Ruth inherited the 'Āina of Victoria Kamamalu, Moses Kekuaiwa, and Namau'u via her father Mataio Kekūanaō'a (who had acquired the 'Āina upon the death of his brother and children).

170. *See infra* chapter 26 for a discussion of the Lunalilo Trust.

5

The Government Lands

The first division of the complex Mahele process was completed in March 1848.[1] Entries in the *Buke Mahele* revealed that more than 240 Ali'i had been granted life estates in approximately 1.5 million acres of land. Although still subject to the rights of native tenants, these lands of the Ali'i and Konohiki could be converted from life estates into freehold fee simple estates of inheritance by paying the Government a "commutation fee" determined by the Privy Council. In return for this fee, payable in money or lands, a Royal Patent would be issued to the landholder.[2]

Following this division with the Ali'i and Konohiki, Kauikeaouli (Kamehameha III) retained about 2.5 million acres, or 60 percent of the Kingdom's lands. He then "commuted" a portion of his lands to the Government to convert his life estate interests into fee simple estates of inheritance. The Mō'ī thus gave 1.5 million acres of his lands to the Government, which became the Government Lands, and he retained about 1 million acres, which became known as the King's Lands and later as the Crown Lands.

On March 8, 1848, the Mō'ī signed and sealed two instruments in the *Mahele Book* that served to give effect to the new land tenure system.[3] The first confirmed that a commutation had been made and that by this instrument Kauikeaouli retained, "for myself and for my heirs and successors forever," lands specifically enumerated and deemed to be the lands of the Mō'ī. The complete text of this first document is as follows:

> Know all men by these presents, that I, Kamehameha III, by the grace of God, King of these Hawaiian Islands, have given this day of my own free will and have made over and set apart forever to the chiefs and people the larger part of my

---

1. *See supra* chapter 4, text at notes 86–90.

2. See W. D. Alexander, "A Brief History of Land Titles in the Hawaiian Kingdom," in *Hawaiian Almanac and Annual,* 105, 116–17 (Thomas G. Thrum, compiler and publisher, 1891). Alexander says that 7,923 Royal Patents confirming Land Commission Awards were issued prior to April 1, 1890.

3. The two instruments were translated into English and included in *In the Matter of the Estate of His Majesty Kamehameha IV,* 2 Hawai'i 715, 723 (1864).

royal land, for the use and benefit of the Hawaiian Government, therefore by this instrument I hereby retain (or reserve) for myself and for my heirs and successors forever, my lands inscribed at pages 178, 182, 184, 186, 190, 194, 200, 204, 206, 210, 212, 214, 216, 218, 220, 222, of this book, *these lands are set apart for me and for my heirs and successors forever, as my own property exclusively.*[4]

The second instrument addressed the status of the Government Lands:[5]

Know all men by these presents, that I, Kamehameha III., by the grace of God, King of these Hawaiian Islands, do, hereby give, make over and set apart forever to the chiefs and people of my Kingdom, and convey all my right, title and interest in the lands situated here in the Hawaiian Islands, inscribed on pages 179 to 225 both inclusive, of this book, to have and to hold to my chiefs and people forever.

These lands are to be in the perpetual keeping of the Legislative Council (Nobles and Representatives) or in that of the superintendents of said lands, appointed by them from time to time, and shall be regulated, leased, or sold in accordance with the will of said Nobles and representatives, for the good of the Hawaiian Government, *and to promote the dignity of the Hawaiian Crown.*[6]

It is instructive to note that, even though these Government Lands were to be administered by the Legislative Council "for the good of the Hawaiian Government," the lands were also designed to be managed "to promote the dignity of the Hawaiian Crown."

Act of June 7, 1848

The Legislature ratified these initiatives of the Mō'ī with the Act of June 7, 1848, "An Act Relating to the Lands of his Majesty the King and of the Government."[7] This important statute can be summarized as follows:

1. The preamble recognized the actions of the Mō'ī in reserving certain lands as his private property, as well as in setting apart the Government Lands to be managed by the House of Nobles and Representatives, or their designees, to promote the prosperity of the Kingdom and the dignity of the Crown.
2. The act acknowledged this benevolent deed of the Mō'ī and affirmed that the "King's Lands,"—that is, the enumerated private lands of King Kamehameha III

4. *Id.* (emphasis added).
5. *Id.* at 723.
6. *Id.* (emphasis added).
7. "Crown, Government and Fort Lands, Enumerated, Etc: An Act Relating to the Lands of His Majesty the King and of the Government," June 7, 1848, L. 1848 at 22, in 2 *Revised Laws of Hawai'i*, 2152–76 (1925). This enactment is also discussed *supra* in chapter 4, text at notes 89–90. *See* appendix 2, *infra*, for the complete text of the act.

"to have and to hold to himself, his heirs, and successors, forever"—were to be "regulated and disposed of according to his royal will and pleasure, subject only to the rights of tenants."

3. The act affirmed the status of the enumerated lands set apart for the Chiefs and People and declared these to be the Government Lands, "subject always to the rights of the tenants."

4. The act empowered the Minister of Interior to manage and dispose of the Government Lands, as provided in the "Act to Organize the Executive Departments" (enacted on April 27, 1845); and with the approval of the King and Privy Council, the Minister of Interior was also empowered to dispose of Government Lands to Hawaiian subjects "for the promotion of agriculture, and the best interests of the Hawaiian Kingdom." This section made no specific mention of promoting the interests or protecting the dignity of "the Hawaiian Crown."[8]

5. Finally, the act set apart "Fort Lands" for the use of the Fort in Honolulu; these Fort Lands, to be "cultivated by soldiers and other tenants," were to be managed under the direction of the Minister of Interior, the Governor of O'ahu, and the native-born Ali'i of the Hawaiian Islands.[9]

The Government Lands

The approximately 1.5 million acres of Government Lands included (1) the lands specified in the Act of June 7, 1848, (2) lands relinquished by Ali'i in lieu of commutation fees, (3) lands purchased by the Government, and (4) all lands forfeited by claimants failing to present claims within the statutory period.[10] The lands were managed by the Minister of Interior, who had to dispose of some of the acreage because of the 1845 "Act to Organize the Executive Ministry"[11] and the need to support the cash-poor Kingdom's increasing number of Government offices.[12] Between 1848 and 1850, about 27,292 acres of Government Lands were sold.[13] By the end of 1857, a total of 182,014 acres had been sold,[14] and by 1873 more than 590,000 acres of the Govern-

---

8. "Disposition of Government Lands: An Act to Organize the Executive Departments of the Hawaiian Islands," April 27, 1845, L. 1846 at 99, part 1, ch. 1, art. II, §§ I–IX : in 2 *Revised Laws of Hawai'i,* 2190–91 (1925).

9. *Id.*

10. Alexander, *supra* note 2, at 118.

11. 1 Ralph S. Kuykendall, *The Hawaiian Kingdom 1778–1854: Foundation and Transformation,* 262–63 (1938, 7th printing, 1989). *See supra* chapter 4, text at notes 18–21 and 45.

12. Jean Hobbs, *Hawai'i: A Pageant of the Soil,* 53 (1935). As early as 1842, certain lands had been set aside to produce revenue for government purposes. *Id.* A Treasury Board comprised of Dr. Gerrit Judd, Timothy Ha'alilo, and John 'Ī'ī accepted taxes paid into the treasury, and by 1846 an accumulated national debt had been paid off as a result of successful management. *Id. See also* Alexander, *supra* note 2, at 118. Although Government property began to be set apart in 1842, the Government continued to have an undivided and undefined claim in all land in the Kingdom until the Mahele.

13. Hobbs, *supra* note 12, at 54, noting that this acreage was sold for $51,086.71, citing "Domestic Intelligence," *The Friend,* May 1, 1850, at 37.

14. Alexander, *supra* note 2, at 118.

ment Lands[15] had been sold, with Royal Patent Grants issued to purchasers.[16] These sales slowed somewhat in 1874, after a statute was enacted that required approval by the Mōʻī and Privy Council for any sale of land valued greater than $5,000.[17] In 1876, responding to concerns that lands were being conveyed to certain favored individuals and companies, a statute was passed requiring that sales of Government Lands take place by public auction after thirty days published notice.[18]

By April 1, 1890, a total of 3,475 "Grants" had been issued documenting Government Land sales.[19] This figure was taken from an index of all Grants issued prior to March 31, 1886, which was published in 1887.[20] Alexander stated that between 1850 and 1860, "nearly all the desirable Government land was sold, generally to natives."[21] Blackman stated similarly that "[b]y 1860 most of the desirable government land had been sold, chiefly to natives, or set apart for the purposes of education."[22] Levy has provided a different picture, reporting that as of 1864, 320,000 acres had been sold to 213 foreigners, as compared to 90,000 acres that were sold to 333 Native Hawaiians.[23] In 1865, the entire island of Niʻihau, containing more than 61,000 acres, was sold to a single foreigner.[24]

In any event, much of this land moved quickly into foreign hands. Blackman reported, for instance, that "[t]he common people were careless of their rights and interests, and easily parted with their holdings. The chiefs fell into habits of extravagance, contracted debts, and mortgaged their estates to the whites, or died without heirs and intestate; and thus their lands were alienated."[25] Because of these transfers, "[a]lready, in 1862, I find it reported that about three-quarters of all the real property on Oahu, except in the district of Waialua, was under the control of the 'foreign element,' and in Waialua about one-half."[26]

In the Act of June 7, 1848, fifty-two ʻIli in the districts of Honolulu, Kalihi, and Waikīkī were identified as the "Fort Lands"—that is, revenue-producing lands

15. Hobbs, *supra* note 12, at 54.

16. "Grants" were recorded in a separate series of volumes from the Royal Patents, which were issued to confirm Land Commission Awards at the Mahele. Alexander, *supra* note 2, at 118–19.

17. Hobbs, *supra* note 12, at 54, citing Act of July 13, 1874.

18. *Id.* at 54–55, citing Act of September 25, 1876.

19. Alexander, *supra* note 2, at 119.

20. *Id.*

21. *Id.*

22. William Fremont Blackman, *The Making of Hawaii: A Study in Social Evolution*, 160 (1906, reprinted 1977).

23. Neil M. Levy, "Native Hawaiian Land Rights," 63 *California Law Review* 848, 859 n.73 (1975), explaining that these figures had been compiled by the author from Commissioner of Public Lands of the Territory of Hawaii, *Indices of Awards* (1929).

24. *Id.*, citing Office of the Commissioner of Public Lands of the Territory of Hawaii, *Indices of Awards*, 10 (1929).

25. Blackman, *supra* note 22, at 160–61.

26. *Id.* at 161, citing 57 *Missionary Herald* 374. Cf. Levy, *supra* note 23, at 857: "By 1852, thousands of acres of prime Hawaiian land were in the hands of foreigners. More importantly, Western property concepts were imposed on the legal structure and would facilitate the rapid, steady takeover of Hawaiian-owned lands during the next several decades."

to support Fort Honolulu.[27] A July 11, 1851, act mandated that portions of Government Lands including these Fort Lands would be sold at auction.[28] The Kuleana Lands within the Fort Lands—whether or not they had been entered with the Land Commission—were excluded from this sale, as were 50 acres upon which the Royal Agricultural Society could continue its research.[29]

Another subdivision of the Government Lands was the School Lands, created pursuant to an act passed on July 9, 1850, stating that "One-twentieth part of all the lands then belonging to the Government should be set apart for the general purposes of Education."[30] Following the 1845 "Act to Organize Executive Departments," the Department of Schools was organized in 1846 and Reverend William Richards was appointed Minister of Public Instruction.[31] The July 9, 1850 act empowered the Minister of Public Instruction "to dispose . . . by sale, lease or otherwise" of the School Lands selected by the Privy Council.[32] By the end of 1881, 3,312 Royal Patent Grants had been issued to purchasers and the revenues received were applied toward the erection and maintenance of buildings and teachers' salaries.[33]

Although most Ali'i adhered to the traditional understanding of Mālama 'Āina, preferring leasing to sales,[34] substantial acreage from the inventory of Government Lands was sold to fund the Government in the new system and to provide lands for those with capital to spend. Sales of Government Land continued during the Provisional Government (1893–94), during the Republic (1894–98), when Government Lands were combined with Crown Lands to make up the Public Lands, in the Territorial period (1898–1959), when these lands were called the Ceded Lands, and after Statehood (1959), when the State of Hawai'i received the majority of the Ceded Lands as a trust.[35]

27. See Hobbs, *supra* note 12, at 55; Alexander, *supra* note 2, at 119; Jon J. Chinen, *Original Land Titles in Hawaii*, 20 (1971).

28. Hobbs, *supra* note 12, at 55.

29. *Id.* The Royal Hawaiian Agricultural Society was organized on August 13, 1850, and remained active through 1856. 1 Ralph S. Kuykendall, *The Hawaiian Kingdom 1778–1854: Foundation and Transformation,* 327 (1989). The purpose of the organization was to promote Hawai'i's agriculture by discussing and addressing problems in meetings and through publications. *Id.* at 328. Its membership included most of the influential foreigners plus a few Native Hawaiians. *Id.*

30. Chinen, *Original Land Titles, supra* note 27, at 33–35; Alexander, *supra* note 2, at 121, citing Act of July 9, 1850.

31. Hobbs, *supra* note 12, at 56.

32. "School Lands Set Apart: An Act to Provide for the Better Support and Greater Efficiency of the Public Schools," July 9, 1850, L. 1850 at 134, in 2 *Revised Laws of Hawai'i,* 2183–84 (1925).

33. Hobbs, *supra* note 12, at 58.

34. The 1864 Minister of Finance's report to the Legislature, prepared by C. De Varigny under Kamehameha V, states that "It is not the policy of our Sovereign nor of his Ministers to favor the sale of what Government lands are now left, but rather to lease them on advantageous terms to the lessees. This principle, however, is not, nor can it be absolute." *Report of the Minister of Finance,* September 15, 1864, at 8 (original on file in the State Archives).

35. *See infra* chapters 17, 18, 20, and 23.

6

The Transfer of Lands from Kauikeaouli to Alexander Liholiho (1854–55)

After the Mahele was complete, Kauikeaouli (Kamehameha III) managed ʻĀina that came to be called the "Crown Lands"—then called simply the "King's Lands"—as an individual would manage private property. Because the Mōʻī did not receive funding from the Government to support his office, Kauikeaouli relied heavily on the King's Lands to finance his royal responsibilities, and throughout his lifetime he leased, sold, and mortgaged portions of these ʻĀina to generate revenue.[1] As the Hawaiʻi Supreme Court later explained, "the crown lands were regarded [in the 1850s] as private lands for many purposes and were often spoken of as such."[2] After Kauikeaouli died on December 14, 1854, the Probate Court struggled with how Kauikeaouli's real and personal property should be dispersed and, in particular, how the King's Lands should be distributed.[3]

Kauikeaouli's estate was submitted to the Probate Court by his executors—Keoni Ana, Judge William Little Lee, Ioane Papa ʻĪʻī, and Mataio Kekūanaōʻa.[4] Kauikeaouli's will of April 2, 1853, consisted of six provisions.[5] First, his hānai (adopted) son Alexander Liholiho was named as heir and successor to the throne. Second, in the event that Liholiho was unable to succeed as monarch, Lot Kamehameha and Victoria Kamāmalu were named as alternates. After arranging for the repayment of any outstanding debts in section three, the fourth provision set aside ʻĀina for Queen

---

1. Lilikalā Kameʻeleihiwa, *Native Land and Foreign Desires: Pehea Lā E Pono Ai?* 310 (1992); *see also* Jean Hobbs, *Hawaii: A Pageant of the Soil,* 64 (1935), explaining that by the time Kauikeaouli died, "a considerable area of the heritage of the ruler had been dissipated."

2. *Kapiolani Estate v. Cleghorn,* 14 Hawaiʻi 330, 332 (1902).

3. *Will of His Majesty Kamehameha III,* First Circuit Probate No. 2410 (1855).

4. The executors of Kauikeaouli's estate were all closely associated with the Mōʻī and affiliated with the government in different capacities. Keoni Ana (John Young II) was the son of Kamehameha's advisor John Young and Kaʻoʻanaʻeha (an Aliʻi Nui of Hawaiʻi lineage) and was a close personal friend of the Mōʻī. He held numerous governmental positions including Minister of the Interior and was a member of the Privy Council. Judge Lee had been the Mōʻī's advisor on most legal matters. *See supra* chapter 4, text at notes 40–74. Respected scholar Ioane Papa ʻĪʻī served the government in a wide range of positions throughout his lifetime and was especially active in the Privy Council. Mataio Kekūanaōʻa was the Kiʻa ʻĀina (Governor) of Oʻahu and an outspoken member of the Privy Council (and was the father of both Kamehameha IV and V). Kameʻeleihiwa, *supra* note 1, at 124, 182, 266, 267, 271.

5. *Will of His Majesty Kamehameha III,* sec. 1, First Circuit Probate No. 2410 (1855).

Kamehameha III
(Kauikeaouli)

Kalama, in substitution of her dower rights. Fifth, all remaining properties, including the King's Lands, were bequeathed to Liholiho. The sixth provision named the executors of the estate and included instructions for filling vacancies.

In accordance with Kauikeaouli's wishes, Liholiho ascended the throne on December 15, 1854, and was proclaimed King Kamehameha IV by his father, Mataio Kekūanaō'a, the Kia 'Āina (governor) of O'ahu.[6] The rest of the will could not be fulfilled as easily, because Kamehameha III had accrued nearly $31,000 in personal debts.[7] Because the Mō'ī did not receive an income from the government but was responsible for the costs of running a Kingdom and maintaining the royal court, his bills mounted quickly. Section three of the will required payment of those bills before the remainder of the estate could be distributed.

After assessing the value of the late King's assets, the executors determined that his personal property was of "trifling value and wholly inadequate to pay the debts," but that his 'Āina could be sold for a profit.[8] After Probate Judge Lorrin Andrews validated the authenticity of the will and ruled that Kauikeaouli was mentally competent when he wrote it, the executors petitioned for permission to liquidate a portion of the King's Lands in order to settle his debts. [9]

---

6. 2 Ralph S. Kuykendall, *The Hawaiian Kingdom 1854–1874: Twenty Critical Years*, 33 (1953, reprinted 1982).

7. *Petition to Probate Judge Andrews from Executors of Kamehameha III's Estate*, March 9, 1855.

8. *Id.*

9. *Will of His Majesty Kamehameha III*, First Circuit Probate No. 2410 (1855), at "Petition from Executors." Judge Andrews had served as a judge of foreign causes, as judge in the court of original and appellate jurisdiction in Honolulu, and as justice of the Supreme Court before being assigned to the Probate Court.

Testimony by Executor William Little Lee on March 9, 1855, that Kauikeaouli's ʻĀina was "extensive" and capable of being sold at a profit and that interest on the debts was mounting convinced the Probate Court to issue an Order of Sale. On March 10, Judge Andrews empowered the executors to "sell, lease or mortgage, as in their discretion may seem best and for the greatest advantage of the estate."[10] Both the Probate Court and the executors of Kauikeaouli's estate allowed parcels of the King's Lands to be sold off in order to satisfy the Mōʻī's obligations. This action was based on the understanding that these lands were the personal possession of the Mōʻī, but they are also consistent with the view that the lands attached to the Crown, because the debts were incurred while the Mōʻī was fulfilling his royal responsibilities to care for his Kingdom (and because as Mōʻī he did not have what others would call a personal or private life). The King's Lands were kept separate and distinct from the Government Lands, and the two types of land were governed differently and served different purposes.

In his will, Kauikeaouli devised "the King's Lands," along with the remainder of his estate, to Alexander Liholiho. In a separate section of the will (and in an earlier public declaration),[11] the Mōʻī also bequeathed his Crown to Alexander Liholiho, who was his hānai son, with Lot Kamehameha and Victoria Kamāmalu as alternates. The Mōʻī's naming of alternate heirs for the throne—but not for the Crown Lands—appears to support the view that Kauikeaouli intended to retain the property for his devisees instead of for the Royal Family or heirs to the Crown,[12] although it is unclear that his intent was this precise since his first choice for the Crown and the lands was the same person—Alexander Liloliho—who was then a teenager in good health.

The fact that Alexander Liholiho did not receive any ʻĀina in the 1848 Mahele is also significant. Some scholars attribute this apparent omission to the fact that Alexander Liholiho was Kauikeaouli's heir to the King's Lands and thus would receive his share of the ʻĀina from his benefactor.[13] If Kauikeaouli intended for Liholiho to

---

Judge Andrews had no "special training" in the field of law and was actually a missionary educator who served as an instructor and principal at Lahainaluna High School on Maui. 1 Ralph S. Kuykendall, *The Hawaiian Kingdom 1778–1854: Foundation and Transformation,* 111, 243–44, 264 (1938, 7th printing 1989).

10. *Will of His Majesty Kamehameha III,* First Circuit Probate No. 2410 (1855), at "Order of Sale."

11. On April 7, 1853, in accordance with Article 25 of the 1852 Constitution, Kauikeaouli had officially proclaimed Alexander Liholiho to be his successor to the throne.

12. The Legislature also acknowledged Kauikeaouli's intention to retain the Crown Lands as his personal private property when it accepted the Mōʻī's grant of roughly 1.5 million acres of land to the Government on June 7, 1848. "Crown, Government and Fort Lands, Enumerated, Etc.," June 7, 1848, 2 *Revised Laws of Hawaiʻi,* 2152 (1925). The legislation itself was entitled "An Act Relating to the Lands of His Majesty the King and of the Government," thus recognizing a distinction between the Crown and Government Lands. The act then goes on to enumerate a list of the Crown Lands "[t]o be the private lands of His Majesty Kamehameha III, to have and to hold to himself, his heirs, and successors forever; and said lands shall be regulated and disposed of according to his royal will and pleasure subject only to the rights of the tenants." *Id.* at 2156. In accepting Government Lands, by contrast, the Legislature noted that the ʻĀina was "made over to the Chiefs and People, by our Sovereign Lord the King, and we do hereby declare those lands to be set apart as the lands of the Hawaiian Government, subject always to the rights of tenants." *Id.* at 2174. *See supra* chapter 4, text at notes 89–90, and chapter 5, text at notes 7–9.

13. Kameʻeleihiwa, *supra* note 1, at 246.

share title to the King's Lands with the Government, he would have provided some independent holdings for his hānai son, especially in light of his anxiety about being left landless in the event of a foreign invasion. [14]

Following Kauikeaouli's example, Alexander Liholiho (after becoming Kamehameha IV) exercised his personal control over the King's Lands even before he received title to them. On May 10, 1855, Alexander Liholiho's Land Agent William Webster petitioned the court for clear title to this 'Āina.[15] Webster urged the court to set aside a portion of the 'Āina to satisfy Kauikeaouli's debt so that the remainder could be "released and conveyed free of encumbrances,"[16] assuring the court that the executors of the estate were in agreement with the petition. He requested that several specific parcels of land be reserved, and that the debts be settled from the unreserved portion of the lands.[17] Webster's petition demonstrates that Alexander Liholiho understood the King's Lands to have been under the control of his foster father, and that they could be used to satisfy Kauikeaouli's obligations. The petition also seems to have been based on the assumption that once the debts were satisfied, the remaining land would become subject to Alexander Liholiho's control.

The fourth clause of Kauikeaouli's will substituted fourteen different 'Ili and Ahupua'a for Queen Kalama's dower rights, subject to her approval. The fact that everyone concerned seems to have accepted the Queen's right to dower presents additional evidence that these King's Lands were viewed as subject to Kauikeaouli's personal control. If these 'Āina had been the property of the office of the Crown as opposed to the property of the individual monarch, they would be considered public property and would not have been subject to any dower claims.

The law of dower in Hawai'i in 1853, when the Mō'ī completed his will, conferred to a wife a life estate (i.e., for as along as she lived) in one-third of all of her husband's property at the time of death.[18] The dower right applied to both real and personal property, based on the assets that remained after all debts were paid.[19] Unless a wife specifically released her interest in writing, she was entitled to demand payment from future purchasers or possessors.[20] An informal assignment of property to

---

14. When discussing the feasibility of and proper framework for the Mahele during a Privy Council meeting on December 18, 1847, Kauikeaouli questioned whether private allodial title would be respected in the event of a takeover by a "Foreign Power," with specific reference to 'Āina he retained: "[W]ould they take possession of [my] lands?" 4 *Privy Council Records* (December 18, 1847) at 304 (May 17, 1847–Aug. 26, 1848).

15. *Will of His Majesty Kamehameha III,* First Circuit Probate No. 2410: William Webster's Petition on behalf of Kamehameha IV, May 10, 1855.

16. *Id.*

17. *Id.* Alexander Liholiho reserved the following lands to ensure that they were not sold: (1) Pu'u Pelekane, (2) Kawananakoa and Kaliu in the District of Honolulu, (3) the Ahupua'a of Waianae in the District of Waianae, and (4) Paumalu and Pupukea in Ko'olauloa. *Id.*

18. Louis Cannelora, *Summary of the Hawaii Law of Dower, Curtesy and Community Property,* 6 (1971), citing *Session Laws 1846,* "Second Act of Kamehameha III," Ch. IV, Sec. IV. *See* further discussion of dower right issues *infra* chapter 8, text at notes 25–26.

19. *Id.* at 7.

20. *Id.*

Queen Kalama

settle a wife's dower rights gave the woman a valid claim to the assigned property.[21] Because of his large debt and his desire to use some of the King's Lands to pay off the debt, the Mōʻī attempted to secure a fee simple interest for his wife by granting her certain choice ʻĀina on Hawaiʻi, Maui, and Oʻahu in place of her dower right.[22]

The Hawaiʻi Supreme Court reported in a later decision that "Queen Kalama declined to accept the lands devised to her by the King's will, in lieu of dower, on the ground that she had received these lands from him in the division of 1848."[23] The Queen had obtained substantial ʻĀina before the Mahele.[24] After her decision

---

21. *Id.* at 34–35. In *Laʻaunui v. Puohu*, 2 Hawaiʻi 161 (1859), the Hawaiʻi Supreme Court ruled that an informal assignment of property to settle a wife's dower rights gives the woman legal title to that parcel. Descendants of Queen Kalama could therefore assert that Kauikeaouli's attempt to settle the Queen's dower claim by providing her with a fee simple interest in certain lots was an informal assignment equivalent to the conveyance of a fee simple interest in those lots.

22. The ʻĀina specified for Queen Kalama in section 4 of Kauikeaouli's will on the island of Hawaiʻi included the Ahupuaʻa of Kula in the Kalana of Puna; the Ahupuaʻa of Kapalaʻalaea in Kona; Kalahuipuaʻa and Anaehoʻomalu in the ʻIli of Waimea in Kohala; and the Ahupuaʻa of Waipiʻo in the Hāmākua District. The ʻĀina on Maui were Kaʻohe, Puhiawaawa, Lemukeʻe, Puʻuohala, and Manienie, all in the ʻIli of Wailuku, and on Oʻahu they included Kailua, Kāneʻohe, and Hakipuʻu, all in the Koʻolaupoko District, and Waikahalulu in the ʻIli of Honolulu.

23. *In the Matter of the Estate of His Majesty Kamehameha IV*, 2 Hawaiʻi 715, 724–25 (1864).

24. Before the Mahele, Queen Kalama held a total of forty-five ʻĀina, most of which (thirty-four) were ʻIli in the Ahupuaʻa of Wailuku on the Moku of Maui. Although she relinquished all of her ʻIli on Maui in the Mahele, which totaled 69 percent of her holdings, the fourteen ʻĀina that she retained included choice areas on Oʻahu and were of considerably greater value. Queen Kalama was not required to pay a commutation fee in order to receive title to these lands. Kameʻeleihiwa, *supra* note 1, at 263–64, 267.

Professor Kameʻeleihiwa has reported that Queen Kalama's ʻĀina included "the entire wharfage of

Kamehameha IV
(Alexander Liholiho)

to decline the lands that purported to be conveyed in the will because of her previous claim to these 'Āina through the Mahele, Alexander Liholiho acknowledged the existence of her dower rights by providing Queen Kalama with a payment for life.[25] In return, she signed a deed to release any additional claims.[26]

Waikahalulu, which fronted part of Honolulu Harbor," stretching from lower Fort Street to Kewalo Basin. *Id.* at 264, citing *Buke Mahele,* 146–47. Kamakau has provided a description of her efforts to sell this land to the Government in 1854, with the support of her husband the Mō'ī, seeking $30,000 for the property. The Legislature said the property was worth $15,000, and a compromise was reached at $20,000. But then Chief Justice William Little Lee challenged the sale, arguing that "the queen had no right to sell the land as it belonged to the government" and contending that if any funds were given to the Queen, it would have to be considered a gift to her. Samuel M. Kamakau, *Ruling Chiefs of Hawaii,* 418 (1961 revised ed. 1992). When others heard that this land was being offered for sale, the British consul offered $80,000, and Dr. Gerrit Judd offered $100,000 on behalf of a consortium of wealthy citizens. The Mō'ī responded that he did not want this important land going to a foreign government and simply wanted "the land of my queen" to be sold "to my own government at a reasonable price." *Id.* at 419. When they realized what was at stake, the Legislature voted to buy the property for the Government for $22,000. *Id.* It is not clear what the basis was for Chief Justice Lee's argument that the land previously belonged to the Government or why the legislative leaders originally supported his position.

    25. *In re Estate of His Majesty Kamehameha IV,* 2 Hawai'i 715, 725 (1864).

    26. *Id.* Although any additional rights were probably extinguished by Queen Kalama's release, the Queen's descendants could have sought to enforce her claims to the fourteen 'Āina specified in Kauikeaouli's will in light of the Hawai'i Supreme Court's ruling in *La'aunui v. Puohu,* 2 Hawai'i 161 (1859). Arguments could have been made that even if Queen Kalama's acceptance of the fourteen parcels in lieu of her dower was not a legal assignment, that the attempted assignment established the Queen's interest in equity, and therefore that she is the rightful holder of the title to those 'Āina.

These events demonstrate that the King's Lands were perceived as being subject to the personal control of the reigning Monarchs during the years that followed the Mahele. Kauikeaouli exhibited this belief in his assignment of lands in his will separately from his designation of the successor to the Crown, and the Supreme Court affirmed it by acknowledging Queen Kalama's interest in dower.

But the nature of the Monarchy was continuing to evolve during this period. In 1850, the House of Representatives was enlarged from seven to twenty-four members, and Cabinet Ministers were authorized to sit in the House of Nobles.[27] The Constitution of 1852, written mostly by Chief Justice William Little Lee, further reduced the power of the Mōʻī. As Blackman explained, the new Constitution "differentiates more fully the legislative, executive, and judicial functions of the government; . . . provides for universal suffrage, without qualification either for representatives or voters; and places important checks on the arbitrary powers of the king. Thus it is to be regarded as a distinct triumph of the 'foreign' over the native influence in the development of Hawaiian political institutions."[28] The changes in the authority of the Mōʻī led over time to changes in the Monarch's relation to the ʻĀina. As the next chapters explain, actions by the Kingdom's Supreme Court and Legislature in the second decade after the Mahele had the effect of transforming these lands from being subject to the Mōʻī's exclusive personal control into lands that had a public trust status to support the Hawaiian Monarchy—and thus to ensure that the Monarch could provide for his people.

---

27. William Fremont Blackman, *The Making of Hawaii: A Study in Social Evolution,* 121 (1906, reprinted 1977).
28. *Id.* at 122.

7

The Passing of Alexander Liholiho (1863)

At 9:15 a.m. on November 30, 1863, the nine-year reign of King Kamehameha IV (Alexander Liholiho) ended unexpectedly and prematurely.[1] Afflicted by chronic asthma and still grieving over the 1862 death of his four-year-old son Prince Albert[2] and perhaps also from his 1859 shooting of his private secretary,[3] Alexander Liholiho died suddenly at the age of 29. The Privy Council,[4] after confirming with Queen Emma that an heir was not to be born posthumously, acted promptly, and at 11 a.m that same day declared thirty-two-year-old Prince Lot Kapuāiwa, the older brother of the late Kamehameha IV, to be heir to the Crown.[5] The twenty-five-year-old Kuhina Nui[6] Victoria Kamāmalu, sister of both Liholiho and Lot, then made a public declaration announcing the Council's decision, and Prince Lot became Kamehameha V.[7]

---

1. 11 *Privy Council Records,* 115, 117 (January 10, 1859–December 11, 1872).

2. On August 27, 1862, the Kingdom mourned the death of four-year-old Prince Edward Albert Kauikeaouli Leiopapa Kamehameha. After the death of the little prince, Kamehameha IV gave Queen Emma the name Kaleleokalani, "the flight of the chief." After the death of Kamehameha IV, Emma took on the name Kaleleonālani, "the flight of the chiefs." 2 Ralph S. Kuykendall, *The Hawaiian Kingdom 1854–1874: Twenty Critical Years,* 124 n. 33 (1953, reprinted 1982); *see generally* George S. Kanehele, *Emma: Hawaii's Remarkable Queen,* 125–43 (1999); Miriam E. Rappolt, *Queen Emma: A Woman of Vision,* 99–112 (1991).

3. In 1859, Alexander Liholiho shot his private secretary Henry Neilson because of suspicions that he might be having an affair with Queen Emma, and Neilson died three years later of complications linked to the shooting. *See, e.g.,* Gavan Daws, *Shoal of Time: A History of the Hawaiian Islands,* 157–58 (1968, reprinted 1974); *see generally* Kanahele, *supra* note 2, at 111–24; Rappolt, *supra* note 2, at 77–88 (1991).

4. Under Articles 49–50 of the 1852 Constitution, the Privy Council consisted of the Mōʻī, the members of the Cabinet, and others appointed by the Mōʻī serving at his pleasure in an advisory capacity. Hawaiian Kingdom Constitutions are available online at http:www.hawaii-nation.org/constitution-1852.html and at http:www.pixi.com/kingdom.

5. 11 *Privy Council Records,* 115, 117 (January 10, 1859–December 11, 1872).

6. Under Articles 43–44 of the 1852 Constitution, the Mōʻī appointed a ranking chief to the position of Kuhina Nui to serve as a check on the King's powers. "All important business for the Kingdom which the King chooses to transact in person, he may do, but not without the approbation of the Kuhina Nui." *Id.* art. 45. During a King's minority or vacancy, the Kuhina Nui was to perform the King's duties and assume all powers vested in the King by the Constitution. *Id.* art. 47. Kamehameha I first bestowed the honor of Kuhina Nui on his favorite wife Kaʻahumanu in 1819. Ralph S. Kuykendall, *Constitutions of the Hawaiian Kingdom: A Brief History and Analysis,* 12 (Hawaiian Historical Society Paper No. 21, 1940, reprinted 1978). Kinaʻu (mother of Victoria Kamāmalu, Liholiho, and Lot) held the position from 1832 to 1839. *Id.* The 1864 Constitution of Kamehameha V abolished the Kuhina Nui office.

7. "It having pleased Almighty God to close the earthly career of King Kamehameha IV at a quarter past

Kamehameha IV (Alexander Liholiho) *(center)* and Kamehameha V (Lot Kapuāiwa) *(right)*, with Dr. Gerritt Judd, 1849

Lot's Ascension to the Throne

Alexander Liholiho's untimely death had left the Kingdom without a designated heir to the throne, and some questioned whether Lot's ascension was in accordance with the Constitution of 1852, especially Articles 25 and 47. Article 25 restricted the Crown as follows:

> The crown is hereby permanently confirmed to His Majesty Kamehameha III during his life, and to his successor. The successor shall be the person whom the King and the House of Nobles shall appoint and publicly proclaim as such, during the King's life; but should there be no such appointment and proclamation, then the successor shall be chosen by the House of Nobles and the House of Representatives in joint ballot.[8]

Because no vote by joint ballot was ever taken by the House of Nobles and the House of Representatives, some opponents charged at the time that Lot did not ascend to the throne legitimately, and some questions are raised even today.

Was Lot's ascension to the throne legitimate or an unconstitutional usurpation of power? Victoria Kamāmalu, as the Kuhina Nui, proclaimed him to be the King

---

nine o'clock this morning, I, as Kuhina Nui, by and with the Advice of the Privy Council of State, hereby proclaim Prince Lot Kamehameha King of the Hawaiian Islands, under the style and title of Kamehameha V. God Preserve the King." 11 *Privy Council Records,* 115, 117 (January 10, 1859–December 11, 1872).

8. 1852 Hawai'i Constitution, art. 25.

and clearly had some power to act pursuant to Article 47 of the 1852 Constitution, which said:

> Whenever the throne shall become vacant by reason of the King's death, or otherwise, and during the minority of any heir to the throne, the Kuhina Nui, for the time being, shall during such vacancy or minority, perform all the duties incumbent on the King, and shall have and exercise all the powers, which by this Constitution are vested in the King.[9]

Although critics questioned whether the Kingdom should have been placed in the hands of the Kuhina Nui until the Legislature elected a King, other individuals reasoned that Victoria Kamāmalu was acting within her official authority when she proclaimed Lot to be Mōʻī, and therefore that his succession was legitimate. According to this view, a vote by joint ballot was unnecessary because a successor was appointed by the Privy Council and publicly proclaimed by the Kuhina Nui.

The matter will remain forever contested because the requirement in Article 25 of a legislative vote was not complied with. Would a vote have produced a different Mōʻī? Although primogeniture (oldest son) selection of the Mōʻī was an established pattern, Kamehameha IV, the adopted son of Kamehameha III, was the *younger* brother of Lot Kapuāiwa. Females were not traditionally excluded from leadership roles, and so Princess Victoria Kamāmalu was eligible, and indeed a small but influential group of the American missionaries—who were supposed to influence the Princess—supported her candidacy.[10] Because Victoria had been educated at the Royal School and had served within the Government, she appears to have been a possible choice.[11] In fact, any of the students educated at the Royal School were eligible, and it is also possible that a new Mōʻī could have been selected from those of Aliʻi lineage who had not attended the Royal School. Princess Ruth Keʻelikolani, half sister of the late Mōʻī, who had not been educated at the Royal School, was one example of such a possibility. Kaʻahumanu, the first Kuhina Nui and foster mother of Princess Ruth, had spoken of her desire that her foster child serve as a future ruler.[12]

Nevertheless, despite these possible alternatives and the failure to comply with the Constitution's requirements, the people greeted the proclamation of Lot as the new Mōʻī with general enthusiasm.[13] In spite of the many changes influenced by Western contact, the makaʻāinana still entrusted the Aliʻi to take care of them. Although mourning the loss of Kamehameha IV, they welcomed the new Mōʻī, Kamehameha V.

---

9. *Id.*, art. 47 (emphasis added).

10. 2 Kuykendall, *supra* note 2, at 125. In a letter dated December 12, 1863, the British Commissioner William W. F. Synge advised his government in writing that foreign residents questioned whether the title of Kamehameha V was "sufficiently clear." *Id.*

11. *See supra* the list of Aliʻi children trained at the Royal School in chapter 3, note 64.

12. Samuel M. Kamakau, *Ruling Chiefs of Hawaii,* 286 (1961, revised ed., 1992).

13. According to Kuykendall, it was universally recognized throughout the Kingdom that in the absence of a direct heir of Kamehameha IV, Prince Lot Kapuāiwa was the rightful successor. 2 Kuykendall, *supra* note 2, at 124. Cf. Meiric K. Dutton, *The Succession of King Kamehameha V to Hawaii's Throne,* 12 (1957), oppos-

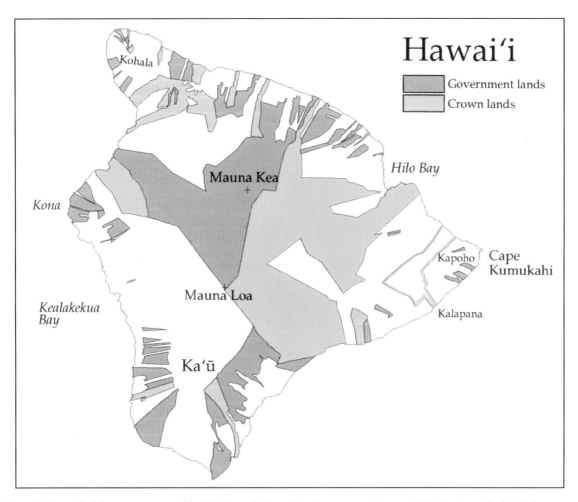

Hawai'i. Compiled from a map traced by F. L. Lowell, Hawaiian Government Survey, 1901. Cartography by Carlos Andrade, 1997.

Note: All place names are given as general locations to facilitate orientation of the reader. Names on the map are not labels of specific land types.

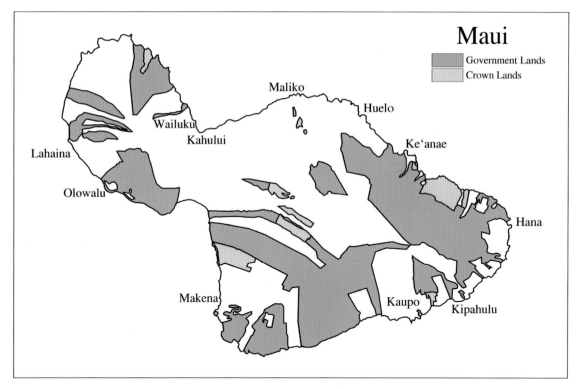

Maui. Compiled from a map by F. S. Dodge, Hawaiian Government Survey, 1885; brought up to date, 1903. Cartography by Carlos Andrade, 1997.

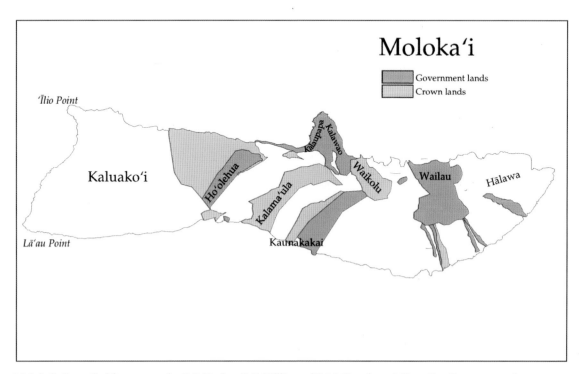

Moloka'i. Compiled from a map by F. S. Dodge, C. J. Willis, and S. M. Kanakanui, Hawaiian Government Survey, 1897. Cartography by Carlos Andrade, 1997.

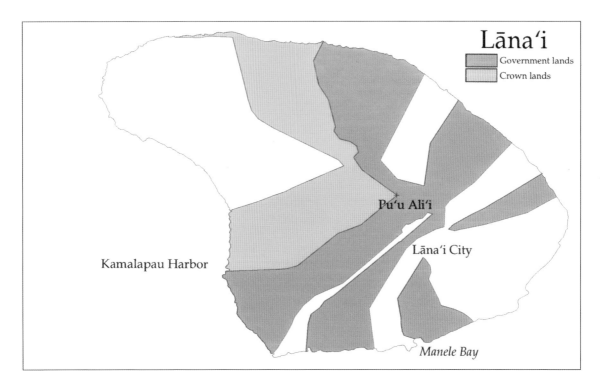

Lānaʻi. Compiled from a map by J. F. Brown and M. D. Monsarrat, Hawaiian Government Survey, 1878. Cartography by Carlos Andrade, 1997.

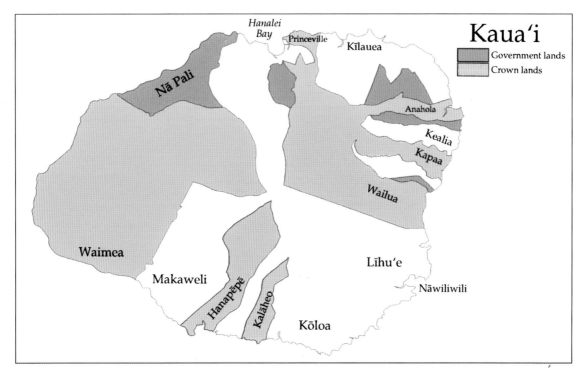

Kauaʻi. Compiled from a map traced by Herbert E. Newton, Hawaiian Government Survey Reg. Map. No. 1398, 1901. Cartography by Carlos Andrade, 1997.

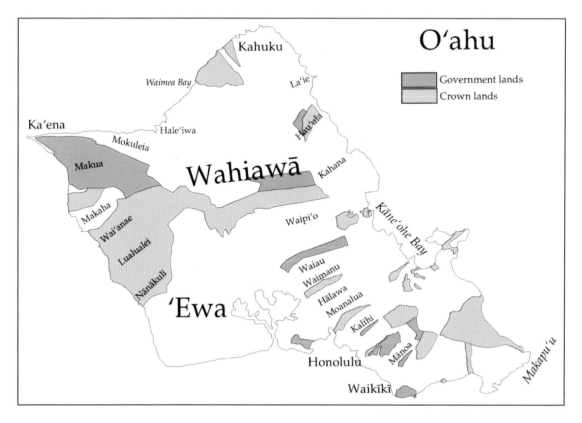

O'ahu. Compiled from a map by C. J. Lyons, finished by Rich'd Covington, Hawaiian Government Survey, 1881. Cartography by Carlos Andrade, 1997.

When Kamehameha IV had ascended to the throne in 1854, he reflected on his predecessor's good intentions and declared that he was going to take a stronger stand to protect Hawaiian sovereignty:

> His majesty Kamehameha III, now no more, was permanently the friend of the foreigner, and I am happy in knowing he enjoyed your confidence and affection. He opened his heart and hand with a royal liberality, and gave till he had little to bestow and you, but little to ask. In this respect I cannot hope to equal him. . . . I therefore say to the foreigner that he is welcome. He is welcome to our shores. Welcome so long as he comes with the laudable motive of promoting his own interests and at the same time respecting those of his neighbor. But if he comes with no more exalted motive than that of building up his own interests at the expense of the Native—to seek our confidence only to betray it—with no higher ambition than that of overthrowing our Government, and introducing anarchy, confusion and bloodshed—then he is most unwelcome![14]

Kamehameha IV and his advisors made continuous efforts to amend the Constitution to restore the King's position of power,[15] but they were relatively unsuccessful. Kamehameha V shared similar ideas concerning Hawaiian nationalism and independence.[16] He has been described as superior to his younger brother "in energy, perseverance and strength of will"[17] and as "the last great chief of the olden type."[18] And when he took office, he refused to take an oath to support the existing 1852 Constitution. The new Mōʻī insisted that it be replaced and instructed his Attorney General, Charles Coffin Harris, to draft a new Constitution reflecting his desire that "the prerogatives of the Crown . . . be more carefully protected . . . and that the influence of the Crown . . . be seen pervading every function of the government."[19] The

---

ing the ascension of Kamehameha V, but nevertheless citing the *Pacific Commercial Advertiser* of December 3, 1863, in which Henry M. Whitney, spokesperson for the American missionaries and the editor of the Advertiser, wrote, "The whole nation looked to him as the constitutional successor, and will greet his accession to the throne with joy even amid grief." In a later issue of the paper, Whitney added that the appointment was made "with a perfect unanimity of sentiment from his subjects" and that "[o]ur late King had proclaimed, according to the Constitution, as far as it was his power to proclaim, that his present Majesty should be his successor." *Id.*, citing the *Pacific Commercial Advertiser,* December 10, 1863.

14. Dutton, *supra* note 13, at 12, citing *The Polynesian,* January 13, 1855.

15. Kuykendall, *Constitutions, supra* note 6, at 21. Kamehameha IV was especially concerned with reducing the powers of the Kuhina Nui, the Privy Council, and the House of Representatives and wanted to reconsider universal suffrage. *Id.*

16. 2 Kuykendall, *supra* note 2, at 125.

17. *Id.* British Commissioner Synge is cited as the source of this description of Kamehameha V. The Commissioner also commented, however, that Kamehameha IV was superior from a Western perspective regarding "refinement, grace of manner, and general culture." *Id.*

18. *Id.*, citing Dr. W. D. Alexander for this description. Blackman described Kamehameha V as "a man of intellectual ability, independence, and pertinacity of purpose, considerable familiarity with foreign politics, and aristocratic and reactionary tendencies. He believed that the people were not fitted for the exercise of political rights, and he was jealous of foreign influence in affairs of state." William Fremont Blackman, *The Making of Hawaii: A Study in Social Evolution,* 122 (1906, reprinted 1977).

19. 2 Kuykendall, *supra* note 2, at 127. The 1864 Constitution greatly strengthened the powers of the Mōʻī. *Id.* at 127–34. Particularly controversial was Article 62 of the 1864 Constitution, which limited voting

new 1864 Constitution did dramatically increase the power of the Mōʻī and remained in effect for twenty-three years until 1887, when King Kalākaua was forced to adopt the "Bayonet Constitution."[20]

Kamehameha V: Selection of Advisors

When Lot Kapuāiwa ascended the throne in 1863, he sought to assume the traditional role of an Ali'i Nui who exercised his power to make the difficult political decisions.[21] It was, therefore, important for him to select the advisors who would best carry out his wishes to benefit his people.[22] The Mōʻī appointed Charles Coffin Harris, an American Episcopalian, as Attorney General, the same position Harris had held under Kamehameha IV.[23] Under Kamehameha V, however, Harris also held a seat in the Cabinet.[24] The Mōʻī selected his own father, Mataio Kekūanaō'a, to replace his sister, Princess Victoria Kamāmalu, as Kuhina Nui.[25] He appointed R. C. Wyllie to be Minister of Foreign Relations and retained Charles de Varigny as Minister of Finance.[26] Elisha H. Allen was appointed Chief Justice, and George M. Robertson, who had been taken from the Supreme Court to become Minister of Interior, was reappointed to be an Associate Justice when it proved difficult to replace him on the bench; Charles G. Hopkins was then made Minister of the Interior for a short period.[27] According to one historian, the strong-willed King served as a unifying factor, successfully bringing together these advisors even though they had sharply diverging views.[28]

---

qualifications to those who met literacy as well as property or income qualifications, a provision that Kamehameha V insisted on in order to protect the Government's "Monarchial character." *Id.* at 131. Although this change was not universally welcomed, in the end the loyalty of the Hawaiian People outweighed any resentment for the actions of the King. *Id.* at 133. According to Professor Kame'eleihiwa, Kamehameha V ruled his people in the traditional pono fashion. He preferred traditional Kahuna healing and licensed these traditional healers to care for his people, and he lifted the ban against the hula. Lilikala Kame'eleihiwa, *Native Land and Foreign Desires: Pehea La E Pono Ai?* 312 (1992).

20. *See infra* chapter 14.

21. The model of a "traditional Ali'i or Mōʻī" was of course Kamehameha I. Kamehameha I understood that the function of a Mōʻī was to "act as source for all the good things in life for Ka Lāhui Hawai'i." Kame'eleihiwa, *supra* note 19, at 59. He set an example for his people by farming and fishing and generously sharing these staples with his Ali'i and maka'āinana. *Id.* The traditional system functioned "with much reciprocal generosity, gift-giving, and aloha." *Id.*

22. 2 Kuykendall, *supra* note 2, at 126.

23. *Id.*

24. *Id.* In 1865, Harris succeeded Varigny as Minister of Finance. *Id.*

25. *Id.*

26. *Id.*

27. *Id.*

28. *Id.*

8

In the Matter of the Estate of His Majesty Kamehameha IV (1864)

This chapter discusses the central event in the evolution of the Crown Lands—the Hawai'i Supreme Court's 1864 decision entitled *In the Matter of the Estate of His Majesty Kamehameha IV,*[1] which addressed whether the lands should pass to the familial heirs of the deceased Mō'ī or to the new Mō'ī. When Kamehameha IV (Alexander Liholiho) died in 1863, the selection of Prince Lot Kapuāiwa as successor to the throne was resolved without delay, as explained in the previous chapter, but the distribution of the King's Lands proved to be much more controversial. The Mō'ī had died without a written will or an oral Kauoha[2] to guide the distribution of his property, and a dispute arose between Queen Emma (widow of Kamehameha IV) and the new Mō'ī (Kamehameha V) regarding the nature and proper distribution of the estate of Kamehameha IV, particularly the 'Āina. Queen Emma argued that the Crown Lands had been the private property of her husband and hence that she should take at least half of these 'Āina as his heir (and another third of the remaining lands as her dower right).[3] Lot argued, on the other hand, that the lands were attached to the Crown, and hence that they had to go to the next Mō'ī, even if he was not the heir by descent of the previous Mō'ī. The decision of the Supreme Court of Hawai'i examined the legal status of these lands and led to a reconfiguration in the relationship between the Mō'ī and the lands.[4]

---

1. *In the Matter of the Estate of His Majesty Kamehameha IV,* 2 Hawai'i 715 (1864).

2. "Kauoha" is defined as "a verbal will; also a command." Lilikalā Kame'eleihiwa, *Native Land and Foreign Desires: Pehea La E Pono Ai?* 390 (1992). Kauoha were used in precontact times to bequeath title and property. *Id.*

3. "It is well known that both Kamehameha III and his immediate successor, Kamehameha IV, dealt with these lands as their private property, selling, leasing, or mortgaging them at pleasure." Letter from Surveyor-General W. D. Alexander to Attorney General W. O. Smith, March 31, 1893, in "Report of Commissioner to the Hawaiian Islands," in 27 *Executive Documents of the House of Representatives for the Second Session of the Fifty-Third Congress, 1893–94,* 199, 200 (1895), originally in *Executive Document No. 47, 53rd Cong., 2d Sess.* (1893) (hereafter cited as "Blount Report").

4. "It seems probable that up to this time no very careful consideration had been given to the exact legal status of the crown lands." Thomas Marshall Spaulding, *The Crown Lands of Hawaii,* 10–11 (University of Hawai'i Occasional Papers No. 1, Oct. 10, 1923). "It is clear that until this particular dispute came about, no careful consideration had been given to the exact legal status of the crown lands." Jean Hobbs, *Hawaii: A Pageant of the Soil,* 65 (1935).

The lawsuit to determine the status of the lands was not brought out of anger. Emma and Lot had been childhood friends since their days together at the Royal School.[5] Some thought that Lot wanted to marry Emma after she had become widowed.[6] Because of his respect for Emma's religious beliefs and her devotion to the memory of her deceased husband, Lot feared rejection and hesitated to propose marriage,[7] although he apparently did later raise the possibility of marriage through an intermediary in 1867 after Queen Emma returned from an extended trip to Europe.[8] Even though they were close friends, they nevertheless both thought that their respective positions were the correct way to characterize the lands, and that it was important to resolve the issue in order to maintain the integrity of the Crown. Both sides presented their arguments vigorously.[9]

The Arguments

Attorney General Charles Coffin Harris argued on behalf of Lot (Kamehameha V). In his writings about his travels in the islands, Mark Twain subsequently skewered Harris as a "feeble personage" who "neglected no opportunity of making himself conspicuous."[10] Twain described Harris as "all jaw, vanity, bombast, and ignorance, a lawyer of 'shyster' caliber, a fraud by nature, a humble worshiper of the scepter above him, a reptile never tired of sneering at the land of his birth or glorifying the ten-acre kingdom that has adopted him—salary, four thousand dollars a year, vast consequence, and no perquisites."[11] But Kuykendall wrote that this characterization was unfair: "It is true that Harris had an unfortunate domineering manner, an air of superiority and condescension that infuriated some people and repelled many others; but he was a man of considerable natural ability, indefatigable industry, and unimpeachable personal integrity."[12] Professor Osorio has reported that "Harris has been described as an obnoxious individual . . . who had little respect for kanaka and an overweening ambition, but in turn they had rather little regard for him."[13]

Harris played a key role in drafting the 1864 Constitution and supported the imposition of a property or income requirement on voters.[14] He later served as Minister of Finance, and in 1867 he drafted a new reciprocity treaty with the United

---

5. *See supra* chapter 3, text at notes 59–65.

6. *See* 2 Ralph S. Kuykendall, *The Hawaiian Kingdom 1854–1874: Twenty Critical Years* 240 (1982).

7. *Id.;* Miriam E. Rappolt, *Queen Emma: A Woman of Vision,* 172–74 (1991).

8. George S. Kanehele, *Emma: Hawai'i's Remarkable Queen,* 184, 227–28 (1999).

9. "Once the issue was actually made, it was not hard for reasonable men to take diametrically opposite views and to make plausible arguments on each side. The character of Kamehameha V, of Queen Emma and of the attorney-general are sufficient evidence that the litigation was an honest attempt to settle an honest difference of opinion." Spaulding, *supra* note 4, at 11.

10. Mark Twain, *Roughing It,* 367 (1871, reprinted 1987, Signet Classic).

11. *Id.* at 362.

12. 2 Kuykendall, *supra* note 6, at 218 n.*.

13. Jonathan Kay Kamakawiwoʻole Osorio, *Dismembering Lāhui,* 143 (2002).

14. 2 Kuykendall, *supra* note 6, at 128–31.

Charles Coffin Harris

States.[15] He was appointed Associate Justice of the Hawai'i Supreme Court in 1874 and was elevated to Chief Justice in 1877, serving until his death in 1881.[16] He was married to the daughter of Elisha H. Allen, who had preceded him as Chief Justice; at the time of Harris' death, his wife was "under restraint in another room of the same house, being hopelessly insane."[17] At some point during his career, Harris received the largest grant of Government Lands that was issued during the Kingdom: 184,298 acres in Ka'ū on the Big Island.[18]

In the important 1864 case, Harris began his argument by asserting that as hereditary successor to the throne, Kamehameha V was entitled to the entire estate of Kamehameha IV, "both real and personal," which Kamehameha IV had inherited from Kamehameha III.[19] But attorneys Asher B. Bates and John Montgomery contended on behalf of Queen Emma that all the property of Kamehameha IV, including the King's Lands, was private property of Kamehameha IV, and must therefore descend in accordance with the Kingdom's general laws of inheritance.[20] Under this

---

15. Gavan Daws, *Shoal of Time: A History of the Hawaiian Islands,* 188 (1968, reprinted 1974).

16. A. Grove Day, *History Makers of Hawaii,* 50 (1984).

17. Liliuokalani, *Hawaii's Story by Hawaii's Queen,* 97 (1997).

18. J. F. Brown, "Estimate of Area Included in All Government Grants (Land Sales) to Date, June 8, 1893," in "Blount Report," *supra* note 3, at 641.

19. *In the Matter of the Estate of His Majesty Kamehameha IV,* 2 Hawai'i 715 (1864).

20. *Id.* at 716.

view, Kingdom law provided that Queen Emma would receive one-half of the estate, after payment of debts,[21] and that she could also claim a one-third dower right in the remaining half.[22]

Chapter 32 of the *Hawai'i Civil Code of 1859* provided that when any person within the Kingdom died intestate (without a will), that person's real and personal property descended to the heirs of the deceased as prescribed by statute.[23] Section 1448 required that one-half of the personal and private property of such an estate would pass to the widow and the other half to any surviving parent of the decedent (if the deceased had no surviving child).[24] Prince Albert, the only child of Kamehameha IV and Queen Emma, had died in 1862 at age four. Queen Emma, therefore, claimed she was entitled to half of her late husband's real and personal property. And because Alexander Liholiho's mother Kīna'u had died, his father Mataio Kekūanaōa was, according to this theory, entitled to the other half.

In addition to Queen Emma's claim to one-half of the estate as a statutory heir, she also claimed a dower right in the other half. "Dower" is a legal doctrine developed in English common law that referred to the legal right or interest a wife acquired in the estate of her husband by marriage but was entitled to claim only upon his death.[25] Section 1299 of Article LIV of the *Hawai'i Civil Code of 1859* provided that a wife who outlived her husband was entitled to a life estate (i.e., for the rest of her life) in one-third of all the lands and personal property owned by her late husband at any time during their marriage, unless she was lawfully barred or had waived her rights to her share.[26] Thus, if Queen Emma was entitled to a right of dower, she was authorized

---

21. *Id.*

22. *See supra* chapter 6, text at notes 18–22, for a discussion of dower rights in the Kingdom.

23. "Of the Descent of Property, Both Real and Personal," *Hawai'i Civil Code,* Ch. XXXII (1859):

> Section 1447: Whenever any person shall die intestate, within this kingdom, his property both real and personal, of every kind and description, shall descend to and be divided among his heirs, as hereinafter prescribed.
>
> Section 1448: . . . If the intestate shall leave no issue, his estate shall descend one half to his widow, and the other half to his father and mother as tenants in common; and if he leave no widow, nor issue, the whole shall descend to his father and mother, or to either of them if only one be alive.

24. *Id.*

25. Louis Cannelora, *Summary of the Hawaii Law of Dower, Curtesy and Community Property,* 1 (1971).

26. "Of Dower," *Hawai'i Civil Code,* Article LIV (1859):

> Section 1299: Every Woman shall be endowed of one-third part of all the lands owned by her husband at any time during marriage, in fee simple, in freehold, or for the term of fifty years of more, so long as twenty-five years of the term remain unexpired, but in no less estate, unless she is lawfully barred thereof; she shall also be entitled, by way of dower, to an absolute property in the one-third part of all his movable effects, in possession, or reducible to possession, at the time of his death, after the payment of all his just debts.
>
> Section 1301: Where any person seized of lands, as aforesaid, shall have executed a mortgage of such lands before marriage, the widow shall, nevertheless, be entitled to dower out of the lands mortgaged, as against every person except the mortgagee and those claiming under him.

> The language from Section 1299 is now codified in Section 533-1 of the *Hawai'i Revised Statutes.* Cannelora has explained that although the language in this statute does not state that the wife's dower inter-

to receive a life estate in one-third of Alexander Liholiho's real and personal property after the payment of all debts.

Opposing this position on behalf of the new Mōʻī, Attorney General Harris contended that as hereditary successor to the throne, Lot was entitled to inherit the entire estate of the previous Mōʻī.[27] Harris cited the Act of June 7, 1848,[28] as well as the history of the Monarchy, as evidence that the Crown Lands reserved by Kauikeaouli (Kamehameha III) at the Mahele were "Royal Domain" annexed to the Hawaiian Crown. According to this view, the Crown Lands were to descend forever to the heirs and successors on the throne and not to other heirs, and, as lands set aside to support the Monarchy, they were not subject to the right of dower.[29]

Harris supported this position by arguing that the history of succession to the throne was evidence that the "Crown of the islands [was] Hereditary and descend[ed] with the blood of the Kamehamehas."[30] He observed that Kamehameha II (Liholiho) had died without a will, and yet Kamehameha III (Kauikeaouli) ascended the throne and took possession of his ʻĀina, in the tradition of the Kālaiʻāina.[31] He explained that this transfer supported his argument that "the property of the dead King did not go to any other than the successor, it went along with the Crown."[32] Harris' assertion that Kamehameha II died without a will ignored, however, Liholiho's issuance of a Kauoha (a verbal will) prior to his trip to London, designating his brother Kauikeaouli as his heir and saying, "Live in peace with the chiefs; these lands which belong to me are yours, the lands given to the chiefs shall be theirs."[33]

Harris' second argument on Lot's behalf focused on the proper translation of the language used in Kauikeaouli's March 1848 statement[34] and the June 7, 1848, statute passed to acknowledge the Mahele.[35] In the March instrument, Kauikeaouli used the phrase "ma kea palapala ke hookoe nei au noʻu iho a no koʻu poe hooilina a no koʻu poe hope a mau loa aku, na aina aʻu i kakauia ma na aoao," which is usually translated as "by this instrument I hereby retain (or reserve) for myself and *for*

---

est is only a "life estate," "the cases have established that in Hawaii, as at common law, the primary dower right gives the widow only a life estate" in one-third of the lands owned by the husband. Cannelora, *supra* note 25, at 15, citing *Keanu v. Kaohi,* 14 Hawaiʻi 142 (1902); *Valentin v. Brunette,* 26 Hawaiʻi 417 (1922); and *Estate of Glover,* 45 Hawaiʻi 569 (1962).

27. *In the Matter of the Estate of His Majesty Kamehameha IV,* 2 Hawaiʻi 715 (1864).

28. "Act Relating to the Lands of His Majesty the King and of the Government, June 7, 1848," 2 *Revised Laws of Hawaiʻi,* 2152 (1925), discussed *supra,* chapter 4, text at notes 89–90; chapter 5, text at notes 7–9; chapter 6, note 12. *See* appendix 2.

29. *Estate of His Majesty Kamehameha IV,* 2 Hawaiʻi 717.

30. "Oral Arguments to *In Re Estate of His Majesty Kamehameha IV,*" 6 (originals on file with the State Archives).

31. *Id.* at 6–7. For a discussion of the Kālaiʻāina, *see supra* chapter 2, text at notes 47–52.

32. "Oral Arguments to *In Re Estate of His Majesty Kamehameha IV,*" 6 (originals on file with the State Archives).

33. Kameʻeleihiwa, *supra* note 2, at 110–11.

34. Kauikeaouli's statement of March 8, 1848, is given in both Hawaiian and English in *Estate of His Majesty Kamehameha IV,* 2 Hawaiʻi at 722–23.

35. "Act Relating to the Lands of His Majesty the King and of the Government, June 7, 1848," 2 *Revised Laws of Hawaiʻi,* 2152 (1925).

my heirs and successors forever, my lands inscribed at pages . . ." (emphasis added). The June 7, 1848, statute contained the similar phrase—"To be the private lands of his Majesty Kamehameha III., to have and to hold to himself, *his heirs and successors forever . . .* " (emphasis added)—subject only to the rights of native tenants.[36]

The attorneys for Queen Emma had asserted that "heirs and assigns" conveyed the proper construction of the June 7, 1848, statute rather than "heirs and successors,"[37] but Harris responded by arguing that the phrase "successors" was the more accurate translation.[38] Harris explained that the 1848 law was originally written in English by John Ricord and was then translated into Hawaiian.[39] He urged therefore that the English version should be used, acknowledging that the Hawaiian version of a law prevailed in cases of "irreconcilable differences" between two texts but also contending that no irreconcilable differences were evident here.[40]

Harris' final argument was based on the principle that all laws of the Kingdom must be interpreted and applied in a manner that is consistent with sound public policy.[41] He explained that it was not consistent with public policy to strip the Crown of its means of existence and dignity, citing Article 36(1) of the 1852 Constitution, which stated that "The King is sovereign of all the Chiefs and of all of the people; the Kingdom is His." In a letter submitted by Harris to Kamehameha V in his Cabinet Council, Harris had asserted that the Act of June 7, 1848, was drawn hastily.[42] The words "private lands," Harris contended, were chosen carelessly and did not mean private property of the King as a private person, but rather property that came under his control as a result of his position. He asserted that the important term "Royal Domain" in the first *whereas* clause of the statute would be undermined and would render the word "successors" void if the word "heirs" was not restricted to the heirs of the throne, thus preventing the estate to pass out of the Crown's control.[43] Harris also pointed out that the King's Lands became the property of Kauikeaouli (Kamehameha III) solely "by reason of his being King. It belonged to him by that reason, and that alone."[44] He contended therefore that the Crown Lands must descend to

36. This is the English translation as it appears in *Estate of His Majesty Kamehameha IV*, 2 Hawai'i at 717.

37. "Oral Arguments to *In Re Estate of His Majesty Kamehameha IV*," 2 (originals on file with the State Archives).

38. *Estate of His Majesty Kamehameha IV*, 2 Hawai'i at 717.

39. "Oral Arguments to *In Re Estate of His Majesty Kamehameha IV*," 8 (originals on file with the State Archives).

40. *Id.*

41. *Id.* at 9.

42. "Harris' Petition to His Majesty in Cabinet Council," at 1, regarding *In Re Estate of His Majesty Kamehameha IV King of the Hawaiian Islands Late Deceased* (originals on file with the State Archives).

43. *Id.* at 1–2.

44. *Id.* at 4. *See also* Spaulding, *supra* note 4, at 11: "It is easy to find contemporary statements that seem to imply that the lands set apart for Kamehameha III in 1848 were ceded to him as absolutely as those assigned to the chiefs were to them, but such remarks were not made as technical legal statements, and too much must not be deduced from them. On the other hand it seems to have been pretty commonly assumed, without any great amount of reflection, that the crown lands would go with the crown."

Kamehameha V in the same manner, that they could not be treated as the estate of a private individual, and that they were not subject to dower.[45]

When it was his turn to present arguments, Attorney John Montgomery argued on behalf of Queen Emma that the Act of June 7, 1848, was simply a confirmation to Kamehameha III (Kauikeaouli) that the lands he had reserved were his private property. From 1848 until his death, Kauikeaouli had leased, mortgaged, or sold these lands in his discretion.[46] If Kauikeaouli had held the Crown Lands as private property, should not his devisee Alexander Liholiho (Kamehameha IV) have held the lands as private property as well?[47] And if the lands in question were the private property of Alexander Liholiho, then his widow and heir Queen Emma was entitled to her claim from her late husband. Montgomery argued that upon the death of Alexander Liholiho, all his personal and real property was subject to distribution under the statutes regulating intestacy, as well as dower.[48]

Montgomery explained that both Alexander Liholiho and Queen Emma treated the King's Lands as private property, to be disposed of as desired, yet subject to Queen Emma's dower interest.[49] Queen Emma joined with her husband to sign all deeds conveying property, demonstrating their understanding that the King's Lands were subject to dower,[50] and that, in order to effect a valid release of dower rights, the Queen was required to join the Mōʻī in the conveyance of property.[51] Although a conveyance by Kamehameha IV without Queen Emma's release of dower would have been valid, a transferee would have taken the land subject to the Queen's dower interest before the conveyance.[52] Just as Kauikeaouli (Kamehameha III) had recognized Queen Kalama's dower right, Alexander Liholiho (Kamehameha IV) and Queen Emma also recognized Queen Emma's right to dower.[53] Although Queen Emma had waived her claim with respect to those properties which she had joined in conveying, her actions waiving her rights in those lands provided evidence of her belief that she held a valid dower interest in the remaining properties.

Montgomery argued that the Act of June 7, 1848, did not deprive Kauikeaouli

45. "Harris' Petition to His Majesty in Cabinet Council," at 1, regarding *In Re Estate of His Majesty Kamehameha IV King of the Hawaiian Islands Late Deceased*, 4–5 (originals on file with the State Archives).

46. *Estate of His Majesty Kamehameha IV*, 2 Hawaiʻi at 724.

47. "Oral Arguments to *In Re Estate of His Majesty Kamehameha IV*," 2–3 (originals on file with the State Archives).

48. *Estate of His Majesty Kamehameha IV*, 2 Hawaiʻi at 716.

49. "Oral Arguments to *In Re Estate of His Majesty Kamehameha IV*," 5 (originals on file with the State Archives).

50. *Estate of His Majesty Kamehameha IV*, 2 Hawaiʻi at 725: "During his Majesty's [Kamehameha IV's] reign, a period of nearly nine years, he constantly dealt with the lands in question as his private property in like manner as his predecessor had done, and her Majesty Queen Emma was always in the habit of joining with him in deeds to individuals, whenever it was necessary that she should do so in order to bar her dower."

51. Section 1308 of the *Civil Code* mandated that a wife's right to dower was barred only by a valid release made "by joining with him [her husband] in the deed conveying the same, . . . or by a separate deed releasing the same, made at the time of conveyance by her husband, or subsequently." *Id.*

52. For more information on dower, *see* Cannelora, *supra* note 25, at 5.

53. "Oral Arguments to *In Re Estate of His Majesty Kamehameha IV*," at 5 (originals on file with the State Archives).

(Kamehameha III) of his fee simple interest,[54] and that in order to translate the act accurately, the "intention and understanding" of Kauikeaouli must not only be determined, "it must control."[55] Montgomery contended that the 1848 act was originally written in Hawaiian, and that no authorized English version of the act existed. To refute Harris' assertion that Kauikeaouli (Kamehameha III) intended the Crown Lands to pass to a "successor on the throne," Montgomery asserted that the proper translation of the phrase "[O]ia na 'Āina ponoi o Kamehameha III, o ko makou 'Ali'i Nui a me ka maikai, nona a no kona poe ho'oilina: a me na hope ana, a mau loa aku, a nolaila, aia no ia ia ka olelo a me ka hooponopono ia mau 'Āina, e like me kona make make 'Ali'i a me kona manao, koe wale no na kuleana o na kanaka e noho ana ma ua mau 'Āina la" was as follows: "To be the private lands of His Majesty Kamehameha III to have and to hold to himself his heirs, and assigns forever, and said lands shall be regulated and disposed according to his royal will and pleasure subject only to the rights of the tenants."[56]

Montgomery explained that in Hawaiian, the same term was used for both "assigns" and "successors," and therefore the court must examine the context and purpose to determine the proper meaning.[57] Montgomery contended that the key word in the Hawaiian phrase must be translated as "assigns," because Attorney General Harris' choice of the word "successors" was "arbitrary" and in conflict with the use and control of these lands by Kauikeaouli (Kamehameha III). Montgomery explained that if the King's Lands passed not to the heirs ("assigns") but to the "successor" (as Mō'ī) of Kauikeaouli, then "he had not the power to divest himself of an atom of it,"[58] because these lands would have to be kept intact for the next Mō'ī. Yet Kauikeaouli had dealt with the King's Lands as his private property during his lifetime by selling, leasing, and mortgaging "a great many of them."[59]

Montgomery maintained that when interpreting an obscure provision in a deed or will, the first thing to ascertain was the intention and understanding of the author of the instrument in question.[60] Article 3 of the *Will of Kamehameha III* instructed his executors to pay his debts out of his property. In Article 4, the Mō'ī recognized his wife's right to dower by granting part of his lands to Queen Kalama in lieu of dower. In Article 5, the Mō'ī bequeathed the remainder of his estate to his hānai (adopted) son, Prince Alexander Liholiho. The *Will of Kamehameha III* thus confirmed his understanding that the King's Lands were his private property, subject to dower and assignable to his heirs.

---

54. *Id.* at 1.
55. *Id.* at 4.
56. "Act Relating to the Lands of His Majesty the King and of the Government, June 7, 1848," 2 *Revised Laws of Hawai'i*, 2152 (1925).
57. "Oral Arguments to *In Re Estate of His Majesty Kamehameha IV*," at 16 (originals on file with the State Archives).
58. *Id.* at 2–3.
59. *Id.*
60. *Id.* at 4.

Montgomery also asserted that the *Will of Kamehameha III* contradicted the view that the King held the lands in trust.[61] The law required that a trust be created by a separate deed, and Kamehameha III had not created a trust by a separate deed. In addition, if the King's Lands were held in trust, then Queen Kalama would have no right to dower.[62]

Montgomery further pointed out that Queen Kalama's dower rights were acknowledged not only by Kauikeaouli but also by Alexander Liholiho (Kamehameha IV), who endowed Queen Kalama with a $2,000-a-year life payment in exchange for the release of any additional dower claim she might have (in addition to the lands she had received).[63] He reasoned that if Queen Kalama had a dower right in the estate of her deceased husband, then Queen Emma must also have a dower right in her husband's estate.

Attorney Asher B. Bates supplemented Montgomery's presentation.[64] In response to Attorney General Harris' arguments that the Kingdom had been a hereditary monarchy, Bates contended that, after the enactment of the Constitution of 1840, the Kingdom no longer had that characteristic.[65] Bates also pointed out that while the *Will of Kauikeaouli* (Kamehameha III) was in probate, Chief Justice William Little Lee had ruled that the estate was to be treated as one of a private individual and required the executors to obtain permission before disposing of any of the King's Lands to pay for the King's debts.[66]

Justice George Morison Robertson

The opinion resolving this heated dispute was written by Justice George M. Robertson. Robertson was born in Huntley, Scotland, in 1821, and left home when he was fifteen with his older brother to move to St. John, New Brunswick, Canada.[67] He later joined the British whaling ship *Peruvian,* which took him to Arctic and Hawaiian waters. He obtained a discharge from the whaling company and returned to Hawai'i on March 30, 1844, when he was twenty-three.[68] He then became a clerk for the firm of Skinner and Company but left that office because he had been "required to perform acts which he considered wrong." [69] He entered the Foreign Ministry, working

---

61. *Id.* at 4.

62. *Id.* at 5.

63. *Id.* at 4.

64. Asher Bates was the brother-in-law of Dr. Gerrit Judd and had served as the Government's legal advisor in the late 1840s. In the 1850s, he served as a member of the Privy Council. Daws, *supra* note 15, at 131, 143.

65. "Oral Arguments to *In Re Estate of His Majesty Kamehameha IV,*" (originals on file with the State Archives).

66. *Id.*

67. Lydia ("Pat") Schaefer Cooke, *The Family of George Morison Robertson and Sarah Symonds Humphreys Robertson after 122 Years—1851–1973,* 7 (Honolulu: Hawaiian Printing Co., 2d ed., 1973).

68. John J. Chinen, *They Cried for Help,* 31 (2002).

69. "Death of Honorable George M. Robertson," *Pacific Commercial Advertiser,* March 16, 1867.

George Morison Robertson and two sons, ca. 1860

for Minister R. C. Wyllie to do his copying, and he subsequently served as a book-keeper and cashier in the Treasury Department in 1846–47 under Dr. Gerrit Judd.[70] He served as a clerk for the recently established Land Commission in 1847[71] and was engaged "in trade" in 1847–48.[72] Robertson achieved some publicity in 1848 when he was serving as clerk in the Ministry of the Interior and brought impeachment charges against Dr. Judd, the Treasury Minister, listing sixteen serious charges (with 175 specifications) for misuse of position, power, and public funds, accusing him of "selfishness, vindictiveness, arrogance, hardheadedness, partiality, and vile hypocrisy" and of being "generally incompetent."[73] He left for California that year to participate in the gold rush and was seen as the clerk in a store in Sacramento in the summer of 1849,[74] "but the venture was not a success and he returned in 1850 to make his permanent home in Hawaii."[75]

---

70. *Id.;* "In Memoriam," *Hawaiian Gazette,* March 20, 1867.

71. Chinen, *They Cried, supra* note 68, at 43.

72. "In Memoriam," *Hawaiian Gazette,* March 20, 1867.

73. Daws, *supra* note 15, at 130, citing "Robertson to Kamehameha III," October 11, 1848, FO & Ex; *Privy Council Records,* November 30, 1848–April 23, 1849.

74. Rev. S. C. Damon, "Sermon Preached at the Death of Hon. G. M. Robertson," republished in *George Morison Robertson,* 44 (Honolulu, 1917).

75. Cooke, *supra* note 67, at 7. *See also* "In Memoriam," *Hawaiian Gazette,* March 20, 1867: "He there also engaged in commercial speculations, which did not prosper."

Upon his return, Robertson was appointed one of the five members of the Land Commission, serving from 1850 to the termination of the Commission on March 31, 1855,[76] and becoming its Vice President on June 27, 1853.[77] He is remembered for his efforts to keep the size of the Kuleana Awards to the makaʻāinana as small as possible.[78] The proceedings of the Commission were informal in nature. Robertson served as hearing officer for some claims[79] and sometimes served as an appraiser to value the land that had been awarded to a claimant.[80]

Robertson served as a member of the House of Representatives from 1851 to 1859 and was Speaker of the House in the 1852, 1853, and 1855 sessions.[81] The House had been expanded from eight to twenty-four members in 1850, and Robertson was elected in 1851 from the Kona District of Oʻahu, where he and the English physician Thomas Charles Byde Rooke[82] defeated Native Hawaiian candidates.[83] With Rooke and Judge William Little Lee, Robertson "introduced a bewildering array of rules and procedures in the first week of the 1851 session [and] the newcomers immediately assumed leadership of the House."[84] In 1852, he continued his attacks on Dr. Gerrit Judd and "engaged Judd in a running argument over his administration of the treasury."[85]

Robertson was elected to the 1864 Constitutional Convention from the Hāmākua District, Hawaiʻi, and was appointed to serve as Vice President of the Convention by Kamehameha V[86] (who had refused to swear to uphold the 1852 Constitution and wanted a document that would strengthen the role of the Mōʻī).[87] Robertson spoke in favor of the ability of this Convention to frame a new Constitution (even though it

---

76. Chinen, *They Cried, supra* note 68, at 31, 172.

77. "In Memoriam," *Hawaiian Gazette*, March 20, 1867.

78. Chinen, *They Cried, supra* note 68, at 32, 126; *see supra* chapter 4, text at notes 135–41. As a member of the House of Representatives, Robertson did assist at least one Konohiki who had missed the deadline for filing a claim by helping to enact legislation in 1854 that granted him additional time. Chinen, *They Cried, supra* note 68, at 82–83, citing 2 *Revised Laws of Hawaiʻi*, 2147 (1925).

79. Robertson was the hearing officer for the claims of the makaʻāinana in Kahana Valley, Oʻahu, in September 1850. Robert H. Stauffer, *Kahana: How the Land Was Lost*, 24–25 (2004).

80. Chinen, *They Cried, supra* note 68, at 59.

81. *Id.* at 31. Another report says that "He was chosen Representative for the District of Kohala, or Hāmākua, for the session of Parliament of the year 1850; and was elected to Parliament for many years in succession." "In Memoriam," *Hawaiian Gazette*, March 20, 1867.

82. Dr. Rooke and his part-Hawaiian wife Grace Kamaʻikuʻi Young were the hānai parents of Emma Naeʻa (who became Queen Emma) and raised her until she was sent off to the Royal School. See Kanahele, *supra* note 8, at 1–4, 9–21; Rappolt, *supra* note 7, at i (1991). In 1858, Alexander Liholiho (Kamehameha IV) appointed Dr. Rooke to the Privy Council, but he died later that year of a heart attack at the age of 52. Kanahele, *Id.,* at 84, 90.

83. Osorio, *supra* note 13, at 68.

84. *Id.* at 75–76.

85. Daws, *supra* note 15, at 144, citing G. P. Judd IV, *Dr. Judd: Hawaii's Friend*, 200 (1960).

86. "A Tribute of Respect to Hon. George M. Robertson, Deceased, Who Was a Justice of the Supreme Court from January 10, 1855 to March 12, 1867 by the Bar of Honolulu, April 21, 1883," reprinted in *George Morison Robertson*, 49 (Honolulu, 1917).

87. *See* Osorio, *supra* note 13, at 110–29.

Kamehameha V
(Lot Kapuāiwa)

departed from the process of amendment found in the 1852 Constitution),[88] and he also spoke in favor of adding a property or income qualification for voters, which the new Mōʻī strongly favored.[89] When that Convention was dissolved by Kamehameha V (because it could not resolve the voting qualification issue), Judge Robertson met with the Mōʻī and his Cabinet for several days to put together what became the 1864 Constitution, which included a property requirement for voting.[90] As a member of the Royal Hawaiian Agricultural Society in 1864, he spoke in favor of importing laborers for the sugar plantations in order to avoid "a rise in wages as would be very detrimental to all the planters." [91]

Robertson was "not a university graduate," but "he knew how to study." [92] Although he was "not a lawyer by profession, he soon by extraordinary zeal and study, became familiar with the rudiments and practice of law, especially in its appli-

---

88. "In Memoriam," *Hawaiian Gazette,* March 20, 1867; 2 Kuykendall, *supra* note 6, at 118. Article 105 of the 1852 Constitution contained "a diabolically complicated method of amendment" requiring approval by each house in two separate legislatures, the second by a two-thirds majority in each house. Osorio, *supra* note 13, at 105–06.

89. 2 Kuykendall, *supra* note 6, at 131. Judge Robertson was elected to the 1864 Constitutional Convention from Hāmākua, on Hawaiʻi Island. "In Memoriam," *Hawaiian Gazette,* March 20, 1867.

90. 2 Kuykendall, *supra* note 6, at 131–32.

91. Osorio, *supra* note 13, at 119, quoting from *Pacific Commercial Advertiser,* April 2, 1864, at 3, cols. 1–2).

92. "A Tribute of Respect," *supra* note 86, at 48.

cation to our local transition society." [93] He was appointed to be a Circuit Judge on the Island of Hawai'i in late 1850,[94] was admitted to the Bar in 1852,[95] and was appointed Police Justice in Honolulu on September 4, 1854.[96]

In 1855 Kamehameha IV (Alexander Liholiho) appointed Robertson an Associate Justice of the Supreme Court.[97] (He was also serving as Speaker of the House of Representatives that year.) This appointment to the Supreme Court was thought by some to be "a very remarkable one" because Robertson had not been trained as a lawyer, but apparently he "demonstrated that he had the first qualification to make a lawyer—a judicial mind [and] for many years before his death, he enjoyed the reputation of being not only an upright Judge, but a sound and discriminating Jurist." [98] Among the important decisions he authored is *Oni v. Meek,*[99] which narrowly construed the 1850 Kuleana Act and restricted the ability of the maka'āinana to utilize the lands of their Ahupua'a.[100] He assisted Chief Justice William Little Lee in producing the *Civil Code* that was adopted by the Legislature in 1859, completing it with Reverend Richard Armstrong after Lee died in 1857.[101] He left the Supreme Court in December 1863, when he was appointed by Kamehameha V as Minister of Interior.[102] But then he was reappointed to the Court by the new Mō'ī two months later in 1864 when it became difficult to find an adequate replacement.[103] He sat as a member of the important Privy Council from 1857 to 1864.[104] On July 27, 1866, he was appointed sole Commissioner of Boundaries for the Kingdom.[105]

---

93. "Death of Honorable George M. Robertson," *Pacific Commercial Advertiser,* March 16, 1867. *See also* "In Memoriam," *Hawaiian Gazette,* March 20, 1867: "As the Land Commission was only a temporary matter, the Judge had the prudence to devote his leisure time to the reading of law."

94. Cooke, *supra* note 67, at 7.

95. "A Tribute of Respect," *supra* note 86, at 47.

96. "In Memoriam," *Hawaiian Gazette,* March 20, 1867.

97. Chinen, *They Cried, supra* note 68, at 31; 2 Kuykendall, *supra* note 6, at 36.

98. "In Memoriam," *Hawaiian Gazette,* March 20, 1867.

99. *Oni v. Meek,* 2 Hawai'i 87 (1858).

100. Justice Robertson rejected a claim to pasture horses on the kula lands of the Ahupua'a, ruling that Section 7 of the 1850 Kuleana Act lists "all the specific rights of the hoaaina (excepting fishing rights) which should be held to prevail against the fee simple title of the konohiki," adding that "it is obvious to us that the custom contended for is so unreasonable, so uncertain, and so repugnant to the spirit of the present laws, that it ought not to be sustained by judicial authority." 2 Hawai'i at 90, 1858 WL 4829, at *3. This issue was revisited by the Hawai'i Supreme Court in *Kalipi v. Hawaiian Trust Co., Ltd.,* 66 Hawai'i 1, 656 P.2d 745 (1982), where the Court agreed that grazing horses was not a customary practice of Native Hawaiians tenants but also explained that traditional activities not mentioned in the Kuleana Act *will be protected* under Hawai'i's Constitution and laws. The Kuleana Act (and Robertson's role in limiting the size of Kuleana Awards) is explained *supra* in chapter 4, text at notes 104–55.

101. *Id.;* Stauffer, *supra* note 79, at 24, explaining that "the *Civil Code* of 1859 abounded with such Western legal concepts as corporate law, wills, probate, and matters relating to private land management" and had the effect of legalizing and codifying "[t]he hereditary accumulation of wealth, ownership and power—as well as private control and ownership of natural resources and the means of production."

102. *Pacific Commercial Advertiser,* December 18, 1863.

103. 2 Kuykendall, *supra* note 6, at 126; "Death of Honorable George M. Robertson," *Pacific Commercial Advertiser,* March 16, 1867; "In Memoriam," *Hawaiian Gazette,* March 20, 1867.

104. Chinen, *They Cried, supra* note 68, at 31.

105. C. J. Lyons, "Land Matters in Hawaii, No. 15," *The Islander,* October 15, 1875, at 223; *Thrum's Hawaiian Annual,* 117 (1891).

Robertson spoke fluent Hawaiian and has been described as a person who was "highly regarded by King Kamehameha IV, and became a close friend and personal advisor of the King."[106] He was thus in the inner circle of leadership and was well acquainted with both litigants in the important 1864 case. Robertson died suddenly on March 12, 1867, of an aneurysm in the aorta,[107] and he was "accorded a public funeral."[108] His youngest son, Alexander G. M. Robertson, born six months after George Robertson's death, was an active member of the group that led the overthrow of the Kingdom in 1893; A. G. M. Robertson played important roles during the Republic of Hawaii and served as Chief Justice of the Hawai'i Supreme Court during the territorial period from 1911 to 1917.[109]

The Opinion

Justice Robertson's decision resolving the dispute over control of the Crown Lands was certainly the most significant of his judicial career.[110] The decision was joined by Associate Justice R. G. Davis, a part-Hawaiian who had recently replaced John Papa 'Ī'ī[111] and who served on the Court from 1864 to 1868.[112] Elisha H. Allen was Chief Justice at the time,[113] but no evidence exists that he participated in the case or joined the opinion.[114]

Robertson's opinion began by describing the Court's careful examination of and reflection on the facts prior to rendering a decision. He emphasized that to give a

106. Cooke, *supra* note 67, at 7.

107. "Death of Honorable George M. Robertson," *Pacific Commercial Advertiser,* March 16, 1867.

108. Cooke, *supra* note 67, at 7.

109. "Brief Illness Fatal to Judge Robertson," *Honolulu Star-Bulletin,* August 21, 1947; "Lengthy Illness is Fatal," *Honolulu Advertiser,* August 21, 1947. *See infra* chapter 22, note 28 and text at notes 37–47 for A. G. M. Robertson's role in the enactment of the Hawaiian Homes Commission Act.

110. "A certain decision of his in regard to the crown lands was far-reaching in its effect, and immortalized his name in the history of the Hawaiian Bench." Ellen McCully Higgins, "Recollections of the Judges of the Earlier Supreme Court," reprinted in *George Morison Robertson,* 50 (Honolulu, 1917).

111. John Papa 'Ī'ī served on the Hawai'i Supreme Court from 1846 to 1864, resigning "to spend the end of his life in 'Ewa in the service of Christian ministry." Sally Engle Merry, *Colonizing Hawai'i: The Cultural Power of Law,* 333 n. 3 (2000).

112. Merry, *supra* note 111, at 103. In 1869, after he left the Court, R. G. Davis opposed the continued importation of plantation workers from China, characterizing them as "uncivilizable coolies" and stating that the Kingdom already had "as many coolies as the courts can take care of." *Id.* at 133, quoting from an 1869 article in the *Pacific Commercial Advertiser* reprinted in Edward C. Lydon, *The Anti-Chinese Movement in the Hawaiian Kingdom 1852–1886,* 37 (San Francisco: R. and E. Research Associates, 1975).

113. The Supreme Court consisted of three justices, appointed by the Mō'ī with the advice of the Privy Council. Elisha H. Allen had been U.S. Consul in Honolulu, and in 1853 he was appointed as Minister of Finance in the Cabinet of Kamehameha III, continuing in that post under Kamehameha IV. *Thrum's Hawaiian Annual,* 65 (1918). He was appointed Chief Justice in 1857 following the death of William Little Lee and served until 1877, when he went to Washington as the first Minister of the Kingdom accredited to the United States. Allen died on January 1, 1883, of a heart attack at a White House reception. 2 Kuykendall, *supra* note 6, at 37; *Thrum's Hawaiian Almanac and Annual,* 59 (1888). Allen played numerous roles in the Kingdom and frequently went on diplomatic missions. *See* 2 Kuykendall, *supra* note 6, at 45–46, 199–200, and 218–220; Daws, *supra* note 15, at 195, discussing Chief Justice Allen's 1873 assignment to negotiate a reciprocity treaty with the United States.

114. The complete file of the 1864 case is found under Probate Court File #2411, Microfilm #52.

just construction to the Act of June 7, 1848, the Court had referred to the two instruments executed by Kamehameha III on March 8, 1848, which were the foundation of the enactment and to "Hawaiian history, custom, legislation and polity, as well as to the records of the Privy Council, and the acts of the parties immediately interested subsequent to the great division."[115]

The Court's decision agreed in some respects with both royal claimants, and yet "differed materially from either."[116] Justice Robertson first explained that Attorney General Harris "was mistaken when he said that the Act of 7th June, 1848, appeared to have been drafted hastily or inadvertently."[117] Chief Justice William Little Lee had prepared the English version of the act and he "knew well the legal import of the language introduced into the Act."[118] Robertson concluded that Kamehameha III (Kauikeaouli) had acted with two separate intentions in carrying out the Mahele in regard to his Crown Lands: (1) He wanted to protect the lands reserved for himself "from the danger of being treated as public domain or Government property," both in order to keep these lands from being confiscated by any foreign power[119] and also to enjoy complete control over them; and (2) he wanted these lands to "descend to his heirs and successors, the future wearers of the crown."[120]

The Court ruled, therefore, that under the Act of June 7, 1848, the Crown Lands could be inherited only by the successors to the throne, but it also ruled that "each successive possessor may regulate and dispose of the same according to his will and pleasure, as private property, in like manner as was done by Kamehameha III."[121] These holdings are somewhat inconsistent, because the first ruling denies the Mōʻī the ultimate power to determine who should inherit the lands, while the second conclusion confirms the power of the Mōʻī to control the Crown Lands in all other respects without supervision or restriction by the Government.

The Court then addressed Queen Emma's dower claim. Justice Robertson first determined that if Queen Emma was entitled as a statutory heir to take one-half of her late husband's estate by inheritance, she could not also take dower in the other half.[122] She could not take both rights in the same estate, for her right to dower would be lost in her superior right to inherit as an heir.[123] Then, based on its ruling that only a Monarch could inherit the lands, the Court rejected Queen Emma's claim of inheritance.

---

115. *In the Matter of the Estate of His Majesty Kamehameha IV*, 2 Hawaiʻi 715, 718 (1864).
116. *Id.*
117. *Id.* at 723.
118. *Id.* at 723–24.
119. *Id.* at 725; *see also Id.* at 722: "The records in the discussion in [Privy] Council show plainly his Majesty's anxious desire to free his lands from the burden of being considered public domain, and, as such, subjected to the danger of confiscation in the event of his islands being seized by any foreign power, and also his wish to enjoy complete control over his own property."
120. *Id.* at 725.
121. *Id.*
122. *Id.* at 716.
123. *Id.*

Queen Emma (looking at a picture of her deceased husband Kamehameha IV), 1863

Finally, in another holding that seems inconsistent, the Court ruled that Queen Emma was entitled to dower rights in these disputed lands.[124] The Court concluded that nothing in the Act of June 7, 1848, took away the Queen's right of dower in the Crown Lands, and hence that she was entitled to dower "except so far as she may have barred her right therein by her own act and deed" by explicitly waiving rights in lands that had been conveyed.[125] The Court reached this conclusion by examining the practices of both Kamehameha III and IV, finding that both had recognized the existence of dower rights in the Crown Lands and had asked their Queens to waive their rights in appropriate cases.[126]

Justice Robertson also concluded that at the time of his death, Kamehameha IV owned real and personal property separate from the Crown Lands.[127] The remainder of the estate of Kamehameha IV was to be distributed in accordance with the general laws of inheritance, and thus Queen Emma and Mataio Kekūanaōa were entitled to split these proceeds after the debts of the Mō'ī had been paid.[128]

The fundamental holdings of this opinion are thus that (1) Lot (Kamehameha

---

124. *Id.* at 726.
125. *Id.* The Court added: "nor is there any law of this Kingdom which renders the matrimonial rights of the wife of the King any less than or any different from those of the wife of any private gentleman." *Id.*
126. *Id.*
127. *Id.*
128. *Id.*

V) and subsequent successors to the throne were entitled to inherit the Crown Lands derived from the lands that Kauikeaouli (Kamehameha III) had claimed as his own in the Mahele, and (2) Lot and his successors as Mōʻī were free to sell, mortgage, or lease the Crown Lands at their will, with the proceeds of these transactions becoming their private property, but upon their deaths the remaining Crown Lands must pass to the next Mōʻī.

This decision has been cited a number of times since it was decided, but the subsequent cases have dealt primarily with laws of inheritance and distribution of property, dower, or land tenure.[129] None of the later cases has questioned the legal basis for the Court's decision or its accuracy. Some commentators have, however, noted the inconsistencies in the Court's conclusions, including Samuel P. King, U.S. District Court Judge for the District of Hawaiʻi, who characterized the grant of a dower interest to Queen Emma as "irrational."[130]

The main inconsistency is that if the Crown Lands were held in trust as property of "the Crown" by Kamehameha IV for the successor Mōʻī, then Queen Emma should not have been entitled to dower, and she need not have executed releases when ʻĀina were transferred. The fact that Queen Emma did join Kamehameha IV in transferring property indicates their belief that the Crown Lands were theirs to alienate. The Court's recognition of her dower rights is consistent with the understanding and practice that occurred at the time of the death of Kauikeaouli (Kamehameha III), where his Queen Kalama did receive payments in lieu of dower,[131] but it is inconsistent with the Court's conclusion that the lands belonged to the Crown and not to the individual who happens to be Mōʻī.

A second fundamental inconsistency in the Court's decision is that if the Crown Lands belonged to the successor to the throne, as opposed to the heirs of the Mōʻī, then the present Mōʻī should have only a possessory interest in the lands for life and should not be able to profit from the sale or transfer of these lands. Thus, Kamehameha IV should not have been able to transfer the lands at all (or grant a right of dower), because he did not own the lands in fee simple or freehold (or have a lease of fifty years or more), the requirement for dower set out by Article LIV, Section 1299 of the 1859 *Hawaiʻi Civil Code* (which Justice Robertson had helped draft).

These inconsistencies cannot be reconciled based on the facts or interpretations logically deduced by the Court. A possible practical explanation is that the members of the Court, who were appointed by the Mōʻī, were faced with a conflict

129. *See, e.g., Estate of Maughan,* 3 Hawaiʻi 262, 269, 1871 WL 6008, at *5 (1871), questioning the "mere obiter dictum" in Justice Robertson's opinion stating that Alexander Liholiho, as the adopted son of Kauikeaouli, would have inherited property in the absence of a will and ruling that adopted children did not have the same inheritance rights as natural children.

130. Samuel P. King, "History of Crown Lands May Determine Their Future," *Honolulu Star-Bulletin,* December 23, 1994, at A-13. *See also Kapiolani Estate v. Cleghorn,* 14 Hawaiʻi 330, 334–35 (1902), questioning the logic of the ruling on dower.

131. *In the Matter of the Estate of His Majesty Kamehameha IV,* 2 Hawaiʻi 715, 724–25 (1864); *see supra* chapter 6, text at notes 18–26.

between "several high personages" and felt compelled to reach an amicable and equitable settlement—a compromise decision that was both agreeable with the Ali'i and sound public policy. Another logical justification is that the Court recognized that, while the lands should pass to the new Mō'ī, a widowed Queen (who had shared the duties of the Crown) needed some revenue to support herself after the death of her husband. The underlying rationale of dower rights justified providing land and resources to the widowed Queen, even if dower would not logically apply to lands that had been held only in trust for a future monarch.

It is also evident that the Ali'i were not in Court merely to add to their personal holdings for selfish motives but rather to fulfill their duties as Ali'i to act on behalf of their people. Queen Emma's altruistic motives were later demonstrated by her decision to use her land holdings to assist the Queen's Hospital to address the people's health needs. Lot (Kamehameha V) concentrated his efforts to pay down the debts incurred by his brother (Kamehameha IV) to ensure a financially sound Kingdom.

The Court's decision was based heavily on the public-policy perspective that each new Mō'ī needs the Crown Lands to have sufficient assets to be a proper Monarch and to satisfy the needs and expenses of the office.[132] The opinion says that it was Kauikeaouli's intent to ensure that the lands should descend to "the future wearers of the crown which the conqueror had won,"[133] indicating that it is simply in the nature of a Monarch to have lands. To have treated the Crown Lands as private in nature and not belonging to the new Mō'ī would have dramatically weakened the Monarchy as an institution. The decision honors the Crown in that sense and also supports the notion that these lands are trust lands designed to benefit all Native Hawaiians. The Ali'i always understood that their control of property carried with it a responsibility to provide for all their people and that their role was essentially that of trustee of the land, with a duty to care for the land (Malama 'Āina) while utilizing it. By linking the lands to the Monarch, the Court reinforced the traditional view that the 'Āina was to be shared.

The decision reflects the changing role of the Mō'ī and confirms the Kingdom's evolution into a true Constitutional Monarchy. It is ironic and regrettable that this important decision was rendered by a Court made up entirely by foreigners. The role of foreigners in this transforming process has continued to be a matter of criticism and concern. In any event, this 1864 opinion marked a turning point in the status and character of the Crown Lands, leading to the legislative changes discussed in the next chapter.

---

132. Kuykendall explained that "[t]here were . . . grave disadvantages in [the] theory" that "the crown lands [were] the king's personal or private property in the same sense that the lands awarded to the chiefs became their private property." 1 Ralph S. Kuykendall, *The Hawaiian Kingdom 1778–1854: Foundation and Transformation,* 288 n.78 (1938, 7th printing, 1989).

133. *In the Matter of the Estate of His Majesty Kamehameha IV,* 2 Hawai'i 715, 725 (1864).

The 1865 Statute Making the Crown Lands Inalienable

As a result of the 1864 Supreme Court decision,[1] it was understood that the Crown Lands passed to the successor of the throne for the Mōʻī's lifetime, but the apparent inconsistencies in Justice Robertson's decision regarding dower and the power of the Mōʻī to sell and transfer Crown Lands remained troublesome. Recognizing the competing interests of the Queen's entitlement to dower on the one hand and the disadvantage of a diminished Royal Domain on the other, the Legislature offered Queen Emma lifetime annual payments of $6,000 if she waived her dower interest in the Crown Lands.[2] She accepted this offer and the Legislature confirmed the matter in "An Act to Make a Permanent Settlement on Her Majesty Queen Emma" on December 3, 1864.[3] The dower question never again became a factor when the lands were later passed to successors to the Crown. [4]

More significantly, the Legislature then eliminated the power of the Mōʻī to sell or transfer ʻĀina that were part of the Crown Lands, dramatically changing the character of these lands and the power of the Mōʻī. Spaulding explained the concern as follows: "The former kings, though they had mortgaged a great deal, had not sold much, but there was nothing to prevent a spendthrift monarch from disposing of every acre to the highest bidder, and leaving nothing to those who came after."[5] This worry was reinforced by Justice Robertson's 1864 opinion, which had interpreted

---

1. *In the Matter of the Estate of His Majesty Kamehameha IV,* 2 Hawaiʻi 715 (1864), described in the previous chapter.

2. Jean Hobbs, *Hawaii: A Pageant of the Soil,* 67–68 (1935).

3. *Id.,* citing *Session Laws,* 1846–74; *Laws of 1864–1865* at 71–72; Thomas Marshall Spaulding, *The Crown Lands of Hawaii,* 12 (University of Hawaiʻi Occasional Papers, No. 1, October 10, 1923). Queen Emma complained periodically about her lack of funds, particularly during her time in Europe in 1865 and 1866. *See, e.g.,* George S. Kanahele, *Emma: Hawaiʻi's Remarkable Queen,* 208–09 (1999). An additional $2,000 a year increase was granted to the Queen in 1882. "An Act to Increase the Permanent Settlement on Her Majesty Queen Dowager Emma," enacted July 5, 1882.

4. The dower issue was not raised again during the terms of Kamehameha V and William Charles Lunalilo, who had remained unmarried. No evidence has been found that it was raised by Queen Kapiʻolani, wife of King Kalākaua. Under the reign of Liliʻuokalani, it would not have been an issue. "Curtesy," the male counterpart, could not have been claimed by her husband, John Owen Dominis, because he predeceased her on August 27, 1891.

5. Spaulding, *supra* note 3, at 12.

the Act of June 7, 1848, to allow each successive Mō'ī to "regulate and dispose of the [lands] according to his will and pleasure, as private property, in like manner as was done by Kamehameha III."[6]

To eliminate this possibility, the Legislature passed "An Act to Relieve the Royal Domain from Encumbrances and to Render the Same Inalienable" on January 3, 1865.[7] This statute established a procedure to pay off the debts and extinguish the remaining mortgages left unsatisfied by the Estate of Kamehameha IV,[8] and then declared that the lands "shall be henceforth inalienable, and shall descend to the heirs and successors of the Hawaiian Crown forever."[9] This enactment also prohibited any lease of Crown Lands for a period longer than thirty years.[10] Although dicta in an 1877 opinion suggested that it might be possible to gain title to 'Āina in the Crown Lands inventory through adverse possession,[11] the Hawai'i Supreme Court ruled decisively during the early territorial period that these lands could not be alienated through that process.[12] The 1865 statute created a three-person Board of Commissioners of Crown Lands, appointed by the Mō'ī (two from his Cabinet Council and a third to act as a land agent), to manage the lands.[13] This Commission was "associated with the government's Interior Department."[14]

This 1865 statute also required that one-fourth of the revenues generated by the Crown Lands be used to pay off the mortgage interest and bond payments,[15] but in fact Kamehameha V, "with rare appreciation of the importance of clearing the burden of debt from the heritage of his successors," actually "voluntarily paid over almost the entire revenue"[16] during the next year and a half. In light of this royal cooperation, the Legislature assumed responsibility for the remaining indebtedness in July 1866.[17] "Thenceforth until the end of the monarchy each king enjoyed the full

---

6. *Estate of Kamehameha IV,* 2 Hawai'i at 725.

7. "An Act to Relieve the Royal Domain from Encumbrances and to Render the Same Inalienable," January 3, 1865, 1 *Session Laws of Hawai'i,* 69 (1851–70), 2 *Revised Laws of Hawai'i,* 2177–79 (1925), 30 *Revised Laws of Hawai'i,* 1226–28 (1905), reprinted in Hobbs, *supra* note 2, at 68–69, in Spaulding, *supra* note 3, at 13–14, *in Liliuokalani v. United States,* 45 Ct. Cl. 418, 431–32, 1909 WL 905 (1910), and in appendix 5 herein, *infra.*

8. Act of January 3, 1865, § 1. The Minister of Finance was authorized to issue up to $30,000 of Exchequer bonds with coupons, setting forth a maximum interest rate and payment schedule, and, along with the Commissioners of Crown Lands, was authorized to negotiate to settle these outstanding mortgages and dispose of the bonds.

9. *Id.,* § 3.

10. *Id.*

11. *Harris v. Carter,* 6 Hawai'i 195, 209 (1877).

12. *Galt v. Waianuhea,* 16 Hawai'i 652, 657, 1905 WL 1371, at *3 (1905), quoting "An Act to Relieve the Royal Domain from Encumbrances and to Render the Same Inalienable," January 3, 1865, 1 *Session Laws of Hawai'i,* 69 (1851–70), and then saying, "No clearer language could be used to indicate that such lands should not and could not be disposed of. And what cannot be disposed of cannot be taken away by adverse possession."

13. Act of January 3, 1865, *supra* note 7, §§ 4 and 6.

14. Robert H. Stauffer, *Kahana: How the Land Was Lost,* 229 (2004).

15. Act of January 3, 1865, *supra* note 7, § 5.

16. Hobbs, *supra* note 2, at 70.

17. Resolution approved July 6, 1866, *Laws 1866–67* at 11, reprinted in *Liliuokalani v. United States,* 45 Ct.Cl. 418, 432–33 (1910). See Hobbs, *supra* note 2, at 70; Spaulding, *supra* note 3, at 14. In this resolution, the

Kamehameha V
(Lot Kapuāiwa), 1865

revenue of the royal lands."[18] The 1866 Legislative Assembly also took steps to survey the Crown and the Government Lands. [19]

The Legislature that enacted the 1865 statute was operating under the new 1864 Constitution, which the new Mōʻī—Kamehameha V (Lot Kapuāiwa)—had promulgated in order to increase the power of the Crown.[20] Under this Constitution, the eighteen members of the House of Nobles and the twenty-seven members of the House of Representatives convened together as a unicameral body to enact legislation. Two future Mōʻī—William Charles Lunalilo and David Kalākaua—were members of the House of Nobles and thus participated in the decision restricting the

Legislature recognized the generosity of the Mōʻī in helping to pay off the indebtedness and also for accepting the limitation on alienation enacted in the 1865 statute: "this Assembly and the nation gratefully appreciate His Majesty's generosity in consenting to the limitation of the royal domain, as at present by law provided."

18. Spaulding, *supra* note 3, at 14.

19. *See* Jonathan Kay Kamakawiwoʻole Osorio, *Dismembering Lāhui: A History of the Hawaiian Nation to 1887,* 139 (2002), discussing the debate on how much to pay the surveyors. Lyons noted in 1875 that the failure to empower the Land Commission to apportion properly the Crown and Government Lands "has created uncertainty all over the group as to boundaries even to this day." C. J. Lyons, "Land Matters in Hawaii, No. 7," *The Islander,* August 13, 1875, at 151.

20. *See generally* 2 Ralph S. Kuykendall, *The Hawaiian Kingdom 1854–1874: Twenty Critical Years,* 127–34 (1982). Queen Liliʻuokalani later explained that the 1840 and 1852 Constitutions "were doubtless drafted under the supervision and advice of the missionaries," and "[s]o when Prince Lot came to the throne in 1863, under the title of Kamehameha V., his first official act was to refuse to take the oath to maintain the existing constitution." Liliuokalani, *Hawaii's Story by Hawaii's Queen,* 20 (1898, reprinted 1997).

powers of the Mō'ī over the Crown Lands. Native Hawaiians dominated this legislative session, with only about nine of the forty-five members being foreign born.[21] The 1866 Legislative Assembly had ten foreign-born members (out of forty-five) plus several part-Hawaiians, the rest being full Hawaiians.[22]

Lot accepted these enactments from his new Legislative Assembly and signed the statutes as Mō'ī, even though they had the effect of restricting his rights to manage the Crown Lands and rendered them inalienable. Lot's father, Mataio Kekūanaō'a, who was Kuhina Nui, also approved the 1865 statute.[23] Although this act restricted the authority of all future Mō'ī, it was consistent with the traditional precontact system whereby Ali'i had only a lifetime interest in their lands because 'Āina were redistributed through Kālai'āina each time a new Mō'ī emerged.[24] It was also compatible with the traditional Mālama 'Āina system, based on the understanding that land was not to be bought and sold but was meant to be utilized wisely, because to mālama the land was to mālama the people. The actions of Lot in consenting to the restrictions on the sale of land coupled with his voluntary contributions to reduce the debt are evidence that he understood his duty to function as a traditional Ali'i, with responsibilities to Akua, the people, the land, the culture, and the Kingdom's sovereignty. The other Ali'i appear also to have accepted the Act of January 3, 1865, perhaps also sharing these traditional understandings and recognizing that rendering the lands inalienable, and thus protected from foreign ownership, was important to the survival of the native culture and of the Kingdom.[25]

---

21. *See* listing of members of the 1864 Legislative Assembly in Osorio, *supra* note 19, at 118.

22. *Id.* at 138. A session of the 1866 Legislature is described in Mark Twain, *Roughing It,* in chapter 67, at 357–58 (1871, reprinted in 1987, Signet Classic).

23. Samuel P. King, "History of Crown Lands May Determine Their Future," *Honolulu Star-Bulletin,* December 23, 1994, at A-13.

24. *See supra* chapter 2, text at notes 47–52.

25. Despite the Act of January 3, 1865, rendering the Crown Lands henceforth inalienable, the Legislature passed the Act of July 21, 1870, entitled "An Act To Enable the Commissioners of Crown Lands to Convey Certain Parcels of Land Belonging to the Royal Domain," which authorized the conveyance of 'Āina from the Crown Lands to five parties:

    1. To Thomas Spencer, lands in Pu'u'eo, in the district of Hilo, Hawai'i for $2,500;

    2. To the Waimea Grazing Company, a certain lot in Waimea, of about seven acres for $100;

    3. To Keahi, a certain piece of land in the Ili of Kapapohaku, in the Ahupua'a of Wailuku, Maui;

    4. To Kanalulu, a tract of land in the 'Ili of Kapa'aloa, in the Ahupua'a of Wailuku, Maui; and

    5. To Kekipi, a parcel of land in the 'Ili of Lamalei also in Wailuku, Maui.

The preamble of the act explained that contracts of sale had been made between these parties and Alexander Liholiho (Kamehameha IV), and consideration had been paid or had been agreed to be paid. The Commissioners of the Crown Lands were authorized to convey the described tracts of lands as though they had been made by Alexander Liholiho in his lifetime.

10

The Ascension of William Charles Lunalilo
to the Throne (1872)

 On December 11, 1872, Lot Kapuāiwa (Kamehameha V) died on his forty-second birthday.[1] Like his younger brother Alexander Liholiho (Kamehameha IV), he had reigned for a nine-year period and had died without naming a successor. William Charles Lunalilo, a cousin of the deceased Mōʻī who also had attended the Royal School, emerged as an early front-runner.[2] Lunalilo was a descendant of Kalaimamahu, a half brother of Kamehameha I.[3] Although his ascension to the throne over his rival, David Kalākaua, preserved the Kamehameha line to some extent, Lunalilo did not consider himself a Kamehameha. At Lunalilo's suggestion, a plebiscite by the male subjects of the Kingdom was held to express their free choice, and Lunalilo was selected overwhelmingly.[4] This decision was then confirmed by the Legislature, as required by the 1864 Constitution.[5] Lunalilo took the oath of office on January 12, 1873,[6] at the age of 37, but he died from tuberculosis and related ailments on February 3, 1874, a little more than a year later.[7]

Queen Liliʻuokalani later described the policy of the Lunalilo Cabinet as "American," seeking links to the United States, instead of being "Hawaiian" and encouraging the prosperity of an independent nation.[8] In contrast to Kamehameha

1. George S. Kanahele, *Emma: Hawaiʻi's Remarkable Queen,* 264 (1999).

2. 2 Ralph S. Kuykendall, *The Hawaiian Kingdom 1854–1874: Twenty Critical Years,* 242 (1953, reprinted 1982). Kuykendall listed the four Aliʻi who were considered for the Crown as Lunalilo, Kalākaua, Ruth Keʻelikolani (Lot's half sister, "because she would place several others in presumptive relation to the Throne"), and Bernice Pauahi Bishop (because she had been the late choice of Kamehameha V). *Id.* at 242–43. Queen Liliʻuokalani suggested that she had also been considered at that time, along with Fanny Kekelaokalani Young (mother of Queen Emma). Liliuokalani, *Hawaii's Story by Hawaii's Queen,* 35 (1898, reprinted 1997). *See also* Kanahele, *supra* note 1, at 264–67.

3. *See* Lilikala Kameʻeleihiwa, *Native Land and Foreign Desires: Pehea La E Pono Ai?* 230 (1992), discussing Lunalilo's relationship to Kamehameha I.

4. 2 Kuykendall, *supra* note 2, at 243–44. Sylvester K. Stevens, *American Expansion in Hawaii 1842–1898,* 92–93 (1945, reissued 1968). Lunalilo received 12,530 votes out of the 12,581 votes cast, with the other fifty-one votes split among David Kalākaua, Queen Emma, Ruth Keʻelikolani, and Bernice Pauahi Bishop. Robert C. Schmitt, *Historical Statistics of Hawaii,* 602 (1977).

5. *Id.;* Constitution of 1864, art. 22.

6. 2 Kuykendall, *supra* note 2, at 245.

7. *Id.* at 259 and 262; Kameʻeleihiwa, *supra* note 3, at 313.

8. Liliuokalani, *supra* note 2, at 37–38.

William Charles
Lunalilo

V, who had distanced himself from men associated with the "missionary" party, King Lunalilo's appointments consisted of Charles Reed Bishop, Minister of Foreign Affairs; Edwin O. Hall, Minister of Interior; Robert Stirling, Minister of Finance; and Albert Francis Judd, Attorney General. Three of these four Ministers were Americans[9] and "two of these four were from families who landed upon our shores with the single intention to teach our people the religion of Christ" and were "seeking to render the Islands a mere dependency, either openly or under sufficient disguise, on the government of the United States."[10]

Lunalilo was ill during most of his brief term and although he sought to be responsive and accountable to his people, policy tended to be made by his Cabinet. The most divisive event of his reign occurred when Lunalilo, pursuant to his Cabinet's advice, offered to cede Pearl Harbor to the United States in exchange for a Reciprocity Treaty that would directly benefit the business community by allowing Hawaiian products, especially sugar, to enter the United States tax free.[11] Because of

9. Gavan Daws, *Shoal of Time: A History of the Hawaiian Islands,* 191 (1968, reprinted 1974).
10. Liliuokalani, *supra* note 2, at 37–38.
11. Kame'eleihiwa, *supra* note 3, at 313; Daws, *supra* note 9, at 191.

the overwhelming opposition by the Ali'i and the general population to the cessation of territory, however, the Mō'ī withdrew the offer before it could be ratified.[12] Charles Reed Bishop reported that every Ali'i, including his own wife (Bernice Pauahi Bishop), was opposed to the Pearl Harbor Plan.[13] Queen Emma wrote, "The reciprocity treaty, giving away land, is much discussed these days. . . . There is a feeling of bitterness against these rude people who dwell on our land and have high handed ideas of giving away somebody else's property as if it was theirs."[14] The debate over this proposal divided the community, and this time those wanting to protect the 'Āina from foreign influences prevailed.

---

12. 2 Kuykendall, *supra* note 2, at 256; Daws, *supra* note 9, at 192–93, explaining that the natives opposed the loss of 'Āina, which they perceived as a preliminary step toward annexation, and bombarded the Mō'ī with angry petitions.

13. 2 Kuykendall, *supra* note 2, at 256; *see* Kame'eleihiwa, *supra* note 3, at 313.

14. 2 Kuykendall, *supra* note 2, at 256, quoting from a letter from Queen Emma to Keliimoewai, August 20, 1873; Kanahele, *supra* note 1, at 271, quoting from the same source.

11

The Transition between the Kamehameha Line and Kalākaua's Keawe-a-Heulu Line

Because King Lunalilo had not named a successor, Article 22 of the 1864 Constitution assigned the task to the Cabinet Council and the Legislative Assembly. The two main candidates were Queen Emma, widow of Kamehameha IV and great-grandniece of Kamehameha I, and David Kalākaua, a descendant of high Aliʻi of Hilo who had supported Kamehameha I.[1] Both had been students at the Royal School,[2] and both were passionate in their quest for the Crown. Kalākaua announced, "My earnest desire is for the perpetuity of the crown and the permanent independence of the government and people of Hawaii, on the basis of equity, liberty, prosperity, progress and protection of the whole people."[3] Queen Emma countered that it had been Lunalilo's "wish and intention" that she reign.[4] Those who supported the interests of the United States and a reciprocity treaty tended to support Kalākaua, while those supporting British interests and opposing the treaty tended to support Emma,[5] but many other complex considerations including genealogy and gender also played roles in this contest.[6] The Legislature's selection of David Kalākaua over Queen Emma by a vote of thirty-nine to six[7] terminated the Kamehameha era and the control of the Crown Lands, which had been personally selected by Kamehameha III, by the Kamehamehas. (The remaining Kame-

---

1. Lilikala Kameʻeleihiwa, *Native Land and Foreign Desires: Pehea La E Pono Ai?* 313 (1992), discussing the candidates' genealogical qualifications.

2. The "serious" candidates were those same individuals considered the year before at the death of Kamehameha V, listed *supra* chapter 10, note 2. 3 Ralph S. Kuykendall, *The Hawaiian Kingdom 1874–1893: The Kalakaua Dynasty,* 4 (1967, reprinted 1987). *See infra* chapter 3, note 64 for a list of the Aliʻi who attended the Royal School.

3. 3 Kuykendall, *supra* note 2, at 8.

4. *Id.*

5. Davianna Pomaikaʻi McGregor, "The Cultural and Political History of Hawaiian Native People," in *Our History, Our Way: An Ethnic Studies Anthology,* 357 (Gregory Yee Mark, Davianna Pomaikaʻi McGregor, and Linda A. Revilla, eds., 1996).

6. Jonathan Kay Kamakawiwoʻole Osorio, *Dismembering Lāhui: A History of the Hawaiian Nation to 1887,* 151–59 (2002); Gavan Daws, *Shoal of Time: A History of the Hawaiian Islands,* 197–99 (1968, reprinted 1974); George S. Kanahele, *Emma: Hawaiʻi's Remarkable Queen,* 274–92 (1999).

7. 3 Kuykendall, *supra* note 2, at 9; Sylvester K. Stevens, *American Expansion in Hawaii 1842–1898,* 93–95 (1945, reissued 1968).

King David Kalākaua

hamehas, however, "such as Bernice Pauahi Bishop and Ruth Keʻelikolani favored David Kalākaua" to become the new Mōʻī,[8] as did Princess Pauahi's husband Charles Reed Bishop.[9]) A riot was sparked by a "howling mob" of Queen Emma's passionate supporters, who "sacked" the courthouse where the vote had occurred, causing extensive property damage, and "assaulted the representatives with clubs," causing the death of one legislator and injuries to others. This fighting continued until 150 armed U.S. forces and 70 British troops landed to reestablish peace.[10]

8. Kanahele, *supra* note 6, at 285.

9. *Id.* at 286.

10. W. D. Alexander, "A Statement of Facts Relating to Politics during Kalākaua's Reign," in "Report of Commissioner to the Hawaiian Islands," in 27 *Executive Documents of the House of Representatives for the Second Session of the Fifty-Third Congress,* 1893–94, originally in H.R. Exec. Doc. No. 47, 53d Cong., 2d Sess. (1893), reprinted in *Foreign Relations of the United States,* 1894, Appendix 2, "Affairs in Hawaii," 179, 180 (1895, preservation photocopy 1992) (hereafter cited as "Blount Report"); 3 Kuykendall, *supra* note 2, at 10. The troops remained in Honolulu for eight days. *Id. See also* Kanahele, *supra* note 6, at 288–92.

Queen Emma

King Kalākaua's ascension to the throne on February 12, 1874, marked the start of the Keawe-a-heulu line.[11] Kalākaua had courted the supporters of U.S. interests and had expressed support for a reciprocity treaty during his campaign to become Mō'ī,[12] but he was committed to maintaining the Kingdom's independence. He understood that the Kingdom's sovereignty depended on the survival of his people and that it was of vital importance to "Ho'oulu Lāhui" (Increase the Race).[13] One his-

---

11. David Kalākaua was born on November 16, 1836, to High Chief Kahanu Kapa'akea and High Chiefess Analea Keohokalole, a great-granddaughter of Keawe-a-heulu. Kristin Zambucka, *Kalākaua: Hawai'i's Last King*, 7 (1983). The founder of the Keawe-a-heulu line was a first cousin to the father of Kamehameha I. Liliuokalani, *Hawaii's Story by Hawaii's Queen*, 105 (1898, reprinted 1997). On February 14, 1874, pursuant to Article 22 of the 1864 Constitution, King Kalākaua appointed his younger brother William Pitt Leleiohoku as his successor. *Id.* at 52. When Leleiohoku died, Lili'uokalani was named heir apparent on April 10, 1877. *Id.* at 55. Princess Ruth Ke'elikolani, adopted mother of the late Leleiohoku, asked the Mō'ī if she could be proclaimed heir apparent, but he declined. *Id.* King Kalākaua's wife Queen Kapi'olani was the granddaughter of Kaumuali'i, the last ruling chief of Kaua'i. Zambucka, *id.*, at 23. Kapi'olani's three nephews were designated Princes: Prince David Kawananakoa, Prince Jonah Kūhiō Kalaniana'ole, and Prince Edward Keliiahonui. *Id. See also infra* chapter 28, text following note 68.

12. McGregor, *supra* note 5, at 357–58.

13. *Id.* at 361; Kame'eleihiwa, *supra* note 1, at 314.

torian commented that Kalākaua was of "makahonu philosophy, believing in the celebration of life."[14] Kalākaua encouraged the revival of traditional practices to instill hope in his dying people. [15]

Trade and relations with the outside world dominated Kalākaua's reign, and he was instrumental in securing the Reciprocity Treaty of January 30, 1875.[16] Queen Liliʻuokalani later wrote that the Mōʻī believed that the Reciprocity Treaty would "enrich or benefit, not one class, but, in a greater or less degree, all his subjects," but she also acknowledged that some had viewed the treaty as the first step toward the loss of independence,[17] even though this version of the treaty did not require the ceding of Puʻuloa (the Pearl River, later Pearl Harbor).

Because of the Reciprocity Treaty and the resulting financial boom, foreigners increasingly desired large parcels of prime land.[18] Some foreigners looked longingly at the Crown Lands, but the Act of January 3, 1865,[19] which prohibited the alienation of the Crown Lands, was in direct conflict with their ambitions. The (Western-dominated) press of the day supported the sale and distribution of the Crown Lands, with one paper noting that "[t]he old and ridiculous notions of primitive times in regard to the effects of alienating territory should have long since been abandoned, and certainly should not be entertained by a government professing enlightenment."[20] A few years later, another paper expressed the same view, arguing that "the moment the Crown Lands become private property, they will become taxable and yield a revenue to the country, so that not only from the private view of the royal family, but from that of the nation at large, the scheme appears to be a good one."[21] The realization that such pressure would always be brought against the integrity of the Crown Lands may have been one reason why Lot (Kamehameha V) had approved the 1865 act that prohibited any alienation of these lands.

Eight years after his election as Mōʻī, Kalākaua turned against the U.S. interests and the "factor-planter-missionary elite" that had dominated the government.[22] He linked his fortunes to the economic initiatives of Claus Spreckels and brought in Walter Murray Gibson as his Prime Minister,[23] seeking to promote a more independent path. The tensions that followed led to the Bayonet Constitution, which was forced upon Kalākaua in 1887, and then in 1893 to the overthrow of the Kingdom.

---

14. Kameʻeleihiwa, *supra* note 1, at 313.

15. *Id.* at 313–14.

16. *See* Liliuokalani, *supra* note 11, at 54; Osorio, *supra* note 6, at 166–73; *see generally* 3 Kuykendall, *supra* note 2, at 17–46; Daws, *supra* note 6, at 202–06.

17. Liliuokalani, *supra* note 11, at 179–80.

18. Jacob Adler, *Claus Spreckels: The Sugar King in Hawaiʻi,* 297 n. 25 (1966).

19. *See supra* chapter 9.

20. Adler, *supra* note 18, at 297 n. 25, quoting *Pacific Commercial Advertiser,* April 1, 1876.

21. *Id.,* quoting *Hawaiian Gazette,* July 4, 1882. *See also* Osorio, *supra* note 6, at 164–66.

22. McGregor, *supra* note 5 at 359.

23. *See generally* Jacob Adler and and Robert M. Kamins, *The Fantastic Life of Walter Murray Gibson: Hawaii's Minister of Everything* (1986); Daws, *supra* note 6, at 220–25.

12

Claus Spreckels, Princess Ruth Keʻelikolani, and the Claim to a Half Interest in the Crown Lands

The California sugar magnate Claus Spreckels came to Hawaiʻi in 1876 on the same steamer that brought word of the Reciprocity Treaty's ratification.[1] On this first trip, Spreckels gathered information on how he could share in Hawaiʻi's future prosperity, and when he returned in 1878, he focused on growing sugar on the plains of central Maui.[2] He brought Hermann Schussler, an engineer who was able to design a ditch system that could transport water from the slopes of Haleakalā.[3] As one of the few in the islands with access to large amounts of cash,[4] Spreckels was able to purchase land, acquire water rights, and attain political influence in the Kingdom.

Spreckels began this effort by purchasing an undivided half interest in 16,000 acres of land from Henry Cornwell in Waikapu commons on Maui and secured a thirty-year lease of 24,000 acres of Crown Lands in the Wailuku plains in central Maui at a rent of $1,000 a year.[5] By 1880, Spreckels had invested $500,000 in an irrigation system to bring water to his otherwise dry lands.[6] Under the terms of the 1865 statute that had rendered the Crown Lands inalienable,[7] thirty years was the maximum permissible length for a lease of these lands, but Spreckels was concerned that this limited time period would not be adequate to recoup his outlays.[8] So, in 1882 he entered into a controversial transaction with Princess Ruth Keʻelikolani, a descendant of the Kamehameha line, which has been described as "an investment in blackmail."[9] Through this maneuver, Spreckels was able to acquire the 24,000 acres of the Wailuku Ahupuaʻa on Maui from the Crown Land inventory.[10]

---

1. Jacob Adler, *Claus Spreckels: The Sugar King in Hawaii,* 3 (1966).
2. *Id.* at 35–36.
3. *Id.*
4. 3 Ralph S. Kuykendall, *The Hawaiian Kingdom 1874–1893: The Kalakaua Dynasty,* 59 (1967, reprinted 1987).
5. Adler, *supra* note 1, at 36, 52.
6. *Id.* at 52.
7. *See supra* chapter 9.
8. Adler, *supra* note 1, at 52.
9. 3 Kuykendall, *supra* note 4, at 61.
10. Jean Hobbs, *Hawaii: A Pageant of the Soil,* 74 (1935).

Claus Spreckels *(standing, second from left)* arriving in Hawaiʻi

This scheme began in September 1880, when Spreckels paid $10,000 for any rights that Princess Ruth had to a "claim" in the Crown Lands.[11] Princess Ruth asserted that because she was of the Kamehameha line, she had inherited a half interest in the Crown Lands.[12] She argued that this interest was not and could not have been taken away by the Act of January 3, 1865, which had rendered the Crown Lands inalienable.[13] In exchange for the $10,000, she gave Spreckels a deed that quitclaimed any rights in the Crown Lands to which she was entitled as heir to Kamehameha III, Kamehameha IV, Kamehameha V, and her father Mataio Kekūanaōʻa.[14] One commentator wrote that if she had possessed a valid title and interest to these lands, it would have been valued at about $750,000.[15]

11. *Id.,* citing a regulation deed dated September 30, 1880.
12. Adler, *supra* note 1, at 296 n. 10.
13. *Id. See supra* chapter 9 for a discussion and analysis of the 1865 act.
14. Adler, *supra* note 1, at 54.
15. *Id.* at 53–54. Adler estimated that at the going rate of about $1.50 an acre in 1880, the Crown Lands were worth about $1,500,000, and hence that Princess Ruth's claim to a half interest, if valid, would have been worth $750,000. *Id.*

Claus Spreckels

In light of the 1864 Supreme Court decision that limited the Crown Lands to "successors of the throne,"[16] as well as the Act of January 3, 1865, which eliminated the Monarch's right to alienate Crown Lands, the claim Spreckels purchased would not appear to have had any legal value whatsoever.[17] Nevertheless, perhaps because some members supported the transfer of Crown Lands into private hands and were

16. *In the Matter of the Estate of His Majesty Kamehameha IV,* 2 Hawai'i 715 (1864); *see supra* chapter 8.

17. Hobbs, *supra* note 10, at 74, saying that Princess Ruth's rights in the Crown Lands in 1880 were "certainly open to question"; 3 Kuykendall, *supra* note 4, at 61, expressing the view that Princess Ruth did not have clear legal title; Adler, *supra* note 1, at 53: "At best, then, her [Princess Ruth's] interest in the crown lands was somewhat shadowy"; Jacob Adler and Robert M. Kamins, *The Fantastic Life of Walter Murray Gibson: Hawaii's Minister of Everything,* 132 (1986): "the decision of the Hawaii Supreme Court seemed to negate any claim Princess Ruth might have had to a vendable title"; Thomas Marshall Spaulding, *The Crown Lands of Hawaii,* 15 (University of Hawai'i Occasional Papers No. 1, October 10, 1923): "As the princess had no estate, right, title or interest of any description in the crown lands, either at law or in equity, this was a singular proceeding"; Jonathan Kay Kamakawiwo'ole Osorio, *Dismembering Lāhui: A History of the Hawaiian Nation to 1887,* 187 (2002): "In the first place, it must be said the [Ruth] Ke'elikolani's *legal* claim was debatable" (emphasis in original).

thus willing to ignore the legal weakness of Spreckels' asserted claim, the Legislature was persuaded to quiet his claim by passing the controversial "Act to Authorize the Commissioners of Crown Lands to Convey Certain Portions of Such Lands to Claus Spreckels in Satisfaction of All Claims He May Have on Such Lands," which King Kalākaua approved on July 21, 1882.[18] As required by the statute, Spreckels signed a quitclaim on August 11, 1882, and the Kingdom conveyed the 24,000 acres to Spreckels to discharge all future claims.[19]

The intervention of the Legislature quieted Spreckels' claim, but many questions were raised regarding this conveyance. Did Spreckels have any plausible legal claim? He was able to obtain favorable legal opinions supporting his claim from Alfred S. Hartwell (an American who was first appointed Attorney General in 1874 and reappointed in 1876, was an Associate Justice of the Hawaiʻi Supreme Court from 1868 to 1874, and later assisted with the overthrow of the Kingdom in 1893),[20] William R. Castle (a Hawaiʻi-born citizen of missionary parents who had been appointed Attorney General on February 15, 1876, was elected to the Legislature in 1878, and later played an active role in obtaining Kuleana Lands in Kahana Valley, Oʻahu,[21] in imposing the 1887 Bayonet Constitution on King Kalākaua, and in overthrowing the Kingdom in 1893),[22] and Edward Preston (who had served as Attorney General from 1878 to 1880, was appointed Attorney General again shortly after he rendered his opinion, serving from 1882 to 1883, and later was an Associate Justice of the Supreme Court).[23]

Did Princess Ruth have an arguably legitimate claim to the Crown Lands? Preston's short May 17, 1882, opinion letter supporting her claim is based on the argument that Princess Ruth's interest in the Crown Lands had somehow already vested before the Supreme Court's 1864 decision and hence that she was entitled to a share of them as heir of Lot (Kamehameha V), despite the 1864 Supreme Court decision and the 1865 statute:

> I feel quite certain that these [Crown] lands were intended to be the private lands of Kamehameha the 3rd and that they descended to his heirs and devisees. . . .
>
> When the lands were divided [in the Mahele] . . . , he retained for his own

---

18. "An Act to Authorize the Commissioners of Crown Lands to Convey Certain Portions of Such Lands to Claus Spreckels in Satisfaction of All Claims He May Have To Such Lands," July 21, 1882.

19. Adler, *supra* note 1, at 64.

20. 3 Kuykendall, *supra* note 4, at 12, 196, 502 n.*, 583–85, and 588.

21. Robert H. Stauffer, *Kahana: How the Land Was Lost*, 145–46 (2004).

22. 3 Kuyendall, *supra* note 4 at 50, 193 n.*, 197, 356, 587, and 605.

23. *Id.* at 200, 254, 267, 371, and 406; Adler, *supra* note 1 at 55–56. Preston was considered to be a "Spreckels man," but Castle and Hartwell were not. *Id.* at 55.

Surveyor-General W. D. Alexander wrote in 1893 that "The correctness of the foregoing settlement [in the Act of January 3, 1865, declaring the Crown Lands to be inalienable] has been contested by some of our best lawyers. They have denied that it carried out the intention of Kamehameha III, and have even held it to have been unconstitutional, and that an action in equity might have been brought in behalf of the heirs of the estate of Kamehameha III [i.e., Princess Ruth]." Letter from Surveyor-General W. D. Alexander to Attorney-General W. O. Smith, March 31, 1893, in "Blount Report," *supra* chapter 11 note 10, at 199, 201.

private use and of his heirs the lands called Crown Lands and disposed of some of them accordingly, devising the residue by Will to his adopted child and heir Kamehameha the 4th, on whose death they descended, as I am of the opinion, to his Queen (Emma) and his father.

The queen has conveyed her rights to the Government and it appears to me that the other moiety descended to Kamehameha the 5th and his Sister Luka [Princess Ruth] who succeeded as heir to her brother on his death intestate in 1872.

Under these circumstances of course, in my opinion the decision of the Supreme Court and the law declaring these lands inalienable are inoperative and void as against Mr. Spreckels' grantor, and I therefore do not hesitate to say that under his conveyance he is entitled to one half of the so called "Crown Lands."[24]

Under today's ethical standards, an attorney who contended in court that an opinion of the highest appellate court and an enactment of the Legislature were "inoperative and void"—without any citations or logical argumentation—would probably be subject to heavy sanctions for presenting a "frivolous" argument.[25] Nonetheless, this opinion was apparently offered with a straight face, and Preston's reward was to be made Attorney General of the Kingdom three days later![26]

Another problem with the claim is that Princess Ruth's complicated genealogy makes it hard to understand even the nature of her claim as heir.[27] Princess Ruth's descent from the Kamehamehas was claimed from her maternal side through her mother, Pauahi.[28] It was unsettled, however, whether Pauahi's father, Pauli Ka'oleioku, was the son of Kamehameha I or of his high-ranking uncle Kalaniopu'u.[29] Thus, it was undetermined whether Princess Ruth was the great-granddaughter or

---

24. Adler, *supra* note 1, at 55–56, quoting from Opinion Letter of Edward Preston, May 17, 1882. *See also* W. D. Alexander, "A Statement of Facts Relating to Politics during Kalākaua's Reign," in "Blount Report," *supra* note 23, at 179, 185 (hereafter cited as "Alexander Statement"), stating that Ruth's claim "had been ignored in the decision of the Supreme Court and the Act of 1865, which constituted the crown lands."

25. If Princess Ruth's interest in the land had "vested" prior to the 1864 decision, then Queen Emma's interest would have similarly vested, and she would have prevailed in the lawsuit. Also, Preston was mistaken in his assertion that Queen Emma had "conveyed her rights to the Government." Queen Emma conveyed her dower rights in exchange for a fixed pension. She did not convey her original claim to the Crown Lands, but the Hawai'i Supreme Court rejected the legitimacy of that claim. *See generally supra* chapter 8.

26. On May 20, 1882, the Gibson Cabinet was appointed, consisting of Walter Murray Gibson, Premier and Minister of Foreign Relations; Simon K. Ka'ai, Minister of Interior; John E. Bush, Minister of Finance; and Edward Preston, Attorney General. Adler, *supra* note 1, at 56. Adler has written that from 1882 to 1886, "the Kalākaua-Gibson-Spreckels triumvirate substantially controlled the Hawaiian government." *Id.* at 58. *See also* Davianna Pomaika'i McGregor, "The Cultural and Political History of Hawaiian Native People," in *Our History, Our Way: An Ethnic Studies Anthology,* 359 (Gregory Yee Mark, Davianna Pomaika'i McGregor, and Linda A. Revilla, eds., 1996): "The Kalākaua-Spreckels-Gibson triumvirate controlled Hawai'i's government until the coup d'etat of 1887." Professor McGregor has explained that Spreckels' financial backing allowed King Kalākaua "to cut off his ties with the traditional haole [factor-planter-missionary] elite and all[y] himself with the [Hawaiian] nationalists." *Id.* at 358.

27. "For one thing her close blood relationship with the Kamehamehas was not accepted universally." Gavan Daws, *Shoal of Time: A History of the Hawaiian Islands,* 228 (1968, reprinted 1974).

28. Kristin Zambucka, *The High Chiefess Princess Ruth Ke'elikolani,* 19 (1992).

29. *Id.* at 14.

Princess Ruth Keʻelikolani (between Samuel Parker [*left*] and
John Cummins [*right*]), ca. 1874–75

great-grandniece of Kamehameha I.[30] Although it was uncertain, therefore, whether
Princess Ruth descended directly from Kamehameha I, her descent from high lin-
eage within the Kamehameha line was not questioned. But Princess Ruth's cousin,
Bernice Pauahi Bishop, also a descendant of the Kamehameha line, was still alive.
Would not Princess Bernice Pauahi have been entitled to a half interest in whatever
lands to which Princess Ruth was entitled?

After Ruth's mother, who was also named Pauahi, died giving birth to Ruth,
Ruth's father, Mataio Kekūanaōʻa, married Kīnaʻu, a daughter of Kamehameha I and
Kuhina Nui in the 1830s.[31] This union produced Moses Kekuaiwa, Lot Kapuāiwa
(Kamehameha V), Alexander Liholiho (Kamehameha IV), and Victoria Kamāmalu.
Kekūanaōʻa did not distinguish between his "Royal Children,"[32] but questions

30. Lilikala Kameʻeleihiwa, *Native Land and Foreign Desires: Pehea La E Pono Ai?* 228 (1992).
31. *Id.* at 101. A genealogy chart shows that Kamehameha II (Liholiho) and Kīnaʻu were children of
Kamehameha I. Liholiho's mother was Keopuolani and Kīnaʻu's mother was Kaheiheimalie.
32. Zambucka, *Ruth, supra* note 28, at 20.

existed whether Princess Ruth was the natural daughter of Mataio Kekūanaō'a or rather of Kahala'ia, a kahu [33] of Kamehameha II.[34] Princess Ruth was thus described as "po'olua," or doubly fathered,[35] a status that was viewed positively by Hawaiians. From a Western perspective, however, if Princess Ruth was not the natural daughter of Kekūanaō'a, then she was not a half sister of Kamehameha IV and Kamehameha V, who were the natural sons of Kekūanaō'a, and thus any claim she might make of being an intestate heir of Kamehameha V would be invalid.

One commentator has suggested that Alexander Liholiho (Kamehameha IV) and Lot (Kamehameha V) believed that Ka'oleioku, Pauahi's father and Princess Ruth's grandfather, was the son of Kalaniopu'u, the high-ranking uncle of Kamehameha I.[36] Under this interpretation, Princess Ruth would not have been a direct descendant of Kamehameha I, unlike the natural children of Mataio Kekūanaō'a and Kīna'u. Perhaps this belief by Lot played a part in his decision not to offer Princess Ruth the throne. Another possible reason was that she was not eligible to reign because she had not been educated at the Royal School, which determined the pool of eligibles.[37] When Lot was on his deathbed on December 11, 1872, he rejected Princess Ruth's request that she be named his successor, because in his judgment she was "not fitted for the position,"[38] and he died without naming the next Mō'ī. This action counters any claim she might have had to the Crown Land as a hereditary or lineal heir, and it is perhaps particularly significant coming from the Mō'ī who had approved the prohibition on alienating the Crown Lands in the Act of January 3, 1865.

Why did Princess Ruth participate in this transaction with Claus Spreckels? Perhaps she did not understand the details of the sale or the claim. It has been suggested by one commentator that her land agent, Simon K. Ka'ai, a Spreckels supporter and a member of the House of Nobles who later supported the 1882 bill transferring the lands to Spreckels, may have misinformed her.[39] Ka'ai served as Minister of Interior, Minister of Finance, and President of the Board of Immigration under King Kalākaua and was generally a strong supporter of the Mō'ī, even when he was

---

33. Mary Kawena Pukui and Samuel H. Elbert, *Hawaiian Dictionary,* 113 (1986) defines "kahu" as "honored attendant, guardian, nurse, keeper."

34. Samuel M. Kamakau, *Ruling Chiefs of Hawai'i,* 347 (1961, revised ed. 1992) identifies Kahala'ia as Princess Ruth's natural father. *See also* Zambucka, *Ruth, supra* note 28, at 9–10.

35. Zambucka, *Ruth, supra* note 28, at 10.

36. *Id.* at 14. "The last ruling Kings of the Kamehameha dynasty, Kamehamehas IV and V held to the view that Kalaniopu'u begat Kaoleioku, so far as their opinions have been expressed in print." Zambucka does not give her source for this statement.

37. See Liliuokalani, *Hawaii's Story by Hawaii's Queen,* 5 (1898, reprinted 1997), stating that attendance at the Royal School was limited to those whose claims to the throne were acknowledged; Princess Ruth did not attend the Royal School. For the list of those who attended the Royal School, *see supra* chapter 3, note 64.

38. See Mary H. Krout, *The Memoirs of Hon. Bernice Pauahi Bishop,* 207–12 (1908). John Dominis, husband of Liliu'okalani, said that on his deathbed, Lot (Kamehameha V) offered Princess Bernice Pauahi Bishop the throne, but she declined and suggested that his sister, Princess Ruth be considered: "it is hers by right." *Id.* at 210. Lot replied, "She is not fitted for the position." *Id.* This story is also told in George S. Kanahele, *Emma: Hawai'i's Remarkable Queen,* 265–66 (1999), citing "Dominis to Bishop," January 7, 1873, as reported in the *Sixth Annual Report of the Hawaiian Historical Society for the Year 1898,* 11–16.

39. Adler, *supra* note 1, at 296 n. 12.

not holding a Cabinet position.[40] The Mōʻī appointed him to the House of Nobles in 1876. In 1880, he defended the Mōʻī for appointing a Cabinet without any Native Hawaiians,[41] but in 1881 he urged that no Caucasians be elected to the Legislature.[42] In 1882, James H. Wodehouse (the British Commissioner to the Kingdom) said that Kaʻai, "although very unscrupulous and very unreliable, has always had great influence with the natives."[43] In 1883, Kaʻai was dismissed as Minister of Finance for "dereliction of ministerial duty" "because of his notorious and persistent intemperance."[44]

If Princess Ruth fully understood or believed that she had an interest in the Crown Lands, then why would she agree to sell for a mere $10,000, since it would have been worth so much more?[45] A possible explanation is that she understood she held no legal claim to the lands but decided that if Spreckels, who should have known better, was willing to give her $10,000 for a meritless claim, she would accept the money.[46] This explanation is supported by the fact that Princess Ruth obtained from Spreckels a $60,000 loan at 6 percent, which enabled her to pay off some existing 12 percent loans.[47] Evidently she was a willing participant in and benefited from her part of the transaction, but whether she supported the Legislature's decision to convey 24,000 acres of the Kingdom's Crown Lands to Spreckels remains speculative.[48]

Did the Legislature, when it conveyed the Wailuku ʻĀina to Spreckels, acknowledge that Ruth had a legitimate right to some or all of the Crown Lands? As described above, Princess Ruth's legal claim was not totally without foundation, but it was quite weak.[49] It is only when one understands Claus Spreckels the man, as well as his financial dominance over the various parties, that it becomes evident that the Legislature's actions were probably motivated more by Spreckels' considerable financial influence than by the legitimacy or strength of his claim.

Spreckels' determined nature was demonstrated by his quest for water. Once he acquired land in Waikapu commons and a leasehold interest in the Wailuku Crown Lands, he focused on using his influence to meet his water needs. On June 24, 1878, Spreckels petitioned King Kalākaua and his Cabinet Ministers to pay $500

---

40. *See generally* 3 Kuykendall, *supra* note 4, at 143, 195 n.*, 200, and 226.

41. *Id.* at 224.

42. *Id.* at 247.

43. *Id.* at 255, citing "Wodehouse to Granville, no. 5, confidential," June 23, 1882, BPRO, FO 58/178.

44. *Id.* at 267, 691 n. 61, citing *Cabinet Council Minute Book,* February 15, 1883; "Daggett to Frelinghuysen, no. 51," February 17, 1883, *USDS, Dispatches, Hawaii,* vol. 21; and "Kaleleonalani (Queen Emma) to Ihilani (Mrs. Pierre Jones)," Feb. 20, 1883, Flora I. Jones Collection. W. D. Alexander later reported that Kaʻai "drank himself to death." "Alexander Statement," *supra* note 24, at 184.

45. By mid-August 1882, Princess Ruth had become suspicious of Kaʻai's handling of her affairs, and she released him from his position several months later. Adler, *supra* note 1, at 66.

46. *See* Lorrin A. Thurston, *Memoirs of the Hawaiian Revolution,* 83 (1936): "Since Princess Ruth never dreamed that she had any interest in the property, the offer was a pickup, and she promptly accepted."

47. Adler, *supra* note 1, at 54.

48. *Id.* at 296 n. 18, citing the *Hawaiian Gazette,* July 26, 1882, for the report that on July 21, the day the land bill was approved, Princess Ruth was being entertained at Spreckelsville on Maui.

49. *See supra* note 17.

a year for the rights to build a 17-mile irrigation system originating on the slopes of Haleakalā.[50] Because his request was not immediately granted, Spreckels arranged to meet with the Mō'ī on July 1 to discuss his concerns.[51] Apparently he offered King Kalākaua a gift of $10,000 and a loan of $40,000 at 7 percent interest to pay off existing notes that required 12 percent interest.[52] This meeting apparently persuaded the Mō'ī to dismiss all of his Cabinet Ministers and to appoint new Ministers who granted Spreckels his water rights on July 8, 1878.[53] This example demonstrates how Spreckels used his revenues to gain political influence.

On July 11, 1882, Premier and Minister of Foreign Relations Walter Murray Gibson informed the members of the Legislature that they would soon be receiving a draft of the "Act to Authorize the Commissioners of Crown Lands to Convey Certain Portions of Such Lands to Claus Spreckels in Satisfaction of All Claims He May Have on Such Lands."[54] When Attorney General Edward Preston formally introduced the bill one week later,[55] Minister of Interior Simon K. Ka'ai advocated that the bill receive priority. The debate, chaired by Charles H. Judd, who was then one of the three members of the Commission of Crown Lands, consumed most of the day on July 18, 1882.[56]

Representative George Washington Pilipo opposed the bill and demanded indefinite postponement.[57] His passionate speech to the governing body made the following points: (1) "This is not a matter that will please the Hawaiian people."[58] (2) This issue "really has no business before this Assembly . . . [and] should be considered in the courts."[59] (3) "I think that taking crown lands away from the crown and giving them to another person is a step toward destroying the independence of the country."[60] Pilipo chastised Ministers Gibson, Preston, and Ka'ai for lobbying selected legislators prior to introducing the bill and denounced Gibson as "a man whose mouth is full of *aloha* for Hawaiians, but whose actions are not."[61] According

50. Adler, *supra* note 1, at 36–37 and 44–51; 3 Kuykendall, *supra* note 4, at 200–01.

51. Adler, *supra* note 1, at 37; 3 Kuykendall, *supra* note 4, at 201.

52. *See generally* Adler, *supra* note 1, at 36–41. In the index to Kuykendall, this transfer is characterized as a "bribe." 3 Kuykendall, *supra* note 4, at 761. Chief Justice Charles Coffin Harris had previously offered to assist Spreckels but expressed outrage at the transfer of funds, saying that "it is the first time money has been used in this Country to procure official favors." Adler, *supra* note 1, at 40, citing a letter from Harris to E. H. Allen, October 4, 1878.

53. 3 Kuykendall, *supra* note 4, at 200. The new Cabinet consisted of Samuel G. Wilder, Minister of Interior; John M. Kapena, Minister of Foreign Relations; Simon K. Ka'ai, Minister of Finance (who later served as Princess Ruth's financial advisor); and Edward Preston, Attorney General (who later issued an opinion supporting Spreckels' claim to the Crown Lands). *Id.*

54. Adler, *supra* note 1, at 59, citing *Journal of Legislative Assembly,* 1882, proceedings of July 11, 1882.

55. *Id.*

56. *Id.* at 63.

57. *Id.* at 59.

58. *Id.*

59. *Id.* at 59.

60. *Id.* at 60, citing *Hawaiian Gazette,* July 26, 1882.

61. *Id.*

to Pilipo, the Ministers had argued that a "conciliatory policy was best, . . . [for] it is better to give this small tract of crown land to prevent trouble." [62] Pilipo emphasized that the Ministers were acting in violation of their oath to support the Kingdom's Constitution. [63] He was especially critical of Simon Kaʻai, Princess Ruth's land agent, saying: "What are we to think of such a native Hawaiian, the same color as myself, whose duty is to watch over and protect the interests of the country?" [64] Pilipo concluded his remarks by asking whether the Ministers were acting on behalf of the interests of a private individual—that is, Spreckels. [65] He asked: "Is it the King? What is the matter with our King? Is he in the power of the same man?" [66]

Attorney General Preston responded by arguing that the land bill was in the best interest of the Kingdom. He acknowledged that he had served as legal advisor for Spreckels but insisted that "I have no retainer from him or any other man in the Kingdom." [67] He emphasized that "[t]his Act has been introduced to settle a claim that might cause trouble for this country" and that Spreckels had been "induced to forego his full demand and accept a compromise as proposed in this bill." [68] Preston asserted that the land bill would save the Kingdom the expense of defending against Spreckels' claim in court, [69] and it would eliminate the risk that Spreckels would prevail in court and acquire not just 24,000 acres, but a half interest in a million acres. [70]

After Pilipo's motion for indefinite postponement was defeated 30 to 8, [71] the entire bill was passed and placed on the calendar for a third reading on July 20. [72] A motion for indefinite postponement was again raised and defeated, this time by a

---

62. *Id.*

63. *Id.* at 61.

64. *Id.* at 60.

65. *Id.* at 61.

66. *Id.*

67. *Id.* at 62, quoting from Preston's presentation to the Legislature.

68. *Id. See also* Spaulding, *supra* note 17, at 15, explaining that Spreckels' "capacity to make trouble was so evident that the Cabinet felt it expedient to buy him off."

69. Some litigation did continue, to determine what lands should be included in the Crown Lands that Princess Ruth had sold her interest in and what lands she could still claim as heir to the lands of her father, Mataio Kekūanaōʻa, who had received some private lands from his son Alexander Liholiho (Kamehameha IV). These issues were complicated because some lands were treated as Crown Lands, even though they were later determined to have been the private lands of the Mōʻī. Although it was pointed out that Princess Ruth had sold to Claus Spreckels her claim, in the terms of the agreement, to "all other lands commonly called, known or reputed to be Crown Lands," the Hawaiʻi Supreme Court noted that it would be illogical to assume that she intended to give up any claims to land later determined to have been the private lands of the Mōʻī that she had received as heir and hence ruled twice that she still retained title to such lands. *Ruth Keelikolani v. Commissioners of Crown Lands,* 6 Hawaiʻi 446, 1883 WL 7056 (1883); *Emma Kaleleonalani and Ruth Keelikolani v. Commissioners of Crown Lands,* 6 Hawaiʻi 454, 1884 WL 6698 (1884).

70. Adler, *supra* note 1, at 62.

71. *Id.* at 63. J. Keau, J. W. Kalua, J. Kamakele, J. Gardner, J. Nawahi, J. M. Kauwila, G. W. Pilipo, and S. Aiwohi voted for indefinite postponement. Voting against postponement were W. M. Gibson, S. K. Kaʻai, J. E. Bush, E. Preston, C. R. Bishop, J. O. Dominis, A. S. Cleghorn, J. P. Parker, P. Isenberg, J. Moanauli, G. Rhodes, J. Mott Smith, E. K. Lilikalani, H. W. Lahilahi, F. Pahia, Frank Brown, S. K. Mahoe, J. Kaluhi, J. L. Kaulukou, L. Aholo, G. E. Richardson, J. Nakookoo, P. Haupu, J. Kauhane, D. H. Nahinu, J. K. Kaunamano, J. Kauai, G. B. Palohau, J. Nakaleka, and J. A. Kaukau. *Id.* at 296 n. 16, citing *Pacific Commercial Advertiser,* July 19, 1882.

72. *Id.* at 63.

vote of 25 to 9, and the bill was then approved. King Kalākaua signed the bill into law the following day, July 21, and also appointed Gibson and Preston to be members of the three-person Commission of Crown Lands.[73]

Some commentators have suggested an additional reason why some of the legislators supported this land bill. Some of the foreigners wanted to remove the restrictions on the sale of Crown Lands, and they looked to the Spreckels' land bill as a step in the right direction.[74] "[B]ecause so much of the Crown lands was among the best agricultural lands in the kingdom, it is easy to see why haole businessmen favored offering them up for sale."[75]

This episode illustrates that the status of the Crown Lands remained somewhat unresolved despite the 1864 Supreme Court decision and 1865 statute designed to provide stability and predictability. The inalienability of these lands proved, before too long, to be based on an insecure foundation, and this principle fell along with the Monarchy in 1893.

The legal issues surrounding Princess Ruth's conveyance of her interest in the Crown Lands continue to be debated occasionally, with some contending that she had some kind of a colorable interest because the Legislature's Act of January 3, 1865 did not explicitly extinguish her interests in the Crown Lands. In a 1987 decision of the Hawai'i Supreme Court, Justice Frank Padgett, writing for the majority, examined this episode and, after discussing Princess Ruth's 1880 deed to Claus Spreckels, stated that "she had no legal right to make" the conveyance.[76] This observation would appear to be correct, but it is not clear that it will be the final word on this odd episode.

---

73. *Id.* at 64.
74. *Id.* at 65.
75. Osorio, *supra* note 17, at 184.
76. *Kohala Corporation v. State,* 69 Hawai'i 54, 62, 732 P.2d 652, 657–58 (1987).

13

The Inalienable Crown Lands (1865–93)

 Except for the episode with Princess Ruth and Claus Spreckels described in the preceding chapter, the Crown Lands were maintained in a relatively stable condition during the twenty-eight years between the 1865 statute and the 1893 overthrow of the Kingdom. The Commissioners of the Crown Lands managed the land, leased the most productive lands (usually to sugar plantations), and conveyed the revenues to the Mōʻī. But this period was a turbulent one for the Kingdom, and the changing demographics and unrelenting efforts of foreigners to acquire ʻĀina led to the 1887 Bayonet Constitution and the 1893 overthrow, as chapters 14 and 16 explain. The Kingdom sold substantial amounts of "choice public land" (from the Government Lands) in a "haphazard fashion" "rapidly during a brief period in the 1850s for an average price of less than two dollars an acre."[1] In five transactions, for instance, the Government sold 353,714 acres.[2] In 1890, 752,931 acres of Government and Crown Lands were leased to seventy-six corporations or individuals, often for pennies per acre.[3] The young Sanford Ballard Dole was arguing in the 1870s that the Crown Lands should be sold for homesteading,[4] and westerners were doing everything they could to obtain lands from all possible sources. This chapter focuses on a few matters affecting the Crown Lands to help complete the story.

1. Robert H. Horwitz, Judith B. Finn, Louis A. Vargha, and James W. Ceaser, *Public Land Policy in Hawaii: An Historical Analysis,* 7 (State of Hawaii Legislative Reference Bureau, Report No. 5, 1969)

2. Sanford B. Dole, "Hawaiian Public Lands," in *Government for the Territory of Hawaii,* H.R. Rep. No. 305, House Comm. on Territories, 56th Cong., 1st Sess., Appendix 1, at 105 (1900); William Fremont Blackman, *The Making of Hawaii: A Study in Social Evolution,* 160 (1906, reprinted 1977).

3. Horwitz et al., *supra* note 1, at 137; Melody K. MacKenzie, "Historical Background," in *Native Hawaiian Rights Handbook,* 10 (Melody Kapilialoha MacKenzie, ed., 1991); Blackman, *supra* note 2, at 160: "The 'crown lands' were leased to planters and ranchers, and the government was administered in their interest rather than in the interest of a peasant proprietorship."

4. S. B. Dole, "The Problem of Population and Our Land Policy," *Pacific Commercial Advertiser,* October 26, 1872, at 2; *see infra* chapter 18, text at notes 1–8.

Sanford Ballard Dole

The Act of July 29, 1872

This statute[5] recognized that the Crown Lands were separate and distinct from the Government Lands.

The 1874 Nonjudicial Mortgage Statute

Many Kuleanas passed from native to foreign hands after the enactment of a non-judicial mortgage and foreclosure law in 1874.[6] This law allowed a lender, in a case where the mortgagee had fallen behind in payments, to auction off the borrower's deed and hence the borrower's land without any judicial oversight.[7] Because interest rates were in the 12–18 percent range, averaging 13 percent, and loans averaged only two-and-a-half years, numerous Kuleana owners were unable to maintain payments or to meet the final balloon payment and thus forfeited their property.[8]

---

5. Act of July 29, 1872.

6. "An Act to Provide for the Sale of Mortgaged Property without Suit and Decree of Sale," *Laws 1874,* Act 33, at 31–32, now codified in *Hawai'i Revised Statutes,* § 667-5; *see generally* Robert H. Stauffer, *Kahana: How the Land Was Lost,* 92–107 (2004).

7. Stauffer, *supra* note 6, at 97.

8. *Id.* at 99.

1876

In 1876, the Legislature enacted a law requiring that all sales and leases of land valued at more than $300 had to take place in a public auction.[9]

Adverse Possession

Many natives lost their lands to sugar plantations and other corporate interests through "adverse possession," which occurred whenever a party utilized a parcel of land against the interest of the title owner for five years. This five-year time period was unusually short. The Hawai'i Supreme Court ruled in 1877 that even the Crown Lands of the Monarchs could be obtained by others through adverse possession,[10] which is contrary to the usual position that adverse possession and statutes of limitation cannot be enforced against the government.[11]

The 1884 Homestead Act

The Homestead Act of 1884 was drafted by Sanford Ballard Dole during the brief time he served in the Legislature.[12] It allowed individuals to obtain plots of up to 20 acres, required them to erect a residence and live on the land for at least three years, and gave them ten years to pay the purchase price,[13] but it attracted few settlers.[14] According to Dole's subsequent explanation, "[t]he administration . . . were so little in sympathy with the policy of this law that no action was taken under it until 1888, when the administration, which had come into power under the [Bayonet] revolution of the previous year, took vigorous measures to carry out its provisions."[15] This statute was amended in minor ways in 1888, 1890, and 1892 (allowing, for instance, a substitute to reside on the land, with the consent of the Minister of Interior).[16] In the years between 1884 and enactment of the Land Act of 1895, about 530 homesteads with a total of about 8,500 acres (averaging 16 acres each) with a total value of about $65,000 were acquired, plus another 3,500 acres, valued at $10,600, subject to special conditions regarding improvements and cultivation without residence.[17]

---

9. *Government for the Territory of Hawaii,* H.R. Rep. No. 305, House Comm. on Territories, 56th Cong., 1st Sess. at 14 (1900).

10. *Harris v. Carter,* 6 Hawai'i 195, 209 (1877).

11. *See, e.g., Kapi'olani Estate v. Cleghorn,* 14 Hawai'i 330, 336 (1902); *Galt v. Waianuhea,* 16 Hawai'i 652, 658–59 (1905), noting that the Act of January 3, 1865, which prohibited alienation of the Crown Lands, "does not appear to have been called to the attention of the court" in *Harris v. Carter,* 6 Hawai'i 195 (1877) and asking how, if the Crown Lands cannot be alienated, "could adverse possession run against those lands on the theory that there had been a grant of the same?"; *Territory v. Puahi,* 18 Hawai'i 649, 650–51 (1908).

12. "An Act to Facilitate the Acquisition and Settlement of Homesteads," August 29, 1884.

13. *Id.* at 64.

14. Linda S. Parker, *Native American Estate: The Struggle over Indian and Hawaiian Lands,* 121 (1989).

15. Dole, "Hawaiian Public Lands," *supra* note 2, at 105–06.

16. *Government for the Territory of Hawaii, supra* note 9, at 64–65.

17. *Id.* at 65, 106.

"Unassigned" Lands

When the Board of Commissioners to Quiet Land Titles (usually called the Land Commission) went out of existence on March 31, 1855,[18] many lands had been overlooked and lacked title,[19] and they became known as "unassigned" lands. These lands were in the possession of third parties, including the Crown Land Commissioners, other branches of the Government, various heirs of Kauikeaouli (Kamehameha III), and various private parties. Many claimants desired to settle the disputes over legal title to these lands.[20]

The 1888 case of *Thurston v. Bishop* involved a suit in ejectment for an "unassigned" land and also addressed broader questions concerning all "unassigned" lands.[21] The Supreme Court sitting en banc (with all members present)[22] ruled by a four-to-one vote (with Justice Sanford Ballard Dole dissenting) that if a claimant had failed to file before the Land Commission within the time for filing such claims, the land in question vested in the Hawaiian Government. The specific question to be addressed was whether the status of Lot Kapuāiwa (Kamehameha V) as a minor exempted him from the requirement that he file claims for his land in the requisite time period and thus prevented the Hawaiian Government from now recovering the land held by the Bishop Estate.[23]

Minister of Interior Lorrin Thurston had claimed the 'Ili of Opu (Makiki, O'ahu) on behalf of the Government.[24] This land was "unassigned" and was in the possession of the Bishop Estate, which had received it upon the death of Lot in 1872.[25]

---

18. "Dissolution of Land Commission; Effect of Awards: An Act to Provide for the Dissolution of the Board of Commissioners to Quiet Land Titles," July 20, 1854, L. 1854 at 21, in 2 *Revised Laws of Hawai'i*, 2146–47 (1925).

19. The letter from W. D. Alexander, Surveyor-General, to Lorrin A. Thurston, Minister of the Interior, dated January 9, 1888 (original on file with the State Archives, Interior Department file), identified 104 'Āina in this class. *Id.* Eighty-eight were located on the island of Hawai'i, twelve on Moloka'i, two on Lāna'i, and two on O'ahu. *Id.*

20. *See, e.g., id.,* discussing the "unassigned" lands held by the Estate of Bernice Pauahi Bishop. Alexander stated that the Minister of Interior was empowered by law to dispose of land in certain cases by quitclaim deeds, or otherwise, "by way of compromise or equitable settlement of the rights of claimants," and had exercised this right in the case of unassigned lands of 'Ōlelomoana and Pāpā 2 in South Kona, Hawai'i. *Id.* at 6. Alexander identified Kaunakakai, Moloka'i, as a similar case and suggested that if the lands were claimed for benevolent or charitable purposes, the Legislature would probably authorize the issuance of a patent to the petitioners. *Id.* at 6–7. In a letter from Thurston to the Bishop Estate Trustees, Thurston declined this suggestion to issue patents for the "unassigned" lands held by the estate. Letter from L. A. Thurston, Minister of the Interior, to Trustees of the Estate of Bernice Pauahi Bishop, 1, February 29, 1888 (original on file with Archives, Interior Department file). Thurston pointed out that other claimants besides the Bishop Estate and the Government had claims, and therefore that the courts were the proper authority to render a decision and that the government would shortly bring a suit in ejectment regarding an "unassigned" land. *Id.*

21. *Thurston v. Bishop,* 7 Hawai'i 421 (1888).

22. The 1888 Supreme Court consisted of Chief Justice A. Francis Judd (son of Dr. Gerrit Judd), Justice Lawrence McCully, Justice Edward Preston, Justice Richard F. Bickerton, and Justice Sanford Ballard Dole.

23. *Thurston v. Bishop,* 7 Hawai'i at 427–28.

24. *Id.* at 422.

25. *Id.* at 422–23.

Lot had received the lands by oral bequest in 1840 from Hoapili.[26] Lot was a minor when the deadline for filing claims before the Land Commission expired February 14, 1848, and he did not become of legal age (twenty years old) until December 11, 1850.[27]

Section 8 of the Act of December 10th, 1845, stated that

> all claims to land as against the Hawaiian Government which are not presented to said Board within the time, at the place, and in the manner prescribed in the notice required to be given in the fifth section of this article, shall be deemed to be invalid, and shall be forever barred in law, unless the claimant be absent from the Kingdom, and have no representative therein.[28]

The Court ruled that the statute made no exception in favor of minors.[29] Lot's failure to present his claim to the Commission did not deprive him of title to lands because he had no title to them—only the right to present a claim for them.[30] The Court noted that Mataio Kekūanaōʻa, Lot's father, had presented other claims to land on his son's behalf and thus ruled that the acts and omissions of Kekūanaōʻa, as father and guardian, bound Lot in respect to claims before the Land Commission.[31]

The Government claimed these lands as public domain, because they were "not awarded or granted to any one."[32] The Court decided that they could not give the private landowners the right of possession of Opu (and the other "unassigned" lands), because to do so would be to give them fee simple title although they never paid a commutation fee to the Government for the lands.[33] They would thus be ruling that a right of possession against the state would be good enough to establish title, which is contrary to the usual rule that adverse possession cannot run against the Government.[34] The Court thus ruled that possessors of "unassigned" lands must yield possession to the Government, which held the title, "since the right of possession follows the title."[35] The Legislature subsequently enacted two statutes, approved by King Kalākaua on November 14, 1890, that adjusted some of these titles, benefiting the Bishop Estate and the Crown Lands, as discussed in the next section.

"An Act to Settle the Title to Certain Unawarded Lands..."

"An Act to Settle the Title to Certain Unawarded Lands, and to Authorize a Compromise with the Trustees under the Will of the Late Bernice Pauahi Bishop" (1890)[36]

26. *Id.* at 423.
27. *Id.* at 436.
28. *Id.* at 429.
29. *Id.* at 434.
30. *Id.* at 433.
31. *Id.* at 434–35.
32. *Id.* at 438.
33. *Id.*
34. *Id.* But compare *Harris v. Carter,* 6 Hawaiʻi 195, 209 (1877), discussed *supra,* text at notes 10–11.
35. *Thurston v. Bishop,* 7 Hawaiʻi at 438.
36. "An Act to Settle the Title to Certain Unawarded Lands, and to Authorize a Compromise with the Trustees under the Will of the Late Bernice Pauahi Bishop," November 14, 1890.

addressed some significant "unassigned" lands possessed by the Estate of Bernice Pauahi Bishop, including the Ahupua'a of Kaunakakai, Moloka'i; the Ahupua'a of Pā'au'au, Ka'ū, Hawai'i; the mauka portion of the 'Ili of Ka'ākaukukui, O'ahu; Ha'ikū 1 and 2, Hilo, Hawai'i; Kaiaakea, Hilo, Hawai'i; Kaluakailio, Hilo, Hawai'i; Kaumana, Hilo, Hawai'i; Kauuiho 1 and 2, Hilo, Hawai'i; Lepoloa, Hilo, Hawai'i; Maulua-iki, Hilo, Hawai'i; Pihā 1 and 2, Hilo Hawai'i; Waikaumalo, Hilo, Hawai'i; Ka'āpoko, Hilo, Hawai'i; Ka'ie'ie, Hilo, Hawai'i; and Mohokea 1 and 2, Ka'ū, Hawai'i. The preamble explained that Bernice Pauahi Bishop was devisee of the estate of her late cousin Ruth Ke'elikolani, who had inherited the private estate of her brother Lot (Kamehameha V). These lands had been continuously held and claimed by Bernice Pauahi Bishop's ancestors and were in possession of the Trustees of the Bishop Estate.

The statute then recognized the generosity of Bernice Pauahi Bishop for the devise of her entire estate for the establishment and maintenance of the Kamehameha Schools, which was acknowledged as "a valuable gift in perpetuity to the public for the promotion of the education of the youth of this Kingdom."[37] It was also recognized that the Trustees of the Bishop Estate extended an offer to the Minister of Interior,[38] whereby the Trustees would quitclaim to the Government the bulk of the disputed lands but would retain for the Trust the Ahupua'a of Pā'au'au, the unawarded portion of the 'Ili of Ka'ākaukukui, and the Ahupua'a of Kaunakakai, where Kamehameha V and his successors had expended large sums toward improvements.[39]

The act then accepted this proposal and authorized the issuance of patents to convey to the Trustees the Ahupua'a of Pā'au'au (2,974 acres, valued at $10,000),[40] the unawarded portion of the 'Ili of Ka'ākaukukui, and the Ahupua'a of Kaunakakai (5,240 acres, valued at $5,000).[41] The remaining identified lands were quitclaimed to the Kingdom. These conveyances served as final settlement of all rights and questions between these parties regarding the disputed lands.

"An Act to Declare Certain Lands to be Part of the Crown Lands . . ."

"An Act to Declare Certain Lands to be Part of the Crown Lands and Royal Domain" (1890)[42] addressed "unassigned" lands held by the Crown Land Commissioners on behalf of King Kalākaua. This statute operated to settle the title questions regarding the following Ahupua'a: Kuli'ou'ou, in the District of Kona, O'ahu; Kea'au, in the Dis-

---

37. *Id.*

38. Charles N. Spencer was the Minister of Interior at the time of this act. *Id.*

39. *Id.*

40. Information taken from *Report of Interior Department for 1890,* 232 (on file in the State Archives).

41. Information taken from a July 22, 1890, letter from W. D. Alexander, Surveyor-General to C. N. Spencer, Minister of the Interior (on file in the State Archives).

42. "An Act to Declare Certain Lands to be Part of the Crown Lands and Royal Domain," November 14, 1890, reprinted in *Liliuokalani v. United States,* 45 Ct.Cl. 418, 434 (1910).

trict of Wai'anae, O'ahu (2,431 acres);[43] Hakalauiki, in the District of Hilo, Hawai'i (614 acres); Manowai'ōpae, in the District of Hilo, Hawai'i (180 acres); Kamoku, on the Island of Lāna'i (3,291 acres); Paoma'i, Lāna'i; Wai'aha, Hawai'i (230 acres); Kapa'akea, Moloka'i (2,178 acres); and Waiohuli, Maui. By this act, these previously "unassigned" lands, held by the Crown Land Commission, were officially declared to be a part of the Crown Lands. As Crown Lands, they became subject to the provisions of the Act of January 3, 1865, which prohibited their alienation.[44]

Notwithstanding the *Thurston v. Bishop* decision,[45] which directed that "lands unawarded by the State are still the property of the State,"[46] these two statutes approved by King Kalākaua on November 14, 1890, served as compromises benefiting the Bishop Estate and the Crown Lands inventory. Although these statutes appear to be gratuitous gestures and pragmatic solutions to complex difficulties, they raise certain issues. If these lands were held by the estate of an Ali'i, why could not the Ali'i hold on to all of these lands? From another perspective, why should these once private lands of Kauikeaouli (Kamehameha III) be transferred to the control of the successors of the Keawe-a-heulu dynasty?[47] Was there authority to add to the Crown Lands inventory?[48] Surveyor-General William D. Alexander opposed doing so because he asserted that under the Act of January 3, 1865, the "Crown Lands, which descend to the successors of the Hawaiian Crown, were expressly limited and designated by name in the Act of June 7, 1848."[49] Alexander knew of no legal authority for adding lands to the Crown Lands list.[50]

Queen Lili'uokalani and the Crown Lands

Shortly after she became Mō'ī, Queen Lili'uokalani instructed the Crown Land Commissioners to "set aside choice sections of crown lands for homestead subdivision in 10 acre lots on a 30 years term for lease and cultivation; first 5 years to be rent free, balance at nominal yearly rent of $1.00 per acre."[51] Her hope was that these lands would go primarily to Hawaiians.[52]

---

43. This acreage figure and those that follow were obtained from the January 17, 1889, letter from Lorrin A. Thurston, Minister of Interior, to W. L. Green, Jonah Austin, and C. P. Iaukea, Commissioners of Crown Lands (on file in the State Archives).

44. "An Act to Relieve the Royal Domain from Encumbrances and to Render the Same Inalienable," January 3, 1865, 1 Sess. Laws of Hawai'i 69 (1851–70). *See supra* chapter 9.

45. *Thurston v. Bishop,* 7 Hawai'i 421 (1888).

46. *Id.* at 438.

47. Interview with Rubellite K. K. Johnson, Honolulu, January 1997, questioning whether these lands should have been transferred to a different family.

48. Prior to the enactment of this statute increasing the Crown Lands, W. D. Alexander questioned whether authority existed to adjust the Crown Lands. Letter from William D. Alexander, Surveyor-General, to Lorrin Thurston, Minister of Interior, July 17, 1889 (on file in State Archives, Interior Department file).

49. *Id.* at 4.

50. *Id.*

51. Helena G. Allen, *The Betrayal of Liliuokalani: Last Queen of Hawaii 1838–1917,* 259 (1982), citing *Thrum's Hawaiian Almanac & Annual* (Bernice Pauahi Bishop Library).

52. *Id.*

14

The 1887 Bayonet Constitution and the Reciprocity/Pearl Harbor Treaty

Preludes to Overthrow

David Kalākaua served as Mōʻī from 1874 to 1891. As King, he strove to maintain the Kingdom's independence and to restore Hawaiian culture despite the continuing decline of the Hawaiian population, the introduction of substantial numbers of foreign contract workers, and increased pressure from the Western business community.

The Reciprocity Treaty of 1875

Through the 1860s, the towns in Hawaiʻi had prospered by serving as "a great general store doing the business of the Pacific whaling fleet in all its details—commission, exchange, supplies, and so forth," but this role "ceased to exist when the ice in the north crushed the whaling fleet" in 1871 and left the Hawaiian economy, according to Sanford Ballard Dole, "now to look up and develop our own resources."[1] King Kalākaua was part of that effort during the first eight years of his reign, and he worked closely with the Americans in the Kingdom who were developing sugar plantations to promote economic prosperity.[2] He traveled to the United States in 1874–75 in order to develop support for what became the Reciprocity Treaty of 1875,[3] which led to "an

---

1. S. B. Dole, "The Problem of Population," *Pacific Commercial Advertiser*, September 28, 1872, 3. The whaling industry was also "ruined" by the U.S. Civil War. Charles Callan Tansill, *Diplomatic Relations between the United States and Hawaii: 1885–1889*, 11 (Fordham University Historical Series No. 1, 1940).

2. Queen Liliʻuokalani referred to this group as the "missionary party" because many in the group were descendants of missionaries. Liliuokalani, *Hawaii's Story by Hawaii's Queen*, 75, 180, 186, 192, 199, 333 (1898, reprinted 1997).

3. "Treaty of Commercial Reciprocity," signed January 30, 1875, entered into force, September 9, 1876, 19 Stat. 625, Treaty Series 161, 8 Charles I. Bevans, *Treaties and Other International Agreements of the United States of America, 1776–1949* (hereafter cited as "1875 Reciprocity Treaty"), 874. Background on the events leading to the adoption of this treaty can be found in Sylvester K. Stevens, *American Expansion in Hawaii 1842–1898*, 85–140 (1945, reissued 1968), and Merze Tate, *Hawaii: Reciprocity or Annexation*, 108–34 (1968).

David Kalākaua

intoxicating increase of wealth"[4] and to the growth in the number of sugar plantations from twenty to sixty-three in five years,[5] but which also was later seen as having
put "in peril the independence of our nation."[6] This treaty did not grant any rights to
the United States regarding the Pearl River Harbor, but the Kingdom did agree not
to "lease or otherwise dispose of . . . any port, harbor, or other territory . . . to any

---

4. Letter from Commissioner James Blount to U.S. Secretary of State W. C. Gresham, July 17, 1893, in
"Report of Commissioner to the Hawaiian Islands," in 27 *Executive Documents of the House of Representatives
for the Second Session of the Fifty-third Congress, 1893–94*, 105 (1895), originally in Executive Document No.
47, 53rd Cong., 2d Sess. (1893) (hereafter cited as "Blount Report").

5. Lawrence H. Fuchs, *Hawaii Pono: A Social History*, 21 (1961, reprinted 1983); *see* Tate, *supra* note 3,
at 117–30, explaining at 119 and 118 that the 1875 Reciprocity Treaty led to "an unprecedented boom in the
Islands" and that "[t]he effects of reciprocity exceeded the most sanguine expectations and the most extravagant predictions."

6. Liliuokalani, *supra* note 2, at 55. Joseph Nawahi also strongly opposed the Reciprocity Treaty, accurately predicting that reciprocity would be "the first step of annexation later on, and the Kingdom, its flag,
its independence, and its people will become naught." Tom Coffman, *Nation Within: The Story of America's
Annexation of the Nation of Hawai'i*, 138 (1998), citing J. G. M. Sheldon, *The Biography of Joseph K. Nawahi*,
167 (Marvin Puakea Nogelmeier, trans., 1908). *See infra* chapter 19, text at notes 25–26.

other power, state, or government."[7] Senator John T. Morgan of Alabama explained later that the treaty "was negotiated for the purpose of securing political control of those islands, making them industrially and commercially a part of the United States, and preventing any other great power from acquiring a foothold there."[8] The Mō'ī also supported the recruitment of contract laborers to work in the sugar fields, which dramatically changed the demographics of the Kingdom's population.[9]

The 1887 Bayonet Constitution

In 1882, however, Kalākaua turned against those who favored closer ties with the United States, supporting instead the growing Hawaiian nationalism led by native political leadership in the Legislature, and the Mō'ī linked his political and economic agenda closely to the activities of Claus Spreckels and Walter Murray Gibson.[10] The American-missionary-planter group regrouped and regained their dominant role in the Kingdom in 1887 when they required the Mō'ī at gunpoint to support the "Bayonet Constitution," which reduced the power of the Monarchy significantly.

Article 34 of the 1864 Constitution had provided that "The King is Sovereign of all the Chiefs and of all the People; the Kingdom is His." Article 34 of the 1887 Constitution deleted the words "the Kingdom is His." Article 31 of the 1864 Constitution had provided that "To the King belongs the Executive power." But this article was revised in the 1887 Constitution to read, "To the King and the Cabinet belongs the Executive power." Article 41 of the 1887 Constitution authorized the Mō'ī to appoint the Cabinet Ministers, but once appointed the Ministers answered to the Legislature, because in the new Constitution a Cabinet Minister could be removed by the Mō'ī only with approval of the Legislature. More importantly, Article 41 also provided that no act of the Mō'ī would have any effect unless it was countersigned by a member of the Cabinet and Article 78 stated that every action taken by the Mō'ī must be "with the advice and consent of the Cabinet." Article 48 of the 1887 Constitution authorized the Mō'ī to veto legislation,[11] but the veto could be overridden by a two-thirds vote of the Legislature. The 1887 Constitution also eliminated the status of the Mō'ī as commander-in-chief and gave control of the military to the Legislature. These changes undercut the authority of the Mō'ī to lead the country.

---

7. "1875 Reciprocity Treaty," *supra* note 3, art. IV; *see generally* Stevens, *supra* note 3, at 125–26.

8. Tansill, *supra* note 1, at 12, citing Chalfant Robinson, *A History of Two Reciprocity Treaties,* 134.

9. 3 Ralph S. Kuykendall, *The Hawaiian Kingdom 1874–1893: The Kalakaua Dynasty,* 117 (1967, reprinted 1987). *See infra* chapter 15.

10. *See supra* chapter 12, text at notes 54–73. For a full discussion of the events that led to the 1887 Bayonet Constitution, *see* 3 Kuykendall, *supra* note 9, at 344–72.

11. The language in the 1887 Constitution was somewhat ambiguous on whether the Mō'ī could veto legislation without the consent of the relevant ministry, but the Hawai'i Supreme Court upheld his right to do so by a 4-1 vote, with Justice Sanford Ballard Dole dissenting. *Everett v. Baker,* 7 Hawai'i 229, 1888 WL 906 (1988). *See* Jonathan Kay Kamakawiwo'ole Osorio, *Dismembering Lāhui: A History of the Hawaiian Nation to 1887,* 241 (2002).

The structure of the Legislature was also revised in the 1887 Constitution. No longer did the Mō'ī appoint members of the House of Nobles, and they began being elected, but only by those voters who could meet the property and income requirements.[12] These requirements (voters had to own property worth $3,000 or have an annual income of $600) were steep enough that the House of Nobles was primarily selected by and composed of westerners, reducing significantly the Hawaiian influence over the governance of the Kingdom.[13]

The Bayonet Constitution was promulgated through the efforts of the Hawaiian League, a secret organization formed to institute "Constitutional, representative Government, in fact as well as in form, in the Hawaiian Islands, by all necessary means."[14] This organization was founded by individuals such as Sanford Ballard Dole, Lorrin Thurston, and William R. Castle, individuals who also played major roles in the 1893 overthrow,[15] and its members were almost all Caucasians.[16] Its executive committee had thirteen members.[17] They opposed Kalākaua's vocal support for Hawaiian nationalism—"Hawaii for the Hawaiians"[18]—and criticized what they characterized as lavish expenditures to build 'Iolani Palace and support his two-week coronation celebration.[19] Some characterized the promotion of Hawaiian culture and the return of the hula as "a retrograde step of heathenism and a disgrace to the age."[20] In addition to their dissatisfaction with Kalākaua, the members of the Hawaiian League also disliked his close associates Walter Murray Gibson and Claus Spreckels. The Hawaiian League (and other citizens of the Kingdom) accused Kalākaua and the Gibson Cabinet of bribery and misuse of funds.[21]

Once the members of the Hawaiian League decided to take action, they increased their clout by uniting secretly with the Honolulu Rifles, an all-Caucasian civil militia.[22] As the Rifles began arming themselves, and as the calls for reform grew louder, King Kalākaua and Prime Minister Gibson recognized that some accommodation would be necessary. In an attempt to pacify the League and its supporters, Kalākaua dismissed Gibson and the rest of the Cabinet in the early morning hours of June 28, 1887.[23] This move was insufficient for the members of the League, however,

---

12. "Hawaii Constitution of 1887," art. 59, limiting voting for the House of Nobles to those with property worth $3,000 or an annual income of $600.

13. 3 Kuykendall, *supra* note 9, at 369–70.

14. *Id.* at 348; Gavan Daws, *Shoal of Time: A History of the Hawaiian Islands,* 243–44 (1968, reprinted 1974); Osorio, *supra* note 11, at 235.

15. 3 Kuykendall, *supra* note 9, at 347.

16. Daws, *supra* note 14, at 244.

17. 3 Kuykendall, *supra* note 9, at 348.

18. *Id.* at 4, 6, stating that Kalākaua "profess[ed] to favor natives for prominent offices."

19. *Id.* at 262, 264.

20. *Id.* at 265, citing *Hawaiian Annual,* 85 (1884) and *Daily Bulletin,* February 27, 1883.

21. *See, e.g., id.* at 353–54.

22. *Id.* at 350–52.

23. *Id.* at 357–58, citing "Merrill to Bayard," No. 135, July 30, 1887, *USDS, Dispatches, Hawaii,* vol. 23.

and they organized a public meeting on June 30 "to take into consideration the present maladministration of public affairs and to consider means of redress." [24] Fearing violence, Kalākaua had the palace doors barricaded and then, playing right into the hands of the Hawaiian League, he called out the Honolulu Rifles to keep the peace.[25] Although they were patrolling the streets under the aegis of the Government, the Rifles were actually taking orders from the Hawaiian League.

The June 30 public meeting was called to order by Judge Sanford Ballard Dole at about two in the afternoon.[26] Speakers read proclamations and denounced the Government, calling for a new Cabinet and a new Constitution.[27] Although the League and its supporters recognized that the only legal way to promulgate a new Constitution was by action of the Legislature, it was clear from the tone of the meeting that the majority of those present wanted a new Constitution as soon possible and did not care how they got it.[28]

The meeting adopted a number of resolutions to that effect, and its participants presented them to the King that same day, putting him in a predicament. For the next night and day, the city was controlled by the Honolulu Rifles, who arrested Gibson on the morning of July 1 and seized a shipment of guns they suspected was going to the King.[29] Kalākaua, knowing he was in danger of losing the Kingdom, called on the ministers of Britain, France, Japan, the United States, and Portugal and attempted to hand the Kingdom over to them for protection. They refused to intervene in this fashion, instructing him to remain in power. Left in a weakened position and apparently in some fear of assassination,[30] the Mō'ī then told the reformers that he would agree to the wishes expressed at the mass meeting.[31]

That afternoon, Kalākaua accepted a new Cabinet, consisting of William Lowthian Green (a merchant who became Premier and Minister of Finance), Lorrin A. Thurston (Minister of Interior), Godfrey Brown (British-born Minister of Foreign Affairs), and Clarence W. Ashford (from Canada, Attorney General),[32] who

---

24. *Id.* at 359.

25. *Id.*

26. Fuchs, without citation, has written that this meeting was attended by "more than 2,500 people, nearly all Caucasians," Fuchs, *supra* note 5, at 29. The number 2,500 is also found in *A Sketch of Recent Events* (Hawaiian Gazette Printers, 1887), reprinted in "Blount Report," *supra* note 4, at 327, 330. Professor Osorio has described the meeting as attended by "members of the Hawaiian League and several hundred other mostly white residents." Osorio, *supra* note 11, at 238. Kuykendall does not estimate the attendance at the meeting but does say that "[s]tores were closed, business came to a halt, and by 2 o'clock the armory was filled to capacity." 3 Kuykendall, *supra* note 9, at 359. Alexander referred to it as "an immense meeting." W. D. Alexander, "A Statement of Facts Relating to Politics During Kalakaua's Reign," in "Blount Report," *supra* note 4, at 179, 196.

27. 3 Kuykendall, *supra* note 9, at 359–62.

28. *Id.* at 361–62.

29. *Id.* at 364, citing "Merrill to Bayard," No. 135, July 30, 1887, *USDS, Dispatches, Hawaii,* vol. 23.

30. Liliuokalani, *supra* note 2, at 181–82; Daws, *supra* note 14, at 244; Rich Budnick, *Stolen Kingdom: An American Conspiracy,* 63 (1992), citing Lorrin A. Thurston, *Memoirs of the Hawaiian Revolution,* 140 (1936).

31. 3 Kuykendall, *supra* note 9, at 364, citing "Merrill to Bayard," No. 135, July 30, 1887, *USDS, Dispatches, Hawaii,* vol. 23.

32. *Id.* at 365.

were "all men of foreign birth" (compared to the previous Cabinet, which had contained three Native Hawaiians)[33] and were all members of the Hawaiian League.[34] Led by Thurston,[35] the members of the Hawaiian League began immediately to draft a new Constitution,[36] completing the Bayonet Constitution on July 6 and presenting it to Kalākaua for his oath and signature. The Mōʻī argued with his new Cabinet for hours, but he eventually gave in and signed the document that would reduce or eliminate most of his powers.[37] The following day, he abrogated the Constitution of 1864 and promulgated the Constitution of 1887.[38] No violence occurred during these very tense days.[39] Although no foreign troops intervened, the U.S. Secretary of State made it clear that "the assistance of the officers of our Government vessels, if found necessary, will . . . be promptly afforded to promote the reign of law and respect for orderly government in Hawaii."[40]

This Bayonet Constitution, written by westerners, governed the Native People of Hawaiʻi for the next six years. In words later written by Queen Liliʻuokalani,

> without any provocation on the part of the king, having matured their plans in secret, the men of foreign birth rose one day *en masse,* called a public meeting, and forced the king, without any appeal to the suffrages of the people, to sign a constitution of their own preparation, a document which deprived the sovereign of all power, made him a mere tool in their hands, and practically took away the franchise from the Hawaiian race."[41]

Liliʻuokalani characterized the Cabinet, under the 1887 Constitution, as "the absolute monarch of the kingdom of the Hawaiian Islands."[42] Professor Osorio has explained that the 1887 Constitution "meant the abrupt and nearly total termination of any executive power or royal authority."[43] The *San Francisco Chronicle* characterized the

---

33. Liliuokalani, *supra* note 2, at 175. Thurston was "Hawaiian by birth," Osorio, *supra* note 11, at 237, but apparently not in the eyes of the Queen.

34. Daws, *supra* note 14, at 248.

35. See 1 Native Hawaiians Study Commission, *Report on the Culture, Needs and Concerns of Native Hawaiians,* 277 (1983), citing Edward Joesting, *Hawaii: An Uncommon History,* 220 (1972) for the proposition that the 1887 Constitution was "written mainly by Lorrin A. Thurston."

36. *Id.;* 3 Kuykendall, *supra* note 9, at 367.

37. 3 Kuykendall, *supra* note 9, at 367, reporting that after he had read the terms of the new constitution, Kalākaua "argued, protested, inquired as to the effect of certain phases of the changes made . . . and for considerable periods appeared to be gazing into space and weighing the probabilities of success in the event of a refusal to comply with the reforms demanded."

38. *Id.* at 368.

39. Letter from the U.S. Minister to Hawaii George F. Merrill to the U.S. Secretary of State Thomas F. Bayard, No. 374 [135], July 30, 1887, reprinted in *Papers Related to the Foreign Relations of the United States for the Year 1887,* 582 (1888).

40. Letter from U.S. Secretary of State Thomas F. Bayard to the U.S. Minister to Hawaii George F. Merrill, No. 372 [52], July 12, 1887, reprinted in *Papers Related to the Foreign Relations of the United States for the Year 1887,* 581 (1888).

41. Liliuokalani, *supra* note 2, at 180–81.

42. *Id.* at 191.

43. Osorio, *supra* note 11, at 240.

government established under the Bayonet Constitution as "a military oligarchy that is more domineering than Kalākaua ever was" and added that "freedom of the press of Honolulu is a myth under the reform party."[44] This Bayonet Constitution, "which set up a Government savoring of the English variety, was a clever device for securing to the [foreigners] the control of the Kingdom."[45]

Pearl River Harbor (Pu'uloa)

While the Kingdom was going through this turmoil, the Supplementary Convention designed to extend the 1875 Reciprocity Treaty was being considered by the U.S. Senate and by the Kingdom's changing Cabinet. (The original treaty had a duration of seven years but continued in force until either side gave notice of abrogation.) On April 14, 1886, after meeting in a closed executive session, the U.S. Senate Foreign Relations Committee recommended ratification but only on the condition that a new article favored by Alabama Senator John T. Morgan and Vermont Senator George F. Edmunds be added:[46]

> Article II: His Majesty the King of the Hawaiian Islands grants to the Government of the United States the exclusive right to enter the harbor of Pearl River in the island of Oahu, and to establish and maintain there a coaling and repair station for the use of vessels of the United States, and to that end the United States may improve the entrance to said harbor and do all other things needful to the purpose aforesaid.[47]

Although some characterized this proposed amendment as calling for a "cession" of the Pearl River Harbor to the United States, others gave it a more limited interpretation, and some apparently felt that the exclusive right given to the United States was "not intended to exclude Hawaiian vessels."[48] The full U.S. Senate spent most of

---

44. Liliuokalani, *supra* note 2, at 375, quoting *San Francisco Chronicle,* September 5, 1887.

45. William A. Russ, *The Hawaiian Revolution: 1893–94,* 20 (1959).

46. Also supporting this amendment was Senator (later President) Benjamin Harrison. Coffman, *supra* note 6, at 112.

47. 3 Kuykendall, *supra* note 9, at 387, citing *Senate Executive Journal* 25, at 5, 419, and Senate Document No. 231, 56th Cong., 2d Sess. Pt. 8, at 244. Senator Morgan's key role has been discussed, e.g., in Tansill, *supra* note 1, at 19: "Senator Morgan, a Democrat, submitted the amendment with reference to Pearl Harbor"; Budnick, *supra* note 30, at 59; "The Hawaiian Treaty: Conditional Ratification by the United States Senate," *Pacific Commercial Advertiser,* February 10, 1887, 2, reporting that Senator Morgan of Alabama and Senator Edmunds of Vermont were "the chief advocates" of the amendment; "The Treaty Debate in the Senate," *Pacific Commercial Advertiser,* March 5, 1887, 2, characterizing Senator Edmunds as "the father of the Pearl River amendment" and stating that he "thought the present Hawaiian Cabinet is hostile to American interests, and that this country ought to receive a lesson to teach it that the United States does not propose to have its good nature imposed upon"; Stevens, *supra* note 3, at 171, quoting a confidential letter from the Kingdom's Minister of the United States, H. A. P. Carter, to Walter Murray Gibson on March 18, 1885 discussing the origins of the discussions about the Pearl River, in the Archives of Hawai'i, Foreign Office and Executive File; Tate, *supra* note 3, at 183–87.

48. 3 Kuykendall, *supra* note 9, at 388, citing letters written in May–July 1886 by the Kingdom's Minister to the United States H. A. P. Carter to the Kingdom's Foreign Minister Walter Murray Gibson and King Kalākaua.

January 19, 1887, in executive session considering the treaty,[49] approved this amendment the following day by a vote of 28 to 21, and then gave its consent to the full Supplemental Convention by a vote of 43 to 11.[50]

This initiative was not the first time that the United States had shown an interest in the potentiality of developing a military facility at the Pearl River. In 1872, a U.S. military mission came to Honolulu, ostensibly on a vacation, investigated the Pearl River area (and other sites) for possible military use, and delivered a report that remained secret until 1897.[51] King William Charles Lunalilo gave serious consideration to the idea of ceding the Pearl River to the United States in exchange for a reciprocity treaty in 1873.[52] When the Reciprocity Treaty of 1875 was finally negotiated, it said that no other nation could be given access to the Pearl River, but, to the great relief of most Native Hawaiians, it did not have any language granting rights to the United States.[53]

The reaction in the Kingdom to the inclusion of the Pearl River in the 1887 Supplemental Treaty was initially strongly negative, but as the political power moved from the Mōʻī and the native leaders to those westerners supporting ties with the United States, a closer look was given to the Pearl River amendment to the Supplementary Convention. An article in the *Pacific Commercial Advertiser* on February 8, 1887, characterized the proposed amendment as calling for the "cession of the Pearl River Harbor" and quoted at length from an analysis in the *San Francisco Bulletin* of January 24, 1887, which explained the potential strategic value of this sheltered harbor, noting also that "it has never been of any practical value to the Hawaiian Kingdom, being unused and practically unknown to a great majority, even of the residents of Honolulu."[54] The *San Francisco Chronicle* sharply opposed extending the Reciprocity Treaty on these terms, saying that it is "for the benefit of the few who derive the profit from so-called reciprocity, and who hold a mortgage upon the Hawaiian Kingdom," adding that the Kingdom is "impoverished," and that the Treaty "is intended to bolster up the fading credit of King Kalākaua and his realm, so that he can play at being King for a few years longer."[55] The *Chronicle*'s analysis noted that it was anticipated that $25,000,000 would be spent to develop the Pearl River into a military harbor, adding that "[i]f the design of the $25,000,000 expen-

---

49. "Pearl River: Renewal of the Project for Its Cession to the United States," *Pacific Commercial Advertiser*, February 8, 1887.

50. 3 Kuykendall, *supra* note 9, at 392–93, citing *Senate Executive Journal* 25, at 690, 694, 705, 708–10.

51. 2 Native Hawaiians Study Commission, *Report on the Culture, Needs and Concerns of Native Hawaiians*, 39 (1983).

52. 2 Ralph S. Kuykendall, *The Hawaiian Kingdom 1854–1874: Twenty Critical Years*, 249–57 (1953, reprinted 1982); Stevens, *supra* note 3, at 116–17; Tate, *supra* note 3, at 82–107. *See supra* chapter 10, text at notes 11–14.

53. *See supra* this chapter, text at notes 3–8.

54. "Pearl River: Renewal of the Project for Its Cession to the United States," *Pacific Commercial Advertiser*, February 8, 1887.

55. "The Hawaiian Treaty: Conditional Ratification by the United States Senate," *Pacific Commercial Advertiser*, February 10, 1887, quoting from *San Francisco Chronicle*.

diture is practically to annex the Hawaiian Islands, practical annexation could be accomplished much more cheaply" by, for instance, loaning the Kingdom $2,000,000 to cover its budget shortfalls.[56] In its issue of February 11, 1887, the *Pacific Commercial Advertiser* stated that Pearl Harbor was "national property, and as such must be conserved in the national interest," and that "the Hawaiian Government will not make any territorial concession to any foreign power, and without its own consent its territorial integrity never will be violated, despite a contrary opinion by American journalists and others who should know better." [57]

In September 1887, the Kingdom's Minister to the United States, Henry A. P. Carter, asked how the amendment would be interpreted, stating that the Kingdom hoped that the amendment "does not and is not intended to invade or diminish in any way the autonomous jurisdiction of Hawaii, while giving to the United States the exclusive rights of use in Pearl Harbor stipulated therein, . . . and further that the article II of the convention and the privileges conveyed by it, will cease and determine with the termination of the treaty of 1875 under the conditions fixed by this [supplemental] convention." [58] The U.S. Secretary of State Thomas F. Bayard responded that the amendment did not call for any "subtraction of Hawaiian sovereignty over the harbor to which it relates" and contained no "language importing a longer duration" for the exclusive rights to the Pearl River Harbor than for the remainder of the treaty.[59]

After this understanding was formalized in an explanatory exchange of notes, the Cabinet recommended approval of the treaty, and King Kalākaua reluctantly signed it on October 20, 1887.[60] In his speech to the Legislature reporting on the treaty, the Mō'ī said that renewal of the 1875 Reciprocity Treaty was "one of the most important events of my reign, and I sincerely believe that it will re-establish the commercial progress and prosperity which began with the Reciprocity Treaty." [61] With regard to the the Pearl River Harbor amendment, he explained that it had been accepted "after mature deliberation, and the interchange between my Government

---

56. *Id.*

57. "Treaty Aftermath," *Pacific Commercial Advertiser,* February 11, 1887, 2. The dredging of the Pearl River did not commence in earnest until after the United States had annexed Hawai'i and was not completed until December 1911. "Pearl Harbor Opening Will Take Place This Morning," *Pacific Commercial Advertiser,* December 14, 1911, at 1, col. 3.

58. "Hawaiian Parliament: Twenty-Ninth Day: Pearl River Harbor," *Pacific Commercial Advertiser,* December 9, 1887, at 2, quoting H. A. P. Carter's September 23, 1887, letter to T. F. Bayard (Letter No. 382); *Foreign Relations of the United States 1887, supra* note 39, at 589–91 (same); 3 Kuykendall, *supra* note 9, at 396; Tansill, *supra* note 1, at 38.

59. "Hawaiian Parliament: Twenty-Ninth Day: Pearl River Harbor," *Pacific Commercial Advertiser,* December 9, 1887, quoting Bayard's September 23, 1887 response to Carter (Letter No. 383); *Foreign Relations of the United States 1887, supra* note 39, at 591 (same); 3 Kuykendall, *supra* note 9, at 396, citing exchanged letters reprinted in Senate Miscellaneous Document No. 64, 50th Cong., 1st Sess, at 204 and Senate Document No. 231, 56th Cong., 2nd Sess. Pt. 8, at 254–58; Tansill, *supra* note 1, at 38; Stevens, *supra* note 3, at 176–82; 1 John Bassett Moore, *A Digest of International Law,* 494 (1906).

60. 3 Kuykendall, *supra* note 9, at 397.

61. "The King's Speech," *Pacific Commercial Advertiser,* November 4, 1887, at 2, quoting the English text of the Mō'ī's speech to the Legislature.

and that of the United States of an interpretation of the said clause whereby it is agreed and understood that it does not cede any territory, or part with, or impair any right of sovereignty, or jurisdiction, on the part of the Hawaiian Kingdom, and that such privilege is co-terminous with the treaty." [62] Minister Carter also tried to explain to the British government that the treaty involved "no cession of Pearl Harbor, but a mere agreement for its use pending the existence of the treaty." [63] President Grover Cleveland formally ratified the treaty on behalf of the United States on November 9, 1887.[64]

Although Kuykendall reported that "some people in the United States professed to believe that the Pearl Harbor concession [based on the 1887 Supplemental Convention] was perpetual," [65] it is clear that those in authority did not, because U.S. officials continued to press for "a permanent right to exclusive occupancy [of Pearl Harbor] as a naval station" [66] and thus "to secure Pearl Harbor in practical perpetuity." [67] This matter was actively debated in the summer of 1892, with Robert W. Wilcox speaking in favor of a "cession of Pearl Harbor for adequate compensation" in order to promote closer relations with the United States and to prevent annexation, arguing that "America does not want another inch of our land." [68] Representative

---

62. *Id.*

63. Tansill, *supra* note 1, at 39, quoting from Memorandum written by U.S. Secretary of State Thomas F. Bayard after a conversation with Carter, November 9, 1887, Bayard manuscript. This same view was conveyed by the Kingdom's Minister of Foreign Affairs Jonathan Austin to the British Commissioner James H. Wodehouse on February 9, 1888, when Austin said, "no cession of territory has been made. . . . The only thing which has been granted to the Government of the United States is the right to make a harbor at its own expense at a place called Pearl River Harbor, and, having so made it, the exclusive privilege of using it during the continuance of the treaty. . . . [T]he convention with the United States Government does not involve any cession of territory to the United States or any release of sovereignty or jurisdiction by this Government. . . . [T]he privileges granted . . . to the United States Government . . . expire with the termination of the treaty." Letter from Austin to Wodehouse, No. 615 [173], February 16, 1888, reprinted in 1 *Papers Relating to the Foreign Relations of the United States for the Year 1888,* 862–63 (1889); *see also* Tansill, *supra* note 1, at 43.

Despite the effort made by the Kingdom's officials to make it clear that the grant of an exclusive right to use Pearl Harbor was only for the duration of the Reciprocity Treaty and did not constitute a cession of territory, subsequent commentators have sometimes characterized the 1887 Supplemental Convention as ceding Pearl Harbor to the United States. *See, e.g.,* "Liliuokalani to Be Guest of Admiral," *Pacific Commercial Advertiser,* December 13, 1911, at 1, col. 1: "The Queen is delighted over the prospect of a trip on the flagship and is looking forward with deep interest to seeing the waterway really open to the navigation of big ships of war, for it was during the reign of her brother, King Kalākaua, that the cession of Pearl Harbor to the United States was made by treaty."

64. "Supplemental Reciprocity Treaty," signed December 6, 1884, entered into force Nov. 9, 1887, 52 Stat. 1399; Treaty Series 163; 8 Bevans, *supra* note 3, at 878; "The Reciprocity Treaty," *Pacific Commercial Advertiser,* November 28, 1887, at 2.

65. 3 Kuykendall, *supra* note 9, at 500 n.*.

66. *Id.* at 501–02, quoting from Sereno E. Bishop, "The Hawaiian Queen and Her Kingdom," 4 *Review of Reviews,* 146–63 (September 1891).

67. *Id.* at 502, quoting from "U.S. Minister to Hawaii John Stevens to U.S. Secretary of State James Blaine," No. 34, October 15, 1891. *See also* Lucien Young, *The Boston in Hawaii,* 295 (1898), arguing that formal annexation of Hawai'i by the United States was necessary because "there are doubts as to the permanency of the title of the United States to [Pearl Harbor]. The Hawaiian government, both the monarchy and the republic, maintains that the United States title to the harbor is coterminus with the existing reciprocity treaty, and that if such is terminated the American rights to Pearl Harbor terminate also. . . . [T]here is no grant of territory by that treaty."

68. 3 Kuykendall, *supra* note 9, at 503, quoting from speeches made by Wilcox on July 9 and 12, 1892.

Joseph Nawahi, the eloquent self-taught attorney from the Big Island who fought for native causes throughout his twenty years in the Legislature,[69] strenuously opposed cession.[70]

The Remainder of King Kalākaua's Reign

After the Bayonet Constitution had been imposed upon him, King Kalākaua continued to shoulder his duties to his people. According to his sister and successor, Queen Lili'uokalani, the Kingdom prospered as a "direct consequence" of Kalākaua's acts, in spite of the restrictions on his power.[71] But the limitations that the 1887 Constitution imposed on native voters and on the Mō'ī "naturally exasperated the Hawaiian people . . . and the country has continued in a constant and growing state of ferment."[72]

On July 30, 1889, Robert W. Wilcox, with Robert Boyd, "made an unsuccessful attempt to overthrow the missionary party"[73] and "to release the king from that hated thraldom under which he had been oppressed."[74] With eighty lightly armed men, Wilcox occupied the grounds of 'Iolani Palace and utilized four cannons that had been stored there to command the four gates to the grounds.[75] But the Mō'ī himself failed to support Wilcox's efforts,[76] perhaps because he feared that Wilcox "intended to depose him and put Liliuokalani on the throne,"[77] or perhaps simply because he feared "open warfare between his Native subjects and the haole" and "had no stomach for war."[78] This "armed insurrection" was "suppressed within eighteen hours," with seven Hawaiians killed and twelve wounded.[79] The United States supported

---

69. *See* Sally Engle Merry, *Colonizing Hawaii: The Cultural Power of Law,* 211–12 (2000).

70. 3 Kuykendall, *supra* note 9, at 503, citing *Pacific Commercial Advertiser,* July 13, 1892, and *Daily Bulletin,* July 13, 1892; *see infra* chapter 19, text at notes 25–26.

71. Liliuokalani, *supra* note 2, at 233.

72. "Statement of Volney V. Ashford" (March 8, 1893), in "Blount Report," *supra* note 4, at 202, 203.

73. Liliuokalani, *supra* note 2, at 199.

74. *Id.* at 198.

75. 3 Kuykendall, *supra* note 9, at 426–27.

76. Osorio, *supra* note 11, at 242: "Having perhaps encouraged Wilcox to take over the palace and 'force' him to abrogate the constitution, the king did not wait for the Native force to arrive, but took refuge in his boathouse, while the surprised ministry reacted with armed men of their own, killing and wounding several of Wilcox's men"; "Volney Ashford Statement," *supra* note 72, at 205–06.

77. 3 Kuykendall, *supra* note 9, at 427, offering this theory as "[o]ne explanation that has been given of the king's absence from the palace," offered by the British Commissioner James H. Wodehouse, Lorrin A. Thurston, and Volney V. Ashford, but adding that "[t]he story is incompatible with other known facts except on the theory of a double cross by Wilcox or the king." *See also* Coffman, *supra* note 6, at 103: "To destroy the Bayonet Constitution was a clear enough goal. What was unclear was whether [Wilcox] also wished to unseat Kalākaua and put Lili'uokalani on the throne."

78. Osorio, *supra* note 11, at 242–43. Professor Osorio has written that "[i]t is difficult to read the king's actions as anything but a betrayal of his own people" and has observed that "he might have demonstrated more spine." *Id.* at 242.

79. Ernest Andrade Jr., *Unconquerable Rebel: Robert W. Wilcox and Hawaiian Politics, 1880–1903,* 58–63 (1996); Davianna Pomaika'i McGregor, "The Cultural and Political History of the Hawaiian Native People," in *Our History, Our Way: An Ethnic Studies Anthology,* 365 (Gregory Yee Mark, Davianna Pomaika'i McGregor, and Linda A. Revilla, eds., 1996); Daws, *supra* note 14, at 256–57.

Robert W. Wilcox,
1889

the Hawaiian Government in its efforts to defeat the insurrection, first by landing a squad of marines from the USS *Adams* to guard the U.S. legation, then by providing 10,000 rounds of rifle ammunition from the *Adams* to the Government, and finally by landing another seventy men armed with machine guns from the *Adams* to assist in maintaining order during the night.[80]

Although the effort of Robert Wilcox failed as a military maneuver, it may have been important symbolically in demonstrating resistence to the "reforms" introduced by the 1887 Bayonet Constitution. In fact, in the elections held in 1890, "the sugar planters and missionary influence combined were downed by the strong will of the natives, allied with the foreign workingmen and mechanics, who opposed the coolie-labor policy of the wealthy class."[81]

King Kalākaua died in 1891 while on a trip to Washington to meet with Minister Henry A. P. Carter regarding the 1890 McKinley Tariff,[82] which had the effect

---

80. 3 Kuykendall, *supra* note 9, at 428; 1 Moore, *supra* note 59, at 495.

81. Hawaiian Patriotic League, "Memorial on the Hawaiian Patriotic League," in "Blount Report," *supra* note 4, at 448, 453. The 1890 election is discussed in 3 Kuykendall, *supra* note 9, at 451–55.

82. "An Act to Reduce the Revenue and Equalize Duties on Imports, and for Other Purposes," October 1, 1890, ch. 1244, 26 Stat. 567.

of nullifying the advantages of the Reciprocity Treaty.[83] Lili'uokalani stated, "So the king went patiently and cheerfully to work for the cause of those who had been and were his enemies."[84] The Queen added that those who supported annexation "were not grateful for a prosperity which must sooner or later, while enriching them, also elevate the masses of the Hawaiian people into a self-governing class, and depose them from that primacy in our political affairs which they chiefly valued."[85]

---

83. Liliuokalani, *supra* note 2, at 206. *See generally infra* chapter 16, text at notes 37–43.
84. Liliuokalani, *supra* note 2, at 206.
85. *Id.* at 233.

15

Population, Voting, and Citizenship in the Kingdom of Hawai'i

 This chapter departs from the chronological approach tracing the historical events relevant to the Crown Lands to examine a relevant and misunderstood topic: What was the nature of the polity or political community in the Kingdom in the years before the 1893 overthrow? This issue is important to modern analysis regarding claims to the Crown Lands, because it is central to the question of who it was that was injured by the overthrow and the accompanying transfer of lands. As the materials that follow demonstrate, this issue has some complexities, but the central answer is not in doubt: Native Hawaiians constituted the overwhelming majority of the political community that participated in decision making in the Kingdom at the time of the 1893 overthrow.

This issue has become important because some commentators have contended that Native Hawaiians had lost control over their lands and the Kingdom's Government before 1893 and hence suffered no injury as a result of the overthrow. Professor Stuart Minor Benjamin has written, for instance, that "[b]y 1890, those descended from pre-1778 inhabitants constituted less than half of the population. A majority of the inhabitants were non-Native Hawaiians; many of them were born in Hawaii, and many were citizens of Hawaii." [1] The late attorney Patrick W. Hanifin, who represented groups challenging programs established for Native Hawaiians before his untimely death in 2003, argued similarly that Native Hawaiians had suffered no injury from the overthrow of the Kingdom, because they no longer controlled the Kingdom and had previously lost effective control of its lands. [2] He asserted that "[t]he government of the Kingdom of Hawaii actively encouraged immigration and offered immigrants easy naturalization and full political rights. Race and ethnicity did not matter." [3] "The Kingdom had thousands of citizens and voters of other ancestries and

---

1. Stuart Minor Benjamin, "Equal Protection and the Special Relationship: The Case of Native Hawaiians," 106 *Yale Law Journal*, 537, 550 (1996).

2. Patrick Hanifin, "Hawaiian Reparations: Nothing Lost, Nothing Owed," 17 *Hawaii Bar Journal,* 107 (1982).

3. Patrick W. Hanifin, "To Dwell on the Earth in Unity: Rice, Arakaki, and the Growth of Citizenship and Voting Rights in Hawaii," 5 *Hawaii Bar Journal* 15, 15 (2002).

their numbers were growing toward a majority."[4] Retired Big Island Circuit Court Judge Paul M. de Silva has contended that "[f]rom the very early years after discovery, Hawaiians welcomed foreigners," that in 1893 "approximately three-fourths of the population protected by the kingdom were not Native Hawaiians," that all the Kingdom's Constitutions protected "people of all races,"[5] and that as of 1893, "anyone born or naturalized in the Republic of Hawaii could be a Hawaiian citizen regardless of race."[6] He has therefore asked that if the Crown and Government Lands "were wrongfully obtained by the United States and if they should be returned, why is it that they should be returned only to people with Hawaiian blood?"[7] Indeed, the U.S. Supreme Court has also given a version of history in its 2000 *Rice v. Cayetano*[8] opinion that provides a distorted view of these matters:

> The conflicts came to the fore in 1887. Westerners forced the resignation
> of the Prime Minister of the Kingdom of Hawaii and the adoption of a new
> Constitution, which, among other things, reduced the power of the monarchy
> *and extended the right to vote to non-Hawaiians.*[9]

Justice Stephen Breyer's concurring opinion in *Rice* is also based on a misunderstanding of Hawaiian history, when he imagines that Hawai'i's population today might contain "individuals who are less than one five-hundredth original Hawaiian (assuming nine generations between 1778 and the present)."[10]

These contentions and factual assertions raise serious issues, and they deserve a serious analysis. If one looks closely at the structure of the Kingdom's Constitutions, one finds a much more complex picture regarding voting and citizenship than those presented above, and a close analysis reveals that some of these assertions are factually incorrect or are seriously misleading. Although it is certainly true that contract laborers were arriving in the Islands in substantial numbers during the twenty-five years that preceded the overthrow, these plantation workers were in the Kingdom on a temporary basis and most had the intention of returning home or going elsewhere when their contracts were completed. "Nearly all of the immigrants considered themselves temporary residents, bound to the terms of their contract and anxious to save some money and return home."[11] The practice in the 1870s was to import for-

---

4. *Id.* at 27.

5. Paul M. de Silva, "Racial-Based Sovereignty Is Unjust," *Honolulu Advertiser,* August 10, 2001, at A-14.

6. Paul de Silva, Letter to the Editor, "Hawaiians: Solution Not in Race-Based Sovereignty," *Honolulu Advertiser,* August 25, 2001, at A-8, col. 4.

7. De Silva, "Racial-Based Sovereignty," *supra* note 5.

8. *Rice v. Cayetano,* 528 U.S. 495 (2000).

9. *Id.* at 504, citing 3 Ralph S. Kuykendall, *The Hawaiian Kingdom 1874–1893: The Kalakaua Dynasty,* 344–72 (1967, reprinted 1987) (emphasis added).

10. *Id.* at 526. See *infra,* chapter 24, note 57.

11. Lawrence H. Fuchs, *Hawaii Pono: A Social History,* 25 (1961, reprinted 1983). *See also* Jonathan Kay Kamakawiwoʻole Osorio, *Dismembering Lāhui: A History of the Hawaiian Nation to 1887,* 281 n. 9 (2002): "most of the new arrivals were not, and did not intend to become, citizens."

eign laborers under three-year contracts "after which they were expected to return home."[12] Lorrin Thurston was very clear in his writings that the Asian laborers were in Hawai'i "temporarily . . . for what they can make out of it," that they "are not citizens," and that "they are not eligible to become citizens."[13] Many of the Japanese laborers left Hawai'i for North America after their contracts were completed.[14] These Asian laborers were excluded from decision-making political circles, as guest workers are excluded from political activity in many countries today, and thus the numbers alone provide an incomplete picture. Although pressure by westerners to wrest control of the Kingdom was intense in the 1887 coup d'etat[15] and eventually successful in the 1893 overthrow,[16] Native Hawaiians continued to play the dominant role in the Kingdom and its Monarchy until the end, and they certainly have a unique and exclusive claim today to the Crown Lands.

Population

Because of introduced diseases that they did not have the necessary immunities to fend off, the population of Native Hawaiians declined dramatically from estimates ranging between 400,000 and 800,000 at the time of Captain James Cook's arrival in 1778 to little more than 40,000 in 1890.[17] Westerners started arriving in the late eighteenth and early nineteenth centuries, but their numbers remained small during those periods. Kamehameha I "and other chiefs were always ready to make an offer to a skilled navigator, sailmaker, blacksmith, armorer, or carpenter. A good trades-man could depend on a gift of land and a native wife or two or three if he stayed."[18] In 1794, sixteen years after Cook's first arrival, "at least 11" foreigners were living in the islands, and by 1818 they numbered in the low hundreds.[19]

In 1820, missionaries began to arrive, leading to substantial changes in social values and land control. Whalers and itinerant travelers came to the islands in small numbers during the next three decades, but no significant changes in the demographics occurred until the introduction of contract laborers to work in the agricultural fields, primarily in the sugar plantations. In 1832, only some 400 foreigners

---

12. Sally Engle Merry, *Colonizing Hawaii: The Cultural Power of Law*, 125 (2000), citing Edward D. Beechert, *Working in Hawaii: A Labor History* (1985).

13. *Id.* at 135, quoting from Lorrin A. Thurston, *A Handbook on the Annexation of Hawaii*, 28 (circa 1897).

14. "After their contracts were finished, thousands of Japanese workers left for the mainland and higher wages. By early 1907 forty thousand Japanese had left Hawai'i for the West Coast. The 1907 order prohibiting Japanese from Hawai'i from going to the mainland trapped many eager emigrants in Hawai'i." Merry, *supra* note 12, at 338 n. 6, citing Ronald Takaki, *Pau Hana Plantation Life and Labor in Hawaii, 1835–1920*, 148 (1989).

15. *See supra* chapter 14.

16. *See infra* chapter 16.

17. *See supra* chapter 3, text at notes 1–30.

18. Gavan Daws, *Shoal of Time: A History of the Hawaiian Islands*, 46 (1968, reprinted 1974).

19. Ralph S. Kuykendall and A. Grove Day, *Hawaii: A History*, 37 (1961).

were residing in the Islands,[20] and by 1844 this number had grown to about 600.[21] The 1850 census reported the total population as 84,165, of whom 82,035 were pure Hawaiian, about 500 were part-Hawaiians, and about 1,600 were "adventurers from all parts of the globe—American and French missionaries, traders and seamen from such widely separated regions as Africa, China, South America, the United States, Scandinavia, the Philippines, and Asia Minor."[22]

The recruitment of foreign workers began in 1852, when about 280 Chinese men were brought to Hawai'i,[23] and the flow of imported laborers continued until 1930. Fewer than 2,000 Chinese came into the Kingdom between 1852 and 1875,[24] but the arrival of workers increased dramatically after the adoption of the Reciprocity Treaty of 1875,[25] which accelerated the growth in the number and size of sugar plantations.[26] Some, including (in 1869) the twenty-five-year-old Sanford Ballard Dole,[27] criticized the early practice of bringing in contract laborers and their treatment once they arrived in the Islands, but after the Reciprocity Treaty and the resulting expansion of the plantations, the momentum behind the importation of workers became unstoppable. In 1876, the population of Hawai'i was about 55,000, of which 46,500 were Hawaiians, 3,000 were part-Hawaiians, 3,500 were Caucasians (including 450 Portuguese laborers), and 2,500 were Chinese.[28] Hawaiians and part-Hawaiians thus made up 89.2 percent of the population as of that date.[29] But in the years that followed, Hawaiians became the numerical minority.

By the time he was twenty-eight, in 1872, Dole started giving strong support to the need to increase Hawai'i's population, writing a series of articles in the *Pacific Commercial Advertiser* explaining his views. He observed that "until our islands

20. Walter F. Judd, *Hawaii Joins the World,* 66 (1999).
21. *Id.* at 156.
22. Andrew W. Lind, *Hawaii's People,* 64 (4th ed., 1990).
23. William Fremont Blackman, *The Making of Hawaii: A Study in Social Evolution,* 194 (1906, reprinted 1977).
24. Merry, *supra* note 12, at 131. "Before the signing of the Reciprocity Treaty, twenty-three hundred immigrants had arrived from Asia, most of them from China, with contracts to work on the plantations." Tom Coffman, *Nation Within: The Story of America's Annexation of the Nation of Hawai'i,* 63 (1998).
25. *See supra* chapter 14, text at notes 3–9.
26. "Faced with the need for a labor force over twice that used before reciprocity, a sharp labor shortage developed which produced a revived demand for foreign immigration." Sylvester K. Stevens, *American Expansion in Hawaii 1842–1898,* 143–44 (1945, reprinted 1968).
27. 2 Ralph S. Kuykendall, *The Hawaiian Kingdom 1854–1874: Twenty Critical Years,* 189 (1953, reprinted 1982), describing a meeting in October 1869 when Dole said that he opposed the contract labor system "from principle," explaining that "[t]ried in the balance of the 'free and equal rights' principle, the contract system is found wanting." After a series of meetings of the economic elites in October 1869, resolutions were adopted stating that "the further introduction into this country of Chinese coolies is undesirable" and that "laws, enforcing contracts to service by penal enactment, tend to injustice, and are contrary to the spirit of the age." *Id.* at 190. Some legislators tried to repeal the law governing contract labor (which had been written earlier by William Little Lee, *see supra* chapter 4, text at notes 40–74), and some adjustments were made to provide laborers some rights and to prohibit married women from entering into labor contracts, but because of planter opposition, "the penal sanctions contained in the masters and servants law were not removed." *Id.* at 191, citing *Laws, 1872,* at 7–8, 20–21, 27–28.
28. 3 Kuykendall, *supra* note 9, at 116.
29. *Id.*

are occupied to their fullest extent, the limit of our productive power will never be reached," and that "with sufficient labor, there would be room for one hundred average sugar plantations here instead of thirty-two at present, and it is probable that this number could be increased to one hundred and fifty." [30] "And there is no less doubt but that, with our lands brought to a state of careful cultivation, and through the economies of a higher civilization than our dusky predecessors could boast, a nation of at least a million might in comfort and plenty occupy our islands, and make them rich and prosperous." [31] "The Hawaiian is not to be displaced, but must be supplemented." [32] He sought "a steady tide of immigration," but favored a mix of immigrants, not just contract laborers, arguing that the Islands needed "settlers and citizens rather than convicts and coolies; that our mountains and our plains must first be planted with men, before they can be profitably and fully planted with cane and rice; that families rather than plantations constitute the true basis of state prosperity, and therefore the first object of our needs." [33]

Dole appears to have made his personal peace with the contract labor system by 1872, explaining that "[a]t present, our contract laborers are, as a rule, highly paid, well fed and cared for, and treated perhaps according to their behavior as well as they deserve, sometimes better." [34] He suggested that plantations should be encouraged to experiment with cooperative arrangements with their workers and profit-sharing deals, stating that with such inducements the workers would "receive high wages, good care and treatment, together with some other circumstances undoubtedly objectionable to an Anglo-Saxon mind, but which would not make any insurmountable obstacle to unsophisticated Mongolians or Malays," because "the life they take up here is immensely superior in a material sense to the life they leave behind." [35]

Between 1872 and 1900, Hawai'i's population almost tripled, growing from 56,896 in 1872 (of whom 51,531 were Hawaiian or part-Hawaiian) to 154,001 in 1900 (of whom only 39,656 were Hawaiian or part-Hawaiian). [36] The plantation owners sought to diversify the labor force: "The need for effective labor control . . . dictated a policy of drawing the workers from a number of different sources." [37] "So large a number of these [contract workers] were Chinese as to arouse alarm and lead to an attempt to encourage Portuguese instead. . . . In 1886 an immigration convention with Japan resulted in increased numbers of this race coming to the Islands." [38] Of the some 154,000 individuals in the Islands in 1900, about 30,000 were pure Hawaiian,

---

30. S. B. Dole, "The Problem of Population," *Pacific Commercial Advertiser*, September 28, 1872, at 3.

31. *Id.*

32. *Id.*

33. S. B. Dole, "Immigration," *Pacific Commercial Advertiser*, October 5, 1872, at 3.

34. S. B. Dole, "Inducements to Immigration," *Pacific Commercial Advertiser*, October 12, 1872, at 2.

35. *Id.*

36. Robert C. Schmitt, *Historical Statistics of Hawaii*, 25 table 1.12 (1977). The importation of plantation laborers continued until about 1930.

37. Lind, *supra* note 22, at 6.

38. Stevens, *supra* note 26, at 145.

10,000 were part-Hawaiian, 27,000 were Caucasian (including 18,000 Portuguese), 26,000 were Chinese, and 61,000 were Japanese.[39]

Despite their numbers, however, the newly arrived laborers played little or no role in political decision making, because the accepted view was that they would earn some money and then return to their homelands.[40] They were viewed by the planter elites as a "necessary evil," because, in their view, "sugar production could not be carried on profitably without cheap labor," and "[t]he attitude of the planters toward this more or less servile labor element came to resemble the Southern philosophy of slavery days toward the negro in the United States."[41] This importation of uneducated "servile" laborers was not the approach preferred by the Kingdom's Government, which had wanted "a high type of immigration capable of repopulating the Islands on a substantial basis," and the U.S. Minister to Hawai'i, Henry A. Peirce, denounced this practice as "the slave trade under another name."[42] In 1896 and 1897, 2,473 individuals were criminally convicted for "deserting or refusing bound service" under the contract labor law,[43] which illustrates how the agricultural workers were controlled.

All told, some 400,000 individuals were brought to Hawai'i for agricultural labor between 1852 and 1930,[44] but a significant percentage went home or continued on to North America. Fuchs reported that although a "minority stayed on," they took "no part in the continuing struggle between haoles and natives for governmental control of the Kingdom."[45] Commissioner James Blount (reporting to President Grover Cleveland after the 1893 overthrow) wrote that "[f]rom 1876 to 1887 there were imported 23,268 Chinese, 2,777 Japanese, 10,216 Portuguese, 615 Norwegians, 1,052 Germans, 1,998 South Sea Islanders, making a total for this one decade of 39,926 immigrants."[46] One author has reported that between 1875 and 1887, 25,497 Chinese moved to the Kingdom (almost all of whom were male) and that 10,196 left to return home,[47] and she also reported that of the 200,000 Japanese who came

---

39. Lind, *supra* note 22, at 34 table 3.

40. Fuchs, *supra* note 11, at 25.

41. Stevens, *supra* note 26, at 144. *See also* Helena G. Allen, *The Betrayal of Liliuokalani: Last Queen of Hawaii 1838–1917*, 212, 304 (1982), stating that the Chinese brought to Hawai'i worked "at slave wage and conditions" and reporting that Queen Lili'uokalani "thought the 'slave labor' on the plantations was 'inhuman.'"

42. Stevens, *supra* note 26, at 144. Peirce served as U.S. Minister to the Kingdom of Hawai'i from 1869 to 1877; after his resignation he became the Foreign Minister of the Kingdom for three months. *Id.* at 148.

43. Blackman, *supra* note 23, at 199.

44. *Rice v. Cayetano*, 528 U.S. 495, 506 (2000); Fuchs, *supra* note 11, at 24; Lind, *supra* note 22, at 6–7, reporting that 180,000 came from Japan and Okinawa, 125,000 came from the Philippines, 46,000 came from South China, 17,500 Portuguese came from the Azores and the Madeira Islands, 8,000 came from Korea, 6,000 came from Puerto Rico, 8,000 came from Spain, 1,300 came from Germany and Galicia, 2,500 came from the Pacific Islands, 2,000 came from Russia, and "numerous other groups [came] in smaller numbers."

45. Fuchs, *supra* note 11, at 25.

46. Letter from Commissioner James Blount to U.S. Secretary of State W. C. Gresham, July 17, 1893, in "Report of Commissioner to the Hawaiian Islands," in 27 *Executive Documents of the House of Representatives for the Second Session of the Fifty-Third Congress, 1893–94*, 105 (1895), originally in Executive Document No. 47, 53rd Cong., 2d Sess. (1893) (hereafter cited as "Blount Report").

47. Merry, *supra* note 12, at 131.

Plantation workers gathering sugarcane on Kaua'i, ca. 1885

between 1885 and 1924, 110,000 went back to Japan and another 40,000 went to the West Coast of the United States.[48] A total of 29,000 of these Japanese arrived in the Islands between 1885 and 1894,[49] leading to an increase in the number of Japanese in Hawai'i from 12,360 in 1890 to 24,407 in 1896[50] and creating challenges both domestically and internationally.[51]

The desire to return home was perhaps particularly strong among those male laborers who came without wives or families. As Lind explained, "[o]wing to the tendency on the part of many of the unmarried immigrants to return to their homeland after the completion of their plantation contracts, the Chinese population actually declined by approximately 1,500 between 1884 and 1890."[52] In 1893, Commissioner Blount reported that 14,522 Chinese males resided in the Islands, but there were only 779 Chinese females, and that "[t]he Japanese men outnumber their women by nearly 5 to 1."[53] Lind has further pointed out that although 46,000 Chinese had

---

48. *Id.* at 338 n. 6, 341–42 n.62, citing Takaki, *supra* note 14, at 148, 169.

49. Coffman, *supra* note 24, at 189.

50. Stevens, *supra* note 26, at 274 n. 14.

51. "[T]he growing influx of Japanese into Hawaii began by this date [1894] to give rise to fears of its consequences." *Id.* at 274; *see also id.* at 283.

52. Lind, *supra* note 22, at 32.

53. Letter from Commissioner James Blount to U.S. Secretary of State W. C. Gresham, June 1, 1893, in "Blount Report," *supra* note 46, at 75.

been brought as laborers, primarily between 1876 and 1885, only 21,674 persons of Chinese ancestry (including some born in the Islands) were counted in the census of 1910.[54] Commissioner Blount reported in 1893 that of the 1,238 "merchants and traders in the entire country . . . 776 are Chinamen and 81 are Americans."[55] Blount observed that it should "not be imagined that the Chinese, Japanese, and Portuguese disappear at the end of their contract term," and reported that "[m]ore than 75 per cent [of the Japanese laborers] may be said to locate here [in Hawai'i] permanently."[56]

The 1890 census counted 40,612 persons of Hawaiian ancestry, who constituted 45 percent of the 89,990 people in the Kingdom,[57] but by the 1896 census the figure had dropped to 36 percent of the 109,020 residents.[58] Hanifin extrapolated that the figure in 1893 was thus "about 40 percent."[59] But these numbers misrepresent the reality of governance in the Islands, because the foreign contract laborers were considered to be temporary visitors and those of Asian ancestry were systematically excluded from participation in the Kingdom's political decision making.

Citizenship

The question of who was eligible to be a citizen of the Kingdom of Hawai'i is complex, because the word "citizen" was not widely used in Kingdom documents. The more typical term used with regard to a kingdom is "subject."[60]

In 1830, Dr. Thomas C. B. Rooke, who had arrived from England the previous year, was allowed to marry the Ali'i Grace Kama'iku'i Young on the understanding that he would swear allegiance to the Mō'ī.[61] The earliest formal consideration of this topic was apparently an August 1838 document called "Alien Laws," which was signed by Kauikeaouli (Kamehameha III) but does not seem to have become formally promulgated as law.[62] The first two articles of this instrument said that the subjects of the Kingdom were those born in the Islands, born to Native Hawaiians living elsewhere, or born on a ship belonging to the Kingdom, and that others were

---

54. Lind, *supra* note 22, at 27. Many of the Spaniards recruited between 1907 and 1913 left Hawai'i for California. *Id.* at 31. "[B]ecause of extensive movement of the single [Filipino] men back to the Philippines or to California, the number of Filipinos left in Hawaii declined by 11,000 in the decade 1930–1940." *Id.* at 32.

55. Blount letter of June 1, 1893, *supra* note 53, at 74.

56. *Id.*; also in letter from Commissioner James Blount to U.S. Secretary of State W. C. Gresham, July 17, 1893, in "Blount Report," *supra* note 46, at 135.

57. Blount letter of June 1, 1893, *supra* note 53, at 73–74.

58. Schmitt, *Historical Statistics, supra* note 36, at 25; Lind, *supra* note 22, at 28.

59. Hanifin, "To Dwell," *supra* note 3, at 26. Judge de Silva's figure of 25 percent is unsupported by any historical data. De Silva, "Racial-Based Sovereignty," *supra* note 5.

60. *See, e.g.,* Hanifin, "To Dwell," *supra* note 3, at 15 n. 4.

61. George S. Kanahele, *Emma: Hawai'i's Remarkable Queen*, 2 (1999).

62. 1 Ralph S. Kuykendall, *The Hawaiian Kingdom 1778–1854: Foundation and Transformation*, 230 n. 17 (1938, reprinted 1989); Osorio, *supra* note 11, at 57, citing Maude Jones, *Naturalization in Hawaii*, 17 (1934).

to be considered aliens unless they took an oath of allegiance to the Kingdom.[63] Two years later, on November 12, 1840, a law was formally enacted that required foreigners who married Hawaiians to "take the oath of allegiance to this government." [64] In 1846, "despite petitions of protests signed by 5,790 Hawaiians," [65] "representing 8 percent of the total adult population of Hawaii in 1845," [66] this procedure was expanded to permit naturalization of foreigners who had lived in the Kingdom for one year.[67] The naturalization process was a flexible one; for instance, John Ricord, the Kingdom's first Attorney General,[68] was naturalized immediately upon landing in the Islands in 1844,[69] but he was released from his oath in 1847 when he departed for other adventures.[70]

This 1846 statute also recognized the category of "denizens," who were specially favored aliens allowed to retain their foreign citizenship but granted the rights and privileges of natives by the Mōʻī.[71] Relatively few were accorded this special status as denizens—only 143 during the half century between 1846 and 1893.[72] The number naturalized was also relatively modest. An 1847 publication estimated that 600 foreigners were living in Honolulu, of whom 146 had become naturalized as subjects of the Kingdom.[73] Another author estimated that about 350 foreigners had become naturalized subjects as of 1846.[74] By 1851, 1,600 foreigners were living in the Kingdom (about 2 percent of the Kingdom's overall population), but only 676 had become naturalized, with 428 of those being from the United States.[75] Between

---

63. Alien males wishing to marry native females who declined to pledge allegiance to the Kingdom would have been required under this law to post a bond of $400, which would be forfeited to help support the family left behind if the male ever left the Islands. Osorio, *supra* note 11, at 57.

64. 1 Kuykendall, *supra* note 62, at 230, citing *Constitution and Laws,* 1842, chapter 10; Hanifin, "To Dwell," *supra* note 3, at 21, citing *Hawaiian Laws 1841–1842,* chapter 10, sec. 9 at 47.

65. Davianna Pomakaʻi McGregor, "An Introduction to the Hoaʻāina and Their Rights," 30 *Hawaiian Journal of History,* 1, 9 (1996).

66. Davianna Pomaikaʻi McGregor, "The Cultural and Political History of Hawaiian Native People," in *Our History, Our Way: An Ethnic Studies Anthology,* 349 (Gregory Yee Mark, Davianna Pomaikaʻi McGregor, and Linda A. Revilla, eds., 1996) (hereafter cited as McGregor, "Cultural and Political History").

67. *Id.* at 22, citing 1 *Statute Laws of Kamehameha III,* sec. 10 at 78.

68. *See supra* chapter 4, note 26.

69. 1 Kuykendall, *supra* note 62, at 236.

70. Osorio, *supra* note 11, at 59. See *supra* chapter 4, note 26.

71. 1 Kuykendall, *supra* note 62, at 266 n. 162, citing 1 *Statute Laws,* 79–80, which said that the denizen was "in all respects accountable to the laws of this kingdom" and had "the like fealty to the king, as if he had been naturalized"; Hanifin, "To Dwell," *supra* note 3, at 22, citing 1 *Statute Laws of Kamehameha III,* sec. 14.

72. Hanifin, "To Dwell," *supra* note 3, at 22, citing H. Arai, *Indices to Certificates of Nationality 1846–1854, Denization 1846–1898, Oaths of Loyalty to the Republic from Oahu 1894, and Certificates of Special Rights of Citizenship 1896–1898* (1991), Hawaiʻi State Archives. A list of the sixty-six men granted "letters patent of denization" between 1883 and 1893 can be found in the "Blount Report," *supra* note 46, at 611–12. Among those given the status of being denizens was Paul Neumann, who had been "a prominent, able lawyer and politician of Bohemian habits" and "was said to be a spokesman for the Spreckels sugar monopoly," who came to Hawaiʻi in 1883 "and within a few days was granted letters of denization by the king and was admitted to the Hawaiian bar" and then quickly became Attorney General. 3 Kuykendall, *supra* note 9, at 267–68.

73. Stevens, *supra* note 26, at 37, citing *The Friend,* January 15, 1847.

74. William D. Alexander, *A Brief History of the Hawaiian People,* 256 (1899, reprinted 2001).

75. Osorio, *supra* note 11, at 52, 67, citing Robert C. Schmitt, *Demographic Statistics of Hawaii,* 25 (1977).

1877 and 1892, 366 persons became naturalized citizens of the Kingdom.[76] By 1893, a total of 3,239 foreigners had become naturalized, including 1,105 Americans, 763 Chinese, 596 British, 242 Portuguese, 230 Germans, 47 French, 68 other Europeans, 136 Pacific Islanders, 27 South Americans, 3 Japanese, and 25 of other ancestry.[77]

The 1850 statute first establishing voter qualifications and the 1852 Constitution granted certain rights to this new category of individuals called denizens. When the *Civil Code* was adopted later in 1859, Article 433 stated that

> It shall be competent for His Majesty to confer upon any alien resident abroad, or temporarily resident in this Kingdom, letters patent of denization, conferring upon such alien, without abjuration of allegiance, all the rights, privileges, and immunities as a native. Such letters patent shall render the denizen in all respects accountable to the laws of this Kingdom, and impose upon him the like fealty to the King as if he had been naturalized as hereinbefore provided.[78]

The distinction between natives and foreigners was recognized and upheld by the Hawai'i Supreme Court in the 1856 decision of *Naone v. Thurston.*[79] Asa G. T. Thurston, son of Asa Thurston (one of the original missionaries) and father of Lorrin Thurston (leader of the 1887 Bayonet Constitution and 1893 overthrow), protested the fact that he was obliged by an 1851 enactment applicable only to persons "born of foreign parentage"[80] to pay a $5 school tax to support schools then being established for children of foreigners. Thurston acknowledged that he was "born of foreign parentage," but claimed that because he was born in the Kingdom he was "a Hawaiian subject by birth."[81] In an opinion written by Justice George M. Robertson, the Hawai'i Supreme Court rejected Thurston's argument, ruling that the statute was not "repugnant either to the letter, or spirit, of the Constitution."[82] Similarly, Section 1st, Chapter 42d of the Kingdom's *Penal Code* prohibited the sale of "any spirituous liquor, or other intoxicating drink or substance" to "any native of this Kingdom," and this provision was also upheld by the Kingdom's Supreme Court, which rejected the argument that this was "class legislation."[83]

---

76. "Blount Report," *supra* note 46, at 614.

77. *Id.*, citing *Index to the Naturalization Record Book for Individuals Naturalized by the Minister of the Interior of the Hawaiian Islands, 1844–1894,* Hawai'i Archives.

78. This provision is quoted in *Aliens and Denizens,* 5 Hawai'i 167, 1884 WL 6673, at *4 (1884).

79. *Naone v. Thurston,* 1 Hawai'i 220, 1856 WL 4225 (1856).

80. "An Act to Provide for the Education of the Children of Foreigners, and Those of Foreign Extraction in the City of Honolulu, and Other Places in the Kingdom," June 28, 1851.

81. *Naone v. Thurston,* 1 Hawai'i 220, 1856 WL 4225, at *1. Asa G. T. Thurston may have been a particularly inappropriate person to make this argument, because apparently his parents "erected a high wall around their compound and prohibited their children from leaving it" in order to "separate their children from Hawaiian children." Merry, *supra* note 12, at 75.

82. *Naone v. Thurston,* 1856 WL 4225, at *3.

83. *Rex v. Booth,* 2 Hawai'i 616, 626–31, 1863 WL 2527, at *7 (1863). In his concurring opinion, Chief Justice Elisha H. Allen mentioned numerous other laws that treated natives differently from nonnatives, such as the 1846 law that severely restricted the enlistment of natives as sailors on foreign vessels and the establishment of specific schools to teach English to Hawaiian youth. *Id.* at 635, 1863 WL 2527, at *11. Chief Justice Allen

Laws that treated natives and nonnatives differently continued to be enacted until the end of the Kingdom and through the Republic period. Juries, for instance, were sometimes formed exclusively of natives, sometimes exclusively of nonnatives, and sometimes rigidly structured with specific numbers of natives and nonnatives. As the Hawai'i Supreme Court later explained,

> [A]s set out in sections 1331 and 1332 of the Civil Laws of 1897, . . . a native Hawaiian, accused of any crime, was entitled to be tried by a jury composed entirely of natives, and a foreigner by a jury composed entirely of foreigners, while in all civil cases in which one party was a native Hawaiian and the other a foreigner (alien or naturalized) the jury was composed of an equal number of natives and foreigners, drawn alternatively from separate boxes.[84]

In 1874, an act was passed requiring those of foreign birth who held Government jobs to take an oath of allegiance to the Constitution and laws of the Kingdom,[85] and the Hawai'i Supreme Court interpreted this provision as requiring that job holders "shall not be an alien." [86]

An act passed in 1882 made it more difficult to become a naturalized citizen, requiring (1) the approval of the King and the Minister of Interior, (2) five years of residence in the Kingdom, (3) ownership of taxable real estate, and (4) good moral character—and excluding those fleeing justice or deserting the military of another country.[87] In 1884, the Hawai'i Supreme Court softened the edge of this provision by ruling that denizens could hold government jobs and that a letter of denization was an effective substitute for an oath of allegiance, pointing out that the Kingdom's first Chief Justice, William Little Lee, was a denizen.[88] These requirements became less significant after the Bayonet Constitution of 1887, which no longer required persons of Hawaiian, American, or European ancestry to be citizens in order to vote.[89]

So, what was the composition of the category of "citizens" or "subjects" of the

---

explained that "[t]he history of our whole legislation shows *that many laws have been passed which applied to the native subjects exclusively,*" *id.* (emphasis added), and concluded by presenting "[m]y own view," which was that "in forming the Constitution it was not the intention of the framers to prohibit legislation exclusively applicable to native subjects." 1863 WL 2527, at *12.

84. *State v. Jones,* 45 Hawai'i 247, 258, 365 P.2d 460, 466 (1961). For purposes of jury formation, a nonnative continued to be classified as a "foreigner" even after naturalization. *See also State v. Johnson,* 51 Hawai'i 195, 456 P.2d 805 (1969) (J. Levinson dissenting), providing a historical summary of the laws impaneling native-only and foreigner-only juries; *Territory v. Ng Kow,* 15 Hawai'i 602, 1904 WL 1294, at *1 (1904), explaining the practice of impaneling Native Hawaiians and "persons of foreign parentage" separately under the jury laws in force at the time of annexation. This practice was not abolished until 1900, with the passage of the Organic Act, Sec. 83, Act of April 30, 1900, c 339, 31 Stat. 141.

85. "An Act to Provide for the Taking of the Oath of Allegiance by Persons in the Employ of the Hawaiian Government," 1874 *Session Laws,* chapter 42, quoted in *Aliens and Denizens,* 5 Hawai'i 167, 1884 WL 6673, at *1 (1884).

86. *Aliens and Denizens,* 5 Hawai'i 167, 1884 WL 6673, at *3.

87. 1882 *Session Laws,* chapter 18, amending Sections 428 and 429 of the *Civil Code,* quoted in *Aliens and Denizens,* 5 Hawai'i 167, 1884 WL 6673, at *4.

88. *Aliens and Denizens,* 5 Hawai'i 167, 1884 WL 6673, at *4.

89. *See infra,* this chapter, text at notes 119–46.

Kingdom at the time of the overthrow in January 1893? Hanifin acknowledged that as of the 1890 census, 84.42 percent of the citizens or subjects were natives and surmised that this figure might have dropped to 80 percent by 1893.[90]

Voting

As just explained, determining whether a person was a "citizen," "subject," or "denizen" of the Kingdom was somewhat complicated, but a further complication was that even persons clearly in one of those categories were not necessarily entitled to vote.[91] Women were never allowed to vote under any of the Kingdom's constitutions, and many men were excluded as well.

The 1840 Constitution created a legislative body, consisting of a House of Nobles with sixteen high Ali'i who were specifically named in the Constitution, plus a "representative body" whose members "shall be chosen by the people, according to their wish, from Hawai'i, Maui, O'ahu and Kaua'i." [92] These members "were initially chosen on the basis of petitions sent to the king." [93] Pursuant to a law enacted in 1842, petitions were circulated, and the seven members of the House of Representatives were those whose petitions had the most signatures (two from Hawai'i, Maui, and O'ahu, and one from Kaua'i).[94] On July 30, 1850, a law was enacted allowing male subjects of the Kingdom (native-born or naturalized) plus male denizens to vote if they were at least twenty years old, had lived for one year in the Kingdom, and were neither insane nor unpardoned felons.[95] A companion statute increased the size of the House of Representatives to twenty-four and gave the Cabinet Ministers seats and the right to vote in the House of Nobles.[96]

The first election for members of the House of Representatives occurred on

---

90. "The 1890 census reported 40,622 ethnic Hawaiians and 7,495 native-born subjects who were not ethnic Hawaiians. . . . The next census, in 1896, reported 39,504 ethnic Hawaiians and 13,733 native-born subjects who were not ethnic Hawaiians. The percentage of native-born subjects who were not ethnic Hawaiians . . . was probably about 20 percent in 1893, midway between the 1890 and 1896 censuses." Hanifin, "To Dwell," *supra* note 3, at 21 n. 55, citing *Thrum's 1900 Hawaiian Annual,* 39.

91. "Under the constitutions of the Hawaiian Kingdom, being a subject was neither necessary nor sufficient to be a voter." *Id.* at 22.

92. *Constitution of 1840,* October 8, 1840.

93. Schmitt, *Historical Statistics, supra* note 36, at 593.

94. Robert C. Schmitt, "Voter Participation Rates in Hawaii Before 1900," 5 *Hawaiian Journal of History,* 50 (1971), citing Lorrin A. Thurston, ed., *The Fundamental Law of Hawaii,* 6, 11, 12 (1904); Hanifin, "To Dwell," *supra* note 3, at 23, citing *Laws of the Hawaiian Islands,* 1842, chapter 2, "Of the Representative Body". Professor Osorio has reported, however, that the lower house was supposed to have eight members but never in fact had more than seven, and it had only five in 1847 and 1849 because of "voting irregularities" and the dissatisfaction of the people on Kaua'i with the political decisions of the representative they had sent previously. Osorio, *supra* note 11, at 66, citing *Journal of the House of Representatives,* April 16, 1851, at 9, and *Journal of the Legislative Council,* May 11, 1847, at 136.

95. 1 Kuykendall, *supra* note 62, at 265–66, citing "An Act to Regulate the Election of Representatives of the People," July 30, 1850; Schmitt, "Voter Participation Rates," *supra* note 94, at 50, citing *Penal Code of the Hawaiian Islands . . . 1850,* at 161–66); Schmitt, *Historical Statistics, supra* note 36, at 594.

96. 1 Kuykendall, *supra* note 62, at 265, citing "An Act to Increase the Number of Representatives of the People in the Legislative Council," July 30, 1850.

January 6, 1851.[97] Even though foreign settlers constituted only 2 percent of the Kingdom's population, seven of the twenty-four representatives elected were Caucasians,[98] including George M. Robertson, William Little Lee, and Thomas C. B. Rooke, and they immediately took control and started changing the procedures followed in the Legislature.[99]

The 1852 Constitution, drafted primarily by William Little Lee,[100] maintained the practice of allowing all male subjects and denizens to vote. Article 78 said that

> Every male subject of His Majesty, whether native or naturalized, and every denizen of the Kingdom, who shall have paid his taxes, who shall have attained the full age of twenty years, and who shall have resided in the Kingdom for one year immediately preceding the time of election, shall be entitled to one vote for the representative or representatives, of the district in which he may have resided three months next preceding the day of election.[101]

Annual elections were held between 1851 and 1856, and thereafter elections were held every two years.[102] The first Kingdom-wide election figures are for the 1858 election, when 12,673 persons cast ballots.

Alexander Liholiho (Kamehameha IV) opposed the universal male suffrage utilized in the elections in the 1850s and sought to amend the 1852 Constitution to add a property requirement.[103] Based on this recommendation, a committee of the House of Representatives drafted an amendment that would have required voters to own $1,000 worth of property or to have an annual income of $1,000, and the committee also drafted an amendment that would have required voters to pass a reading test.[104] Although these proposals were originally supported, because of the procedural complexities required to amend the 1852 Constitution and because of public concern about these requirements, the amendments were never formally ratified.[105]

But the 1864 Constitution, developed according to the instructions of the new Mōʻī—Lot (Kamehameha V)[106]—did eliminate universal male suffrage, which Lot

---

97. Schmitt, *Historical Statistics, supra* note 36, at 593.

98. Osorio, *supra* note 11, at 67–69.

99. *Id.* at 75–76. "Among the twenty-four members elected to the house of representatives of 1851 were several naturalized haoles of excellent ability." 1 Kuykendall, *supra* note 62, at 266.

100. Osorio, *supra* note 11, at 85.

101. This section excluded those who were "insane" or who "have been convicted of any infamous crime," unless their vote had been restored through a pardon. The 1852 Constitution has been "regarded as a distinct triumph of the 'foreign' over the native influence in the development of Hawaiian political institutions." Blackman, *supra* note 23, at 122.

102. Schmitt, "Voter Participant Rates," *supra* note 94, at 51, citing *Civil Code of the Hawaiian Islands,* 187 (1859).

103. Ralph S. Kuykendall, *Constitutions of the Hawaiian Kingdom: A Brief History and Analysis,* 23 (Hawaiian Historical Society Paper No. 21, 1940, reprinted 1978).

104. *Id.*

105. *Id.* at 24–25.

106. The Constitutional Convention established to produce a new Constitution deadlocked over the issue of property and income qualifications, and so Lot dissolved the body and worked with those favoring such qualifications to produce the Constitution of 1864, which was promulgated by the Mōʻī without approval of the Legislature or the public. 2 Kuykendall, *supra* note 27, at 131–32.

viewed as detrimental to monarchial power. Article 62 required voters to own property of at least $150, or a leasehold with rent of at least $25/year, or to have an annual income of $75/year, and it also required voters to be able to read and write if they were born after 1840. One had to be a "male subject of the Kingdom" to vote under this provision, which eliminated denizens from eligibility.[107] The egalitarian phrase in Article I of the 1852 Constitution proclaiming that "God hath created all men free and equal" was also removed from the 1864 document.[108]

The dramatic impact of these restrictive requirements can be seen by examining the number of voters in Honolulu, which maintained voting records during this period. In January 1860, 1,776 votes were cast in Honolulu, increasing to 2,962 in January 1862 and then decreasing somewhat to 2,408 in January 1864.[109] But in January 1866, when the election was governed by the new 1864 Constitution, only 218 votes were cast, with the number slowly rising to 607 in February 1868, to 921 in February 1870, to 1,275 in February 1872, and then to 1,336 in February 1874.[110] Professor Osorio has quoted the *Pacific Commercial Advertiser* as stating that only 500 of the nearly 5,000 adult males in the District of Honolulu had voted in the January 1866 election, even though 3,500 of them were taxpayers, confirming its views that the changes in the 1864 Constitution were "unjust" because "only a few government officials and rich persons" were allowed to vote.[111]

After Lot (Kamehameha V) died in 1872, William Charles Lunalilo sought public approval of his ascension to the Crown, and on January 1, 1873, an election of "all the male subjects of the kingdom"[112] was held, which he won overwhelmingly. He then promoted the repeal of the property/income requirement for all elections, which occurred in 1874.[113] But the wealth requirements were reinstated in 1887, along with an onerous literacy requirement, for electors casting votes for the House of Nobles.[114] The 1874 repeal of the property requirements apparently did not have much of an impact on voting practices, because only 1,402 votes were cast in Honolulu in February 1876, 1,179 in February 1878, 1,490 in February 1880, 1,451 in February 1882, 1,942 in February 1884, and 2,157 in February 1886.[115]

About one-ninth of the qualified voters in Honolulu in 1884 were Caucasian, although this percentage might have been substantially higher "if all of them had

107. See Osorio, *supra* note 11, at 125, reporting that Lot "wanted to confine the franchise to actual subjects of the kingdom," and at 134: "Denizens . . . were disenfranchised."

108. *Constitution of 1852*, art. 1; *Constitution of 1864*, art 1; Osorio, *supra* note 11, at 132–33.

109. Schmitt, *Historical Statistics, supra* note 36, at 597 table 24.1.

110. *Id.*

111. Osorio, *supra* note 11, at 142, 275 n. 89, citing and quoting from *Pacific Commercial Advertiser*, January 6, 1866, at 1.

112. 2 Kuykendall, *supra* note 27, at 243.

113. See Kuykendall, *Constitutions, supra* note 103, at 42–43, discussing the amendments to Articles 62 and 63 of the 1864 Constitution.

114. Schmitt, *Historical Statistics, supra* note 36, at 594.

115. *Id.* at 597.

paid their taxes and claimed their privileges."[116] The jump in numbers to 3,619 for the September 1887 election[117] is attributable to the provision in the 1887 Constitution allowing Portuguese laborers to vote, discussed below.

The 1887 Constitution

The 1887 Constitution, drafted by Lorrin A. Thurston and the other westerners who led a coup d'etat[118] against the Mō'ī,[119] converted the House of Nobles into an elected rather than appointed body, made the number of Nobles equal to the number of Representatives (they met in a unicameral body), and imposed different voting qualifications for the House of Nobles and for the House of Representatives. To vote for the Nobles, one had to be a taxpaying male resident twenty years of age "of Hawaiian, American or European birth or descent" who could "read and comprehend an ordinary newspaper in either Hawaiian, English or some European language,"[120] who had resided in the Kingdom for three years or more, and who met the "stiff property qualification"[121] of owning at least $3,000 in taxable property or having an annual income of $600/year.[122] The same requirements applied to voters for the House of Representatives, except that the property/income requirement was eliminated.

The literacy rules requiring the ability to read Hawaiian, English, or another European language had the effect of allowing immigrant laborers from Portugal and Puerto Rico to vote—but not those from Asia, even if they had become naturalized citizens of the Kingdom. The property/income requirements, which were substantially higher than those utilized in the 1864 Constitution, had the effect of giving westerners almost complete control of the House of Nobles.[123] As one commentator explained, the Bayonet Constitution, "which set up a Government savoring of the English variety, was a clever device for securing to the [foreigners] the control of the Kingdom."[124] "Considering that the annual income of the highest paid Hawaiian

---

116. Osorio, *supra* note 11, at 279 n. 76, quoting from *Pacific Commercial Advertiser,* February 9, 1884, at 3, col. 4.

117. Schmitt, *Historical Statistics, supra* note 36, at 597.

118. *See* Hanifin, "To Dwell," *supra* note 3, at 25.

119. *See supra* chapter 14.

120. *1887 Constitution,* art. 62.

121. Hanifin, "To Dwell," *supra* note 3, at 25.

122. *1887 Constitution,* art. 59. The literacy and three-year residency requirements were waived for persons residing in the Kingdom as of 1887 if they registered to vote for the first election following its promulgation. The Constitution stated that the twenty-four Nobles (who previously had served for life) would have six-year terms; to be a Noble, one had to be twenty-five years old, have resided in the Kingdom for three years, and be able to meet the same property requirements that applied to voters for the House of Nobles. *Id.,* art. 56. Perhaps inadvertently, this article did not require Nobles to be male or to be able to read.

123. William A. Russ, *The Hawaiian Revolution: 1893–94,* 20 (1959); 3 Kuykendall, *supra* note 9, at 370: "many of the native Hawaiians were excluded by the high property qualification"; Fuchs, *supra* note 11, at 29: "The House of Nobles was thus converted from an instrument of the King to the legislative voice of the haoles."

124. Russ, *supra* note 123, at 20.

free laborer was $248," [125] fewer than half of those eligible to vote for the House of Representatives could vote for the Nobles in Honolulu, and in the other islands only about one-third of those who could vote for the House of Representatives could vote for the Noble representing them. [126]

In the 1887 election, 14,598 were registered to vote, but only 2,997 were eligible to vote for the House of Nobles. [127] In 1890, 13,593 were registered to vote, [128] 11,671 actually voted in the election for House of Representatives, but only 3,187 votes were cast for the House of Nobles. The Native Hawaiians and part-Hawaiians registered to vote numbered 9,554, [129] another 2,091 registered voters were Portuguese, 637 were American, 505 were British, and 382 were German. In 1892, 14,217 male individuals were registered to vote, of whom 9,931 were Hawaiians. [130]

Citizenship or holding a letter of denization was no longer a requirement for voting. Only 8 of the 10,216 Portuguese contract workers brought to the Islands between 1878 and 1886 became naturalized citizens, but all who were adult males were allowed to vote if they signed a document indicating that they would support the Bayonet Constitution and the laws of the Kingdom. This document also stated that the individual was "[n]ot hereby renouncing, but expressly reserving, all allegiance and citizenship now owing or held by me" to Portugal. [131] In late September 1887, U.S. Secretary of State Thomas Bayard told the U.S. Minister to the Kingdom George Merrill that U.S. citizens "could take an oath to support the new Hawaiian Constitution, vote, and hold office without losing American citizenship." [132]

Professor Osorio has observed that "[t]he Bayonet Constitution allowed the whites political control without requiring that they swear allegiance to the king. Indeed, the constitution removed every paradox that had previously confounded haole citizens and other white residents by making the nation belong to them without requiring that they belong to the nation." [133] Or, as John Bassett Moore wrote in 1906,

> While government was more securely conducted under [the 1887 Constitu-tion], yet a certain native antagonism was exhibited toward it, not only because it curtailed the powers of the native king but also because it increased the politi-cal privileges of the foreign residents, who were allowed to enjoy political rights without renouncing their foreign allegiance and citizenship. [134]

---

125. McGregor, "Cultural and Political History," *supra* note 66, at 363.

126. For voting statistics during this period, *see* Schmitt, *Historical Statistics, supra* note 36, at 597.

127. Samuel P. King, "The Federal Courts and the Annexation of Hawaii," 2 *Western Legal History*, 1, 8 (1989), citing a 1971 research study by the Hawai'i State Statistician.

128. Liliuokalani, *Hawaii's Story by Hawaii's Queen*, 237 n. 1 (1898, reprinted 1997).

129. McGregor, "Cultural and Political History," *supra* note 66, at 365.

130. King, *supra* note 127, at 7.

131. Blount letter of July 17, 1893, *supra* note 53, at 112.

132. Rich Budnick, *Stolen Kingdom: An American Conspiracy,* 69 (1992), citing "Bayard to Merrill," September 30, 1887, and "Blount Report," 1168–69.

133. Osorio, *supra* note 11, at 197.

134. 1 John Bassett Moore, *A Digest of International Law,* 496 (1906).

This "native antagonism" led to a failed attempt to remove the "reform" government through arms in 1889[135] and then to the more successful electoral effort in 1890, which voted out the "reform" Cabinet.[136]

One of the most significant aspects of the 1887 Constitution was that it introduced "a racial requirement" by limiting voting by nonnatives to those of European or American ancestry. Aliens of Asian ancestry had no opportunities to participate in political decision making, even if they had become naturalized citizens. In 1884, 18,254 Chinese were in the Kingdom, some of whom were qualified to vote under the 1864 Constitution by having been born or naturalized in the Kingdom. More than 400 Chinese had become naturalized between 1850 and 1887.[137] But after the 1887 Constitution, none of those who had become citizens through naturalization could continue to vote.[138] In an 1892 opinion written by Justice Sanford Ballard Dole, the Hawai'i Supreme Court upheld the "radical change" introduced by the 1887 Constitution, "which substituted the race requirement for the old condition of citizenship" and thus prohibited a naturalized citizen of Chinese ancestry from voting.[139] A male of Chinese ancestry born in the Kingdom was deemed to be of "Hawaiian" birth under the language in the 1887 Constitution,[140] but he still had to establish that he could read a newspaper in Hawaiian, English, or another European language before he could vote. This arrangement was actively opposed by the Chinese and Japanese in the Kingdom,[141] and by the Japanese government,[142] and it "gave to the *haoles* as a group a greatly increased power in the government and reduced the Hawaiians to a position of apparent and, for a while, actual inferiority in the political life of the country."[143]

The carefully crafted language in the 1887 Constitution did allow persons of European ancestry to vote if they could read a newspaper in any European language, a provision designed explicitly to allow those of Portuguese ancestry to vote. Thurston and the others who wrote the 1887 Constitution deduced that the 10,000 laborers of Portuguese ancestry[144] would support their efforts, and, in fact, "[i]t was the

135. *See supra* chapter 14, text at notes 73–80.

136. *See infra* this chapter, text at notes 154–60.

137. Osorio, *supra* note 11, at 281 n. 8, citing Jones, *supra* note 62.

138. See Schmitt, "Voter Participation Rates," *supra* note 94, at 56, reporting that the 1890 census stated that persons of Chinese and Japanese ancestry accounted for 51.8 percent of all males of voting age, but that none were registered to vote.

139. *Ahlo v. Smith*, 8 Hawai'i 420, 1892 WL 1076, at *2 (1892).

140. 3 Kuykendall, *supra* note 9, at 407 n.*.

141. *Id.* at 406.

142. "[T]he Japanese Government now claims for its citizens equal rights with other foreigners." "Statement of the Hawaiian Patriotic League," in "Blount Report," *supra* note 46, at 448, 454.

143. 3 Kuykendall, *supra* note 9, at 370.

144. By 1884, 10,000 Portuguese were in the Islands. Osorio, *supra* note 11, at 281 n. 9, citing Robert C. Schmitt, *Demographic Statistics of Hawaii*, 25 (1977). Reflecting the anti-Asian sentiments of the time, Thurston characterized the Chinese and Japanese contract workers as "an undesirable population from a political standpoint, because they do not understand American principles of government" and because they sought to return home "[a]s soon as they accumulate a few hundred dollars." He favored the Portuguese immigrants, calling them "a hard-working industrious, home-creating and home-loving people who would be of advantage

votes of foreigners including the Portuguese, enfranchised by the new constitution, that gave the Reform Party [which was dominated by westerners] its decisive victory" in the election held September 12, 1887.[145] Chief Justice Albert Francis Judd later told Commissioner James Blount that "the reason that the Portuguese were allowed to vote was to balance the native vote."[146]

But the Native Hawaiians still played an active and usually dominant role in the politics of the islands, because "[t]hough the new [1887] Constitution increased the political power of the large foreign property-holders in various ways, . . . the suffrage was still in native hands."[147] The 1890 census reported that 13,593 were registered to vote, and of these 8,777 were listed as "natives" and another 777 were "half-castes"—that is, part-Hawaiians.[148] Of the remainder, half (2,091) were Portuguese laborers.[149]

In 1890, the Legislature approved amendments to the Constitution to reduce the amount of property one had to own to vote for the Nobles from $3,000 to $1,000, to allow only "subjects" instead of mere "residents" to vote, and to require Nobles to be male.[150] But these provisions were never adopted, because the 1892 Legislature did not reconsider and confirm them, as required by Article 82 of the 1887 Constitution.[151] It is not altogether clear whether denizens would have been excluded from voting by the requirement that voters must be "subjects."

The Constitution drafted by Queen Lili'uokalani, which she was prepared to present to her subjects in January 1893, would have included the provision proposed in 1890 to limit the electorate to male "subjects" (those born in Hawai'i or naturalized), would have changed the House of Nobles to become a body of twenty-four individuals appointed by the Monarch for life (rather than being a group elected for three-year terms by those with property), and would have increased the number in the House of Representatives from twenty-four to forty-eight.[152] She later defended

---

to any developing country. They constitute the best laboring element in Hawaii." Merry, *supra* note 12, at 135, quoting from Lorrin A. Thurston, *A Handbook on the Annexation of Hawaii*, 28 (circa 1897). Commissioner James Blount was less enthusiastic about the 10,216 Portuguese contract laborers imported from Madeira and the Azores Islands, describing them as "the most ignorant of all imported laborers and reported to be very thievish. They are not pure Europeans, but a commingling of many races, especially the negro. . . . Very few of them can read and write. . . . It is wrong to class them as Europeans." Blount Letter of June 1, 1893, *supra* note 53, at 74.

145. 3 Kuykendall, *supra* note 9, at 410, citing *Daily Bulletin,* September 16, 1887 (letter of "One Who Voted Straight Reform").

146. Blount Letter of July 17, 1893, *supra* note 53, at 110, 113.

147. Stevens, *supra* note 26, at 146.

148. Blount Letter of July 17, 1893, *supra* note 53, at 132.

149. *Id.*

150. Kuykendall, *Constitutions, supra* note 103, at 51; 3 Kuykendall, *supra* note 9, at 465. Another proposed amendment would have given the Legislature the right to limit and control the activities of the contract laborers brought into the Kingdom. *Id.*

151. Kuykendall, *Constitutions, supra* note 103, at 51–52.

152. 3 Kuykendall, *supra* note 9, at 586; Blount Letter of July 17, 1893, *supra* note 53, at 115. *See infra* chapter 16, text at notes 5–12.

the change that would have limited voting to "subjects" of the Kingdom by explaining that she "had thought it wise to limit the exercise of suffrage to those who owed allegiance to no other country" and that this approach is no "different from the usage in all other civilized nations on earth."[153]

As explained above,[154] 13,593 men were registered and eligible to vote in the February 1890 election,[155] and of these, 9,554 were of Hawaiian ancestry;[156] "about two-thirds of the voters for representatives were Hawaiians and . . . Hawaiians comprised more than a third of the voters for nobles."[157] In the February 1890 election, the National Reform Party, led by Robert W. Wilcox, who voiced the dissatisfaction of the Native Hawaiians about the 1887 Constitution and rallied their political enthusiasm, particularly in Honolulu, won fourteen out of the twenty-four seats in the House of Representatives and took all nine of the seats for Nobles on Oʻahu (but lost the other fifteen seats on the neighbor islands).[158] The National Reform Party was able to organize the Legislature (the Nobles and Representatives met together as one body), elect its President and control its committees,[159] and force the members of the "reform" Cabinet, led by Lorrin Thurston, to resign.[160]

The February 1892 election did not break down along racial lines.[161] "The elections of 1892 produced a strange assembly, in which no party had a majority."[162] Wilcox and his group formed the Liberal Party, along with people like the Ashford Brothers, who had been active in promoting the Bayonet Constitution, and they were critical of Queen Liliʻuokalani and called for a constitutional convention. Three conservative parties supported the Queen and stability, generally opposing a constitutional convention and supporting a new free trade agreement with the United States. The Liberal Party won only thirteen seats, with the other parties holding thirty-five.[163] Native Hawaiians held twenty-five of the forty-eight seats in the House of Representatives and House of Nobles in the Legislature that met during 1892–93.[164] These results certainly do not indicate that the Native Hawaiians had lost control of the Kingdom. Even with the limiting property and income restrictions governing the voting for the Nobles, Native Hawaiians continued to play the dominant role in decision making, and the election also confirmed that the Queen continued to have broad support.

---

153. Liliuokalani, *supra* note 128, at 237.
154. *See supra* this chapter, text at notes 148–49.
155. Liliuokalani, *supra* note 128, at 363 n. 1.
156. McGregor, "Cultural and Political History," *supra* note 66, at 365.
157. 3 Kuykendall, *supra* note 9, at 453, citing *Pacific Commercial Advertiser,* November 22, 1889.
158. *Id.* at 454.
159. *Id.* at 459.
160. *Id.* at 461.
161. *Id.* at 514–22.
162. Daws, *supra* note 18, at 267.
163. 3 Kuykendall, *supra* note 9, at 521.
164. Clinton R. Ashford, "Who Were the Victims of the Overthrow?" *Honolulu Advertiser,* August 20, 1995, at B-1, col. 1.

Conclusions

Those who have claimed that the Kingdom was a multiethnic pluralistic place where everyone was welcome and everyone was treated equally are misrepresenting history. Patrick Hanifin was wrong when he wrote that "[t]he government of the Kingdom of Hawaii . . . offered immigrants easy naturalization and full political rights. Race and ethnicity did not matter."[165] In fact, after the 1887 Constitution, the immigrants who came from Asia, as most did, were granted no political rights whatsoever and were completely barred from political participation because of their race and ethnicity, even if they became naturalized citizens. Similarly, the U.S. Supreme Court misrepresented reality in *Rice v. Cayetano* when it said that the 1887 Constitution "extended the right to vote to non-Hawaiians,"[166] and it was particularly insensitive for the Court to have ignored the blatant racial discrimination against those of Asian origins promoted by the "Reform Party" in a case in which the Court purported to condemn classifications based on ancestry.[167]

Lorrin Thurston and the others who drafted the 1887 Constitution gave the Portuguese laborers advantages over other immigrant workers because they thought the Portuguese voters would benefit their political agenda. Judge de Silva was technically correct that all immigrants could have become naturalized citizens, but such a status would not have benefited the vast majority who were of Asian ancestry because they would still have been denied the right to vote. The Kingdom during this difficult period was occupied by numerous ambitious political opportunists playing hardball, and Native Hawaiians were struggling to maintain their heritage, sovereignty, and lands and culture against a better-resourced and unrelenting opposition.

In her protest to the annexation treaty being promoted by the Western revolutionaries that had led the January 1893 overthrow, Queen Lili'uokalani stated that "My people constitute four-fifths of the legally qualified voters of Hawaii, and excluding those imported for the demands of labor, about the same proportion of the inhabitants."[168] Although this statement claims a percentage of native voters somewhat higher than the 70 percent reported in other sources,[169] it presents a relatively accurate description of the political community of the Kingdom at the time of the overthrow. In the 1890 election, Native Hawaiians had effectively wrested control of the Kingdom from those who had foisted the Bayonet Constitution on the Kingdom, and efforts were underway during the years that followed to reassert a stronger role for the Monarchy. Those who now claim that the Native Hawaiians had lost control of the Kingdom prior to the 1893 overthrow are wrong.

---

165. Hanifin, "To Dwell," *supra* note 3, at 15.

166. *Rice v. Cayetano*, 528 U.S. 495, 504 (2000). *See infra* chapter 24, note 13.

167. *Id.* at 514–17.

168. Liliuokalani, *supra* note 128, at 355, quoting from the Queen's official protest to the proposed 1893 annexation treaty.

169. *See supra* this chapter, text at notes 155–57.

16

The 1893 Overthrow of the Kingdom

Following King Kalākaua's death in San Francisco in January 1891 at the age of 54, the Crown passed to his sister, Lili'uokalani, pursuant to the requirements of Article 22 of the 1887 Constitution.[1] As Queen, Lili'uokalani continued her brother's fight to preserve an independent Kingdom and, in particular, sought to roll back the "reforms" of the 1887 Bayonet Constitution. Kalākaua had sought in 1890 to convene a Constitutional Convention, and this proposal had widespread support of the native population and of native leaders such as Joseph Nawahi and Robert Wilcox.[2] In 1892, "[p]etitions poured in from every part of the Islands for a new constitution" restoring the Monarch's power,[3] meetings were held to discuss the development of a new Constitution, and drafts were circulated.[4] The Queen asked the Legislature to call a Constitutional Conven-

---

1. See 3 Ralph S. Kuykendall, *The Hawaiian Kingdom 1874–1893: The Kalakaua Dynasty,* 470–78 (1967, reprinted 1987). Article 22 stated that "The Crown is hereby permanently confirmed to His Majesty Kalakaua, and to the Heirs of His body lawfully begotten, and to their lawful Descendants in a direct line; failing whom, the Crown shall descent to Her Royal Highness the Princess Liliuokalani, and the heirs of her body, lawfully begotten, and their lawful descendants in a direct line."
2. *Id.* at 461–65. "In the legislative session of 1890 and in that of 1892 strong efforts were made to pass a bill to provide for the holding of a constitutional convention. . . . The history of the movement indicates that it was carefully organized and managed and had the support of a large part of the native population." Ralph S. Kuykendall, *Constitutions of the Hawaiian Kingdom: A Brief History and Analysis,* 54 (Hawaiian Historical Society Paper No. 21, 1940, reprinted 1978). Joseph Nawahi, then vice president of the recently formed Liberal Party, stated in January 1892 that "the crowning ambition of the party was to have a new constitution." 3 Kuykendall, *supra* note 1, at 520, citing *Daily Bulletin,* January 8, 1892. *See also* Helena G. Allen, *The Betrayal of Liliuokalani: Last Queen of Hawaii 1838–1917,* 261 (1982).
3. Liliuokalani, *Hawaii's Story By Hawaii's Queen,* 230 (1898, reprinted 1997). The Queen reported that she had received an estimated 6,500 petitions requesting a new constitution, a number that was two-thirds of the 9,500 persons registered to vote, *id.* at 231, 237, and was "the entire population of native or half-native birth." *Id.* at 239. The "Blount Report" included a statement submitted by Hui Kalaiaina (the Hawaiian Political Association) stating that these petitions contained 8,000 names. "Report of Commissioner to the Hawaiian Islands" (hereafter cited as "Blount Report") at 18, originally in H.R. Exec. Doc. No. 47, 53d Cong., 2d Sess., reprinted in *Foreign Relations of the United States, 1894,* Appendix 2, "Affairs in Hawaii" (hereafter cited as "Affairs in Hawaii"), 483–84 (1895, preservation photocopy 1992). "The petition still exists, apparently in two different formats. The more formal, printed petition has about 1,600 names, mostly male, reflecting the Western practice of restricting political participation to men. A simpler format has several thousand more names." Tom Coffman, *Nation Within: The Story of America's Annexation of the Nation of Hawai'i,* 120 (1998).
4. Coffman, *supra* note 3, at 119–20; Allen, *Betrayal, supra,* note 2, at 281–82 (1982), explaining that the Queen was working as early as August 1892 with Joseph Nawahi, Sam Nowlein, and William White to develop the text of a new Constitution and had presented copies of a draft to members of the Cabinet.

tion,[5] but the Legislature refused, and the Mōʻī then attempted to promulgate a new Constitution by decree on January 14, 1893,[6] following the 1864 example of her predecessor Lot (Kamehameha V) and using a draft based on his 1864 Constitution.[7] The Queen's proposed Constitution would have allowed her to remove members of the Cabinet, would have allowed the Monarch to appoint members of the House of Nobles for life, would have limited voters to male subjects of the Kingdom (i.e., those born in Hawaiʻi or naturalized) "in distinction from temporary residents,"[8] would have allowed the Monarch to dismiss the Cabinet, and would have eliminated the requirement that the Monarch's actions be confirmed by the Cabinet.[9] From her perspective, based on the history and customs of the Native Hawaiians, "the promulgation of a new constitution, adapted to the needs of the times and the demands of the people, has been an indisputable prerogative of the Hawaiian monarchy,"[10] and she was acting "to restore some of the ancient rights of my people."[11] Her native supporters in the Hawaiian Patriotic League (Hui Hawaiian Aloha ʻĀina) explained further that "it was only because the immortal principles of justice, liberty, and equality were violated or ignored in the Bayonet Constitution of 1887 that the Queen to satisfy her own people undertook to suggest to her constitutional advisers, the cabinet, the promulgation of a new constitution embodying these desirable features and addressed to the masses, not to a mere faction."[12]

Although the Queen agreed to set aside her proposed Constitution (at least for

---

5. *See, e.g.,* Allen, *Betrayal, supra* note 2, at 261. Article 47 of the Constitution of 1887 provided that "The Legislature has full power and authority to amend the Constitution as hereinafter provided; and from time to time to make all manner of wholesome laws, not repugnant to the Constitution." This provision allowing the Legislature to amend the Constitution easily and giving the Mōʻī no role in the process reflected the dramatic turnaround that had occurred in earlier periods, when each new Mōʻī would exercise broad power, including reallocation of lands through the Kālaiʻāina (*see supra* chapter 3, text at notes 47–50), and from the less distant past when Lot (Kamehameha V) had promulgated the new Constitution of 1864 on his own initiative after he assumed the Crown (*see supra* chapter 7, text at notes 15–19).

6. 3 Kuykendall, *supra* note 1, at 582.

7. *See supra* chapter 7, text at notes 15–19. Queen Liliʻuokalani described the actions taken by Lot in Liliuokalani, *supra* note 3, at 20–21.

8. Liliuokalani, *supra* note 3, at 237.

9. Letter from Special Commissioner James H. Blount to U.S. Secretary of State W. Q. Gresham, July 17, 1893, (hereafter cited as Blount Letter of July 17, 1893) in "Blount Report," *supra* note 3, at 115, reprinted in "Affairs in Hawaii," *supra* note 3, at 581; 3 Kuykendall, *supra* note 1, at 586; Allen, *Betrayal, supra* note 2, at 284; William Fremont Blackman, *The Making of Hawaii: A Study in Social Evolution,* 131–32 (1906, reprinted 1977). Although Article 62 of the version of the Constitution published in Commissioner James H. Blount's report contains a requirement that voters own property of $150 or earn $75 per year, the members of her Cabinet reported that the version of the Constitution they had seen on January 14, 1893, had not contained such a requirement. Blount letter of July 17, 1893, *supra,* in "Affairs in Hawaii," *supra* note 3, at 581.

10. Liliuokalani, *supra* note 3, at 21. *See also id.* at 238, explaining that "[t]he right to grant a constitution to the nation has been, since the very first one was granted, a prerogative of the Hawaiian sovereigns" and noting that all the previous constitutions had been promulgated without approval of the people or voters, and that, in particular, the 1887 Constitution had been imposed by "aliens determined to coerce my brother."

11. *Id.* at 237.

12. "Statement of the Hawaiian Patriotic League to President Grover Cleveland," July 15, 1893, in "Blount Report," "Affairs in Hawaii," *supra* note 3, at 483–84.

the time being) after the members of her Cabinet refused to sign it and other opposition emerged,[13] her initiative provided the opportunity that the wealthy Western businessmen and sugar planters in the Annexation Club[14] had been waiting for—to move toward the annexation of Hawai'i by the United States. Some also believed that abrogation of the Monarchy would open up the Government and Crown Lands for exploitation.[15] One hundred years later, in 1993, the U.S. Congress acknowledged that U.S. military and diplomatic officials had played an essential role in ensuring the success of the overthrow and that this role had been "illegal" and in violation of international law and issued a formal apology for the activities of the United States.[16]

Earlier Relations between the United States and the Kingdom of Hawai'i

As explained previously in chapter 3, the Kingdom of Hawai'i was formally established in the early 1800s under Kamehameha I, who united the islands. Hawai'i was thereafter recognized as an independent nation and as a full member of the family of nations.[17] It entered into four treaties of friendship, commerce, and navigation with the United States[18] and exchanged diplomats with the United States and other

---

13. The Queen's explanation of the events during this period are in her statement to the Blount Commission, which is reprinted in Liliuokalani, *supra* note 3, at 376, 383–89.

14. The secret origins and early activities of the small (approximately seventeen-member) Annexation Club are summarized in Sylvester K. Stevens, *American Expansion in Hawaii 1842–1898*, 206–07 (1945, reprinted 1968); *see also* 3 Kuykendall, *supra* note 1, at 532–41. After the overthrow in January 1893, the size of this group grew. *See, e.g.,* Ernest Andrade Jr., *Unconquerable Rebel: Robert W. Wilcox and Hawaiian Politics, 1880–1903,* 126 (1996), explaining that Robert Wilcox attended an organizational meeting of the Annexation Club in March 1893 attended by about 800 persons, and "was almost the only non haole present."

15. As early as 1872, Sanford Ballard Dole had argued that keeping the Crown Lands inalienable was a "mistaken policy" that had prevented the development of "a comprehensive homestead system of settlement." Sanford B. Dole, "The Problem of Population and Our Land Policy," *Pacific Commercial Advertiser,* October 26, 1872, at 2. *See supra* chapter 13, text at note 4, and *infra* chapter 18, text at notes 1–8.

16. *See* "Joint Resolution to Acknowledge the 100th Anniversary of the January 17, 1893 Overthrow of the Kingdom of Hawaii," Sec. 2, Pub. L. 103-150, 107 Stat. 1510 (1993) (hereafter cited as "Apology Resolution").

17. *See, e.g.,* Karen Blondin, "A Case for Reparations for Native Hawaiians," 16 *Hawaii Bar Journal,* 13, 20–22 (winter 1981); Jennifer M. L. Chock, "One Hundred Years of Illegitimacy: International Legal Analysis of the Illegal Overthrow of the Hawaiian Monarchy, Hawai'i's Annexation, and Possible Reparations," 17 *University of Hawai'i Law Review,* 463–66 (1995); David Keanu Sai, "American Occupation of the Hawaiian State: A Century Unchecked," 1 *Hawaiian Journal of Law and Politics,* 46, 53–56 (2004), available at http://www2.hawaii.edu/~hslp/journal_vol1.html (last visited September 22, 2006).

18. (1) "Treaty with Hawaii on Commerce," December 23, 1826, United States–Hawaii, 8 *Department of State, Treaties and Other International Agreements of the United States of America 1776–1949,* 861 (C. Bevans, comp. 1968), reprinted in Robert H. Stauffer, "The Hawai'i–United States Treaty of 1826," 17 *Hawaiian Journal of History,* 40, 55–58 (1983). Article I of this treaty stated that the "peace and friendship" between the United States and the people of Hawai'i "are hereby confirmed, and declared to be perpetual." This treaty was never ratified by the United States Senate, 1 John Bassett Moore, *A Digest of International Law,* 476 (1906), but "for more than a decade, after Captain Jones had secured the signatures of Kaahumanu and Kalanimoku to this abortive treaty, American officials and residents of the Hawaiian Islands were seeking to impress upon the perplexed chiefs the sanctity of this agreement which the government of the United States had refused to accept." Harold W. Bradley, "Thomas ap Catesby Jones and the Hawaiian Islands, 1826–1827," in *Thirty-Ninth Annual Report of the Hawaiian Historical Society,* 17, 25 (1931). *See generally* Stauffer, *id.,* at 53, 58–59, confirming that

nations.[19] The first U.S. representative in the Islands was John C. Jones, who was appointed on September 19, 1820, to serve as "agent of the United States for commerce and seamen."[20]

In 1842, after the Kingdom's emissaries to Washington (Timothy Ha'alilio and W. H. Richards) had met with Secretary of State Daniel Webster and various legislators, President John Tyler issued a statement called the Tyler Doctrine recognizing the "independent existence" of Hawai'i[21] and "declaring the Monroe Doctrine to include the Hawaiian Islands"[22] by saying that the United States would oppose "the adoption of an opposite policy by any other power."[23] Congress subsequently provided $3,000 to enable a diplomatic agent to reside in the Kingdom, and President Tyler then appointed George Brown to be "Commissioner of the United States for the Sandwich Islands."[24] The Tyler Doctrine was reaffirmed in 1849 by President Zachary Taylor, who stated that the U.S. policy was "that the islands may maintain their independence and that other nations should concur with us in this sentiment."[25] The U.S. Congress has summarized this period by stating that from 1826 until 1893, the United States recognized the independence of the Kingdom of Hawai'i, extended full and complete diplomatic recognition to the Kingdom of Hawai'i, and entered into

---

the 1826 treaty was treated by both sides as a binding agreement; *Rice v. Cayetano,* 528 U.S. 495, 504 (2000), characterizing the 1826 agreement as "articles of arrangement."

(2) "Treaty with Hawaii on Friendship, Commerce and Navigation," December 20, 1849, United States–Hawaii, ratified by the United States on February 4, 1850, 9 Stat. 977, T.S. No. 160. Article 1 stated that "There shall be perpetual peace and amity between the United States and the King of the Hawaiian Islands, his heirs and his successors." Other articles enunciated rules of commerce and navigation based on the principle of equality. (On March 26, 1855, the Hawaiian Nation acceded to the Convention of July 22, 1854 between the United States and Russia, guaranteeing the rights of neutrals at sea. 7 Miller 121.)

(3) "Treaty with Hawaii on Commercial Reciprocity," January 30, 1875, United States–Hawaii, 19 Stat. 625, T.S. No. 161, discussed *supra* in chapter 14, text at notes 1–8.

(4) "Treaty with Hawaii on Commercial Reciprocity," December 6, 1884, entered into force as amended November 9, 1887, United States–Hawaii, 25 Stat. 1399, T.S. No. 163, discussed *supra* in chapter 14, text at notes 46–70.

19. *See* Chock, *supra* note 17, at 464, listing treaties between the Kingdom of Hawai'i and numerous other nations.

20. 1 Moore, *supra* note 18, at 475.

21. 1 Ralph S. Kuykendall, *The Hawaiian Kingdom 1778-1854: Foundation and Transformation,* 195 (1938, reprinted 1989), citing Sen. Exec. Doc. No. 77, 52d Cong., 2d Sess., at 35–37.

22. Stauffer, *supra* note 18, at 54.

23. 1 Kuykendall, *supra* note 21, at 195, citing Sen. Exec. Doc. No. 77, 52d Cong., 2d Sess., at 35–37; 1 Moore, *supra* note 18, at 476–77.

24. 1 Kuykendall, *supra* note 21, at 196.

25. Stevens, *supra* note 14, at 49, quoting from President Taylor's annual message of December 4, 1849, in 5 James D. Richardson, *A Compilation of the Messages and Papers of the Presidents,* 17 (1896–99). President Taylor explained the importance of Hawai'i to the United States as follows *(id.):*

> The position of the Sandwich Islands with reference to the territory of the United States on the Pacific, the success of our persevering and benevolent citizens who have repaired to that remote quarter in Christianizing the natives and inducing them to adopt a system of government and laws suited to their capacity and wants, and the use made by our numerous whale ships of the harbors of the islands as places of resort for obtaining refreshments and repairs all combine to render their destiny peculiarly interesting to us.

treaties and conventions of friendship with the Kingdom of Hawai'i Monarchs to govern commerce and navigation described above.[26]

During the years that followed, the economic and social links between Hawai'i and the United States grew in intensity, with the interest of the Western sugar planters to develop and protect markets for their crops in the United States and the interest of the United States in developing a port at Pearl Harbor driving this relationship.[27] The Reciprocity Treaty of 1875 brought prosperity to the Islands, but it also put the Kingdom at the mercy of the United States, which could restrict the opportunity to sell sugar in the United States. Hawai'i developed a relationship with the United States that might be described as that of a vassal state or tributary state, much like the relationship of some of the Caribbean and Central American countries in the early part of the twentieth century. An example of the intertwined relations between the United States and the Kingdom is provided by the resignation in 1877 of Henry Peirce as the U.S. Minister to the Kingdom and his subsequent appointment as the Kingdom's Foreign Minister.[28] As the U.S. Supreme Court subsequently explained, "The United States was not the only country interested in Hawaii and its affairs, but by the later part of the [nineteenth] century, the reality of American dominance in trade, settlement, economic expansion, and political influence became apparent."[29] Many Native Hawaiians recognized that "reciprocity was leading directly toward annexation . . . and protests against the growing Americanization of the Islands became so common as to alarm the American Minister."[30]

In July 1887, just after Kalākaua acceded to the Bayonet Constitution, the U.S. Secretary of State Thomas F. Bayard wrote to the U.S. Minister in Honolulu, George W. Merrill, that the United States and Hawai'i had, as a result of the Reciprocity Treaty, "commercial relations more intimate in their nature and of incomparably greater volume and value than Hawaii had or ever can have with any other government."[31] In order to protect against any "obstruction to the channels of legitimate commerce" and to protect the property of U.S. citizens, "the assistance of the officers of our Government vessels, if found necessary, will therefore be promptly afforded to promote the reign of law and respect for orderly government in Hawaii."[32] In 1874, U.S. troops had landed in Honolulu to bring order to the turmoil that occurred

---

26. See "Apology Resolution," *supra* note 16, whereas para. 3; "Native Hawaiian Education Act of 1994," 20 U.S.C. § 7512 (Supp. I 2002), "Findings," para. 4 (hereafter cited as "1994 Education Act"); "The Native Hawaiian Health Care Improvement Act of 1992," 42 U.S.C. § 11701 (1994), "Findings," para. 6 (hereafter cited as "1992 Health Care Act"); "An Act Relating to Hawaiian Sovereignty," ch. 359, 1993 Haw. Sess. Laws 1009, "Findings," para. 4; "Omnibus Indian Advancement Act, Title II," which may be cited as "Hawaiian Homelands Homeownership Act of 2000," Public Law No. 106-568, (2000), § 202(12).

27. See supra chapter 14, text at notes 46–70.

28. Stevens, *supra* note 14, at 148. *See supra* chapter 15, text at note 42.

29. *Rice v. Cayetano*, 528 U.S. 495, 504 (2000).

30. Stevens, *supra* note 14, at 149.

31. Letter from Thomas F. Bayard to George W. Merrill, July 12, 1887, reprinted in *Foreign Relations of the United States, 1887*, 580–81.

32. *Id.*

after the Legislature selected Kalākaua to be Mōʻī rather than Queen Emma,[33] and in July 1889, when Robert W. Wilcox and Robert Boyd rose up in arms to try to restore the Monarchy to the position it had held before the 1887 Bayonet Constitution, U.S. marines from the USS *Adams* landed to protect people and property and help restore order.[34] As the U.S. Supreme Court later explained, "The presence of American military forces in Hawaii helped to discourage these efforts" to restore the Monarch's powers.[35]

The Overthrow of the Kingdom

In the early 1890s, Honolulu had become a lively and gracious town, with modern amenities, such as "a complete electrical plant with an installation equal to that of any city, and [a] telephone system [that] is the best I have ever seen, with a corps of operators that cannot be excelled in politeness."[36] But Hawai'i was facing an uncertain economic future during this period. The McKinley Tariff Bill,[37] passed by the U.S. Congress in 1890 and taking effect on April 1, 1891, removed the tariffs on all sugar entering the United States and granted a subsidy of two cents a pound to U.S. growers,[38] thus nullifying the advantage that the Reciprocity Treaty had given to Hawaiian sugar growers and sharply limiting the amount of sugar exported from the Kingdom.[39] This enactment had the effect of causing a "depression"[40] and "sense of panic"[41] in the Kingdom.

---

33. 3 Kuykendall, *supra* note 1, at 10.

34. 1 Moore, *supra* note 18, at 495. *See supra* chapter 14, text at notes 73–80.

35. *Rice v. Cayetano,* 528 U.S. 495, 504 (2000).

36. Lucien Young, *Real Hawaii: Its History and Present Conditions Including the True Story of the Revolution (American Imperialism)* (a revised and enlarged edition of *The* Boston *at Hawaii* [1898]), 38–39 (1970).

37. "An Act to Reduce the Revenue and Equalize Duties on Imports, and for Other Purposes," October 1, 1890, ch.1244, 26 Stat. 567. *See supra* chapter 14, text at notes 82–83.

38. The "McKinley Tariff Act," characterized as a "masterpiece in the art of political logrolling," was enacted "under the direction of [Ohio Senator and later President] William McKinley" after the Republicans returned to power on March 4, 1889. Stevens, *supra* note 14, at 188; *see also* Jacob Adler, *Claus Spreckels: The Sugar King in Hawaii,* 218 (1966); Andrade, *supra* note 14, at 86–87.

39. U.S. Minister John Stevens warned of the potential impact of the "McKinley Tariff Act" in May 1890, a year before it took effect, explaining that "[i]n the opinion of all well-informed persons, to place sugar on the free list would be the virtual annulment of the reciprocity treaty and the destruction of the prosperity of the islands." Stevens, *supra* note 14, at 188, quoting from a letter from Minister Stevens to the U.S. State Department, May 20, 1890, reprinted in *Foreign Relations of the United States, 1894,* 319. For the view that the failure to protect Hawai'i's economy in this bill may have been a deliberate effort by U.S. Secretary of State James Blaine "to use the vulnerability of Hawai'i's cash economy to take perpetual control of Hawai'i," *see* Coffman, *supra* note 3, at 107. Congress passed "An Act Relating to the Treaty of Reciprocity with the Hawaiian Islands," March 3, 1891, Ch. 534, 26 Stat. 844, which said that the "McKinley Tariff Act" did not "repeal or impair the provisions" of the 1887 Reciprocity Treaty, but this short statute did nothing to reestablish the advantages that Hawaiian exporters had previously held.

40. 3 Kuykendall, *supra* note 1, at 541; *see also* Allen, *Betrayal, supra* note 2, at 258 ("Because of the United States' McKinley Tarriff Bill, the country was in a state of depression"); Gavan Daws, *Shoal of Time, A History of the Hawaiian Islands,* 268 (1968, reprinted 1974), reporting that in January 1893, "[t]he depression caused by the McKinley Act was at its lowest point"; Stevens, *supra* note 14, at 189: "The business depression continued in 1892 before any partial recovery was noticeable."

41. Coffman, *supra* note 3, at 107.

Lorrin Thurston, 1890   John L. Stevens, 1893

President Benjamin Harrison acknowledged on December 1, 1890, that the Tariff Act imposed a "wrong" on the Kingdom, which he was "bound to presume was wholly intentional," and he urged Congress to "repair what might otherwise seem to be a breach of faith on the part of this Government."[42] The price of sugar plummeted from $100 a ton to $60 a ton, causing some producers to sell sugar at less than the cost of production.[43] Although some of the Western planter-elites had been unenthusiastic about annexation because of their fear that "under the terms of the United States constitution the Hawaiian system of labor contracts could no longer be enforced,"[44] they came to understand that annexation by the United States was the only way to protect their economic interests and were concerned that the Queen's initiative to promulgate a new constitution to strengthen the Monarchy would reduce the value of their investments.[45] The "leading spirit"[46] of this move-

42. Merze Tate, *Hawaii: Reciprocity or Annexation*, 219 (1968), quoting from President Harrison's second annual message on December 1, 1890, in 9 James D. Richardson, *A Compilation of the Messages and Papers of the Presidents*, 10 (1896–99).

43. Adler, *supra* note 38, at 221, quoting from an analysis written by Lorrin A. Thurston to U.S. Secretary of State James G. Blaine, May 27, 1892; Tate, *supra* note 42, at 219, citing a communication from Minister John Stevens to U.S. Secretary of State John W. Foster, November 20, 1892, No. 74, *USDS, Dispatches, Hawaii*, vol. 25, in H.R. Exec. Doc. No. 48, 53d Cong., 2d Sess., *reprinted in* "Affairs in Hawaii", *supra* note 3, at 377.

44. Adler, *supra* note 38, at 221, quoting from an analysis written by Lorrin A. Thurston to U.S. Secretary of State James G. Blaine, May 27, 1892; *see also* Coffman, *supra* note 3, at 123: "some historians have noted . . . that sugar planters were not indisputably supportive of the coup. They wanted their two-cent bonus for sugar, but they did not want to lose their control over low-cost labor, which would occur as soon as they came under U.S. law."; Lawrence H. Fuchs, *Hawaii Pono: A Social History*, 30 (1961, reprinted 1983): "A number of planters feared that the destruction of the monarchy would lead to annexation and the elimination of the contract-labor system."

45. Melody K. MacKenzie, "Historical Background," in *Native Hawaiian Rights Handbook*, 11 (Melody Kapilialoha MacKenzie, ed., 1991).

46. Blount Letter of July 17, 1893, *supra* note 9, at 117, in "Affairs in Hawaii," *supra* note 3, at 583.

ment, Lorrin A. Thurston,[47] went to Washington to lobby for support and was told by the U.S. Secretary of the Navy that President Benjamin Harrison had authorized the Secretary "to say to you that, if conditions in Hawaii compel you to act as you have indicated [i.e., to overthrow the Hawaiian Monarchy], and you come to Washington with an annexation proposition, you will find an exceedingly sympathetic administration here."[48]

U.S. Minister John L. Stevens

Their annexation goal was also "zealously promoted"[49] by the U.S. Minister to the Kingdom of Hawai'i, John L. Stevens, who had a "well-known hostility"[50] and an "intense antagonism for the continuation of the Kingdom."[51] Stevens had been a minister in the Unitarian Church (known for his opposition to slavery) and a coeditor and coproprietor of the *Kennebec Journal* in Augusta, Maine (with James G. Blaine), a member of the Maine Legislature (1865–70) (where he led a successful campaign to abolish capital punishment), and had served as U.S. ambassador to Paraguay and Uruguay and later to Sweden and Norway before arriving in Hawai'i in 1889.[52] "At first [he] professed to favor a protectorate rather than outright annexation. . . . But in either event Stevens was unabashed in announcing his belief that America must control Hawai'i."[53] Stevens' willingness to intervene in the Kingdom's activities was

---

47. Lorrin A. Thurston was the grandson of Asa Thurston on his father's side and Lorrin Andrews on his mother's side, both among the early missionaries. His background and central role in the overthrow and annexation of Hawai'i are described in Coffman, *supra* note 3, at 72–90, 115–27; *see also* Daws, *supra* note 40, at 242–44, 265–67; Thurston Twigg-Smith, *Hawaiian Sovereignty: Do the Facts Matter?* 138–47 (1998). One commentator has written that he "was not really a representative of the wealthy or planter interests. He was rather a 'radical' representing non-Hawaiians who were not especially men of property." Adler, *supra* note 38, at 219; *see also* Stevens, *supra* note 14, at 206, reporting that Thurston did not "represent the larger economic interest of the Islands. Primarily a lawyer and a small planter with some other minor business connections, he would not come under the classification of the 'planter interest' in any important sense." "Imbued as he was with the idea that only whites could rule the islands efficiently, he was able to consider this a form of patriotism." Stephen Kinzer, *Overthrow: America's Century of Regime Change from Hawaii to Iraq*, 16 (2006). After annexation, Thurston became publisher of the *Pacific Commercial Advertiser* and pursued economic interests involving agriculture and railroads.

48. Lorrin A. Thurston, *Memoirs of the Hawaiian Revolution*, 230–32 (1936).

49. Grover Cleveland, "President's Message Relating to the Hawaiian Islands," December 18, 1893, at VI, in H.R. Exec. Doc. No. 47, in "Affairs in Hawaii," *supra* note 3, at 448. Kuykendall noted that "when Stevens went to Hawaii he believed firmly that the future of the Hawaiian Islands was linked to that of the United States" and "apparently thought it was his mission to see that the island kingdom did not stray from the path of its American destiny." 3 Kuykendall, *supra* note 1, at 567–68.

50. Letter of U.S. Secretary of State W. Q. Gresham to President Grover Cleveland, October 18, 1893 (hereafter cited as Gresham letter), in "Blount Report" at xx, reprinted in "Affairs in Hawaii," *supra* note 3, at 462.

51. Coffman, *supra* note 3, at 39.

52. *Id.* at 76–77, 93, 97–100. Profiles of Stevens can also be found in 3 Kuykendall, *supra* note 14, at 566–73; and Rich Budnick, *Stolen Kingdom: An American Conspiracy*, 76–77 (1992).

53. Coffman, *supra* note 3, at 101. *See also* William S. Dudley, "The Fall of the Monarchy and Annexation of Hawaii," in 1 Native Hawaiians Study Commission, *Report on the Culture, Needs and Concerns of Native Hawaiians*, 289, 294 (Report issued pursuant to Pub. L. 96-565, Title III, 1983): "Stevens . . . had held strong annexation views from the beginning, and this was well known in the Hawaiian community."

Landing of U.S. troops from USS *Boston,* January 17, 1893

U.S. troops from USS *Boston,* commanded by Lucien Young, at the grounds of the Arlington Hotel, January 17, 1893

evident earlier when he agreed to bring U.S. troops into Honolulu to control disorders anticipated on election day in 1890.[54] In November 1889, he had asked the U.S. State Department to send additional naval forces to the islands "for the prompt protection of American interests, should occasion arise,"[55] and in August 1891, he asked Washington to station a warship in Honolulu indefinitely "to render things secure" and ensure "proper regard for American interests."[56] The USS *San Francisco* was sent to the Islands, and it was replaced on August 24, 1892,[57] "to Lili'uokalani's dismay,"[58] by the USS *Boston*, which was

> one of the most formidable cruisers of the new [U.S.] navy, of the superstructure class, of three thousand tons displacement and a maximum speed of fifteen and a half knots per hour. Her crew consisted of 280 officers and men, well organized and drilled. The main battery consisted of two 8-inch central pivot high-powered guns mounted in echelon, and six 6-inch high-powered guns mounted in broadside pivots. The secondary battery consisted of two 6-pounder, two 3-pounder, and 1-pounder rapid-fire guns; two 47 mm., two 37 mm. revolving cannon; Gatling guns, torpedo outfit, and small arms.[59]

In March 1892, Stevens asked the U.S. Secretary of State for permission to land U.S. troops in the Islands, in anticipation of a revolution, acknowledging that such action would "deviate from established international rules and precedents" but noting that "the relations of the United States to Hawaii are exceptional."[60] On November 19, 1892, he wrote a long letter to the Secretary of State making the case for the annexation of Hawai'i and arguing that the Kingdom's Monarchy was "an absurd anachronism" that stood as "an impediment to good government—an obstruction to the prosperity and progress of the islands."[61]

---

54. 3 Kuykendall, *supra* note 1, at 453. This landing did not take place because of protests by the Kingdom's Cabinet ministers, and no disorders occurred. *Id.* at 453–54.

55. Stevens, *supra* note 14, at 191.

56. Davianna Pomaika'i McGregor, "The Cultural and Political History of Hawaiian Native People," in *Our History, Our Way: An Ethnic Studies Anthology*, 367 (Gregory Yee Mark, Davianna Pomaika'i McGregor, and Linda A. Revilla, eds., 1996), quoting from a letter from Minister Stevens in August 1891, in Gillis, *The Hawaiian Incident*, 6.

57. Young, *supra* note 36, at 3, 50.

58. Coffman, *supra* note 3, at 112; *see also* Young, *supra* note 36, at 34, reporting that "the presence of the American Minister [Stevens] and of the United States ship *Boston* was a source of disquietude to the Queen and her supporters."

59. Young, *supra* note 36, at 2–3.

60. Cleveland, *supra* note 49, at 7, quoting from a letter from Minister Stevens to the U.S. Secretary of State, March 8, 1892, in "Affairs in Hawaii," *supra* note 3, at 449.

61. *Id.* at 6, quoting from a letter from Minister Stevens to the U.S. Secretary of State, Nov. 19, 1892, in "Affairs in Hawaii," *supra* note 3, at 448. *See also* letter from E. C. MacFarlane to Commissioner James H. Blount, May 6, 1893, in "Blount Report," *supra* note 3, at 430: "Shortly after the commencement of the last session of the Legislature, it was an open secret that the Volney-Ashford-Wilcox party were planning a revolutionary movement, which had the support of the annexationist element, and that the latter element had the sympathy of the United States minister [John Stevens]."

Members of the Committee of Safety (and the Provisional Government): Henry E. Cooper (chair) *(center)*, Henry Waterhouse *(clockwise, from top)*, Lorrin A. Thurston, Ed Suhr, F. W. McChesney, John Emmeluth, William R. Castle, William O. Smith, J. A. McCandless, C. Bolte, W. C. Wilder, Andrew Brown, and Theodore F. Lansing

On January 16, 1893, the members of the Annexation Club's Committee of Safety[62] asked Minister Stevens to land armed forces to protect their life, liberty, and property. Minister Stevens promptly ordered 160 "well-armed"[63] marines from the U.S. naval vessel *Boston* to enter Honolulu[64] and to position themselves near the Government buildings and the 'Iolani Palace to intimidate Queen Lili'uokalani, her very limited military force,[65] and her Government.[66] As U.S. Secretary of State W. Q. Gresham later explained, "The troops were landed, not to protect American life and property, but to aid in overthrowing the existing government. Their very presence implied coercive measures against it."[67] "[T]here is no doubt that their presence [the American forces] provided a psychological support for the revolutionists."[68] On the afternoon of January 17, the Committee of Safety took possession of a Government

---

62. The Committee of Safety's thirteen members were William O. Smith (born in the Islands of U.S. ancestry), Lorrin A. Thurston (born in the Islands of U.S. ancestry), William R. Castle (born in the Islands of U.S. ancestry), A. S. Wilcox (born in the Islands of U.S. ancestry), William C. Wilder (U.S. citizen), Crister Bolte (naturalized citizen of German ancestry), Henry Waterhouse (naturalized citizen from Tasmania), Andrew Brown (a Scot, never naturalized), H. F. Glade (German citizen), Henry E. Cooper (U.S. citizen), F. W. McChesney (U.S. citizen), Theo. F. Lansing (U.S. citizen), and John A. McCandless (U.S. citizen). Blount Letter of July 17, 1893, *supra* note 9, at 121–22, in "Affairs in Hawaii," *supra* note 3, at 584; Helena G. Allen, *Sanford Ballard Dole: Hawaii's Only President*, 287 (1988). No person of Native Hawaiian ancestry was on the Committee. Four of the thirteen were born in Hawai'i of American parents and another three were naturalized citizens of the Kingdom; the remaining six included four U.S. citizens, one citizen of Great Britain, and one citizen of Germany. During the days of the overthrow, one of the Hawaiian citizens of American ancestry (Wilcox) returned to Kaua'i and was replaced by John Emmeluth, a U.S. citizen, and Glade resigned (because he was the German consul) and was replaced by Ed Suhr, another German citizen. 3 Kuykendall, *supra* note 1, at 587; Allen, *Betrayal, supra* note 2, at 287 and 415. Nine of the thirteen members were U.S. citizens or of American ancestry. Budnick, *supra* note 52, at 105. In President Cleveland's December 1893 "Message to Congress," he said that a majority (seven members) of the Committee "were foreign subjects, and consisted of five Americans, one Englishman, and one German." Cleveland, *supra* note 49, at 8, in "Affairs in Hawaii," *supra* note 3, at 450. *See generally* Twigg-Smith, *supra* note 47, at 135–66, providing short biographical sketches of the leaders of the 1893 revolution.

63. Gresham Letter, *supra* note 50, at 17–18, in "Affairs in Hawaii," *supra* note 3, at 459–60.

64. Ralph S. Kuykendall and A. G. Day, *Hawai'i: A History from Polynesian Kingdom to American Commonwealth*, 178 (1948); 3 Kuykendall, *supra* note 1, at 593–96.

65. Historical sources differ on the number of troops that the Queen might have mustered. In President Cleveland's statement, he reported that Lili'uokalani had 500 armed men and several pieces of artillery at her command. Cleveland, *supra* note 49, at 11, in "Affairs in Hawaii," *supra* note 3, at 453. *See also* Dudley, *supra* note 53, at 295, reporting that "the government had a force of five hundred men, ten Gatling guns, and twelve pieces of artillery at its disposal." U.S. Navy Lieutenant Lucien Young, an officer on the *Boston,* wrote subsequently, however, "that I was cognizant of the exact number [of the Kingdom's armed men], which was only one hundred and forty-five." Young, *supra* note 36, at 251.

66. President Cleveland later explained that the placement of the troops made it clear that they had not been landed "for the security of American life and property," because if that had been the goal, the troops would have been placed "in the vicinity of such property and so as to protect it, instead of at a distance and so as to command the Hawaiian Government building and palace." Cleveland, *supra* note 49, at 9, in "Affairs in Hawaii," *supra* note 3, at 451.

67. Gresham letter, *supra* note 50, at 20, in "Affairs in Hawaii," *supra* note 3, at 462. "[E]very evidence indicates that the early landing of American forces from the *Boston* and their station in proximity to the government buildings gave undue aid and comfort to the revolutionists and discouraged the existing monarchical government from effectively coping with the situation." Stevens, *supra* note 14, at 222, citing Julius W. Pratt, *Expansionists of 1898: The Acquisition of Hawaii and the Spanish Islands*, 94–109 (1936).

68. Dudley, *supra* note 53, at 296.

office building and proclaimed the abrogation of the Monarchy [69] and the establishment of a Provisional Government until the terms of annexation with the United States could be negotiated.[70]

Minister Stevens, "pursuant to prior agreement, recognized this government within an hour after the reading of the proclamation, and before five o'clock, in answer to an inquiry on behalf of the Queen and her cabinet, announced that he had done so." [71] The U.S. representative in the Kingdom thus recognized the Provisional Government "before any demand for surrender had even been made on the Queen or on the commander or any officer of any of her military forces at any of the points where her troops were located," [72] "when it had little other than a paper existence, and when the legitimate government was in full possession and control of the palace, the barracks, and the police station." [73]

This "overeagerness to recognize the new government" [74] by Minister Stevens "placed the Government of the Queen in a position of most perilous perplexity." [75] Rather than risk the lives of her people, Queen Liliʻuokalani surrendered in protest, stating that she "yielded to the superior force of the United States . . . until such time as the Government of the United States shall upon facts being presented to it undo the action of its representative and reinstate me in the authority which I claim as

---

69. The proclamation purporting to announce the abrogation of the Monarch was issued by a "dozen or so foreigners, who had been previously assured of a recognition by the United States minister as soon as provisional government was proclaimed," and who read their announcement to an audience that included themselves and "the native janitor." Prince J. K. Kalanianaole, "The Story of the Hawaiians," 21 *Mid-Pacific Magazine*, 117, 129 (February 1921).

70. Cleveland, *supra* note 49, at 10, in "Affairs in Hawaii," *supra* note 3, at 452. As explained *infra* in chapter 17, because annexation was blocked by U.S. President Grover Cleveland, the Provisional Government was succeeded by the Republic of Hawaii on July 4, 1894, with Sanford Ballard Dole declared president.

71. Cleveland, *supra* note 49, at 11, in "Affairs in Hawaii," *supra* note 3, at 453. Recognition by other governments followed. On January 18, 1893, Austro-Hungary, Belgium, Chile, Denmark, France, Germany, Italy, Mexico, the Netherlands, Peru, Portugal, Russia, and Spain recognized the Provisional Government, and on January 20, Great Britain and Japan recognized the new government. McGregor, *supra* note 56, at 373.

72. Blount Letter of July 17, 1893, *supra* note 9, at 120, in "Affairs in Hawaii," *supra* note 3, at 586.

73. Gresham Letter, *supra* note 50, at 20, in "Affairs in Hawaii," *supra* note 3, at 462. Stevens' role and the support he received from Washington were crucial to the success of the overthrow:

Thurston overthrew the Hawaiian monarchy with a core group of fewer than thirty men. They may have thought they made the Hawaiian revolution, and in a sense they did. Without the presence of Stevens or another like-minded American minister, however, they might never have even attempted it. A different kind of minister would have reprimanded the rebels in Hawaii rather than offer them military support. . . .

Although Stevens was an unabashed partisan, he was no rogue agent. He had been sent to Hawaii to promote annexation, and the men who sent him, President Harrison and Secretary of State Blaine, knew precisely what that must entail. . . . [H]e was doing what the president and the secretary of state wanted (Kinzer, *supra* note 47, at 30).

74. 3 Kuykendall, *supra* note 1, at 629. *See also* Stevens, *supra* note 14, at 222, stating that Minister Stevens' "recognition of the Provisional Government was hasty and not justifiable upon the grounds which he later defended it."

75. Cleveland, *supra* note 49, at 11, in "Affairs in Hawaii," *supra* note 3, at 453.

the Constitutional Sovereign of the Hawaiian Islands." [76] Commissioner Blount was explicit in stating that Minister Stevens had acted improperly, pointing out that Stevens had "consulted freely with the leaders of the revolutionary movement from the evening of the 14th" and had "promised them protection," noting also that the rebels "needed the [U.S.] troops on shore to overawe the Queen's supporters and government" because "[t]hey had few arms and no trained soldiers. They did not mean to fight." [77] The U.S. Congress later declared that Minister Stevens' actions had violated treaties between the two nations and international law, [78] and that without the support of the U.S. troops and diplomatic efforts, the insurrection would have failed for lack of popular support and insufficient arms. [79]

The United States played another crucial role two weeks after the initial overthrow. As William F. Quinn (who was Governor of Hawai'i at the time of statehood) later explained,

> Two weeks later there were rumors of counter-revolt. The Provisional Government's small military force would not be effective and a formal request was made to Stevens to protect the government pending negotiations toward annexation by the United States. He promptly complied. The flag of the United States was raised over the government building and custody was given to the United States Marines. Stevens' actions were approved by the State Department who commended his course of action in giving protection to life and property from apprehended disorder. [80]

On February 1, 1893, Minister Stevens declared Hawai'i to be a protectorate of the United States. [81] Although President Cleveland disavowed the protectorate when he took office in early March, the U.S. flag flew over the Government buildings and the U.S. troops remained on guard in Honolulu until Commissioner James Blount

---

76. Her complete statement was as follows (*see* "Apology Resolution," *supra* note 16, whereas para. 9):

I, Liliuokalani, by the Grace of God and under the Constitution of the Hawaiian Kingdom, Queen, do hereby solemnly protest against any and all acts done against myself and the Constitutional Government of the Hawaiian Kingdom by certain persons claiming to have established a Provisional Government of and for this Kingdom.

That I yield to the superior force of the United States of America whose Minister Plenipotentiary, His Excellency John L. Stevens, has caused United States troops to be landed at Honolulu and declared that he would support the Provisional Government.

Now to avoid any collision of armed forces, and perhaps the loss of life, I do this under protest and impelled by said force yield my authority until such time as the Government of the United States shall, upon facts being presented to it, undo the action of its representatives and reinstate me in the authority which I claim as the Constitutional Sovereign of the Hawaiian Islands.

77. Blount Letter of July 17, 1893, *supra* note 9, at 128, in "Affairs in Hawaii," *supra* note 3, at 594.
78. "Apology Resolution," *supra* note 16, whereas para. 8; "1992 Health Care Act," *supra* note 26, "Findings," para. 8.
79. "Apology Resolution," *supra* note 16, whereas para. 10.
80. William F. Quinn, "Native Hawaiian Claims: The Issue of the '80s," 10–11 (essay delivered to the Social Science Association, May 7, 1984).
81. Cleveland, *supra* note 49, at 8, in "Affairs in Hawaii," *supra* note 3, at 587.

President Benjamin Harrison, 1888

ordered them taken down on April 1.[82] Stevens was subsequently recalled from his diplomatic post, and Commander Gilbert C. Wiltse (commanding officer of the *Boston*) was disciplined and forced to resign his commission.[83] Two U.S. warships remained in Honolulu Harbor "because of the continued agitation among people of certain classes."[84]

The revolutionary group rushed a five-member delegation to Washington and quickly negotiated a treaty with President Harrison, which was signed on February 14, 1893, and sent the next day to the U.S. Senate for its advice and consent.[85] The Republican Benjamin Harrison was a lame-duck president with only a few more weeks in office, however, because Democrat Grover Cleveland had beaten him in the

---

82. *Id.;* Allen, *Betrayal, supra* note 2, at 302; Young, *supra* note 36, at 208–10. Rear Admiral Joseph S. Skerett, the Commander in Chief of Naval Forces in the Pacific, who had arrived in Honolulu on February 10, 1893, on the USS *Mohican* and had assumed command from Captain Gilbert C. Wiltse (who then left Honolulu on February 28), "exhibited unmistakable signs of irritation and humiliation" when learning that Commissioner Blount had ordered the U.S. flags to be removed and the troops to leave Honolulu, "and afterwards wrote a complaint to the Navy Department." Young, *supra* note 36, at 216, 246–47. But see 3 Kuykendall, *supra* note 1, at 624, reporting that Admiral Skerrett "had told Stevens as early as March 16 that he could see no reason for the further presence of the troops on shore" and that "Skerrett's advice obviously convinced Blount that their presence was unnecessary."

83. "Apology Resolution," *supra* note 16, whereas para. 13.

84. 3 Kuykendall, *supra* note 1, at 624, citing Admiral Skerrett's transmittals to the Navy Department.

85. *See* Chock, *supra* note 17, at 465, citing Sen. Exec. Doc. No. 76, 52d Cong., 2d Sess. (1893), reprinted in *Foreign Relations of the United States, 1894.* In President Harrison's message transmitting the treaty to the Senate, he asserted "that the overthrow of the monarchy was not in any way promoted by the United States, but had its origin in what seemed to be a reactionary and revolutionary policy on the part of Queen Liliuokalani, which put in serious peril not only the large and preponderating interests of the United States in the islands, but all foreign interests, and indeed the decent administration of civil affairs and the peace of the islands." 1 Moore, *supra* note 18, at 496.

James Blount and wife Eugenie W. Blount

November 1892 election and Cleveland was slated to take office on March 4, 1893. The U.S. Senate debated the annexation issue, but the two-thirds vote required to advise and consent to a treaty could not be obtained,[86] and when President Grover Cleveland took office, he withdrew the treaty.[87] President Cleveland then appointed former Representative James H. Blount of Georgia to conduct an investigation into the overthrow. Blount, a former Confederate officer, had served as a Democrat in the House of Representatives for eighteen years until March 4, 1893, had previously chaired the House Foreign Affairs Committee, and "had no connection with the Islands and no obvious view on annexation prior to his appointment."[88] After spending more than four months in the Islands,[89] Blount concluded that the United States diplomatic and military representatives had abused their authority and were responsible for the change in government.[90]

---

86. 3 Kuykendall, *supra* note 1, at 616.

87. MacKenzie, *supra* note 45, at 12.

88. 2 Native Hawaiians Study Commission, *Report on the Culture, Needs and Concerns of Native Hawaiians,* 70 (Report issued pursuant to Pub. L. 96-565, Title III, 1983).

89. Blount arrived in Honolulu March 29, 1893, and remained until August 1. Blackman, *supra* note 9, at 136; McGregor, *supra* note 56, at 374.

90. "Blount Report," *supra* note 3. Commissioner Blount conducted extensive interviews, including ones with many of those who supported and participated in the overthrow. Some historians have criticized Blount, complaining that he did not interview any members of the Committee of Safety or the officers on the *Boston.* 3 Kuykendall, *supra* note 1, at 628; Dudley, *supra* note 53, at 299. But Blount did conduct extensive interviews

President Grover Cleveland, 1888

The "Blount Report" stated that "the presence of the American troops, who were landed without permission of the existing government, was used for the purpose of inducing the surrender of the Queen, who abdicated under protest with the understanding that her case would be submitted to the President of the United States."[91] The members of the Provisional Government also acknowledged at the time that their rebellion against the Queen would not have succeeded without the presence of the U.S. Marines.[92] U.S. Secretary of State W. Q. Gresham wrote to President Grover Cleveland on October 18, 1893, that the Provisional Government "was established by the action of the American minister [Stevens] and the presence of the troops landed from the *Boston*" and that it was clear that the majority of those eligible to vote under the 1887 Constitution did not favor "the existing authority or annexation to this or any other country. They earnestly desire that the government of their choice shall be restored and its independence respected."[93] He thus recommended

---

with Henry Waterhouse and Crister Bolte, both members of the Committee of Safety, on May 2 and May 5, 1893, "Blount Report," *supra* note 3, at 47–56 and 249–65, in "Affairs in Hawaii," *supra* note 3, at 715–31, and he received a detailed report from another member, William O. Smith, which is in the form of a discussion between Smith and Henry E. Cooper (another member of the Committee of Safety) and James B. Castle, dated July 15, 1893. *Id.* at 489–503, in "Affairs in Hawaii," *supra* note 3, at 955–69; 2 Native Hawaiians Study Commission, *supra* note 88, at 71. Apparently, "key members of the Provisional Government refused to be interviewed." *Id.* at 70–71.

91. 1 Moore, *supra* note 18, at 499.

92. *Id.* at 500, citing the response of the Provisional Government to President Cleveland's report to the Queen, in H.R. Exec. Doc. No. 70, 53d Cong., 2d Sess., in "Affairs in Hawaii," *supra* note 3, at 1276–82.

93. Gresham letter, *supra* note 50, at 20, in "Affairs in Hawaii," *supra* note 3, at 462.

that the United States should not annex Hawai'i "by force and fraud," but rather should respect its independence.[94]

In his December 18, 1893, report to Congress, President Cleveland made it clear that he was "unimpressed and indeed offended by the actions of the American Minister."[95] He described the actions of Minister Stevens and the U.S. Marines as an "act of war, committed with the participation of a diplomatic representative of the United States and without authority of Congress," and expressed regret that by such acts the government of a peaceful and friendly people had been overthrown.[96] President Cleveland had no doubt that the actions by U.S. diplomats and troops were crucial to the success of the revolution, stating that "the provisional government owes its existence to an armed invasion by the United States"[97] and that the overthrow of the Kingdom "is directly traceable to and dependent for its success upon the agency of the United States acting through its diplomatic and naval representatives."[98]

The annexationists remained determined, however, and persuaded the Senate Foreign Relations Committee, then under the leadership of the "ardent annexationist"[99] Senator from Alabama, John Tyler Morgan, to conduct a second investigation into the overthrow. The Committee held hearings in Washington from December 27, 1893, through February 26, 1894, but unlike the Blount investigation sent no one to visit the Islands. This report, signed only by Senator Morgan because "[t]he Committee was unable to reach a majority opinion,"[100] did not disagree with the factual summary reached by Commissioner Blount. Both reports agreed that "Stevens, Wiltse and the military presence of the United States were the prime cause for the success of the overthrow."[101] But they disagreed on whether the actions of Minister Stevens

---

94. *Id.* at 21, in "Affairs in Hawaii," *supra* note 3, at 463.

95. *Rice v. Cayetano,* 528 U.S. 495, 505 (2000).

96. Cleveland, *supra* note 49, at 14, in "Affairs in Hawaii," *supra* note 3, at 462. President Cleveland further concluded that a "substantial wrong has thus been done which a due regard for our national character as well as the rights of the injured people requires we should endeavor to repair" and called for the restoration of the Hawaiian Monarchy. *Id. See also* "Apology Resolution," *supra* note 16, whereas paras. 14–15.

97. Cleveland, *supra* note 49, at 12, in "Affairs in Hawaii," *supra* note 3, at 454.

98. *Id.* at 13, in "Affairs in Hawaii," *supra* note 3, at 455. Although the "Morgan Report" and some commentators have suggested that the role of the U.S. diplomats and military forces may not have been crucial to the success of the overthrow (*see, e.g.,* Andrade, *supra* note 14, at 118–24), it is clear, in the words of the U.S. Supreme Court's historical summary, that the Western rebels had "the active assistance of John Stevens, the United States Minister to Hawaii, acting with United States armed forces." *Rice v. Cayetano,* 528 U.S. 495, 505 (2000).

99. Andrade, *supra* note 14, at 135. Senator Morgan had long been interested in Hawai'i and was referred to by Kuykendall as "Hawaii's Senator." 3 Kuykendall, *supra* note 1, at 616. In 1887, for instance, he promoted the amendment to the Supplemental Reciprocity Treaty that gave the United States control of the Pearl River Harbor (*see supra* chapter 14, text at notes 40–50) and offered the view to U.S. Secretary of State Thomas F. Bayard that King Kalākaua and Walter Murray Gibson were criminals and that the Hawaiian Monarchy was afflicted with "moral bankruptcy." Charles Callan Tansill, *Diplomatic Relations between the United States and Hawaii: 1885-1889,* 26 (Fordham University Historical Series No. 1, 1940), citing "John T. Morgan to Secretary Bayard," April 8, 1887, in Bayard MS.

100. 2 Native Hawaiians Study Commission, *supra* note 88, at 74.

101. *Id.* at 23.

Queen Liliʻuokalani

and Captain Wiltse were proper and authorized. "Where Blount found fault, Morgan offered praise." [102]

Senator Morgan's report condoned Minister Stevens' actions, characterizing U.S. relations with Hawaiʻi as unique and not to be judged by normal rules of international law because "Hawaii has been all the time under a virtual suzerainty of the United States." [103] He explained that the United States has "always exerted the privilege of interference in the domestic policy of Hawaii to a degree that would not be justified, under our view of the international law, in reference to the affairs of Canada, Cuba, or Mexico," and that "the attitude of the United States toward Hawaii was in moral effect that of a friendly protectorate." [104]

Because of this politically charged division of views in Washington, annexation was blocked, but President Cleveland's efforts to restore the Hawaiian Monarchy also

---

102. *Id.* at 7.

103. *Report of the Committee on Foreign Relations*, S. Rep. 277, 53rd Cong., 2d Sess., at 21 (1894) (hereafter cited as "Morgan Report"). The "Morgan Report" also stated that "Hawaii is an American state and is embraced in the American commercial and military system. . . . The United States has assumed and deliberately maintained toward Hawaii a relation which is entirely exceptional and has no parallel in our dealings with any other people." *Id.* at 20. *See also* Robert H. Stauffer, *Kahana: How the Land Was Lost,* 73 (2004): "It can also be argued that the government that was overthrown in 1893 had, for much of its fifty-year history, been little more than a *de facto* unincorporated territory of the United States. The kingdom's government was often American-dominated if not American-run."

104. "Morgan Report," *supra* note 103, at 21; 2 Native Hawaiians Study Commission, *supra* note 88, at 75.

failed. On February 7, 1894, the U.S. House of Representatives "resolved that there should be neither restoration of the Queen nor annexation to the United States,"[105] and on May 31, 1894, the U.S. Senate adopted a resolution stating that "the people of the Hawaiian Islands" had the right "to establish and maintain their own form of government and domestic polity; that the United States ought in no wise to interfere therewith; and that any intervention in the political affairs of these islands by any other government will be regarded as an act unfriendly to the United States."[106]

In its 1993 "Apology Resolution," the U.S. Congress formally apologized for the participation of U.S. diplomats and military personnel in the 1893 overthrow, characterizing this action as having violated "treaties between the two nations and . . . international law."[107] It explained that "without the active support and intervention by the United States diplomatic and military representatives, the insurrection against the Government of Queen Liliuokalani would have failed for lack of popular support and insufficient arms."[108] It acknowledged that this action denied to the Native Hawaiian People their "inherent sovereignty through self-government and . . . their right to self-determination, their lands, and their ocean resources."[109] The "Apology Resolution" also acknowledged that the United States had received 1.8 million acres of land, which had been the Crown, Government, and Public Lands of the Kingdom of Hawai'i, without "the consent of or compensation to the Native Hawaiian people of Hawai'i or their sovereign government."[110] U.S. District Court Judge Susan Oki Mollway has summarized the findings of Congress in the "Apology Resolution" by saying, "On January 17, 1893, the United States overthrew the Kingdom of Hawaii. A century later, Congress acknowledged that this overthrow was illegal, and that it deprived native Hawaiians of their right to self-determination."[111] U.S. District Judge Alan C. Kay has stated similarly that "Congress has made repeated findings in numerous legislative enactments that the Hawaiian Monarchy was unlawfully overthrown with the aid of the United States."[112]

The Hawai'i State Legislature has similarly characterized the 1893 overthrow as having occurred "without the consent of the native Hawaiian people or the lawful Government of Hawaii in violation of treaties between the [United States and the Kingdom of Hawai'i] and of international law."[113] It further stated that the 1898 annexation of Hawai'i to the United States occurred "without the consent of or com-

---

105. 2 Native Hawaiians Study Commission, *supra* note 88, at 74.

106. Andrade, *supra* note 14, at 136, quoting from 26 *Congressional Record*, 5499–5500.

107. "Apology Resolution," *supra* note 16, whereas para. 8.

108. *Id.*, whereas para. 10.

109. *Id.*, whereas para. 23.

110. *Id.*, whereas para. 25.

111. *Arakaki v. Cayetano*, 198 F.Supp.2d, 1165, 1170 (D. Hawai'i 2002), aff'd in part and reversed in part, 477 F. 3d 1048 (9th Cir. 2007).

112. *Doe v. Kamehameha Schools*, 295 F.Supp.2d, 1141, 1150 (D. Hawai'i 2003), citing "Apology Resolution," *supra* note 16, and other congressional statutes.

113. Hawai'i State Legislature, "A Bill Relating to Hawaiian Sovereignty," Act 359 (1993).

pensation to the indigenous people of Hawaii or their sovereign government," and that because of this action "the indigenous people of Hawaii were denied the mechanism for expression of their inherent sovereignty through self-government and self-determination, their lands, and their ocean resources." Hawai'i's Intermediate Court of Appeals stated in 1994 that the Hawai'i State Legislature "has tacitly recognized the illegal overthrow." [114]

---

114. *State v. Lorenzo,* 77 Hawai'i 219, 221, 883 P.2d 641, 643 (Haw. App. 1994).

17

The Republic of Hawaii (1894–98)

 The small group of westerners who engineered the overthrow of the Kingdom in January 1893, with the crucial help of U.S. military and diplomatic personnel, wanted the United States to annex the islands immediately. The Republican President Benjamin Harrison supported this effort and sought to rush an annexation treaty through the Senate after the takeover.[1] But Harrison had been defeated in the November 1892 election by Democrat Grover Cleveland, who took office on March 4, 1893, and Cleveland withdrew the proposed annexation treaty almost immediately after his inauguration.

After this setback, the Legislature of the Provisional Government set up by the Western revolutionaries in Hawai'i passed a law on March 15, 1894, to convene a Constitutional Convention, which met from May 30 to July 5, 1894, to adopt a Constitution for the "Republic of Hawaii"[2] through a process that had no popular legitimacy.[3] "Insurrection leader Sanford Dole personally selected 19 of the 37 delegates so that the insurrectionists would have a majority and retain control of Hawai'i. The remaining delegates were elected, but many of the previously qualified voters were excluded by strict voting requirements."[4] The nineteen appointed members consisted of the five members of the Provisional Government's Executive Council and fourteen members of its Advisory Council.[5] All delegates were required to give an

---

1. Tom Coffman, *Nation Within: The Story of America's Annexation of the Nation of Hawai'i,* 141 (1998).

2. See A. F. Judd, "Constitution of the Republic of Hawaii," 4 *Yale Law Journal* 53 (1893); 1 John Bassett Moore, *A Digest of International Law,* 501 (1906).

3. The Western revolutionaries based their authority to convene the 1894 Constitutional Convention on the Proclamation issued by the Provisional Government on January 17, 1893, which stated that "All Hawaiian Laws and Constitutional principles not inconsistent herewith shall continue in force until further order of the Executive and Advisory Councils." Judd, *supra* note 2, at 53–54.

4. Jennifer M. L. Chock, "One Hundred Years of Illegitimacy: International Legal Analysis of the Illegal Overthrow of the Hawaiian Monarchy, Hawai'i's Annexation, and Possible Reparations," 17 *University of Hawai'i Law Review,* 463, 490 (1995); *see also* Gavan Daws, *Shoal of Time: A History of the Hawaiian Islands,* 281 (1968, reprinted 1974). The members of the Republic's Constitutional Convention are pictured in Thurston Twigg-Smith, *Hawaiian Sovereignty: Do the Facts Matter?* (1998), between pages 216 and 217.

5. Sylvester K. Stevens, *American Expansion in Hawaii 1842–1898,* 271 (1945, reissued 1968). Professor Andrade has reported that only five were Hawaiians and only two were Portuguese. Ernest Andrade, Jr.,

Sanford Ballard Dole

oath of allegiance to the Provisional Government and to oppose reestablishment of the Monarchy.[6] Twenty-one of the delegates were of U.S. ancestry, seven were of English descent, six were Native Hawaiians, and three were Portuguese.[7]

The Constitution of 1894, prepared primarily by Sanford Ballard Dole[8] and Lorrin A. Thurston,[9] was declared to be the law of the land effective July 4, 1894, by proclamation,[10] and Dole became the President of this "Republic."[11] The Repub-

---

Unconquerable Rebel: Robert W. Wilcox and Hawaiian Politics, 1880–1903, 141 (1996), citing *Hawaiian Star,* May 5, 1894, and *Pacific Commercial Advertiser,* May 5, 1894.

6. Stevens, *supra* note 5, at 271.

7. *Id.*

8. Judd, *supra* note 2, at 54. Background on Dole can be found in Helena G. Allen, *Sanford Ballard Dole: Hawaii's Only President 1844–1926* (1988), and in Coffman, *supra* note 1, at 69–72, 145–46.

9. Coffman, *supra* note 1, at 148–63; William Fremont Blackman, *The Making of Hawaii: A Study in Social Evolution,* 141 n. 1 (1906, reprinted 1977), explaining that Dole and Thurston each prepared drafts independently and then, according to Dole, they "fused the two, taking such parts from both as we thought best."

10. "[E]ven those few thousand voters who had elected the delegates who had approved the constitution could not be trusted to endorse it, and so the constitution became law not by plebiscite but by proclamation." Daws, *supra* note 4, at 281.

11. Melody K. MacKenzie, "Historical Background," in *Native Hawaiian Rights Handbook,* 13 (Melody Kapilialoha MacKenzie, ed., 1991), citing William A. Russ, *The Hawaiian Republic 1894–1898,* 36 (1961).

lic of Hawai'i functioned for four years until annexation was finally accomplished under the administration of a new U.S. President, Republican William McKinley, who signed the Joint Resolution of Annexation on July 7, 1898.[12]

Article 91 of the 1894 Constitution stated that this new Constitution was the "Supreme Law of the Republic" and that all previous Constitutions of the Hawaiian Islands and all inconsistent laws were abrogated and deemed to be null and void. Section 1 of Article 92 declared that all statutes and all rights, actions, prosecutions, judgments, and contracts would continue unless inconsistent with the 1894 Constitution or specifically abrogated or addressed. Section 2 stated that statutes referring to the "King," the "Kingdom," or the "Provisional Government" should be construed to refer to the "President" or to the "Republic of Hawaii."

Article 15 of the 1894 Constitution stated that the Republic's territory included the land that previously made up "the Kingdom of the Hawaiian Islands, and the territory ruled over by the Provisional Government of Hawaii or which may hereafter be added to the Republic." The status of the Crown Lands was addressed in Article 95:

> That portion of the public domain heretofore known as Crown Land is hereby
> declared to have been heretofore, and now to be, the property of the Hawaiian
> Government, and to be now *free and clear from any trust* of or concerning the
> same, and from all claim of any nature whatsoever, upon the rents, issues and
> profits thereof. *It shall be subject to alienation* and other uses as may be provided
> by law. All valid leases thereof now in existence are hereby confirmed [emphasis
> added].

By this provision, the Republic took possession of the Crown Lands, which in 1894 consisted of about 971,463 acres and were valued (in terms of the value of the dollar at that time) at $2,314,250.[13] Most were under long-term leases, generating rental revenues of $49,268.75 per year.[14] Subsequent commentators have characterized this seizure as an expropriation without compensation.[15] Table 1 shows how the Crown

---

12. "Joint Resolution to Provide for Annexing the Hawaiian Islands to the United States," ch. 55, 30 Stat. 750, 751 (1898).

13. C. P. Iaukea, *Biennial Report of the Commissioners of Crown Lands, 1894,* 8 (1894) (hereafter cited as *Crown Lands Report*). The Crown Lands were reported to have consisted of about 984,000 acres in 1855. Arthur Y. Akinaka and James M. Dunn, *A Land Inventory and Land Use Study for the Department of Hawaiian Home Lands,* 21 (December 18, 1972).

14. U.S. Hawaiian Commission, *The Report of the Hawaiian Commission,* 5 (1898) (hereafter cited as *Hawaiian Commission Report*).

15. *See, e.g.,* MacKenzie, *supra* note 11, at 3, 13: "Under the republic's constitution, the republic also expropriated the Crown Lands, without compensation to the monarch"; *Expressing the Policy of the United States Regarding the United States Relationship with Native Hawaiians and to Provide a Process for the Recognition by the United States of the native Hawaiian Governing Entity, and for Other Purposes,* Senate Comm. on Indian Affairs, S. Rep. No. 107-66, at 13 (2001): "The Republic also claimed title to the Government Lands and Crown Lands without paying compensation to the monarch."

TABLE 1. Crown Lands by island (1894)

Island	Acres	Value
Hawai'i [a]	642,852	$992,300
Maui [b]	69,121	180,500
Moloka'i [c]	20,892	25,000
Lāna'i [d]	17,369	17,000
O'ahu [e]	66,593	518,450
Kaua'i [f]	154,636	581,000
TOTALS	971,463	$2,314,250

[a] See Table 2a
[b] See Table 2b
[c] See Table 2c
[d] See Table 2d
[e] See Table 2e
[f] See Table 2f

Lands were distributed by island.[16] Table 2 presents a more detailed listing of these lands, along with a description of them prepared in 1894 by C. P. Iaukea.[17]

Through Article 95 of the 1894 Constitution, the "crown lands were lumped in with the government lands, which together became the 'Public Lands of the Provisional Government and Republic.' Thus what Kamehameha III had 'set aside for me and my heirs and successors forever, as my property exclusively,' was transmuted into part of the general land holdings of the government of Hawaii."[18] The leaders of the Republic thereby decreed that the Crown Lands could be sold, accomplishing a goal they had long sought[19] and reversing the Act of January 3, 1865,[20] which had rendered the Crown Lands inalienable. This constitutional provision also declared that the Crown Lands were to be viewed as free and clear of any trust, it confirmed the earlier confiscation of Queen Lili'uokalani's annual Crown Land revenue of approxi-

---

16. *Crown Lands Report, supra* note 13, at 8. In a report issued May 11, 1893, W. D. Alexander, Surveyor-General, reported somewhat lower figures, listing 589,473 acres on the island of Hawai'i, 68,248 on Maui, 21,383 on Moloka'i, 17,370 on Lāna'i, 64,178 on O'ahu, and 154,636 on Kaua'i, for a total acreage of Crown Lands of 915,288. "Report of Theo. C. Porter to Commissioner James Blount, May 11, 1893," in "Report of Commissioner to the Hawaiian Islands," in 27 *Executive Documents of the House of Representatives for the Second Session of the Fifty-third Congress, 1893–94,* 607 (1895), originally in Executive Document No. 47, 53rd Cong., 2d Sess. (1893) (hereafter cited as "Blount Report"). *See also* Jean Hobbs, *Hawaii: A Pageant of the Soil,* 108 (1935), citing *Hawaiian Star,* May 18, 1893, at 5, for the view that the Crown Lists consisted of "985,000 acres, more or less, of which 650,000 acres were located on the island of Hawaii, 66,000 on Maui, 22,000 on Molokai, 23,000 on Lanai, 70,000 on Oahu, and 154,000 on Kauai. Besides these . . . crown lands, the government lands comprised some 828,000 acres."

17. *Crown Lands Report, supra* note 13, at 57–73, table E.

18. Samuel P. King, "History of Crown Lands May Determine Their Future," *Honolulu Star-Bulletin,* December 23, 1994, at A-13.

19. *See supra* chapters 12–13.

20. *See supra* chapter 9.

Table 2a. Crown Lands: Island of Hawai'i

District	Name of Tract	Area Acres	No. of Lease	Lease Expires	Annual Rental	Estimated Value	Remarks
Kona	Puuwaawaa	40,000	186	Aug. 1918	$1,210	$15,000	Good grazing, makai portion extremely rocky. Area approximate.
	Haleohiu	1,000	—	—	—	$1,500	Rocky. Portions suitable for coffee.
	Waiaha II	200	—	—	—	$1,000	Rocky. Good coffee land.
	Puaa	859	—	—	—	$1,000	Rocky. Small portion suitable for coffee.
	Onouli	367	—	—	—	$500	Dense forest.
	Honomalino	6,000	132	Jan. 1904	$405	$15,000	Coffee, grazing, and woodland. Large portion suitable for coffee.
Kau	Kapalapala	172,780	106	Jul. 1907	$1,200	$85,000	Grazing.
	Waiohinu	15,210	151	Apr. 1914	$600	$35,000	About 150 acres cane. Has valuable water springs.
Puna	Olaa	54,260	—	—	—	$200,000	About 30,000 acres of good coffee land.
	Apua	9,420	40	Feb. 1902	$30	$5,000	Dry grazing wood, &c.
	Kehena	1,000	—	—	—	$1,000	Dry grazing. Kauaula was given in exchange for this land.
	Waiakolea	313	—	—	—	$800	Dry grazing. Fishpond.
	Kaimu	5,000	—	—	—	$5,000	Dry grazing. Large portion suitable for coffee.
Hilo	Waiakea	95,000	124	Jun. 1918	$2,000	$200,000	3,000 acres cane land with considerable coffee land. Has valuable fishing rights.
	Ponahawai	2,946	—	—	$475	$8,000	Woodland. A few small pieces in Hilo town. Good coffee land at edge of woods.
	Piihonua	57,236	—	—	$2,900	$95,000	Grazing, forest, & c. Several valuable lots in Hilo Town about 300 acres cane land.
Hamakua	Humuula	101,000	75	Apr. 1908	$1,000	$75,000	High table land and especially adapted for sheep raising. Between 400 and 500 acres cane land near lower end.
	Hakalau-iki	577	56	Oct. 1908	$500	$15,000	Nearly all cane land.
	Manowaiopae	180	180	Apr. 1908	$180	$3,500	About 100 acres cane land.
	Kalopa	6,600	101	Jul. 1913	$1,033	$55,000	Between 800 to 1,000 acres cane land. Remainder fine grazing.
	Honokaia	5,186	55	Jul. 1913	$305	$50,000	600 to 800 acres cane land. Cane land reverts to Crown Commissioners Oct. 1898.
	Lalakea	—	—	—	—	—	Sold by Kamehameha IV.
	Kaohia	12					In Waipio Valley. Rice land.
	Pohakumauluulu	26	107	Jul. 1912	$75	$5,000	In Waipio Valley. Rice land.
	Muliwai	5,000	—	—	—	—	About 40 acres in Valley, remainder above.
	Waimanu	5,000	—	—	—	$5,000	Deep valley. Taro land. Formerly leased at $600 per annum.

District	Name of Tract	Area Acres	No. of Lease	Lease Expires	Annual Rental	Estimated Value	Remarks
Kohala	Pololu	1,343	80	Jul. 1904	$600	$5,000	Deep valley; 100 acres rice land.
	Aamakao	—	—	—	—	—	Sold to J. Wight by Kamehameha IV.
	Iole	—	—	—	—	—	Sold to E. Bond by Kamehameha IV.
	Kaauhuhu	1,737	43	May 1897	$250	$10,000	About 150 acres cane land. Good grazing.
	Kawaihae	13,000	0	Jul. 1913	$1,050	$25,000	Dry grazing.
	Waimea	41,600	113	—	$1,285 }	$75,000	Grazing. Makai portion very rocky.
	Puukapu	—	—	—	$1,527 }		Homesteads. Nearly all good grazing land. Area included in that of Waimea.

Total Area of Crown Lands on Hawai'i: 642,852 Acres

TABLE 2b. Crown Lands: Island of Maui

District	Name of Tract	Area Acres	No. of Lease	Lease Expires	Annual Rental	Estimated Value	Remarks
Lahaina	Mala	2,807	160	Apr. 1913	$700	$10,000	Equivalent to Wahikuli.
	Alamihi	9	—	—	—	—	Includes fishpond.
	Kuholilea	—	—	—	—	—	Probably none remaining.
	Kahua, 1 & 2	3	96	Jan. 1896	$713	—	Lease No. 96 covers Wainee, Kahua, Puehuehu, Waianae & Polapola. Also taro land in Honokawai.
	Lapakea	1,346	134	Jan. 1904	$134	—	26–100 in Lahaina town. Lease No. 134 covers Alamihi, Lapakea, Ilikahi, and Mokuhinia.
	Ilikahi	—	—	—	—	$5,000	A few small pieces. 51–100 acres.
	Opaeula	—	—	—	—		Probably none remaining.
	Polapola	—	—	—	—		In Lahaina town. 61–100 acres.
	Waianae	—	—	—	—		2 35–100.
	Wainee, 1 & 2	40	—	—	—	—	Includes "Mokuhinia Pond."
	Puehuehu	28	—	—	—	—	—
	Kauaula	—	—	—	—	—	Given in exchange for "Kehena" Puna.
Olowalu	Olowalu	6,000	51	Jul. 1908	$700	$20,000	300 acres cane land.
	Ukumehame	11,040	177	Nov. 1907	$250	$15,000	About 75 acres cane land. Remainder dry grazing.
	Aweoweo	—	—	—	—	—	Ili of Ukumehame.

(continued on next page)

TABLE 2b. Crown Lands: Island of Maui (continued)

District	Name of Tract	Area Acres	No. of Lease	Lease Expires	Annual Rental	Estimated Value	Remarks
Kula	Keokeo	5,332 }	168	Nov. 1911	$1,500	$60,000	All below road, good grazing.
	Waiohuli	11,734 }					About 3,000 acres above fine corn and potato land.
	Kealahou 1 & 2	217	115	Jan. 1908	$ 100	$ 2,500	Grazing.
Hana	Waiohinu	310	61	Jan. 1900	$ 200	$ 5,000	125 acres cane land.
	Wailua	300	135	Jan. 1904	$ 60	$ 3,500	Valuable for the water supply.
Koolau	Wailua 1 & 2	3,000	81	Jul. 1894	$ 300	$ 8,000	100 acres rice. Principally mountain land.
	Keanae	11,148	82	Jul. 1894	$ 300	$10,000	Taro land, about 100 acres. Principally mountain land.
	Honomanu	3,260	52	Jul. 1908	$ 500	$15,000	Deep valley. Valuable for its water rights.
Napoko	Wailuku	—	—	—	—	—	Transferred to C. Spreckels. Grant 3343.
	Polipoli	70	134a	Jan. 1904	$ 100	$ 3,000	Cane land. At Waihee.
Kahakuloa	Kahakuloa	10,523	33	Jan. 1896	$ 300	$10,000	Dry grazing.
	Waiokila	—	15	Jul. 1913	$ 100	$ 2,000	Area included in Kahakuloa.
Kaanapali	Napili	300	145	Jan. 1904	$ 275	$ 1,500	—
	Polua	—	—	—	—	—	Grazing. Taro land.
	Honokawai	4,000	159	Apr. 1912	$ 750	$10,000	—
	Ahoa	—	—	—	—	—	—

Total Area of Crown Lands on Maui: 69,121 Acres

TABLE 2c. Crown Lands: Island of Moloka'i

District	Name of Tract	Area Acres	No. of Lease	Lease Expires	Annual Rental	Estimated Value	Remarks
Kona	Ualapue	709	—	—	—	$ 5,000	Good grazing with valuable fishpond. Formerly leased for $360 per annum.
	Kalamaula	6,747	—	—	—	—	Dry grazing.
	Palaau	11,258 }	117	Jan. 1918	$1,200	$20,000	Dry grazing.
	Kapaakea	2,178 }					Dry grazing.

Total Area of Crown Lands on Moloka'i: 20,892 Acres

Table 2d. Crown Lands: Island of Lāna'i

District	Name of Tract	Area Acres	No. of Lease	Lease Expires	Annual Rental	Estimated Value	Remarks
	Kalulu	—	—	—	—	—	Transferred to Hawaii Government.
	Kamoku	8,291 }	167	Jan. 1916	$500	$17,000	Grazing land.
	Paomai	9,078 }					Grazing land.

Total Area of Crown Lands on Lāna'i: 17,369 Acres

Table 2e. Crown Lands: Island of O'ahu

District	Name of Tract	Area Acres	No. of Lease	Lease Expires	Annual Rental	Estimated Value	Remarks
Kona	Kahauiki	1,344	126	Jan. 1913	$800	$20,000	Grazing, banana, & c.
Kapalama	1/2 Kamookahi	—	150	—	$50	$400	1.88 acres. Taro, banana. (Kaulahea, tenant at will).
	1/2 Kamookahi	—	184	—	$175	$750	3.44 acres in 6 small pieces.
	Kuwiliwili	—	120	—	$275	$1,000	Rice land and fishpond.
	1/2 Nauwala	—	—	—	—	—	Uncertain.
	1/2 Paepaealii	—	—	—	—	—	Sold to W. Buckle.
	Kumupali	—	—	—	—	—	Probably none remaining.
Honolulu	Kawaiiki	—	—	—	$100	$1,500	6 4-10 acres. Taro land. Government, tenant at will.
	Haukaukoi	—	—	—	—	—	Uncertain.
	Kahookane	—	—	—	$40	$1,000	1.14 acres. Mauka of reservoir. Nuuanu.
	Laukaha	2,220	41	Apr. 1907	$300	$45,000	Upper Nuuanu Valley.
	1/2 Kawananakoa	—	—	—	—	$10,000	About 4 acres. Mausoleum premises.
	Kukanaka	—	—	—	—	—	Uncertain.
	Kapalua	10	127,172	Apr. 1906	$475	$1,700	Pauoa valley, taro land.
	Kahehuna	—	—	—	—	—	Uncertain.
	Auwaiolimu	500	71, 170	Aug. 1912	$250	$60,000	Valuable building lots west slope Punchbowl Hill.

(continued on next page)

TABLE 2e. Crown Lands: Island of Oʻahu (continued)

District	Name of Tract	Area Acres	No. of Lease	Lease Expires	Annual Rental	Estimated Value	Remarks
Waikiki	Pawaa	—	—	—	—	—	Loi Ili, uncertain.
	Pukele	198 }	136	Jan. 1904	$585	$ 5,000	Grazing, in 2 sections.
	Waiomao	748 }					Grazing. Palolo valley.
	1/2 Kahaumakaawe	—	108a	Sept. 1897	$100	$ 500	Taro land.
	Halelena	—	—	—	—	—	Remnant. Manoa valley.
	Puahia	32 }					—
	Piliamoo	14 }	70	Jul. 1912	$220	$ 4,000	Taro land. Manoa valley.
	Hamana	2 }					—
	Mookahi 1 & 2	5	—		—	—	2 secs. Rice land.
	Kaloi iki	—	—		—	—	Not determined.
	Kaalawai	—	—		—	—	Uncertain.
	Kaluaolohe	—	—		—	—	Uncertain.
	1/2 Poloke	—	—		—	—	1/2 acre Makiki valley.
	Kahalauluhine	—	—		—	—	Uncertain.
	Kaneloa	171	74,157	Sept. 1919	$330	$80,000	Most of this land in Kapiolani Park. Portion rice land. The Park lots very valuable.
	1/2 Wailupe	41	109	Nov. 1902	$200	$ 1,600	Crown has fishpond.
	Kuliouou	518	173	Jul. 1911	$100	$ 4,000	Dry grazing.
Koolaupoko	Waimanalo	6,500	165	Nov. 1920	$1,500	$75,000	About 1,200 acres cane land. Good grazing.
Kailua	Kawailoa	525	114	Feb. 1903	$400	$ 5,000	Good grazing. Includes small island.
Kaneohe	Kaluapuhi						Rice, grazing and fishponds.
	Waikalua	1,486 }	—	—	$1,987	$16,000	In 14 sections. Covered by sundry leases.
	Halekou						
	Kanohouluiwi }						
	Keaahala	379	183	May 1913	$300	$ 5,000	Cane land.

	Land	Acres		Date			Remarks
	Kahalekauila	—	—	—	—	—	Sold to Parker.
	Kuou	—	—	—	—	—	Sold.
	Kahaluu	—	—	—	—	—	Sold to Stewart.
	Maluaka	—	—	—	—	—	Sold to Parker.
	Makawai }	1,261	—	—	$780	$10,000	Rice land and grazing.
	Hopekea						Covered by sundry leases.
	Kualoa 1 & 2	—	—	—	—	—	Sold to Judd.
Koolauloa	Hauula	1,576	9	Jun. 1904	$200	$3,500	Grazing land.
	Kahuku	—	—	—	—	—	Sold.
	Kawela	—	—	—	—	—	Sold.
	Waialee	733	3	Sept. 1901	$175	$3,000	Grazing and taro land.
	Paumalu	2,010	5	Feb. 1902	$150	$5,000	Grazing and taro land.
	Pupukea	2,353	6	Feb. 1902	$150	$5,000	Grazing and taro land.
Waianae	Waianae-kai	6,143	60	Jul. 1909	$1,200 }	$75,000	500 acres cane land. Coffee.
	Waianae-uka	14,678	68	Jan. 1912	$500		Good grazing land.
	Keaau	2,431	110	Nov. 1902	$400	$8,000	Grazing. Portion good coffee land.
	Lualualei	14,772	2	Aug. 1901	$700	$45,000	500 acres cane. Remainder superior grazing land.
	Nanakuli	3,431	69	Feb. 1912	$570	$10,000	Fine grazing land.
Ewa	Ohua Waikaka-lava	490	—	—	—	$1,000	Grazing. Included in Lease No. 68 to Dowsett.
	Papaa	—	—	—	—	—	Sold to Hunt.
	1/2 Pouhala	810	—	—	—	$3,000	Grazing. Portion covered in lease to Dowsett. Fishpond.
	Weloka	21	130	Jan. 1918	$100	$3,000	Fishpond.
	Honokawailani }	11	128	Jan. 1909	$75	$1,500	Kula and rice land.
	Kauhihau						Grazing and taro.
	Aiea	1,175	66	Jan. 1912	$250	$8,000	Grazing and taro.
	Puukahua	5	—	—	—	—	Kula. Included in Lease No. 130.
	Hoaeae	—	—	—	—	—	None remaining.

Total Area of Crown Lands on Oʻahu: 66,593 Acres

(continued on next page)

TABLE 2f. Crown Lands: Island of Kaua'i

District	Name of Tract	Area Acres	No. of Lease	Lease Expires	Annual Rental	Estimated Value	Remarks
Kona	Kalaheo	4,045	13	Feb. 1909	$330	$15,000	Mostly grazing and wood land. Valuable fishpond.
	Hanapepe	8,000	53	Dec. 1917	$1,000	$50,000	Good grazing with valuable water rights.
	Waimea	92,462	112	Dec. 1917	$1,400	—	Cane, grazing & c. The rental includes $100 for water, taken from the Waimea River for irrigation purposes.
Waimea	Kekaha Pokii Waiawa Mokihana Milolii Nuololo Mana	—	415	Jan. 1920	$4,000	$175,000	Good cane land about 1,500 acres. Area included in that of Waimea.
Halelea	Hanalei	16,400	—	1906	$1,179	$45,000	About 800 acres cane land. Valuable fishery. Good grazing.
Koolau	Anahola	6,237	44	—	—	—	500 acres cane land & 100 acres rice. About 40 acres rice land under lease for $250 per an. See Lease No. 178.
Puna	Kapaa	7,237		May 1907	$600	$121,000	1,200 acres cane land. 200 acres rice land available.
	Wailua-uka	17,455	1,086	Oct. 1917	$1,200	$175,000	650 acres cane land. Has valuable water rights, several hundred acres cane land in the upper portion might be made available. At Wailua-kai there are several acres of rice land. Good grazing.
	Wailua-kai	2,800	171	July 1921	$800		

Total Area of Crown Lands on Kaua'i: 154,636 Acres

mately $50,000,[21] and it purported to deprive the Queen of any recourse through the courts of the new government.

During the brief reign of the Republic, its Supreme Court interpreted land laws in a manner that favored landlords over the common tenants (makaʻāinana), thus continuing to limit the land rights of Native Hawaiians. In *Dowsett v. Maukeala*,[22] for instance, the Court made it difficult for a commoner to obtain title through adverse possession by presuming that a tenant was residing permissively, thus tolling the time needed to elapse for an adverse possession claim.

Voting in the Republic of Hawaii

The 1894 Constitution of the Republic of Hawaii carefully limited voting rights to ensure that westerners would be able to maintain control of the Islands. Voting was limited (a) to male citizens of the Republic, but those naturalized prior to January 17, 1893, were denied the right to vote unless they were "a native of a country having, or having had, treaty relations with Hawaii,"[23] which was designed "to exclude Japanese and Chinese from the franchise";[24] (b) to males who had received a "certificate of service" from the Minister of Interior for having "rendered substantial service" in the formation or functioning of the Provisional Government;[25] and (c) to males holding a letter of denization.[26] Those in these categories could vote if they were at least twenty years old, but they also had to take an oath that they would "support the Constitution, Laws and Government of the Republic of Hawaii; and will not, either directly or indirectly, encourage or assist in the restoration or establishment

---

21. The 1894 *Crown Lands Report* determined that the annual revenue generated by the Crown Lands for that period was approximately $49,268.75. *Crown Lands Report, supra* note 13, at 9. Another source reported the annual income from the Crown Lands to be $48,769.75. Helena G. Allen, *The Betrayal of Liliʻuokalani,* 318 (1982), citing State doc. #1313; 1384. Queen Liliʻuokalani reported that she did not receive a cent from the Provisional Government or from the Republic. Liliuokalani, *Hawaii's Story by Hawaii's Queen,* 260 (1898, reprinted 1997). Beginning in 1912, the Territorial Government paid Queen Liliʻuokalani an annual pension of $12,000. Allen, *Betrayal, id.,* at 372.

22. *Dowsett v. Maukeala,* 10 Hawaiʻi 166, 1895 WL 1503 (Hawaii Republic, 1895).

23. *Constitution of the Republic of Hawaii,* July 3, 1894, art. 74(1).

24. Daws, *supra* note 4, at 281. Lorrin Thurston explained in his *Handbook on the Annexation of Hawaii,* a pamphlet circulated around 1897 to promote annexation, that "the Chinese and Japanese in Hawaii . . . are not citizens, and by the Constitution of Hawaii, they are not eligible to become citizens; they are aliens in America and aliens in Hawaii; annexation will give them no rights which they do not now possess, either in Hawaii or in the United States." Quoted in Sally Engle Merry, *Colonizing Hawaii: The Cultural Power of Law,* 135 (2000). A report issued in 1898 stated that "[t]here are about 700 Chinese who have been naturalized into the Hawaiian Republic." *Hawaiian Commission Report, supra* note 14, at 3 (1900).

"In December 1893, the Japanese warship *Naniwa* returned to Honolulu Harbor, and in March 1894 Japan formally requested that the Constitution being prepared by the Republic of Hawaii grant Japanese nationals the same voting rights given to other foreign nationals, particularly Americans." Twigg-Smith, *supra* note 4, at 224. This request was rejected "[b]ecause Japanese subjects outnumbered American citizens of the Republic more than ten to one" and because "the Republic also realized that Japanese voting rights probably would preclude Annexation to the United States." *Id.* at 224–25. *See also* Coffman, *supra* note 1, at 192–204.

25. *Constitution of the Republic of Hawaii,* July 3, 1894, arts. 17(2) and 74(1).

26. *Id.,* arts. 19 and 74(1).

of a Monarchical form of Government in the Hawaiian Islands."[27] The Republic awarded its certificate of service and letters of denization to 362 aliens during its brief existence.[28]

The phrasing in Article 74 prohibiting persons from voting if they had become naturalized before 1893 and if they came from a country without a naturalization treaty with Hawai'i excluded most Asians from the electorate. The provision governing naturalization also produced this result, because it limited this procedure to citizens or subjects "of a country having express treaty stipulations with the Republic of Hawaii concerning naturalization"[29] and further required such persons to "be able understandingly to read, write and speak the English language"[30] and to "be able intelligently to explain, in his own words, in the English language, the general meaning and intent of any article or articles of this Constitution."[31]

Voters must have paid their taxes,[32] and, except for those with certificates of service, they were obliged to demonstrate that they could read and write English or Hawaiian.[33] The House of Nobles was renamed the "Senate." To vote for the members of this body, voters had to meet the additional requirement of demonstrating that they owned real property worth $1,500 or personal property worth $3,000 or had an income of $600 for the previous year.[34] To serve in the Senate a person had to own property worth at least $3,000 or have earned $1,200 during the previous year,[35] which made the Senate "a fairly exclusive club."[36] Even to serve in the House of Representatives, one had to own property worth at least $1,000 or have earned at least $600 during the previous year.[37] The President was to be selected by the Legislature (for a six-year term) rather than by popular vote and was not eligible to be reelected for a second consecutive term.[38] The President and the four Cabinet members formed

---

27. *Id.*, arts. 74(1) and 101.

28. Patrick W. Hanifin, "To Dwell on the Earth in Unity: Rice, Arakaki, and the Growth of Citizenship and Voting Rights in Hawaii," 5 *Hawaii Bar Journal,* 15, 29 (2002), citing H. Arai, *Indices to Certificates of Nationality 1846–1854, Denization 1846–1898, Oaths of Loyalty to the Republic from Oahu 1894, and Certificates of Special Rights of Citzenship 1896–1898.*

29. *Constitution of the Republic of Hawaii,* July 3, 1894, art. 18(2)(5).

30. *Id.,* art. 18(2)(3).

31. *Id.,* art. 18(2)(4).

32. *Id.,* art. 74(6).

33. *Id.,* art. 74(7). This section also includes a requirement that voters (unless they had the certificate of service given to those who have supported the Provisional Government) "be able to read and write, with ordinary fluency, any section or sections of the Constitution." This provision was suggested by Lorrin Thurston, who noticed similar language in the 1891 Mississippi Constitution, where it was used for decades to exclude African-Americans from voting. Coffman, *supra* note 1, at 148, 156, 161. It was "designed largely to bar Asiatics from the suffrage." Stevens, *supra* note 5, at 272, citing Donald Rowland, "Orientals and the Suffrage in Hawaii," 27 *Pacific Historical Review.*

34. *Constitution of the Republic of Hawaii,* July 3, 1894, art. 76.

35. *Id.,* art. 56.

36. Twigg-Smith, *supra* note 4, at 237.

37. *Constitution of the Republic of Hawaii,* July 3, 1894, art. 58. Voting for Representatives was according to the cumulative voting system. *Id.,* art. 73.

38. *Id.,* art. 24.

an Executive Council.[39] Cabinet members could be removed from office by the President only with the concurrence of the other three members.[40] A Council of State consisting of five Senators, five Representatives, and five Presidential appointees had the power to take certain actions between legislative sessions.[41]

In the May 2, 1894, election of delegates to the Provisional Government's Constitutional Convention (in which most candidates ran unopposed),[42] 4,477 individuals were registered to vote,[43] but only 745 Native Hawaiians were among those who voted, compared to 14,217 registered voters (of whom 9,931 were Hawaiian) in the last election held by the Kingdom in 1892.[44] Most Hawaiians would not declare an oath to the Provisional Government, and at a meeting attended by about 2,000 on April 9, 1894, those continuing to support the Monarchy agreed to boycott the election for delegates to the Constitutional Convention.[45] In the first election held by the Republic after the 1894 Constitution had been promulgated, on October 29, 1894, 1,917 persons were registered to vote, "of whom 509 were Hawaiians, 466 Americans, 274 British, 362 Portuguese, 175 Germans, and 131 of other nationality."[46]

In the 1896 election, 3,196 persons voted for members of the House of Representatives and 2,017 voted for members of the Senate.[47] Native Hawaiians and part-Hawaiians numbered 39,400 in the 1896 census, constituting 36 percent of the population of 109,010, but only 1,126 of the Hawaiians were willing to take an oath of allegiance to the Republic's Constitution and vote in the 1897 election for the Republic's Legislature,[48] and the total number of registered voters in that election was only 2,687.[49]

Chief Justice A. F. Judd explained that a parliamentary government and suffrage for women would be appropriate for a "civilized and enlightened constituency" but would be "unsafe" in Hawai'i's "heterogeneous" and "polyglot" communities.[50] Attorney General William O. Smith observed that "[t]hese islands are totally unfit for

---

39. *Id.*, art. 21.

40. *Id.*, art. 27.

41. *Id.*, art. 81.

42. Andrade, *supra* note 5, at 141.

43. *Id.;* Liliuokalani, *supra* note 21, at 363.

44. Samuel P. King, "The Federal Courts and the Annexation of Hawaii," 2 *Western Legal History,* 1, 7 (1989); Davianna Pomaika'i McGregor, "Kupa'a I Ka 'Āina: Persistence on the Land," 34 (University of Hawai'i Ph.D. dissertation, December 1989, citing *Government for the Territory of Hawaii,* Report No. 305 to Accompany H.R. 2972, U.S. Cong. House Comm. on Territories, 56th Cong., 1st Sess., February 12, 1900, at 9.

45. Andrade, *supra* note 5, at 139. *See also* Lawrence H. Fuchs, *Hawaii Pono: A Social History,* 32 (1961, reprinted 1983), reporting that "about 2,500 persons" were at this meeting.

46. Andrade, *supra* note 5, at 147, citing *Honolulu Bulletin,* October 10, 1894, and *Pacific Commercial Advertiser,* October 10, 1894.

47. Liliuokalani, *supra* note 21, at 363.

48. *Government for the Territory of Hawaii,* Report No. 305 to Accompany H.R. 2972, U.S. Cong. House Comm. on Territories, 56th Cong., 1st Sess., February 12, 1900, at 9.

49. 1 Native Hawaiians Study Commission, *Report on the Culture, Needs and Concerns of Native Hawaiians,* 307 (report issued pursuant to Pub. L. 96-565, Title III, 1983), citing 31 *Congressional Record,* 6,702 (1898)). The figure of 2,693 registered voters for the 1897 election is used in King, *supra* note 44, at 7.

50. Judd, *supra* note 2, at 55, 57.

an ideal Republic" and asserted that the Government had therefore "to combine an oligarchy with a representative form of government." [51] Lorrin A. Thurston had written in November 1893 that "I favor not less than 5 years for a readjustment and settling down period, before elections take place." [52] Thurston Twigg-Smith, grandson of Lorrin Thurston, wrote subsequently that "[t]he Republic was a hard-nosed form of government, giving up aspects of civil liberties and the universal voting rights its people would secure later under Annexation, to assure its control until an administration sympathetic to Annexation took over the U.S. presidency." [53]

Population Policies of the Republic of Hawaii

During the Republic's few years of existence, immigrant labor was imported into the Islands in huge numbers, because "with annexation imminent, it became necessary to assure the labor supply for a number of years ahead, before immigration restrictions applicable in the United States might be exercised in Hawaii." [54] Between January 1, 1895, and June 1900, 64,284 Japanese were brought to the Islands, of whom 52,457 were adult males, 9,930 were females, and 1,897 were children.[55]

U.S. Acquiescence

On August 15, 1894, President Cleveland informed a delegation representing Queen Lili'uokalani that his earlier efforts to rectify the wrong done to the Kingdom had "failed" and that he had turned "the entire subject to the Congress of the United States." [56] Because, he continued, Congress had "signified that nothing need be done touching American interference with the overthrow of the Government of the Queen," he would not provide any "present or future aid or encouragement . . . to restore any government heretofore existing in the Hawaiian Islands." [57] Tom Coffman has explained that President Cleveland sought expanding markets "in response to America's deepening economic trouble" [58] and that for these reasons Cleveland "abandoned his active, moralistic objections to acquiring territory." [59] Also in 1894, the U.S. Congress enacted the Wilson-Gorman Act, which was a new tariff bill

---

51. Daws, *supra* note 4, at 280, citing Smith to Thurston, February 18, 1894, Minister & Envoys.

52. Twigg-Smith, *supra* note 4, at 232, quoting from a November 19, 1893, letter written by Thurston to Sanford Ballard Dole.

53. *Id.* at 128.

54. Hobbs, *supra* note 16, at 115.

55. *Id.*, referring to the annual files of the Hawaiian Sugar Planters' Association.

56. Letter from President Grover Cleveland to H. A. Widemann, J. A. Cummins, and Samuel Parker, August 15, 1894.

57. *Id.*

58. Coffman, *supra* note 1, at 164, citing William Appleman Williams, *The Tragedy of American Diplomacy,* 31 (1955, reprinted 1988) and William Appleman Williams, *The Roots of the Modern American Empire,* 366 (1969).

59. *Id.* at 165.

"restoring the cane sugar industry of Hawaii to its privileged position of equal treatment with American growers." [60]

Hawaiian Resistance

In January 1895, an effort was undertaken to restore the Queen with military force, but it was suppressed. Queen Lili'uokalani was arrested, tried, and convicted of "misprison of treason," imprisoned in the 'Iolani Palace for eight months and kept under house arrest for another five months.[61] She was forced to abdicate her throne formally in order to protect her supporters from execution and long prison terms.[62] Commissioner James Blount had observed on July 31, 1893, that the Provisional Government "can only rest on the use of military force, possessed of most of the arms in the islands, with a small white population to draw from to strengthen it. Ultimately it will fall without fail. It may preserve its existence for a year or two, but no longer." [63] Because of the support it found in the U.S. Congress, the Government established by "the small white population" proved to be more resilient that Blount had predicted.

---

60. *Id.* at 165, 191.

61. *See generally, Trial of a Queen: 1895 Military Tribunal* (Hawai'i Judicial History Center, 1995).

62. Daws, *supra* note 4, at 281–84; Coffman, *supra* note 1, at 168–77; Andrade, *supra* note 5, at 149–68; Blackman, *supra* note 9, at 142–44; Allen, *supra* note 8, at 321–50 (1982); "Joint Resolution to Acknowledge the 100th Anniversary of the January 17, 1893 Overthrow of the Kingdom of Hawaii," whereas para. 21, Pub. L. 103–150, 107 Stat. 1510 (1993).

63. Letter from Commissioner James Blount to Secretary of State W. C. Gresham (July 31, 1893), in "Blount Report," *supra* note 16, at 164.

18

The 1895 Land Act

 As early as 1872, when Kamehameha V (Lot) was still King, Sanford Ballard Dole (then only twenty-eight years old) had attacked the restrictions that kept the Crown Lands from being freely sold. In a newspaper commentary, he argued that restrictions on distribution of "the Crown lands, inalienable and generally farmed out on long terms," as well as the "prejudice" against selling the Government Lands (which were alienable, but in fact were "mostly farmed out to tenants like the Crown lands") were a "mistaken policy . . . which forms perhaps the greatest obstacle to a comprehensive homestead system of settlement."[1] He specifically argued that the Act of January 3, 1865,[2] which had prohibited the sale of the Crown Lands, should be repealed and that the Crown Lands should be made available to persons seeking homesteads: "As to the Royal Domain, the evident policy to be pursued is to repeal the act of 1865, which made them inalienable, and vest them, with a few proper reservations in the government, to be thrown open as needed to settlers."[3]

Although Dole recognized that such a step "would be at first received in some quarters with extreme disfavor," nonetheless "there is nothing in it inconsistent with intelligent loyalty and patriotism."[4] Such a change in policy might lead to "an increase of the subjects of the Kingdom," and "[t]he 'glory of the King is in the number of his people' not in the number of his acres."[5] He continued to develop these views in the following decades, helping to pass the Homestead Act of 1884,[6] for instance, during

---

1. S. B. Dole, "The Problem of Population and Our Land Policy," *Pacific Commercial Advertiser,* October 26, 1872, at 2, col 2. *See* discussion in 2 Ralph S. Kykendall, *The Hawaiian Kingdom 1854–1874: Twenty Critical Years,* 193 (1953, 4th printing, 1982); Ethel M. Damon, *Sanford Ballard Dole and His Hawaii,* 326–27 (1957). *See also supra* chapter 13, text at note 4.

2. "An Act to Relieve the Royal Domain from Encumbrances, and to Render the Same Inalienable," January 3, 1865, 1 *Sess. Laws of Hawai'i,* 69 (1851–70), discussed *supra* chapter 9.

3. Dole, "Problem," *supra* note 1, at 2. *See also* S. B. Dole, "Systems of Immigration and Settlement," *Pacific Commercial Advertiser,* November 16, 1872, at 2, suggesting that the Kingdom needed "to open suitable tracts of Government and Crown lands to settlers, as it should be needed."

4. Dole, "Problem," *supra* note 1, at 2.

5. *Id.*

6. "An Act to Facilitate the Acquisition and Settlement of Homesteads," August 29, 1884; *see supra* chapter 13, text at notes 12–17.

Sanford Ballard Dole,
April 23, 1926

his first year in the Legislature, and arguing again in 1891 that the best approach for Hawaiʻi would be to promote "the development of a hardy, intelligent, peaceful agricultural population" by "the opening up of public lands to settlers."[7] Twenty-two years later, in 1894, when Dole became President of the "Republic of Hawaii," he finally had an opportunity to implement these youthful ideas.[8]

Sanford Ballard Dole was born in Honolulu in 1844, the son of Daniel and Emily Dole, who had arrived in the Islands from Maine in 1841. Daniel Dole was a missionary who later became the first head of Punahou School.[9] Sanford Ballard Dole attended Williams College in Massachusetts, studied with an attorney in Washington, D.C., for a year, was admitted to the practice of law in Suffolk County, Massachusetts, in 1867, and then returned to the Islands to establish a law practice. He was elected to the Kingdom's Legislature in 1884 and drafted the Homestead Law enacted that year.[10] He was appointed as Associate Justice of the Hawaiʻi Supreme Court in 1886, played a prominent role in the movement that imposed the Bayonet Constitution on King Kalākaua in 1887, and was a key member of the group

---

7. Robert H. Horwitz, Judith B. Finn, Louis A. Vargha, and James W. Ceaser, *Public Land Policy in Hawaii: An Historical Analysis,* 5 (State of Hawaiʻi Legislative Reference Bureau, Rep. No. 5, 1969), quoting from Sanford B. Dole, "The Political Importance of Small Land Holdings in the Hawaiian Islands" (paper presented to the Honolulu Social Science Association, March 23, 1891).

8. As the quotes from the 1872 article indicate, Dole was concerned about the "underpopulation" problem and the inevitable threat to political and social stability if alien immigration continued. *See supra* chapter 15, text at notes 30–35.

9. *See generally* Helena G. Allen, *Sanford Ballard Dole: Hawaii's Only President* (1988); A. Grove Day, *History Makers of Hawaii,* 35–36 (1984).

10. *See supra* chapter 13, text at notes 12–17.

that overthrew the Monarchy in 1893. After serving as President of the Republic of Hawaii from 1894 to 1898, he was appointed Governor of the Territory of Hawai'i by President McKinley and served in that role until 1903. He was appointed a U.S. District Judge for the Territory that year and held that position until 1916. Dole passed away in 1926.

Those who admired Dole emphasized his sincerity, honesty, and public speaking abilities.[11] "He had an easy manner of speech, and his style of debate was described as calm, deliberate, and even magnetic."[12] At times he expressed concern about the labor conditions of the contract workers imported to work on the sugar plantations[13] and took some actions intended to improve the conditions of Native Hawaiians.[14]

Others in the group that overthrew the Kingdom in 1893 and established the Republic in 1894 agreed with Dole's views regarding the opening up of the Crown and Government Lands, and changing the land policies of the Islands became a high priority for the new Government. In contrast, the envoys sent by Queen Lili'uokulani to Washington after the overthrow—the attorney Paul Neumann and Prince David Kawananakoa—sought to promote support for the Queen by arguing that "the revolutionists had stolen the Crown lands."[15]

William D. Alexander, who had become Surveyor-General, wrote in the statement he presented to Commissioner James Blount in July 1893 that some in the 1890 Legislature had promoted the idea "that the vested rights of the reigning Sovereign in the crown lands should be provided for by issuing bonds, the interest upon which should be equal to his annual receipts from said land, and which should expire at his death."[16] This approach would liberate these "valuable lands, embracing about 876,000 acres," which then could be opened "to settlement by industrious farmers of small means." The 1890 Legislature declined to adopt this plan, but Alexander continued to promote the idea after the overthrow, arguing that

> it would seem that, upon the abolition of the office for which the revenues of the Crown Lands were appropriated, the lands would escheat to the Government,

---

11. Horwitz et al., *supra* note 7, at 2.

12. *Id.,* citing "Biography: Sanford B. Dole," MS, Taylor Collection, Public Archives of Hawai'i, Box 1, Document No. 33, at 1.

13. 2 Kuykendall, *supra* note 1, at 189, quoting from speech made by Dole in October 1870 criticizing the contract labor system as one designed to promote "plantation profits," which ignores "the prosperity of the country, the demands of society, [and] the future of the Hawaiian race." *See supra* chapter 15, note 27 and text at notes 34–35.

14. Horwitz et al., *supra* note 7, at 3, referring to "Dole's championship of the cause of native Hawaiians."

15. 3 Ralph S. Kuykendall, *The Hawaiian Kingdom 1874–1893: The Kalakaua Dynasty,* 618 (1967, reprinted 1987).

16. Letter from Surveyor-General W. D. Alexander to Attorney General W. O. Smith, March 31, 1893, delivered to Commissioner James H. Blount, July 18, 1893, reprinted in "Report of Commissioner to the Hawaiian Islands" (hereafter cited as "Blount Report"), originally in H.R. Exec. Doc. No. 47, 53d Cong., 2d Sess., at 199, 201, reprinted in *Foreign Relations of the United States, 1894,* Appendix II, "Affairs in Hawaii" (hereafter cited as "Affairs in Hawaii") at 665, 667 (1895, preservation photocopy 1992).

TABLE 3. Crown Lands available for lease, 1894

Island	District	Name of tract	Acres	Description
Hawaiʻi	Kona	Puʻuwaʻawaʻa	35,000	Very rocky and dry grazing
		Haleohiu	1,000	Rocky and dry grazing
		Waiʻaha	200	Rocky and dry grazing
		Puaʻa	859	Rocky and dry grazing
		Onouli	367	Rocky and dry grazing
	Puna	Olaʻa	47,000	Good agricultural land
		Waiʻākōlea	300	Rocky and dry grazing
		Kaimū	2,000	Rocky and dry grazing
	Hāmākua	Waimanu	5,000	Leap Valley
Oʻahu	Koʻolau	Makawai/Hopekea	1,200	Kula Land
	Ewa	Pouhala	43	Kula Land
Molokaʻi		Malapue	1,200	Rocky and dry grazing
TOTAL			94,169	

and it would then be in order for the Legislature to repeal the act of January 3, 1865, and to use the said lands thenceforth for the purpose of building up a class of industrious and thrifty farmers, owning their lands in fee simple. Such a class is the mainstay of every free country.

As documented in the previous chapter, the Crown Lands were determined in 1894 to consist of 971,463 acres, but only 94,169 of these acres were available for lease, sale, or homestead because most of the lands had been placed under thirty-year leases during the Kalākaua reign. Of these available lands, only the ʻĀina in the Puna District of the Big Island was suitable for agriculture. Table 3 shows the lands unencumbered by leases.[17] Because this acreage was limited, the Provisional Government looked for ideas "to secure surrender from the present holders of large leases by offering such terms as will better pay them than what the income of their lands is at present."[18]

An April 1895 editorial in *Paradise of the Pacific* stated that the lands formerly "known as Crown Lands . . . are very extensive, capable of improvement that would greatly increase their value, and while hitherto the income has been one of the perquisites of royalty, it is now proposed, as rapidly as possible, to divide this vast estate into homesteads."[19] Sanford Ballard Dole wrote to his brother several weeks after he became President of the Republic of Hawaii in July 1894 explaining that the next step to be taken was "to pass a new land law providing for the management and disposition of government lands including Crown Lands. I intend to provide for different

17. Minister of Finance Theo. C. Porter, "Crown Lands Available for Lease, Sale, or Homestead," in "Report of Finance Minister Theo. C. Porter to Commissioner James H. Blount," May 11, 1893, in "Blount Report," *supra* note 16, at 604, 608, in "Affairs in Hawaii," *supra* note 16, at 1076, 1078.

18. Jean Hobbs, *Hawaii: A Pageant of the Soil,* 108 (1935), quoting from *Hawaiian Star,* May 18, 1893, at 5.

19. 8 *Paradise of the Pacific* 4:54 (Frank L. Hoogs, ed., April 1895).

methods of furnishing land to settlers, and to make it well nigh impossible for specu-
lators to get a chance at the public lands." [20]

A year later, on August 14, 1895, President Dole signed the Land Act of 1895,[21]
a comprehensive statute relating to Public Lands, which had been drafted to address
many of his concerns,[22] and which he later called a "great advance on all previous
land legislation." [23] The act explicitly repealed the 1865 Act, thus allowing the Crown
Lands to be sold, and it established a program to encourage homesteading patterned
after American family farming.[24] Lands could be sold only in parcels of 1,000 acres
or less, with no more than 600 acres available for purchase on an installment plan.[25]
General leases on Public Lands could not be longer than twenty-one years, and they
contained a clause allowing the Government to retake possession of the leased land to
promote homesteading settlement.[26] Because the program was open only to citizens,
denizens, and those holding special rights of citizenship,[27] it was intended to benefit
primarily Native Hawaiians and immigrants from the United States and Europe.[28]

The 1895 Land Act formally merged the Crown Lands with the Government
Lands,[29] declared that these "Public Lands" would now be alienable,[30] and thus led
directly to a reduction in the Crown Lands inventory.[31] Utilizing the various pro-

---

20. Helena G. Allen, *The Betrayal of Liliuokalani: Last Queen of Hawaii 1838–1917*, 319–20 (1982),
quoting from S. B. Dole letter to his brother, July 26, 1894, in Dole Collection (Stodieck).

21. The Land Act of 1895, enacted August 14, 1895, was the short title for "An Act Relating to the Public
Lands, and Amending Sections 36, 39, and 40 of the Civil Code, Relating to the Care of Government Lands;
Section 42 of the Civil Code, Chapter 44 of the Laws of 1876, Chapter 5 of the Laws of 1878, and Act 48 of the
Laws of the Provisional Government of the Hawaiian Islands, relating to the Disposition of Government Lands;
Sections 43 and 44 of the Civil Code, relating to the Conveyances of Government Lands; Section 45 of the Civil
Code, relating to Surveys and Maps of Government Lands; Section 46 and 47 of the Civil Code, relating to Land
Agents; and Chapter 87 of the Laws of 1892, relating to Homesteads, and Repealing an Act entitled 'An Act
to Create a Sinking Fund,' approved December 31st, 1864, and an Act Entitled 'An Act to Relieve the Royal
Domain from Encumbrances and to render the same Inalienable, Approved on January 3d, 1865.'" Act 26,
[1895] *Hawai'i Laws* Spec. Sess. 49–83.

22. Horwitz et al., *supra* note 7, at 5, quoting from Sanford B. Dole, "Hawaiian Land Policy," *Hawaiian
Almanac & Annual* (Thomas G. Thrum, compiler and publisher, 1898).

23. *Id.*, quoting from Dole, "Hawaiian Land Policy," *supra* note 22, at 126.

24. *Id.* at 3. Dole preferred "family farming" over plantations worked by aliens. *Id.*

25. Land Act of 1895, § 17; Lawrence H. Fuchs, *Hawaii Pono: A Social History*, 33 (1961, reprinted
1983); Hobbs, *supra* note 18, at 110.

26. *Id.;* Davianna Pomaika'i McGregor, "Kupa'a I Ka 'Āina: Persistence on the Land," 36 (1989)
(unpublished Ph.D. dissertation, Univ. of Hawai'i) (on file in the Hawaiian-Pacific Collection, University of
Hawai'i Library).

27. *See supra* chapter 17, text at notes 23–31.

28. Neil M. Levy, "Native Hawaiian Land Rights," 63 *California Law Review*, 848, 863 n. 115 (1975):
"The constitution [of 1894, arts. 17–18] provided citizenship for only those Orientals born or naturalized in the
Republic of Hawaii. The effect of this naturalization requirement was to exclude most Orientals from home-
steading eligibility."

29. The Land Act of 1895 defined Public Lands to include "all lands heretofore classed as Government
Lands, all lands heretofore classed as Crown lands, and all lands that may hereafter come into the control of the
government by purchase, exchange, escheat, or by the exercise of the right of eminent domain or otherwise."
Laws of Hawai'i 1895, § 445.

30. Land Act of 1895, August 14, 1895, Part I, § 2.

31. As explained above, however, more than 90 percent of the former Crown Lands inventory was not
immediately available to be sold to homesteaders, because it was still subject to thirty-year leases that had been
negotiated during the Kalākaua reign.

TABLE 4. Special Agreements

| | 1896–97 | | | 1898–99 | | |
	No.	Acres	Value	No.	Acres	Value
1st District (Hilo, Puna, Hawaiʻi)	31	2,255	$13,143	15	893.70	$10,497.80
2nd District (Hāmākua, Kohala)	19	1,279	$10,691	31	550.68	$ 3,386.00
3rd District (Kona, Kāʻu)	4	164	$ 3,820	4	184.23	$ 460.25
4th District (Maui, Molokaʻi, Lānaʻi)	16	1,525	$ 6,330	3	251.96	$ 3,045.00
5th District (Oʻahu)	—	—	—	—	—	—
6th District (Kauaʻi)	—	—	—	—	—	—
Total	70	5,223	$33,984	53	1880.57	$17,389.50

grams described below, about 800 individuals obtained title to more than 40,000 acres of these lands between 1895 and 1899.[32] A report in 1900 stated that 9,960 of these acres had come from the Crown Lands, at a valuation of $36,400.[33] To some extent, this act seemed designed to gain support for the Republic from the common (and frequently landless) Hawaiians. It had the effect in some areas of clustering Hawaiians into limited locations and encouraging them to abandon their scattered Kuleana holdings.

The act provided that a three-member Board of Commissioners (the Minister of Interior and two others appointed by the President with the approval of the Cabinet, one of whom was designated "the Agent of Public Lands") would control and manage these lands.[34] Their goal was to distribute as much land as possible, but they were constrained by the long-term leases that remained on most of the best lands, by the lack of access to some of the arable lands that might have been used, for instance, for coffee cultivation, and by their realization that indiscriminate cutting of native forests would lead to erosion and destruction of arable lowlands.[35] The commissioners were empowered to make "special homestead agreements," setting terms of sale, payments, and conditions regarding residence and improvements at their discretion.[36] One commentator observed that these "special homestead agreements" primarily benefited westerners who had cash plus credit.[37] From 1896 to 1899, 123 special agreements were issued affecting about 7,104 acres of land valued at $51,373.05.[38] These transactions are summarized in Table 4.[39]

Under the 1895 Act, qualified citizens were eligible for three separate homestead programs: the Right-of-Purchase Lease, the Cash Freehold, and the 999-Year

32. John H. Bay and Jane vanSchaick, *Analysis of the 999 Year Homestead Lease Program: Current Problems and Possible Solutions,* 12 (1994).
33. "Report of J. F. Brown, Agent of Public Lands" (August 29, 1898), in U.S. Hawaiian Commission, *Report of the Hawaiian Commission,* 46 (1898).
34. Land Act of 1895, August 14, 1895, Part III, § 6.
35. Horwitz et al., *supra* note 7, at 12.
36. *Id.* at 8.
37. Levy, *supra* note 28, at 863 n. 117.
38. Horwitz et al., *supra* note 7, at 9, 13, citing *Report of the Commissioners of Public Lands for 1896–1897* and *1898–1899* respectively.
39. *Id.*

TABLE 5. Right of Purchase Leases

| | 1896–97 | | | 1898–99 | | |
	No.	Acres	Value	No.	Acres	Value
1st District (Hilo, Puna, Hawai'i)	132	6,007	$44,167	87	5,229.24	$38,601.13
2nd District (Hāmākua, Kohala)	78	3,018	$24,426	8	268.25	$2,533.69
3rd District (Kona, Kā'u)	10	429	$1,824	2	377.00	$668.22
4th District (Maui, Moloka'i, Lāna'i)	46	3,907	$10,504	13	1,268.00	$5,451.00
5th District (O'ahu)	—	—	—	—	—	—
6th District (Kaua'i)	—	—	—	—	—	—
Total	266	13,361	$80,921	114	7,228.14	$47,531.64

Homestead Lease.[40] Under the Right-of-Purchase Lease,[41] a lessee obtained a twenty-one-year lease with an annual lease rental based on 8 percent of the appraised land value.[42] At any time after the third year of compliance with home maintenance, residency, and cultivation requirements, the lessee was entitled to receive a government Land Patent signifying fee simple ownership.[43] A total of 380 Right-of-Purchase Leases were entered into from 1896 to 1899 involving 20,589.14 acres valued at $128,452.64.[44] These transactions are summarized in Table 5.[45]

Those individuals who had capital could take advantage of the Cash Freehold program, which made lots available at public auction. Under this installment plan, 25 percent of the purchase price was required as a down payment.[46] After three additional annual payments, a homesteader in compliance with home residence and cultivation requirements was entitled to a Land Patent signifying ownership of the fee simple interest.[47] Some 23 Cash Freehold transactions taking up 783.82 acres (valued at $4,117.54) were entered into from 1896 to 1899.[48] These transactions are summarized in Table 6.[49]

The 999-Year Homestead Lease program was best suited for the Native Hawaiians because it provided homesteads at little cost.[50] The program was available to any "citizen by birth or naturalization and any person who [had] received letters of denization, and any person who has received special rights of citizenship, over eighteen

---

40. Section 19 of the Land Act of 1895 empowered the commissioners to enter into general leases of Public Lands not to exceed twenty-one years.

41. Levy, *supra* note 28, at 863 n. 117, stating that this program was designed for "impoverished potential agricultural entrepreneurs."

42. Land Act of 1895, § 61.

43. *Id.,* § 64.

44. Horwitz et al., *supra* note 7, at 9, 13, citing *Report of the Commissioners of Public Lands for 1896–1897* and *1898–1899* respectively.

45. *Id.*

46. Land Act of 1895, sec. 68.

47. *Id.*

48. Horwitz et al., *supra* note 7, at 9, 13, citing *Report of the Commissioners of Public Lands for 1896–1897* and *1898–1899* respectively.

49. *Id.*

50. Levy, *supra* note 28, at 863. Upon application, a $2 fee was required.

TABLE 6. Cash Freeholds

| | 1896–97 | | | 1898–99 | | |
	No.	Acres	Value	No.	Acres	Value
1st District (Hilo, Puna, Hawaiʻi)	14	564	$3,493	—	—	—
2nd District (Hāmākua, Kohala)	4	144	$ 360	4	67.82	$ 169.54
3rd District (Kona, Kāʻu)	1	8	$ 95	—	—	—
4th District (Maui, Molokaʻi, Lānaʻi)	—	—	—	—	—	—
5th District (Oʻahu)	—	—	—	—	—	—
6th District (Kauaʻi)	—	—	—	—	—	—
Total	19	716	$3,948	4	67.82	$ 169.54

TABLE 7. Homestead Lease Program

| | 1896–97 | | 1898–99 | |
	No.	Acres	No.	Acres
1st District (Hilo, Puna, Hawaiʻi)	—	—	—	—
2nd District (Hāmākua, Kohala)	9	47	—	—
3rd District (Kona, Kāʻu)	29	466	10	228.63
4th District (Maui, Molokaʻi, Lānaʻi)	19	395	40	414.89
5th District (Oʻahu)	10	26	1	2.79
6th District (Kauaʻi)	—	—	—	—
Total	67	934	51	646.31

years of age." [51] To be eligible, an applicant could not be delinquent in taxes, could not already own land in Hawaiʻi (other than wetland taro or rice land), and could not have applied for lands from any other program in the act.[52] An applicant could, however, apply for one lot plus one additional lot of wetland if the wetland was in close proximity.[53]

Successful applicants first received a Certificate of Occupation for a parcel of Public Land. If dwelling, residency, cultivation, and tax requirements were successfully complied with during a six-year probationary period, then a 999-year Homestead Lease with its restrictions could be issued.[54] Lands held under a Certificate of Occupation or under a Homestead Lease plan were subject to taxes as fee simple estates.[55] The Homestead Lease was inalienable and could not be transferred by will, but only according to statutory descent.[56] The acreage under the Homestead Lease program was limited to 45 acres of pastoral-agricultural land, 16 acres of agricultural land, and only 1 acre of wetland requiring considerable water.[57] Approximately 118

---

51. Land Act of 1895, sec. 31.

52. *Id.* An applicant was also ineligible if the spouse owned land (other than 1 acre of wetland) or was an applicant for land under this act. *Id.*

53. *Id.*

54. *Id.,* § 32, 35.

55. *Id.,* § 50.

56. *Id.,* § 43.

57. *Id.,* § 28; *see generally* Hobbs, *supra* note 18, at 111–12.

TABLE 8. Homesteads distributed under the 1895 Land Act

Nationality	Number of Homesteads	Acres
American	103	7,446
Portuguese	130	4,092
Hawaiian (including a "few" persons born in Hawai'i of foreign parents)	223	8,382
British	21	1,359
Russian	10	844
German	17	835
Norwegian	11	586
Japanese	3	186
French	2	189
Italian	1	20
TOTALS	521	24,749

Homestead Lease transactions involving 1,580.31 acres were entered into from 1896 to 1899.[58] These transactions are summarized in Table 7.[59]

According to a chart compiled a few years later by Yale Professor William Fremont Blackman, the various homesteads distributed under the 1895 Land Act went to ethnic groups as shown in Table 8.[60]

Somewhat different figures are found in the 1969 *Report of the Legislative Reference Bureau,* which are apparently based on *Reports of the Commissioners of Public Lands for the Period 1896–97 and 1898–99* and are shown in Table 9.[61]

The annexation of Hawai'i by the United States in 1898 did not immediately affect these homesteading programs. According to a later study,[62] the various programs remained operative until the passage of the Hawaiian Homes Commission Act (HHCA) in 1921,[63] but few homesteads were established under them after 1899.[64] This study reported that between 1895 and 1921, about 750 Certificates of Occupation were issued under the Homestead Lease Program. About 265 were converted to Homestead Leases, but by 1950, only 130–200 Homestead Leases and Certificates of Occupation remained.[65] The factors contributing to the cancellation or

---

58. Horwitz et al., *supra* note 7, at 9, 13, citing *Report of the Commissioners of Public Lands for 1896–1897* and *1898–1899* respectively.

59. *Id.*

60. William Fremont Blackman, *The Making of Hawaii: A Study in Social Evolution,* 163 (1906, reprinted 1977); *see also* Hobbs, *supra* note 18, at 114.

61. Horwitz et al., *supra* note 7, at 11, 14. The chart for 1898–99 did not include the category of Hawaiian-born of non-Hawaiian ancestry, so this group may have been included in the "Hawaiian" category for that period.

62. Bay and vanSchaick, *supra* note 32, at 7.

63. Act of July 9, 1921, 67 Pub. L. 34, 42 Stat. 108 (1921). The background and nature of this statute are discussed *infra* in chapter 22.

64. When the Hawaiian Homes Commission Act was passed, sugarcane lands were eliminated from the inventory available for homesteading. Levy, *supra* note 28, at 865. The general desire for homestead lands, therefore, ceased. *Id.* at 865–66.

65. Bay and vanSchaick, *supra* note 32, at 8.

TABLE 9. Homesteads according to *Report of the Legislative Reference Bureau* (1969)

Nationality	1896–97		1898–99		Total	
	Holdings	Acres	Holdings	Acres	Holdings	Acres
American	79	5,520	60	4,564	139	10,084
Hawaiians	129	3,873	101	2,629	230	6,502
Non-Hawaiians born in Hawai'i	50	3,120	—	—	50	3,120
Portuguese	106	4,144	37	975	143	5,119
British	20	1,256	8	514	28	1,770
Russian	9	794	4	347	13	1,141
German	13	595	9	545	22	1,140
Norwegian	11	586	1	90	12	676
Japanese	2	137	1	48	3	185
French	2	189	—	—	2	189
Swedish			1	111	1	111
Italian	1	20	—	—	1	20
TOTAL	422	20,234	222	9,823	644	30,057

surrender of most of the Certificates of Occupation and Homestead Leases included "[a]bandonment, failure to pay taxes, failure to meet the cultivation or residency requirements, and lessees dying without legal heirs."[66]

The Homestead Lease program was formally discontinued in 1950, and in order to phase out the program, holders of Homestead Leases and Certificates of Occupation were given the right to purchase their fee simple interest at fair market value.[67] About sixty-five to seventy-five holders of Leases and Certificates acquired the fee interest,[68] and the leases remained in effect for those not exercising this option.[69]

In 1994, about forty-six Homestead Leases and five Certificates of Occupation remained,[70] occupying about 167 acres[71] of Ceded Lands (including Crown Lands), with a total assessed land value of almost $14 million.[72] These holdings were located as shown in Table 10.[73]

Because public resources are required to administer the remaining Homestead Leases, some officials have favored a quick phaseout of the program.[74] But many of the remaining leaseholders face financial, legal, and emotional obstacles, frustrating their ability to obtain the fee interest.[75] One suggested solution has been to offer the

66. *Id.*
67. *Id.* at 7.
68. *Id.* at 53.
69. *Id.* at 7.
70. *Id.* at 8.
71. *Id.* at 23.
72. *Id.*
73. Chart taken from *id.* at 23.
74. *Id.* at 71.
75. *Id.* at 72.

TABLE 10. Homestead leases remaining in 1994

Island	No. of leaseholds	Total acreage	Approximate total value assessed
Oʻahu	25	60	$11,689,000
Maui and Molokaʻi	9	48	$717,000
Kauaʻi	12	28	$1,273,000
Hawaiʻi	5	41	$234,000
Total	51	167	$13,948,000

sale of fee simple ownership for a nominal or reduced "leased fee" conversion price, instead of a fair market price, and to provide financial assistance.[76] Although this approach appears to be an enlightened one, it may not be altogether fair to those who paid market value in the past.

The fact that most of the remaining lessees are of Hawaiian ancestry adds to the complexity of this issue.[77] Historically, the Homestead Lease, Right of Purchase Lease, Cash Freehold, and Special Agreement programs established by the Land Act of 1895 reduced the Public Lands, including the Crown Lands inventory. Continued depletion is especially inappropriate now when Native Hawaiians seek to preserve the Ceded Lands as a land base for their emerging sovereign nation. But because these lands have a special link to the individuals and ʻohana who have been living and working on them for many decades, these families appear to have a unique claim to continued occupation and use of the lands.

Summary and Conclusion

It was reported in 1899 by J. F. Brown, Agent of Public Lands for the Republic of Hawaiʻi, that a total of 46,594 acres of Government and Crown Lands had been alienated under the 1895 Land Act by the Republic of Hawaii.[78] As he looked back on the results of the 1895 Land Act in 1898 at the time of annexation, Sanford Ballard Dole stated that "The results have been somewhat disappointing."[79] He expressed regret that "[i]n proportion to their numbers comparatively few Hawaiians have taken up homestead leases or lands under any of the methods provided in the act."[80] The 1896

---

76. *Id.* at 74–76. Another option would be to terminate the fee purchase option first extended in 1950. *Id.* at 79.

77. *Id.* at 24.

78. U.S. Dept. of the Interior and U.S. Dept. of Justice, *From Mauka to Makai: The River of Justice Must Flow Freely,* 53 (Report on the Reconciliation Process between the Federal Government and Native Hawaiians, October 23, 2000), citing *Hawaiian Land Systems and Transactions Thereunder,* Senate Comm. on Foreign Relations, S. Doc. No. 72, 56th Cong., 1st Sess. (1899).

79. Sanford B. Dole, "Hawaiian Public Lands," in *Government for the Territory of Hawaii,* H.R. Rep. No. 305, House Comm. on Territories, 56th Cong., 1st Sess., Appendix I, at 105, 107.

80. *Id.*

census revealed that 57 percent of all the taxable land was controlled by persons of European or American ancestry,[81] who had taken "over most of Hawai'i's land . . . and manipulated the economy for their own profit."[82]

Dole observed that Hawaiians appeared to be much more comfortable with "a communal form" of "land proprietorship" and "have been slow to appreciate the importance to themselves of permanent holdings."[83] Toward the end of his political career, Dole thus seemed to recognize the deep differences in values between the Hawaiians and the westerners who took control of the Islands from them. Dole served as the first Governor of the Territory of Hawai'i for a few years, but in 1903 he left the political arena and became a judge once again.

81. Blackman, *supra* note 60, at 161, citing the 1896 census as reported in "Blount Report," at 77; Sally Engle Merry, *Colonizing Hawaii: The Cultural Power of Law,* 95 (2000), citing Theodore Morgan, *Hawaii: A Century of Economic Change 1778–1876,* at 139 n. 59 (1948).

82. Levy, *supra* note 28, at 858.

83. Dole, "Hawaiian Public Lands," *supra* note 79, at 107.

19

Annexation by the United States (1898)

 The end of the nineteenth and beginning of the twentieth century was a time of turmoil and transition, when perspectives of idealism and limitless progress clashed with the old-fashioned habits of greed, selfishness, great-power competition, and imperialism. The United States had fulfilled its self-image of "Manifest Destiny," had stretched its borders across North America, was emerging as a land of opportunity and innovation, and was becoming more active in world affairs.

In November 1896, William McKinley, a Republican Senator from Ohio, defeated Democrat Grover Cleveland as President, and he took office four months later in March 1897. This transition was followed by the Spanish-American War in 1898, which was the central event in a period of imperialistic expansion by the United States. After the mysterious explosion of the USS *Maine* in Havana harbor, U.S. public sentiment—fanned by a jingoistic press campaign—turned sharply against Spain. Even though Spain agreed to every condition laid down by President McKinley with respect to Cuba, McKinley nonetheless sought and obtained authority from the U.S. Congress to send troops against Spanish land and naval forces in Cuba. After about four months of fighting in the Caribbean and the Philippines, the United States prevailed, and Spain agreed to cede Puerto Rico, Guam, and the Philippines to the United States and to withdraw its forces from Cuba. The United States emerged from this episode as a world power with political and economic interests in distant areas. The annexation of Hawai'i also occurred in 1898 and must be seen as part of this spasm of U.S. global expansion.[1]

---

1. Comprehensive discussions of the facts and issues raised by the U.S. annexation of Hawai'i can be found in, *e.g.,* Tom Coffman, *Nation Within: The Story of America's Annexation of the Nation of Hawai'i* (1998); Rich Budnick, *Stolen Kingdom: An American Conspiracy* (1992); and Thomas J. Osborne, *Annexation Hawaii: Fighting American Imperialism* (published as *Empire Can Wait* in 1981, republished under present title in 1998).

President William McKinley,
June 7, 1898

Earlier Discussions of Annexation

The possibility of U.S. annexation of the Hawaiian Islands was discussed on a periodic and regular basis throughout the nineteenth century. Liholiho (Kamehameha II) was initially reluctant to allow the missionaries who arrived in 1820 to settle in the Islands, because the Mōʻī "worried that the Americans intended to take possession of the islands."[2] Two U.S. warships came to the Islands in 1826 to investigate and enforce debts incurred by Aliʻi to U.S. merchants,[3] and, as disagreements over debts increased in the late 1820s and early 1830s, natives became concerned that the Kingdom might be taken over by the United States.[4] On December 19, 1842, however, U.S. President John Tyler issued a formal message recognizing the "independent existence" of the Kingdom of Hawaiʻi and stating that the United States would oppose "the adoption of an opposite policy by any other power."[5]

---

2. Sally Engle Merry, *Colonizing Hawaii: The Cultural Power of Law,* 61 (2000), citing *Missionary Herald,* 119 (1821).

3. 1 Ralph S. Kuykendall, *The Hawaiian Kingdom 1778–1854: Foundation and Transformation,* 91–92 (1938, reprinted 1989).

4. Samuel M. Kamakau, *Ruling Chiefs of Hawaii,* 285 (1961, revised ed., 1992); *see also* Merry, *supra* note 2, at 77.

5. 1 John Bassett Moore, *A Digest of International Law,* 477 (1906); *see supra* chapter 16, text at notes 21–26.

Theodore Roosevelt surrounded by the "Rough Riders" in the Spanish-American War, 1898

Despite this apparently definitive statement, talk of annexation resurfaced within a few years. Beginning about 1851, Kauikeaouli (Kamehameha III) gave some thought to the idea of annexation by the United States because of his concern about the imperialist designs of the European powers, and he thought annexation by the United States might protect the Monarchy.[6] Representatives of France, in particular, were "menacing" and imposing demands on the Kingdom, leading the Mō'ī and his Privy Council to pass a proclamation on March 10, 1851, placing the Islands provisionally under the protection of the United States.[7] Two of the King's Ministers delivered this document the next day to the U.S. Minister to the Kingdom, Luther Severance,[8] in a sealed envelope with instructions that it was "to be opened and acted

<hr>

6. Merry, *supra* note 2, at 89–90, citing Laura Fish Judd, *Honolulu: Sketches of Life in the Hawaiian Islands from 1828 to 1861*, 218–19 (Dale E. Morgan, ed., 1966); *see generally* 1 Kuykendall, *supra* note 3, at 407–27; Sylvester K. Stevens, *American Expansion in Hawaii 1842–1898*, 54–76 (1945, reissued 1968).

7. W. D. Alexander to James H. Blount, July 18, 1893, in "Report of Commissioner to the Hawaiian Islands," in 27 *Executive Documents of the House of Representatives for the Second Session of the Fifty-Third Congress, 1893–94*, 141, 146 (1895), originally in Executive Document No. 47, 53rd Cong., 2d Sess. (1893) (hereafter cited as "Blount Report").

8. Luther Severance was the founder and editor of the newspaper the *Kennebec Journal* in Augusta, Maine, and was later appointed U.S. Commissioner to the Kingdom of Hawai'i by President Zachary Taylor. Coffman, *supra* note 1, at 58. In the 1850s, James G. Blaine (who served as U.S. Secretary of State in the early 1880s and again under President Benjamin Harrison beginning in 1889) and John L. Stevens were coeditors and proprietors of the *Kennebec Journal*, which had a long record of supporting the annexation of Hawai'i by the United States. *Id.* at 72, 76–77.

upon only in case of an emergency"—that is, an attack by France.[9] Three months later, on June 21, 1851, the Kingdom's Legislature passed a joint resolution confirming that the King should "place the Kingdom under the protection of some friendly state" if France should continue to make its "unjust" demands, which are "clearly . . . contrary to the law of nations and to treaty."[10]

In response to these actions, U.S. Secretary of State Daniel Webster wrote to Minister Severance on July 14, 1851, that the United States "was the first to acknowledge the national existence of the Hawaiian Government, and to treat with it as an independent state," adding that the United States "still desires to see the nationality of the Hawaiian Government maintained, its independent administration of public affairs respected, and its prosperity and reputation increased."[11] Webster wrote that the United States expected other nations—specifically naming France—to act with similar respect for Hawai'i's independence and emphasized that the United States had always had and was destined to continue to have the dominant relationship with the Islands: "The Hawaiian Islands are ten times nearer to the United States than to any of the powers of Europe. Five-sixths of all their commercial intercourse is with the United States, and these considerations . . . have fixed the course which the Government of the United States will pursue in regard to them."[12] Webster's successor as Secretary of State, William L. Marcy, observed in 1853 that Hawai'i would at some point become a protectorate of some foreign power and that, although the United States did not want to accelerate such a process, "the United States would rather acquire their sovereignty than see it transferred to any other power."[13]

This matter came into greater focus in February 1854, when the Mō'ī instructed his Foreign Minister Robert C. Wyllie "to ascertain on what terms a treaty of annexation could be negotiated to be used as a safeguard to meet any sudden danger that might arise."[14] In April 1854, U.S. Minister to Hawai'i David L. Gregg received instructions from Secretary of State Marcy authorizing him to negotiate a treaty of

9. Alexander to Blount, *supra* note 7, at 141.

10. "Joint Resolution," enacted June 21, 1851, approved by the King, August 4, 1851, in "Blount Report," *supra* note 7, at 149.

11. 1 Moore, *supra* note 5, at 480–81 (1906), quoting from Webster to Severance, July 14, 1851, *Foreign Relations 1894,* App. II, 99–101.

12. *Id.* at 481.

13. *Id.* at 482, summarizing a letter from U.S. Secretary of State William L. Marcy to U.S. Minister to Hawai'i David L. Gregg, Sept. 22, 1853. In August 1853, "[n]ineteen of the most respectable and affluent merchants and planters of the islands . . . presented a memorial to the king" arguing that it was in "the true interest of the king and his people to promote annexation to the United States which could be accomplished at this time with greater advantage than at any future period." Merze Tate, "Great Britain and the Sovereignty of Hawaii," 31 *Pacific Historical Review,* 327, 330 (1962) (hereafter cited as Tate, "Great Britain"), citing "Enclosure with Miller to Clarendon," No. 18, Sept. 3, 1853, F.O. 58/76. In December 1853, Marcy inquired of the U.S. Minister in Paris whether France would take any effective action "in case of an attempt on the part of the United States to add these islands to our territorial possessions by negotiation or other peaceable means." Charles Callan Tansill, *Diplomatic Relations Between the United States and Hawaii: 1885–1889,* 10 (Fordham University Historical Series No. 1, 1940), citing Marcy to John Mason, December 16, 1853, *France Instructions,* vol. 15, MS Dept. of State.

14. Alexander to Blount, *supra* note 7, at 144. *See generally* Gavan Daws, *Shoal of Time: A History of the Hawaiian Islands,* 147–53 (1968, reprinted 1974).

annexation.[15] Wyllie and Judge William Little Lee met with Gregg and explained the Kingdom's terms for annexation, which included "guarantying to the Hawaiian subjects all the rights of American citizens, providing for the admission of the Hawaiian Islands as a State into the Union, for a due compensation to the King and chiefs, and a liberal sum for the support of schools."[16] Gregg apparently took these discussions seriously, because at the Fourth of July celebration held in Honolulu in 1854, his oration referred "to the prospect that a new star would soon be added to the constellation of States."[17] It was clear to others, however, that the U.S. President "would never have approved of a treaty admitting the islands into the Union as a *State*."[18] The United States was obsessed during this period with the issue of slavery, and U.S. politicians and the U.S. press speculated that the annexation of Hawai'i would lead to the introduction of slavery into the Islands.[19] Because of this concern, Judge Lee wrote to Wyllie explaining that "it was the wish of the King and chiefs to be admitted as a *State*, and they must not be deceived by any ambiguity in the phraseology of the treaty. They wish by this article to shield the nation from *slavery*, and it would be dishonorable to leave so vital a question involved in any doubt."[20] Crown Prince Alexander Liholiho was unenthusiastic about the annexation proposal but did not publicly oppose it until the death of Kauikeaouli on December 15, 1854, whereupon Alexander Liholiho became Kamehameha IV and formally quashed further discussion of annexation.[21]

The United States expressed interest in annexation again in 1867 (the year the United States purchased Alaska from Russia), when U.S. Secretary of State William H. Seward wrote to the U.S. Minister to the Kingdom Edward M. McCook that "a lawful and peaceful annexation to the United States, with the consent of the people of the Sandwich Islands [Hawai'i], is deemed desirable by this Government; and that if the policy of annexation should really conflict with the policy of reciprocity, annexation is in every case to be preferred."[22] This proposal was raised in 1871 by the U.S. Minister to the Kingdom[23] and in 1873 by U.S. Secretary of State Hamilton Fish.[24]

---

15. 1 Moore, *supra* note 5, at 483, citing Marcy to Gregg (April 4, 1854), *Foreign Relations 1894,* App. II, 121).

16. Alexander to Blount, *supra* note 7, at 144.

17. *Id.*

18. *Id.* at 146, referring to a statement attributable to U.S. Secretary of State William L. Marcy (emphasis in original); 1 Moore, *supra* note 5, at 483, citing *Foreign Relations 1894,* App. II, 121–31; Tansill, *supra* note 13, at 10, explaining that Marcy also opposed the provision in the draft treaty that would have required payments of $300,000 to the Mō'ī and Ali'i.

19. Alexander to Blount, *supra* note 7, at 145, referring to a letter written by Senator Sumner and an article in the *New York Tribune* on July 20, 1854. *See* Merze Tate, "Slavery and Racism as Deterrents to the Annexation of Hawaii, 1854–1855," 47 *Journal of Negro History,* 1 (1962).

20. Alexander to Blount, *supra* note 7, at 145 (emphasis in original). *See also* Merry, *supra* note 2, at 89–90.

21. Alexander to Blount, *supra* note 7, at 146.

22. 1 Moore, *supra* note 5, at 483, quoting from Seward to McCook, September 12, 1867, *Foreign Relations 1894,* App. II, 143; *see generally* Stevens, *supra* note 6, at 95–107.

23. 1 Moore, *supra* note 5, at 484, citing Pierce to Fish, February 25, 1871, *Foreign Relations 1894,* App. II, 17; *see generally* Stevens, *supra* note 6, at 110–11.

24. 1 Moore, *supra* note 5, at 484–85, citing Fish to Pierce, March 25, 1873, *Foreign Relations 1894,* App. II, 19; *see generally* Stevens, *supra* note 6, at 112–13.

After the 1875 Reciprocity Treaty,[25] the economic links between the United States and the Islands became much more profound, and the annexation possibility was discussed regularly. Hawaiian legislator Joseph Nawahi recognized this aspect of the treaty and "spoke eloquently against the Reciprocity treaty . . . saying it would lead to annexation."[26] U.S. Secretary of State James Blaine recognized in 1881 that Hawai'i held a geographic position of unique importance to the United States, similar to that of Panama and Cuba, and that the increase in Asian workers in Hawai'i could affect the stability, independence, and neutrality of the Kingdom. He wrote that if Hawai'i drifted

> from their independent station it must be toward assimilation and identification with the American system, to which they belong by the operation of natural laws and must belong by the operation of political necessity. . . . [I]f, through any cause, the maintenance of such a position of neutrality should be found by Hawaii to be impracticable, this Government would then unhesitatingly meet the altered situation by seeking an avowedly American solution for the grave issues presented.[27]

After the aborted military efforts led by Robert Wilcox in 1889 to reverse the changes imposed by the 1887 Bayonet Constitution and restore the powers of the Crown, and in particular after both Kalākaua and Princess Lili'uokalani appeared to disavow support for the risks he took on their behalf (about a dozen Hawaiians were killed in this effort),[28] it was said that "Wilcox has ever since been an advocate of annexation to the United States, although his idea was to accomplish this end by first establishing an independent republic, and proceeding as in the case of Texas."[29] Wilcox's political ally John E. Bush (who was also part-Hawaiian) "sometimes hinted [in his newspaper] that he would welcome annexation to the United States on the condition that Hawaii should be admitted as a state on an equality with the other states."[30]

The westerners who had imposed the Bayonet Constitution on the Mō'ī were also thinking intensely about annexation, and in 1889–90 they attempted to negotiate a treaty with the United States, sometimes called the Carter-Blaine Treaty (after the Kingdom's Minister to the United States H. A. P. Carter and U.S. Secretary of State James Blaine), which would have established "an American protectorate" over

---

25. "Treaty of Commercial Reciprocity," signed January 30, 1875, entered into force, September 9, 1876, 19 Stat. 625, Treaty Series 161, 8 Charles I. Bevans, *Treaties and Other International Agreements of the United States of America, 1776–1949,* 874; *see supra* chapter 14, text at notes 1–8.

26. Merry, *supra* note 2, at 212; *see supra* chapter 14, text at notes 69–70.

27. 1 Moore, *supra* note 5, at 489, citing Blaine's letter to U.S. Minister to Hawai'i Comly, December 1, 1881, *Foreign Relations 1881,* 635. *See also* Coffman, *supra* note 1, at 100: "Blaine had openly endorsed the idea of taking over Hawaii and stated his willingness to abandon American tradition in order to do so."

28. *See supra* chapter 14, text at notes 73–80.

29. *Statement of Volney V. Ashford* (March 8, 1893), in "Blount Report," *supra* note 7, at 202, 206.

30. 3 Ralph S. Kuykendall, *The Hawaiian Kingdom 1874–1893: The Kalakaua Dynasty,* 509 (1967, reprinted 1987).

Hawai'i "similar to that later created in Cuba by the Platt amendment."[31] This treaty would have "extended complete commercial reciprocity to Hawai'i . . . [and would have] meant that a sugar bounty adopted in the United States would apply equally to Hawai'i."[32] The proposed treaty would also have included "a special clause, now known as the 'bayonet clause,' [that would have] allowed them to call at any time for the landing of the United States troops, to protect them and any cabinet they might uphold."[33] King Kalākaua's trip to California in late 1890 "gave rise to a rash of reports that he was going to arrange for the annexation of his kingdom to the United States," even though "[t]here was, in fact, not a scintilla of truth in the report."[34] In October 1891, President Benjamin Harrison wrote to his Secretary of State James G. Blaine emphasizing "the necessity of maintaining and increasing our hold and influence in the Sandwich Islands."[35]

In short, the idea of annexation by the United States was never very far in the background during the half century before the overthrow. Although this possibility never commanded the support of a majority of the population, it was talked about repeatedly by leaders across the political spectrum. Nonetheless, it cannot be said that annexation was inevitable. The way it eventually occurred was, to say the least, unorthodox, and, according to several commentators, in violation of the procedures required by the U.S. Constitution,[36] and, as later acknowledged by Congress, the end result of a process that violated principles of international law.[37]

The Push for Annexation after the 1893 Overthrow

The westerners who united with U.S. Minister John L. Stevens to overthrow the Monarchy in 1893 wanted the United States to annex the Islands immediately, and their efforts probably would have been successful had not Democrat Grover Cleveland defeated Republican Benjamin Harrison in the 1892 election. Immediately after the January 1893 overthrow, the Provisional Government pushed for the ratification of a treaty to annex Hawai'i to the United States, and on February 14, 1893, such a treaty was signed by Harrison's Secretary of State John W. Foster and the five commissioners sent to Washington by the Provisional Government. But before the U.S. Senate could act, Harrison was replaced by Cleveland, who withdrew the treaty on March 9, 1893, a few days after he was sworn into office.[38]

---

31. Stevens, *supra* note 6, at 197.

32. *Id.*

33. Hawaiian Patriotic League, "Memorial on the Hawaiian Crisis," in "Blount Report," *supra* note 7, at 448, 453.

34. 3 Kuykendall, *supra* note 30, at 471.

35. Coffman, *supra* note 1, at 112, quoting from Harrison to Blaine, October 14, 1891, in *The Correspondence Between Harrison and Blaine, 1882–1893,* 206 (Albert T. Volwiler, ed., 1940).

36. *See infra* this chapter, text at notes 54–62, 83–86.

37. "Joint Resolution to Acknowledge the 100th Anniversary of the January 17, 1893 Overthrow of the Kingdom of Hawaii," Pub. L. 103-150, 107 Stat. 1510 (1993) (hereafter cited as "Apology Resolution").

38. Osborne, *supra* note 1, at 10–16. *See supra* chapter 16, text at notes 85–87.

As explained in chapter 16, when Cleveland took office in March 1893, he sent James H. Blount to Honolulu to investigate the situation. Blount reported that the U.S. Minister and the U.S. military authorities in the Islands had acted improperly and that annexation did not have the support of the residents of the Islands. Cleveland's Secretary of State, W. Q. Gresham,[39] reported that those who supported the overthrow did not claim "that a majority of the people, having the right to vote under the constitution of 1887, ever favored the existing authority [the Provisional Government] or annexation to this or any other country. They earnestly desire that the government of their choice shall be restored and its independence respected."[40] Gresham's letter to President Cleveland went on to report that

> Mr. Blount states that while at Honolulu he did not meet a single annexation-ist who expressed willingness to submit the question to a vote of the people, nor did he talk with one on that subject who did not insist that if the Islands were annexed suffrage should be so restricted as to give complete control to foreigners or whites. Representative annexationists have repeatedly made similar statements to the undersigned.[41]

Among those who provided testimony for this view was Samuel Parker, Queen Lili'uokalani's Foreign Minister, who told Commissioner Blount that 8,500 of the 9,500 voters of Hawaiian ancestry would have voted to support restoration of the Monarchy had an election been held in 1893, and that perhaps one-fourth of the 4,000 non-Hawaiian voters also would have been for restoration of the Queen.[42]

In the United States, a variety of views were also voiced during this period about the benefits and costs of annexation. Those favoring annexation pointed to the historical, cultural, and commercial ties between the United States and Hawai'i, the strategic political and military advantages that possession of Hawai'i would provide to the United States, and, in particular, the need to address the threat posed by the possibility that Japan might try to annex or impose control over Hawai'i, in light of the dramatic increase in Japanese contract-labor immigration to the Islands.[43] Those opposing annexation argued that it would be immoral and imperialistic to absorb a

---

39. Gresham was a Republican who was "begged" by President Cleveland (a Democrat) to be Secretary of State and proceeded, with regard to Hawai'i, "to undo the accomplishments of his bitter political opponent from Indiana, Benjamin Harrison," at least temporarily. 3 Kuykendall, *supra* note 30, at 620.

40. Letter from Secretary of State W. Q. Gresham to President Grover Cleveland, October 18, 1893, in "Blount Report," *supra* note 7, at xvii, xx.

41. *Id.*

42. Interview with Samuel Parker (April 6, 1893), in "Blount Report," *supra* note 7, at 437, 443.

43. William Fremont Blackman, *The Making of Hawaii: A Study of Social Evolution,* 145–46 (1906, reprinted 1977); Lucien Young, *The Boston at Hawaii,* 284–97 (1898); Cushman K. Davis, U.S. Senate Comm. on Foreign Relations, *Annexation of Hawaii: Report to Accompany S.R. 127,* S.Rep. No. 55-681 (2d Sess., March 16, 1898); Robert R. Hitt, U.S. House of Representatives Comm. on Foreign Affairs, *Annexation of the Hawaiian Islands: Report to Accompany H. Res. 259,* H.R. Rep. No. 55-1355 (2d Sess. May 17, 1898) (hereafter cited as *Hitt Report*); Coffman, *supra* note 1, at 205–06, 213–17, 222–24, 245, 249, 258. "Japanese outnumbered Americans in 1897 in Hawaii by roughly twelve to one. The number of Japanese men arriving in a single year often far outnumbered the entire colony of white males." *Id.* at 259.

small and militarily defenseless nation whose residents did not want to be annexed,[44] that it would lead to foreign policy complications, that supporting and defending the Islands would drain U.S. resources, that Hawaiian sugar would imperil the U.S. sugar beet industry,[45] that "the population of the islands, being largely of inferior or Asiatic stock, would add still further elements of discord and debility to a nation already too heterogeneous,"[46] and that establishing a protectorate over Hawai'i would achieve the advantages of annexation without all of its disadvantages.[47]

Those westerners in Hawai'i favoring annexation worked to counter the opposition, both in the Islands and in the United States. On March 21, 1893, they transformed the Annexation Club, which had been "a closely held, small, secret group"[48] prior to the overthrow,[49] into an inclusive and public body with branches throughout the Islands.[50] By September 30, 1893, it was claiming a membership of 6,596 individuals, of whom 1,449 were reported to be American, 2,386 Portuguese, 1,671 Hawaiian, and 1,090 of other ancestry.[51] These numbers apparently resulted, at least in part, because "many plantation laborers and native officials were influenced rather by persuasion and threats than by annexationist sympathies in joining this club."[52] In early 1894, the Annexation Club transformed itself once again, this time into the American Union Party.[53]

Expansionism under President McKinley

The 1897–98 annexation process was contentious and controversial, because deep divisions remained regarding the propriety of the U.S. role in the overthrow and the appropriateness of the annexation. A new annexation treaty between the United States and the Republic of Hawaii was concluded on June 16, 1897, three months after McKinley took office,[54] but it was never approved by the U.S. Senate and its sup-

---

44. The *New York Times* had written an editorial in 1893 arguing that under the principles of democracy embraced by the United States, the inhabitants of the Hawaiian Islands had the right to determine their own political destiny. Editorial, "To Convey a Stolen Kingdom," *New York Times,* July 28, 1893, at 4.

45. Blackman, *supra* note 43, at 146–47.

46. *Id.* at 147.

47. *Id.* at 147; Melody K. MacKenzie, "Historical Background," in *Native Hawaiian Rights Handbook,* 14 (Melody Kapilialoha MacKenzie, ed., 1991); 2 Native Hawaiians Study Commission, *Report on the Culture, Needs and Concerns of Native Hawaiians,* 102–03 (Report issued pursuant to Pub. L. 96-565, Title III, 1983).

48. Thurston Twigg-Smith, *Hawaiian Sovereignty: Do the Facts Matter?* 85 (1998).

49. *See supra* chapter 16, note 14.

50. Blackman, *supra* note 43, at 144.

51. *Id.*

52. *Id.*

53. *Id.*

54. In his message promoting this treaty, President McKinley argued that it was designed to formalize a union that was "the inevitable consequence of the relation steadfastly maintained with that mid-Pacific domain for three-quarters of a century . . . thus realizing a purpose held by the Hawaiian people and proclaimed by successive Hawaiian governments through some seventy years of their virtual dependence upon the benevolent protection of the United States." 1 Moore, *supra* note 5, at 503, quoting from Senate Exhibit 5, 5th Cong., 1st Sess.

porters concluded by March 1898 that they would not be able to assemble the two-thirds majority necessary for ratification.[55] "After much debate and many delays, the chances of the treaty receiving a two-thirds majority in the Senate appeared slim."[56]

The 1898 Newlands Resolution

With the coming of the Spanish-American War in 1898, particularly after the U.S. Navy's victory in Manila on May 1, 1898, the military advantages of annexing Hawai'i came into clearer focus. Even though the United States had previously acquired rights to Pearl Harbor,[57] annexationists in the United States argued that those rights might be abrogated and that only annexation would secure the U.S. interests.[58] On May 4, 1898, nine days after fighting commenced in the Spanish-American War, Representative Francis G. Newlands of Nevada introduced in the House of Representatives a joint resolution to annex the Hawaiian Islands to the United States, seeking to obtain approval through the vote of a simple majority in both the House and the Senate. Despite arguments challenging the constitutionality of acquiring Hawai'i by a legislative act that would usurp the treaty powers of the Senate, the House approved the Newlands Resolution by a vote of 209 to 91 on June 15, 1898.[59] Three weeks later, on July 6 (after a series of secret debates),[60] while the four-month Spanish-American War was still flaring, the Senate passed this joint resolution by a vote of 42 to 21, with 26 abstentions.[61] President McKinley signed the annexation resolution into law the following day, July 7, 1898.[62]

Opposition by the Native Hawaiian People

Throughout this process, Native Hawaiians offered virtually no support to the Provisional Government, to the Republic of Hawaii, or for annexation, because their loyalty remained with Queen Lili'uokalani.[63] The deposed Queen and the Hawaiian Patriotic League, representing the Native Hawaiians, petitioned the United States for

---

55. 1 Native Hawaiians Study Commission, *Report on the Culture, Needs and Concerns of Native Hawaiians*, 301 (Report issued pursuant to Pub. L. 96-565, Title III, 1983); Julius W. Pratt, *Expansionists of 1898: The Acquisition of Hawaii and the Spanish Islands*, 225 (1936).

56. 1 Native Hawaiians Study Commission, *supra* note 55, at 300.

57. *See supra* chapter 14, text at notes 46–70.

58. MacKenzie, "Historical Background," *supra* note 47, at 14, citing 55th Cong., 2d sess. *Congressional Record*, 5982 (June 15, 1898); Appendix at 669–70 (June 13, 1898).

59. 31 *Congressional Record*, 6018 (1898); 2 Native Hawaiians Study Commission, *supra* note 47, at 105.

60. Associated Press, "Secret Debate on U.S. Seizure of Hawaii Revealed," *Honolulu Star-Bulletin*, February 1, 1969, A-1.

61. 31 *Congressional Record*, 6712 (1898).

62. "Joint Resolution to Provide for Annexing the Hawaiian Islands to the United States," 30 Stat. 750 (1898).

63. *See generally* Coffman, *supra* note 1, at 235–44. The efforts of Native Hawaiians and Queen Lili'uokalani to oppose annexation are described in detail in Noenoe K. Silva, *Aloha Betrayed: Native Hawaiian Resistance to American Colonialism*, 123–203 (2004, reprinted 2005).

restoration of the Monarchy, but this petition was not acted upon. In January 1895, a group of Lili'uokalani's supporters attempted to restore her to power militarily, but rumors of the planned attack had made their way through Honolulu and the westerners were able to intercept the weapons and quell the uprising.[64] After this aborted attempt, Lili'uokalani was arrested along with two hundred supporters, trials were held before a military commission in a martial law context, and she was forced to abdicate her throne and pledge allegiance to the Republic of Hawaii in order to protect the others.[65]

After McKinley's election in 1896, when the pressure toward annexation increased once again, Native Hawaiians mounted a campaign in opposition and conducted a petition drive in which some 21,000 people (98 percent of whom were Native Hawaiians) registered their views against annexation.[66] This effort was coordinated by three native groups—Hui Aloha 'Āina, Hui Kālai'āina, and the Women's Patriotic League—whose members traveled throughout the Islands identifying local representatives to collect signatures.[67] On October 8, 1897, a rally against annexation was held in Honolulu attended by a crowd estimated to have been between 800 and 2,000 by the pro-annexation *Pacific Commercial Advertiser* and to have been between 4,000 and 5,000 by the anti-annexation *Ke Aloha 'Āina.*[68] Four leaders of the petition drive left Hawai'i on November 20, 1897, to take the 556 pages of their documents to Washington.[69] These signed pages were described as a "monster petition" in the *Congressional Record*[70] and elsewhere,[71] but ultimately they did not achieve the desired goal of derailing the momentum toward annexation. Lorrin Thurston tried to discredit the petitions, noting that many signatures were of women (who could not vote) and almost 5,000 were of persons between fourteen and twenty years of age (who were also ineligible to vote).[72] His efforts to counter the petitions could not undercut their value as evidence "that Native Hawaiians actively and continuously opposed annexation, and that they had not become any more friendly to the idea the longer they had lived with it."[73] Lili'uokalani spent much of her time in 1897

---

64. Ralph S. Kuykendall, *Hawaii: A History,* 185 (1948); 1 Moore, *supra* note 5, at 502.

65. Kuykendall, *History, supra* note 64, at 185–86; Liliuokalani, *Hawaii's Story by Hawaii's Queen,* 262–99 (1898, reprinted 1997).

66. Dan Nakaso, "Anti-Annexation Petition Rings Clear," *Honolulu Advertiser,* August 5, 1998, at 1.

67. Coffman, *supra* note 1, at 277.

68. *Id.*

69. *Id.* at 279–80.

70. *Id.* at 280.

71. Another source has referred to "the so-called 'monster petition' of 1897 signed by approximately 29,000 native Hawaiians protesting annexation by the United States" and has explained that although a "subsequent report indicated that many names on it were fraudulent," "[a] large portion of the 29,000 names on the list remained . . . and they represented the vast majority of the 31,000 'native Hawaiians' living on the islands." 1 Native Hawaiians Study Commission, *supra* note 55, at 307 (1983), citing 31 *Congressional Record* 6702, 5787 (1898) and S. Rep. No. 55-681, at 43 (1898).

72. Coffman, *supra* note 1, at 280–81: "The implication was that the reader should discount the opinions of minors who were not voters, which was a curious line of attack because it ignored the fact that adult Hawaiians had been effectively disenfranchised."

73. *Id.* at 281.

and 1898 in the United States arguing against annexation,[74] and her efforts—along with the petitions—appear to have had the effect of blocking ratification of the 1897 treaty. Two decades later, Prince Jonah Kūhiō Kalanianaʻole explained that Native Hawaiians "did not want to be annexed to this country [the United States], and it was through the connivance of this country, through the help of the American minister that we became a part of this country."[75]

During this period, Japan also opposed the U.S. annexation of Hawaiʻi, arguing in late 1897 that "the maintenance of the status quo in Hawaii was essential to the good understanding of the powers having interests in the Pacific" and that the rights and claims of Japanese subjects residing and working in Hawaiʻi might be jeopardized (adding also that it entertained no designs itself to the Islands).[76] This expression of Japanese concern was followed by U.S. assurances to the Japanese government that Japanese subjects would be treated fairly and without discrimination in an annexed Hawaiʻi.[77] In December 1897, "Japan withdrew its protest against annexation and ultimately settled its difficulties with the Republic [of Hawaiʻi] in return for an indemnity of $75,000, after Washington had exerted pressure to end the disagreement prior to annexation."[78]

During the debate on the Newlands Resolution, Senator Augustus O. Bacon of Georgia (who opposed annexation) introduced an amendment requiring a plebiscite open to all adult males, but this initiative was rejected by a vote of 42 nays to 20 yeas, with 27 abstentions, because it was clear from the vast numbers of Native Hawaiians who signed opposing petitions that the vote would go against annexation.[79] "Congressional debate on annexation is filled with comments to the effect that it was known that most, if not all, native Hawaiians opposed annexation."[80] After Congress' passage of the Newlands Resolution, "[t]he natives were desperately gloomy."[81] Princess Kaʻiulani had written to her aunt (Queen Liliʻuokalani) "that she had never seen her people in worse condition."[82]

---

74. Helena G. Allen, *The Betrayal of Liliuokalani: Last Queen of Hawaii 1838–1917,* 361 (1982); Coffman, *supra* note 1, at 263–71, 284.

75. "Hawaiian Homes Commission Act, 1920, Hearings on H.R. 13500 before the Senate Comm. on Territories," 66th Cong., 3rd Sess., 137 (December 14, 1920): Statement of Prince Jonah Kalanianaʻole, Delegate, Territory of Hawaiʻi.

76. 1 Moore, *supra* note 5, at 504; Stevens, *supra* note 6, at 287.

77. 1 Moore, *supra* note 5, at 505–09. Great Britain did not issue "a single protest" or even ask an "annoying question" at the time of the 1898 annexation, apparently because of "the growing identity of interests between her and the United States." Tate, "Great Britain," *supra* note 13, at 348.

78. Stevens, *supra* note 6, at 288.

79. Osborne, *supra* note 1, at 114, 159 n. 17, citing 31 *Congressional Record,* 6709–10 (July 6, 1898). *See* Twigg-Smith, *supra* note 48, at 235–38, defending the decision to deny the Hawaiian People the opportunity to vote on annexation.

80. 1 Native Hawaiians Study Commission, *supra* note 55, at 307–08, citing 31 *Congressional Record,* 6014, 6337, 6404, and 6469 (1898).

81. Allen, *supra* note 74, at 361.

82. *Id.* at 362.

Annexation by Joint Resolution

During the debates over annexation in the 1890s, many argued that territory could not be acquired without a treaty[83] and questioned the legitimacy under U.S. constitutional law of the method by which the United States acquired Hawai'i, which remains a matter of substantial dispute even today.[84] Among the opponents of annexation was University of Michigan Law Professor Thomas M. Cooley, author of one of the leading constitutional law treatises of the time. Writing in 1893 with regard to the first proposed annexation treaty, Cooley argued that the rebels running the Provisional Government did not have the authority to convey the Hawaiian Islands to the United States and that the United States did not have the authority under its own Constitution to accept territory that would be an "outlying colony" rather than land area that was destined to become a state in the Union.[85] When the Newlands Resolution was being debated in 1898, Georgia Senator Augustus O. Bacon argued that the U.S. Constitution did not permit the acquisition of territory through joint resolution and would allow it only through a consensual treaty between nations.[86]

Special Recognition Given to the Public Lands

The opening "whereas" clause of the Joint Resolution declared that the Republic of Hawaii had agreed to cede "absolutely and without reserve" all rights of sovereignty to the United States and also to cede and transfer to the United States "the absolute

---

83. See MacKenzie, "Historical Background," *supra* note 47, at 15, 24 n. 100.

84. See, e.g., Douglas W. Kmiec, "Legal Issues Raised by Proposed Presidential Proclamation to Extend the Territorial Sea," 1 *Territorial Sea Journal* 1, 20–21 (1990), stating that whether the awkward manner in which Hawai'i was annexed "demonstrates the constitutional power of Congress to acquire territory is certainly questionable" and that "[i]t is therefore unclear which constitutional power Congress exercised when it acquired Hawaii by joint resolution") (Professor Kmiec was Assistant Attorney General in the Office of Legal Counsel of the U.S. Justice Department when he wrote this memorandum, which was originally submitted on October 4, 1988).

85. Thomas M. Cooley, "Grave Obstacles to Hawaiian Annexation," 15 *The Forum*, 389, 392 (1893).

86. Jennifer M. L. Chock, "One Hundred Years of Illegitimacy: International Legal Analysis of the Illegal Overthrow of the Hawaiian Monarchy, Hawai'i's Annexation, and Possible Reparations," 17 *University of Hawai'i Law Review*, 463, 492–93 (1995), citing 31 *Congressional Record*, 6138, 6149, 6516, 6518 (1898), and also discussing the opposition of other Senators.

A constitutional law treatise written some years later said that "[t]he constitutionality of the annexation of Hawaii, by a simple legislative act, was strenuously contested at the time both in Congress and by the press. The right to annex by treaty was not denied, but it was denied that this might be done by a simple legislative act." 1 W. Willoughby, *The Constitutional Law of the United States*, §239, at 427 (2d ed., 1929), quoted in Kmiec, *supra* note 84, at 20. This issue has also been raised regarding the annexation of Texas in 1846. *See, e.g.,* Ralph H. Brock, "'The Republic of Texas Is No More': An Answer to the Claim that Texas Was Unconstitutionally Annexed to the United States," 28 *Texas Tech Law Review*, 679, 724–34 (1997). The U.S. Supreme Court gave tacit recognition to the legitimacy of the annexations of Texas and Hawai'i by joint resolution, when it said in *De Lima v. Bidwell*, 182 U.S. 1, 196 (1901), that "territory thus acquired [by conquest or treaty] is acquired as absolutely as if the annexation were made, as in the case of Texas and Hawaii, by an act of Congress." *See also Texas v. White*, 74 U.S. (7 Wall.) 700 (1868), stating that Texas had been properly admitted as a state in the United States.

fee and ownership of all public, Government or Crown lands, public buildings or edifices, ports, harbors, military equipment, and all other public property of every kind." About 1.75 million acres of the former Crown and Government Lands,[87] estimated to be worth $5.5 million at the time,[88] were thus "ceded" to the United States.

The second operative paragraph of the Resolution recognized that Hawai'i's Public Lands were unique and declared that federal public land policies would not be applicable to them: "The existing laws of the United States relative to public lands shall not apply to such lands in the Hawaiian Islands, but the Congress of the United States shall enact special laws for their management and disposition." Although revenues from other federal lands are normally put into the general federal fund, the Joint Resolution required that revenues from Hawai'i's Public Lands be put into a separate fund for the "inhabitants of the Hawaiian Islands for educational and other purposes."[89] This provision recognized the unique legal status of these lands, the special rights of the Native Hawaiian People to these lands and their revenues, and the continuing obligations of the United States toward Native Hawaiians, which have also been acknowledged by Congress in the 1900 Organic Act,[90] in the Hawai-

87. The figures used at the time varied from 1,744,713 to 1,782,500. U.S. Hawaiian Commission, *Report of the Hawaiian Commission,* 45, 51 (appendix 1, 1898).

88. Blackman, *supra* note 43, at 164. But see Lorrin Thurston, *A Handbook of the Annexation of Hawaii,* 20 (circa 1897), estimating the amount of land at 1,740,000 acres, valued at $4,389,550 in 1894 (hereafter cited as Thurston, *Handbook*). This lower figure is also found in *Hitt Report, supra* note 43, at 43.

89. The 1898 Newlands Resolution and the 1900 Organic Act did not "identify Native Hawaiians as a separate political entity, for to do so would have been inconsistent with the overall policy of destroying indigenous political sovereignty." Gavin Clarkson, "Not Because They Are Brown, But Because of Ea: Why the Good Guys Lost in *Rice v. Cayetano,* Why They Didn't Have to Lose," 7 *Michigan Journal of Race & Law,* 317, 326 (2002). But U.S. policy has changed and now recognizes the importance of supporting the separate political status of native communities; see, e.g., "President Nixon's Special Message to Congress on Indian Affairs of July 8, 1970," [1970] Public Papers 564 (Richard M. Nixon), and the references to "inhabitants" in the 1898 Newlands Resolution and the 1900 Organic Act are now seen to have recognized the special political status of Native Hawaiians. *See infra* chapter 20, text at note 18, referring to the 1982 Attorney General letter stating that the reference to "inhabitants" was meant to refer to "the indigenous population." Any ambiguity concerning the term "inhabitants" has been cleared up in the "Apology Resolution," *supra* note 37, whereas clause 25, where the Congress referred only to the "Native Hawaiian people" when it recognized that the "crown, government and public lands" were ceded to the United States "without the consent of or compensation to the Native Hawaiian people of Hawaii or their sovereign government." *See also Expressing the Policy of the United States Regarding the United States Relationship with Native Hawaiians and to Provide a Process for the Recognition by the United States of the Native Hawaiian Governing Entity, and for Other Purposes,* Senate Comm. on Indian Affairs, S. Rpt. No. 107-66, at 12 (2001): "Commencing with the Joint Resolution for Annexation, the United States has repeatedly recognized that, as a result of the above-recited history, it has a special relationship with the Native Hawaiian people and a trust obligation with respect to the public lands of Hawaii." "Just as it had with regard to the Pueblo, Navajo, and California Indians after the war with Mexico and the subsequent treaty of Guadalupe-Hidalgo, the United States also inherited a trust responsibility with regard to Native Hawaiians at the moment of annexation." Clarkson, *id.,* at 328. An 1899 opinion of the United States Attorney General interpreted this provision as subjecting the Public Lands to "a special trust, limiting the revenue from or proceeds of the same to the uses of the inhabitants of the Hawaiian Islands for educational and other purposes." 22 Op. Att'y Gen. 574 (1899).

90. "Act of April 30, 1900," §73(e), 31 Stat. 141 (1900): "All funds arising from the sale or lease or other disposal of public land shall be appropriated by the laws of the government of the Territory of Hawaii and applied to such uses and purposes for the benefit of the inhabitants of the Territory of Hawaii as are consistent with the joint resolution of annexation, approved July 7, 1898."

ian Homes Commission Act,[91] in the 1959 Admission Act,[92] and more recently in the 1993 "Apology Resolution."[93]

Article IV of the Joint Resolution declared that "The public debt of the Republic of Hawaii . . . including the amount due to depositors in the Hawaiian Postal Savings Bank, [was] assumed by the . . . United States; but the liability in this regard shall in no case exceed $4,000,000." This assumption of the public debt of the Republic of Hawai'i did not constitute compensation for the Ceded Lands. In his *Handbook of the Annexation of Hawaii,* Lorrin Thurston responded to the objection that "under the proposed treaty of annexation, the United States assumes the Hawaiian public debt without receiving in return the means or property with which to pay it."[94] Thurston stated that the net debt of the Republic was approximately $3,900,000, and that the Republic's saleable property was about $7,938,000, and thus that the United States would be left with a net profit of approximately $4,000,000.[95] The United States gained substantial assets in this transaction, and the 1993 "Apology Resolution" acknowledged that "1,800,000 acres of crown, government and public lands of the Kingdom of Hawaii" were ceded without "the consent of or compensation to the Native Hawaiian people of Hawaii or their sovereign government."[96]

The 1900 Organic Act

Congress's adoption of the Newlands Resolution in 1898 was followed in 1900 by its enactment of Hawai'i's Organic Act,[97] signed by President McKinley on April 30, 1900, which established a government for the Territory of Hawai'i. This enactment defined the political structure and powers of the territorial government and its relationship to the United States, again without any participation or approval of the Hawaiian People or any compensation to them.[98]

The Organic Act confirmed cession of the former Crown and Government Lands to the United States and authorized the Territory of Hawai'i to administer these lands. Section 91 of the Organic Act stated that

> except as otherwise provided, the public property ceded and transferred to the
> United States by the Republic of Hawaii under the joint resolution of annexa-
> tion . . . shall be and remain in the possession, use, and control of the government

91. See discussion *infra* in chapter 22; *see also* discussion in Melody K. MacKenzie, "The Ceded Lands Trust," in *Native Hawaiian Rights Handbook,* 26–42 (Melody Kapilialoha MacKenzie, ed., 1991).

92. "Admission Act of March 18, 1959," Pub. L. No. 86-3, 73 Stat. 4 (1959).

93. "Apology Resolution," *supra* note 37.

94. Thurston, *Handbook, supra* note 88, at 38.

95. *Id.* Thurston added that this excess did not include the profit from sources such as customs, rents, and post office revenues. *Id.* These figures were also published in *Hitt Report, supra* note 43, at 59.

96. "Apology Resolution," *supra* note 37.

97. "Organic Act of April 30, 1900," ch. 339, 31 Stat. 141 (1900).

98. "Apology Resolution," *supra* note 37, whereas para. 30.

of the Territory of Hawaii, and shall be maintained, managed, and cared for by it, at its own expense, until otherwise provided for by Congress, or taken for the uses and purposes of the United States by direction of the President or of the governor of Hawaii.[99]

Section 99 of the Organic Act followed the language in Article 95 of the Republic's 1894 Constitution and asserted that the Public Lands (including the Crown Lands) could be sold and that Queen Lili'uokalani no longer had any legal claim to the Crown Lands:

> [T]he portion of the public domain heretofore known as Crown Land is hereby declared to have been, on the twelfth day of August, eighteen hundred and ninety-eight, and prior thereto, the property of the Hawaiian government, and to be *free and clear from any trust of or concerning the same,* and from all claim of any nature whatsoever, upon the rents, issues, and profits thereof. *It shall be subject to alienation* and other uses as may be provided by law.[100]

Section 73(4)(e) reaffirmed, however, that the Public Lands were impressed with a "trust" status under the federal government's ownership: "All funds arising from the Territory's sale or lease or other disposal of public land shall be . . . applied to such uses and purposes for the benefit of the inhabitants of the Territory of Hawaii as are consistent with the joint resolution of annexation."

Between annexation and statehood in 1959, despite the existing fiduciary duty between the United States and the "inhabitants" of the Territory, the federal government under provisions of the Organic Act "set aside" large parcels of land for defense purposes,[101] and the Territory of Hawai'i exercised its administrative control and disposed of some of the Public or Ceded Lands, without providing any direct benefits to the Native Hawaiian People.[102]

---

99. "Organic Act," *supra* note 97, sec. 91.

100. *Id.,* sec. 99 (emphasis added).

101. Robert H. Horowitz, Judith B. Finn, Louis A. Vargha, and James W. Ceaser, *Public Land Policy in Hawaii: An Historical Analysis,* 20 (State of Hawai'i Legislative Reference Bureau Report No. 5, 1969).

102. *See infra* chapter 20.

20

The Crown Lands during the
Territorial Period (1898–1959)

How Much ʻĀina Was Actually "Ceded" to the United States?

In the documents written around the time of annexation, the exact acreage of the Crown and Government Lands "ceded" to the United States varied, and modern authors tend to report that "about 1,750,000 acres" or "approximately 1,800,000" acres were transferred.[1] In a report written for the House of Representatives Committee on Territories in February 1900, the figure used was 1,751,400 acres, of which 31,346 acres were in "lots taken up, but not yet patented," leaving 1,720,055 acres.[2] These ʻĀina constituted almost half of the 4,112,000 acres in the eight main Hawaiian Islands.[3] And most of this land was leased; in 1898, 1,384,903 acres were leased to sixty-five corporations and individuals.[4]

A recent report of the Interior and Justice Departments has pointed out that another 254,418.10 acres of "emerged and submerged lands of the Northwestern Hawaiian Islands" were also "ceded" to the United States.[5] The land area of the Northwestern Hawaiian Islands constitutes only 5.2 square miles (about 13.2 square

---

1. *See, e.g.,* Robert H. Horwitz, Judith B. Finn, Louis A. Vargha, and James W. Ceaser, *Public Land Policy in Hawaii: An Historical Analysis,* 63 (State of Hawaii Legislative Reference Bureau Report No. 5, 1969); "Joint Resolution to Acknowledge the 100th Anniversary of the January 17, 1893 Overthrow of the Kingdom of Hawaii," whereas clause 25, Pub. L. 103-150, 107 Stat. 1510 (1993); *Rice v. Cayetano,* 146 F.3d 1075, 1077 (9th Cir. 1998), *rev'd on other grounds,* 528 U.S. 495 (2000).

2. *Government for the Territory of Hawaii,* House Comm. on Territories, Rpt. No. 305, 56th Cong., 1st Sess., at 16 (1900).

3. Dept. of Business and Economic Development, *State of Hawaii Data Book: A Statistical Abstract,* 198 (1987). On the next page, the same document gives the total acreage of the state (excluding the Northwestern Hawaiian Islands) as 4,141,300.

4. Horwitz et al., *supra* note 1, at 137.

5. U.S. Dept. of the Interior and U.S. Dept. of Justice, *From Mauka to Makai: The River of Justice Must Flow Freely,* 30 n.3 (Report on the Reconciliation Process between the Federal Government and Native Hawaiians, October 23, 2000) (hereafter cited as *Mauka to Makai*).

kilometers or about 3,262 acres),[6] so most of these additional acres are submerged lands. It has been recognized that "all submerged lands surrounding each [Hawaiian] island to one marine league seaward (three miles)" are included in the Public Land Trust,[7] and if the acreage of the submerged lands within 3 nautical miles of the eight main islands were included the resulting figure would be still larger. Lands that are newly created, either through lava flows that create land extensions or through erosion that creates new submerged lands, have also been deemed to be part of the "ceded lands" and the Public Land Trust, because the Republic of Hawaii ceded territory that "may hereafter be added to the Republic" as well as presently existing public land.[8]

The Ceded Lands Have Been Held in Trust since 1898

The language in the Newlands Resolution,[9] enacted by Congress in 1898 to formalize the annexation of Hawai'i, described the lands and properties being transferred as "absolute fee and ownership of all public, Government or Crown lands, public buildings or edifices, ports, harbors, military equipment, and all other public property of every kind and description belonging to the Government of the Hawaiian Islands, together with every right and appurtenance thereunto appertaining."[10] But it was clear to all that these lands were not properties that could be freely disposed of, because of their special history and meaning. "At the time of annexation, the United States implicitly recognized the unique nature of the Government and Crown Lands."[11] These lands were not to be merged with other public lands of the United States, but rather, "[t]he existing laws of the United States relative to public lands shall not apply to such land in the Hawaiian Islands; but the Congress of the United States shall enact special laws for their management and disposition."[12] The 1898 Resolution went on to say "that all revenue from or proceeds of the same, except as regards such part thereof as may be used or occupied for the civil, military, or naval purposes of the United States, or may be assigned for the use of the local government, shall be used solely for the benefit of the inhabitants of the Hawaiian Islands for

6. Jon M. Van Dyke, Joseph R. Morgan, and Jonathan Gurish, "The Exclusive Economic Zone of the Northwestern Hawaiian Islands: When Do Uninhabited Islands Generate an EEZ?" 25 *San Diego Law Review,* 425, 466 (1988).

7. *Napeahi v. Paty,* 921 F.2d 897, 900 (9th Cir. 1990), citing *Bishop v. Mahiko,* 35 Hawai'i 608, 642–45 (1940); *see also* Letter from Deputy Attorney General William M. Tam (approved by Attorney General Tany S. Hong) to Susumu Ono, Chair, Board of Land and Natural Resources, June 24, 1982 (hereafter cited as 1982 AG Letter).

8. *Napeahi v. Paty,* 921 F.2d, 902–03, citing *County of Hawaii v. Sotomura,* 517 P.2d 57, 61 (Hawai'i 1973), *cert. denied,* 419 U.S. 872 (1974), and *State v. Zimring,* 58 Hawai'i 106, 566 P.2d 725, 735–39 (1977).

9. "Joint Resolution of Annexation of July 7, 1898," 30 Stat. 750.

10. *Id.,* opening paragraph. An opinion letter from the Department of the Attorney General later ruled that this phrase included the submerged lands around Hawai'i's islands. 1982 AG Letter, *supra* note 7, at 5.

11. Melody K. MacKenzie, "The Ceded Lands Trust," 4:6 *Hawaii Bar Journal,* 6 (June 2000).

12. "Joint Resolution of Hawaiian Annexation of July 7, 1898," 30 Stat. 750 (1898), para. 13.

educational and other public purposes." [13] The U.S. Attorney General wrote in 1899 that the Resolution had created a "special trust" for the benefit of Hawai'i's people. [14] The Hawai'i Supreme Court explained in 1977 that by virtue of the language in the 1900 Organic Act, "Congress provided that the United States would have no more than naked title to the public lands other than those set aside for federal uses and purposes," [15] adding also that "[t]he beneficial ownership of the people of Hawaii was again acknowledged in the Admission Act." [16] Hawai'i's Attorney General explained later in 1982 that these provisions, taken together, meant that "while the U.S. held the naked title to the lands, the beneficial uses were severed and allowed to remain with Hawaii's people." [17] This Attorney General letter stated further that the reference to "inhabitants" was meant to refer to "the indigenous population." [18]

Land Alienation after Annexation

Almost immediately after annexation, and before Congress had taken any action to create a government for Hawai'i or determine how the lands should be managed, officials acting on behalf of the new territory began to sell and dispose of these Public Lands. [19] After about a year, legal opinions [20] persuaded President William McKinley that these transactions lacked legal authority, and on September 28, 1899, he issued an executive order suspending any further land transactions in the Islands. [21] Before this order was issued, 254 parcels totaling 15,334 acres valued at $78,127 had been conveyed under Land Patents and Right-of-Purchase leases. [22] When the Organic Act was passed the following year, it contained a provision authorizing the President to

---

13. *Id.,* para. 3.

14. *Hawaii—Public Lands,* 22 U.S. Op. Atty. Gen 574, 1899 WL 577 (1899).

15. *State v. Zimring,* 58 Hawai'i 106, 124, 566 P.2d 725, 737 (1977).

16. *Id.* at 125, 566 P.2d at 737.

17. 1982 AG Letter, *supra* note 7, at 5.

18. *Id. See also* "The Prince's Plan is Co-Opted," *Wall Street Journal,* September 9, 1991, at A-4, col. 1: "When the Hawaiian islands were later annexed to the United States [in 1898], the islands' government [the Republic of Hawaii] acknowledged that this acreage belonged to native Hawaiians, and ceded it to the United States with the stipulation that it be held in trust for native Hawaiians."

19. Horwitz et al., *supra* note 1, at 19. The justification for these sales is found in *Government for the Territory of Hawaii, supra* note 2, at 15:

   The act of annexation provided that "the existing laws of the United States relative to public lands shall not apply," and also that "the municipal legislation of the Hawaiian Islands not inconsistent with this act ... shall remain in force until the Congress of the United States shall otherwise provide."

   As municipal legislation embraced land laws, the government of Hawaii believed that it was authorized to execute these laws.

20. *See, e.g., Hawaii—Public Lands,* 22 U.S. Op. Atty. Gen 574, 575, 1899 WL 577 (1899), explaining that the officers of the Territorial Government "have no authority to sell or otherwise dispose of the public lands in the Hawaiian Islands, and that any such sales or agreements to sell will be absolutely null and void as against the Government of the United States."

21. Horwitz et al., *supra* note 1, at 19. These transactions were also ratified in Section 73(c) of the Organic Act, "Act of April 30, 1900," ch. 339, 31 Stat. 141 (1900).

22. *Government for the Territory of Hawaii, supra* note 2, at 15, 68.

ratify and confirm the transactions that had taken place during the 1898–99 period.[23] The Organic Act also contained provisions like those in the Newlands Resolution, stating that the Public Lands in Hawai'i should be kept separate from those in the rest of the United States[24] and that the revenues from these lands must be used for the inhabitants of Hawai'i.[25]

U.S. military officials moved quickly to acquire two large tracts of lands on O'ahu that were being leased for agricultural purposes. On July 20, 1899, President McKinley issued an executive order to "set aside" for army use more than 15,000 acres of Public Land,[26] and this action led to the condemnation of the private leases and the conversion of these areas into Schofield Barracks and Fort Shafter. President McKinley issued at least four other executive orders between November 2, 1898, and January 5, 1900, setting aside Public Land in Hawai'i for the use of the federal government,[27] and about 20,000 acres were set aside during this period.[28] The plans leading to the transformation of the Pearl River area into the Pearl Harbor Naval Base also began to be developed during this period.[29]

The Organic Act,[30] which was designed to establish a government for the Territory of Hawai'i, to confirm the cession of lands to the United States, and to provide specific laws governing these lands, was adopted by the Senate on April 25, 1900, by a voice vote, but the vote in the House was surprisingly unenthusiastic, with 138 voting Yea, 54 voting Nay, 21 voting Present, and 138 not voting at all.[31] Only 39 percent of the Representatives actually supported this measure. "The congressional debate over passage of the Organic Act had revealed considerable concern about the Islands' concentration of land ownership and the plantation system, with its reliance on 'hordes of alien laborers.'"[32] This enactment reinforced the recognition found in the 1898 Newlands Resolution that the lands transferred at the time of annexation "were impressed with a special trust under the federal government's proprietorship."[33] The Board of Commissioners of Public Lands was replaced by a single Commissioner

---

23. Organic Act, "Act of April 30, 1900," ch. 339, 31 Stat. 141, sec 91.

24. *Id.,* sec. 99.

25. *Id.,* sec. 73: "All funds arising from the sale or lease or other disposal of such lands (i.e. all ceded lands) shall be appropriated by the laws of the government of the Territory of Hawaii and applied to such uses and purposes for the benefit of the inhabitants of the Territory of Hawaii as are consistent with the joint resolution of annexation, approved July seventh, eighteen hundred and ninety-eight."

26. Horwitz et al., *supra* note 1, at 19–20, reporting that "President McKinley's executive order consisted simply of his signature of endorsement on the back of the War Department letter."

27. *Id.* at 179 n. 34, reporting that other executive orders or presidential proclamations were issued on November 2, 1898, November 10, 1899, December 18, 1899, and January 5, 1900.

28. *Id.* at 62.

29. *Id.* at 20. *See infra* this chapter, text at notes 46–49.

30. Organic Act, "Act of April 30, 1900," ch. 339, 31 Stat. 141 (1900).

31. Samuel P. King, "The Federal Courts and the Annexation of Hawaii," 2 *Western Legal History,* 1, 13 (1989).

32. Horwitz et al., *supra* note 1, at 21.

33. MacKenzie, *supra* note 11, at 6.

TABLE 11. Leased Crown Lands by year of expiration (1900)

Year	Hawai'i	Maui	Moloka'i Lāna'i	O'ahu	Kaua'i	Total
1900		370		1		371
1901	3		15,505			15,508
1902	9,421			6,843		16,263
1903	7,343			55		7,398
1904		600		4,008	17,284	21,982
1906					6,354	6,354
1907	172,780	11,040				183,820
1908	102,015	9,477				111,492
1909				6,154	4,045	10,199
1911	18	17,066	23	540		17,647
1912	5,038	3,200		20,322		28,560
1913	62,200	3,316		2,542		68,058
1914	15,210					15,210
1916			17,369			17,369
1917					117,917	117,917
1918	135,000		20,183	26	7,237	162,446
1919	744					744
1920				6,970		6,970
1921	57,236				2,800	60,036
TOTAL	567,007	45,069	37,575	62,966	155,637	868,254

of Public Lands, who was given broad responsibility to administer the lands.[34] New leases of Public Lands were limited to five years in duration,[35] and corporations could not "acquire and hold real estate in Hawaii in excess of 1,000 acres," [36] both apparently "to inhibit the further expansion of Hawaii's plantations." [37]

Most of the Crown Lands, even after annexation, remained under long-term leases and hence were not available for use or transfer. Table 11 is based on a chart published in 1900 showing Crown Lands and the year their leases would expire.[38]

By the end of the territorial period, in 1959 when Hawai'i became a state, a total of 227,972 acres had been "set aside" by federal pronouncements for national parks (on the islands of Maui and Hawai'i) and another 59,106 acres had been set aside for other purposes, mostly for military installations.[39] The federal government had purchased 28,235 acres from the Public Lands and was using another 117,413 acres of these lands under licenses from the Territory.[40]

34. Horwitz et al., *supra* note 1, at 21.
35. Organic Act, "Act of April 30, 1900," ch. 339, 31 Stat. 141, sec. 73 (1900).
36. *Id.*
37. Horwitz et al., *supra* note 1, at 21.
38. *Government for the Territory of Hawaii, supra* note 2, appendix D, at 57.
39. Horwitz et al., *supra* note 1, at 68.
40. *Id.* at 68, 105.

Early Challenges to the Legitimacy of the Territory's Control of the Crown Lands

The status of the Crown Lands continued to be an issue during this period. As described in the next chapter, Queen Liliʻuokalani continued to argue that she had rights to these lands, and other challenges were made in other contexts. In both *Territory v. Kapiʻolani Estate*[41] and *Territory v. Puahi,*[42] the Hawaiʻi Supreme Court ruled that such challenges were nonjusticiable political questions because they involved policy decisions rather than judicial ones. In *Territory v. Kapiʻolani Estate,* the Court refused to consider a claim that action taken by the Republic of Hawaii in Article 95 of the 1894 Constitution[43] and in the 1895 Land Act[44] merging the Crown and Government Lands was "confiscatory in its nature," ruling that such a claim "does not present a judicial question" and "this court has no authority to declare it to be invalid."[45]

Pearl Harbor

Within a few years after annexation, the United States started developing the mouth of the Pearl River into what is now one of the world's premier naval bases. In 1901, Congress appropriated funds to enable the Secretary of the Navy to acquire the land surrounding the lochs, and 719 acres were thereafter acquired by condemnation from the Bishop Estate and five owners of smaller parcels.[46] In 1902, a contract was awarded to begin the excavation of a channel into the harbor 200 feet wide, 30 feet deep, and 2,085 feet long.[47] The work of "dredging the channel, constructing a dry dock, barracks, warehouses, an ammunition depot, a submarine base, a radio center, and a hospital" began in earnest in 1908.[48] The harbor was formally opened several years later in a substantial ceremony attended by Queen Liliʻuokalani. "By 1930, the harbor was a major industrial base for the servicing of the United States Pacific Fleet."[49]

Homesteading in the Early Years of the Territory

During the first few years of the Territory, "the homesteading movement in Hawaii made little net progress."[50] "[W]hile approximately 200 citizens took up land under

---

41. *Territory v. Kapiʻolani Estate*, 18 Hawaiʻi 640 (1908).

42. *Territory v. Puahi*, 18 Hawaiʻi 649 (1908).

43. *See supra* chapter 17, text at notes 12–13, 18.

44. *See supra* chapter 18.

45. *Territory v. Kapiʻolani Estate*, 18 Hawaiʻi 640, 646 (1908).

46. Joseph D. VanBrackle, "Pearl Harbor from the First Mention of 'Pearl Lochs' to Its Present Day Usage," 21–26 (undated manuscript on file in Hawaiian-Pacific Collection, Hamilton Library, University of Hawaiʻi at Mānoa).

47. *Id.* at 21.

48. *Mauka to Makai, supra* note 5, at 31.

49. *Id.*

50. Horwitz et al., *supra* note 1, at 23.

the general provisions of the Land Act of 1895, other family farmers abandoned their holdings or sublet them. Thus there was little or no net gain in the number of homesteaders in the Territory."[51] After Sanford Ballard Dole resigned as Governor in 1903, he was replaced by George R. Carter, a prominent financier, who favored promoting large plantations rather than the small homesteads Dole had favored.[52] Carter's most controversial move occurred in 1907, when he approved the trade of 40,000 acres of excellent agricultural land from the Public Lands on Lāna'i to the rancher Charles Gay in exchange for 293.5 acres of forest reserve land in the Tantalus area above Honolulu plus 3 acres for school sites in Honolulu.[53] This transfer to an individual was apparently designed, in part, to get around the prohibition on transfers of more than 1,000 acres to corporations, because Gay immediately obtained a $192,279 mortgage from William Irwin, an old partner of Claus Spreckels[54] and a director of one of the large sugar factors, to cover the transaction. Irwin later took possession of the Lāna'i land from Gay.[55] This dubious deal was challenged in a case that went all the way to the Hawai'i Supreme Court.[56]

The next Governor, Walter Francis Frear, was able to persuade Congress in 1908 to amend the Organic Act's five-year limitations on land leases to allow leases of fifteen years.[57] This move allowed the sugar plantations to extend the leases that were expiring, but it also led to further frustration on the part of the Hawaiians, who were seeing "that their land, their country, and their government had been usurped by the *haoles* who had initially been welcomed to their Islands," and that the Territorial Governors had done "pathetically little . . . for the Hawaiian people."[58]

Congress adopted amendments to the homesteading program in 1910, modestly favoring homesteaders by requiring homesteads to be drawn by lot instead of by bidding, "thus eliminating excessive bidding;" imposing qualifications on homesteaders, thereby "making it possible to eliminate the more undesirable and unfit applicants;" and prohibiting the sale or transfer of a homestead to aliens (unless they had declared their intent to become a U.S. citizen) or to anyone who already owned more than 80 acres of land (without authorization of the Land Commis-

---

51. *Id.* at 23–24.

52. *Id.* at 26.

53. *Id.* at 28, 180 n. 150; *see generally* Robert H. Horwitz, *Public Land Policy in Hawaii: Land Exchanges,* 14–29 (State of Hawaii Legislative Reference Bureau, Report No. 2, 1964); *Mauka to Makai, supra* note 5, at 36.

54. Gavan Daws, *Shoal of Time: A History of the Hawaiian Islands,* 311 (1968, reprinted 1974).

55. "[I]n 1923, one corporation first purchased the 48,000 acres that had previously been removed from the Ceded Lands through an exchange of lands. . . . The corporation then acquired ownership to most of the remaining lands on Lanai (totaling 98 percent of the island) through a series of quiet title and other legal proceedings, including adverse possession, by 1928." *Mauka to Makai, supra* note 5, at 37.

56. *McCandless v. Carter,* 8 Hawai'i 221 (1907). McCandless also petitioned to the U.S. Supreme Court. *See* Horwitz et al., *supra* note 1, at 62 n. 19, citing Petition No. 109, Supreme Court of the United States, October Term, 1908.

57. Horwitz et al., *supra* note 1, at 29, citing "An Act to Amend Section Seventy-Three of the Act to Provide a Government for the Territory of Hawaii," April 2, 1908, ch. 124, 35 Stat. 56.

58. *Id.* at 31.

sioner and Governor).[59] This enactment also required that lands held under a lease be made available for sale whenever a group of twenty-five or more eligible citizens so requested.[60] This provision "opened the door for breaking the sugar planter's grip on the best agricultural lands leased from the territory,"[61] and Governor Lucius Pinkham actively resisted implementing it in 1916,[62] when a number of sugar leases were expiring. This tension led in part to the enactment of the Hawaiian Homes Commission Act of 1921,[63] which set aside some lands for Hawaiians but eliminated any right to claim leased sugar lands.

Continued Loss of Kuleanas

The loss of their Kuleanas by the Native Hawaiian makaʻāinana continued during the early territorial period. These losses occurred primarily (1) because many of the Kuleanas were "under mortgage with no prospect of redemption,"[64] and (2) because Kuleanas leased to sugar plantations literally could not be found later, because the lands and their surroundings had been physically transformed to become unrecognizable. A writer in 1915 explained that "[t]he boundary hedges or fences, were cut down, the ku-aunas or dykes, were leveled off, the ditches were filled up, the fruit trees sacrificed, and when the middle-aged owner came back from Honolulu to the place which was dear to him from childhood, he simply couldn't find it!"[65] This writer said that "I doubt whether more than one-third of the original 937 Kuleanas granted on the island of Kauai, are now in the actual possession of hands in any way akin to the original owners, and for the purposes originally intended."[66] A congressional report issued in 1920 stated that "the tax returns for 1919 show that only 6.23 per centum of the property [in private hands, measured by value] of the Islands is held by native Hawaiians and this for the most part is lands in the possession of approximately a thousand wealthy Hawaiians, the descendants of the chiefs."[67]

---

59. "An Act to Amend an Act Entitled 'An Act to Provide for a Government for the Territory of Hawaii' Approved April Thirtieth, Nineteen Hundred, May 27, 1910," 36 Stat. 443, ch. 258, sec. 5 (cited hereafter as "Act of May 27, 1910"); *see* Jean Hobbs, *Hawaii: A Pageant of the Soil,* 121–22 (1935); Melody K. MacKenzie, "Historical Background," in *Native Hawaiian Rights Handbook,* 17 (Melody Kapilialoha MacKenzie, ed., 1991).

60. "Act of May 27, 1910," *supra* note 59, sec. 5.

61. Alan Murakami, "The Hawaiian Homes Commission Act," in *Native Hawaiian Rights Handbook,* 43, 45 (Melody Kapilialoha MacKenzie, ed., 1991).

62. Marylyn M. Vause, "The Hawaiian Homes Commission Act, 1920: History and Analysis," 19 (University of Hawaiʻi Masters' Thesis, June 1962) (on file in the University of Hawaiʻi Library), citing *Report of the Governor of Hawaii to the Secretary of Interior,* 1916, 3.

63. "Hawaiian Homes Commission Act, 1920," 67 Pub.L. 34, 42 Stat. 108 (1921).

64. J. M. Lydgate, "The Vanishing Kuleana," in *Hawaiian Almanac and Annual,* 103, 109 (Thomas G. Thrum, compiler and publisher, 1915).

65. *Id.* at 107.

66. *Id.* at 109.

67. *Rehabilitation of Native Hawaiians,* H.R. Rpt. No. 839, House Comm. on Territories, 66th Cong., 2nd Sess. (April 15, 1920), at 6, quoted in *Rice v. Cayetano,* 528 U.S. 495, 503–04 (2000).

Citizenship and Voting during the Territorial Period

The 1900 Organic Act stated that everyone who had been a citizen of the Republic of Hawaii would become citizens of the Territory of Hawai'i and of the United States.[68] But this provision excluded almost all the Asian immigrants living in the Islands.[69]

Although one commentator has written that "[a]nnexation to the United States led to full democratic government in Hawaii" and "eliminated the option of re-writing the voting laws to exclude voters that the ruling faction disliked,"[70] Hawai'i did not in fact become an egalitarian political community after annexation. "[F]ederal legislation supported by Mainland racial attitudes excluded from citizenship and participation in the political life of the Territory large portions of the residents of Oriental ancestry. It was not until after World War II that a major shift in the nation's conception of itself on the world scene brought the laws that significantly reduced this form of racial discrimination."[71] Women also could not vote, and a statute allowing them to vote in territorial elections was not passed until 1930, ten years after the passage of the Nineteenth Amendment gave women the right to vote in the states. Efforts were also made to limit the voting clout of Native Hawaiians by retaining a property requirement,[72] but Congress would not support this initiative. The 1900 Organic Act ended property requirements but maintained a literacy requirement, requiring voters to be able to read and write English or Hawaiian.[73] In the 1900 election, 11,216 men were registered to vote, many more than during the Republic, but lower than the 14,300 who were registered for the Kingdom's last election in 1892.[74]

The Organic Act also extended U.S. laws governing immigration to the Territory, confirming the application of the Chinese exclusion laws[75] and effectively end-

---

68. Organic Act, "Act of April 30, 1900," ch. 339, 31 Stat. 141, sec. 4 (1900).

69. At the time of annexation, about 25,000 Japanese and 21,500 Chinese resided in the Islands, but only 700 of the Chinese and virtually none of the Japanese were citizens. Ernest Andrade, Jr., *Unconquerable Rebel: Robert W. Wilcox and Hawaiian Politics, 1880–1903,* 276 (1996), citing 32 *Congressional Record,* 2614.

70. Patrick W. Hanifin, "To Dwell on the Earth in Unity: Rice, Arakaki, and the Growth of Citizenship and Voting Rights in Hawaii," 5 *Hawaii Bar Journal,* 15, 29 (2001).

71. Andrew W. Lind, *Hawaii's People,* 8 (1955, reprinted 1980).

72. "Those who had supported annexation wanted to continue the system of a limited franchise as established under the former republic because they wanted to make certain that the Hawaiian voting majority could not be rebuilt to become a threat to a stable government sympathetic to the growth of business." Andrade, *supra* note 69 at 181–82 (1996).

The five-member Hawaiian Commission set up to propose laws for the Territory, which included Senators John T. Morgan and Shelby M. Cullom of Illinois, Representative R. R. Hitt of Illinois, Sanford Ballard Dole, and Hawai'i Supreme Court Justice Walter M. Frear as members, had "recommended that candidates for office and voters in elections for the Hawaiian senate should have to meet a property qualification," but "Congress disagreed." Daws, *supra* note 54, at 294.

73. Organic Act, "Act of April 30, 1900," ch. 339, 31 Stat. 141, secs. 60, 62 (1900).

74. Andrade, *supra* note 69, at 197, citing *Hawaiian Gazette,* October 16, 1900.

75. The 1898 Joint Resolution of Annexation, 30 Stat. 750, had explicitly prohibited Chinese immigration: "There shall be no further immigration of Chinese into the Hawaiian Islands, except upon such conditions as are now or may hereafter be allowed by the laws of the United States; and no Chinese, by reason of anything herein contained, shall be allowed to enter the United States from the Hawaiian Islands." *See* Andrade, *supra* note 69, at 185. For a summary of the political dynamics of the early years of the Territorial Government, *see* Tom Coffman, *The Island Edge of America: A Political History of Hawai'i,* 7–14 (2003).

ing the contract labor system, thus putting "the finishing touches to the problem of Asian immigration" into the Islands.[76] After annexation, most of the agricultural workers brought to the Islands were from the Philippines, with others coming from Portugal, Spain, Puerto Rico, and Russia.[77]

The Hawaiians continued to play an active role in the political life of the Islands in the early decades of the Territory. Because the Japanese and Chinese immigrants were ineligible for citizenship, these communities had to wait until children born in Hawai'i came of voting age before they could play an active role in local politics. The Hawaiians registered to vote at a much higher rate than other ethnic groups, with 73 percent of the eligible Hawaiians registering for the 1920 election, compared to 52 percent of the Caucasians and 45 percent of the Portuguese.[78] The Hawaiians remained the numerical majority of voters until the 1924 election, when they fell below the 50 percent mark.[79]

Suppression of Hawaiian Culture

Although the Native Hawaiians had some political successes in the early elections held in the Territory, the Territorial government made every effort to stamp out the unique qualities of the Hawaiian culture. As U.S. District Judge Alan C. Kay later explained,

> Western systems and values were . . . imposed on the Native Hawaiians. The implementation of a western-style school system focused on general world information and the development of basic math and literacy skills in an effort to westernize Native Hawaiian society. It did not account for the Native Hawaiian customary method of learning, nor for the unique Native Hawaiian culture and heritage. The use of the Hawaiian language as an instructional medium was banned in the schools from 1896 until 1986. The school system furthermore operated essentially as a dual-tracked system, with most Native Hawaiians receiving training suitable only for vocational and low paying jobs. Education thus operated generally to further marginalize Native Hawaiians.[80]

Put more dramatically, "[o]nce Hawaii became an American territory in 1900, foreigners prohibited Hawaiian language and beat Hawaiian children for speaking it. As a result, we became ashamed to be Hawaiian."[81] "Native Hawaiians tell of being

---

76. Andrade, *supra* note 69, at 183.

77. Hobbs, *supra* note 59, at 120–21.

78. Robert Littler, "Hawaiian Vote Here Strongest," *Honolulu Star-Bulletin,* May 21, 1927, at 2, col. 4.

79. *Id.*

80. *Doe v. Kamehameha Schools,* 295 F.Supp.2d, 1,141, 1,150 (D. Hawai'i 2003) (citations omitted).

81. Lilikala Kame'eleihiwa, *Native Land and Foreign Desires: Pehea La E Pono Ai?* 316 (1992). *See also* 1 Native Hawaiians Study Commission, *Report on the Culture, Needs and Concerns of Native Hawaiians,* 173–203 (1983) (Report issued pursuant to Pub.L. 96-565, Title III), describing the suppression and importance of the Hawaiian language; *see generally* Maenette Kape'ahiokalani, Padeken Ah Nee Benham, and Ronald H. Heck, *Culture and Educational Policy in Hawai'i: The Silencing of Native Voices* (1998).

punished as children for speaking Hawaiian and of teachers going to homes and discouraging the use of Hawaiian."[82]

The Hawaiian spirit was not crushed altogether, however, as evidenced by the Hawaiians' continued recognition of the wrongs they had suffered and by their unrelenting quest for some form of justice and compensation. In 1918, for instance, focusing in particular on the Crown Lands whose leases to the sugar companies were expiring, Senator John Wise sought to promote homesteading by introducing Senate Concurrent Resolution Number 2 in the Territorial Legislature, which was supported by a committee report containing the following language:

> As the lands of Hawaii in the Great Mahele of 1848 were cut up one-third to the Chief, one-third to the people, and one-third to the Crown, which said Crown lands are not held in trust for the benefit of the people, this resolution seeks to have portions of same set aside for the benefit of the people of the Hawaiian race.[83]

It is significant that the Hawaiians viewed themselves as the proper beneficial owners of the Crown Lands and understood that their rights to these lands should be recognized.

---

82. *From Mauka to Makai, supra* note 5, at 29.
83. Vause, *supra* note 62, at 26, quoting from *Senate Journal,* 10 Legislature, at 1,044–45.

21

Liliuokalani v. United States
(1910)

 In the years following the 1893 overthrow, Queen Liliʻuokalani worked relentlessly to try to restore her Kingdom and to block annexation. And in the debates over annexation and in the years following the 1898 annexation she (and others) asserted claims to the Crown Lands. On June 17, 1897, for instance, in the protest Liliʻuokalani issued the day after the draft treaty of annexation was submitted to the U.S. Senate, she included in her protest the concern about the Crown Lands, contending that these Lands have

> in no way been heretofore recognized as other than the private property of the constitutional monarch, subject to a control in no way differing from other items of a private estate. . . . [I]t is proposed by said treaty to confiscate said property, . . . those legally entitled thereto, either now or in succession, receiving no consideration whatever for estates, their title to which has been always undisputed, and which is legally in my name at this date.[1]

These claims were debated during the congressional deliberations preceding the 1898 Newlands Resolution[2] and the 1900 Organic Act,[3] but Congress decided to leave the issue to the courts.

In the book she wrote in 1898, Liliʻuokalani stressed the unique nature of the Crown Lands (and the trust responsibility recognized by the Monarchs), explaining that the amount of $50,000 generated annually by these lands was designed to generate revenue so that "the reigning sovereign . . . might care for his poorer people."[4] "They are by legislative act and the rulings of the Supreme Court my own property

---

1. Liliuokalani, *Hawaii's Story by Hawaii's Queen,* 355 (1898, reprinted 1997); William Fremont Blackman, *The Making of Hawaii: A Study in Social Evolution,* 149 (1906, reprinted 1977), quoting from the Queen's protest, issued June 17, 1897, the day after the proposed treaty of annexation was submitted to the U.S. Senate.

2. "Joint Resolution of Hawaiian Annexation of July 7, 1898," 30 Stat. 750 (1898). *See supra* discussion in chapter 19.

3. Organic Act, "Act of April 30, 1900," ch. 339, 31 Stat. 141 (1900). *See supra* discussion in chapter 20.

4. Liliuokalani, *supra* note 1, at 260.

Queen Lili'uokalani

at this day," she explained, adding sadly that no revenue had been transferred to her because "the doctrine that might makes right seems to prevail." [5]

The five-member Hawaiian Commission established by Congress after annexation to recommend legislation for the new Territory (which included Sanford Ballard Dole and John T. Morgan as members) did not support Lili'uokalani's legal claim to the Crown Lands, but "did say that the U.S. government could nevertheless award her a sum as compensation, based upon considerations of justice, fairness, and policy." [6] While the Organic Act was being debated, several bills were introduced in Congress in 1900 to appropriate $250,000 to the former Queen in exchange for her relinquishing her claim to the Crown Lands, but none were adopted.[7] An attempt to delete the provision in Section 99 of the Organic Act stating that the Crown Lands

---

5. *Id.* at 260–61.

6. Ernest Andrade Jr., *Unconquerable Rebel: Robert W. Wilcox and Hawaiian Politics, 1880–1903,* 230 (1996), citing 1 "Staff of Senate Subcomm. on Pacific Islands and Porto Rico, Report on Hawaiian Investigation," 82 (1903) (hereafter cited as 1 "Hawaiian Investigation"); 2 "Staff of Senate Subcomm. on Pacific Islands and Porto Rico, Report on Hawaiian Investigations," 7–8 (1902) (hereafter cited as 2 "Hawaiian Investigation").

7. Andrade, *supra* note 6, at 282 n. 44, citing 33 *Congressional Record,* 2513–20, 2704, 2900–04 (1900).

were free and clear of any trust or claim, in order to allow Liliʻuokalani to pursue her claim in the courts, also failed.[8]

The 1901 Territorial Legislature, which was controlled by the Home Rule Party and dominated by Hawaiians, enacted an appropriation of $250,000 "in full payment and satisfaction of all claims and demands of Her Majesty Liliuokalani against the Republic of Hawaii and the Territory of Hawaii,"[9] but this bill was pocket-vetoed by Governor Sanford Ballard Dole.[10] During the extra session held that year, the Legislature appropriated $15,000 to Liliʻuokalani,[11] but this payment "was not considered as compensation for the lands but simply a grant."[12]

Between 1900 and 1909, Liliʻuokalani made five more trips to Washington to protest the manner in which the Crown Lands were being handled.[13] In 1902, for instance, she explained to the Senate Subcommittee on the Pacific Islands and Puerto Rico the basis for her claim.[14] In 1903, Theresa Owana Keohelelani Wilcox and Elizabeth Kekaaniau Pratt petitioned the Senate Subcommittee on the Pacific Islands and Puerto Rico to support the petition of Liliʻuokalani seeking compensation for the taking of the Crown Lands.[15] In 1905, Liliʻuokalani filed a formal petition offering to relinquish her claim in exchange for a settlement of $10,000,000, which she considered to be half the value of the Crown Lands.[16] Then in 1910, seventeen years after the overthrow and twelve years after annexation, she filed a claim in the United States Court of Claims to recover a "vested equitable life interest" in the Crown Lands, which the Republic of Hawaii had "ceded" to the United States with annexation.[17] Her attorney, Sidney M. Ballou,[18] asserted that although the Queen had been divested of the Crown Lands by the United States, she retained a vested life estate interest in them.

8. Davianna Pomaikaʻi McGregor, "Kupaʻa I Ka ʻĀina: Persistence on the Land," 40 (1989) (unpublished Ph.D. dissertation, University of Hawaiʻi) (on file in the Hawaiian-Pacific Collection, Hamilton Library, University of Hawaiʻi at Mānoa), citing "Congressional Debates on Hawaii Organic Act, Together with Debates and Congressional Action on Other Matters Concerning the Hawaiian Islands," 33 *Congressional Record,* 2449 (pt. 3, 1900).

9. Andrade, *supra* note 6 at 230 (1996), citing 1 "Hawaiian Investigation," *supra* note 1, at 96.

10. *Id.* at 230.

11. *Id.* at 212, 230.

12. *Id.* at 230.

13. Helena G. Allen, *The Betrayal of Liliuokalani: Last Queen of Hawaii 1838–1917,* 370 (1982).

14. 2 "Hawaiian Investigation," *supra* note 6, at 453–488.

15. "Crown Land Compensation Claim," presented to 95th Cong., 1st Sess. (1977), at 43; *see generally* chapter 28 *infra.*

16. McGregor, *supra* note 8, at 83 n. 33, citing a petition in Delegate Kalanianaʻole's petitions file.

17. *Liliuokalani v. United States,* 45 Ct. Cl. 418, 1909 WL 905 (Ct. Cl. 1910).

18. Sidney Miller Ballou, 1870–1929, was a prominent Honolulu attorney of the day. He issued two books in 1897 compiling the civil and penal laws of Hawaiʻi and wrote several books about the practice of law. Sidney M. Ballou, *Civil Laws of the Hawaiian Islands* (1897); Sidney M. Ballou, *Penal Laws of the Hawaiian Islands* (1897); Sidney M. Ballou, *Appeals and Exceptions in Hawaiian Courts* (1900). He served as lobbyist for the Hawaiʻi Sugar Planters' Association and had become a judge by 1913. H. Brent Melendy, "The Controversial Appointment of Lucius Eugene Pinkham, Hawaii's First Democratic Governor," 17 *Hawaiian Journal of History,* 185, 192 (1983). In 1899, Ballou's home in Honolulu was described as one of the "very beautiful homes" that had recently been constructed. 25 *Hawaiian Almanac and Annual,* 136 (Thomas G. Thrum, compiler and publisher, 1899).

According to Ballou's argument, Hawai'i's history and laws established that the Crown Lands, which previously were the fee simple private lands of Kauikeaouli (Kamehameha III), had evolved into a "vested equitable life interest" held by the reigning Monarch.[19] This life interest, or "life estate," he argued, entitled each Monarch to the use and the revenues of the Crown Lands for the duration of the Monarch's life.

Ballou thus asserted that when Lili'uokalani became Mō'ī on January 20, 1891, she acquired such a vested life interest in the Crown Lands, and he contended that this interest was equivalent to a private property interest in an existing trust. He urged that, pursuant to universally accepted rules regarding trusts, when the United States acquired legal title to the Crown Lands, it also acquired notice of the existing trust and became a trustee for the beneficiary, Lili'uokalani.[20] He argued that when property has been converted, if its identity can be traced, it must be deemed to be subject to the rights of the original owner.

The Queen's attorney argued next that Article 95 of the Republic of Hawaii's 1894 Constitution[21]—which had declared that the Crown Lands were "to be now free and clear from any trust of or concerning the same"—acknowledged that a trust had existed in favor of the reigning Monarch. The word "now" demonstrated, he contended, that the provision intended to confiscate Lili'uokalani's rights to a "claim of any nature whatsoever upon the rents, issues, and profits thereof."[22] Ballou also attacked Article 95 of the 1894 Constitution, explaining that it was specifically designed to bar her claim in the courts of the Republic and that the language of Article 95 stating that the Crown Lands were "heretofore . . . the property of the Hawaiian Government" was false unless "heretofore" was restricted to the eighteen months of the Provisional Government.[23] He noted that prior to 1893 the Crown Lands were not considered to be property of the government and were not part of the public domain, citing the language of the Acts of 1848[24] and 1865[25] in support of his claim.[26]

Ballou's arguments on behalf of Lili'uokalani assumed that her life interest

---

19. *Liliuokalani v. United States*, 45 Ct.Cl. at 419–20, 424.

20. *Id.* at 421–22.

21. *See supra* chapter 17, text at notes 12–13, 19–21, for the text and analysis of Article 95 of the 1894 Constitution.

22. *Liliuokalani v. United States*, 45 Ct.Cl. at 423, 428.

23. *Id.* at 423.

24. *Id.* The text says "1845," but it must have been intended to refer to the Act of "1848." *See* discussions of the "Act Relating to the Lands of His Majesty the King and of the Government, June 7, 1848," L. 1848 at 22, in 2 *Revised Laws of Hawai'i*, 2152 (1925), *supra* in chapter 4, text at note 89; chapter 5, text at notes 7–9; chapter 6, note 12; and chapter 8, text at note 28.

25. "An Act to Relieve the Royal Domain from Encumbrances and to Render the Same Inalienable," January 3, 1865, 1 *Sess. Laws of Hawai'i*, 69 (1851–70), 2 *Revised Laws of Hawai'i*, 2,177–79 (1925), 30 *Rev. Laws of Hawai'i*, 1226–28 (1905), reprinted in Jean Hobbs, *Hawaii: A Pageant of the Soil*, 68–69 (1935); in Thomas Marshall Spaulding, *The Crown Lands of Hawaii*, 13–14 (University of Hawai'i Occasional Papers No. 1, October 10, 1923); in *Liliuokalani v. United States*, 45 Ct. Cl. 418, 431–32, 1909 WL 905 (1910), and in appendix 8 herein, *infra;* this statute is discussed *supra* in chapter 9.

26. *Liliuokalani v. United States*, 45 Ct. Cl. at 423.

had been acknowledged, and he argued that her claim turned on two questions: (1) whether her rights were "extinguished" or "merely suspended" by Article 95 of the 1894 Constitution of the Republic of Hawaii, and (2) whether her rights were extinguished by the "confiscatory" language in Article 99 of the Organic Act.[27] He submitted that justice required the answer to the first question be that her rights were merely suspended, because of Lili'uokalani's "acknowledged equitable right" to the lands that had been taken.[28] The second question, he argued, had to be answered in the negative, because the confiscatory declaration in Section 99 of the Organic Act unconstitutionally deprived Lili'uokalani of her property without due process of law.[29]

It is also significant to note, as we look back upon this case, that Ballou invoked international law principles in his arguments on behalf of the former Queen. He cited Chief Justice John Marshall's decision in *United States v. Percheman,*[30] for the proposition that "even in cases of conquest," "[t]he modern usage of nations, which has become law, would be violated . . . and . . . the whole civilized world would be outraged if private property should be generally confiscated and private rights annulled."[31] He noted the analogy between the annexation of Hawai'i and the United States' acquisition of the Panama Canal Zone,[32] acknowledging that it was not up to the courts to question "the necessity or propriety" of the transaction but arguing that the courts were obliged to adjudicate "the rights of private property" and protect from "confiscation" "any inconvenient rights of private property," because otherwise "it may readily be imagined to what length" conquering governments might go in the future to acquire property from private owners.[33]

Judge Fenton W. Booth[34] of the United States Court of Claims[35] rejected Ballou's arguments on May 16, 1910, holding that Lili'uokalani was not entitled to

---

27. *Id.,* referring to the 1900 Organic Act, *supra* note 2. Section 99 of the 1900 Organic Act is reprinted *supra* in chapter 19, text at note 100.

28. *Liliuokalani v. United States,* 45 Ct. Cl. at 423–24.

29. *Id.* at 424.

30. *United States v. Percheman,* 32 U.S. (7 Pet.) 51 (1833).

31. *Id.* at 86–87.

32. *Liliuokalani v. United States,* 45 Ct. Cl. at 420, explaining that "[w]hen the manifest destiny of the United States demanded the acquisition of certain rights in the Isthmus of Panama" just as it had "demanded the possession of the strategic outpost controlling the North Pacific [Hawai'i]," the United States had not taken the desired territory from the existing government, but rather "[i]n both cases there was a domestic revolution, and the revolutionary government turned over to the United States the sovereignty desired."

33. *Id.* at 420–21.

34. Fenton Whitlock Booth served on the U.S. Court of Claims for thirty-four years, the last eleven as its Chief Justice. He was born in Illinois in 1869, the son of a merchant. His uncle (Newton Booth) served as Governor of and later U.S. Senator for California; a first cousin (Booth Tarkington) was a distinguished author. He served as a Republican member of the Illinois Legislature and was a delegate to the 1904 Republican National Convention before being appointed to the Court of Claims (upon the recommendation of the Speaker of the House of Representatives Joe Cannon) in 1905 (at age thirty-five) by President Theodore Roosevelt. 1 Marion T. Bennett, *The United States Court of Claims: A History,* 103–05 (1976).

35. The Court of Claims consisted of five justices at the time of this decision, and although no other names are listed on the opinion, apparently all five sat on all cases presented to the court. The other justices were Chief Justice Stanton Judkins Peelle (from Indiana), Charles Bowen Howry (from Mississippi), George Wesley Atkinson (from West Virginia), and Samuel Stebbins Barney (from Wisconsin). All except Howry were Republicans. *Id.* at 86–90, 92–96, 106–13.

recover the value of or income from the Crown Lands because she held no property rights in these lands. He acknowledged that in the years immediately after the 1848 Mahele, "[t]he title to the crown lands was vested in the Sovereign; he leased and alienated the same at his pleasure; the income and profits therefrom were his without interference or control."[36] But the statute enacted on January 3, 1865,[37] changed this situation, and "provided against their alienation, and put their management and control in the hands of commissioners as provided in the act."[38] Judge Booth observed that the "nature and extent" of the Monarch's title in the Crown Lands had been "squarely"[39] before the Hawai'i Supreme Court in its 1864 decision *In re Estate of Kamehameha IV,*[40] and he relied heavily on Justice George M. Robertson's "exhaustive"[41] and "exceedingly able opinion,"[42] which he characterized as having concluded that the Crown Lands formed an estate "presumably vested in fee simple in so far as the Crown is concerned, as distinguished from the personality of the Sovereign, and yet limited as to possession and descent by conditions abhorrent to a fee-simple estate absolute."[43]

Based on the 1864 holding, Judge Booth concluded that the Act of 1865 specifically limited the legal title of the Mō'ī over the lands to those activities that were necessary to support and maintain the Crown.[44] The court concluded that this 1865 statute, which had been enacted with the approval of King Kamehameha V (Lot), "expressly divested the King of whatever legal title or possession he theretofore had in or to the Crown lands."[45] Judge Booth reasoned that even earlier, as explained in Judge Robertson's 1864 opinion, the Crown Lands "belonged to the office and not to the individual"[46] and were designed to provide "the support and maintenance of the Crown."[47] The Court of Claims thus ruled that "the Hawaiian Government in 1865 by its own legislation determined what the court is now asked to determine."[48]

---

36. *Liliuokalani v. United States,* 45 Ct. Cl. at 425.

37. "Act of January 3, 1865," *supra* note 25.

38. *Liliuokalani v. United States,* 45 Ct. Cl. at 425.

39. *Id.* at 426.

40. *In re Estate of His Majesty Kamehameha IV,* 2 Hawai'i 715, 1864 WL 2485 (1864), discussed *supra* in chapter 8.

41. *Liliuokalani v. United States,* 45 Ct. Cl. at 424.

42. *Id.* at 426.

43. *Id.* Judge Booth quoted from the Hawai'i Supreme Court's 1864 decision that "the lands descended in fee, the inheritance being limited, however, to the successors to the throne, and each successive power *[sic]* may regulate and dispose of the same according to his will and pleasure, as private property, in like manner as was done by Kamehameha III." *Id.* at 426, quoting from *In re Estate of Kamehameha IV,* 2 Hawai'i at 725, 1864 WL 2485, at *7). Judge Booth misquoted the earlier opinion slightly, using the word "power" where the 1864 opinion had said "possessor."

44. *Liliuokalani v. United States,* 45 Ct. Cl. at 427.

45. *Id.* at 426–27, citing *Harris v. Carter,* 6 Hawai'i 195, 208, 1877 WL 7591 (1877).

46. *Id.* at 427.

47. *Id.,* explaining that although the Monarch retained "certain attributes pertaining to fee-simple estates, such as unrestricted power of alienation and incumbrance, there were likewise enough conditions surrounding the tenure to clearly characterize it as one pertaining to the support and maintenance of the Crown, as distinct from the person of the Sovereign."

48. *Id.*

In upholding the legitimacy of the confiscation of the Crown Lands, Judge Booth concluded that

> It seems to the court that the crown lands acquired their unusual status through a desire of the King to firmly establish his Government by commendable concessions to his chiefs and people out of the public domain. The reservations made were to the Crown and not the King as an individual. The crown lands were the resourceful methods of income to sustain, in part at least, the dignity of the office to which they were inseparably attached. When the office [of the Monarch] ceased to exist, they became as other lands of the Sovereignty and passed to the defendants [the United States] as part and parcel of the public domain.[49]

Although the Hawai'i Supreme Court had recognized Queen Emma's right of dower, it was "clear from the opinion that the crown lands were treated not as the King's private property in the strict sense of the term."[50]

Several other points in the Court of Claims' opinion are intriguing and relevant to earlier chapters in this volume. Judge Booth mentioned the July 1882 transaction between Princess Ruth Ke'elikolani and Claus Spreckels[51] and cited it as support for the view that the Crown Lands "belonged to the office [of the Monarch] and not to the individual."[52] Judge Booth found persuasive that when Princess Ruth Ke'elikolani (sister and heir of Lot Kapuāiwa [Kamehameha V]) conveyed to Spreckels (for $10,000) any and all of her interest in the Crown Lands, the "sovereign authorities" (i.e., the Legislature) stepped in to resolve the dispute.[53] By subsequent legislation in which Spreckels agreed to relinquish any claims to the Crown Lands in exchange for the Ahupua'a of Wailuku, Maui, the sovereign authorities "restored the attempted conveyance to the general body of the crown lands."[54]

Judge Booth also ventured into the difficult question of the motives of Kauikeaouli (Kamehameha III) when he divided the land in the Mahele. Lili'uokalani's attorney had emphasized Justice Robertson's acknowledgment in his 1864 opinion that Kauikeaouli had created the Crown Lands as his own private lands to protect them from being taken in the event of a foreign invasion—"a desire to prevent the impoverishment of the Sovereign in the event of a successful foreign invasion"[55]— but Judge Booth dismissed this statement as "not in harmony" with the rest of Justice Robertson's opinion.[56] The court found more persuasive Robertson's statement that "[i]t was the imperative necessity of separating and defining the rights of the several

---

49. *Id.* at 428, citing *O'Reilly de Camera v. Brooke*, 209 U.S. 45 (1908); *Hijo v. United States*, 194 U.S. 315 (1904); *Sanchez v. United States*, 216 U.S. 167 (1910).

50. *Id.* at 427.

51. *See* discussion of this episode *supra* in chapter 12.

52. *Liliuokalani v. United States*, 45 Ct. Cl. at 427.

53. *Id.*

54. *Id.*

55. *Id.*, citing *In re Estate of Kamehameha IV*, 2 Hawai'i at 722, 1864 WL 2485, at *5.

56. *Id.*

parties interested in the lands which led to the institution of the board of land commissioners, and to the division made by the King himself, with the assistance of his privy council,"[57] adding the cynical and insensitive observation that "[i]t was in fact the usual contest between the monarch and his people."[58]

Toward the end of his opinion, Judge Booth posed the following rhetorical question: If Kamehameha III had been "deposed" by a "pretender for the throne [who] had successfully established his claim," "[i]s it possible that Kamehameha III could have recovered the rents and profits from the crown lands during the remainder of his life" as Lili'uokalani was claiming?[59] In Judge Booth's mind, Kamehameha III had made the crucial decisions that these lands should support the Crown, and hence that a deposed Monarch would have no remaining rights to their profits.

Because of its holding that Queen Lili'uokalani held no vested rights in the Crown Lands, the Court of Claims did not even address the merits of Ballou's argument that Section 99 of the 1900 Organic Act constituted a taking of property without due process of law.[60] But Judge Booth did add a final note to his opinion suggesting that the six-year statute of limitations would have barred the Queen's "taking" claim if it had been meritorious: "The organic act of 1900 puts an end to any trust—if the same possibly existed—and the petition herein was not filed until January 20, 1910, more than six years thereafter."[61]

Judge Booth's opinion contains several inconsistencies that should have merited further discussion. In considering the 1882 "Spreckels incident,"[62] Judge Booth failed to address the full complexity of this situation. The action taken by the "sovereign authorities" (i.e., the Legislature) in resolving the dispute could have been construed as acknowledging that Princess Ruth had some sort of a valid personal claim to the Crown Lands separate from the office. The court failed to consider the possibility (because Princess Ruth was not the Mō'ī) that the Legislature's action had acknowledged an existing property right, distinct from the "royal office" of the throne. The Court of Claims may not have understood that the Spreckels' land transaction was a complicated anomaly and aberration that arose from the politics and personalities of the time.

Judge Booth viewed the Crown Lands through Western eyes, without any understanding of or sympathy for the Hawaiian concepts of Aloha 'Āina, Mālama 'Āina, and the reciprocal rights and obligations that formed the trust relationships

57. *Id.* at 427–28, quoting from *In re Estate of Kamehameha IV,* 2 Hawai'i at 719, 1864 WL 2485, at *3.
58. *Id.* at 428.
59. *Id.*
60. *Id.* at 429.
61. *Id.* This conclusion ignores the fact that the claim to the Crown Lands had been presented, albeit in other forums, immediately after the annexation and had been actively debated during the deliberations by Congress that led to the 1900 Organic Act and then pursued in other venues.
62. *See* discussion *supra* in chapter 12.

between the Ali'i and the maka'āinana. He quoted the provision in the 1840 Constitution stating that the land "belonged to the chiefs and the people in common,"[63] but he does not appear to have recognized the significance of this acknowledgment that the 'Āina was shared. Judge Booth's short historical summary characterized the history of precontact Hawai'i as "the usual story of conquest,"[64] described the traditional land tenure system as a "feudal system,"[65] and disparaged the authority of Kamehameha I as "the usual one of conquest."[66] Although praising the distribution of lands by Kauikeaouli (Kamehameha III) as "commendable,"[67] Judge Booth's opinion displayed no understanding of the sense of responsibility and sharing that animated the actions of the Ali'i or how their view of 'Āina differed from the Western approach toward landownership.[68] Justice Robertson's 1864 opinion gave at least some recognition to these unique Hawaiian perspectives through his recognition of Queen Emma's right to dower,[69] which would not logically have existed under Judge Booth's view of the status of the Crown Lands. Although Judge Booth purported to rely upon Justice Robertson's 1864 reasoning, he failed to explain how the Hawai'i Supreme Court could have concluded that dower rights existed in these lands if they were not in some sense the private property of the Mō'ī.[70]

More significantly, Congress' 1993 enactment of the "Apology Resolution"[71] has raised substantial questions about and appears to have undercut the legal basis for the Court of Claims' decision. Congress has acknowledged that the 1893 overthrow of the Kingdom of Hawai'i was an "illegal" act and has apologized for the "participation of agents and citizens of the United States, and the deprivation of the rights of Native Hawaiians to self-determination." The Resolution also recognized that the subsequent transfer of the Kingdom's land to the Republic and then to the United States was without "compensation to or the consent of the Native Hawaiian people." The Court of Claims reasoned that Lili'uokalani's rights to the Crown Lands ceased when her office ceased to exist, but if the overthrow of the Kingdom was illegal, then the subsequent transfer of Hawai'i's "public domain" to the United States must also have been of questionable legality.

A distinguished scholar of Indian law has analyzed the Court of Claims decision as follows:

---

63. *Liliuokalani v. United States,* 45 Ct. Cl. at 425, quoting from the 1840 Constitution.

64. *Id.* at 426.

65. *Id.* at 424.

66. *Id.* at 426.

67. *Id.* at 428.

68. *See supra* chapters 2–3.

69. *See supra* chapter 8, text at notes 25–29, 49–53, 122–26, 131.

70. 45 Ct. Cl. at 427: "although the court sustained the right of dower in the widow of the King it is clear from the opinion that the crown lands were treated not as the King's private property in the strict sense of the term."

71. "Joint Resolution to Acknowledge the 100th Anniversary of the January 17, 1893 Overthrow of the Kingdom of Hawaii," Sec. 2, Pub. L. 103-150, 107 Stat. 1510 (1993).

The court in *Lili'uokalani* generally analyzed Hawaiian property law correctly: the crown lands, at least since legislation in 1865, were to be held and used by the monarch, but not as individual property. They were permanent assets of the kingdom for the benefit of all the Hawaiian people that descended to successors to the throne. It would appear, then, that the proper claimants for loss of those lands would be all the descendants of the people of the Hawaiian Kingdom.[72]

The Crown Lands belonged to the Native Hawaiian Mō'ī and were administered to enable the Mō'ī to govern and to provide for the Native Hawaiian people. It would thus appear that the future of these lands must be decided by the Native Hawaiian people. A logical way to ensure this result would be to transfer these Lands to the Native Hawaiian Nation, when it is reestablished, so that these lands can continue to provide benefits for the Native Hawaiian people in accordance with their own decisions.

Beginning in 1912, the Territorial Legislature began giving the ex-Queen an annual pension of $12,000,[73] recognizing her unique status and providing a modest compensation for her losses.[74] "[U]ntil her death on November 11, 1917," Queen Lili'uokalani "never ceased to hope that the rights she claimed would be recognized by the government of the United States."[75] At her death, she decreed that her personal lands be utilized for the benefit of her people,[76] and she would surely be pleased if the Crown Lands were to become the core of the lands of the restored Native Hawaiian Nation.

72. David Getches, "Alternative Approaches to Land Claims: Alaska and Hawaii," in *Irredeemable America: The Indians' Estate and Land Claims,* 301, 329 (Imre Sutton, ed., 1985).

73. Allen, *Betrayal, supra* note 13, at 372.

74. Representative Johnson said in the February 1920 hearings on the Hawaiian Homes Commission Act that he believed the United States "treated [Queen Lili'uokalani] rather shabbily in not giving her an annuity or a pension." "Rehabilitation and Colonization of Hawaiians and Other Proposed Amendments to the Organic Act of the Territory of Hawaii and on the Proposed Transfer of the Buildings of the Federal Leprosy Investigation Station at Kalawao on the Island of Molokai, to the Territory of Hawaii," *Hearing before the House Comm. on the Territories,* 66th Cong., 2nd Sess., at 165 (1920).

75. Hobbs, *supra* note 25, at 123.

76. *See infra* chapter 26, text at notes 78–103.

22

The Hawaiian Homes Commission Act (1921)

On July 9, 1921, Congress enacted the Hawaiian Homes Commission Act (HHCA),[1] which set aside about 203,500 acres of what had been part of the Crown and Government Lands inventory to provide ninety-nine-year homestead leases of land at a nominal fee for residences and farm lots for Native Hawaiians.[2] This statute was passed for a variety of diverse and complex reasons and was the result of a compromise of conflicting goals.[3] Certainly the goal of the Native Hawaiian proponents and some of the federal officials in the Interior Department was to reverse the native population's progressively declining numbers and thus to "rehabilitate" the race.[4]

The statute's enactment marked an important recognition of the federal government's trust obligation to Native Hawaiians.[5] Those supporting the bill consid-

---

1. "Hawaiian Homes Commission Act, 1920," 67 Pub. L. 34, 42 Stat. 108 (1921), reprinted in 1 *Hawai'i Revised Statutes,* 191 (1993) (hereafter cited as HHCA).

2. In the HHCA, "native Hawaiians" are defined as persons with at least 50 percent Hawaiian blood. *Id.,* § 201(7). A recent amendment has permitted a person with 25 percent Hawaiian blood to take over a lease as heir. *Id.,* § 209(a).

3. The most comprehensive analysis of the conflicting forces that produced this statute is Marylyn M. Vause, "The Hawaiian Homes Commission Act, 1920: History and Analysis," (1962) (unpublished Master's thesis, University of Hawai'i) (on file in the University of Hawai'i Library); *see also* Neil M. Levy, "Native Hawaiian Land Rights," 63 *California Law Review,* 848, 865 (1975).

4. *See, e.g., Ahuna v. Department of Hawaiian Home Lands,* 64 Hawai'i 327, 336 n.10, 640 P.2d 1161 (1982), quoting Territorial Senator John H. Wise, an author of the Hawaiian Homes Commission Act as saying (in H.R. Rep. No. 839, 66th Cong., 2d Sess. 4 [1920]), "The Hawaiian people are a farming people and fishermen, out-of-door people, and when they were frozen out of their lands and driven into the cities they had to live in the cheapest places, tenements. That is one of the reasons why the Hawaiian people are dying. Now, the only way to save them, I contend, is to take them back to the lands and give them the mode of living that their ancestors were accustomed to and in that way rehabilitate them."

5. During the hearings that led to the passage of the Hawaiian Homes Commission Act, federal officials analogized the relationship between the United States and Native Hawaiians to the relationship that had been established between the United States and American Indians. *See, e.g.,* Statement of Secretary of Interior Franklin K. Lane that "the natives of the islands . . . are our wards . . . and for whom in a sense we are trustees." "Rehabilitation of Native Hawaiians," H.R. Rep. No. 839, House Comm. on Territories, 66th Cong., 2d Sess. (April 15, 1920) (hereafter cited as H.R. Rep. 66-839), at 4. *See also Ahuna v. Dept. of Hawaiian Home Lands,* 64 Hawai'i 327, 336, 640 P.2d 1161 (1982): "The legislative history at the inception of the HHCA strongly suggests that the federal government stood in a trusteeship capacity to the aboriginal people"; *Rice v. Cayetano (II),* 963 F. Supp. 1547, 1553 (D. Hawai'i 1997), *rev'd on other grounds,* 528 U.S. 495 (2000), explaining that Native

ered the constitutionality of passing legislation for one racial group and concluded that such an enactment would be constitutional because it was analogous to the special legislation that had been enacted for Indians since the founding of the country.[6]

Of particular importance to our present understanding of the status of the Crown Lands was the argument presented repeatedly during the debates on the Hawaiian Homes Commission Act that Hawaiians were entitled to a share of the Public Lands because they were denied their fair share of the lands distributed during the 1848 Mahele and had a continuing claim to the Crown Lands. This view can be found, for instance, in a 1918 committee report of the Territorial Senate's Committee on Public Lands:

> As the lands of Hawaii in the Great Mahele of 1848 were cut up one-third to the Chief, one-third to the people, and one-third to the Crown, *which said Crown lands are now held in trust for the benefit of the people,* this resolution seeks to have portions of same set aside for the benefit of the people of the Hawaiian race.[7]

Hawaiians "developed their own trust relationship with the Federal Government as demonstrated by the passage of the [Hawaiian Homes Commission Act], and because Native Hawaiians were not being excluded from beneficial legislation in the same manner as unacknowledged mainland United States Indian tribes."

6. "Rehabilitation and Colonization of Hawaiians and Other Proposed Amendments to the Organic Act of the Territory of Hawaii and on the Proposed Transfer of the Buildings of the Federal Leprosy Investigation Station at Kalawao on the Island of Molokai, to the Territory of Hawaii," House Comm. on the Territories, 66th Cong., 2d Sess., at 152 (1920), containing a statement by Chair Charles F. Curry, in response to doubts about the constitutionality of enacting legislation for Native Hawaiians, stating that "Congress does pass laws giving preference to soldiers and to Indians. It makes land allotments to Indians. . . . The law could give preference to the Hawaiians for homesteading if Congress would enact it"; at 259–60, containing a statement by Secretary of the Interior Franklin K. Lane stating that "I have not thought there was any serious . . . constitutional difficulty. . . . We have got the right to set aside these lands for this particular body of people because I think the history of the islands will justify that before any tribunal in the world. . . . It would be an extension of the same idea [established in dealing with the Indians]"; at 260, where Chair Curry stated that "the United States Government has just as much right—to provide lands for the Hawaiians as it has to provide lands for the Indians"; at 260–61, containing a written analysis by the Solicitor of the Interior Department stating that "an act of Congress setting apart a limited area of the public lands of the Territory of Hawaii for lease to and occupation by native Hawaiians" "would not" "be unconstitutional" based on the many precedents whereby lands have been distributed to Indians and other groups; at 299, where Chair Curry stated, "And the Indians received lands to the exclusion of other citizens. That is certainly in line with this legislation, in harmony with this legislation"; and at 300, where Chair Curry, in response to questions from Representative Dowell about whether Native Hawaiians are entitled to the same status as Indians, stated that "the Hawaiians were deprived of their lands without any say on their part, either under the kingdom, under the republic, or under the United States Government." In response to Representative Dowell's concern that the situation in Hawai'i might be different because "we have no government or tribe or organization to deal with," Chair Curry stated that "We have the law of the land of Hawaii from ancient times right down to the present where the preferences were given to certain classes of people." *Id.* at 300. The Territorial Attorney General, Harry Irwin, also submitted a written opinion concluding that the enactment of the Hawaiian Homes Commission Act would not violate any provisions of the U.S. Constitution. *Id.* at 292–94; "Hawaiian Homes Commission Act, 1920: Hearings on H.R. 13500: A Bill to Amend an Act Entitled 'An Act to Provide a Government for the Territory of Hawaii,' Approved April 30, 1900, as Amended to Establish an Hawaiian Homes Commission, and for Other Purposes," Senate Comm. on Territories, 66th Cong., 3d Sess., at 134–36 (December 14, 1920) (hereafter cited as "December 1920 Senate Hearings").

The committee report concluded that "the legislation is based upon a reasonable and not an arbitrary classification and is thus not unconstitutional class legislation" and that "there are numerous congressional precedents for such legislation in previous enactments granting Indians and soldiers and sailors special privileges in obtaining and using the public lands." H.R. Rep. No. 66-839, *supra* note 5, at 11.

7. Vause, *supra* note 3, at 26, quoting from *Senate Journal,* 10 Legislature, 1,044–45.

Prince Jonah Kūhiō
Kalanianaʻole

The group Aha Hui Puʻuhonua O Na Hawaiʻi (Hawaiian Protective Association) filed a petition with Congress during this period explaining the importance of "the soil" and "returning to mother earth" for the Hawaiians and arguing that "the Crown Lands, in particular, were the special birthright of the common people." According to their submission to Congress, although "Kamehameha III had recognized that the common people had one-third interest in the lands of Hawaiʻi at the time of the Mahele . . . the common people only received 0.8 percent of the land on an individual fee simple basis and the remaining portion of the lands were held in trust by the monarchy." [8]

This perspective was also promoted regularly by Prince Jonah Kūhiō Kalanianaʻole, who was the Delegate from the Territory of Hawaiʻi in the Congress during the deliberations that led to the enactment of the Hawaiian Homes Commission Act. Prince Kūhiō contended strenuously that the common Hawaiians were entitled to a share of the lands that had been "ceded" from the Republic of Hawaii to the United

8. Davianna Pomaikaʻi McGregor, "Kupaʻa I Ka ʻĀina: Persistence on the Land," 103 (1989) (unpublished Ph.D. dissertation, University of Hawaiʻi) (on file in the Hawaiian-Pacific Collection, Hamilton Library, University of Hawaiʻi at Mānoa), paraphrasing Aha Hui Puʻuhonua O Na Hawaiʻi, "Memorial to Congress" (Hawaiʻi State Archives, Delegate Kalanianaʻole File)).

States in 1898 because they had not obtained their fair share of the lands distributed during the Mahele.[9] He explained that the Mō'ī and the Land Commissioners and others developing the distribution process had recognized that "three classes" had interests in the lands of Hawai'i that "were about equal in extent": (1) "the King or Government," (2) "the chiefs," and (3) "the common people."[10] But the common Hawaiians—the maka'āinana—received only some 28,600 acres, a tiny percentage of what they should have received under the original plan.[11] As Prince Kūhiō explained, "The King and chiefs received for their portion 1,619,000 acres; the Government 1,505,460 acres; the balance, amounting to approximately 984,000 acres, was not conveyed to the common people, but reverted to the Crown."[12] The common people thus "assumed that these lands were being held in trust by the crown for their benefit,"[13] and the lands remained in the hands of Monarchs as part of the Crown Lands until the 1893 overthrow. Prince Kūhiō also explained how Article 95 in the 1894 Constitution of the Republic of Hawaii, which purported to eliminate the trust status of the Crown Lands and combine them with the Government Lands, was another example of "the injustice done the common people by those in power."[14] Because these lands had become part of the Public Lands of the United States, administered by the Territory of Hawai'i, and because the "one-third interest of the common people had been recognized, but ignored in the division,"[15] the Prince explained, the common people were now entitled to these lands through the Hawaiian Home Lands Program.

Prince Kūhiō expressed these views directly to Congress in his testimony supporting the homestead program. He explained that "[i]n the first constitution of Hawaii, promulgated by the King in 1840, it was there said that the common people had a community right, that they had an equal interest in the lands of the Kingdom with the chiefs and the King. In the law of 1845 it was again recognized by the board

---

9. This position is explained in detail in Prince J. K. Kalaniana'ole, "The Story of the Hawaiians," 21 *Mid-Pacific Magazine* 117 (February 1921).

10. *Id.* at 126. This position is supported by principles promulgated by the Land Commission in 1846, which said in their preface that "there are but three classes of persons having vested rights in the land—1st, the government (the King), 2nd, the landlord, and 3rd, the tenant." "Principles Adopted by the Board of Commissioners to Quiet Land Titles in Their Adjudication of Claims, Presented to Them, and Approved by the Legislative Council," October 26, 1846, in 2 *Revised Laws of Hawai'i*, 2126 (1925). The plan developed by Judge William Little Lee the following year was to allow the King to retain his private lands "subject only to the rights of the tenants," and then to divide the remaining land into thirds—"one-third to the Hawaiian government, one-third to the chiefs and konohiki, and the final third to the tenant farmers, 'the actual possessors and cultivators of the soil.'" Melody K. MacKenzie, "Historical Background," in *Native Hawaiian Rights Handbook*, 7 (Melody Kapilialoha MacKenzie, ed., 1991), citing 4 *Privy Council Records*, 296–306 (1847)). *See also* the discussion of this issue *supra* in chapter 4, text at notes 84, 104-12.

11. *See supra* chapter 4, text at notes 120–34.

12. Kalaniana'ole, *supra* note 9, at 126; *see also* speech made by Prince Kūhiō in 61 *Congressional Record*, 7452 (May 21, 1920).

13. Kalaniana'ole, *supra* note 9, at 126.

14. *Id.* at 126, 129. *See supra* chapter 17, text at notes 12–13, 18–21 for the text and analysis of Article 95 of the 1894 Constitution.

15. *Id.* at 129.

William H. Cornwell, John Wise, David Kawananakoa, John Dominis Holt II, and Clarence W. Ashford *(left to right)* in San Francisco during their trip to the Democratic National Convention in Kansas City, 1904

of royal commissioners that the common people had a one-third interest in the lands of the Kingdom."[16] Speaking later before the full U.S. House of Representatives, Prince Kūhiō said that at the time of the Mahele, "a one-third interest of the common people had been recognized, but ignored in the division, and . . . had reverted to the Crown, presumably in trust for the people," thus focusing explicitly on the Crown Lands, and he further explained that these specific lands "were taken over by the Republic of Hawaii" after the 1893 overthrow.[17] As a result of these unfulfilled promises and subsequent transfers, Kūhiō said, "[p]erhaps we have a legal right, certainly we have a moral right, to ask that these lands be set aside. We are not asking that what you are to do be in the nature of a largesse or as a grant, but as a matter of justice—belated justice."[18]

Territorial Senator John H. Wise echoed this position, explaining to the House Committee on the Territories that the makaʻāinana "knew that some day they would have some of that land [the Crown Lands], and that is ground into them even to-

---

16. "December 1920 Senate Hearings," *supra* note 6, at 68–69 (statement of Prince Jonah Kūhiō Kalanianaʻole). *See generally id.* at 67–77.

17. *Congressional Record*, 7452 (1920) (statement of Prince Jonah Kūhiō Kalanianaʻole).

18. *Id.* at 7453.

day." [19] Wise explained that the Crown Lands remained available because "King Kalakaua . . . went to work and leased these lands under long term leases, and these leases now are expiring or are about to expire, and they are the only lands we have to homestead." [20] Because the maka'āinana had received only 28,000 acres of the one-third of the lands that had been set aside for them, they "believed that the Crown lands represented the remainder of these lands held in trust for them. Considering the expiration of leases on former Crown lands, [Wise] believed that as a matter of equity, Hawaiians should be given preference to these lands." [21]

Senator Wise was a key player in the events leading to the adoption of the Hawaiian Homes Commission Act.[22] He was born in 1869 in Kohala on the Big Island, the son of Julius A. Wise, a native of Germany, and Rebecca Nawaa. He was in the first class of the Kamehameha School for Boys and then graduated from theological seminary in Oberlin, Ohio. He spent a year in prison for his participation in the 1895 effort to overthrow the Republic of Hawaii and reinstate the Monarchy.[23] He was originally a Democrat, he seconded the nomination of William Jennings Bryan at the 1900 Democratic National Convention, and he cast the deciding vote putting Bryan's silver doctrine into the Democratic platform.[24] In 1905 he became a Republican and attended the Republican National Convention in 1912.[25] During his time in the Territorial Senate (as a Republican), he was viewed skeptically by the planter elite. In 1918, the *Honolulu Star-Bulletin* characterized him as the "radical leader" of the Senate,[26] and the *Pacific Commercial Advertiser* said that he "smells to high heaven." [27]

Another Hawaiian who testified that the Hawaiians had an entitlement to the lands was Reverend Akaiko Akana, pastor of the Kawaiaha'o Church in Honolulu, who spoke on behalf of Ahahui Pu'uhonua O Na Hawai'i . He explained that "The bill before us does not ask others to help us. *The land involved is our own, by moral*

---

19. "Hearings before the House Committee on the Territories on the Rehabilitation and Colonization of Hawaiians and Other Proposed Amendments to the Organic Act of the Territory of Hawaii," February 3, 4, 5, 7, and 10, 1920 (hereafter cited as "February 1920 House") at 158 (statement of Senator John H. Wise).

20. Vause, *supra* note 3, at 49, quoting "February 1920 House Hearing," *supra* note 19, at 31–32.

21. *Id.* at 45, citing "1920 House Hearing," *supra* note 19, at 88–90. *See also* Senator Wise's testimony to the U.S. House Committee on Territories:

> The Hawaiian people, those of Hawaiian blood, have rights to these Crown lands, for the governments of the United States and the Territory of Hawaii have given them these rights. We feel that we have not got all that is coming to us.
>
> . . . the Crown lands were a portion of the lands given out in the Great Mahele of 1848 that were [held] in trust for the common people.

Vause, *supra* note 3, at 113, citing "February 1920 House Hearing," *supra* note 19, at 32, 47.

22. Among the other members of the delegation that went to Washington to lobby for the enactment of the Hawaiian Homes Commission Act in 1921 were Harold W. Rice and Charles A. Rice, the direct ancestor (and his brother) of Harold "Freddy" Rice, who brought the claim in *Rice v. Cayetano,* 528 U.S. 495 (2000), described *infra* in chapter 24.

23. A. Grove Day, *History Makers of Hawaii,* 130 (1984).

24. Vause, *supra* note 3, at 35 n. 2, citing *Honolulu Advertiser,* February 22, 1929.

25. *Id.,* citing *Honolulu Star-Bulletin,* August 30, 1948.

26. *Id.* at 24, quoting from *Honolulu Star-Bulletin,* December 7, 1918.

27. *Id.* at 24 n. 20, quoting from *Pacific Commercial Advertiser,* October 6, 1918.

equity, and the money with which to finance the project comes from the rental of this land." [28]

This view was understood and accepted by the legislators crafting the Hawaiian Homes Commission Act, and the Chair of the House Committee on the Territories, Charles F. Curry, made several key statements accepting the important view that the Crown Lands had been held in trust by the Monarchs for the common Hawaiians (makaʻāinana). After Senator Wise put forward the view that "the crown lands belong to the common people . . . of the Hawaiian race," Chair Curry said: "There is an equity and justice in saying that these crown lands belonged to the Hawaiian people." [29]

Addressing Senator Wise, Chair Curry observed that "from your standpoint these crown lands never really vested in the Federal Government except in trust for the common people. . . . [T]hey were placed in trust for the common people when in possession of the king, and just as we have provided land for the Indians, we may use these lands to provide for the Hawaiian race." [30] Secretary of the Interior Franklin K. Lane agreed that "the natives, were not treated fairly in the division of the lands that was made in 1848." [31] Using the same words that Prince Kūhiō had utilized when addressing the Congress, Secretary Lane told the House Committee on Territories that passage of the Hawaiian Homes Commission Act "should not be done in the nature of largesse or as a grant to these people. It should be done as a matter of justice—belated justice." [32]

The statements accepting the legitimacy of the claims of Native Hawaiians to the Crown Lands made by Chair Curry and other key players in the enactment of the Hawaiian Homes Commission Act are particularly significant, because a contrary view was presented to them with some vigor by Harry Irwin, the Attorney General of the Territory of Hawaiʻi, which the members of Congress rejected. In his substantial written opinion, Irwin acknowledged that "the native Hawaiian population did not receive anything like a proper proportion of the public lands under the Great Mahele," [33] that it was "amazing" that the common people received only 28,000 acres of lands in which they "undoubtedly had very extensive rights," [34] and that they had a "quasi equitable" or "moral equity" claim to these lands. [35] Nonetheless he contended that the Hawaiians had no legally enforceable claim to the Crown Lands under equity

---

28. "December 1920 Senate Hearing," *supra* note 6, at 54. Reverend Akana also said it was "surprising" to hear the testimony of A. G. M. Robertson opposing the Hawaiian Homes Commission Act, summarized *infra* this chapter, text at notes 37–41, because Robertson was "married to a Hawaiian girl" and had "greatly benefited by the good will of the Hawaiians." *Id.*

29. "February 1920 House Hearing," *supra* note 19, at 162.

30. *Id.* at 163 (statement of Chair Curry).

31. *Id.* at 251.

32. *Id.* at 253. Prince Kūhiō's language is quoted *supra* this chapter, text at note 18.

33. "February 1920 House Hearing," *supra* note 19, at 288.

34. *Id.*

35. *Id.* at 312.

Alexander George Morison
Robertson

or law, because these lands had been conveyed to the United States "free and clear of any trust whatever." [36]

In addition, Alexander George Morison Robertson, son of Justice George Morison Robertson [37] and himself Chief Justice of the Territory from 1911 to 1917, also testified (as attorney for the Parker Ranch) in strident and forceful terms against the theory that "the Crown lands . . . were held by the King in trust for the common people," stating that "there is absolutely nothing in that, either in law, fact, or history. The common people never had any claim in these Crown lands of any character." [38] "I say without any hesitation they [the Hawaiian people] had no equitable interest in those lands; that those lands, as decided by the Senate Subcommittee in 1903, and as decided by the Court of Claims in 1910, went from the hand of the Monarch to the Federal Government, free and clear of any equitable claim by anybody." [39] In the strongest possible terms, Robertson stated that "I am absolutely opposed to this bill,

---

36. *Id.* at 292, 312; *see generally* Vause, *supra* note 3, at 83, 113–14.

37. Associate Justice George M. Robertson was author of the opinion in *In the Matter of the Estate of His Majesty Kamehameha IV,* 2 Hawai'i 715 (1864), which led to the transformation of the Crown Lands; *see supra* chapter 8.

38. "December 1920 Senate Hearings," *supra* note 6, at 22.

39. *Id.* at 33. A. G. M. Robertson also testified forcefully that "[t]he common people got their full share of the very cream of the lands in 1848 under the act of 1845." *Id.* at 32. *See also id.* at 19, where Robertson said that "when the common people received their 28,000 acres of land . . . they were given the very cream of the entire group." Prince Jonah Kūhiō Kalaniana'ole responded to this assertion by pointing out that "[t]he most valuable lands to-day are the sugar lands, and the natives never got any of that land." *Id.* at 69.

and I believe it is un-American and unconstitutional," [40] adding also that "[t]here are hundreds of white men out there [in Hawai'i] who feel they are absolutely against this bill and that they are being discriminated against by it who can not send representatives to Washington." [41]

Judge Robertson's views were challenged by Senator John F. Nugent of Idaho, who asked, "Why should not these Hawaiians have the monopoly of their own land in their own country?" [42] Robertson replied that "[i]t is not their own land," but Senator Nugent insisted that the natives needed their own land, adding that "[t]he only thing that the civilization of the white man has brought to any of these aboriginal races is whisky and the diseases of the white man. I think the blackest page of American history is that of the treatment of the Indians by the United States Government." [43] Robertson responded by arguing that "[t]he Hawaiians are not Indians," [44] stating that the Indians were "a roving, nomadic race of people" and that "[t]hey did not take to civilization the way the Hawaiians did," [45] and asserting that "[t]he Hawaiians took to civilized customs there like a trout to a fly." [46]

The views of Attorney General Irwin and Judge Robertson did not persuade the federal legislators and executive officials. Secretary of Interior Lane concluded that "the natives, were not treated fairly in the division of the lands that was made in 1848." [47] And the report issued by the U.S. House Committee on Territories explained that "the second great factor demanding passage of this bill" was the inequitable land distribution system resulting from the Mahele and the continuing claim held by the Native Hawaiians, as Prince Kūhiō had explained:

> But *having been recognized as owners of a third interest in the lands of the kingdom,* the common people, believing that in the future means were to be adopted

40. *Id.* at 12.

41. *Id.* In support of his argument that the bill was unconstitutional, Judge Robertson contended that it was "a flagrant case of class legislation. No one would have the hardihood to deny that it is absolutely class legislation, drawn on what seems to me the viscious [sic] line of race. This bill cleaves the Hawaiian community in two, separating the whites from Hawaiians and Part-Hawaiians, taxing one for the benefit of the other, discriminating against the one and favoring the other according to the color of his skin and the kind of blood that God has put in his veins." *Id.* at 14; *see also id.* at 33–36, where Robertson gives his constitutional analysis in more detail.

Prince Jonah Kūhiō Kalaniana'ole, Hawai'i's delegate to Congress, objected to Robertson's statement that moneys to support the Home Lands Program "are to come out of the white taxpayers' pockets of the Territory. That is not correct. They are to come out of leases of the cane lands—that is, if the land board sees fit to lease them. If they do not, we have to find some other means of raising money to help the Hawaiians." *Id.* at 10, 129. Prince Kūhiō was correct in observing that taxpayer funds were not utilized for decades to support the Home Lands Program, and it was historically notoriously underfunded. *See generally* Alan Murakami, "The Hawaiian Homes Commission Act," in *Native Hawaiian Rights Handbook,* 43–76 (Melody Kapilialoha MacKenzie, ed., 1991).

42. "December 1920 Senate Hearings," *supra* note 6, at 23.

43. *Id.* 23–24. Senator George E. Chamberlain of Oregon immediately added, "I agree with you." *Id.* at 24.

44. *Id.* at 30.

45. *Id.* at 31.

46. *Id.*

47. H.R. Rep. No. 66-839, *supra* note 5, at 4.

to place them in full possession of these lands, *assumed that the residue was being held in trust by the Crown for their benefit.* However, *the lands were never conveyed to the common people,* and after a successful revolution, were *arbitrarily seized,* and by an article in the Hawaiian constitution became the public lands of the Republic of Hawaii.[48]

The delegates to Hawai'i's 1950 Constitutional Convention also understood that the establishment of the Hawaiian Home Lands Program was justified because the westerners who gained control of Hawai'i had failed to protect the lands of the Hawaiian people and that this program served "to preserve *only a very small part . . . of the domain* for the Hawaiians."[49] During the floor debate, Delegate Flora K. Hayes, Chair of the Committee on the Hawaiian Homes Act, explained that the package of provisions accepting and protecting the Hawaiian Home Lands Program "continues the recognition by the people of Hawaii of the justice of the original enactment of the Hawaiian Homes Commission Act as of 1920."[50]

The Hawaiian Homes Commission Act preserved "only a very small part . . . of the domain" the Hawaiians were entitled to because of the pressure from the Western sugar interests in the Islands. Because the Western elites wanted to keep the best lands available for lease by their sugar plantations, the lands eventually chosen for the homestead program had only marginal agricultural potential.[51] Many of the plantations' long-term leases of public lands were expiring,[52] and so the planter elites sought to exclude lands with sugar potential from those that would be offered to the Hawaiians through the federal statute. They also worked hard to raise the "blood quantum" necessary to be eligible for a homestead, in order to limit the number of beneficiaries and thus to minimize the act's impact.[53]

The statute is entitled "Hawaiian Homes Commission Act, 1920," but it was actually passed by Congress in July of 1921. The Senate in Hawai'i's Territorial Legislature was controlled by Caucasians by a majority of one in 1919 and 1920,[54] and this group proposed eliminating the valuable lands from those that would be assigned to the Hawaiian Homes Commission and to increase the blood quantum requirements for eligible Hawaiians. Nationally, the Republicans controlled the House of Representatives by a 240–192 margin and the Senate by a 49 to 47 margin in the 66th Con-

---

48. *Id.* at 5 (emphasis added).

49. Standing Committee Report No. 33, 1 *Proceedings of the Constitutional Convention of Hawaii, 1950,* 170–71 (1960) (emphasis added).

50. 2 *Proceedings of the Constitutional Convention of Hawaii, 1950,* 672 (1961).

51. MacKenzie, *supra* note 10, at 17–18; Levy, *supra* note 3, at 877–78.

52. During the period 1918–22, about twelve major sugar leases on Public Lands expired and the sugar interests feared these lands would be lost to homesteaders. Robert H. Horwitz, Judith B. Finn, Louis A. Vargha, and James W. Ceaser, *Public Land Policy in Hawaii: An Historical Analysis,* 38–39 (State of Hawaii Legislative Reference Bureau Report No. 5, 1969). *See also* Vause, *supra* note 3, at 52, 65–72.

53. "But no sooner did Prince Kūhiō float his plan in Congress than it was co-opted by sugar and pineapple planters, who saw it as a way to secure their own uncertain futures. Their leases on 26,000 prime acres were about to expire and a general homesteading law threatened to transfer their lucrative holdings to other hands." "The Prince's Plan Is Co-Opted," *Wall Street Journal,* September 9, 1991, at A-4, col. 1.

54. "December 1920 Senate Hearings," *supra* note 6, at 87 (statement of Delegate Kalaniana'ole).

gress (1919–21) when the hearings on the bill were being held, and they increased their control dramatically in the 67th Congress (1921–23) to a 311–126 margin in the House (which also contained four members of the Progressive Party and one member of the Socialist Party) and to a 60–36 margin in the Senate.[55] The Republican candidate for the presidency, Warren G. Harding, also won the 1920 election.

The Republicans thus dominated the national government in 1921, and the sugar planters in Hawai'i found receptive ears in the executive and legislative branches for their concerns. Although original proposals would have allowed a much larger number of Native Hawaiians to obtain homesteads (Prince Kūhiō and Senator Wise both supported a 1/32 blood quantum requirement),[56] the bill as enacted restricted eligible homesteaders to those with 50 percent blood quantum.[57] Those unenthusiastic about the program pressed for this high percentage because they hoped that, with the rapid decline of the Hawaiian population, the program could be phased out and the lands could be released to others in a relatively short period of time.[58] Both daily newspapers had criticized the 1/32 qualifying fraction "as an absurdity" and found the 50 percent requirement "much more acceptable."[59] This high blood quantum restriction has minimized the act's effectiveness and has also had the effect of imposing an artificial barrier that has divided the Hawaiians as a people.

Because of the successful efforts of Hawai'i's sugar interests to keep most of the agriculturally productive lands out of the Home Lands Program, Section 203 excluded most agricultural lands from the "available lands":

> All public lands of the description and acreage as follows, *excluding* (a) all lands within any forest reservation; (b) *all cultivated sugarcane lands,* and (c) all public lands held under certificate of occupation, homestead lease, right of purchase lease, or special homestead agreement, are hereby designated, and hereinafter referred to, as "available lands."[60]

---

55. *See* Party Division History, U.S. Senate Homepage, http://www.senate.gov/pagelayout/history/one_item_and_teasers/partydiv.htm; and http://en.wikipedia.org/wiki/67th_Congress (sites visited Nov. 19, 2006).

56. Vause has explained that the 1/32 figure came from a casual remark made by Senator Wise to the House Committee on Territories on February 3, 1920. Senator Wise was asked, "I notice in the resolution that you provide for those of Hawaiian blood. . . . How far do you go with that?" His answer was, "I contend that anybody, even to the thirty-second degree should be included." Vause, *supra* note 3, at 73 n.4, citing "February 1920 House Hearing," *supra* note 19, at 175. A 1/32 blood requirement would include everyone with a Hawaiian ancestor within the past five generations, and Senator Wise may have thought that it would essentially include everyone with some Hawaiian blood.

57. The increase to the 50 percent blood quantum requirement gained impetus from Senate Concurrent Resolution No. 8, enacted by the 1921 Territorial Legislature, which advocated this change, as well as a requirement that the program initially be an experimental five-year program, focusing on 37,900 acres on Hawai'i and Moloka'i and that the limitation on corporations owning more than 1,000 acres be repealed. Murakami, *supra* note 41, at 47; Vause, *supra* note 3, at 90–91.

58. *See, e.g.,* "Rehabilitation Should Be Limited to Hawaiians of Pure Blood, Says Governor," *Honolulu Star-Bulletin,* April 23, 1921, at 1.

59. Vause, *supra* note 3, at 132, citing *Honolulu Star-Bulletin,* July 22, 1920, and April 18, 1921; *Pacific Commercial Advertiser,* October 13, 1920.

60. HHCA, *supra* note 1, sec. 203 (emphasis added).

The lands assigned to this program were thus "in remote locations far from urbanized areas, on the dry, leeward side of each island, generally with poor soils and rough terrain, more difficult and costly to develop."[61] "Almost all of the lands lacked water for irrigation or domestic use. Most of the lands were rough, rocky and dry, 55,000 acres were covered with barren lava. Another 7,800 acres were the steep parts of mountains."[62] In an oft-quoted remark, State Representative William Jarrett denounced the proposals being made by Territorial Governor Charles J. McCarthy and the sugar planters by describing the lands being offered to the Hawaiians as "lands that a goat couldn't live on."[63] Nonetheless, the Hawaiian leaders who had promoted the program worked to make the initial five-year trial phase of the program a success, and in 1926 Congress gave approval to expand the program to the entire 203,500 acres, on a permanent basis.[64]

Table 12 shows the original inventory of "available lands" assigned to the Home Lands Program by island (and their derivation where it can be determined).[65]

HHCA Section 203 provided that in addition to the expressly named lands, the Commission was to select acreages out of larger parcels. These selections are given in Table 13.[66]

As a condition of statehood, the U.S. Congress in the 1959 Admission Act[67] required the new State of Hawai'i to take responsibility for administering the Hawaiian Home Lands Program, and the State accepted this responsibility as part of its Constitution.[68] Some provisions in the original act can still be amended only with the approval of the U.S. Congress. According to Congress' subsequent explanation of this action, the United States "reaffirmed the trust relationship which existed

---

61. Office of the Governor, *Report on the Hawaiian Home Lands Program: Progress Report on the Implementation of Recommendations of the Federal-State Task Force III-4* (Submitted to the U.S. Senate Committee on Energy and Natural Resources, January 1992). These lands have also been characterized as "'fourth-class' lands." "The Prince's Plan Is Co-Opted," *Wall Street Journal*, September 9, 1991, at A-4, col. 2.

62. McGregor, *supra* note 8, at 297.

63. Vause, *supra* note 3, at 89, quoting from *Honolulu Star-Bulletin*, April 23, 1921. *See also* Linda S. Parker, *Native American Estate: The Struggle over Indian and Hawaiian Lands*, 154 (1989): "By removing the sugar-producing lands from use as homelands, the bill left only the poorer agricultural and pastoral lands. Much of the available land was marginal because of a lack of water or soil unsuited for farming. Most attempts to farm these lands failed"; MacKenzie, *supra* note 10, at 17–18: "Homesteading was originally conceived of as an agricultural experiment, but since the lands were arid and of marginal agricultural quality, virtually none of the homestead areas designed for diversified agriculture were successful." Title III of the Hawaiian Homes Commission Act also served the interests of the sugar planters by annulling the provision allowing twenty-five citizens to make claims to leased lands suitable for the cultivation of sugar. Vause, *supra* note 3, at 110.

64. McGregor, *supra* note 8, at 299–300, citing Felix Keesing, "Hawaiian Homesteading on Molokai," in *University of Hawaii Research Publications*, vol. 1, no. 3, 7–9 (January 1936).

65. Information regarding "Lands" and "Acreage" is taken from Arthur Y. Akinaka and James M. Dunn, *A Land Inventory and Land Use Study for the Department of Hawaiian Home Lands*, 2–3 (December 18, 1972). "Derivation" information was also provided. *Id.* at 24–25. Akinaka and Dunn have reported that the "Derivations" for most of the lands appear by name in the *Buke Mahele*. *Id.*

66. Information regarding the Commission's selection and derivation of these lands is from *id.* at 16, 24–25.

67. "Hawaii Statehood Admission Act," 86 Pub. L. 3, 73 Stat. 4 (1959).

68. *Hawai'i State Constitution*, art. XII, § 1. *See infra* chapter 24, text at notes 141–49.

TABLE 12a. Hawaiian Home Lands: Island of Hawai'i

Lands	Acreage —more or less	Derivation
Kamaoa-Puueo	1,000	Government
(Kamaoa) Puukapu	12,000	Crown
Kawaihae 1	10,000	Crown
Pauahi	750	
Kamoku-Kapulena	5,000	Government – commutation from W.C. Lunalilo
Waimanu	200	Crown
Nienie	7,350	
Hamakua District	53,000 to be selected from Humuula Mauka	
Panaewa, Waiakea	2,000	Crown
(Waiakea)	2,000	
Waiakea-Kai or Keaaukaha		
Piihonua	2,000 acres of agricultural lands to be selected	
Kaohe-Makuu	2,000 acres to be selected by Commission	Government (Makuu)

TABLE 12b. Hawaiian Home Lands: Island of Maui

Lands	Acreage —more or less	Derivation
Kahikinui	25,000	Government commutation from Lot Kamehameha.
Kula public lands	6,000	

TABLE 12c. Hawaiian Home Lands: Island of Moloka'i.

Lands	Acreage —more or less	Derivation
Palaau	11,000	Crown
Kapaakea	2,000	Crown former unassigned land adjusted in 1890.
Kalamaula	6,000	
Hoolehua	3,500	Government Crown
Kamiloloa I and II	3,600	
Makakupaia	2,200	Government
Kalaupapa	5,000	

TABLE 12d. Hawaiian Home Lands: Island of O'ahu:

Lands	Acreage —more or less	Derivation
Nanakuli	3,000	
Lualualei	2,000	
Waimanalo	4,000 excepting the military reservation & the beach lands	Crown

TABLE 12e. Hawaiian Home Lands: Island of Kaua'i

Lands	Acreage —more or less	Derivation
Waimea	15,000	Crown
Moloaa	2,500	Government
Anahola & Kamalomalo	5,000	Crown (Anahola)

TABLE 13. Hawaiian Home Lands acreages selected from larger parcels

Lands	Acreage Total	Year	Derivation
Panaewa	2,000	1924	
Keaukaha	2,000	1924	
Waiohuli-Keokea	6,000	1926	Crown, former unassigned land adjusted in 1980 (Waiohuli)
Humuula	49,100	1929	
Piihonua	2,000	1929	
Kaohe-Makuu	2,000	1929	Government (Makuu)
Waimanalo	192	1931	Crown

between the United States and the Hawaiian people by retaining the exclusive power to enforce the [Hawaiian Home Lands] trust, including the power to approve land exchanges, and legislative amendments affecting the rights of beneficiaries under such Act."[69]

Although the State has made some efforts recently to improve the administration of the Hawaiian Home Lands Program, it has historically suffered from serious structural problems,[70] including the limitation that the lands were subject to "exclusions" of Section 203, the vague "more or less" quantifications in the act that do not provide clear guidance regarding which lands are actually to be included, the inadequate surveys, the underfunded and mismanaged administration,[71] and the subse-

69. "Native Hawaiian Health Care Improvement Act of 1992," 42 U.S.C. § 11701(15). "The Findings in the 1994 Native Hawaiian Education Act," 20 U.S.C. §§ 7512(1),(7)-(13), reconfirm that "Native Hawaiians are a distinct and unique indigenous people," that the Kingdom of Hawai'i was overthrown with the assistance of officials of the United States, that the United States had apologized for "the deprivation of the rights of Native Hawaiians to self-determination" (emphasis added) and that "Congress had affirmed the *special relationship* between the United States and the Native Hawaiians" through the enactment of the Hawaiian Homes Commission Act, 1920, the 1959 Admission Act, and other listed statutes.

70. Murakami, *supra* note 41, at 43: "the track record of HHCA administrators has been dismal," 51–52; U.S. Dept. of the Interior and U.S. Dept. of Justice, *From Mauka to Makai: The River of Justice Must Flow Freely,* 35 (Report on the Reconciliation Process Between the Federal Government and Native Hawaiians, October 23, 2000) (hereafter cited as *Mauka to Makai*): "implementation of the HHCA can only be described as a dismal failure." *See generally* Hawaii Advisory Committee to the United States Commission on Civil Rights, *A Broken Trust—The Hawaiian Homelands Program: Seventy Years of Failure of the Federal and State Governments to Protect the Civil Rights of Native Hawaiians* (December 1991).

71. Office of the Governor, *Report on the Hawaiian Home Lands Program, supra* note 61, at 3–4 lists the improper actions of the Federal Government as including "(1) no funding; (2) limitation on revenues derived from trust assets; (3) alienation of land; (4) public use of trust lands without compensation; (5) permanent

quent deletions and adjustments made by the Federal and State Governments. At least four of the nine commissioners governing this program must be at least one-fourth Hawaiian,[72] but all are appointed by the Governor of the State of Hawai'i, and hence they are not directly accountable to the Native Hawaiian beneficiaries. The program has historically been underfunded,[73] and many of its lands remain undeveloped and unavailable for the many waiting applicants.[74] "[D]uring the Territorial period (1921–1959) and the first two decades of statehood (1959–1978), inadequate funding forced the Department of Hawaiian Home Lands to lease its best lands to non-Hawaiians in order to generate operating funds."[75] In 1996, the Hawai'i Supreme Court ruled that the practice of leasing lands to non-Hawaiians violated the Hawaiian Homes Commission Act.[76]

About 7,000 Native Hawaiians hold leases on the lands managed by the Department of Hawaiian Home Lands,[77] and some 20,000 are on the wait list, hoping someday to receive a lease from the department.[78] Some have been waiting for several decades.

Although the original goal of the Hawaiian Homes Commission Act was to transfer 200,000 acres to Native Hawaiian homesteaders, the actual amount was always less because of the vague definitions given to some of the lands and because some lands were removed during the Territorial years to be used for other purposes.[79] A survey undertaken in 1972 reported that 189,878 acres were in the program,[80] and a government report in 1986 stated that 187,597 acres were included (of which only 32,528 acres were being used for homesteads, with the rest being leased to raise revenues).[81]

In the last few years, the Department of Hawaiian Home Lands has been undertaking serious efforts to make the trust whole. "Since 1984, the State of Hawai'i has

---

reservation of trust lands without compensation or land exchange; and (6) the discriminatory denial of federal dollars on the basis of race." Two improper State actions are also identified: "(1) alienation of land; and (2) public use of trust land without compensation." *Id.* at 4.

72. HHCA, *supra* note 1, § 202(a).

73. *See* Murakami, *supra* note 41, at 43, 51–56.

74. MacKenzie, *supra* note 10, at 18.

75. *Expressing the Policy of the United States Regarding the United States Relationship with Native Hawaiians and to Provide a Process for the Recognition by the United States of the Native Hawaiian Governing Entity, and for Other Purposes,* Report 107-66 of the Senate Committee on Indian Affairs, 107th Cong, 1st Sess., at 14 (September 21, 2001).

76. *Bush v. Watson,* 81 Hawai'i 474, 918 P.2d 1130 (1996).

77. Department of Business and Economic Development, *State of Hawaii Data Book: A Statistical Abstract,* 202 (2000). This figure has increased from 5,765 (1,166 agricultural and 4,599 residential) in 1986. Department of Business and Economic Development, *State of Hawaii Data Book: A Statistical Abstract,* 208 (1987), citing Department of Hawaiian Home Lands, *'Āina Ho'opulapula: Annual Report, FY 1986,* 19–21, 24.

78. This figure has increased from 12,041 (3,915 agricultural and 8,126 residential) in 1986. Department of Business and Economic Development (1987), *supra* note 77, at 208.

79. *See* Akinaka and Dunn, *supra* note 65, at 14–18.

80. *Id.* at 2.

81. After a 16,518-acre land transfer from the Public Land Trust and several smaller transactions, the land total has risen to 200,176 acres. Department of Business and Economic Development (2000), *supra* note 77, at 202; Department of Business and Economic Development (1987), *supra* note 78, at 208.

acted to address some of these issues by canceling twenty-four Executive Orders, nine forest reserves, and seven proclamations, returning 42,806 acres of previously withdrawn lands, to the Home Lands Trust."[82] During the administration of Governor John Waihe'e (1987–95), 16,518 acres were added to the lands of the department to compensate for lands that had been transferred out during earlier periods. In 1995, as a result of litigation and a protracted negotiating period, the Hawai'i State Legislature approved a $600 million settlement to the Department of Hawaiian Home Lands to compensate for lands improperly conveyed from the department during the Territorial period, to be paid in $30 million increments over a twenty-year period.[83] Also in 1995, "the United States acted to resolve [its] withdrawal of [Hawaiian Home Lands] by enacting the Hawaiian Home Lands Recovery Act (HHLRA) and in 1998, [by] signing a Memorandum of Agreement with the State of Hawaii that provided for the return of 960 acres to the Home Land Trust."[84]

In 1988, Hawai'i's Legislature enacted the Native Hawaiian Trusts Judicial Relief Act,[85] to provide some opportunities to resolve controversies related to breaches of trust committed against beneficiaries of the Hawaiian Home Lands Trust since statehood. Then in 1991, the Legislature enacted another statute to establish the Hawaiian Home Lands Trust Individual Claims Review Panel to evaluate such claims and make recommendations to the Legislature for appropriate resolution of them.[86] The panel received more than 4,300 claims and had evaluated 2,050 of them by the end of 1998, recommending payments of more than $16,000,000 to the more than 400 successful claimants.[87] In its 1999 session, the Legislature enacted a bill designed to extend the panel's life to allow it to evaluate the remaining claims,[88] but Governor Benjamin Cayetano vetoed this bill,[89] and the panel thus went out of business and no claimants received any payments. The claimants then filed a class action, claiming that the State's action in terminating this program violated the Contract Clause of the U.S. Constitution.[90] The trial judge, Victoria Marks, certified the plaintiff class and granted the plaintiffs their motion for summary judgment in August 2000. On June

82. *Mauka to Makai, supra* note 70, at 43; "Broken Promise: Hawaiians Wait in Vain for Their Land," *Wall Street Journal,* September 9, 1991, at A-4, col. 4.

83. *See* "An Act Relating to Hawaiian Home Lands," act 14, §§ 6, 8, 1995 *Hawai'i Sess. Laws,* 696, 700, 701; Department of Hawaiian Home Lands, *1995 Annual Report,* 1 (1995); *Mauka to Makai, supra* note 70, at 43.

84. *Mauka to Makai, supra* note 70, at 36.

85. "An Act Relating to Right to Sue by Native Hawaiian and Hawaiian Individuals and Organizations," act 395, 1988 *Hawai'i Sess. Laws,* 942, codified as *Hawai'i Revised Statutes,* chapter 673.

86. "An Act Relating to Individual Hawaiian Home Lands Trust Claims," act 323, 1991 *Hawai'i Sess. Laws,* 990.

87. *See* Hawaiian Home Lands Trust Individual Claims Review Panel, *Report to the Governor and the Hawaii Legislature* (1997), and Hawaiian Home Lands Trust Individual Claims Review Panel, *Report to the Governor and the Hawaii Legislature* (1999).

88. H.B. 1675, H.D. 1, S.D.1, C.D.1.

89. Governor Cayetano vetoed this bill in June1999. Pat Omandam, "Hawaiians Rip Veto Blocking Land Claims," *Honolulu Star-Bulletin,* June 17, 1999.

90. *Kalima v. State of Hawaii,* Civ. No. 99-4771-12 VSM (Haw. 1st Cir.).

30, 2006, the Hawai'i Supreme Court ruled that the beneficiaries had a right to sue, and thus allowed the case to go forward.[91]

The Hawaiian Home Lands Program has been important because it demonstrates that the U.S. Government has accepted a trust responsibility toward Native Hawaiians and considers them to have a status comparable to that of other Native Americans. The program has helped some Native Hawaiians, but many others remain on the outside waiting to obtain some benefit from it.

For purposes of this study, the most important perception that emerged from the debates creating the Hawaiian Home Lands Program was the understanding that the Crown Lands were lands that the Hawaiian Monarchs held in trust for all the Native Hawaiian People, and that the common Hawaiians had a continuing claim to these lands because they received such a minimal amount of land during and after the 1848 Mahele. Congress acted in 1921 to return some of these lands back to the maka'āinana, but it was only a modest amount and the lands had marginal agricultural value. Native Hawaiians have a continuing claim to these lands. Returning all of the remaining Crown Lands to the Native Hawaiian Nation would be a constructive way to correct the injustices that have occurred and the 'Āina selected by Kamehameha III would allow Native Hawaiians to continue their renaissance.

---

91. *Kalima v. State of Hawai'i,* III Hawai'i 84, 137 P. 3d. 990 (2006).

23

Statehood (1959 to Present)

On August 21, 1959, Hawai'i became the Fiftieth State of the United States.[1] The vote of the people of Hawai'i in favor of statehood was an overwhelming 94 percent in favor, but this vote has been criticized by some because it did not list other self-determination options as possibilities, including independence or a freely associated status.[2]

Becoming a state of the United States was a topic that had been discussed in the Islands for more than a hundred years. In the early 1850s, Kauikeaouli (Kamehameha III) instructed his advisors to negotiate a treaty of annexation with the United States on the condition that Hawai'i be admitted as a state in the Union.[3] After annexation occurred in 1898, statehood was a regular topic of discussion among the Hawaiian leaders of the time. Prominent Hawaiians such as D. Kalauokalani, Robert Wilcox, J. K. Kaulia, and John Wise formed a new political party in June 1900 called Home Rula Ku'oko'a (The Independent Home Rule Party), which had as one of its central tenets the goal of securing statehood for Hawai'i.[4] In 1903, the Territorial Legislature,

---

1. "Admission Act of March 18, 1959," Pub. L. No. 86-3, 73 Stat. 4 (1959), reprinted in 1 *Hawai'i Revised Statutes,* 90 (1993).

2. Some Native Hawaiians have challenged the legitimacy of the 1959 vote because the only options given to the voters were (1) to become a state or (2) to remain a territory; they have argued that the option of becoming independent or a freely associated state should also have been given to the voters. Others have argued that the United States violated international law by allowing large numbers of non-Hawaiians to immigrate to the Islands, thus depriving Native Hawaiians of their unique right to exercise self-determination in their native islands. *See, e.g.,* Eric Steven O'Malley, "Irreconcilable Rights and the Question of Hawaiian Statehood," 89 *Georgetown Law Review,* 501, 515–17 (2001); Jon M. Van Dyke, Carmen Di Amore-Siah, and Gerald W. Berkley-Coats, "Self-Determination for Nonself-Governing Peoples and for Indigenous Peoples: The Cases of Guam and Hawai'i," 18 *University of Hawai'i Law Review,* 623, 624–25 n. 3 (1996).

3. *See supra* chapter 19, text at notes 6–21.

4. Wilcox said in July 1901, when he was serving as the first Delegate from the Territory of Hawai'i to the U.S. Congress, that

> when the Congress meets in December the first bill I shall introduce will be one to admit Hawaii to statehood. Of course I realize that such a measure will meet with opposition on the ground that we have but recently been incorporated as a Territory and should wait. Be that as it may, I will introduce the bill, because I know that the sooner we start to work in such matters the sooner our efforts will meet with regard.
> Some day Hawaii will be a state and it will not be many years.

"Bill to Make Hawaii a State: Delegate Wilcox Declares His Views in Plain Terms," *Evening Bulletin,* July 12, 1901, at 1.

Robert W. Wilcox,
first delegate to the
U.S. Congress from the
Territory of Hawai'i

with 70 percent Native Hawaiian members, voted unanimously to petition Congress for statehood.[5] "Prince Jonah Kūhiō Kalaniana'ole, Hawai'i's delegate to Congress, introduced the first statehood bill in the House of Representatives in 1919, and the second in the next session."[6] Delegate Victor S. K. Houston introduced another statehood bill in the early 1930s.[7] In January 1935, Delegate Samuel Wilder King introduced a different type of bill, seeking authorization to frame a state constitution.[8]

At the hearings Congress held in 1935, seventeen Hawaiians testified or submitted letters, with fifteen supporting statehood, one expressing opposition, and one other expressing conditional opposition.[9] Hearings were held again in 1937, this time with nine Hawaiians testifying in support and one expressing opposition.[10] David K. Trask, an important Hawaiian leader who served in the Territorial Senate and later as Sheriff of the Territory, and who was a member of the Democratic Party's central committee for ten years, had long been a foe of statehood, but he changed his posi-

5. Lawrence H. Fuchs, *Hawaii Pono: A Social History,* 406 (1961, reprinted 1983).

6. Gavan Daws, *Shoal of Time: A History of the Hawaiian Islands,* 333 (1968, reprinted 1974).

7. *Id.*

8. *Id.*

9. Davianna Pomaika'i McGregor, "Are Native Hawaiians Also Native American?" 15 (handout distributed at presentation given at the University of Hawai'i at Mānoa, November 30, 2000).

10. *Id.*

tion in 1940 after attending the national Democratic Party convention that year.[11] A plebiscite was held in the Territory in 1940, in which the voters supported the idea of statehood by a 2 to 1 margin, 46,174 voting in favor and 22,428 voting no.[12] Congressional hearings were held again in 1946, with eleven Hawaiians testifying in support, two in opposition, and two giving conditional support.[13] In the 1947 hearings, three Hawaiians testified in support, none in opposition.[14] In 1948, sixteen Hawaiians testified in support, one in opposition.[15] In 1950, eight Hawaiians testified in support of statehood, and one (John Hoopale) asked Congress "to restore the independence of our beloved land."[16]

In 1950, 85 percent of the voters cast ballots for delegates to the Constitutional Convention to draft a state constitution.[17] Twelve of the sixty-three delegates elected to the 1950 Con Con were of Hawaiian ancestry, including Trudy M. Akau, Samuel K. Apoliona Jr., J. Pia Cockett, Flora Kaai Hayes, William H. Heen, Charles E. Kauhane, Samuel Wilder King, Richard J. Lyman Jr., Arthur K. Trask,[18] and James K. Trask. The Constitution drafted by these delegates was approved by the voters in November 1950 by a 3-1 margin, with 82,788 in favor and 27,109 opposed.[19] Heen went to Washington in 1954 to lobby for statehood and served as Vice Chair of the Hawai'i Statehood Commission.[20]

William S. Richardson, who later served as Lieutenant Governor and Chief Justice of the State of Hawai'i, was another prominent Hawaiian who traveled to

11. "David Trask Rites Set for Tomorrow," *Honolulu Star-Bulletin,* October 13, 1950.

12. Robert C. Schmitt, *Historical Statistics of Hawaii,* 602 (1977); Daws, *supra* note 6, at 383–84. The ballot used in the 1940 election asked the question, "Do you favor statehood?" in both English and Hawaiian. Some 80 percent of the eligible voters cast their ballots, and the support for statehood was greater on the neighbor islands (where more than 70 percent voted yes) than on O'ahu (where 63 percent voted yes). Opponents of statehood were primarily Caucasians concerned that persons of Japanese ancestry would come to dominate the politics of the Islands. *See generally* Roger Bell, *Last Among Equals: Hawaiian Statehood and American Politics,* 73–74 (1984).

13. McGregor, "Are Native Hawaiians Also Native American?" *supra* note 9, at 15. Most of these hearings were held in Honolulu.

14. *Id.*

15. *Id.*

16. *Id.* Hoopale's testimony was the only voice for independence. Most of the other Hawaiians opposing statehood expressed concern that the new state would be controlled by persons of Japanese ancestry. A "commonwealth" option, similar to that of Puerto Rico, was promoted by former Governor Ingram M. Stainback, but all of the candidates in his Commonwealth Party "were beaten badly in the 1958 election." Fuchs, *supra* note 5, at 412. *See also* Kevin Dayton, "From Simple Dreams to Grand Challenges," *Honolulu Advertiser,* August 18, 1999, at 2, col. 2.

17. Schmitt, *supra* note 12, at 384.

18. Arthur K. Trask also served on a commission promoting statehood. In 1999, he said he favored sovereignty for Native Hawaiians but also felt he was right to press for statehood: "I've always favored sovereignty. To me, we had to have statehood first as a preliminary step to get to Congress and to get to the American people on an equal basis. We had to be a state, and talk man to man. Otherwise, we couldn't do it. We didn't have a vote in Congress." Kevin Dayton, "From Simple Dreams to Grand Challenges," *Honolulu Advertiser,* August 18, 1999, at 2, col. 1.

19. Schmitt, *supra* note 12, at 384.

20. Bob Dye, "Long Era of Public Duty by Heens Comes to End," *Honolulu Advertiser,* April 22, 2001, at B-3, col. 5.

Washington to lobby for statehood in the 1950s. As he later explained, those who were outside the central corridors of power (including most Hawaiians) favored statehood, because it offered a chance for local control and local leadership, while those with wealth and close ties to the Washington leadership opposed statehood because it would undercut their control over Island affairs.[21]

All told, Hawai'i's Territorial Legislature had made at least seventeen attempts to obtain statehood for the Islands since 1903, some sixty-six bills had been introduced into Congress since 1920, and more than twenty-two congressional investigations looked into the topic after 1935.[22] When the opportunity for statehood finally appeared on the horizon in 1959, "[n]ot a single important political figure politically disagreed."[23] In March 1959, after Congress voted for statehood, the bells at Kawaiaha'o Church in Honolulu rang for three hours[24] and Reverend Abraham Akaka presided over a special statehood service at the church.[25]

The 1959 Admission Act

When statehood finally came in 1959, it was supported by most Native Hawaiians, because it enabled them to have at least some say over decisions governing their Islands. The vote across the Islands favored statehood by a 17-1 margin of approval, 132,938 (94 percent) in favor and 7,854 opposed, and support seemed to come from all communities on all islands.[26] The primary focus of the Hawaiians during the run-up to statehood was on protecting the Hawaiian Home Lands Program and in protecting their claims to the Public Lands held by the Federal Government. A separate ballot question was offered on the Hawaiian Home Lands Program, and it passed also by a similar overwhelming margin.

The 1959 Admission Act transferred the Hawaiian Home Commissions Act to the new State, but the Federal Government retained certain oversight responsibilities, and some provisions of the act can be amended only with the approval of the Federal Government.[27] The Admission Act also transferred most of the lands in the Public Land Trust to the State and attached explicit trust responsibilities to these lands. In Section 5(b) of the 1959 Admission Act, Congress transferred about 1.4 million of

21. Interviews with William S. Richardson, Honolulu, May 2001. *See also* Fuchs, *supra* note 5, at 407: "But not all of the citizens of Hawaii wanted statehood. Until 1935, the overwhelming majority of the *kamaaina* oligarchy of the Islands were steadfastly opposed."

22. Sheryl L. Miyahira, "Hawaii's Ceded Lands," 3 *University of Hawai'i Law Review,* 101, 124 (1981), citing 105 *Congressional Record,* 3,858 (1959) and H.R. Rep. No. 32, 86th Cong., 1st Sess., Appendix B, at 68–69 (1959).

23. Fuchs, *supra* note 5, at 414.

24. Dayton, *supra* note 18, at 2 col. 6.

25. Fuchs, *supra* note 5, at 447; Mary Adamski, "Hawaiian Pastor's Influence Endures," *Honolulu Star-Bulletin,* at A-4, col. 4.

26. "The only one of the Islands' 240 precincts to reject statehood was tiny Ni'ihau, all of whose 107 registered voters were Hawaiian or part-Hawaiian." Fuchs, *supra* note 5, at 414.

27. "Admission Act," *supra* note 1, sec. 4.

the roughly 1.75 million acres of Public Lands (the former Crown and Government Lands) to the new State of Hawai'i (which included the Hawaiian Home Lands).[28] But the State of Hawai'i received only "naked" title to these Public Lands, along with the fiduciary responsibilities of a trustee.[29] In Section 5(f) of the Admission Act, Congress stated explicitly that these transferred lands are to be held as a "public trust" by the State and that the revenues generated by these lands are to be used for the following five specific purposes:

> for the support of the public schools and other public educational institutions, *for the betterment of the conditions of native Hawaiians, as defined in the Hawaiian Homes Commission Act, 1920, as amended,* for the development of farm and home ownership on as widespread a basis as possible[,] for the making of public improvements, and for the provision of lands for public use. (Emphasis added.)

These carefully crafted provisions were based on the clear recognition that Native Hawaiians had continuing claims to these lands and that they must be held in trust until those claims are finally resolved.[30]

In 1992, the Congress explained that the United States had "reaffirmed the trust relationship which existed between the United States and the Hawaiian people by retaining the legal responsibility of the State for the betterment of the conditions of native Hawaiians under section 5(f) of the [Admission Act]."[31] Hawai'i's first State Constitution, which had been drafted in 1950, explicitly accepted these trust responsibilities and committed the new State to comply with them.[32] The Federal Government retained some 373,720 acres of lands, including the national parks on the islands of Maui and Hawai'i and the federal military bases, which are mainly on O'ahu.[33]

---

28. This approach of transferring vast amounts of land to the State "differed significantly from the legal treatment of lands in other states admitted to the Union, where only a small portion of the land was allocated to the new state." Melody K. MacKenzie, "Historical Background," in *Native Hawaiian Rights Handbook,* 18 (Melody Kapilialoha MacKenzie, ed., 1991). Small amounts of "surplus" land were transferred from the Federal to State Government in 1964 and thereafter pursuant to Section 5(e) of the Admission Act. *See* Robert H. Horwitz, Judith B. Finn, Louis A. Vargha, and James W. Ceaser, *Public Land Policy in Hawaii: An Historical Analysis,* 70–71, 93–95, 97–99, 102–03, 105–06 (Legislative Reference Bureau Report No. 5, 1969). In 1963, Congress enacted Pub. L. No. 88-233, 77 Stat. 472, authorizing the Federal Government to continue to return unneeded lands to the State and stating that these lands would be subject to the trust obligations spelled out in Section 5(f) of the Admission Act. Between 1981 and 1987, for instance, the Federal Government transferred nine parcels containing 721 acres from the Ceded Lands Trust to the State, plus another four parcels containing 119 acres of lands that the Federal Government had purchased and held in fee. Letter from Deputy Attorney General William M. Tam (approved by Attorney General Warren Price III) to State Senator Andrew Levin, October 16, 1987.

29. *State v. Zimring,* 58 Hawai'i 104, 124, 566 P.2d 725, 737 (1977).

30. "The ceded lands of the native Hawaiian commoners, meantime, were still being held in trust by the federal government. With statehood in 1959, the U.S. required that this land and the revenues it generated be used for 'the betterment' of native Hawaiians, but that never happened." "The Prince's Plan Is Co-Opted," *Wall Street Journal,* September 9, 1991, at A-4, col. 2.

31. "Native Hawaiian Health Care Improvement Act of 1992," 42 U.S.C. sec. 11701 (16).

32. *Hawai'i Constitution,* Article XIV(7) (1950), now *Hawai'i Constitution,* Article XVI(7).

33. U.S. Dept. of the Interior and U.S. Dept. of Justice, *From Mauka to Makai: The River of Justice Must Flow Freely,* 37 (Report on the Reconciliation Process between the Federal Government and Native Hawaiians, October 23, 2000) (hereafter cited as *Mauka to Makai*).

The 1978 Constitutional Convention

Until Hawai'i's 1978 Constitutional Convention, the State of Hawai'i interpreted the provisions in the 1959 Admission Act described above as allowing it to use the revenue received from the Public Lands for any one of the five purposes listed in Section 5(f),[34] and the State devoted almost all of the revenue to public education and allocated no funds specifically to benefit Native Hawaiians.[35] Because of this neglect, the delegates to the 1978 Convention proposed a series of constitutional amendments that were subsequently ratified by the voters and added to Hawai'i's Constitution. These amendments stated that the general public and Native Hawaiians were the beneficiaries of the Public Lands Trust,[36] they created the Office of Hawaiian Affairs (OHA),[37] they required the State Legislature to allocate a pro rata share of the revenues from the Public Lands to OHA to be used explicitly for the betterment of Native Hawaiians,[38] they stated that Hawaiian should be one of the official languages of the State (along with English),[39] they clarified the funding for the Department of Hawaiian Home Lands,[40] and they imposed limits on the ability to claim land through adverse possession.[41]

OHA is a "self-governing corporate body,"[42] "independent from the executive branch and all other branches of government,"[43] established not only to receive and manage assets on behalf of Native Hawaiians but also to facilitate self-government and self-determination for them.[44] The report of the 1978 Constitutional Convention explained that OHA was created "to provide Hawaiians the right to determine the priorities [that would] effectuate the betterment of their condition and welfare and promote the protection and preservation of the Hawaiian race" and, in general, to "unite Hawaiians as a people."[45] In 1980, the Hawai'i Legislature determined

---

34. MacKenzie, "Historical Background," *supra* note 28, at 19.

35. *Rice v. Cayetano,* 146 F.3d 1075, 1077 (9th Cir. 1998): "no benefits actually went to native Hawaiians until the state constitution was amended in 1978."

36. *Hawai'i Constitution,* Article XII(4), stating that the Ceded Lands transferred by the Federal Government to the State of Hawai'i "shall be held by the State as a public trust for Native Hawaiians and the general public." This amendment was designed to provide greater emphasis to the Native Hawaiian claims and to rectify the past inequities. Some of the dynamics of the 1978 Constitutional Convention are described in Tom Coffman, *The Island Edge of America: A Political History of Hawai'i,* 305–16 (2003).

37. *Hawai'i Constitution,* Article XII(5).

38. *Id.,* Article XII(6).

39. *Id.,* Article XV(4).

40. *Id.,* Article XII(1).

41. *Id.,* Article XVI(12).

42. *Trustees of the Office of Hawaiian Affairs v. Yamasaki,* 69 Hawai'i 154, 163, 737 P.2d 446, 452 (1987).

43. Committee on Hawaiian Affairs, Standing Comm. Rpt. No. 59, 1 *Proceedings of the 1978 Constitutional Convention,* 645 (1980).

44. Committee on Hawaiian Affairs, Standing Comm. Rpt. No. 59, and Committee of the Whole, Rpt. No. 13, 1 *Proceedings of the 1978 Constitutional Convention,* 644 and 1,018 (1980); *see generally* Jon M. Van Dyke, "The Constitutionality of the Office of Hawaiian Affairs," 7 *University of Hawai'i Law Review,* 63 (1985).

45. Committee of the Whole, Rpt. No. 13, *supra* note 44, at 1,018.

that the appropriate pro rata share of the revenues from the Public Land Trust that should go to OHA was 20 percent.[46] This figure apparently seemed appropriate to the legislators at the time both because the "betterment of the conditions of native Hawaiians" was one of five purposes listed in Section 5(f) of the Admission Act and also because persons of Hawaiian ancestry constituted about 20 percent of the population of the State.

These important decisions led to further conflict and confusion because of the difficulty in agreeing on what lands were included in the Public Land Trust and how "revenues" should be defined.[47] The OHA Trustees brought a lawsuit against several State agencies in the mid-1980s to challenge the State's interpretation of these terms, but the Hawai'i Supreme Court ruled in 1987 that this dispute was a "political question" that was not appropriate for judicial resolution and that the political branches of government should try harder to address and resolve their differences.[48] The administration of Governor John Waihe'e then entered into negotiations with the OHA Trustees and in 1990 agreed to a formula that defined the Public Land Trust and divided revenues into two categories: (1) "sovereign revenues," which come from activities unique to a government, such as collecting taxes, fines, or tuition at the State's university or receiving federal grants; and (2) "proprietary revenues," which come from revenue-enhancing uses of land that any landowner could engage in, such as leases to agricultural concerns, issuing licenses for mineral exploitation, or operating airports or other profitable enterprises. It was agreed that OHA would receive 20 percent of the proprietary revenues but would not receive any pro rata share of the sovereign revenues. The Legislature agreed to this formula in its 1990 legislative session,[49] and the State paid almost $135 million to OHA for revenues it had received in the 1980s but had not shared with OHA.[50]

In 1994, OHA brought a lawsuit against the State for the revenues the State receives from the stores operated by Duty Free Shoppers in Waikīkī. Because the customers receive their purchases when they depart at the Honolulu International Airport, which is partially on lands that are part of the Public Land Trust, and because the stores could not operate without this airport delivery, OHA argued that it was entitled to a pro rata share of these revenues. Once again, the Hawai'i Supreme Court refused to reach the merits of this case, ruling that it presented a nonjusticiable political question that must be resolved by the Legislature.[51] In its closing, it nonetheless acknowledged "that the State's obligation to native Hawaiians is firmly established in our con-

---

46. "Act 273" (1980), codified at *Hawai'i Revised Statutes,* Sec. 10-13.5.

47. *See generally* Melody K. MacKenzie, "The Ceded Lands Trust," in *Native Hawaiian Rights Handbook,* 26–42 (Melody Kapilialoha MacKenzie, ed., 1991).

48. *Trustees of the Office of Hawaiian Affairs v. Yamasaki,* 69 Hawai'i 154, 737 P.2d 446 (1987). *See generally* Michael M. McPherson, "*Trustees of Hawaiian Affairs v. Yamasaki* and the Native Hawaiian Claim: Too Much of Nothing," 21 *Environmental Law,* 427 (1991).

49. "Act 304," 1990 *Hawai'i Session Laws.*

50. Melody K. MacKenzie, "The Ceded Lands Trust," *Hawaii Bar Journal,* June 2000, 6, 7, citing House Standing Comm. Rpt. No. 602 on H.B. No. 2207, H.D. 1 (February 14, 1997).

51. *Office of Hawaiian Affairs v. State,* 96 Hawai'i 388, 31 P.3d 901 (2001).

stitution," and that "it is incumbent upon the legislature to enact legislation that gives effect to the right of native Hawaiians to benefit from the ceded lands trust."[52]

In 2006, the Hawai'i Supreme Court again declined to address and resolve a case brought by OHA for revenues,[53] ruling that the 1990 agreement described above was not an enforceable contract[54] and that the claim brought by OHA was barred by its failure to give written notice to the State sixty days prior to filing its lawsuit[55] and by its failure to file within the two years established by the governing statute of limitations.[56] In this case, as in previous ones, the Court affirmed once again that the State of Hawai'i has "continuing trust obligations to native Hawaiians"[57] and that "it is incumbent upon the legislature to enact legislation that gives effect to the right of native Hawaiians to benefit from the ceded lands trust . . . [and] we trust that the legislature will . . . enact legislation that most effectively and responsibly meets those obligations."[58] During the 2006 legislative session, the Legislature approved a partial settlement of this disputed revenue flow, agreeing that OHA should receive $15,100,000 annually and should receive $17,500,000 to compensate for the underpayment received by OHA during the 2001–05 cycles.[59]

OHA has also brought a lawsuit, along with individual Hawaiians, against the State's Housing Financing Development Corporation (HFDC), which later became the Housing and Community Development Corporation of Hawaii (HCDCH), to prevent the State from selling or transferring any of the lands in the Public Land Trust until the claims of the Native Hawaiian People are addressed and resolved.[60] This claim was based on actions taken in the late 1960s to protect the claims of the natives in Alaska[61] and those of the Maori in New Zealand (Aotearoa).[62] This case

52. *Id.* at 401, 31 P.3d at 914, citing *Hawai'i Constitution,* Article XVI, sec. 7.

53. *Office of Hawaiian Affairs v. State,* 110 Hawai'i 338, 133 P.3d 767 (2006).

54. *Id.* at 351–54, 133 P.3d at 780–83. The Court acknowledged that "the legislative history behind Act 304 [implementing the 1990 agreement] utilizes the terms 'settlement' and 'resolution'" but concluded nonetheless that the Legislature had not provided the "'clear and unambiguous' intent required to contractually bind the State." *Id.* at 353–54, 133 P.3d at 782–83.

55. *Id.* at 358–59, 133 P.3d at 787–88.

56. *Id.* at 359–66, 133 P.3d at 788–95.

57. *Id.* at 366, 133 P.3d at 795, citing *Office of Hawaiian Affairs v. State,* 96 Hawai'i 388, 401, 31 P.3d, 901, 914 (2001).

58. *Id.,* citing *Office of Hawaiian Affairs v. State,* 96 Hawai'i 388, 401, 31 P.3d, 901, 914 (2001).

59. S.B. No. 2948, S.D.1, H.D.2, C.D.1 (2006). In this enactment, "[t]he legislature acknowledges that the State's obligation to native Hawaiians is firmly established in the state constitution." *Id.,* sec. 1, citing Article XII of the *Hawai'i Constitution.* The statute says that "immediate action should be taken to clearly designate the pro rata share of revenues derived from the public land trust that the Office of Hawaiian affairs is to receive annually," *id.,* sec. 1, but also states that this bill should not be viewed as the settlement of this dispute: "Nothing in this Act shall resolve or settle, or be deemed to acknowledge the existence of, the claims of native Hawaiians to the income and proceeds of a pro rata portion of the public land trust under article XII, section 6, of the state constitution." *Id.,* sec. 7.

60. *Office of Hawaiian Affairs v. Housing and Community Development Corporation of Hawaii,* Civ. No. 94-4207-11 (1st Cir. Ct. Hawai'i).

61. *See, e.g., Alaska v. Udall,* 420 F.2d 938 (1969), *cert. denied,* 397 U.S. 1076 (1970).

62. *See, e.g., New Zealand Maori Council v. Attorney General* (1987) 1 NZLR, 641, blocking the New Zealand Government from transferring public lands, even to a state-owned enterprise, until the rights of the Maori people to those lands had been fully protected.

went to trial before Circuit Judge Sabrina McKenna in November 2001, and she ruled on December 5, 2002 that although the substantive claims of the Native Hawaiians were well founded in law and in fact, she was blocked from ruling in their favor by the procedural doctrines of sovereign immunity, laches, estoppel, and the political question doctrine.[63] This case is now pending on appeal before the Hawai'i Supreme Court.[64]

Although disputes continue regarding the proper way to settle the claims of the Native Hawaiian People, Hawai'i's political leaders agree that these claims are well founded and must be settled in a fair manner. The State has acknowledged on several occasions that Native Hawaiians have valid claims to the Ceded Lands. A major example can be found in the Findings in Section 1 of Act 359 (1993), where the Hawai'i State Legislature recognized that

> (9) In 1898, Hawai'i was annexed to the United States through the Newlands Res-
> olution *without the consent of or compensation to the indigenous people of Hawai'i
> or their sovereign government.* As a result, *the indigenous people of Hawai'i were
> denied* the mechanism for expression of their inherent sovereignty through self-
> government and self-determination, *their lands,* and their ocean resources.[65]

In his 1998 statement outlining his plans for his second four-year administration, Governor Benjamin J. Cayetano gave similar recognition to the Native Hawaiian claim by stating that "we will settle the ceded lands issue before the end of my second term. This complex and most difficult issue must be resolved in a manner which is fair to all."[66] When he left office, Governor Cayetano listed his inability to settle the dispute over Ceded Lands as one of the failures of his time as Governor.[67]

Governor Linda Lingle has similarly recognized the importance of addressing and resolving the claim of the Native Hawaiian People for an appropriate share of the Ceded Lands. In her State of the State address to the Legislature on January 21, 2003, she said,

> Here at home in Hawai'i I will continue to work with you and with the Hawaiian
> community *to resolve the ceded lands issue* once and for all. Our joint decision
> to make the $10.3 million payment *is a good first step, but that is all it is.* Like so
> many other issues we currently face, the ceded lands issue is one that did not

---

63. *Office of Hawaiian Affairs v. Housing and Community Development Corporation of Hawaii,* Civ. No. 94-4207-11-SSM (1st Cir. Ct. Hawaii, December 5, 2002).

64. *Office of Hawaiian Affairs v. Housing and Community Development Corporation of Hawaii (HCDCH),* S.C. No. 25570.

65. "An Act Relating to Hawaiian Sovereignty," ch. 359, sec. 1(9), 1993 *Hawai'i Session Laws,* 1,009 (emphasis added).

66. "The Next Four Years: Completing the Vision," *Honolulu Advertiser,* October 16, 1998, at A-13, col. 3.

67. Pat Omandam, "Governor Admits Failure over OHA," *Honolulu Star-Bulletin,* January 6, 2002, at A-6, col. 6.

occur overnight, and will not be resolved overnight. It is as complicated as it is emotionally charged. But until we get it resolved, our community can never really come together as one.[68]

Another significant development was the State Legislature's creation in 1993, "in response to a groundswell of support for Hawaiian Sovereignty,"[69] of the Hawaiian Sovereignty Advisory Commission,[70] which was modified in 1994 to become the Hawaiian Sovereignty Elections Council.[71] The preamble to the 1993 State statute characterized the 1893 overthrow as having occurred "without the consent of the native Hawaiian people or of the lawful Government of Hawaii in violation of treaties between the [United States and the Kingdom of Hawai'i] and of international law." It further stated that the 1898 annexation of Hawai'i by the United States occurred "without the consent of or compensation to the indigenous people of Hawaii or their sovereign government," and that because of this action "the indigenous people of Hawaii were denied the mechanism for expression of their inherent sovereignty through self-government and self-determination, their lands, and their ocean resources." This language is similar to and in some sections identical to that used in the 1993 "Apology Resolution" passed by the U.S. Congress.[72] The 1994 Hawai'i State legislation established a process designed to facilitate efforts of the Native Hawaiians "to restore a nation of their own choosing."[73]

Although challenged on various theories,[74] the Hawaiian Sovereignty Elections Council held a plebiscite in 1996 asking the question, "Shall the Hawaiian people elect delegates to propose a Native Hawaiian government?" Some 30,423 Hawaiians returned their ballots in this mail-in election, with 22,294 (73 percent) voting "Yes" and 8,129 (27 percent) voting "No."[75] Eighty-five delegates were subsequently selected in a vote conducted by the nonprofit organization Ha Hawai'i, and they drafted two proposed constitutions: one for a nation-within-a-nation governing entity and the other for an independent nation.[76] This effort was criticized by some,

---

68. Governor Linda Lingle's State of the State speech, State Legislature, January 21, 2003 (emphasis added).

69. *Mauka to Makai, supra* note 33, at 44.

70. "Act 359" (1993), 1993 *Hawai'i Session Laws,* 1,009, recognizing in Section 1(6) that "Native Hawaiians are a distinct and unique indigenous people" whose lands and sovereignty were illegally taken from them. The Commission issued its *Final Report* on February 18, 1994.

71. "Act 200" (1994). The Council issued its *Final Report* in December 1996.

72. "Joint Resolution to Acknowledge the 100th Anniversary of the January 17, 1893 Overthrow of the Kingdom of Hawaii," Pub. L. No. 103-150, 107 Stat. 1510 (1993) (hereafter cited as "Apology Resolution").

73. "Act 200" (1994), sec. 2. *See generally* Noelle M. Kahanu and Jon M. Van Dyke, "Native Hawaiian Entitlement to Sovereignty: An Overview," 17 *University of Hawai'i Law Review,* 427 (1995), and Van Dyke, Di Amore-Siah, and Berkley-Coats, *supra* note 2.

74. *Rice v. Cayetano (I),* 941 F.Supp. 1529, 1535 (D. Hawai'i 1996), *rev'd on other grounds,* 528 U.S. 495 (2000).

75. Hawaiian Sovereignty Elections Council, *Final Report,* 28 (December 1996).

76. Hawaii Advisory Committee to the U.S. Commission on Civil Rights, "Reconciliation at a Crossroads: The Implications of the Apology Resolution and *Rice v. Cayetano* for Federal and State Programs Benefiting Native Hawaiians" (June 2001), citing http://www.hawaiianconvention.org.

Senator Daniel Akaka

however, because of the low turnout in the vote for delegates,[77] and recent activities have focused on an effort that would be facilitated by the Federal Government under the "Akaka Bill," described below. In 1997, Hawai'i's Legislature continued to address the claims of Native Hawaiians by enacting a statute that again referred to the 1993 congressional "Apology Resolution" as an accurate recounting of "the events of history relating to Hawaii and Native Hawaiians" and called for a "lasting reconciliation" and "a comprehensive, just, and lasting resolution."[78]

Inconsistent Federal Actions

While the State of Hawai'i was seeking to fulfill its duties under the 1959 Admission Act to "better the conditions of Native Hawaiians,"[79] the Federal Government was

---

77. Only 8,867 persons cast ballots for delegates in a special election out of a possible 101,000 eligible Hawaiian voters. *Mauka to Makai, supra* note 33, at 44.

78. "An Act Relating to the Public Land Trust," ch. 329, 1997 *Hawai'i Session Laws,* 2,072, 2,073. To achieve this goal, the Legislature provided partial funding to undertake a complete inventory of the Public Lands and established a joint committee consisting of representatives of the Governor, the Legislature, and OHA to determine "whether lands should be transferred to the Office of Hawaiian affairs in partial or full satisfaction of any past or future obligations under article XII, section 6 of the Hawaii Constitution." *Id.,* Section 3.

79. "Admission Act," *supra* note 1, sec. 5(f).

acting erratically with regard to its relationship with the Native Hawaiian People. On August 27, 1979, the Department of Interior Solicitor's Office issued an opinion letter explaining that the United States continued to have a trust relationship with Native Hawaiians even though the State of Hawai'i was successor trustee and principal title holder to most of the Trust Lands.[80] In 1980, Congress enacted a statute to establish a Native Hawaiians Study Commission to "conduct a study of the culture, needs and concerns of the Native Hawaiians," consisting of nine members, three of whom had to be from Hawai'i.[81] On his last full day in office, January 19, 1980, President Jimmy Carter appointed nine individuals to this Commission, but President Ronald Reagan first sought to abolish the Commission, and when he learned that he could not ignore a congressional statute altogether, he replaced Carter's nine nominees with nine of his own.[82] Six were mid-level bureaucrats from federal agencies, and the other three were Native Hawaiian Republicans.[83] This group met for many months but divided when they issued their final report on June 23, 1983, with the six federal bureaucrats issuing a report acknowledging that the Hawaiians had suffered terribly in the years since Western contact but concluding that the Federal Government could not be held responsible for these tragic consequences.[84] The three Hawaiian Republicans issued a strong minority report examining the key events surrounding the overthrow and annexation and reaching the opposite conclusion, explaining that the United States Government bore the central responsibility for the overthrow of the Kingdom and the taking of land and resources from the Hawaiians.[85]

During the two Reagan terms and the term of the first President Bush, a group of attorneys in the Justice Department opposed to affirmative action worked to oppose any efforts to protect or expand the programs established for Native Hawaiians, arguing that such programs promoted invidious racial distinctions.[86] On the

---

80. Letter from Interior Department Deputy Solicitor Frederick Ferguson to the Western Regional Office of the U.S. Commission on Civil Rights, August 27, 1979.

81. Pub.L. No. 96-565, Title II, 94 Stat. 3324 (December 22, 1980).

82. *See* Hawaii Advisory Committee to the U.S. Commission on Civil Rights, *supra* note 76, at 20.

83. The federal officials appointed by President Reagan to this Commission were Stephen P. Shipley (who served as Vice Chair), Carl A. Anderson, Carol E. Dinkins, James C. Handley, Diane K. Morales, and Glenn R. Schleede. The three Hawai'i Republicans were Kina'u Boyd Kamali'i (who served as Chair), Winona K. D. Beamer, and H. Rodger Betts.

84. 1 Native Hawaiians Study Commission, *Report on the Culture, Needs and Concerns of Native Hawaiians* (report issued pursuant to Pub. L. 96-565, Title III, 1983). *See generally* Melody MacKenzie and Jon Van Dyke, The Hawaii Study Commission—a Bizarre Charade, *Honolulu Star-Bulletin,* April 21, 1983, at A-23, col.1.

85. 2 Native Hawaiians Study Commission, *Report on the Culture, Needs and Concerns of Native Hawaiians* (report issued pursuant to Pub. L. 96-565, Title III, 1983).

86. Lisa Cami Oshiro, "Recognizing Na Kanaka Maoli's Right to Self-Determination," 25 *New Mexico Law Review,* 65, 76 (1995), citing "Statement by President Ronald Reagan upon Signing H.J. Res. 17 into Law," 22 *Weekly Compilation Presidential Documents,* 1,462, *1986 U.S. Code Congr. & Admin. News,* 5,253 (October 27, 1986); and "Statement by President George H. W. Bush upon Signing the Hawaiian Homes Commission Act Amendments," Pub. L. 102-398, 28 *Weekly Compilation Presidential Documents,* 1,876, *1992 U.S. Code Congr. & Admin. News,* 1,337 (October 6, 1992). *See also* Carl C. Christensen, "Native Hawaiians and the Constitution: Can the Indian Commerce Clause Cross the Pacific?" 27 (paper for Indian Law Seminar, Harvard Law School, Spring 1997): "The administrations of Presidents Reagan and Bush followed a political agenda of opposing any

last day in office of the first President Bush, January 19, 1993, the Solicitor to the Department of Interior, Thomas Sansonetti, issued an opinion letter denying that the Federal Government owed any trust obligations to Native Hawaiians under either the Hawaiian Homes Commission Act or the 1959 Admission Act.[87] This letter was withdrawn on November 15, 1993, by John D. Leshy, the Solicitor to the Department of the Interior during the Clinton Administration.[88]

The 1993 "Apology Resolution"

On the occasion of the 100th anniversary of the illegal overthrow of the Kingdom of Hawai'i,[89] the U.S. Congress adopted a joint resolution (a) apologizing to Native Hawaiians on behalf of the people of the United States for the overthrow of the Kingdom of Hawai'i on January 17, 1893, with the participation of agents and citizens of the United States, and for the deprivation of the inherent rights of Native Hawaiians to self-determination and sovereignty, (b) supporting, recognizing, and commending the reconciliation efforts of the State of Hawai'i with Native Hawaiians, and (c) "urg[ing] the President of the United States to . . . acknowledge the ramifications of the overthrow of the Kingdom of Hawaii and to support reconciliation efforts between the United States and the Native Hawaiian people."[90] The U.S. Congress concluded in this enactment, which has the equivalent status to any other statute enacted by Congress,[91] that the overthrow of the Kingdom of Hawai'i was in viola-

---

'affirmative action' programs that provided 'race-based' benefits to particular disadvantaged ethnic groups. This carried over into the area of Indian law as against state governments and to restrict the scope of the class of Native Americans eligible for special treatment under the Indian Commerce Clause."

87. Memorandum M-36978 from Thomas L. Sansonetti, Solicitor, U.S. Department of the Interior, to Counselor to the Secretary and Secretary's Designated Officer, Hawaiian Homes Commission Act, January 19, 1993.

88. Statement of John D. Leshy, November 15, 1993, also "disclaiming any future Departmental reliance on an August 27, 1979, letter of the Deputy Solicitor," attached to a letter from Secretary of Interior Bruce Babbitt to Senator Daniel K. Akaka, November 15, 1993; *Mauka to Makai, supra* note 33, at 39.

89. *See supra* chapter 16.

90. *See* "Apology Resolution," *supra* note 72, whereas para. 37 and Sec. 1: "Acknowledgment and Apology," paras. 1 and 3.

91. The "Apology Resolution" is a statute of the United States, and the courts have taken judicial notice of its findings. *See, e.g., State v. Lorenzo,* 77 Hawai'i 219, 221, 883 P.2d, 641, 643 (Haw. App. 1994): "The United States Government recently recognized the illegality of the overthrow of the Kingdom and the role of the United States in that event. P.L. 103-150, 107 Stat. 1510 (1993)." The "Apology Resolution" was formally enacted by the U.S. Congress, passing the Senate by a roll-call vote of 65 to 34, and it was signed by President Clinton on November 23, 1993. A "joint resolution" enacted by Congress as a public law and signed by the President is a statute of the United States and has the same effect as any other law enacted by Congress. *See, e.g., Ann Arbor R. Co. v. United States,* 281 U.S. 658, 666 (1930), treating a joint resolution just as any other legislation enacted by Congress; Hans Linde, *et al., Legislative and Administrative Processes,* 110 (1981): "The prescribed form of a proposal for a statute is generally called a bill, *although Congress also uses the form of a joint resolution to enact legislation*" (emphasis added); Read, MacDonald, et al., *Materials on Legislation,* 129 (4th ed., 1982), quoting from R. M. Gibson, "Congressional Concurrent Resolutions: An Aid to Statutory Interpretation," 37 *American Bar Association Journal,* 421, 422–23 (1951): "In recent years much major legislation has taken the form of a joint resolution; it is now rather generally conceded that *a joint resolution of Congress is just as much a law as* a bill after passage and approval" (emphasis added); Jack Davies, *Legislative Law and Process in a Nutshell,* 66 (2d

tion of treaties between the Kingdom and the United States and of international law, that it could not have been accomplished without the assistance of U.S. agents, and that the subsequent "cession" of these lands to the United States in 1898 was "without the consent of or compensation to the Native Hawaiian people of Hawaii or their sovereign government":

> Whereas, *without the active support and intervention by the United States diplomatic and military representatives,* the [January 1893] insurrection against the Government of Queen Liliuokalani *would have failed* for lack of popular support and insufficient arms; . . .
>
> Whereas the Republic of Hawaii also ceded *1,800,000 acres of crown, government and public lands* of the Kingdom of Hawaii, *without the consent of or compensation to the Native Hawaiian people of Hawaii or their sovereign government;* . . .
>
> The Congress—
>
> (1) on the occasion of the 100th anniversary of *the illegal overthrow* of the Kingdom of Hawaii on January 17, 1893, acknowledges the historical significance of this event *which resulted in the suppression of the inherent sovereignty of the Native Hawaiian people.* (Emphasis added.)

Congress thus expressed its commitment to acknowledge the ramifications of the overthrow of the Kingdom of Hawai'i in order to provide a proper foundation for reconciliation between the United States and the Native Hawaiian People.[92]

Although the "Apology Resolution" does not itself "serve as a settlement of any claims against the United States,"[93] "result in any changes in existing law,"[94] or itself create a claim, right, or cause of action,[95] it does confirm the factual foundation for the previously asserted claims of the Native Hawaiian People to some or all of the Crown and Government Lands that were "ceded" to the United States at the time of the 1898 annexation.[96]

An important step in the reconciliation process occurred in 2000, when the Interior and Justice Departments issued a report describing the history and current condition of the Native Hawaiians, acknowledging that Native Hawaiians are indig-

---

ed., 1986): "a joint resolution originates in one house and, with the concurrence of the other house, has the force of official legislative action"; L. Harold Levinson, "Balancing Acts: Bowsher v. Synar, Gramm-Rudman-Hollings, and Beyond," 72 *Cornell Law Review,* 527, 545 (1987): "Courts have consistently held that the legal effect of a joint resolution is identical to that of an enacted bill"; Goehlert and Martin, *Congress and Law-Making: Researching the Legislative Process,* 42 (2d ed., 1989): "In reality there is little difference between a bill and a joint resolution, as a joint resolution goes through the same procedure as a bill and has the force of law."

92. *See* "Apology Law," *supra* note 72, sec. 1: "Acknowledgment and Apology," paras. 4–5.

93. *Id.,* sec. 3.

94. S. Rep. No. 103-126 (1993) at 35.

95. *Rice v. Cayetano (I),* 941 F.Supp. 1529, 1546 n. 24 (D. Hawai'i 1996), *rev'd on other grounds,* 528 U.S. 495 (2000).

96. *See, e.g., State v. Lorenzo,* 77 Hawai'i 219, 221, 883 P.2d 641, 643 (Haw. App. 1994), citing the "Apology Resolution," *supra* note 72, for the proposition that "[t]he United States Government recently recognized the illegality of the overthrow of the Kingdom and the role of the United States in that event."

President William Clinton signing the "Apology Resolution," November 23, 1993, with *(from left to right)* Noelle Kahanu, Vice President Al Gore, Senator Daniel Inouye, Patricia Zell, Representative Patsy Mink, John Mink, Representative Neil Abercrombie, Senator Daniel Akaka, Esther Kiaaina, and Robert Ogawa

enous people, recognizing the trust responsibilities of the United States with regard to Native Hawaiians, and making recommendations, including the following key proposal: [97]

> It is evident from the documentation, statements, and views received during the reconciliation process undertaken by Interior and Justice pursuant to Public Law 103-150 (1993), that the Native Hawaiian people continue to maintain a distinct community and certain governmental structures and they desire to increase their control over their own affairs and institutions. *As [a] matter of justice and equity, this report recommends that the Native Hawaiian people should have self-determination over their own affairs within the framework of Federal law, as do Native American tribes.* For generations, the United States has recognized the rights and promoted the welfare of Native Hawaiians as an indigenous people within our nation through legislation, administrative action, and policy statements. To safeguard and enhance Native Hawaiian self-determination over their lands,

---

97. *Mauka to Makai, supra* note 33.

cultural resources, and internal affairs, the Departments believe Congress should enact further legislation to clarify Native Hawaiians' political status and to create a framework for recognizing a government-to-government relationship with a representative Native Hawaiian governing body.[98]

Perhaps even more importantly, this report of the Interior and Justice Departments acknowledged once again that the Crown and Government Lands claimed by the Provisional Government in 1893 included "lands that were impressed with a trust for the Native Hawaiian common people."[99] The Justice Department also reaffirmed the relationship between the United States and the Native Hawaiian People in the amicus curiae brief submitted by the Solicitor General in *Rice v. Cayetano*.[100]

Kahoʻolawe

One of the important accomplishments of the Native Hawaiian renaissance has been to end the U.S. Navy's bombing of the island of Kahoʻolawe, which lies southwest of Maui. The Navy had used this 30,000-acre island for target practice since the early 1940s. After a variety of protests and occupations in the 1970s and 1980s,[101] the United States finally announced during the administration of the first President Bush that the bombing would stop. The Congress then appropriated $400,000,000[102] to clear the island of unexploded ordinance, and in November 2003 it was formally turned over to the State of Hawaiʻi to hold until the Native Hawaiian Nation is reconstituted.[103] In its enactment accepting temporary control of Kahoʻolawe as trustee, the Legislature stated the following:

> Transfer. Upon its return to the State, the resources and waters of Kahoʻolawe shall be held *in trust* as part of the public land trust; provided that *the State shall transfer management and control of the island and its waters to the sovereign native Hawaiian entity* upon its recognition by the United States and the State of Hawaii.[104]

---

98. *Id.* at 4, 17 (emphasis added).

99. *Id.* at 1.

100. "Brief of the United States as *Amicus Curiae* Supporting Respondent," *Rice v. Cayetano*, No. 98-818, July 1999. This important brief explained that

> Congress has identified Native Hawaiians as a distinct indigenous group within the scope of its Indian affairs power, and has enacted dozens of statutes on their behalf pursuant to its recognized trust responsibility. . . . Congress does not extend services to Native Hawaiians because of their race, but because of their unique status as the indigenous people of a once-sovereign nation as to whom the United States has established a trust relationship.

Id. at 9–10.

101. *See generally United States v. Mowat*, 582 F.2d 1194 (9th Cir. 1978).

102. "Fiscal Year 1994 Dept. of Defense Appropriations Act," Title X, sec. 10001(a), Pub.L. No. 103-139, 107 Stat. 1418 (1994).

103. *Hawaiʻi Revised Statutes*, chap. 6K.

104. *Id.*, sec. 6K-9 (emphasis added).

Retained Federal Lands

The Federal Government currently controls about 370,000 acres of the lands that were ceded to the United States at the time of annexation in 1898. More than 220,000 of these acres are in the national parks on Maui and the Big Island, and the rest are in military bases scattered around the Islands, including Schofield Barracks, Fort Shafter Military Reservation, Hickam and Wheeler Air Force Bases, Marine Corps Base Hawaii (Kāne'ohe), Lualualei Ammunition Depot, Bellows Air Force Station,[105] and Makua Valley on O'ahu, Bonham Air Force Base on Kaua'i, and the Pohakuloa training area on the Big Island. Hawai'i's Attorney General Shiro Kashiwa issued an opinion a year after statehood, on October 18, 1960, stating that "The Legislative History [of the 1959 Admission Act] indicates that Congress intended to compensate the State of Hawaii for the possession and use of ceded lands which it retains under section 5(c) and the free use of additional areas now under permit, license or permission, written or verbal, which it may withdraw under section 5(d)."[106] But no such compensation has ever been provided.

The "Akaka Bill"

Since 2001, the U.S. Congress has been considering the "Akaka Bill,"[107] which would constitute a major step in the "reconciliation" called for in the 1993 "Apology Resolution."[108] This bill would formally recognize the Native Hawaiian People as indigenous people under U.S. law and would lead to negotiations that would return lands and resources to a reestablished autonomous Native Hawaiian Nation. This law would thus comply with the road map set forth in Section IV(A) of the *Rice v. Cayetano* opinion,[109] where Justice Kennedy cited the Menominee Restoration Act[110] and the Indian Reorganization Act[111] as examples of appropriate congressional enactments to establish quasi-sovereign political entities within which natives-only votes are permissible.

If enacted, the "Akaka Bill" would reaffirm the rights of Native Hawaiians as indigenous people and grant formal "federal recognition" to the Native Hawaiian governing entity, would facilitate a process for establishing this Native Hawaiian governing entity and set in motion a negotiating process for pursuing the additional

---

105. *See* Miyahira, *supra* note 22, at 137–38.
106. "Interpretation of Section 5 of the Hawaii Statehood Act (Public Law 86-3), Approved March 18, 1959," memorandum issued by Attorney General Shiro Kashiwa, October 18, 1960, at 31.
107. The "Akaka Bill" was formally entitled "Native Hawaiian Government Reorganization Act" and was numbered S.147 and then S.3064 during the 2005–06 Congress. *See generally* John Heffner, "Between Assimilation and Revolt: A Third Option for Hawaii as a Model for Minorities World-Wide," 37 *Texas International Law Journal*, 591, 600–01 (2002).
108. "Apology Resolution," *supra* note 72, Section 1(5).
109. *Rice v. Cayetano*, 528 U.S. 495, 520 (2000).
110. 25 U.S.C. sec. 903b.
111. 25 U.S.C. sec. 476.

claims the Hawaiian People have for the lands and resources that were taken from them, and would thereby protect the existing programs that the Federal and State Governments have established for them. Some Hawaiians have viewed this bill as an inadequate compromise, but it would not require any Native Hawaiians to give up any rights or claims they presently possess and would lead to Native Hawaiian autonomy and the return of land and resources.

The most significant part of the "Akaka Bill" is that it would provide formal federal recognition of Native Hawaiians as indigenous people entitled to a legal status similar to that of other natives in the United States.[112] Although Congress has enacted many previous laws that have included "findings" stating that Native Hawaiians have this status, the 2000 decision of the U.S. Supreme Court in *Rice v. Cayetano*[113] concluded that Congress still had not "determined that native Hawaiians have a status like that of Indians in organized tribes," so some new more formal and more specific enactment appears to be needed.

The "Akaka Bill" would facilitate a process leading to the creation of a Native Hawaiian governing entity, which would have the legitimacy to negotiate for the return of land and resources. Although Native Hawaiians could reestablish a government without the "Akaka Bill," any governmental body established by a group of Native Hawaiians might still be subject to attack by other Native Hawaiians who did not participate in the process or opposed it. Without the "Akaka Bill," therefore, it would be difficult to enter into a serious negotiation for the return of lands and resources, because the Federal and State Governments are unlikely to transfer valuable lands and resources unless they are sure they are negotiating with the legitimate representatives of the Native Hawaiian People. The U.S. Supreme Court's 2004 opinion in the *Lara* case[114] strongly confirms Congress' power to legislate for native people and thus gives strong support for the conclusion that the "Akaka Bill" would be found to be a constitutional exercise of congressional power under the Indian Commerce Clause.

---

112. The Findings in Section 1 say that Native Hawaiians are "indigenous, native people of the United States," that the United States has "a special trust relationship" with the Native Hawaiian People, that the Native Hawaiian People were once represented by a separate and independent nation recognized by the United States through treaties and diplomatic relationships, that Congress has repeatedly acted in recognition of this special relationship to protect and promote the rights of the Native Hawaiian People, that Native Hawaiians have maintained their "separate identity as a distinct native community," and that Native Hawaiians have worked to give "expression to their rights as native people to self-determination and self-governance" through activities such as their participation in OHA. It is also important that the Findings confirm that "Congress has also delegated broad authority to administer a portion of the federal trust responsibility to the State of Hawaii," because the *Rice* opinion questioned whether Congress "may, and has, delegated to the State a broad authority to preserve" the "native" status of Native Hawaiians. *Rice v. Cayetano*, 528 U.S. 495, 518 (2000). The Statement of Policy in Section 3 also confirms these conclusions, in explicit and unambiguous terms.

113. *Rice v. Cayetano*, 528 U.S. 495 (2000).

114. *United States v. Lara*, 541 U.S. 193 (2004). *See also Kahaiwaiolaa v. Norton*, 386 F.3d 1271 (9th Cir. 2004), explaining that "in the end, we must commit this question to Congress to apply its wisdom in deciding whether or not native Hawaiians should be included among those eligible to apply for federal tribal recognition. The *Kahaiwaiolaa* case is discussed *infra* chapter 24, text at notes 74–89.

Section 8(c)(2) of the "Akaka Bill" would empower federal courts to hear claims "over any existing claim against the United States arising under [existing] Federal law . . . and relating to the legal and political relationship between the United States and the Native Hawaiian governing entity." Although this is a limited grant of jurisdiction, it does allow at least certain types of claims to be brought that cannot now be pursued, and it grants a twenty-year period during which such claims can be brought.

Those advocating independence assert that the "Akaka Bill" will undercut their efforts. But Section 8(c)(1) of the revised "Akaka Bill" explicitly states that it does not involve the settlement or relinquishment of any claims: "Nothing in this Act serves as a settlement of any claim against the United States." In its revised "findings" in Section 2(13), the bill now reaffirms that "the Native Hawaiian people never directly relinquished to the United States their claims to their inherent sovereignty as a people over their national lands, either through the Kingdom of Hawaii or through a plebiscite or referendum." Working to implement the procedures that would be established under the "Akaka Bill" would not involve "acquiescing" to the illegal overthrow of the Kingdom of Hawai'i in 1893. It is a historical fact that the Kingdom was overthrown illegally in 1893 and that lands were taken without the consent of or compensation to Native Hawaiians. The "Akaka Bill" would begin the process of providing some long-overdue compensation and would allow those favoring independence to continue to promote their cause. But even if Hawai'i were to become independent at some time in the future, the Native Hawaiian People would be a numerical minority in the Islands, and they would still need something like the "Akaka Bill" to protect their unique claims to their land and resources.

The "Akaka Bill" may not be the complete solution, but it would provide further protection for existing programs designed to serve Native Hawaiians, and it would begin the process of addressing and resolving the long-festering claims of the Native Hawaiian People. If Congress passes this bill, it would open a new era for Native Hawaiians and lead to a better and more prosperous Hawai'i for everyone. On June 8, 2006, the U.S. Senate took a vote to impose cloture and thus enable the bill to be voted up or down on its merits. The vote was 56 in favor of cloture and 41 against, thus failing to achieve the 60 votes needed to cut off debate. In 2007, the Bill was reintroduced and is under active consideration as this book is being published.

Summary

To summarize this chapter, steps have been taken during the past two decades to correct some of the wrongs that occurred in the nineteenth century and to recognize that the Crown Lands—and indeed the Public Land Trust as a whole—should be a source of revenue and strength for the Native Hawaiians. These steps have been awkward and inconsistent, and further efforts are needed before justice will have been served and reconciliation achieved. For more than 100 years, the Crown Lands have been intermingled with the Government Lands and other Public Lands. Even though they have all been held in trust since 1898, these lands have been poorly administered and have been managed and sometimes transferred and dissipated without concern for the needs and claims of the Native Hawaiian People. It is time to recognize once again the special character of the Crown Lands. They were selected by Kauikeaouli (Kamehameha III) as his unique personal holdings and they then evolved into lands designed to support the dignity and needs of the Hawaiian Monarchs as they struggled to lead their people in the late nineteenth century. These lands are distinct from the Government Lands, which were designed to be "public" in the more classic sense of the term, and they were selected to provide for the full range of needs of the people and their Government. The Crown Lands have a uniquely Hawaiian heritage and appear to be the logical choice to form the corpus of lands for the emerging Native Hawaiian Nation. This conclusion would be consistent with the suggestion made by Prince Kūhiō and Aha Hui Puʻuhonua O Na Hawaiʻi during the deliberations that led to the enactment of the Hawaiian Homes Commission Act in 1921—that the Crown Lands should be set aside for the Native Hawaiian People.[115]

---

115. *See supra* chapter 22, text at notes 16–21.

24

The "Painful Irony" of *Rice v. Cayetano* (2000)

 The efforts of Native Hawaiians to recover their lost lands, resources, and governmental authority were frustrated in February 2000, when the U.S. Supreme Court issued its opinion in *Rice v. Cayetano*,[1] declaring unconstitutional the provision in Hawai'i's Constitution limiting those who could vote for the Trustees of the Office of Hawaiian Affairs (OHA) to those of Native Hawaiian ancestry. OHA had been established pursuant to a constitutional provision[2] added to Hawai'i's Constitution in 1978 in order to provide a forum for Native Hawaiians to discuss issues of common concern and to facilitate the process of self-determination leading to self-governance.[3] The U.S. Supreme Court mishandled the case of *Rice v. Cayetano*, refusing to accept the unique status of Native Hawaiians as Hawai'i's first people and failing to understand the role that OHA has played for the Native Hawaiian people in their quest for self-determination.

The *Rice* Opinions

Justice Kennedy's Majority Opinion

The majority opinion in *Rice v. Cayetano* described in substantial detail the history of the Native Hawaiian people,[4] acknowledged explicitly the major role of U.S. diplomats and troops in the 1893 overthrow of the Kingdom of Hawai'i,[5] and cited the 1993 congressional "Apology Resolution,"[6] which described the overthrow as

---

1. *Rice v. Cayetano*, 528 U.S. 495 (2000). The term "painful irony" in the title to this chapter comes from Justice Stevens' dissent, where he wrote that "it is a painful irony indeed to conclude that native Hawaiians are not entitled to special benefits designed to restore a measure of self-governance because they currently lack any vestigial native government—a possibility of which history and the actions of this nation have deprived them." 528 U.S. at 535.

2. *Hawai'i Constitution*, Article XII, secs. 4–6.

3. *See supra* chapter 23, text at notes 37–50, 61–66.

4. *Rice*, 528 U.S. at 499–510.

5. *Id.* at 504–05: "A so-called Committee of Safety, a group of professionals and businessmen, *with the active assistance of John Stevens, the United States Minister to Hawaii, acting with United States armed forces,* replaced the monarchy with a provisional government." (Emphasis added.)

6. *Id.* at 505, citing "Joint Resolution to Acknowledge the 100th Anniversary of the January 17, 1893 Overthrow of the Kingdom of Hawaii," Pub. L. 103-150,107 Stat. 1510 (1993) (hereafter cited as "Apology Resolution").

Justice Anthony M. Kennedy

"illegal" and acknowledged that the U.S. acquisition of 1.8 million acres of land was "without the consent of or compensation to the Native Hawaiian people."[7] But the opinion then declared unconstitutional the steps taken by all the people of Hawai'i to establish the Office of Hawaiian Affairs, which was designed to facilitate the reestablishment of a self-governing Native Hawaiian political body and the return of lands and resources to the Native Hawaiian People.[8] Perhaps because it was blinded by a lack of enthusiasm about affirmative action programs, the Supreme Court's majority failed to appreciate that when the people of Hawai'i established OHA as a vehicle to facilitate Native Hawaiian self-determination they were acting consistently with steps the United States has taken for many of its native people and consistently with its obligations under international law.[9]

Justice Anthony Kennedy's majority opinion began by detailing the modern history of the Hawaiian Islands. It described the dramatic changes in landownership

---

7. "Apology Resolution," *supra* note 6, Sec. 1(1) and Whereas para. 25.

8. Background explaining the historical developments that led to the creation of the Office of Hawaiian Affairs can be found in Jon M. Van Dyke, "The Constitutionality of the Office of Hawaiian Affairs," 7 *University of Hawai'i Law Review,* 63, 68–69 (1985) (hereafter cited as Van Dyke, "OHA"), and Jon M. Van Dyke, "The Political Status of the Native Hawaiian People," 17 *Yale Law & Policy Review,* 95, 101–10 (1998) (hereafter cited as Van Dyke, "Political Status").

As explained *supra* in chapter 23, text at notes 26–46, the establishment of OHA was undertaken by the State of Hawai'i in response to its responsibilities under the Admission Act of 1959, Pub.L. No. 86-3, 73 Stat. 4, reprinted in 15 *Hawai'i Revised Statutes Ann.,* 107 (Michie 1997), which had transferred about 1.4 million acres of land to the new State in trust for the Native Hawaiian People and the general public and was consistent with the action taken by the Federal Government to assist other Native Americans and the Alaska Natives through the 1971 Alaska Native Claims Settlement Act (ANSCA), Pub L. No. 92-203, 85 Stat. 688 (codified as amended at 43 U.S.C. secs. 1601–29).

9. *See* Van Dyke, "OHA," *supra* note 8, at 68–69, and *infra* this chapter, note 49.

during the nineteenth century, combined with the "constant efforts" of "the United States and European powers" "to protect their interests and to influence Hawaiian political and economic affairs in general." [10] The opinion mentioned four of the treaties between the United States and the Kingdom of Hawai'i and acknowledged "the reality of American dominance in trade, settlement, economic expansion, and political influence." [11] It noted the actions by westerners forcing the Bayonet Constitution on King Kalākaua in 1887, which "reduced the power of the monarchy and extended the right to vote to non-Hawaiians." [12] Then, in 1893, these westerners "with the active assistance of John Stevens, the United States Minister to Hawaii, acting with United States armed forces, replaced the monarchy with a provisional government." [13] President Grover Cleveland refused to support the efforts of these revolutionaries to annex the Islands to the United States, but President William McKinley had no such qualms, and annexation occurred in 1898.[14]

The majority opinion cited the 1993 congressional "Apology Resolution" [15] but failed to take any significant note of the admissions made by Congress in this important enactment and the conclusions that logically follow from these admissions. Section II of the majority opinion explained the 1921 enactment of the Hawaiian Homes Commission Act,[16] the 1959 admission of Hawai'i as the Fiftieth State,[17] the 1978 creation of the Office of Hawaiian Affairs,[18] and the efforts of Harold "Freddy" Rice beginning in 1996 to challenge the provision in Hawai'i's Constitution that limited voting for OHA Trustees to persons of Native Hawaiian ancestry.[19] Although one can point out serious problems with many of the details listed in the Court's historical summary and the way it presented them,[20] it is significant nonetheless that the

---

10. *Rice,* 528 U.S. at 504.

11. *Id.*

12. *Id.,* citing 3 Ralph Kuykendall, *The Hawaiian Kingdom 1874–1893: The Kalakaua Dynasty,* 344–372 (1967, reprinted 1987). This statement from the Court's majority opinion greatly oversimplified the changes in voting rights, as explained *supra* in chapters 15 and 17. It is misleading to say that the 1887 Constitution "extended the right to vote to non-Hawaiians." It extended the right to vote to certain non-citizens of Portuguese ancestry but cut back on the rights of poor Hawaiians to vote and continued to exclude most residents of Asian ancestry. *See supra* chapter 15, text at notes 166–67. The great-grandfather of the plaintiff in the *Rice* case, William Hyde Rice, was part of the group that imposed the Bayonet Constitution on King Kalākaua in 1887.

13. *Rice,* 528 U.S. at 505.

14. "Joint Resolution to Provide for Annexing the Hawaiian Islands to the United States, July 7, 1898," ch. 55, 30 Stat. 750 (1898). *See supra* chapter 19.

15. *Rice,* 528 U.S. at 505, citing "Apology Resolution," *supra* note 6; *see supra* chapter 23, text at notes 81–88.

16. "Hawaiian Homes Commission Act, 1920," Pub.L. No. 67-34, 42 Stat. 108 (1921), reprinted in 15 *Hawai'i Revised Statutes Ann.,* 331 (Michie 1997) (hereafter cited as HHCA).

17. Admission Act, *supra* note 7.

18. *Rice,* 528 U.S. at 508–10.

19. *Id.* at 510–11.

20. *See, e.g.,* Eric K. Yamamoto and Chris Iijima, "The Colonizer's Story: The Supreme Court Violates Native Hawaiian Sovereignty—Again," 3:2 *ColorLines* (Summer 2000), at http://www.arc.org/C_Lines/CLArchive/story3_2_01.html, explaining that "[t]he Court's decision grossly distorted the history of Hawai'i" by giving little attention to U.S. colonialism, using "patronizing and stereotypic language" and making "no mention of the long history of white racism in Hawai'i"; Sharon Hom and Eric K. Yamamoto, "Collective Memory, History, and Social Justice," 47 *UCLA Law Review,* 1747, 1771–77 (2000) (same).

Court's majority acknowledged the enormous social dislocation that Native Hawaiians experienced[21] and the crucial role that the United States and its citizens played in undermining Hawaiian culture, overthrowing the Hawaiian Government, and annexing Hawai'i as a colony of the United States.

But then, Sections III and IV of Justice Kennedy's majority opinion, which analyzed the efforts of the State of Hawai'i to address this historical disaster, completely ignored the history summarized in Sections I and II and accepted no sense of obligation or responsibility on the part of the United States or the State of Hawai'i for the events described. Hawai'i did not, of course, exist as a state when those events occurred, but it now controls, as trustee, 1.4 million acres of land acquired as a result of the illegal[22] overthrow of the Hawaiian Kingdom "without the consent of or compensation to the Native Hawaiian people."[23]

Justice Kennedy explained that the people of the State of Hawai'i established the Office of Hawaiian Affairs in 1978 pursuant to their fiduciary duties—duties that had been transferred in part from the United States to the State in the 1959 Admission Act.[24] In a statewide election in which voters of all races participated, the electorate amended Hawai'i's Constitution in 1978 to establish OHA in order to enable the Hawaiian People to determine their priorities, "promote the protection and preservation of the Hawaiian race," and "unite Hawaiians as a people."[25] The creation of this organization was, in short, undertaken to fulfill the responsibility that the State of Hawai'i had to facilitate self-determination by the Native Hawaiian people.[26] The 1993 congressional "Apology Resolution" said that the Native Hawaiian people are "indigenous,"[27] that they have "inherent sovereignty,"[28] that they have "rights . . . to self-determination,"[29] and that a process of "reconciliation" must be pursued to rec-

---

21. The majority opinion also described "the tragedy inflicted on the early Hawaiian people by the introduction of western diseases and infectious agents," which led to "mortal illnesses" and "despair, disenchantment, and despondency" among their descendants. 528 U.S. at 506, citing Laurence H. Fuchs, *Hawaii Pono, A Social History* 13 (1961).

22. The overthrow is described as "in violation of treaties . . . and of international law" and "illegal" on five separate occasions in the "Apology Resolution,"*supra* note 6, Whereas paras. 8, 14, 19, 36 and Section 1(1).

23. *Id.*, Whereas para. 25.

24. *Rice*, 528 U.S. at 507–08.

25. *Id.* at 508, quoting from Committee of the Whole Rep. No. 13, 1 *Proceedings of the Constitutional Convention of Hawaii of 1978,* 1,018 (1980). For additional background about the establishment of OHA, *see* Van Dyke, "OHA," *supra* note 7, at 68–69.

26. The delegates to Hawai'i's 1978 Constitutional Convention explained that the goal of creating the Office of Hawaiian Affairs was to enable the Native Hawaiian People to determine, through their own elected officials, the path they wished to follow to reestablish a self-governing political entity similar to those established by other Native Americans. Committee of the Whole Rep. No. 13, 1 *Proceedings of the Constitutional Convention of Hawaii of 1978,* 1,019 (1980), quoted in Van Dyke, "OHA," *supra* note 7, at 68.

The responsibility to facilitate the self-determination of native people exists under U.S. and international law. *See* Van Dyke, "Political Status," *supra* note 7, at 138–40.

27. "Apology Resolution,"*supra* note 6, Whereas para. 29.

28. *Id.*, Whereas para. 28 and Section 1(1).

29. *Id.*, Section 1(3).

tify the wrongs suffered by the Native Hawaiian People.[30] The State was acting, there-fore, in a manner consistent with the goals and instructions of the U.S. Congress.

The Supreme Court ruled, nonetheless, that one aspect of the efforts of the State of Hawai'i to facilitate the self-determination efforts of the Native Hawaiians was unconstitutional, holding that the provision in Hawai'i's Constitution that lim-ited those who could vote for OHA's nine trustees to persons of Hawaiian ancestry violated the Fifteenth Amendment.[31] The Court was careful to avoid undercutting the many precedents that allow Congress to "fulfill its treaty obligations and its respon-sibilities to the Indian tribes by enacting legislation dedicated to their circumstances and needs."[32] But it concluded that the restrictions on voting for OHA Trustees did not qualify under this doctrine because the OHA election was administered by the State to elect "public officials" rather than being an election run by the natives them-selves to select their leaders, which would be "the internal affair of a quasi-sover-eign."[33] In reaching this conclusion, the Court ruled that a governmental body can-not facilitate the process of reestablishing a "quasi-sovereign" native political entity by conducting an election for the natives, even though it cited statutes in which the United States government had done just that—"the Menominee Restoration Act, 25 U.S.C. sec. 903b, and the Indian Reorganization Act, 25 U.S.C. sec. 476"[34]—without apparently recognizing that it was striking down a practice that the U.S. Government had engaged in repeatedly.

In any event, the Court's majority acknowledged that the outcome of the *Rice* case would have been different if the Native Hawaiians had formed a "quasi-sover-eign" political entity and had conducted election of their leaders themselves, because it was on this basis that Justice Kennedy distinguished the OHA election from the many elections across the country in which natives select their leaders.[35] The Court thus provided a road map for Native Hawaiians to follow.

The *Rice* holding is limited in its scope, resting solely on the Fifteenth Amend-ment and carefully avoiding any broad pronouncements about the status of the separate and preferential programs that have been established for Native Hawaiians to provide partial compensation for their unresolved and festering claims.[36] As U.S. District Judge David A. Ezra said when the case was remanded back to his court-room, the Supreme Court's "decision was a narrow one, restricted to the single issue of state-sponsored Hawaiian-only elections. The suggested precedential value of the

---

30. *Id.,* Section 1(5).

31. *Rice,* 528 U.S. at 499, 524.

32. *Id.* at 519–20, citing *Morton v. Mancari,* 417 U.S. 535 (1974), and its extensive progeny.

33. *Id.* at 520. *See also id.* at 522: "the elections for OHA trustee are elections of the State, not of a sepa-rate quasi-sovereign, and they are elections to which the Fifteenth Amendment applies."

34. *Id.* at 520.

35. *Id.* at 519–21.

36. The majority opinion was careful to say that "As the court of appeals did, we assume the validity of the underlying administrative structure and trusts, without intimating any opinion on that point." *Id.* at 521–22. In his dissent, Justice Stevens (joined by Justice Ginsburg) wrote that the majority's "assumption is surely correct." *Id.* at 529.

United States Supreme Court's decision in other contexts is problematic and specu-
lative at best." [37]

It should also be noted that Justice Kennedy's *Rice* opinion repeatedly acknowledged that Native Hawaiians are indigenous, aboriginal, and native by referring regularly and without qualification or limitation to "the native Hawaiian people," "the
native Hawaiian population," [38] and "the native population." [39] Justice Kennedy also
acknowledged that these "people" share a common "culture and way of life," that
they have experienced a common "loss" that has had effects that have "extend[ed]
down through generations," and that it has been appropriate for the State of Hawai'i
"to address these realities." [40] The *Rice* majority opinion thus provides the essential
underpinning for the conclusion that Native Hawaiians are entitled to the same legal
status as other native people within the United States, and that rational-basis (rather
than strict scrutiny) judicial review should apply to programs for Native Hawaiians.

But the *Rice* opinion contains dicta that have encouraged individuals opposed
to the programs that have been established for Native Hawaiians—such as the Hawaiian Home Lands Program and OHA—to file lawsuits challenging their constitutionality. Referring to the statutory definition of "Hawaiian" as "any descendant of the
aboriginal peoples inhabiting the Hawaiian Islands which exercised sovereignty and
subsisted in the Hawaiian Islands in 1778, and which peoples thereafter have continued to reside in Hawaii," [41] the Court said that "Ancestry can be a proxy for race. It is
that proxy here. . . . The State, in enacting the legislation before us, has used ancestry
as a racial definition and for a racial purpose." [42] This conclusion would normally
require the State to justify its programs under the strict-scrutiny/compelling-state-
interest/least-drastic-alternative level of judicial review. But the State argued that the
more deferential rational-basis level of judicial review applied under *Morton v. Mancari*,[43] because Congress and the State and federal courts have repeatedly recognized
the Native Hawaiians as having the same legal status as other Native Americans.[44]

The Supreme Court carefully avoided addressing this argument, ruling that

37. "Transcript of Proceedings before Chief United States District Judge David Alan Ezra," *Rice v. Cayetano* (D. Hawai'i, April 7, 2000), at 7–8. *See also American Federation of Government Employees (AFL-CIO) v.
United States*, 195 F.Supp.2d 4, 19 (D.D.C. 2002): "*Rice* only dealt with the right to vote, which is a fundamental
right evoking strict scrutiny review. Moreover, *Rice* involved neither a Fifth Amendment due process claim nor
a Fourteenth Amendment equal protection claim"; *Arakaki v. Lingle*, 305 F.Supp.1161, 1170 n. 7 (D. Hawai'i
2004), *reversed on other grounds*, 477 F.3d 1048 (9th Cir. 2007), *certiorari petition pending*, explaining that *Rice*
was "distinguishable" because it involved a race-based challenge to an election "under the Fifteenth Amendment, not preferences and/or benefits being provided to native populations allegedly based on their political,
as opposed to racial, status."

38. 528 U.S. at 507.

39. *Id.* at 506.

40. *Id.* at 524.

41. *Id.* at 515, quoting from *Hawai'i Revised Statutes*, sec. 10-2.

42. *Id.* at 514–15.

43. *Morton v. Mancari*, 417 U.S. 535 (1974).

44. *See* Van Dyke, "Political Status," *supra* note 7, at 104–10 and 119–26, summarizing such statutes
and judicial decisions.

even if the *Mancari* rational-basis standard governed programs enacted for Native Hawaiians that were challenged under the Fourteenth Amendment, this case was different because the OHA voting restriction was challenged under the Fifteenth Amendment. The Fifteenth Amendment, it explained, is not affected by *Mancari* and establishes an absolute prohibition on the use of racially based categories, and thus it does not permit Congress to "authorize a State to establish a voting scheme that limits the electorate for its public officials to a class of tribal Indians, to the exclusion of all non-Indian citizens."[45] Because judicial review under the Fifteenth Amendment is not affected by the deferential rational-basis review applicable to challenges under the Fourteenth Amendment under *Mancari,* the Court avoided reaching any conclusions regarding the level of judicial review applicable to programs established by the State of Hawai'i for Native Hawaiians, noting that this matter was complex and that it could "stay far off that difficult terrain."[46]

The Court also expressed concern whether "the voting classification [for OHA Trustees] is symmetric with the beneficiaries of the programs OHA administers."[47] They were not precisely symmetrical, it is true, but the lack of an exact fit was purposeful, because the creators of OHA wanted to allow the Hawaiian People to revisit the definitions of "native Hawaiian" and "Hawaiian" governing the various trusts and then to reach their own conclusions on the appropriate meaning of these words. As explained above in chapter 22, the definition of "native Hawaiian" in the Hawaiian Homes Commission Act became a person with 50 percent Hawaiian blood after intense lobbying from the sugar industry in Hawai'i to reduce the number of individuals eligible for homesteads. Even the Hawaiians involved in the effort to pass this law had favored a 1/32 Hawaiian blood quantum requirement.[48] The 50 percent

---

45. *Rice,* 528 U.S. at 520.

46. *Id.* at 519. To resolve that question, the Court explained, would require addressing whether Congress "has determined that native Hawaiians have a status like that of Indians in organized tribes, and [whether] it may, and has, delegated to the State a broad authority to preserve that status." *Id.* at 518. The Court added that "[i]t is a matter of some dispute . . . whether Congress may treat native Hawaiians as it does the Indian tribes." *Id.,* citing Van Dyke, "Political Status," *supra* note 7, and Stuart Minor Benjamin, "Equal Protection and the Special Relationship: The Case of Native Hawaiians," 106 *Yale Law Journal,* 537 (1996).

The State of Hawai'i had argued that Congress had previously determined that Native Hawaiians have a political and legal status similar to that of other Native Americans. In the 1993 "Apology Resolution," *supra* note 6, Whereas clause 28, Congress made the explicit finding that "the indigenous Hawaiian people never directly relinquished their claims to their inherent sovereignty as a people or over their national lands to the United States," and in the 1994 Native Hawaiian Education Act, 20 U.S.C. secs. 7512(1) and (8) (formerly sec. 7902[1]), Congress found that "Native Hawaiians are a distinct and unique indigenous people" and that there is a "special relationship between the United States and the Native Hawaiians." Some of the many congressional statutes grouping Native Hawaiians with other Native Americans or establishing special programs for Native Hawaiians are listed in Van Dyke, "Political Status," *supra* note 7, at 106 n. 67, and the complete list is found in Appendix A in the amicus curiae brief of Hawai'i's congressional delegation in *Rice v. Cayetano.* Laws passed by Congress after the *Rice* decision that reaffirm that Native Hawaiians have a similar status to that of other Native Americans are discussed *infra* this chapter, text at notes 62–64.

47. *Rice,* 528 U.S. at 523.

48. HHCA, *supra* note 16, sec. 201(a)(7). *See supra* chapter 22, text at notes 56–59. Prince Jonah Kūhiō Kalaniana'ole, Hawai'i's delegate to the Congress at that time, testified in favor of a 1/32nd blood quantum level. In this book, the terms "Native Hawaiian" and "Hawaiian" are used interchangeably to refer to all persons descended from the Polynesians who lived in the Hawaiian Islands when Captain Cook arrived in 1778, following the practice found in all federal statutes enacted since 1970.

blood-quantum requirement has served to divide the Hawaiian People, and, especially in light of the more recent federal statutes defining "Native Hawaiian" more broadly, the delegates to Hawai'i's 1978 Constitutional Convention authorized all persons of Hawaiian ancestry, without a blood-quantum limitation, to vote for the OHA Trustees, in order to allow all Hawaiians to come together to consider this question.[49]

Justice Kennedy's majority opinion closed by explaining that the "essential ground" for the Court's holding is that any classification utilizing a racial criteria is "demeaning," that it is improper to assume that a non-Hawaiian would "not cast a principled vote" on the selection of leaders to make decisions regarding Native Hawaiian resources and policies, and that the State of Hawai'i's initiative to promote Native Hawaiian self-governance by facilitating their election of their own leaders "would give rise to the same indignities, and the same resulting tensions and animosities, [that] the [Fifteenth] Amendment was designed to eliminate."[50] This characterization appears to have been based either on an ideological perspective that rejects the value of diversity in our pluralistic country and the obligation to rectify the injustices or on a complete misunderstanding of the careful balance that has been achieved in Hawai'i—based on the respect and honor that all races have toward the Native Hawaiians—and the widespread support that exists in Hawai'i for a just resolution of the claims of the Native Hawaiian people.[51]

Justice Breyer's Concurring Opinion

Justice Stephen Breyer (joined by Justice David Souter) concurred with the result reached by the Court's five-member majority but disagreed "with the critical rationale that underlies that result."[52] The concurring opinion was substantially more sympathetic to the claims of the Native Hawaiians and acknowledged that "Native

---

49. The delegates to Hawai'i's 1978 Constitutional Convention recognized that the 50 percent blood quantum requirement in the Hawaiian Homes Commission Act "has proved to be a factor in dividing the Hawaiian community—mothers and fathers from their children, cousins from cousins, friends from friends," that "the time has come to include all native Hawaiians regardless of blood quantum, for the number of descendants is increasing," and that "the removal of blood qualification will be in line with the current policy of the federal government to extend benefits for Hawaiians to all Hawaiians regardless of blood quantum." Standing Comm. Rep. No. 59, 1 *Proceedings of the Constitutional Convention of Hawaii of 1978,* 647 (1980). The convention delegates were "tempted to change this outmoded rule from the 1920s," but instead concluded that "this responsibility should be assumed by" those of Hawaiian ancestry working through OHA and thus determined that everyone of Hawaiian ancestry should vote for OHA's Trustees. *Id.*

50. *Rice,* 528 U.S. at 523–24.

51. In a poll of 429 Hawai'i voters conducted September 5–9, 2000, for instance, those expressing an opinion supported the "Akaka Bill" (*see supra* chapter 23, text at notes 99–106) by a two-to-one margin (49 percent in favor, 25 percent opposed; 27 percent expressed no opinion). Pat Omandam, "Most Isle Voters Plan to Take Part in OHA Ballot," *Honolulu Star-Bulletin,* September 15, 2000, at A-1, col. 1.

52. *Rice,* 528 U.S. at 524. U.S. District Judge David A. Ezra noted when the case was remanded that "The majority opinion was achieved with a bare five justices agreeing to its central premise. Two other justices concurred in the result of the case but did not accept the full breadth of Justice Kennedy's reading of the Fifteenth Amendment." "Transcript of Proceedings before Chief United States District Judge David Alan Ezra," *Rice v. Cayetano* (D.Hawai'i, April 7, 2000), at 6.

Justice Stephen G. Breyer

Hawaiians, considered as a group, may be analogous to tribes of other Native Americans."[53] But the two concurring judges joined in the result reached by the majority because of their concern about the fact that the OHA electorate consisted of 130,000 persons of Hawaiian ancestry with less than 50 percent Hawaiian blood, in addition to the 80,000 persons who met the 50 percent blood quantum definition of "native Hawaiian" found in the Hawaiian Homes Commission Act of 1920.[54] Justice Breyer was thus concerned that the OHA electorate was not structured in a way that is "analogous to membership in an Indian tribe."[55] Not only were those voting for the OHA Trustees not required to enroll as members of a native tribe, village, or community, as other natives are required to do, but also no limit defined the minimum quantum of Hawaiian blood a person had to have to vote for the OHA Trustees. At two points[56] in his short opinion, Justice Breyer expressed concern that persons with only

---

53. *Rice,* 528 U.S. at 526 (Breyer, J., concurring).
54. *Id.,* referring to the definition of "native Hawaiian" found in section 201(a)(7) of the HHCA, *supra* note 16.
55. 528 U.S. at 526.
56. *Id.* at 526 and 527.

"one five-hundredth original Hawaiian" blood could vote for the OHA Trustees and asserted that this expansive definition has no parallel among other native groups.[57]

The delegates to Hawai'i's 1978 Constitutional Convention left the definition of "Native Hawaiian" unresolved because they sought to have the Hawaiians themselves define the term through OHA.[58] Justice Breyer acknowledged that each native group has "broad authority to define its membership."[59] How else can the Native Hawaiians exercise that power except by bringing together all people who have Hawaiian lineage into an organization designed to allow them to debate and decide how to define themselves? In any event, Justice Breyer's opinion was a limited one, and it includes strong hints that he would look more favorably upon limitations on voting for Native Hawaiian leaders if the Native Hawaiians were organized in a manner approved by Congress and more closely analogous to the governmental structure of other native communities.

Justice Kennedy's majority opinion also indicates that a Hawaiians-only vote would be constitutional if undertaken within a congressionally approved quasi-sovereign political entity. His opinion recognized that a wrong had been done to the

---

57. *Id.* at 526, illustrating the variety of definitions used by native communities but also asserting that all have some outside minimum of required native blood. Justice Breyer's "one-five hundredth" figure is based on the possibility that a birth from a Hawaiian and non-Hawaiian mating might have occurred shortly after Western contact in 1778, and then nine generations might have followed without any further Hawaiian blood being introduced into the line. *Id.* Although this scenario is theoretically possible, it must be extremely rare because the migration of other races to Hawai'i did not begin in any real numbers until the 1860s. *See supra* chapter 15, text at notes 17–59. In 1860, the population of Hawai'i was 94.05 percent full-blooded Hawaiian, plus another 1.92 percent part-Hawaiian. Office of Hawaiian Affairs, *Native Hawaiian Data Book,* 4 (1998). As a practical matter, the maximum dilution of Hawaiian blood is thus five or at most six generations, and the minimum amount of Hawaiian blood that one is likely to find today is 1/32, or rarely 1/64.

In fact, contrary to Justice Breyer's assertion, examples can be found of native groups that define their membership without reference to a specific blood quantum. The Maori in Aotearoa (New Zealand), for instance, have no minimum amount of native blood that a person must have before being considered a Maori. Similarly, membership in the Chickasaw Nation and in the Choctaw Nation of Oklahoma is open to all "lineal descendants" of persons whose names appeared on the final rolls of the Chickasaw Nation and Choctaw Nation of Oklahoma, respectively, in 1906. *Constitution of the Chickasaw Nation,* art. II; *Constitution of the Choctaw Nation of Oklahoma,* art. II(1). Members of the Citizen Potawatomi Nation are those who are descendants of persons enrolled in the tribe in 1937. *Constitution of the Citizen Potawatomi Nation,* art. 3(b). Membership in the Wampanoag Tribe of Gay Head (Aquinnah) includes all persons of "direct descent from a specifically identified Gay Head Wampanoag Indian on the 1870 census roll of the tribe compiled by Richard L. Pease and included in a report submitted to the State of Massachusetts on May 22, 1871." *Constitution of the Wampanoag Tribe of Gay Head (Aquinnah),* art. II(2). Membership in the Miami Tribe of Oklahoma is open to any "blood descendant" of a "person of Miami Indian blood . . . who relocated to Kansas." *Constitution of the Miami Tribe of Oklahoma,* art. III(f).

Curiously, Justice Breyer cites the Choctaw Constitution while criticizing the voting criteria for OHA Trustees, noting that it refers to persons "having had an ancestor whose name appeared on a tribal roll—but in the far less distant past." 528 U.S. at 526. Apparently, Justice Breyer did not realize that one could appear on the Choctaw roll in 1906 even if one had only 1/32nd Choctaw blood, "as many did." Gavin Clarkson, "Not Because They Are Brown, But Because of Ea: Why the Good Guys Lost in *Rice v. Cayetano,* and Why They Didn't Have to Lose," 7 *Michigan Journal of Race & Law,* 317, 343 (2002). Professor Clarkson has also observed that the Cherokee Nation of Oklahoma has members with as little as 1/4,096th Indian blood. *Id.* at 344 n. 183, citing "Native American Roots, Once Hidden, Now Embraced," *Washington Post,* April 7, 2001, at A-1.

58. *See supra* this chapter, note 49.

59. *Rice,* 528 U.S. at 527 (*citing Santa Clara Pueblo v. Martinez,* 436 U.S. 49, 72 n.32 (1978)).

Justice John Paul Stevens

Native Hawaiians.[60] If a wrong occurred, a constitutional remedy must be possible.[61] It would be too absurd to conclude that the Court has imposed a "Catch-22" situation on the Native Hawaiians whereby any effort to address the taking of their lands and sovereignty would violate the U.S. Constitution. The matter must be correctable, and the enactment of the "Akaka Bill" would provide the statutory framework to address and provide redress for the injuries suffered by the Native Hawaiian People.

Subsequent Acts of Congress

Congress has not been deterred by the *Rice* decision and has continued to enact legislation including Native Hawaiians in programs for Native Americans and acknowledging their status as the indigenous people of Hawai'i. Although the "Akaka Bill" is still pending, a number of other bills have been passed into law since the *Rice* decision. Among the most significant are the Hawaiian Homelands Homeowner-

---

60. *Rice,* 528 U.S. at 504–05: "A so-called Committee of Safety, a group of professionals and businessmen, with the active assistance of John Stevens, the United States Minister to Hawaii, acting with United States armed forces, replaced the monarchy with a provisional government."

61. *See infra* this chapter, text following note 109.

ship Act of 2000 [62] (which restated the findings that had previously appeared in the 1993 "Apology Resolution" and in other statutes confirming the indigenous status of Native Hawaiians and the losses they have experienced) and the 2002 Native Hawaiian Education Act [63] (stating that "Native Hawaiians are a distinct and unique indigenous people" and that "the political status of Native Hawaiians is comparable to that of American Indians and Alaska Natives"). [64] In 2004, Congress established the Office of Native Hawaiian Relations in the Office of the Secretary of the Interior with the responsibility to "continue the process of reconciliation with the Native Hawaiian people." [65]

Subsequent Judicial Controversies

Because of the dicta in the *Rice* majority opinion, a number of challenges have been mounted to dismantle the (limited and inadequate) programs that have been established for the Native Hawaiian People. The first skirmish, *Arakaki v. State of Hawai'i*,[66] concerned the requirement in Hawai'i's Constitution that the OHA Trust-

---

62. "Hawaiian Homelands Homeownership Act of 2000," sec. 201 of "Omnibus Indian Advancement Act," Pub. L. 106-568, 114 Stat. 2868 (December 27, 2000).

63. "Native Hawaiian Education Act," Pub. L. 107-110, 115 Stat. 1425 (2002), 20 U.S.C. sec. 7512(1) and (12).

64. One of the most explicit recent examples of Congress' recognition that Native Hawaiian communities have a comparable status to Indian tribes can be found in the preferential program established in Section 8014(3) of the "Fiscal Year 2002 Defense Appropriations Act," Pub. L. No. 107-117, 115 Stat. 2230, 2272 (2002), and the "Fiscal Year 2001 Defense Appropriations Act," Pub. L. No. 106-259, 114 Stat. 656, 677 (2000), which defined those Native American organizations eligible for the preference as "an Indian tribe, as defined in 25 U.S.C. 450b(e), or a Native Hawaiian organization, as defined under 15 U.S.C. 637(a)(15)." In other words, Congress has explicitly referred to a "Native Hawaiian organization" as the equivalent to an "Indian tribe," thus confirming once again the political status of the Native Hawaiians and the "special relationship" that exists between the United States and them.

65. In the "Consolidated Appropriations Act of 2004," Pub. L. 108-199, 118 Stat. 3, div. H, sec. 148 (2004), Congress established the Office of Native Hawaiian Relations within the Office of the Secretary of the Interior, in order to

1. effectuate and implement the special legal relationships between the Native Hawaiian people and the United States;
2. continue the process of reconciliation with the Native Hawaiian people; and
3. fully integrate the principle and practice of meaningful, regular, and appropriate consultation with the Native Hawaiian people by assuring timely notification of and prior consultation with the Native Hawaiian people before any federal agency takes any actions that may have the potential to significantly affect Native Hawaiian resources, rights, or lands.

This Office was established by the Secretary of the Interior in Order No. 3254, June 24, 2004. Congress has also continued to include Native Hawaiians in many programs designed to assist Native Americans. For instance, in the "Consolidated Appropriations Act of 2004," Pub.L. 108-199, 118 Stat.3, div. G, title II, Congress authorized financial assistance for "programs benefiting Alaska Native Corporations and Native Hawaiians" and $9,500,000 for Native Hawaiian housing under Title VIII of the "Native American Housing Assistance and Self-Determination Act of 1996."

66. *Arakaki v. State of Hawai'i*, Civ. No. 00-00514 HG-BMK ("Order Granting Plaintiff's Motion for Summary Judgment," D. Hawai'i September 19, 2000).

ees be of Native Hawaiian origin.[67] U.S. District Judge Helen Gillmor ruled that the reasoning in *Rice* required her to conclude that it was unconstitutional to exclude non-Hawaiians from running to become OHA Trustees, basing her decision on both the Fifteenth and the Fourteenth Amendments.[68] The U.S. Court of Appeals for the Ninth Circuit affirmed the decision, but it was careful to rest its affirmance solely on the Fifteenth Amendment and instructed Judge Gillmor to reissue her opinion without its discussion on the Fourteenth Amendment.[69]

Barrett and *Carroll*

Patrick Barrett and John Carroll filed separate cases alleging that the operations of the Office of Hawaiian Affairs and the Department of Hawaiian Home Lands (DHHL) denied them their constitutional rights as Caucasians because they were excluded from benefiting from the programs of these agencies. Neither Barrett nor Carroll had formally sought benefits from OHA, so U.S. District Judge David A. Ezra ruled that they lacked standing to challenge OHA's programs. Barrett had applied for a lease on Hawaiian Home Lands, but the District Court ruled that he could not proceed with his challenge against DHHL because he had not joined the United States, which was an indispensable party (and had not agreed to be sued). The Ninth Circuit[70] affirmed Judge Ezra's conclusions, ruling that Barrett and Carroll did not have standing to challenge the Office of Hawaiian Affairs because they could not demonstrate any personal injury resulting from its programs, and their challenges thus represented only "generalized grievances." With regard to Barrett's challenge of the Hawaiian Home Lands Program, the court acknowledged that his application for a homestead lease gave him the requisite injury to trigger standing, but it nonetheless affirmed the dismissal because Barrett had not joined the United States as a defendant. In an important sentence, the court said that "Article XII of the Hawaiian Constitution cannot be declared unconstitutional without holding [Section 4] of the Admission Act unconstitutional."[71] This language is significant because it supports the position that OHA has been trying to develop in related litigation: that the trust responsibility assigned to the State of Hawaiʻi at the time of statehood constituted a partial settlement of the claims of the Native Hawaiian People, and thus that the Hawaiian Home Lands Program and the responsibility to use revenues from the Ceded Lands "for the betterment of the conditions of Native Hawaiians"[72] cannot be declared unconstitu-

---

67. Article XII, sec. 5 of the *Hawaiʻi Constitution* requires that all nine members of OHA's Board of Trustees be of Hawaiian ancestry.

68. *See Arakaki v. State of Hawaiʻi*, 314 F.3d 1091, 1097 (9th Cir. 2002) (Summarizing Judge Gillmor's decisions).

69. *Arakaki v. State of Hawaiʻi*, 314 F.3d 1091 (9th Cir. 2002). Judge Gillmor issued a "Second Amended Order" following the Ninth Circuit's instructions on August 22, 2003.

70. *Carroll v. Nakatani*, 342 F.3d 934 (9th Cir. 2003).

71. *Id.* at 944.

tional without disrupting that carefully crafted settlement and putting the statehood of Hawai'i into question.[73]

Kahawaiolaa v. Norton

This case[74] involved a claim brought by Hawaiians that the Department of Interior regulations excluding natives in Hawai'i from seeking federal recognition as Indian tribes[75] violated the Equal Protection Clause of the Fourteenth Amendment. U.S. District Judge Alan C. Kay ruled that the claim was barred by the political question doctrine, explaining that "Adjudication of Plaintiffs' claims would directly place the Court in the shoes of Congress and the Executive Branch in determining whether Native Hawaiians should be recognized and acknowledged as an Indian tribe."[76] Judge Kay also explained that if the challenge to these regulations were justiciable, a rational-basis standard of judicial review would apply,[77] and that it was rational for Congress to exclude Native Hawaiians from the recognition regulations.[78]

In an opinion written by Judge Sidney R. Thomas, the U.S. Court of Appeals for the Ninth Circuit affirmed the dismissal of the lawsuit—but on different grounds. Judge Thomas' opinion explained that the dispute was justiciable and was not barred by the political question doctrine,[79] but then he agreed with Judge Kay's alternative conclusion that courts must give deferential rational-basis scrutiny to federal actions treating one group of natives differently from other groups.[80] The court noted that "[a]t first blush, even under rational basis review, a geographic exception to an otherwise uniform federal regulation appears problematic,"[81] but it nonetheless concluded that "the origin of the acknowledgment regulations and the unique history of Hawaii provide sufficient basis to sustain the regulation against an equal protection challenge under the highly deferential rational basis review."[82] The Ninth Circuit's opinion then summarizes this "unique history of Hawaii," explaining that in January

---

72. Admission Act, *supra* note 7, sec. 5(f).

73. *See infra* this chapter, text at notes 160–61.

74. *Kahawaiolaa v. Norton*, 222 F.Supp.2d 1213 (D.Hawai'i 2002), *affirmed on other grounds*, 386 F.3d 1271 (9th Cir. 2004).

75. 25 C.F.R. sec. 83.3(a) says that native groups eligible for federal recognition as Indian tribes are limited to "those American Indian groups indigenous to the continental United States."

76. 222 F.Supp.2d at 1219.

77. *Id.* at 1223 n. 14, explaining that the rational basis standard used in *Morton v. Mancari*, 417 U.S. 535, 555 (1974) would apply to federal activities involving Native Hawaiians, citing *United States v. Nuesca*, 945 F.2d 254, 257 (9th Cir. 1991), and *Price v. State of Hawaii*, 764 F.2d 623, 626-27 (9th Cir. 1985), for support of this conclusion.

78. *Id.* at 1223 n. 14.

79. 386 F.3d at 1275–77.

80. *Id.* at 1279, explaining that "[t]he racial classification of native Hawaiians in *Rice* does not apply to this case" because "at its core, *Rice* concerned the rights of individuals, not the legal relationship between political entities," and "the recognition of Indian tribes remains a political, rather than racial determination" and thus is "not subject to heightened scrutiny."

81. *Id.* at 1280.

82. *Id.*

1893 U.S. Minister John L. Stevens "conspired to overthrow the existing government in Hawaii and positioned armed naval forces to effectuate his plan,"[83] that "indigenous Hawaiians . . . were once subject to a government that was treated as a co-equal sovereign alongside the United States until the governance over internal affairs was entirely assumed by the United States,"[84] and therefore that "[i]t is rational for Congress to provide different sets of entitlements—one governing native Hawaiians and another governing members of American Indian tribes."[85] Judge Thomas' opinion concluded by saying that "we recognize that, in many ways, the result is less than satisfactory,"[86] noting that it would have been preferable "if the Department of Interior had applied its expertise to parse through history and determine whether native Hawaiians, or some native Hawaiian groups, could be acknowledged on a government-to-government basis."[87] Nonetheless, the court explained, "in the end, we must commit this question to Congress to apply its wisdom in deciding whether or not native Hawaiians should be included among those eligible to apply for federal tribal recognition."[88] This statement provides strong indication that the federal courts will conclude that the "Akaka Bill,"[89] which would grant federal recognition to the reorganized Native Hawaiian governing entity, will be found to be constitutional if it is enacted by Congress.

Arakaki v. Lingle

Fourteen residents of Hawai'i brought this claim as taxpayers, arguing that the Department of Hawaiian Home Lands and the Office of Hawaiian Affairs were "race-based" programs that violated the Equal Protection Clause of the Fourteenth Amendment. U.S. District Judge Susan Oki Mollway ruled in March and in May 2002 that, as taxpayers, their standing was limited to challenging general fund expenditures that supported DHHL and OHA, and that the plaintiffs could not challenge any of their other revenue sources or their expenditures and programs.[90] In November 2003, Judge Mollway dismissed the claims against DHHL, following the Ninth Circuit's ruling in *Carroll v. Nakatani* that the United States is an indispensable defendant to any challenge to the Hawaiian Homes Program and that because the United States has not consented to being sued, the claim against the State regarding DHHL must be dismissed.[91] Then, on January 14, 2004, the District Court dismissed the remaining claims brought by Appellants against the OHA Appellees, ruling that they presented

---

83. *Id.* at 1281–82, citing the "Apology Resolution,"*supra* note 6.
84. *Id.* at 1282.
85. *Id.* at 1282–83.
86. *Id.* at 1283.
87. *Id.*
88. *Id.*
89. *See supra* chapter 23, text at notes 107–14.
90. *Arakaki v. Cayetano*, 198 F.Supp.2d 1165, 1175–76 and 299 F.Supp.2d 1090, 1106–07 (D. Hawai'i 2002).
91. *Arakaki v. Lingle*, 299 F.Supp.2d 1114 and 299 F.Supp.2d 1129 (D. Hawai'i 2003).

a nonjusticiable political question that should be resolved by the political branches of the Government.[92]

On appeal,[93] the U.S. Court of Appeals for the Ninth Circuit agreed that most of the claims filed by the *Arakaki* plaintiffs were properly dismissed, including the claims against DHHL (because the United States was an indispensable party to such a claim) and the challenges to OHA's programs funded by revenues from the Public Land Trust (because the plaintiffs as taxpayers did not have the necessary "nexus" to programs funded from revenues that were not related to State tax revenue). But, in an opinion written by Judge Jay Bybee, the Ninth Circuit also ruled that the *Arakaki* plaintiffs did have standing as taxpayers to challenge the constitutionality of the OHA programs funded by revenues from the State's general funds, because the required nexus existed in that situation. In reaching that conclusion, Judge Bybee relied on the Circuit Court's earlier decision of *Hoohuli v. Ariyoshi,*[94] which had allowed State taxpayers to challenge OHA's use of general-fund revenues.[95]

On May 15, 2006, the U.S. Supreme Court issued an opinion in the *DaimlerChrysler* case[96] that made it clear that *Hoohuli* had been wrongly decided and explained that State taxpayers do not have standing to challenge State expenditures of tax moneys, because no nexus exists between such expenditures and the amount of taxes that any taxpayer will have to pay to the State. The taxpayers in *DaimlerChrysler* had asserted that they were burdened because the tax money used to lure DaimlerChrysler to establish a plant in Ohio depleted funds that could have been used to provide programs for their benefits. But the Supreme Court explained that even if the taxpayers won the lawsuit, they would probably be required to pay the same amount of tax in future years: "A taxpayer-plaintiff has no right to insist that the government dispose of any increased revenue it might experience as a result of his suit by decreasing his tax liability or bolstering programs that benefit him."[97]

The Court stated clearly that "we hold that state taxpayers have no standing under Article III to challenge state tax or spending decisions simply by virtue of their status as taxpayers."[98] In fact, the Court specifically cited the Ninth Circuit's *Arakaki v. Lingle* opinion in its footnote 4, making it clear that the Ninth Circuit's conclusion allowing taxpayer standing was inconsistent with the holding that it was issuing. In 2007, the Ninth Circuit ruled that the *Arakaki* taxpayer plaintiffs did not have stand-

---

92. *Arakaki v. Lingle,* 305 F.Supp.2d 1,161, 1,171–74 (D. Hawai'i 2004).

93. *Arakaki v. Lingle,* 423 F.3d 954 (9th Cir. 2005),

94. *Hoohuli v. Ariyoshi,* 741 F.2d 1169 (9th Cir. 1984).

95. In response to the argument made by OHA that *Hoohuli* was inconsistent with the rulings of other circuits and of the U.S. Supreme Court, Judge Bybee explained that his three-judge panel was still bound by the 1984 *Hoohuli* ruling and that "[o]ur decision in *Hoohuli* remains the law of the circuit until our court, sitting en banc, overrules it, or until the Supreme Court, in a majority opinion, plainly undermines its principles." 423 F.3d at 969.

96. *DaimlerChrysler v. Cuno,* 126 S.Ct. 1854 (2006).

97. *Id.* at 1863.

98. *Id.* at 1864.

ing to challenge state expenditures to support OHA and DHHL, and the case was then dismissed completely based on the *DaimlerChrysler* ruling.[99]

Doe v. Kamehameha Schools

This case challenging the Hawaiians-only admission policy of the Kamehameha Schools is described in the next chapter.[100]

The Strict-scrutiny Test

The attorneys representing the State of Hawai'i and those representing OHA and other Hawaiian programs under attack have consistently argued that the deferential rational-basis level of judicial review should apply to such programs under *Morton v. Mancari*,[101] and that they are constitutional because they are rationally related to the self-government, self-sufficiency, and cultural integrity of the Native Hawaiians.[102] State and federal courts have repeatedly agreed that this is the standard of judicial review that should be applied,[103] but if some court in the future were to apply the strict-scrutiny level of judicial review, the programs established for Native Hawaiians should be able to meet this high standard.

Although the *Rice* holding was carefully limited to the Fifteenth Amendment, some of the dicta in the opinion invited challenges under the Fourteenth Amendment to programs for Native Hawaiians because it contained language saying that

---

99. *Arakaki v. Lingle,* 477 F. 3d 1048 (9th Cir. 2007), and 2007 WL 1248916 (D. Hawai'i 2007).

100. *See infra* chapter 25, text following note 72.

101. *Morton v. Mancari,* 417 U.S. 535 (1974).

102. *See* Van Dyke, "Political Status," *supra* note 7, at 141–45.

103. *Id.* at 119–26, summarizing such cases. Other cases agreeing that rational-basis review should apply to judicial scrutiny of governmental programs established for Native Hawaiians include the following:

1. *Kahawaiolaa v. Norton,* 222 F.Supp.2d 1213 (D.Hawai'i 2002), *affirmed on other grounds,* 386 F.3d 1271 (2004), where District Judge Alan C. Kay concluded—two years after the Supreme Court's opinion in *Rice v. Cayetano,* 528 U.S. 495 (2000)—that "[t]he appropriate standard of review" for a "constitutional challenge" to governmental decisions regarding programs for Native Hawaiians "if justiciable, would be the rational basis standard." 222 F.Supp. at 1223 n. 14, citing *Morton v. Mancari,* 417 U.S. 535, 555 (1974); *United States v. Nuesca,* 945 F.2d 254, 257 (9th Cir. 1991); and *Duro v. Reina,* 860 F.2d 1463, 1467 (9th Cir. 1988). Judge Sidney R. Thomas, writing for the Ninth Circuit on appeal, explained that courts should utilize "the highly deferential rational basis review" to scrutinize Congress' decision to enact legislation for Native Hawaiians different from the legislation enacted for other Native Americans. 386 F.3d at 1,280.

2. *Arakaki v. Lingle,* 305 F.Supp.2d 1161, 1171 n. 8 (D.Hawai'i 2004), *affirmed in part and reversed in part,* 477 F.3d 1048 (9th Cir. 2007), explaining that the analysis utilized in *Morton v. Mancari, supra,* would apply to a challenge to the Hawaiian Home Lands Programs, and that it would not matter that Native Hawaiians had not been formally recognized under the 1978 Department of the Interior's regulations "as Congress itself appears to have recognized native Hawaiians as needing the United States' protection." *See also* Annmarie M. Liermann, Comment, "Seeking Sovereignty: The Akaka Bill and the Case for the Inclusion of Hawaiians in Federal Native American Policy," 41 *Santa Clara Law Review,* 509, 538–43 (2001), concluding that rational-basis review should apply to legislation concerning Hawaiians.

the limitation of OHA voting to persons of Hawaiian ancestry was a "race-based voting qualification,"[104] and that the reference to Hawaiian ancestry was "a proxy for race."[105] This conclusion is significant, because the Supreme Court's decisions in *City of Richmond v. J. A. Croson Co.*[106] and *Adarand Constructors v. Pena*[107] require all racial classifications to meet the strict-scrutiny test, whereby the Government must establish that the goal it is seeking to achieve is "compelling" and that the means it has selected to achieve that goal is "the least drastic alternative" that could have been chosen to achieve that goal.[108]

Programs for Native Hawaiians Can Meet the Test

Programs for Native Hawaiians can meet the "strict-scrutiny/compelling-state-interest/least-drastic alternative" test. The primary "goals" or "interests" of governmental programs designed to provide separate or preferential programs for Native Hawaiians are (1) to acknowledge their status as native, aboriginal, and indigenous people and to facilitate and support their quest for self-determination and self-governance and (2) to provide compensation for their loss of land and resources or to promote the return of those lost lands and resources. These interests are certainly "compelling" under our legal system, because they involve providing redress for the loss of the most essential rights recognized under U.S. and international law. And limiting these programs to persons of Hawaiian ancestry will frequently be the "least drastic alternative," because it is these people and their ancestors who have suffered the losses and who uniquely have the right to self-determination and self-government.

This historical basis of the claims of the Native Hawaiian People is detailed in the previous chapters of this volume and has also been retold many times by the

---

104. *Rice,* 528 U.S. at 517.

105. *Id.* at 514.

106. *City of Richmond v. J. A. Croson Co.,* 488 U.S. 469 (1989).

107. *Adarand Constructors v. Pena,* 515 U.S. 200 (1995).

108. In her opinion for the *Adarand* majority, Justice O'Connor was careful "to dispel the notion that strict scrutiny is 'strict in theory, but fatal in fact.'" *Id.* at 237. Citing *United States v. Paradise,* 480 U.S. 149 (1987), as an example of case where "a narrowly tailored race-based remedy" was justified, she wrote that "[w]hen a race-based action is necessary to further a compelling interest, such action is within constitutional constraints if it satisfied the 'narrow tailoring' test this Court has set out in previous cases." Other examples when the strict-scrutiny test has been met in a racial context include *Grutter v. Bollinger,* 539 U.S. 306 (2003), upholding the admissions policy utilized by the University of Michigan Law School, which used race as a relevant admission factor, and stressing that "context matters" even "when reviewing race-based governmental action under the Equal Protection Clause"; *Local 28, Sheet Metal Workers v. EEOC,* 478 U.S. 421 (1986), permitting a race-conscious remedy after a finding of past discrimination; *Lee v. Washington,* 390 U.S. 333 (1968), allowing racial segregation of prison inmates because of racial unrest; *Regents of the University of California v. Bakke,* 438 U.S. 265 (1978), allowing race to be utilized as a "plus" factor in admissions to achieve the compelling governmental interest of educational diversity but prohibiting the use of a racial quota; *Hunter v. Regents of the Univ. of California,* 190 F.3d 1061 (9th Cir. 1999), ruling that the race-based admission policy of UCLA's research elementary school served the compelling interest of promoting research on urban educational issues and was narrowly tailored as the best alternative to serve that interest; *Williams v. Babbitt,* 115 F.3d 657, 665 n.8 (9th Cir. 1997): "We have little doubt that the government has compelling interests when it comes to dealing with Indians. In fact, *Mancari's* lenient standard may reflect the Court's instinct that most laws favoring Indians serve compelling interests"; *Wittmer v. Peters,* 87 F.3d 916, 919 (7th Cir. 1996), holding that effective operation of prison boot camps is a compelling governmental interest.

U.S. Congress and federal courts.[109] The United States Congress has explicitly found on numerous occasions that Native Hawaiians are an indigenous people and that their political status under U.S. law is comparable to that of American Indians.[110] Although in earlier periods the United States had entered into explicit treaties with native people whose land was taken, after the passage of the Appropriations Act of 1871,[111] the United States entered into no further formal treaties.[112] The history of the status and treatment of Native Hawaiians (like that of the Alaska Natives) is thus different from that of American Indians in the forty-eight contiguous states. Native Hawaiians "developed their own trust relationship with the Federal Government as demonstrated by the passage of the [Hawaiian Homes Commission Act,] and because Native Hawaiians were not being excluded from beneficial legislation in the same manner as unacknowledged mainland United States Indian tribes."[113]

The State of Hawai'i gained only formal "naked"[114] title to the Ceded Lands by

---

109. An accurate description of the illegal overthrow of 1893 and the annexation of 1898 can be found in the 1993 "Apology Resolution," *supra* note 6, which the Hawai'i Legislature has referred to as sound. (In "An Act Relating to the Public Land Trust," ch. 329, 1997 *Hawai'i Session Laws,* 2,072, Hawai'i's Legislature referred to Congress' 1993 "Apology Resolution" as an accurate recounting of "the events of history relating to Hawaii and Native Hawaiians" and called for a "lasting reconciliation" and "a comprehensive, just, and lasting resolution." *Id.* at 2,073.) The U.S. Congress provided another accurate summary of these events in the "Findings of the Native Hawaiian Health Care Improvement Act Amendments of 1992," Pub. L. No. 102-396, 106 Stat. 1948 (1992), codified at 42 U.S.C. sec. 11701 (1994). Accurate descriptions can also be found in the opinions of the District Court and the Court of Appeals in *Rice v. Cayetano,* 963 F. Supp., 1547, 1551–52 (D.Hawai'i 1997), and 146 F.3d 1075, 1077-78 (9th Cir. 1998), and the Supreme Court's summary of the history in Section I of *Rice v. Cayetano,* 528 U.S. at 499–507 is accurate in describing the role of the United States in the overthrow of the Kingdom and the transfer of lands.

110. *See, e.g.,* "Apology Resolution," *supra* note 6, referring to Native Hawaiians as an "indigenous . . . people"; "Native Hawaiian Education Act of 1994," 20 U.S.C. secs. 7902-12 (West Supp., 1998), acknowledging the special relationship that exists between the United States and the Native Hawaiian people; "Hawaiian Homelands Homeownership Act of 2000," Pub. L. 106-568, 114 Stat. 2868 (2000), sec. 202(13); "2002 Native Hawaiian Education Act," Pub. L. 107-110, 115 Stat. 1425, 20 U.S.C. sec. 7512(1) (Supp.I 2002): "Native Hawaiians are a distinct and unique indigenous people." The Congress has affirmed this status repeatedly by treating Native Hawaiians as Native Americans and by including Native Hawaiians in legislation and programs designed to assist Native Americans, as listed, for instance, in Section 202(14)-(15) of the "Hawaiian Homelands Homeownership Act of 2000" and in the "2002 Native Hawaiian Education Act," 20 U.S.C. sec. 7512(13). *See also supra* this chapter, note 64.

See also "Native American Graves Protection and Repatriation Act," Pub. L. No. 101-601, 104 Stat. 3048, 25 U.S.C. sec. 3001-13, which designates "Native Hawaiian organizations," as defined in 25 U.S.C. sec. 3001(11), as having the same rights as Indian tribes to claim culturally important remains and items. Senate Report No. 101-473 at 6 explained that "there are over 200 tribes and 200 Alaskan Native villages and Native Hawaiian communities, each with distinct cultures and traditional and religious practices that are unique to each community."

U.S. District Judge Alan C. Kay has recently explained that Congress "has made legislative findings that the United States has a political relationship with and a special trust obligation to Native Hawaiians as the indigenous people of Hawaii." *Doe v. Kamehameha Schools,* 295 F.Supp.2d 1141, 1150 (D.Hawai'i 2003), *aff'd,* 470 F. 3d 827 (9th Cir. en banc 2006), citing the "Native Hawaiian Education Act," 20 U.S.C. sec. 7512 , and the "Native Hawaiian Health Care Improvements Act," 42 U.S.C. sec. 11701.

111. "Appropriations Act of 1871," ch. 120, sec. 1, 16 Stat. 544, 566, codified at 25 U.S. C. sec. 71.

112. *See generally* Felix S. Cohen's *Handbook of Federal Indian Law,* 105–07 (Rennard Strickland et al., eds., 1982 edition); *Rice v. Cayetano (II),* 963 F.Supp., 1547, 1553 (D.Hawai'i 1997), *reversed on other grounds,* 528 U.S. 495 (2000).

113. *Rice v. Cayetano (II),* 963 F.Supp., 1547, 1553 (D. Hawai'i 1997), citing HHCA, *supra* note 16.

114. *State v. Zimring,* 58 Hawai'i 106, 124, 566 P.2d 725, 737 (1977).

virtue of the 1959 Admission Act, where the United States transferred these Ceded Lands to the State in trust, and it holds these lands as trustee pending the resolution of the claims of Native Hawaiians to these lands. Because Native Hawaiians are named beneficiaries to these lands and have a substantial pending claim to ownership of the Ceded Lands, which the State has recognized and is in the process of addressing, the Native Hawaiians are in a position similar to that of the Alaska Natives in the late 1960s while their land claims were pending[115] and to that of the Maoris in New Zealand (Aotearoa) in the 1970s while the Waitangi Tribunal was evaluating their claims.[116] As the quotations from State and federal legislation discussed above in

---

115. The "Alaska Statehood Act," Pub. L. No. 85-508, 72 Stat. 339 (1958), codified at 48 U.S.C. sec. 21 (1982), recognized the rights of Eskimos, Indians, and Aleuts to their lands but did not define the boundaries of the land. In order to protect their aboriginal lands, the Alaska Natives were compelled to file land claims on vast amounts of acreage and petitioned Secretary of Interior Stewart Udall to impose a moratorium on all land transfers until the claims of the Natives were resolved. Secretary Udall imposed an informal freeze on land transfers in 1966 and converted the freeze into a formal executive order in 1969. Shannon D. Work, Comment, "The Alaska Native Claims Settlement Act: An Illusion in the Quest for Native Self-Determination," 66 *Oregon Law Review*, 195, 207(1987), citing Mary Clay Berry, *The Alaska Pipeline: The Politics of Oil and Native Land Claims*, 49, 60 (1975). Although Governor Walter J. Hickel had opposed this land freeze while he served as Governor, he was nominated by President Nixon to succeed Udall as Secretary of the Interior, and, during his confirmation hearings, he agreed "to retain the freeze for two more years or until the claims were settled, whichever occurred first." Berry, *supra*, at 61. The freeze remained in place until the passage of the "Alaska Native Claims Settlement Act of 1971," 85 Stat. 688 (1971), codified in 43 U.S.C. sec. 1601 *et seq.*

116. The Maori in Aotearoa (New Zealand) are the Polynesian cousins of the Native Hawaiians, and their efforts to recover land, resources, and autonomy parallels in many ways the efforts of the Native Hawaiians. The Maori are considerably farther along in this struggle, however, and the courts of their country have acted repeatedly to protect and effectuate their rights.

The Waitangi Tribunal was established to examine claims that the British Crown failed to fulfill its obligation under the 1840 Treaty of Waitangi to protect Maori land and resources. When the New Zealand Government opposed the Maori claims before the Waitangi Tribunal, the Maori proceeded to court and won a succession of ten cases against the Government. One of the most significant cases was *New Zealand Maori Council v. Attorney General* (1987) 1 NZLR 641, where the New Zealand Court of Appeals declared that it would be unlawful for the New Zealand Government to transfer any public lands, even to state-owned enterprises, without ensuring that the rights of the Maori people to those lands were fully protected. The court stated that because the New Zealand Government owed "fiduciary" duties to the Maori, the Government's responsibility was "not merely passive but extends to active protection of the Maori people in the use of their lands and waters to the fullest extent practicable." *Id.* at 642.

This key 1987 decision was followed by others that also blocked the Government's sale of lands claimed by the Maori. Two of the most important cases involved the Tainui challenge to the sale of land by the state-owned Coalcorp and the challenge to the transfer of crown land to state-owned enterprises. See Ranginui J. Walker, "Maori Issues," in 5 *Contemporary Pacific*, 156, 158 (1993).

In the CoalCorp situation, the Tainui argued that the sale of CoalCorp's North Island mines would pre-empt their claim before the Waitangi Tribunal. The court agreed, and its decision also had the effect of blocking the sale and development of new coal fields in the South Island. *Coal Week International*, vol. 10, no. 36 (September 5, 1989), 1989 WL 2100147. Also in 1989, the New Zealand Government had to put on hold the sale of state forests to private investors. The sale of the timberlands, estimated to be $4 billion in value, could not proceed until the complex web of Maori claims on the lands was resolved. "New Zealand Forest Sale Stalled," *Los Angeles Times*, May 22, 1989, 1989 WL 2296115.

Subsequently, the Maori in the North Island were successful in stopping the use of crown land to establish a national park in their area until their claims to the lands proposed for the park have been settled. The Waitangi Tribunal investigated the dispute and recommended that large areas be returned to the tribes, but the Government was slow to accept these recommendations. Until the Government reached a settlement regarding the Maori claims, its effort to transfer lands to establish a park were blocked. *See* Margaret Mutu, "Maori Issues," in 7 *Contemporary Pacific*, 152, 154–55 (1995).

chapter 23 illustrate,[117] the State of Hawai'i and the United States Government have acknowledged on several occasions that Native Hawaiians have cognizable claims to the Ceded Lands.[118] The Native Hawaiian People thus have a collective property right that is cognizable under U.S. law.[119]

The Public Land Trust

The validity of the underlying trusts that formed the basis for the establishment of the Office of Hawaiian Affairs and the Department of Hawaiian Home Lands was not presented to the Court in *Rice v. Cayetano*,[120] but the historical basis for this trust is

---

117. Illustrative of the State's acknowledgment of the validity of the claims of the Native Hawaiian people are the Findings in Section 1 of "An Act Relating to Hawaiian Sovereignty," ch. 359, 1993 *Hawai'i Session Laws,* 1009, where the Hawai'i State Legislature recognized (in language closely paralleling that found in the "Apology Resolution," *supra* note 6) that

> (9) In 1898, Hawai'i was annexed to the United States through the Newlands Resolution *without the consent of or compensation to the indigenous people of Hawai'i or their sovereign government.* As a result, *the indigenous people of Hawai'i were denied* the mechanism for expression of their inherent sovereignty through self-government and self-determination, *their lands,* and their ocean resources. (Emphasis added.)

Also in 1993, the Hawai'i Legislature recognized that the State of Hawai'i holds federally returned Ceded Lands in temporary trust, and that ultimately the proper entity to control these lands is the Native Hawaiian Nation once it is restored. In its enactment accepting temporary control of Kaho'olawe as trustee, the Legislature stated that

> Transfer. Upon its return to the State, the resources and waters of Kaho'olawe shall be held *in trust* as part of the public land trust; provided that *the State shall transfer management and control of the island and its waters to the sovereign native Hawaiian entity* upon its recognition by the United States and the State of Hawai'i.

H.R.S. Section 6K-9 (emphasis added).

118. Another example can be found in a letter written by Hawai'i's Attorney General Robert Marks on September 24, 1994, to Clayton Hee, OHA Chair, agreeing to include the following language in OHA's acceptance of any funds for land transfers:

> By agreeing and accepting the provisions set out in the August 29, 1994 letter from Joseph K. Conant, Executive Director, Housing Finance and Development Corporation, State of Hawai'i, and, in the future, accepting payment of the sum specified as payable to the Office of Hawaiian Affairs by the Corporation in that letter, the Chairperson, and members of the Board of Trustees of the Office of Hawaiian Affairs, and the Office of Hawaiian Affairs, act solely for the purpose of implementing the provisions of Act 318, SLH 1992, and only on behalf of the Office of Hawaiian Affairs, and in no manner do they waive or otherwise act in furtherance or diminution of any claim the Hawaiian people may have to the land comprising the site of the Villages of Leiali'i project.

119. *See, e.g.,* Alani Apio and Robert A. Alm, "Let's Open a Second Dialogue," *Honolulu Advertiser,* December 26, 1999, at B-4, col.4:

> At one of the [dialogue] sessions, a Hawaiian said to the non-Hawaiians present: "You, personally, did not cause the pain, we know that. But you are the beneficiaries of the system that caused harm to us and you must be part of the solution." And, in fact, the non-Hawaiians in the room, many of whom work downtown, or for the government, or for the university, are major beneficiaries of the fact that this is now America. A nation, land and all, was stolen.
> Someone lost and somebody gained.

For the development of the argument that the Hawaiian claim should be articulated as a "property right," *see, e.g.,* Clarkson, *supra* note 57, at 346, 349.

120. *Rice,* 528 U.S. at 521 (2000): "As the Court of Appeals did, we assume the validity of the underlying administrative structure and trusts, without intimating any opinion on that point."

well grounded in State and federal statutes.[121] The State of Hawai'i's role as trustee of the Public Land Trust for the benefit of Native Hawaiians is spelled out in Hawai'i's Constitution[122] and was explained by the District Court in its *Rice* decisions.[123] The Hawai'i Supreme Court has stated that "Article XII, § 4 [of the Hawai'i State Constitution] imposes a fiduciary duty on Hawaii's officials to hold ceded lands in accordance with the § 5(f) trust provisions, and the citizens of the state must have a means to enforce compliance."[124] The State as trustee of the Public Land Trust is held to the same strict standards applicable to private trustees, and "the beneficiaries of this trust should not be left powerless to prevent the State from allegedly neglecting its obligations."[125]

Governmental Duties as Trustee for Native Lands

The nature of the responsibilities of the State and Federal Governments regarding these trust lands can be illustrated by decisions regarding comparable native land in North America.[126] U.S. Supreme Court decisions indicate that the Government's power to control and manage Native American lands in good faith "show that this power is subject to constitutional limitations and does not enable the government to . . . deal with them as its own."[127] The Court has held that if Congress takes Indian

---

121. It is sometimes contended that Justice Stephen Breyer, in his concurring opinion in *Rice,* denied that a trust existed, but this view misunderstands the point he was trying to make. When Justice Breyer said "there is no 'trust' for native Hawaiians here," 528 U.S. at 525, he was not saying that no trust exists, but rather that the electorate for the Office of Hawaiian Affairs was not congruent with the trusts that had previously been established. Justice Breyer's meaning and intent become clear from the paragraphs that follow, which emphasized that OHA received funds from several sources and that its membership was not limited by a defined blood quantum.

Justice Breyer also noted that the trust established by Section 5(f) of the 1959 Admission Act is for the betterment of the general public as well as of Native Hawaiians. The people of Hawai'i made that sharing explicit in Article XII, Section 4 of the *Hawai'i Constitution,* which was added in 1978 and which identified Native Hawaiians and the general public as the two distinct named beneficiaries of the Public Land Trust. The fact that two beneficiaries are named does not, of course, diminish the rights of either named beneficiary. Each has rights under the trust. In 1980, the Hawai'i Legislature determined that OHA should receive 20 percent of the revenues generated from the Public Land Trust to be used for the benefit of Native Hawaiians. *Hawai'i Revised Statutes Ann.,* secs. 10–13.5 (Michie, 1997).

122. *Hawai'i Constitution,* Article XII, sec. 4.

123. *Rice v. Cayetano (II),* 963 F. Supp. 1547, 1554 (D.Hawai'i 1997): "the trust obligation owed and directed by Congress and the State of Hawai'i", and *Rice v. Cayetano (I),* 941 F. Supp. 1529, 1543 (D.Hawai'i 1996): "The State . . . [is] trustee of the public trust created by the federal government in the Admission Act," both *rev'd on other grounds,* 528 U.S. 495 (2000).

124. *Pele Defense Fund v. Paty,* 73 Hawai'i 578, 605, 837 P.2d 1247, 1264 (1992).

125. *Id.* at 605 n. 18, 837 P.2d at 1264 n. 18 (citations omitted); *see also Ahuna v. Department of Hawaiian Home Lands,* 64 Hawai'i 327, 640 P.2d 1161 (1982). *See, in general,* Slade, *Putting the Public Trust Doctrine to Work* (1990), chap. 11, sec. 2: "The Duties of Private Trustees as Guidance for Public Trustees," *Restatement (Second) of Trusts,* § 164, 169–185 (1959).

126. These issues are also discussed in Mark A. Inciong, "The Lost Trust: Native Hawaiian Beneficiaries under the Hawaiian Homes Commission Act," 8 *Arizona Journal of International & Comparative Law,* 171 (1991).

127. *Chippewa Indians v. United States,* 301 U.S. 358, 375–76 (1937) (citations omitted). *See also United States v. Creek Nation,* 295 U.S. 103, 109–10 (1935).

property for non-Indian use, the United States is liable under the Fifth Amendment of the Constitution for payment of compensation and an uncompensated taking may be enjoined.[128]

The interests that Native Hawaiians and other Native Americans hold in real property represent a unique form of property right in the American legal system. That right has been shaped by the federal trust over these lands and the statutory restraints against alienation. The property right is a form of "ownership in common," held for the benefit of all members of the tribe. The rights of native peoples to property are "as sacred as the fee-simple title of the whites."[129]

Fifth Amendment protection extends to Indian property rights "recognized" by Congress.[130] As explained above, Congress has recognized in both the 1959 Admission Act, Section 5(f), and the 1993 "Apology Resolution" that Native Hawaiians are beneficiaries of the illegally taken Ceded Lands. When a valid trust is created, the beneficiaries become the owners of the equitable or beneficial title to the trust property.[131]

The application of ordinary trust standards to Government officials is commonplace, as illustrated by the significant Federal District Court decision, *Pyramid Lake Paiute Tribe v. Morton*,[132] where the court struck down a regulation allowing diversions of water for a federal reclamation project that adversely affected a downstream lake on an Indian reservation. Although the diversions violated no specific statute or treaty, the court found them to be in violation of the Federal Government's trust responsibility. The court held that the Secretary of the Interior—as trustee for the tribe—was required by his trust responsibility to administer reclamation statutes in a manner that did not interfere with Indian rights. Trustees are obliged to adhere strictly to standard fiduciary principles. This responsibility includes a duty of loyalty and the duty of trustees to put the interests of their beneficiaries before their own interests.

As explained above, both the Federal and State Governments have recognized that the overthrow of the Kingdom of Hawai'i was illegal and that the taking of the Ceded Lands was without the consent of or compensation to the Native Hawaiian People.[133] Moreover, the 1959 Admission Act, the Hawai'i State Constitution, and

---

128. *Lane v. Pueblo of Santa Rosa*, 249 U.S. 110 (1919); *Pyramid Lake Paiute Tribe v. Morton*, 354 F. Supp. 252 (D.D.C., 1973). *See also Shoshone Tribe v. United States*, 299 U.S. 476, 498 (1937): "Spoliation is not management."

129. *Mitchell v. United States*, 34 U.S. (9 Pet.) 711, 746 (1835).

130. *See, e.g., Sioux Nation of Indians v. United States*, 601 F.2d 1157 (Claims Ct. 1979); *Fort Berthold Reservation v. United States*, 390 F.2d 686 (Claims Ct. 1968).

131. *See, e.g., City of Mesquite v. Malouf*, 553 S.W.2d 639 (Tex. Civ. App. 1977); *Rheinstrom v. Commissioner of Internal Revenue*, 105 F.2d 642 (8th Cir. 1939); *Parrish v. Looney*, 194 S.W.2d 419 (Tex. Civ. App. 1946): "The trustee is only the depository of the bare legal title," citing Bogert, *Trusts & Trustees* (2d ed.), Sec. 146, p. 45 (1945).

132. 354 F.Supp. 252 (D.D.C., 1972).

133. *See supra* chapter 23, text at notes 69–73, 89–96.

relevant sections of the *Hawai'i Revised Statutes* must all be construed in light of the canon of construction that enactments passed for the benefit of Native Americans should be liberally construed in their favor.[134] As a result, the Native Hawaiian claim must be accepted as constituting a valid property right.[135] And protecting a legitimate property right is certainly a compelling interest for a government to pursue.

The Right to Self-Determination and Self-Governance

Protecting the right of the Native Hawaiian People to self-determination and self-governance is an equally compelling governmental interest. As the material above explains, Congress and the Hawai'i State Legislature have repeatedly said that Native Hawaiians have this right, and that it has been illegally taken from them. In the 1993 "Apology Resolution," Congress said that the Hawaiian people "never directly relinquished their claims to their inherent sovereignty as a people" and listed among the wrongs done to them "the deprivation of the rights of Native Hawaiians to self-determination."[136] The right to self-determination is the most basic of human rights under federal and international law,[137] and efforts to facilitate the exercise of this right are mandated by fundamental principles of human rights and human decency.

---

134. *See, e.g., Antoine v. Washington,* 420 U.S. 194, 199 (1975); *Wilson v. Omaha Indian Tribe,* 442 U.S. 653, 666 (1979); *Alaska Pacific Fisheries Co. v. United States,* 248 U.S. 78, 89 (1918).

135. In two cases after the U.S. Supreme Court's *Rice* decision, the Hawai'i Supreme Court has recognized the continuing validity of the traditional and customary Native Hawaiian rights recognized in Article XII, sec. 7 of the *Hawai'i Constitution,* which have always been viewed in Hawai'i as property rights. *In the Matter of the Water Use Permit Applications, Petitions for Interim Instream Flow Standard Amendments, and Petitions for Water Reservations for the Waiahole Ditch Combined Contested Case,* 94 Hawai'i 97, 137, 9 P.3d 409, 449 (2000); *Ka Pa'akai o Ka 'Āina v. Land Use Commission,* 94 Hawai'i 31, 45, 7 P.3d 1068, 1082 (2000).

136. "Apology Resolution,"*supra* note 6, Whereas para. 29 and Sec. 1(3); similar language is in the 1994 "Native Hawaiian Education Act," which reconfirmed that "Native Hawaiians are a distinct and unique indigenous people" and that the United States had apologized for "the deprivation of the rights of Native Hawaiians to self-determination." 20 U.S.C. sec. 7902(1), 7902(8).

137. *See generally* S. James Anaya, "The Native Hawaiian People and International Human Rights Law: Toward a Remedy for Past and Continuing Wrongs," 28 *Georgia Law Review,* 309 (1994); Jon M. Van Dyke, Carmen Di Amore-Siah, and Gerald W. Berkley-Coats, "Self-Determination for Nonself-Governing Peoples and for Indigenous Peoples: The Cases of Guam and Hawai'i," 18 *University of Hawai'i Law Review,* 623 (1996). In a report commissioned by the U.N. Sub-Commission on the Prevention of Discrimination and Protection of Minorities, Special Rapporteur Jose Martinez Cobo described the right of indigenous peoples to self-determination as follows:

> Self-determination, in its many forms, must be recognized as a basic precondition for the enjoyment by indigenous peoples of their fundamental rights and the determination of their own future. . . .
> . . . [S]elf-determination constitutes the exercise of free choice by indigenous peoples, who must to a large extent create the specific content of this principle, in both its internal and external expressions, which do not necessarily include the right to secede from the State in which they may live and to set themselves up as sovereign entities. The right may in fact be expressed in various forms of autonomy within the State.

Jose Martinez Cobo, *Study of the Problem of Discrimination against Indigenous Populations,* U.N. ESCOR, Comm'n on Hum. Rts., Sub-Comm'n on Prevention of Discrimination and Protection of Minorities, 36th Sess., Agenda Item 11, at 74, U.N. Doc. E/CN.4/Sub.1983/21/Add.8, paras. 580–81, U.N. Sales No. E.86.XIV.3 (1983).

Lower Courts Ruled That the Limitation on OHA Voting
Met the Strict-Scrutiny Test

If further evidence were needed that compelling interests exist to provide separate and preferential programs for Native Hawaiians, one need only look at the opinions of the District Court and Court of Appeals in *Rice v. Cayetano* to find such substantiation. Although these decisions were reversed by the Supreme Court's *Rice* opinion, the application of the strict-scrutiny test was not addressed by the Supreme Court, and the views of the lower court judges on this topic have substantial persuasive value.

Both the District Court for the District of Hawai'i and the U.S. Court of Appeals for the Ninth Circuit ruled in *Rice* that the Hawaiians-only vote for OHA Trustees need only meet the rational-basis level of judicial review, because Native Hawaiians had been viewed by the U.S. Congress as comparable to other Native Americans. But both courts also commented on whether this approach would also meet the strict-scrutiny test, perhaps in anticipation of this issue being addressed on appeal. U.S. District Court Judge David Ezra said that the State's interest in limiting the voting to persons of Hawaiian ancestry when it conducted the 1996 Native Hawaiian Vote (to determine views on sovereignty) was "rationally related to, *and perhaps even compelling* in light of, the state's unique obligation to Native Hawaiians as demonstrated by its constitution and the [Hawaiian Homes Commission Act]." [138]

The Ninth Circuit went into this subject in more detail and explicitly addressed the argument that the Hawaiians-only voting scheme for OHA Trustees violated the strict-scrutiny test mandated by *Adarand Constructors v. Pena*. [139] In an opinion written by Judge Pamela Rymer, the court said that it did not think the strict-scrutiny test should apply, but then it concluded without hesitation that the Hawaiians-only vote could meet that test. Judge Rymer's language on this issue is quoted in full because of its importance to this discussion:

> However, even if the voting restriction must be subjected to *strict judicial scrutiny* because the classification is based explicitly on race, it survives because the restriction is rooted in the special trust relationship between Hawaii and descendants of aboriginal peoples who subsisted in the Islands in 1778 and still live there—which is not challenged in this appeal. Thus, *the scheme for electing trustees ultimately responds to the state's compelling responsibility to honor the trust,* and the restriction on voter eligibility is *precisely tailored* to the perceived value that a board "chosen from among those who are interested parties would be the best way to insure proper management and adherence to the needed fiduciary

---

138. *Rice v. Cayetano (I)*, 941 F.Supp. 1529, 1544 (D.Haw. 1996), *reversed on other grounds*, 528 U.S. 495 (2000).

139. *Adarand Constructors v. Pena*, 515 U.S. 200 (1995).

The 2000 U.S. Supreme Court Justices *(left to right)* Antonin G. Scalia, Ruth Bader Ginsburg, John Paul Stevens, David H. Souter, William Rehnquist, Clarence Thomas, Sandra Day O'Connor, Stephen G. Breyer, Anthony M. Kennedy

principles." 1 *Proceedings of the Constitutional Convention of Hawaii of 1978*, Standing Comm. Rep. No. 59, at 644.

Given the fact that only Hawaiians and native Hawaiians are trust beneficiaries, *there is no race-neutral way to accord only those who have a legal interest in management of trust assets a say in electing trustees except to do so according to the statutory definition by blood quantum which makes the beneficiaries the same as the voters.* We therefore conclude that because Hawaiians and native Hawaiians have the right to vote as such, not just because they are Hawaiian, that the Equal Protection Clause does not preclude Hawaii from restricting the voting for trustees to Hawaiians and excluding all others.[140]

The Least-Drastic-Alternative Requirement
The second paragraph quoted above is especially important, because it addresses the question of whether a "less drastic alternative" can be devised to meet the Government's compelling interests, and the Court of Appeals concludes that one cannot be

---

140. *Rice v. Cayetano,* 146 F.3d 1075, 1082 (9th Cir. 1998) (emphasis added), *reversed on other grounds,* 528 U.S. 495 (2000).

developed because of the close and essential link between the Native Hawaiian People and their assets. Judge Rymer explained in her opinion for the Ninth Circuit[141] that *the assets being managed by the OHA Trustees belong to the Native Hawaiian People,* and that it is an essential underpinning of fundamental notions of property law that individuals and groups are entitled to manage and control their own property.[142]

Delegating Responsibilities to the State of Hawai'i

The Supreme Court's majority opinion in *Rice* suggested that it is still an open question whether Congress "may, and has, delegated to the State [of Hawai'i] a broad authority to preserve that status,"—that is, the status of Native Hawaiians "like that of Indians in organized tribes."[143] Commentators have thought that this should not be a troublesome issue, because "[p]resumably the United States can also fulfill its trust obligations to Native Hawaiians by delegating duties to the state of Hawaii to the same extent that it can delegate its duties towards Indians to mainland states."[144]

The U.S. Congress recently explained in the Hawaiian Homelands Home-ownership Act of 2000[145] and in the 2002 Native Hawaiian Education Act[146] that "Congress has also delegated broad authority to administer a portion of the Federal trust responsibility to the State of Hawaii." As is explained in more detail below,[147] this delegation constituted an explicit condition of statehood which the State was obliged to accept—Congress required the new State of Hawai'i to adopt the Hawaiian Homes Commission Act as a "compact" between the United States and the State and required the State to manage the Ceded Lands as a public trust for, among other things, "the betterment of the conditions of native Hawaiians."[148] The language in the Admission Act is not permissive, and the State of Hawai'i does not have the option of avoiding or ignoring these delegated responsibilities. The State has accepted these duties[149] and has recognized the claims of Native Hawaiians[150] and the importance of settling these claims in a fair and honorable manner.[151] The State of Hawai'i's trust obligations to Native Hawaiians are particularly important because they stem

---

141. "[T]here is no race-neutral way to accord only those who have a legal interest in management of trust assets as say in electing trustees except to do so according to the statutory definition of blood quantum which makes the beneficiaries the same as the voters." *Id.* at 1082.

142. For commentary agreeing that programs established exclusively for Native Hawaiians would survive strict-scrutiny judicial review, *see* Robert J. Diechert, "The Fifteenth Amendment at a Crossroads: *Rice v. Cayetano,*" 32 *Connecticut Law Review,* 1075, 1076, 1120–25 (2000).

143. *Rice,* 528 U.S. at 518.

144. Cohen's *Handbook, supra* note 111, at 803–04, citing Public Law 280, which delegated "jurisdiction over Indians to several mainland states."

145. "Hawaiian Homelands Homeownership Act of 2000," sec. 202(13), Pub. L. No. 106-568, 114 Stat. 2868 (2000).

146. "2002 Native Hawaiian Education Act," 20 U.S.C. sec. 7512(12)(C).

147. *See infra* this chapter, text at notes 158–66.

148. Admission Act, *supra* note 7, secs. 4, 5(f).

149. *See supra* chapter 24, text at notes 34–74.

150. *See infra* this chapter, text at notes 154–57.

151. *See supra* chapter 24, text at notes 66–68.

from the congressional enactment admitting Hawai'i to statehood. When Congress imposes trust responsibilities in statutes admitting territories into the Union as states, Article VI of the U.S. Constitution requires the states to defer to those admission enabling acts and to comply with the trust responsibilities.[152]

The State's role as trustee of the "public trust" for the benefit of Native Hawaiians is acknowledged expressly in Article XII, Section 4 of Hawai'i's Constitution, and Article XII, Section 6 recognizes that Native Hawaiians are entitled to "income and proceeds from that pro rata portion of the trust referred to in section 4 of this article for native Hawaiians."[153]

---

152. *See, e.g., Gladden Farms v. State,* 633 P.2d 325, 327 (Arizona 1981), striking down the transfer of lands from one state agency to another because it did not comply with the requirements of the "Enabling Act" admitting Arizona to statehood, which required all such sales to be by public auction; *Kadish v. Arizona State Land Department,* 747 P.2d 1183, 1185 (Arizona 1987), interpreting the trust responsibilities laid down by Congress in the "New Mexico–Arizona Statehood Enabling Act" strictly and thus forbidding the state from making nonhydrocarbon mineral leases without appraisal or for less than their true value; *Branson v. Romer,* 958 F. Supp. 1501, 1514–16 (D. Colorado 1997), interpreting the congressional statute admitting Colorado to the Union as creating an enforceable perpetual trust in favor of the public schools, *aff'd sub nom. Branson School District RE-82 v. Romer,* 161 F.3d 619 (9th Cir. 1998), explaining that although the "Colorado Enabling Act" did not use the word "trust," the explicit restrictions on how lands could be managed or disposed evidenced Congress' intent to create trust duty; *Alamo Land & Cattle Co. v. Arizona,* 424 U.S. 295, 302 (1976), reaffirming "the Court's concern for the integrity of the conditions imposed" by the "New Mexico–Arizona Statehood Enabling Act" on the lands conveyed to the states, which "has long been evident"; *Lassen v. Arizona ex rel Arizona Highway Dept.,* 385 U.S. 458, 469 (1967), affirming the importance of maintaining the value of the trust corpus established by the "New Mexico–Arizona Statehood Enabling Act," even when trust lands are needed for highway purposes, and requiring Arizona to "actually compensate the trust in money for the full appraised value of any material sites or rights of way which it obtains on or over trust lands"; *Ervien v. United States,* 251 U.S. 41, 47 (1919), strictly enforcing the language in "Arizona's Statehood Enabling Act" and stating that the enumeration of public land trust purposes in the statute is "necessarily exclusive of any other purpose"; *United States v. New Mexico,* 536 F.2d 1324 (10th Cir. 1976), requiring New Mexico to adhere strictly to the terms of the "Statehood Enabling Act," which had conveyed 50,000 acres to the state to support 'miners' hospitals for disabled miners"; *United States v. 11.2 Acres of Land, More or Less, in Ferry County, Washington,* 293 F. Supp 1042 (1968), holding that a Washington statute that conveyed public trust lands that had been received at statehood to the United States for irrigation purposes without compensation was unconstitutional and in violation of the trust responsibilities established in the "Statehood Enabling Act"; *United States v. 78.61 Acres of Land in Dawes and Sioux Counties, Nebraska,* 265 F. Supp. 564 (1967), striking down the Nebraska Legislature's grants of rights-of-way over school lands to the United States for transmission lines without compensation because such a conveyance was in conflict with the terms of Nebraska's "Statehood Enabling Act of 1864"); *County of Skamania v. State,* 685 P.2d 576 (Washington 1984), striking down a statute passed by Washington's Legislature to assist the timber industry in a period of economic hardship because the enactment violated the state's obligations under its statehood enabling act to manage its public lands in trust for its public schools and universities.

153. Court decisions that have recognized the State's trust duties include *Office of Hawaiian Affairs v. State,* 96 Hawai'i 388, 401, 31 P.3d 901, 914 (2001), explaining that the State of Hawai'i's obligation to Native Hawaiians is firmly rooted in the State Constitution and recognizing the "right of native Hawaiians to benefit from the ceded lands trust"; *Pele Defense Fund v. Paty,* 73 Hawai'i 578, 605, 837 P.2d 1247, 1264 (1992), explaining that "the ceded lands trust" is "held for the benefit of native Hawaiians and members of the public" and that beneficiaries have standing to sue to challenge alleged breaches of trust obligations; *Rice v. Cayetano,* 146 F.3d 1075, 1080 (9th Cir. 1998): "Hawaii acknowledged a trust obligation toward native Hawaiians as a condition of admission to the union"; *Rice v. Cayetano,* 528 U.S. 495, 521–22 (2000): "As the court of appeals did, we assume the validity of the underlying administrative structure and trusts, without intimating any opinion on that point"; *Arakaki v. Cayetano,* 324 F.3d 1078, 1087 (9th Cir. 2003), observing that "[t]he State and HHC/DHHL defendants are directed by section 4 of the Admission Act, and Article XII of the Hawai'i Constitution to provide benefits to native Hawaiians."

The Hawai'i State Legislature has repeatedly recognized the State's delegated trust responsibility to Native Hawaiians and its duty to facilitate a complete settlement of their claims.[154] In 1993, the Hawai'i Legislature "recognized that the Native Hawaiian people were "denied . . . their lands."[155] In 1997, the Hawai'i Legislature "accepted" the "Apology Resolution" and called for "lasting reconciliation" and "a comprehensive, just, and lasting resolution."[156] The State Legislature has also decreed that the island of Kaho'olawe and its waters shall be transferred "to the sovereign Native Hawaiian entity upon its recognition by the United States and the State of Hawai'i."[157]

The Admission Act

The Admission Act constitutes a compact between the United States and the Native Hawaiian People. The 1959 Admission Act required the State of Hawai'i to administer the Hawaiian Home Lands Program[158] and also to use some of the revenue from the Public Land Trust "for the betterment of the conditions of native Hawaiians."[159] If setting aside lands for Hawaiians and establishing the Office of Hawaiian Affairs to utilize the Public Lands revenues for their betterment were to be held to be unconstitutional, would the Admission Act itself then be unconstitutional, and would Hawai'i cease to be a state? It is clear from the historical events that led to statehood that protecting the special rights and claims of the Native Hawaiian People was an integral part of the statehood package and was an essential underpinning for the support that the Native Hawaiians gave to statehood. Under well-established principles of severability,[160] therefore, if the provisions of the Admission Act governing the Hawaiian Home Lands Program and revenue for Hawaiians should be found to be unconstitutional, the entire Admission Act would fall.[161]

---

154. *See, e.g.,* H.R.S. 10-1: "The people of the State of Hawai'i and the United States of America as set forth and approved in the Admission Act established a public *trust* which includes among other responsibilities, betterment of conditions for native Hawaiians. The people of the State of Hawai'i reaffirmed their *solemn trust obligation and responsibility to native Hawaiians* and furthermore declared in the State Constitution that there be an office of Hawaiian affairs to address the needs of the aboriginal class of people of Hawai'i." (Emphasis added.)

155. "An Act Relating to Hawaiian Sovereignty," ch. 359, 1993 *Hawai'i Session Laws,* 1009.

156. "An Act Relating to the Public Land Trust," ch. 329, 1997 *Hawaii'i Session Laws,* 956.

157. *Hawai'i Revised Statutes,* sec. 6K-9.

158. Admission Act, *supra* note 7, sec. 4. The research and analysis in this section was developed by Melody K. MacKenzie in connection with memoranda filed in the *Arakaki v. Lingle* litigation, discussed *supra,* this chapter, text at notes 90-99.

159. *Id.* sec. 5(f).

160. Under standard severability analysis, if a part of a statute is unconstitutional, the entire statute must be struck down unless it is evident that the Legislature would have enacted the constitutional provisions without the unconstitutional provisions. Because the maintenance of the Hawaiian Home Lands Program was a central focus of the statehood discussion, it is not at all clear that the people of Hawai'i would have voted for statehood without this program being protected.

161. *See* Eric Steven O'Malley, "Irreconcilable Rights and the Question of Hawaiian Statehood," 89 *Georgetown Law Review,* 501, 535 (2001): "If OHA violates the Fourteenth Amendment's Equal Protection Clause, does not the state constitution that led to its creation also violate Equal Protection?"

In § 5 of Hawai'i's Admission Act, Congress conveyed most of the Ceded Lands to the new State of Hawai'i with the condition that Hawai'i hold these lands and their income and proceeds as a "public trust" for one or more of five purposes, including "the betterment of the conditions of native Hawaiians, as defined in the Hawaiian Homes Commission Act, 1920, as amended." Then, in Section 7(b) of the same statute, Congress explicitly required the people of Hawai'i to affirm by vote that "the terms or conditions of the grants of land or other property therein made to the State of Hawaii are consented to fully by said State and its people." And, just to reinforce the importance of these conditions, Congress added in this same section a statement that if a majority of the people of Hawai'i did not vote to accept these conditions, "the provisions of this Act shall cease to be effective." In other words, Hawai'i would not have become a state if the people of Hawai'i had not agreed by vote to the requirement that the revenues from the Ceded Lands be used, in part, for "the betterment of the conditions of native Hawaiians." In case any doubt might have remained, Congress reiterated in Section 7(c) that the President must "find that the propositions set forth in the preceding subsection have been duly adopted by the people of Hawaii" before "Hawaii shall be deemed admitted into the Union."

Based on drafts of earlier statehood bills, the people of Hawai'i had anticipated that such a condition would be attached to statehood and to the transfer of lands, and they put an explicit provision into the 1950 Constitution accepting any conditions of trust that Congress might put on the Public Lands transferred to the State of Hawai'i. This language was in Article XIV, section 7 of the 1950 Constitution, and is now found in Article XVI, Section 7: "Any trust provisions which the Congress shall impose, upon the admission of this State, in respect of the lands patented to the State by the United States or the proceeds and income therefrom, shall be complied with by appropriate legislation." [162] It is significant that Congress reviewed this language (and the rest of the 1950 Constitution, which also accepted responsibility for administering the Hawaiian Homes Commission Act, 1920) and stated explicitly in Section 1 of the 1959 Admission Act that Hawai'i's Constitution "is hereby found to be republican in *form and in conformity with the Constitution of the United States* and the principles of the Declaration of Independence, and is hereby accepted, ratified, and confirmed." (Emphasis added.)

The legislative history of the Admission Act reveals that the members of Congress understood that the transfer of the Hawaiian Home Lands Program to the State of Hawai'i and the requirement that revenues from the Ceded Lands be used for the "betterment of the conditions of native Hawaiians" were not duplicative but served two separate purposes, settling in part the unresolved and festering claims of

---

162. In 1978, the voters of Hawai'i approved an amendment adding an additional sentence to this provision reinforcing the State's commitment to protect the rights of Native Hawaiians: "Such legislation shall not diminish or limit the benefits of native Hawaiians under Section 4 of Article XII."

the Native Hawaiian People.[163] Similarly, the legislative record in Hawai'i also demonstrates that the delegates to the 1950 Constitutional Convention understood that the revenues for Native Hawaiians from the Ceded Lands would be an additional effort to resolve their claims, over and above the benefits provided from the Hawaiian Homes program.

Two separate committees—(1) the Committee on Agriculture, Conservation and Land and (2) the Committee on the Hawaiian Homes Commission Act (HHCA)—reported out provisions dealing with the acceptance of trust responsibilities. The HHCA Committee presented proposals that eventually became Article XI, §§ 1 and 2 of the 1950 Constitution[164] relating to the Hawaiian Home Lands Program, and the Committee on Agriculture, Conservation and Land reported out separate provisions relating to the Public Lands that were expected to be transferred from the Federal Government to the new State. This committee first considered a provision that was very similar to § 5(f) of the Admission Act, in order to make Hawai'i's Constitution conform to the version of the statehood bill then pending before Congress.[165]

But in the Committee of the Whole, this more specific trust language was replaced by the more general language that became Article XIV, sec. 7, and is now the

163. *See, e.g.,* statement of Hawai'i's Delegate Joseph R. Farrington that the reason for using revenues from the Ceded Lands for the "betterment of the conditions of native Hawaiians" "is the very strong feeling that you find in Hawaii that the Hawaiians did not do so well when the land was divided in the 'great mahele' of 1848. And that feeling is particularly among the Hawaiians themselves. After all, they have something of a prior consideration as to the use of the receipts of the land." U.S. Senate Committee on Interior and Insular Affairs, 81st Cong., 2d Sess, *Hearings on H.R. 49, S. 156, and S.1782,* May 1, 2, 3, 4, and 5, 1950, at 354.

Senator Guy Cordon from Oregon expressed full support for the view explained by Delegate Farrington, recognizing and explaining to the other members that the Native Hawaiians had an unresolved claim to the lands then held by the Federal Government:

> I agree with the Delegate [Farrington] when he suggests that there is a feeling that perhaps the Hawaiians have not been wholly justly dealt with here. I have that feeling. The so-called public lands . . . those lands are in no sense public lands as that term is understood in the United States. They were initially crown lands, and went from the status of crown ownership into that of public ownership of a republic which succeeded the monarchy. From my viewpoint the United States of America has not any interest in them whatever, except to transmit them to the people of Hawai'i. If I could transmit a portion of them and get a good job for the Hawaiians of Hawai'i I would like to do it.

Id. (Senator Cordon later chaired the *Hearings of the Senate Subcommittee on Territories and Insular Affairs of the Committee on Interior and Insular Affairs* on March 6, 1953.)

In hearings held in 1955, the chief counsel for the House Committee on Interior and Insular Affairs (Mr. Abbott) explained to Representative B. F. Sisk of California that the goal of the language of the provision that became Section 5(f) of the Admission Act was to provide revenues for two "separable" beneficiaries: (a) for the general public through "support of the public schools . . . and other public educational institutions" and (2) for "the betterment of conditions of native Hawaiians." House Committee on Interior and Insular Affairs, *Hearings on H.R. 2535 and H.R. 2536, Bills "To Enable the People of Hawaii and Alaska Each to Form a Constitution and State Government and to be Admitted into the Union on an Equal Footing with the Original States," and related Bills H.R. 49, H.R. 185, H.R. 187, H.R. 248, H.R. 511, H.R. 555, and H.R. 2531,* 84th Cong., 1st Sess., Jan. 31, 1955.

164. Renumbered and amended in 1978 as Article XII, §§ 1 and 2 of the *Hawai'i Constitution.*

165. 1 *Proceedings of the Constitutional Convention of 1950,* 234–35 (1960).

first sentence in Article XVI, sec. 7.[166] It is significant that this provision did not find its genesis in the HHCA Committee and was not specifically related to the Hawaiian Home Lands Program. The Constitutional Convention's adoption of the language in Article XIV, sec. 7 (now Article XVI, sec. 7) indicates that the trust referred to in Hawai'i's Constitution is the 5(f) trust.

It cannot be doubted, therefore, that the State and the Federal Government entered into a bilateral compact regarding the revenues from these lands and that an essential part of that compact was that the State would transfer part of the revenues from these lands to the Native Hawaiian People in order to resolve, in part, the claims that Native Hawaiians have regarding these lands. Congress required the State and its people to agree to use lands and revenues for the Native Hawaiian People because of its recognition of the claims of the Native Hawaiian people and the need to make progress in resolving these claims. The provisions in the Admission Act thus constitute a settlement of part of the claim, and the State's decision in 1978 to create the Office of Hawaiian Affairs and then to allocate 20 percent of the income generated from the trust lands for programs for Native Hawaiians unquestionably falls within the scope of the State's compact with the United States to utilize the trust lands and income "for the betterment of the conditions of native Hawaiians."

Conclusion

In the closing paragraph of Justice Kennedy's opinion for the Court in *Rice v. Cayetano,* he acknowledged that the "culture and way of life" of the Native Hawaiians were "all but engulfed by a history beyond their control," and that "their sense of loss may extend down through generations." [167] But then he said, oddly, that any attempt to address these losses must be through "the political consensus that begins with a sense of shared purpose" because "[t]he Constitution of the United States, too, has become the heritage of all the citizens of Hawaii." [168] The statement is odd because the Office of Hawaiian Affairs was created through a "political consensus" and "a sense of shared purpose." It was created by the 1978 Constitutional Convention and approved by all the voters of Hawai'i in the November 1978 election. The reference to the U.S. Constitution is also odd, because the U.S. Constitution explicitly recognizes the separate status of the native people, [169] and that separate status has always

---

166. The Committee explained that "Although this section seemed to put full trust in the Congress of the United States, this was believed justified since in the past Congress has always been very fair in its dealings with the Territory, and the members believed Congress would continue to deal in this way with the State of Hawai'i." 1 *Proceedings of the Constitutional Convention of 1950,* 337–38 (1960).

167. *Rice,* 528 U.S. at 524.

168. *Id.*

169. The "Indian Commerce Clause," Article I, sec. 8, cl. 3, groups "Indian tribes" together with foreign nations, obviously recognizing their separate status, and Article I, sec. 2, cl. 3 says that "Indians not taxed" shall not be counted for purposes of apportionment, again recognizing that Indians were outside the U.S. political

been part of our constitutional tradition. Native Hawaiians are different culturally from other Native Americans, who themselves span a wide cultural spectrum, but it is impossible and illogical to consider Native Hawaiians as different from other Native Americans in a legal or constitutional sense. The misguided *Rice* decision has not, however, stopped the momentum toward the reemergence of the Native Hawaiian Nation. Congress has continued to pass important legislation recognizing the status of Native Hawaiians as indigenous people, and the Justice and Interior Departments have concluded that *Rice* "should not stand as an obstacle to the Federal Government's ongoing efforts to work with the Native Hawaiian community in furtherance of 'reconciliation' under the Apology Resolution." [170] U.S. District Judge David A. Ezra observed when the *Rice* case was remanded to his courtroom that the Supreme Court had reversed itself in previous situations and that "[w]hen you have a large and expensive ship, the wise captain does not call for it to be abandoned at the first sight of a small leak but, rather, gathers the crew in a cooperative effort to fix and save the vessel." [171]

---

community. Even after the adoption of the Fourteenth Amendment, which granted citizenship generally to all persons born in and "subject to the jurisdiction" of the United States, Indians were not granted citizenship unless a specific treaty granted them this status. Not until 1924 were all Indians in the United States given citizenship. "Act of June 2, 1924," ch. 233, 43 Stat. 253. *See generally* Cohen's Handbook, *supra* note 111, at 642–45.

170. U.S. Dept. of the Interior and U.S. Dept. of Justice, *From Mauka to Makai: The River of Justice Must Flow Freely* (Rpt. on the Reconciliation Process Between the Federal Government and Native Hawaiians, Oct. 23, 2000).

171. "Transcript of Proceedings before Chief United States District Judge David Alan Ezra," *Rice v. Cayetano* (D. Hawai'i, April 7, 2000), at 9; Pat Omandam, "Judge Takes No Further Action on Rice," *Honolulu Star-Bulletin*, April 7, 2000, at A-3, col. 1.

25

The Kamehameha Schools

This chapter and the one that follows depart from the Crown Lands to look at the four main trusts established by Aliʻi Nui in the late nineteenth and early twentieth centuries. Although the ʻĀina and assets examined in these chapters were never part of the Crown Lands, their story is relevant to the central themes of this book because these ʻĀina became part of the private lands of leading Aliʻi at the Mahele in 1848—at the same time Kamehameha III (Kauikeaouli) took charge of the Crown Lands (then called "the King's Lands")—and the ways in which these four central Aliʻi treated their ʻĀina helps us to understand the relationship between the Mōʻī and the Crown Lands.

Schools for Native Hawaiians

On October 31, 1883, Princess Bernice Pauahi Bishop, great-granddaughter of Kamehameha I, signed and sealed her will,[1] creating what is known today as the Kamehameha Schools.[2] This important will was drafted with the assistance of her husband Charles Reed Bishop, a prominent Honolulu banker and entrepreneur, who helped to administer the Bishop Estate after her death and who tried throughout his life to promote his wife's vision of a better life for her people. After bequeathing sums of money and life estates in land to various individuals in the first twelve provisions of her will,[3] Pauahi left "all the rest, residue and remainder of my estate real and personal, wherever situated" to support the establishment of schools "giving

1. Two codicils were also added, on October 4 and 9, 1884, affecting the management of the Estate. Bernice P. Bishop Estate, *Wills and Deeds of Trust,* 21–27 (3rd ed., 1957). *See generally* Jon M. Van Dyke, "The Kamehameha Schools/Bishop Estate and the Constitution," 17 *University of Hawaiʻi Law Review,* 413 (1995).

2. In response to the turmoil in the 1990s (discussed *infra* this chapter, text at notes 53–64), on January 1, 2000, the Interim Trustees renamed what had been called "the Kamehameha Schools Bernice Pauahi Bishop Estate" to simply "Kamehameha Schools." Sally Apgar, "Trust Enters New Era," *Honolulu Advertiser,* December 19, 1999, at A-8.

3. *See* "Will of Bernice Pauahi Bishop" (October 31, 1883), in *The Kamehameha Schools/Bernice Pauahi Bishop Estate, Excerpts from the Will and Codicils of Princess Bernice Pauahi Bishop and Facts About the Kamehameha Schools/Bernice Pauahi Bishop Estate,* 3 (1976) (hereafter cited as "Excerpts from Pauahi's Will"). In the first twelve provisions in the will and in subsequent codicils, Bernice Pauahi Bishop conveyed payments

Princess Bernice Pauahi Bishop

the preference to Hawaiians of pure or part aboriginal blood."[4] Although the wording in the will says only that a "preference" should be given to children of Hawaiian blood, contemporaneous and subsequent statements and documents confirm that the goal of Princess Pauahi was to create a school for Native Hawaiians and that the word "preference" was included only because of concerns that insufficient numbers of children of Hawaiian ancestry might someday be available to attend the schools.

---

and life estates in properties to various individuals, but the title to these properties reverted back to the Bernice Pauahi Bishop Estate upon their death.

    Her will also conveyed several life estates to her husband, Charles Reed Bishop. Property now popularly known as the Molokaʻi Ranch and parcels in Waikīkī were devised to Charles Reed Bishop by the ninth provision of Pauahi's will; property in Waiʻalae Nui, Waiʻalae Iki, Maunalua, and the ʻIli of Kaʻakopua were devised to him by the third provision of the first codicil. *Wills and Deeds of Trust: Bernice P. Bishop Estate, Bernice P. Bishop Museum, Charles R. Bishop Trust*, 10–11, 14 (rev. ed., 1927). In 1890, Charles Reed Bishop conveyed the 29,069 acres he had inherited back to the Bernice Pauahi Bishop Estate. Harold W. Kent, *Charles Reed Bishop: Man of Hawaii*, 166 (1965). Bishop then deeded an additional 64,619 acres of his own lands to the Estate. *Id.*

    4. "Excerpts from Pauahi's Will," *supra* note 3, at 3. The wording in the first three paragraphs of the thirteenth provision of the will is as follows:

> Thirteenth. I give, devise and bequeath all of the rest, residue and remainder of my estate real and personal, wherever situated unto the trustees below named, their heirs and assigns forever, to hold upon the following trusts, namely: to erect and maintain in the Hawaiian Islands two schools, each for boarding and day scholars, one for boys and one for girls, to be known as, and called the Kamehameha Schools.
>
>   I direct my trustees to expend such amount as they may deem best, not to exceed however one-half of the fund which may come into their hands, in the purchase of suitable premises, the erection of

Charles Reed Bishop

Princess Pauahi's concern for her people was well known. "The dominating idea of Mrs. Bishop was the enlightenment and elevation of the Hawaiian race."[5] In 1884 Pauahi had been suffering from an unknown sickness, and she traveled to San Francisco, where doctors discovered cancer and recommended an operation.[6] She prepared herself for the worst, but "expressed a strong desire that she might live, and go back to Honolulu, 'to do more for her people.'"[7] Pauahi was able to recover sufficiently to return to Honolulu in June of 1884,[8] but her health continued to fail and she passed away on October 16, 1884. Just eight days before her death, she told a close friend that "a lady said to her once that she must be very happy as she had so

---

school buildings, and in furnishing the same with the necessary and appropriate fixtures furniture and apparatus.

I direct my trustees to invest the remainder of my estate in such manner as they may think best, and to expend the annual income in the maintenance of said schools; meaning thereby the salaries of teachers, the repairing buildings and other incidental expenses; and to devote a portion of each years income to the support and education of orphans, and others in indigent circumstances, *giving the preference to Hawaiians of pure or part aboriginal blood;* the proportion in which said annual income is to be divided among the various objects above mentioned to be determined solely by my said trustees they to have full discretion. (Emphasis added.)

Some have occasionally argued that the will was not designed to create schools for Native Hawaiians because the language "giving the preference to Hawaiians of pure or part aboriginal blood" is found in the third paragraph, immediately following the reference to orphans and indigents. But a more careful reading of the three paragraphs reveals that they must be read as a whole and that the language regarding the "preference" is meant to refer to the Schools as a whole. This reading is confirmed by the subsequent statements made by Charles Reed Bishop, as explained in the text that follows.

5. Mary H. Krout, *The Memoirs of Hon. Bernice Pauahi Bishop,* 238 (1908, reprinted in 1958).

6. *Id.* at 220–21.

7. *Id.*

8. *Id.*

much property. [Princess Pauahi's reply was that] happiness is not money, for having so much she felt responsible and accountable."[9]

Because of her status as Ali'i and the privilege of her high rank, Pauahi's vision to create a school for Hawaiian children was almost instinctual. Duty and responsibility prompted the last heroic act of a loving sovereign to use the bounty of land gifted her to save her people from complete annihilation. At the time, no one doubted the intent of Pauahi or the reason why the schools were to be established for pure or part-Hawaiian children, many of whom had lost one or both parents to disease and many of whom were living in squalor. At the opening ceremony for the school for boys, a light rain fell over the mountains and "[t]he older Hawaiians smiled contentedly: 'It is an omen. As the water Kane refreshes the land, so will this gift from our Princess restore life to our people.' "[10]

At the inaugural Founder's Day on December 19, 1887, Charles Reed Bishop gave the keynote speech, explaining his wife's sorrow over the destruction of her people and her hope that through the Kamehameha Schools her people would be ready and able to compete against the flood of foreigners that would inevitably come.[11] He made it clear that the Schools were designed for children of Hawaiian ancestry, explaining that "Hawaiians have the preference [in admission], and [that Pauahi] hoped [the students] would value and take the advantages of [the Schools] as fully as possible."[12] In a letter written ten years later, on February 11, 1897, to Charles Hyde, a fellow Trustee on the first board of the Bernice Pauahi Bishop Estate, Charles Reed Bishop wrote, "There is nothing in the will of Mrs. Bishop excluding white boys or girls from the Schools, *but it is understood by the Trustees that only those having native blood are to be admitted at present,* that *they are to have the preference so long as they avail themselves of the privileges open to them to a reasonable extent.*"[13]

In a letter to Trustee Samuel Damon dated February 20, 1901, later included in the Minutes of Trustees, Charles Reed Bishop wrote, "According to the reading of Clause 13 on Page 8 of the Will as published, the preference to Hawaiians having aboriginal blood applied only to the education of orphans and others in indigent circumstances; *but it was intended and expected that the Hawaiians having aboriginal blood would have preference,* provided that those of suitable age, health, character, and intellect should apply in numbers sufficient to make up a good school."[14] In a

---

9. Cobey Black and Kathleen Dickenson Mellen, *Princess Pauahi and Her Legacy,* 87–88 (1965), recounting a conversation of October 8, 1884, with Juliette Cooke, teacher and confidant of Pauahi.

10. *Id.* at 99.

11. Kent, *supra* note 3, at 152–54.

12. *Id.* at 153. Bishop also explained that "[i]f the youth of native blood fall off in numbers, or stand off in any improper way the youth of other races will be taken in, of course, on terms suited to the conditions which then exist." *Id.* at 163.

13. *Id.* at 162 (emphasis added).

14. *Id.* at 163 (emphasis added). In this letter, Bishop explains why the will does not explicitly say that the schools should be exclusively for those of Hawaiian ancestry: "The Schools were intended to be perpetual, as it was impossible to tell how many boys and girls of aboriginal blood would in the beginning or thereafter qualify and apply for admissions, those of other races were not barred or excluded." *Id.*

Kamehameha Schools

letter written a decade later, on October 9, 1911, again to Trustee Samuel Damon, Bishop explained, "It is decidedly my wish that the native Hawaiians of pure and part aboriginal blood shall . . . take advantage of the preference given them by the Will, with the understanding, of course, that they shall be obedient to the rules and conditions made by the Trustees under the Will; if they do not do so, they cannot expect that others not of their class shall be permanently excluded. *So long as the number of applicants keeps up as it has done so far, it seems to me better that the young people of other nationalities should not be admitted.*" [15]

The ʻĀina That Supports the Schools

The appropriateness of giving Native Hawaiians the preference in admission to the Kamehameha Schools becomes apparent when the nature of the lands that support these Schools is understood. These lands constituted much of the ʻĀina that had been allocated to the Kamehameha Aliʻi in the 1848 Mahele. Princess Pauahi had accumulated the bulk of the ʻĀina still held by the Kamehamehas because she was one of the last recognized heirs of this line. At the January 22, 1886, meeting of the Trustees, the Bernice Pauahi Bishop Estate was determined to hold 375,569 acres, almost one-tenth of the acreage in the eight main Hawaiian islands.[16] Although she had received some ʻĀina from her parents, Abner Pākī and Laura Konia, and from her aunt ʻAkahi, Pauahi received the largest portion of her lands when her cousin Ruth Keʻelikolani died in 1883, just one year before Pauahi's own death.[17]

---

15. *Id.* at 164 (emphasis added).

16. *Id.* at 148. As noted *supra,* this chapter note 3, Charles Reed Bishop returned all of his life estate interest, or 29,069 acres, to the Estate (which brought the Estate's acreage to 375,569) and then added 64,619 acres of his own property, which brought the total land holdings of the Estate to 440,188 acres. *Id.* at 166. Today Kamehameha Schools owns 366,458 acres spread across the islands of Kauaʻi, Oʻahu, Molokaʻi, Maui, and Hawaiʻi.

17. George Kanahele, *Pauahi: The Kamehameha Legacy,* 189 (1986).

Princess Pauahi received her first 5,811.84 acres [18] of land upon the death of her father Abner Pākī in 1855.[19] Although Pākī's grandfather, Kamehamehanui, was a former Mō'ī of Maui, Pākī was not closely related to Kamehameha I and was thus a Kaukau Ali'i, or chief of lesser rank.[20] Nonetheless, at the time of the Mahele, he was allocated six 'Āina.[21]

Pākī disapproved of his daughter's courtship with and marriage to Charles Reed Bishop.[22] Both he and Pauahi's birth mother, Konia, hoped she would marry one of the princes—Alexander Liholiho (who became Kamehameha IV) or Lot Kapuāiwa (who became Kamehameha V).[23] In fact, at an early age, Pauahi was promised in marriage to Lot by her hānai mother Kīna'u.[24] But Pauahi had her own ideas and emotions and expressed her strong personal preference for Charles Reed Bishop.

Pauahi first approached her hānai father, Mataio Kekūanaō'a, and later her birth parents Pākī and Konia, expressing her wish to break her engagement to Lot and to marry Charles.[25] Because of her parents' opposition, she also approached Lot with her dilemma. Lot eventually released Pauahi from their engagement, but these events strained Pauahi's relationship with her parents.[26]

Pauahi later reconciled with her parents, and Abner Pākī left his daughter a considerable estate upon his death. These lands included fourteen small plots in downtown Honolulu, plus substantial acreage in He'eia and Wai'alae Iki on the island of O'ahu.[27] Pauahi also received title to her parent's home, Hale'akalā, on King Street.[28] Table 14 lists the lands and their acreages.[29]

Two years after the death of her father, Pauahi's birth mother Laura Konia died at the age of 49. Konia was either the granddaughter or grandniece of Kamehameha I.[30] Because Konia was Ali'i Nui at the time of the Mahele in 1848, she received eleven 'Āina.[31] Of the land received in the first division of the Mahele, Konia left her daugh-

---

18. *Id.* at 82.

19. *Id.* at 77.

20. Lilikala Kame'eleihiwa, *Native Land and Foreign Desires: Pehea La E Pono Ai?* 267 (1992).

21. *Id.* at 268, table 17.

22. Krout, *supra* note 5, at 99–100.

23. *Id.* at 97–98.

24. Kanahele, *supra* note 17, at 56.

25. *Id.* at 65–68.

26. *Id.* at 68–69.

27. *Id.* at 77.

28. *Id.* Kanahele reported that the correct spelling of the house was Hale'akala, or "Pink House," rather than Haleakalā, which translates as "House of the Sun." *Id.* at 75.

29. *Id.* at 82.

30. Kame'eleihiwa, *supra* note 20, at 228. Konia's father, Pu'uli Ka'oleioku, was said to be po'o lua ("had two fathers"), *id.;* it was an accepted practice among high-ranking chiefs for both the mother's husband and the actual sire to be the legitimate fathers of a child for legacy purposes. Mary Kawena Pukui and Samuel H. Elbert, *Hawaiian Dictionary,* 342 (1986). Pu'uli Ka'oleioku's mother was Kanekapolei, and his father was either Kamehameha I or the King's brother, Kalani'opu'u. Thus, Konia was either the granddaughter or grandniece of Kamehameha I. Kame'eleihiwa, *supra* note 20, at 228.

31. Kame'eleihiwa, *supra* note 20, at 229, table 6.

TABLE 14. ʻĀina Received from Abner Pākī

Location (Oʻahu)	Acreage
Ahupuaʻa of Heʻeia	4,172.00
Waiʻalaeiki	1,608.20
Punchbowl	0.84
Pualoalo, Nuʻuanu	1.24
Kapohuluhulu	2.40
Kalawahine	0.43
King Street (Haleʻakalā)	2.11
Richards Street	0.75
Hotel and Fort Streets	0.10
Queen and Punchbowl Streets	0.98
Kaumakapili	0.26
Alakea and Queen Streets	0.55
Corner of Nuʻuanu and King St.	0.55
Laimi	6.15
Laimi	12.63
Beretania and Nuʻuanu Streets	2.65
TOTAL	5,811.84

TABLE 15. ʻĀina Received from Laura Konia

Location	Acreage
Kauaʻi	
Ahupuaʻa of Lumahaʻi in Haleleʻa	3,150
Oʻahu	
Kaonohi in ʻEwa	1,603
Hawaiʻi	
Ahupuaʻa of Keʻei in South Kona	5,478
TOTAL	10,231

ter 10,231 acres of land on Kauaʻi, Oʻahu, and Hawaiʻi (Table 15).[32] Thus Pauahi received a total of 16,042.84 acres from her two birth parents.[33]

In 1877 Pauahi's Aunt ʻAkahi died, leaving her an additional 9,557 acres of land on Oʻahu and Hawaiʻi.[34] ʻAkahi's great-grandfather, Keuua, was the father of Kamehameha I, who in turn was the great-grandfather of Pauahi.[35] Because ʻAkahi died without children, she bequeathed her lands to her niece as her "closest kin and

32. Kanahele, *supra* note 17, at 82.
33. *Id.*
34. *Id.* at 152.
35. *Id.*

TABLE 16. 'Āina Received from 'Akahi

Location	Acreage
O'ahu	
Kaipu, Mānoa	10.25
Hawai'i	
Kealia, South Kona	7,300
Makalawena, North Kona	656
Ke'eiiki, North Kona	1,106
Pu'uwepa, Kohala	466
Ulupa'alua, Kohala	19.49
TOTAL	9,557

legitimate heir," [36] bringing Pauahi's holdings to 25,600.58 acres.[37] Table 16 lists the lands from 'Akahi.[38]

On May 24, 1883, Ruth Ke'elikolani died, leaving her cousin Pauahi about 353,000 acres of land on Kaua'i, O'ahu, Moloka'i, Maui, and Hawai'i.[39] Ruth was the granddaughter of Ka'oleioku, who was also Konia's father.[40] As explained earlier in chapter 12, Ruth's relation to Kamehameha was similar to Konia's, because it is unclear whether she was the great-granddaughter or great-grandniece of Kamehameha I.[41] Regardless, Ruth was an Ali'i Nui and was allocated twelve 'Āina in the Mahele.[42] Although these lands were only a small portion of the 'Āina she would eventually deed to Pauahi, Ruth was among the ten Ali'i Nui of the Mahele to receive the most 'Āina.[43] Ruth later inherited 'Āina from other Ali'i who had received 'Āina at the Mahele—from her first husband Lelei'ohoku, from her father Mataio Kekūanaō'a, from her half brother Lot Kapuāiwa (Kamehameha V), and from her half sister Victoria Kamamalu—to form a massive collection of lands.[44]

Ruth's husband Lelei'ohoku had received the sixth-largest number of 'Āina in the Mahele among the Ali'i Nui.[45] Because they had no children, Ruth inherited all of her husband's property upon his death in 1848.[46] When her father Mataio Kekūanaō'a died on November 24, 1868,[47] Ruth inherited all of his property as well. Although Mataio had received only six 'Āina in the Mahele, he had inherited extensive holdings upon the death of his children Victoria Kamāmalu, Lot Kapuāiwa (Kamehameha V),

36. *Id.* at 153.
37. *Id.* at 152.
38. *Id.*
39. *Id.* at 165.
40. Kame'eleihiwa, *supra* note 20, at 246.
41. *Id.* at 228; *see supra* this chapter, note 30.
42. Kame'eleihiwa, *supra* note 20, at 229, table 6.
43. *Id.* at 227–28.
44. *Id.* at 310.
45. *Id.* at 229, table 6.
46. *Id.* at 291, table 22.
47. *Id.*

and Moses Kekuiwa.[48] Mataio also received the ʻĀina of his brother Nueku Namauʻu upon his death in 1848.[49] All of these ʻĀina were left by Ruth to Pauahi, who in turn included them in the lands that formed the corpus of Estate supporting the Kamehameha Schools.

When Pauahi acquired ʻĀina from her parents and later from her aunt, she took an active role in the administration of her properties. Although she (like her father) relied upon Konohiki (land managers) to assist her in the day-to-day management of the lands, she accepted overall responsibility and participated in negotiating leases.[50] She was conscientious in fulfilling her role and obligations as an Aliʻi, she sought to use her ʻĀina to better the living conditions of the makaʻāinana, and she was generous with her Konohiki.[51] Although she declined the dying offer of Lot Kapuāiwa (Kamehameha V) to succeed him as Mōʻī on December 11, 1872,[52] Pauahi encumbered her ʻĀina with the responsibilities of her rank, and she continues to provide for her people through the lands that now support the Kamehameha Schools.

The Kamehameha Schools control the largest collection of lands in Hawaiʻi today except for those administered by the State Government. Its holdings were once the private domain of the various Aliʻi in the Kamehameha ʻohana, which had been distributed to them in the Mahele of 1848 by Kauikeaouli (Kamehameha III) to try to keep the ʻĀina in Native Hawaiian hands in the event sovereignty over the Hawaiian Islands was lost to a foreign power. Even though the lands the Mōʻī had set aside for himself (the Crown Lands) did not stay in Native Hawaiian hands and were treated as Public Lands by the foreign power (the United States) that eventually took over the Islands, Kamehameha III was more successful with regard to the Aliʻi ʻĀina that ultimately accumulated into the hands of Princess Pauahi and are now controlled by the Kamehameha Schools for the benefit of Native Hawaiian children.

Recent Developments Involving the Kamehameha Schools

The legacy of Princess Pauahi has been tested in recent years. In 1997, five community leaders authored a long article entitled "Broken Trust,"[53] criticizing the manage-

---

48. *Id.*

49. *Id.*

50. Kanahele, *supra* note 17, at 83–84.

51. *Id.* at 91.

52. 2 Ralph S. Kuykendall, *The Hawaiian Kingdom 1854–1874: Twenty Critical Years,* 241 (1982).

53. Samuel King, Charles Kekumano, Walter Heen, Gladys Brandt, and Randall Roth, "Broken Trust," *Honolulu Star-Bulletin,* August 9, 1997, at B-1.

Samuel P. King was Senior Federal District Court Judge; Charles Kekumano was Chair of the Queen Liliʻuokalani Trust, a retired Catholic priest, and former chair of the Police Commission; Walter Heen was a retired judge of the State Intermediate Court of Appeal, a former State legislator, and a former member of the City Council; Gladys Brandt was former principal of Kamehameha School for Girls, former director of the Secondary Division of Kamehameha Schools, and former chair of the University of Hawaiʻi Board of Regents; and Randall Roth was Professor of Law at the William S. Richardson School of Law, University of Hawaiʻi at Mānoa. Two of these authors subsequently provided a summary and overview of their efforts and the events during this period in Samuel P. King and Randall W. Roth, *Broken Trust: Greed, Mismanagement and Political Manipulation at America's Largest Charitable Trust* (2006).

ment style, political ties, and personal enrichment of the Estate's Trustees.[54] Many alumni, parent groups, and community leaders supported this critique, prompting the Governor to request the State Attorney General to investigate the allegations of fiduciary misconduct.[55] At the same time, the Internal Revenue Service was conducting a separate audit into the propriety of the Trustees' investment habits, putting the Schools' valuable tax-exempt status as an educational institution in danger.[56] The result of the two investigations was the temporary removal of four of the five Trustees (the fifth had voluntarily resigned),[57] and by 1999, all five had tendered resignations.[58] One of the five, Lokelani Lindsay, subsequently served six months in federal prison for bankruptcy fraud.[59]

One of the community's concerns about the Bishop Estate was the selection of the Trustees by the members of the Hawai'i Supreme Court. This process appeared to many to create conflicts of interest,[60] especially since the selections were made without any definable qualification standards and seemed on some occasions to be based on political links rather than merit. The fourteenth provision of Princess Pauahi's will had instructed that "vacancies [for Trustees] shall be filled by the choice of a majority of the Justices of the Supreme Court."[61] Whether the Supreme Court accepts such assignments is, however, totally at its discretion, as was evidenced when it declined in 1989 to pick the trustees of a charitable trust created by a woman named Sadie Smith.[62] In response to the groundswell of criticism by the community to the apparent conflict of interests in selecting Trustees, four of the five Justices announced in December 1997 that they would no longer make Bishop Estate Trustee selections.[63] A new process was established that involves a seven-member committee to screen applications and present a list to the Probate Court judge, who then makes an appointment from the names on that list.[64] Terms are now also limited to two five-year appointments, rather than the lifetime terms previously granted to Trustees.[65]

---

54. The Bishop Estate Trustees were Gerard Jervis, Lokelani Lindsey, Henry Peters, Oswald Stender, and Richard "Dickie" Wong.

55. Paul M. Barrett, "Tempest Erupts over Secretive Hawaiian Trust," *Wall Street Journal,* October 10, 1997, at B-1.

56. *Id.*

57. Trustee Oswald Stender submitted a temporary resignation to Probate Court Judge Kevin Chang on May 7, 1999, and had "earlier said he would step down when the other former trustees are removed." Ken Kobayashi, "Ousted Trustees to Fight Final Removal," *Honolulu Advertiser,* August 25, 1999, at A-1, A-7.

58. Apgar, *supra* note 2, at A-8.

59. King and Roth, *supra* note 53, at 265.

60. *See* Van Dyke, *supra* note 1, at 422–23.

61. "Excerpts from Pauahi's Will," *supra* note 3, at 4.

62. King, Kekumano, Heen, Brandt, and Roth, *supra* note 53, at B-1.

63. Ken Kobayashi, "Judge Launches New Era at Kamehameha Schools, Seven-Member Committee Named to Select Trustees," *Honolulu Advertiser,* January 7, 2000, at A-8.

64. *Id.* at A-1.

65. In recent years, the Trustees had lifetime terms until they turned seventy years old. *Id.* The Trustees as of June 2007 were J. Douglas Ing, Robert K. U. Kihune, Corbett Kalama, Diane J. Plotts, and Nainoa Thompson.

The second serious challenge to the Kamehameha Schools has concerned its practice of admitting only students of Hawaiian ancestry. Some had expressed concern about the constitutionality of Princess Pauahi's vision of a school for native children in light of the U.S. Supreme Court's 2000 decision in *Rice v. Cayetano*.[66] Perhaps because of that concern and perhaps out of concern for the Schools' tax-exempt status as a charitable nonprofit educational trust,[67] the new Trustees offered a non-Hawaiian child admission to attend classes in the new Maui campus in 2002.[68] This decision was denounced by many in the Native Hawaiian community.[69] Despite the tax-exemption concern,[70] what hit a nerve in the Hawaiian community was the intimation that there were not enough qualified Native Hawaiian applicants to fill all the spots for the Maui campus,[71] because many students of Hawaiian ancestry were being denied admission to the Schools.

The admissions policy was challenged more directly in 2003, this time in the form of lawsuits filed in Federal District Court by two non-Hawaiian applicants. In one awkward case, the Trustees permitted Brayden Mohica-Cummings, who had been provisionally admitted when it was thought he was of Hawaiian ancestry, to stay at Kamehameha Schools through the twelfth grade in exchange for his agreement to drop his lawsuit.[72] The second case involved a direct challenge to the Hawaiians-only admissions policy of the Schools.[73]

U.S. District Court Judge Alan C. Kay upheld this policy, finding a "legitimate justification for [the Kamehameha Schools'] admissions policy, which serves a legitimate remedial purpose, and [ruling] that the policy relates to that purpose,"[74]

---

66. *Rice v. Cayetano*, 528 U.S. 495 (2000), discussed *supra* chapter 24.

67. Walter Wright, "Decision Viewed as Appeasement to IRS," *Honolulu Advertiser*, July 16, 2002, at A-6.

68. Timothy Hurley and Walter Wright, "Non-Hawaiian Given Campus Spot," *Honolulu Advertiser*, July 12, 2002, at A-1. Since 1887, the Kamehameha Schools had operated only one campus on O'ahu, first at what is now the Bishop Museum, and then after a process of transition between 1930 and 1950 in Kapālama Heights. *See* Ke Alii Pauahi Foundation, "About the Foundation," at http://www.pauahi.org/AboutUs.php (visited November 19, 2006). As part of a strategic plan to expand its educational mission, Kamehameha Schools has opened additional campuses on the islands of Maui and Hawai'i during the past decade.

69. Adam Liptak, "School Set Aside for Hawaiians Ends Exclusion to Cries of Protest," *New York Times*, July 27, 2002, at A-9, citing comment made by Hawaiian Studies Professor Haunani-Kay Trask of the University of Hawai'i: "It really hurt people . . . and the pain was so palpable you could almost smell the anger."

70. In an attempt to protect against a constitutional attack on its admissions policies, the Trustees had already cut programs that were supported by federal taxpayer dollars at Kamehameha Schools, including ROTC, lunch support, and drug education programs, leaving its tax-exempt status as the only remaining federal link to the operation of the Schools. *Id.*

71. In response to the admission of a non-Hawaiian to the Maui campus, the CEO of Kamehameha Schools at the time, Hamilton McCubbin, was reported to have said that "when all the accepted applicants of Hawaiian ancestry meeting the admission criteria have been exhausted, qualified non-Hawaiian applicants may be considered for admittance on a space-available basis." Hurley and Wright, *supra* note 67, at A-1.

72. Rick Daysog, "Schools Let Non-Hawaiian Stay," *Honolulu Star-Bulletin*, November 29, 2003, at A-1.

73. *Doe v. Kamehameha Schools/Bernice Pauahi Bishop Estate*, 295 F.Supp.2d, 1141 (D. Hawai'i 2003), *aff'd*, 470 F. 3d 827 (9th Cir. en banc 2006).

74. *Id.* at 1,146.

emphasizing that the Kamehameha Schools receives no federal funding and is a private educational institution, created with "unique historical context."[75] After providing a detailed history of the disastrous effect of Western contact on the native population, culture, and self-governance, Judge Kay noted that the Schools fulfill the same educational needs and goals for Native Hawaiian children that Congress has seen fit to provide in a myriad of other remedial legislation for the benefit of Native Hawaiians, in recognition of the trust relationship that the United States has with the Native Hawaiians.[76] In response to the plaintiff's claim that the admissions policy violated federal antidiscrimination law, the opinion explained that Congress had recognized the Kamehameha Schools as a "significant resource" in the education of Native Hawaiians, citing a May 14, 2000, report by the House Committee on Education and the Workforce urging the Bishop Trust to *"redouble its efforts to educate native Hawaiian children."*[77] Thus, the remedial efforts of the Kamehameha Schools to give preference in education to Native Hawaiian children, coupled with the intent and actions of Congress to do the same, proved that the Kamehameha Schools' admissions policy served a legitimate interest related to the goal of providing for the education of Native Hawaiians.

In its brief to the Ninth Circuit Court urging affirmance, the Kamehameha Schools emphasized the remedial mission of the Schools, its private status, the congressional enactments supporting the Schools' mission, and its limited resources, supporting the conclusion that "so long as the critical needs to Native Hawaiians far exceed the available supply of student openings at Kamehameha, it is appropriate and necessary to serve Native Hawaiians first and foremost."[78] After analyzing prior case law and the purpose of the 1866 Civil Rights Act, the brief stated that the appropriate level of scrutiny is a deferential one, requiring "only that a private school's preferential admissions policy have a reasonable relationship to a legitimate purpose."[79] Kamehameha Schools thus urged the court to consider the nature of its preference-based admissions policy as a reasonable tool to aid the still-struggling Native Hawaiian population, through which education is but one way to elevate them above their current low socioeconomic status.

The three-judge panel that first heard this appeal ruled by a 2-1 vote that the Schools' policy of admitting only persons of Hawaiian ancestry violated the 1866 Civil Rights Act.[80] The majority opinion, written by Judge Jay Bybee, character-

---

75. *Id.* at 1166.

76. *Id.* at 1167–68.

77. *Id.* at 1168 (emphasis in original), citing H.R. Rep. No. 107-63(I) at 732 (2001).

78. "Appellee's Answering Brief," *Doe v. Kamehameha Schools/Bernice Pauahi Bishop Estate,* WL 1394616, at *36–37 (9th Cir. 2004) (No. 04-15044).

79. *Id.* at 15.

80. *Doe v. Kamehameha Schools/Bernice Pauai Bishop Estate,* 416 F.3d 1025 (9th Cir. 2005), *decision vacated pending rehearing en banc,* 441 F.3d 1029 (9th Cir. 2006). The panel's majority opinion, written by Judge Jay Bybee, was joined by Judge Robert Beezer. The 1866 Civil Rights Act, now codified in 42 U.S.C. sec. 1981, says that "All persons within the jurisdiction of the United States shall have the same right in every State and Territory to make and enforce contracts . . . as is enjoyed by white citizens."

ized the Kamehameha Schools as having admitted "that its admissions process is premised upon an express racial classification"[81] and said that the Schools had not attempted "to justify its admissions policy by appealing to a First Amendment right to freedom of association" and had not "explicitly argue[d] for a relaxed level of scrutiny by appealing to the political nature of classifications premised on membership in a federally recognized Indian tribe."[82] Judge Bybee stated that the issue thus became "whether the Schools can articulate a legitimate nondiscriminatory reason justifying this racial preference."[83] The majority opinion acknowledged that Congress had approved "scattered statutes adopted specially for the benefit of native Hawaiians," but it declined to try to harmonize those laws with the 1866 statute "[f]or reasons both of separation of powers and our own sanity."[84] Judge Bybee also acknowledged that "Congress has expressly and repeatedly, determined that the United States wrongfully participated in the demise of the Hawaiian Monarchy, . . . the harmful consequences of which in terms of the decimation and suffering wrought on the native Hawaiian people and culture, are well documented."[85] These many findings by Congress were, however, irrelevant, Judge Bybee concluded, because of the Schools' "explicit concession that the preference at issue constitutes discrimination on the basis of race."[86]

Judge Susan Graber dissented, arguing that the many statutes passed by Congress for the benefit of Native Hawaiians were "part of the statutory context into which Section 1981 was reenacted" in 1991 and that the Kamehameha Schools' "exclusive educational preference for Native Hawaiians . . . was motivated by the need to remedy abysmal socioeconomic and educational conditions and by the United States government's unique relationship with and responsibility for Native Hawaiians."[87] She concluded:

Because the statutory context demonstrates that Congress did not intend for Section 1981 to bar all exclusive preferences to remedy the severe educational deficits suffered by Native Hawaiians, a population unique within this country, and because Kamehameha Schools has amply demonstrated that its admission

---

81. 416 F.3d at 1,030. This conclusion of the panel's majority is directly contrary to the conclusion of the District Court, which found as a factual matter that "[t]he preference provided by the admissions policy is not perpetual nor an absolute bar to the admittance of other races to Kamehameha Schools." *Doe v. Kamehameha Schools/Bernice Pauahi Bishop Estate,* 295 F.Supp.2d, 1141, 1146 (D. Hawai'i 2003). The District Court opinion written by Judge Alan Kay explained that the admissions preference given by the Schools to students of Native Hawaiian genealogy or ancestry is based on a "political" classification rather than a "racial" one, because the United States has recognized repeatedly that it "has a political relationship with and a special trust obligation to Native Hawaiians as the indigenous people of Hawaii." *Id.* at 1150, citing 20 U.S.C. sec. 7512 and 42 U.S.C. sec. 11701.
82. 416 F.3d at 1029.
83. *Id.* at 1039–40.
84. *Id.* at 1042.
85. *Id.* at 1046.
86. *Id.* at 1047.
87. *Id.* at 1050.

preference is regularly reviewed and currently required to combat those deficits, I respectfully dissent from the majority's contrary conclusion.[88]

The panel's opinion was quickly characterized as "flawed" in a casenote published in the *Harvard Law Review,*[89] which emphasized that the panel should have considered "the need to preserve Native Hawaiian culture and identity," explaining that the Schools "provide an environment uniquely conducive to reconnecting students with their cultural heritage."[90] The note concluded that "the Ninth Circuit should have factored in the historical context, real need, and practical limitations facing Native Hawaiians and Kamehameha Schools to reach a more considered and equitable conclusion."[91]

On February 22, 2006, the Ninth Circuit announced that the panel's opinion had been vacated and that the court would rehear the case before a fifteen-judge en banc session of the court.[92] Oral argument was held on June 20, 2006, and a new opinion was issued December 5, 2006, reversing the panel's conclusion by an 8-7 vote and upholding the policy of the Kamehameha Schools giving preference to students of Native Hawaiian ancestry.[93]

In her opinion for the majority, Judge Graber noted that the Schools are "a purely private entity that receives no federal funds" and that "[t]he Supreme Court has never applied strict scrutiny to the actions of a purely private entity."[94] She then explained that the Schools' admission policies met federal statutory standards (1) because they responded to a "manifest imbalance . . . in the K-12 educational arena in the state of Hawaii, with Native Hawaiians falling at the bottom of the spectrum in almost all areas of educational progress and success;"[95] (2) because they do not "unnecessarily trammel" the rights of non-Hawaiians who have "no expectation of admission" to these Schools, which "were established when Hawaii was a sovereign nation, and . . . were built on the Hawaiian monarchy's land;"[96] and (3) because the policies have been applied flexibly and are limited in duration "only for so long as is necessary to remedy the current educational effects of past, private and government-sponsored discrimination and of social and economic deprivation."[97] Judge Graber also explained that the 1866 Civil Rights Act was reenacted in 1991, at a time when Congress had recognized repeatedly "the special relationship that the United States has with Native Hawaiians" and was active in passing legislation to support special

---

88. *Id.* at 1,051.

89. "Civil Rights—Section 1981: Ninth Circuit Holds That Private School's Remedial Admissions Policy Violates Section 1981—*Doe v. Kamehameha Schools,*" 416 F.3d, 1025 (9th Cir. 2005), 119 *Harvard Law Review,* 661, 661 (2005).

90. *Id.* at 668.

91. *Id.*

92. *Doe v. Kamehameha Schools/Bernice Pauahi Bishop Estate,* 441 F.3d, 1029 (9th Cir. 2006).

93. *Doe v. Kamehameha Schools/Bernice Pauahi Bishop Estate,* 470 F.3d, 827 (9th Cir. en banc 2006).

94. *Id.* at 839.

95. *Id.* at 843.

96. *Id.* at 845.

97. *Id.* at 846.

and preferential programs for Native Hawaiians.[98] It would be "incongruous," therefore, to hold that Congress sought to restrict the ability of the Kamehameha Schools to grant preferences for Native Hawaiians at the same time it "was repeatedly enacting remedial measures aimed exclusively at Native Hawaiians."[99] "Accordingly," she concluded, "the most plausible reading of Section 1981 [the 1866 Civil Rights Act] . . . is that Congress intended that a preference for Native Hawaiians, in Hawaii, by a Native Hawaiian organization, located on the Hawaiian monarchy's ancestral lands, be upheld because it furthers the urgent need for better education of Native Hawaiians, which Congress has repeatedly identified as necessary."[100]

Judge William Fletcher wrote a concurring opinion, for himself and four other judges, stressing that a "narrower ground" also supported upholding the admission policies of the Kamehameha Schools.[101] This additional rationale rested on the conclusion that "'Native Hawaiian' is not merely a racial classification" but "is also a political classification" and hence that Congress is free to legislate on behalf of Native Hawaiians and to authorize the "Kamehameha Schools to give preferential treatment to Native Hawaiians."[102] Judge Fletcher supported this view by noting the Congressional recognition of the "special trust relationship" between Native Hawaiians and the United States,[103] by explaining that "[i]n other contexts, the Supreme Court has not insisted on continuous tribal membership, or tribal membership at all, as a justification for special treatment of Indians,"[104] and by observing that the Supreme Court's opinion in *Rice v. Cayetano*[105] "was careful to confine its analysis to voting rights under the Fifteenth Amendment"[106] and "never questioned the validity of the special relationship doctrine under the Fourteenth Amendment, and never even hinted that its Fifteenth Amendment analysis would apply to the many benefit programs enacted by Congress for Native Hawaiians, Alaska Natives, and American Indians."[107] Judge Fletcher's opinion then reviewed the many Congressional enactments that provided exclusive and preferential programs for Native Hawaiians, especially in the area of education, and concluded by noting that "[i]t would be deeply ironic for us to hold that Section 1981 [the 1866 Civil Rights Act] forbids private institutions from giving Native Hawaiians educational benefits when, at the same time, Congress itself provides such benefits and provides public funds for private organizations to do the same."[108]

Judge Bybee wrote the main dissenting opinion, restating the views expressed

98. *Id.* at 848.
99. *Id.* at 849.
100. *Id.*
101. *Id.* (Fletcher, J., concurring).
102. *Id.* at 853.
103. *Id.* at 850.
104. *Id.* at 851 (citing *United States v. John*, 437 U.S. 634 (1978), and *Delaware Tribal Business Committee v. Weeks*, 430 U.S. 73 (1977)).
105. *Rice v. Cayetano*, 528 U.S. 495 (2000).
106. 470 F.3d at 852 (Fletcher, J., concurring).
107. *Id.* at 853.
108. *Id.* at 856.

in his majority opinion for the three-judge panel in 2005 and sharply criticizing the analysis found in the opinions of Judges Graber and Fletcher. [109] He addressed Judge Fletcher's "political classification" argument by noting first that it had not been presented by the Kamehameha Schools "on appeal, and it was not briefed by either party" and hence was "waived." [110] He then contended that the "political classification" argument must fail because "Native Hawaiians have never been accorded federal recognition as a Native American tribe, and while the 'special trust relationship' between Congress and Native Hawaiians bears many similarities to the relationship between Congress and Native American tribes, the two relationships are not identical." [111] In addition, the special status of a "political classification" "would still not benefit Kamehameha because that doctrine does not apply to private parties." [112] Judge Bybee agreed that the goals of the Kamehameha Schools have been "noble" and that its admission policy "seeks to remedy a significant problem in a community that is in great need," but he nonetheless concluded that it should be declared invalid because it is inconsistent "with the Supreme Court's requirement for a valid affirmative action plan." [113]

Judge Bybee's dissenting conclusion was joined by six other judges, but they all wrote separately (or joined separate dissenting opinions) expressing their frustrations with this conclusion. Judge Pamela Rymer (writing for herself and four others) declared that her view that the School's admission policy violated the 1866 Civil Rights Law was "altogether infelicitous." [114] She expressed frustration with the decisions of the Supreme Court that have held that this law can be invoked by whites against nonwhites,[115] she noted that she had "difficulty understanding how Section 1981 applies to a purely private, philanthropically-endowed, non-profit educational institution," [116] and she stated that "because education is the greatest inheritance of all, I have difficulty understanding what business it is of the federal government to tell a Native Hawaiian that she can't choose to help other Native Hawaiians whom

---

109. Judge Bybee referred to arguments presented in the majority opinions as "absolutely wrong" (*id.* at 869) and "either demonstrably wrong or utterly irrelevant" (*id.* at 873).

110. *Id.* at 880 (Bybee, J., dissenting).

111. *Id.* at 881. In his footnote 21, Judge Bybee asserted that "there is cause to question whether such an act [granting federal recognition to Native Hawaiians] would be within Congress's constitutional power," but he assumed for the purpose of this case "that Congress has the power to formally recognize Native Hawaiians and to treat them as any other federally recognized tribe" (*id.* at 881 n. 21). At another point in the opinion, Judge Bybee appeared to have accepted the authority of Congress to enact separate and preferential programs for Native Hawaiians, because he noted "[t]hat when Congress wishes to give Native Hawaiians special treatment, it knows how to do so—and is not shy about it" (*id.* at 878).

112. *Id.* at 882.

113. *Id.* at 885.

114. *Id.* at 885 (Rymer, J., dissenting). *Webster's Seventh New Collegiate Dictionary* defines "infelicitous" as "not appropriate in application or expression," 432 (1963), or, in other words, something that makes one unhappy.

115. *Id.* at 885 (noting her frustration with the holdings of *McDonald v. Santa Fe Trail Transp. Co.,* 427 U.S. 273 (1976), and *Rice v. Cayetano,* 528 U.S. 495 (2000)).

116. *Id.* at 885.

she believes particularly need it." [117] Because of her view of "precedent," however, she concluded that the law did not permit "Kamehameha Schools to justify its preferential admissions policy on the footing that the policy redresses past societal discrimination against Native Hawaiians." [118]

Judge Andrew Kleinfeld (writing for himself and two others) also expressed frustration with his view of the governing law, noting that "we are not free to make a social judgment about what is best for Hawaiians. We are stuck with a case that is before us in our capacity as judges and we have to follow the law." [119] He acknowledged that he "might have preferred to avoid deciding this case, if some jurisdictional defect existed," but no jurisdictional barrier could be found. [120] "Employment law, Indian law, our admiration for Kamehameha Schools, and our sentiments about public policy are irrelevant." [121] Because he felt bound by confining judicial precedents, Judge Kleinfeld joined the dissent.

Judge Alex Kozinski, writing solely for himself, suggested that the Kamehameha Schools could escape from the 1866 Civil Rights Act—which prohibits "private discrimination in the making and enforcing of *contracts*" [122]—if the Schools were to waive tuition payments: "I don't believe section 1981 would apply at all if the schools were run entirely as a philanthropic enterprise and allowed students to attend for free. . . . I have found no case where section 1981 has been applied to a charity." [123]

After this narrow victory for the admissions policies of the Kamehameha Schools, the attorney for the non-Hawaiian student challenging these policies filed a petition for certiorari to the U.S. Supreme Court, but on May 14, 2007, the lawsuit was settled and the petition was withdrawn. [124] The result of this settlement is that the en banc decision of the Ninth Circuit stands as the governing law and the Schools are able to maintain their admissions policies.

---

117. *Id.* at 886.
118. *Id.*
119. *Id.* at 888 (Kleinfeld, J., dissenting).
120. *Id.*
121. *Id.*
122. *Id.* at 888 (Kozinski, J., dissenting; emphasis in original).
123. *Id.* at 888–89.
124. Thomas Yoshida, "Kamehameha Schools and 'John Doe' Settle Admissions Lawsuit," Kamehameha Schools Web site, May 14, 2007, at <http://www.ksbe.edu/article.php?story=20070514073144797> (visited June 18, 2007).

26

The Other Aliʻi Trusts

The first division in the 1848 Mahele was between the Mōʻī and the Aliʻi. As explained in chapter 4, the most extensive tracts of the 1.5 million acres allocated to the Aliʻi were distributed to the ten highest and most prestigious chiefs, the Aliʻi Nui. They paid the commutation fee by assigning one-third of their lands back to the Government and then used these lands to support themselves and the thousands of native tenants who lived within their boundaries. As the previous chapter explained, ʻĀina from six of the ten Aliʻi Nui were passed down to Bernice Pauahi Bishop, who established the Estate that now supports the Kamehameha Schools.

The other Aliʻi also recognized their fiduciary responsibility to their people, who were battling Western diseases and social upheaval, and they also established trusts to help Native Hawaiians during this period of turmoil. This chapter examines the history, failures, and successes of the three largest Native Hawaiian charitable trusts (after the Kamehameha Schools) still existing today: the King Lunalilo Trust, the Queen Emma Trust, and the Queen Liliʻuokalani Trust.

The Lunalilo Trust

The tragic history of the Lunalilo Trust mirrors the plight of Native Hawaiians past and present. Like many other Aliʻi, William Charles Lunalilo sought guidance from and placed his trust in individuals who understood the Western system, but his decision led to an unhappy result. Lunalilo was elected Mōʻī and took office in January 1873 amidst much enthusiasm and hope, but he served for less than thirteen months, dying in February 1874 when he was only thirty-seven of tuberculosis and related ailments.[1]

In 1871 (before he had any assurance that he would later become Mōʻī), Lunalilo wrote a will to bequeath his personal ʻĀina to establish the first Aliʻi trust for the

---

1. *See supra* chapter 10.

The Other Ali'i Trusts

benefit of the Native Hawaiian People.[2] His goal was to create a home benefiting the "poor, destitute and infirm people of Hawaiian (aboriginal) blood or extraction, giving preference to old people."[3] Lunalilo's vast landholdings, if they had not been sold off, would have provided ample revenues to preserve the Lunalilo Home's financial security in perpetuity. But those entrusted with carrying out Lunalilo's intentions decided to sell off the 'Āina he bequeathed to the trust, resulting in a tragedy not only to the memory of the Mō'ī but also to the intended Native Hawaiian beneficiaries.

William Charles Lunalilo was the only child of Miriam Kahahaika'ao'aokapuoka Kekāuluohi-o-mano (Kekāuluohi) and Charles Kana'ina, and he received his estate from lands passed from his mother's side.[4] Kekāuluohi received her lands from her mother Kaheiheimalie Kaniu Kalākaua Hoapiliwahine (Kaheiheimalie) and her father Kalaimamahu, a younger half brother of Kamehameha I.[5] Kaheiheimalie, a younger sister of Ka'ahumanu, was also a wife of Kamehameha I.[6] Although Ka'ahumanu was the favorite wife of Kamehameha I, she did not have any children. The union of Kamehameha I and Kaheiheimalie (who was of Maui lineage) produced offspring, which should have insured stability in the Kingdom,[7] but when Kaheiheimalie died in January 1842, her three children by Kamehameha I had already died, and therefore her 239 'Āina (mostly on Maui) were left to her only surviving child, Kekāuluohi.[8] Upon Kekāuluohi's death on June 7, 1845, the property left by her mother combined with lands from her father, Kalaimamahu, as well as those collected by Kekāuluohi as Kuhina Nui (1839–45), were left to her minor son, William Charles Lunalilo, who was under the guardianship of his father Charles Kana'ina.[9]

Prior to the Mahele, Lunalilo's personal holdings were second only to those of Kauikeaouli (Kamehameha III).[10] During the Mahele, Lunalilo relinquished 173

---

2. *Will of William Charles Lunalilo,* June 7, 1871. Lunalilo's Will provided first that upon his death, his real estate should pass for a life term to his father, Kana'ina. If he married and had children, his lands would benefit them after his father's death. If he had no children, upon Kana'ina's death, his lands would pass to His Majesty Kamehameha V for his natural life. After the death of Kana'ina and Kamehameha V, and if he had no issue, the lands would revert to Lunalilo's Trust. *Id.*

3. *Id.*

4. Lilikala Kame'eleihiwa, *Native Land and Foreign Desires: Pehea La E Pono Ai?* 125 (1992). According to Professor Kame'eleihiwa, Kana'ina was a Kaukau Ali'i. Kekauluohi intended that Charles Kana'ina, of low genealogy, not receive any lands but serve as guardian for his higher-ranking son. *Id.* The "Partial List of Lands Agreed upon by the Mahele . . ." does, however, award lands to Charles Kana'ina separately from William Charles Lunalilo. See Office of the Commissioner of Public Lands of the Territory of Hawaii, "Partial List of Lands Agreed upon by the Mahele to Belong to the More Important Aliis and Chiefs and Confirmed to Them by Awards of the Commission To Quiet Land Titles," in *Indices of Awards Made by the Board of Commissioners to Quiet Land Titles in the Hawaiian Islands,* 65 (1929).

5. Kame'eleihiwa, *supra* note 4, at 124–25.

6. *Id.*

7. Kaheiheimalie's children by Kamehameha I included Kamehameha Kapuāiwa Iwi, Kamehamalu Kekuaiwaokalani, and Kaho'anoku Kīna'u (Kīna'u). *Id.* at 125. Kīna'u was the wife of Mataio Kekūanaō'a and mother of Davida Kamehameha, Mosese Kekuaiwa, Alexander Liholiho (Kamehameha IV), Lot Kapuāiwa (Kamehameha V), and Victoria Kamāmalu. *Id.* at 123.

8. *Id.* at 124–25.

9. An exact list of Kekauluohi's 1845 'Āina does not exist. *Id.* at 127. William Charles Lunalilo was born on January 31, 1835, *id.* at 291, and thus was thirteen in 1848, the central year of the Mahele.

10. *Id.* at 243.

325

TABLE 17. Real property granted to William C. Lunalilo in the Mahele

Land Commission Award	Royal Patent	Land and Location	Acreage
8559-B	7394	Kawela, Hamakua, Hawaii	1,255.00
8559-B	—	Waikoekoe, Hamakua, Hawaii	
8559-B	—	Makapala, Kohala, Hawaii	
8559-B	7680	Kehena, Kohala, Hawaii	
8559-B	—	Puhau, Kohala, Hawaii	
8559-B	—	Puako, Kohala, Hawaii	
8559-B	7534	Honuainonui, Kona, Hawaii	262.00
8559-B	7819	Puapuanui, Kona, Hawaii	379.00
8559-B	7536	Lehuulanui, Kona, Hawaii	
8559-B	7455	Lehuulanui, Kona, Hawaii	2,840.00
			290.00
8559-B	7454	Kawanui, Kona, Hawaii	380.00
8559-B	7456	Lanihaunui, Kona, Hawaii	302.00
8559-B	7374	Pakiniiki, Kau, Hawaii	2,357.00
8559-B	7049	Honuapo, Kau, Hawaii	2,200.00
8559-B	8030	Kahaualea, Puna, Hawaii	26,000.00
8559-B	8088	Keahialaka, Puna, Hawaii	5,562.00
8559-B	8094	Keahialaka, Puna, Hawaii	
8559-B	7223	Keaau, Puna, Hawaii	64,275.00
8559-B	7192	Makahanaloa, Hilo, Hawaii	7,600.00
8559-B	7192	Pepeekeo, Hilo, Hawaii	7,600.00
8559-B	—	Kaapahu, Kipahulu, Maui	
8559-B	—	Waiehu (2), Waiehu, Maui	
8559-B	—	Ahikuli, Waiehu, Maui	
8559-B	7664	Pepee, Wailuku, Maui	255.70
8559-B	8129	Honolua, Kaanapali, Maui	3,860.00
8559-B	8396	Kalimaohe, Lahaina, Maui	
8559-B	8395	Polanui, Lahaina, Maui	
8559-B	8397	Kuholilea, Lahaina, Maui	
8559-B	7655	Waialua, Molokai	
8559-B	7656	Kawela, Molokai	14,787.00
8559-B	8193	Pau, Waikiki, Oahu	
8559-B	8311	Pau, Waikiki, Oahu	
8559-B	8416	Pau, Waikiki, Oahu	
8559-B	7635	Kamoku, Waikiki, Oahu	
8559-B	7652	Kaluakou, Waikiki, Oahu	
8559-B	8124	Kapahulu, Waikiki, Oahu	
8559-B	8165	Kapahulu, Waikiki, Oahu	2,184.44
8559-B	7531	Kaalaea, Koolaupoko, Oahu	
8559-B	—	Kapaka, Koolauloa, Oahu	
8559-B	7494	Laiewai, Koolauloa, Oahu	6,194.00
8559-B	7494	Laiemaloo, Koolauloa, Oahu	
8559-B	5688	Pahipahialua, Koolauloa, Oahu	704.00

(continued on next page)

TABLE 17. Real property granted to William C. Lunalilo in the Mahele (continued)

Land Commission Award	Royal Patent	Land and Location	Acreage
8559-B	8323	Kahili, Koolau, Kauai	1,789.00
8559-B	8173	Kalihiwai, Koolau, Kauai	8,600.00
8559-B	7060	Pilaa, Koolau, Kauai	1,520.00
8559-B	—	Manuahi, Kona, Hawaii	
8559-B	7373	Waipouli, Puna, Hawaii	
8559-B	5637	House Lot, Paunau, Lahaina	
8364		Maui	
8559-B	5639	House Lot, Aki, Lahaina, Maui	
8559-B	5699	House Lot, Loinui, Lahaina, Maui	
247	5695	Lot, Beretania St., Honolulu, Oahu	.543
247	5636	Lot, King St., Honolulu, Oahu	.13
247	5636	Lot, King St., Honolulu, Oahu	.28
247	5695	Lot, King St., Honolulu, Oahu	.92
247	—	Lot, King St., Honolulu, Oahu	
247	110	Lot, Merchant St., Honolulu, Oahu	.10
247	5695	Lot, Queen St., Honolulu, Oahu	.51
247	5635	Lot, Punchbowl St., Honolulu, Oahu	.13
247	5695	Lot, Punchbowl St., Honolulu, Oahu	.24
247	—	Lot, Fort St., Honolulu, Oahu	.11
247	—	Lot, Palace Walk, Honolulu, Oahu	
247	—	Lot, Palace Walk, Honolulu, Oahu	
247	7521	Lot, Kakaako, Honolulu, Oahu	.25
277	5638	Lahaina (3), Lahaina, Maui	
277	5640	Lot, Puunoa, Lahaina, Maui	
277	8364	Lot, Paunau, Lahaina, Maui	
277	—	Lot, Paeohi, Lahaina, Maui	

'Āina, or about 73 percent of his holdings,[11] but his remaining lands were still vast—some 68 'Āina totaling about 161,200 acres on the islands of Hawai'i, Maui, Moloka'i, O'ahu, and Kaua'i. Table 17 lists real property granted to William C. Lunalilo in the Mahele.[12] These 'Āina were further reduced in 1850 to 43 parcels as a result of an additional commutation to the Government.[13]

When Lunalilo was a minor, his father Charles Kana'ina managed his son's lands, and the father continued to keep his eye on the lands even after Lunalilo reached his majority. In fact, in 1858, Charles Kana'ina was so concerned that his twenty-four-year-old son was not properly managing his affairs and might lose his

11. *Id.*

12. This information is taken from *Indices of Awards, supra* note 4, at 77–79. "Acreage" figures and additional "Royal Patent" figures are included if identified within the *Indices.*

13. Kame'eleihiwa, *supra* note 4, at 243.

'Āina that he petitioned the court to place Lunalilo under a guardianship.[14] The court agreed that Lunalilo was a "spendthrift," [15] and guardians were appointed.[16]

Lunalilo's Will, dated June 7, 1871, as well as a codicil dated January 31, 1874, were both drafted by attorney Albert Francis Judd.[17] The will empowered a majority of the Supreme Court Justices to nominate and appoint three trustees. On March 16, 1877, the Court appointed Sanford Ballard Dole, Edwin O. Hall, and John Mott-Smith as the first Trustees of the Lunalilo Trust.[18] It is instructive and revealing to note that of the first nine trustees to control Lunalilo's holdings, at least six were future members of the Committee of Safety and the subsequent Provisional Government. It should also be remembered that Sanford Ballard Dole supported breaking up and selling off the Crown Lands in his 1872 newspaper articles in order to promote American-style family farming.[19] Dole's enthusiasm for selling the lands in the Lunalilo Estate followed logically from his lifelong position favoring the sale of the Crown Lands.

The breakup of the Lunalilo Estate can be traced through three court decisions, beginning with the 1874 case contesting the validity of Lunalilo's Will.[20] At issue was whether Lunalilo's Will was void, because he was under guardianship as a "spendthrift" when he wrote the will. The Hawai'i Supreme Court consisted then of Chief Justice Elisha H. Allen and Associate Justices Charles C. Harris and Albert Francis Judd. Justice Judd recused himself from this litigation, having "drawn the will and codicil" of the late Mō'ī.[21] The remaining two justices affirmed a probate judge's decision that the will was valid.[22] The Court held that although Lunalilo was under guardianship, he was not incapacitated from making a will.[23]

The next case occurred five years later in 1879.[24] Lunalilo's Will said that his lands were to be utilized to support elderly impoverished Hawaiians and expressed his concern that providing a building for these needy individuals was a priority.

---

14. *Id.* at 308–09.

15. *In the Matter of the Estate of His Late Majesty Lunalilo, Deceased,* 3 Hawai'i 519 (1874).

16. *See* Kame'eleihiwa, *supra* note 4, at 309. According to Professor Kame'eleihiwa, Lunalilo agreed to his father's "prudent" request.

17. *See In re Estate of Lunalilo,* 3 Hawai'i 519 (1874), which states that Judge Judd recused himself from this case because he had written Lunalilo's Will and Codicil. It is interesting to note that the June 7, 1871, will is signed by Lunalilo and witnessed by its drafter, A. Francis Judd, plus John Paty. The January 31, 1874, codicil is not signed by Lunalilo but by A. F. Judd alone, "in the presence of Lunalilo and by His express direction." In the codicil, the first section addresses the disposal of articles of silverware inherited through his mother. This section is incomplete, without a designated beneficiary.

18. "William Charles Lunalilo Estate Trustees and Terms," a handout provided by Greg Meyer, General Manager at Lunalilo Home, lists the first nine Trustees from 1877 to 1906 as Sanford Dole, E. O. Hall, John Mott-Smith, William O. Smith, Mary S. Parker, W. C. Parke, Henry Waterhouse, Ernest Mott-Smith, and Lorrin Thurston.

19. *See* discussion *supra* in chapter 13, text at note 4, and in chapter 18, text at notes 1–8.

20. *In re Estate of Lunalilo,* 3 Hawai'i 519 (1874).

21. *Id.*

22. *Id.* at 522.

23. *Id.* at 520.

24. *In the Matter of the Estate of His Late Majesty Lunalilo,* 4 Hawai'i 162 (1879).

The Trustees had already sold portions of the Estate, accumulating thereby a sum of \$28,228.90, and they appeared before the Supreme Court for instructions on whether they were obliged to expend the entire sum immediately on the buildings and its grounds or could invest a portion to generate a revenue stream for future maintenance of the building and support of the residents.[25] In 1879, the Supreme Court consisted of Chief Justice Harris, Associate Justice Lawrence McCully, and Associate Justice Albert Francis Judd, who declined to recuse himself this time.[26]

The Court observed that it was evident that Lunalilo "did not suppose that his real property would be so valuable as it has since proved to be."[27] The Court also explained that Lunalilo "appears to have thought it quite possible that it would not realize upon sale so much as \$25,000."[28] Despite these comments, the Court held that Lunalilo had commanded in his will that once \$25,000 was accumulated, it was to be spent "to purchase the ground and erect the buildings required."[29]

The third case, handed down by the Supreme Court in 1881,[30] had the most profound negative impact on Lunalilo's desire to provide a home for elderly and needy Hawaiians. The Court was again comprised of Chief Justice Harris and Associate Justices McCully and Judd, and once again Justice Judd declined to recuse himself.[31] The Trustees sought the Court's direction regarding their authority to negotiate and execute leases of lands in the ʻIli of Pau on Oʻahu, lands at Keaʻau on Hawaiʻi, and the fishery of Waiehu on Maui.[32] They also wanted to purchase a small parcel within the ʻIli of Pau to enhance the value of their surrounding lands.[33]

The Trustees argued that the leases were not only advantageous but also were justified by the will, which stated, "I hereby order and direct that the said trustees shall apply the net rents, issues and profits arising from the principal sum, etc."[34] The Trustees submitted to the Court their view that the word "rents" contemplated that some land might be leased.[35] They further contended that even if the Court found that the will did not explicitly give them the authority to the lease lands, it should nonetheless "ratify and justify" the leases.[36]

The Court rejected this seemingly logical position, however, ruling that the Trustees had no power to lease land and had even less authority to buy lands because,

---

25. *Id.* at 162–63.

26. *Id.* at 162.

27. *Id.* at 163.

28. *Id.*

29. *Id.* at 165. The Court also explained that if third parties made contributions "so that there will be either the whole or a part of the whole \$25,000 remaining, then and not till then, the rents, issues and profits of the sum so remaining shall be devoted to the repair or improvement of the buildings and the maintenance of inmates." *Id.* at 164–65.

30. *In the Matter of the Estate of His Late Royal Majesty Lunalilo,* 4 Hawaiʻi 381 (1881).

31. *Id.*

32. *Id.*

33. *Id.*

34. *Id.* at 382.

35. *Id.*

36. *Id.*

in the Court's view, it was Lunalilo's intention to sell and dispose of the lands of his Estate.[37] The Court concluded, "The answer is that *the whole land is devised to the trustees, not to hold, but to sell,* so that money may be procured wherewith to aid the infirm. The testator did not wish to invest in land; his wish was to invest in an Infirmary, and to obtain the means of maintaining that Infirmary and its occupants." [38]

The Court thus decided that once the $25,000 sum was accumulated for the buildings, Lunalilo did not want the sale of lands to stop.[39] The Court reasoned that "the whole tenor of the will [was] to the effect that *the whole of the real estate shall be turned to ready money,* which can readily be used, to found this Infirmary." [40] In light of this interpretation of Lunalilo's intentions, the Court ordered the Trustees to sell all of the land of the Estate! [41]

King Kalākaua granted to the Lunalilo Estate 21 acres in Kewalo, Makiki, O'ahu, on which to build,[42] and the first Lunalilo Home officially opened to the first ten residents in March 1883. But because of this 1881 Supreme Court decision, the lands Lunalilo had left to his Estate were virtually depleted, and subsequent unsuccessful investments left the Estate not only land-poor but without income.

The Lunalilo Home was relocated to a 20-acre lot in what is now Hawai'i Kai on O'ahu in 1927 because of the urban development of the Makiki area and safety concerns for the residents.[43] In 1969 the Trustees increased the Estate's revenues by developing 15 of these Hawai'i Kai acres into a leasehold residential tract. In 1983 these lots had to be sold to the lessees under Hawai'i's leasehold-to-fee conversions law.[44]

Today, Lunalilo Home is located at 501 Kekāuluohi Street in Hawai'i Kai and has a maximum capacity of fifty-six beds.[45] The home and the approximately 5 acres of 'Āina it sits upon are the primary remaining assets of the Estate.[46] In recent years, with no outside revenue stream, the home has faced dire financial straits. It was forced to close down in 1997 to engage in fund-raising for renovations necessary to improve the structure and to comply with the requirements of the federal Americans with Disabilities Act. The home reopened in 2001, and in 2004 it was nearing the completion of the four-and-a-half-year, $4.5 million remodeling and restructuring

37. *Id.* at 382–83.
38. *Id.* (emphasis added).
39. *Id.* at 383.
40. *Id.* (emphasis added).
41. *Id.*
42. Telephone interview with Greg Meyer, General Manager of Lunalilo Home, Hawai'i Kai, Hawai'i (July 16, 1996).
43. Catherine Kau, "Native Hawaiian Charitable Trusts," in *Native Hawaiian Rights Handbook,* 281, 287 (Melody Kapilialoha MacKenzie, ed., 1991).
44. *Id.*
45. *In the Matter of the Estate of William Charles Lunalilo,* Petition for Instructions Regarding Renovations; Exhibits "A" – "C" filed with the Circuit Court of the First Circuit on October 30, 1996.
46. *Id.* at 2. The trust's assets include an investment portfolio of securities. *Id.* As of 1996, the net assets of the trust were valued at about $6,700,000. *Id.*

process. As of 2004, thirty-seven Hawaiians resided at Lunalilo Home, which also operates an elderly day care program.[47]

Lunalilo relied on his father to manage his lands during his minority and continued to rely on his father and other guardians for all but a handful of his adult years. He turned to Attorney Albert Francis Judd to draw up his will and to preserve his land in trust to benefit the poor and infirm elderly among his people under the Western legal system. Judd had a fiduciary duty to find out what Lunalilo intended, to make sure Lunalilo understood the nature of his holdings and his options, and to create a document that expressed and effectuated Lunalilo's desires.

Surely Lunalilo would have wanted his Trust to last in perpetuity. And certainly the link that Hawaiians have to their 'Āina should have led to the conclusion that as much of the land within the Estate as possible should have been preserved. In a capitalist system, a secure land base provides stability and assists in insuring a regular revenue stream. From a Hawaiian perspective, leasing is always preferable to sale, because it ensures that 'Āina will be available for future generations. But from the perspective of the Western Supreme Court Justices and the Western Trustees of the Estate, sale was preferable because it promoted economic development and allowed persons with greater entrepreneurial instincts (i.e., non-Hawaiians) to exploit and develop the land.

Was this just a case of a poorly written will and codicil? Judd's actions in preparing the will and codicil and then in participating subsequently in the decision that required the Trustees to sell the Estate's lands raise serious legal, ethical, and moral questions. It appears that these three court decisions and the depletion of the Lunalilo Estate were part of a plan by a group of Western settlers to break up the Ali'i landholdings and make them available to the general public (especially their peers) to the detriment of the intended beneficiaries.[48] As the first and least stable of the Ali'i trusts, the Lunalilo Trust provided a vivid example of the potential problems involved in creating and administering such a trust.

The Queen Emma Trust

Queen Emma Kaleleonalani was the wife of Alexander Liholiho, who reigned as Kamehameha IV from December 1854 until his death on November 30, 1863.[49] During their reign, both the Mō'ī and his Queen devoted much of their energy to the

---

47. Rosemarie Bernardo, "Lunalilo Home Plans Day Care for Adults," *Honolulu Star-Bulletin,* February 1, 2004, http://starbulletin.com/2004/02/01/news/story7.html.

48. Two years after the 1893 overthrow of the Kingdom of Hawai'i, an article in *Paradise of the Pacific* reported that some people believed that the landholdings of the Bishop Estate should be broken up and sold for farming and small industries. 8 *Paradise of the Pacific* 4:54 (Frank L. Hoogs, ed., April 1895). The article added that the Government Lands were already being leased and sold for these purposes and proposed that the Crown Lands be similarly subdivided as soon as possible. *Id.*

49. 2 Ralph S. Kuykendall, *The Hawaiian Kingdom 1854–1874: Twenty Critical Years,* 33, 124 (1953, reprinted 1982); *see supra* chapters 6 and 7.

Queen Emma in England

needs of their people. After the death of her husband at the young age of twenty-nine (less than a year after the death of their four-year-old son Prince Albert),[50] Queen Emma continued to use both her influence and her personal funds to provide for the medical, religious, and educational interests of her people. She was instrumental in procuring funds for the establishment of Queen's Hospital, and she also assisted in founding Saint Andrew's Priory on O'ahu.[51] Many of the properties placed in trust by Queen Emma to provide funding for the Priory scholarships and for the hospital were devised to her by Ali'i claimants of the *Buke Mahele.* Of the first seven parcels placed in trust, at least four may be traced to Ali'i Nui or Kaukau Ali'i claims.[52]

On October 21, 1884, Queen Emma created a trust establishing four $150 scholarships at Saint Andrew's Priory and financial support for the hospital that she and her husband founded in 1859.[53] In Paragraph 13 of her will, Queen Emma placed seven parcels of land on Kaua'i and O'ahu in trust with Alexander Cartwright for the maintenance of the four scholarships and lifetime annuities to four individuals.[54]

---

50. *See supra* chapter 7.

51. Russell E. Benton, *Emma Naea Rooke: Beloved Queen of Hawaii,* 37–38 (1988).

52. *See supra* chapter 4.

53. *Will of Queen Emma Kaleleonalani,* October 21, 1884 (First Circuit Probate File 1787, Hawai'i State Archives). The scholarship allowance was increased to $1,400 by Trustee Bruce Cartwright, with approval of the court, on May 29, 1935. The Court in *Hite v. Queen's Hospital,* 36 Hawai'i 250, 291 (1942), later changed the annual payment back to $600 as originally directed by Queen Emma in her will.

54. *Will of Queen Emma Kaleleonalani,* October 21, 1884 (First Circuit Probate File 1787, Hawai'i State Archives). Paragraph 11 established lifetime annuities (paid in monthly installments) in the sum of $900 for Lucy Peabody, $600 to Hikoni, $300 for Grace Kahoali'i, and $300 for Mary Lewai. *Id.*

TABLE 18. Parcels designated for Queen's Hospital in Queen Emma's Will

Location	Aliʻi Award (Mahele)
Kauaʻi	
Ahupuaʻa of Lawai	James Young Kanehoa
Oʻahu	
Hanaia Kamalama, Nuʻuanu	Keoni Ana
Huehue, Honolulu	Kauikeaouli
Kaluaokau, Waikiki, Kona	W. C. Lunalilo
Mahinui & Ao, Kaneʻohe	?
Mauna Kea Street	?
Half of Ahupuaʻa of Halawa, Ewa	Grace Kamaikui

The provisions of the trust directed Cartwright to use the income from the properties for the payment of the annuities and scholarships. Upon the death of the annuitants, Queen Emma empowered the trustee to sell the properties "provided the real estate remaining will, in the opinion of the Supreme Court, produce a yearly income sufficient to provide for the aforesaid scholarships." [55] Queen Emma also specified that the proceeds of any sale were to be invested, with any remaining profits split evenly between Queen's Hospital and a trust for Queen Emma's cousin Albert Kuniakea.[56]

In Paragraph 14 of her will, Queen Emma conveyed several pieces of property to Queen's Hospital.[57] In the next paragraph, she set aside five parcels of land in trust for her cousin Albert. Upon his death, the will mandated the conveyance of the properties to Albert's "lawful" children.[58] If Albert died without legitimate children living, the remainder of his interests were to pass to Queen's Hospital.[59] Table 18 lists the parcels designated for Queen's Hospital in the Queen's Will.[60]

Because Albert Kuniakea died without legal issue, the five parcels placed in trust for him were turned over to Queen's Hospital by Cartwright in 1903.[61] Like those in Paragraph 13 of the will, these properties may also be traced to the Aliʻi Awards of the *Buke Mahele.* Table 19 lists the parcels designated for Albert.[62]

---

55. *Id.,* para. 13.

56. Albert's mother Gini (Jane) Lahilahi Young and Queen Emma's birth-mother Pane (Fanny) Kekelaokalani Young were sisters. Dorothy B. Barrère, *The King's Mahele: The Awardees and Their Lands,* 9 (1994).

57. *Will of Queen Emma Kaleleonalani,* October 21, 1884, para. 14 (First Circuit Probate File 1787, Hawaiʻi State Archives).

58. *Id.,* para. 15.

59. *Id.,* para. 16.

60. This list is derived from *Will of Queen Emma Kaleleonalani,* October 21, 1884 (First Circuit Probate File 1787, Hawaiʻi State Archives); telephone interview with Keith Lee, Queen Emma Foundation (January 9, 1997); and Barrère, *supra* note 56, at 9, 212, 245, 430–34.

61. "Fat Legacy is Paid to Hospital," *Hawaiian Gazette,* March 31, 1903, at 5, col. 6.

62. This list is assembled from *Will of Queen Emma Kaleleonalani,* October 21, 1884 (First Circuit Probate File 1787, Hawaiʻi State Archives); telephone interview with Keith Lee, Queen Emma Foundation (January 9, 1997); and Barrère, *supra* note 56, at 7, 114, 258, 401.

TABLE 19. Parcels designated for Albert Kuniakea

Location	Ali'i Award (Mahele)
Hawai'i	
Ahupua'a of Kawaihae, Kohala	Keoni Ana
Ahupua'a of Kealahewa, Kohala	Kaoanaeha
Ahupua'a of Waikahekahe, Puna	Gini (Jane) Lahilahi Young
Ahupua'a of Kamoamoa, Puna	Kaoanaeha
Maui	
Halaka'a, Lahaina	Joshua Kaeo

Although the 'Āina placed in trust by Queen Emma shared the same origin as the Crown Lands (in the sense that they were awarded to Ali'i in the Mahele), her 'Āina was respected as private property and distributed largely in accordance with her wishes—for the benefit of her people. Her lands thus had a different fate than the Crown Lands, which came to be viewed as the property of the office of the Crown and were commingled with the Government Lands after the 1893 overthrow, when they lost their distinctive status altogether.

Since the early 1900s, Queen's Hospital has made numerous efforts to obtain the remainder of the revenues generated by the properties (after the payment of scholarships) as well as the properties themselves.[63] Several attempts were also made to dissolve the trust and distribute what remained of the Estate, most of which were resisted by other beneficiaries as well as by the Trustees.[64]

On March 11, 1939, Acting Trustee Bruce Cartwright died, and Charles M. Hite was appointed to fill the position on April 20.[65] Soon thereafter, Hite filed a petition asking the Circuit Court to review the manner of distribution and use of funds from the Queen Emma Trust and to determine whether the monies given to the hospital had to be used solely for the accommodation and treatment of Native Hawaiians or could be used for other purposes.[66] The Hawai'i Supreme Court eventually ruled that Queen's Hospital was founded "for the use alike of indigent Hawaiians and such foreigners and others who might choose to avail themselves of the same,"[67] and it could be used to service both.

Despite the Court's conclusion on this matter, the question remained whether the trust should be dissolved altogether. Beneficiaries questioned whether a trust was necessary to collect revenues from the properties and distribute income, especially in

---

63. Kau, *supra* note 43, at 289.

64. "Plan Afoot to End Queen Emma Trust May Stir Trouble: Kamaaina Group Headed by John Wilson, Opposes Any Liquidation," *Honolulu Advertiser,* November 14, 1944, at 7, col. 2.

65. "Queen's Hospital Faces Huge Suit: Hite Asks Court Decide Whether Queen Emma Bequests Are Misused," *Honolulu Advertiser,* July 12, 1939, at 7, col. 1.

66. *Hite v. Queen's Hospital et. al.,* 36 Hawai'i 250, 260–61 (1942).

67. *Id.* at 268.

light of the Trustee's fees.[68] Many members of the local community, however, including Attorney General C. Nils Tavares, opposed attempts to dissolve the trust.[69]

After negotiations between the Trustees of Queen's Hospital and the Priory directors and after a partial distribution of the Trust's Estate in 1950,[70] Judge Allen Hawkins terminated the Queen Emma Trust in 1967.[71] After determining that it was "illogical"[72] to maintain a trust to provide for $600 in scholarships, the hospital received the remaining two lots at Queen and Richards Streets, valued at roughly $1 million, and gave the priory $25,000 to maintain the scholarships.[73]

Today, the funds for the Priory scholarships have been exhausted.[74] The Queen Emma Foundation continues to manage the lands left by the late Queen and other properties owned by the Queen's Health Systems (formerly Queen's Hospital) to help "support and advance health care in Hawaiʻi."[75] The Foundation also operates a community grant program to increase Native Hawaiian cultural awareness and pride in Koʻolauloa, one of the areas with the highest proportion of Native Hawaiians and one of the last rural areas on Oʻahu.[76] The Foundation operates on the revenues derived from its 12,000 acres of land. Of the Foundation's property, the most valuable land is 18.5 acres located in Waikīkī, including the land where the International Marketplace sits. In September of 2003, the Foundation announced its plan to capitalize on this landholding by closing down the Marketplace and constructing a low-rise retail and entertainment complex to be completed by 2008.[77]

---

68. "Plan Afoot to End Queen Emma Trust May Stir Trouble: Kamaʻaina Group Headed by John Wilson, Opposes Any Liquidation," *Honolulu Advertiser,* November 14, 1944, at 1, col. 1. The estate's Trustee was then receiving about $1,400 per year. "Queen Emma Trust Abolished," *Honolulu Advertiser,* March 8, 1967, at A-2, col. 3.

69. "Tavares Objects to Termination of Queen's Trust," *Honolulu Star-Bulletin,* January 30, 1945, at 4, col. 4.

70. In *Hite v. Queen's Hospital,* 38 Hawaiʻi 494 (1950), the Court ruled that the Trustee should ascertain how much property was necessary to maintain the priory scholarships and transfer the "excess" real estate to the hospital. *Id.* at 520. The Court had been adamant in its position that the hospital's land—which, as explained above in the text, originated from Aliʻi lands distributed in the Mahele that had been devised to the hospital in Queen Emma's Will—was private property. "None of the purposes for which The Queen's Hospital was organized included the administration of powers of the sovereign, nor were its assets owned by the sovereign. . . . On the contrary it was endowed by private, benevolently-inclined persons, and the fund subscribed and contributed by them was the financial nucleus of its establishment. The property of the hospital is private property." *Id.* at. 271.

71. The Trustees of Queen's Hospital initially offered the Priory directors a lump-sum payment of $20,000 to maintain the yearly scholarships, with the hospital gaining title to the two lots remaining in the estate. The directors of the Saint Andrew's Priory rejected the offer and made a counteroffer of $25,000, which was accepted. "Plan Afoot to End Queen Emma Trust May Stir Trouble: Kamaʻaina Group Headed by John Wilson, Opposes Any Liquidation," *Honolulu Advertiser,* November 14, 1944, at 1.

72. "Queen Emma Trust Abolished," *Honolulu Advertiser,* March 8, 1967, at 1, col. 6.

73. *Id.*

74. Telephone interview with Suann Wilson, Saint Andrew's Priory Admissions (January 9, 1997).

75. "The Queen's Health Systems, 1996 Overview" (on file with author).

76. Sandra Janoff, "Hawaiian Community Uses FS to Reconnect with Traditional Values," *Future Search* (2003), available at http://www.futuresearch.net/method/applications/world/north_america/hawaiin_values.cfm (visited November 19, 2006).

77. Kelli Abe Trifonovitch, "Bring the Locals Back: The Queen Emma Foundation's Mike Hastert Says

Queen Lili'uokalani,
ca. 1863–64

Queen Lili'uokalani's Trust

Queen Lili'uokalani, the last reigning Mō'ī, is remembered for many things—but especially for her personal strength and dignity. As the Hawaiian Kingdom and the Crown Lands were stripped from her control, she persisted in trying to set things right. She also persisted in trying to carry out her traditional responsibility as an Ali'i to mālama (care for) her people. She focused her concern on orphaned and destitute Hawaiian children, because they were particularly vulnerable as the changing legal and social system led to the decline of the traditionally supportive 'ohana system. By a trust deed dated December 2, 1909, Lili'uokalani set aside her private landholdings to benefit these Hawaiian children.[78] Section VII of the trust reads as follows:

> From and after the death of the Grantor, all of the property of the trust estate, both principal and income, which shall not be required for any of the special provisions or payments in this instrument before mentioned, shall be used by the Trustees for the benefit of orphan and other destitute children in the Hawaiian Islands, the preference to be given to Hawaiian children of pure or part aboriginal blood.[79]

---

the Redevelopment of the International Marketplace is a Part of Reinventing Waikīkī," *Hawaii Business,* April 2004, available at http://www.hawaiibusiness.com (visited November 19, 2006).

78. *Trust Deed of Liliuokalani,* December 2, 1909.

79. The *Trust Deed of Liliuokalani,* December 2, 1909, was amended on October 22, 1911. Changes included inserting "and other destitute children" after the word "orphans" in this first paragraph of Section VII.

Schedules A, B, and C of the trust deed listed the property included in the trust conveyance. Schedule A provided the long inventory of the lands that had been conveyed to Lili'uokalani by deed (including properties in Waikīkī that have proven to be quite valuable), as follows:

1. Deed of A. Keohokalole, et al., dated May 13, 1859, Liber 12, page 26; Hamohamo, Waikiki, Oahu;

2. Deed of Hiikua, dated May 7, 1864, Liber 18, page 145; the Ahupua'a of Puelelu, Kona, Molokai;

3. Deed of Umalele, June 17, 1864, Liber 18, page 218; Apanas 1, 2, and 3 of R.P. 2284, Waialae-iki, Oahu;

4. Deed of Administrator Est. of C. Kapaakea, August 3, 1867, Liber 24, page 198; Apana 2 of R.P. 4449, Kamookahi, Waikiki, Oahu;

5. Deed of Richard H. Stanley, April 21, 1870, Liber 31, page 27; Ahupua'a of Honohina, Hilo, Hawaii;

6. Deed of Makanahelehele, et al., April 17, 1873, Liber 36, page 489; L.C.A. 2085, R.P. 2828, at Kaneloa, Waikiki, Oahu;

7. Deed of Kailikole, dated December 27, 1873, Liber 38, page 406; L.C.A. 2492, R.P. 2795, Hamohamo, Waikiki, Oahu;

8. Deed of Hokii, September 2, 1876, Liber 46, page 348; L.C.A. 1446, R.P. 6239, Waikiki, Oahu;

9. Deed of Kalela et al., November 1, 1880, Liber 66/476; house lot at Hamohamo, Waikiki, L.C.A. 1433, R.P. 1272;

10. Deed of S.W. Mahelona, March 12, 1881, Liber 159/402; land at Kamookahi, Waikiki, Oahu;

11. Deed of D. Malo, March 26, 1881, Liber 68/118; Apanas 1 and 2 of L.C.A. 1926, R.P. 2590, Kolowalu Manoa, Waikiki, Oahu;

12. Deed of Haumea, June 7, 1861, Liber 67/454; L.C.A 11047, R.P. 6391; L.C.A 7397, R.P. 7045; L.C.A. 6176, R.P. 5698; Keauhou, Kona, Hawaii, and Waikiki, Kona, Oahu;

13. Deed of Mary Ann Conradt, October 1, 1881, Liber 75/83; L.C.A. 1437, R.P. 3920, Kalia; L.C.A. 1437 at Pahupahupua'a; Waikiki, Oahu;

14. Deed of M. Kuaea, May 2, 1862, Liber 74/136; L.C.A. 8183, R.P. 1321 at Hauula, Koolauloa, and land described in Liber 66/605 at Haleaha, Koolauloa, Oahu;

15. Deed of D.K. Fyfe, Com'r of Estate of W. L. Moehonua, ded'd, November 29, 1882, Liber 82/248; Apanas 1, 2, 3, and 4 of L.C.A. 5230, Lahaina, Maui;

16. Deed of Sarah Kahookaamoku, March 5, 1883, Liber 78/418; L.C.A. 2557 at Kamookahi, Oahu;

17. Deed of Herman Kockemann, March 26, 1883, Liber 77/404; land at Hamohamo, Waikiki, Oahu;

18. Deed of Kalanialii, June 23, 1883, Liber 81/149; R.P. 2557, Kamookahi, Oahu;

19. Deed of Kuhinia, September 1, 1883, Liber 82/406; in the Kuleana of Ohuohu, L.C.A. 1451, R.P. 6123, and L.C.A. 1450, R.P. 6805; Hamohamo, Waikiki, Oahu;

20. Deed of D.W. Pauahi et al., January 26, 1884, Liber 84/437; Apana 2 of L.C.A. 1468, R.P. 2508, Waikiki, Oahu;

21. Deed of Tamar Kuaea, Admx. Estate of M. Kuaea, August 15, 1887, Liber 89/264; land at Waikahalulu, Honolulu, Oahu;

22. Deed of Albert G. Bliss, December 3, 1884, Liber 90/342-3; land at Kapalama, Honolulu;

23. Deed of Kapunani et al., April 9, 1885, Liber 109/82; Apana 2 of L.C.A. 2027, R.P. 2575, Hamohamo, Waikiki, Oahu;

24. Deed of Chas. B. Wilson, Feb. 11, 1886, Liber 96/482; and also by deed of Cecil Brown, June 17, 1896, Liber 159/431; lots Nos. 9 and 11 of Macfarlane lots on Young Street, Honolulu;

25. Deed of J. Aea, July 17, 1886, Liber 108/23; land on upper side of public road at Waikahalulu, Honolulu, (see Liber 72/377);

26. Deed of Deborah Mahoe, December 20, 1886, Liber 98/467; Apanas 1 and 2 in the Ili of Kapahaha and Keoneula, on King Street, Honolulu;

27. Deed of Ioela Kane et al., March 18, 1887, Liber 107/11; land near Kapiolani Park, Kapahulu;

28. Deed of Kalawaia, April 14, 1887, Liber 104/157; land at Kauluwela, Honolulu, portion of Apana 49 of L.C.A. 7713; land at Nahiku, Maui, R.P. 1818; land at Kapalama, Honolulu, L.C.A. 1081, R.P. 2491;

29. Deed of Emma Buchanan, Guardian, July 25, 1887, Liber 108/189; L.C.A. 1452, R.P. 5060, Hamohamo, Waikiki, Oahu;

30. Deed of Puu et al., May 28, 1886, Liber 110/334; Apana 1 of L.C.A. 1475, R.P. 1275, at Hamohamo, Waikiki, Oahu;

31. Deed of Keamalu et al., October 1, 1888, Liber 112/213; L.C.A. 2030, R.P. 5585, at Kauluwela, Honolulu;

32. Deed of John Kaelele, October 12, 1888, Liber 113/306; L.C.A. 2030, R.P. 5585, at Kauluwela, Honolulu;

33. Deed of Wm. R. Castle, August 31, 1889, Liber 118/314; Palolo; Oahu; Kuleanas of: Mahoe, R.P. 2545; Kalakuaole, R.P. 3480; Kilohana, R.P. 2413;

34. Deed of A.S. Cleghorn, January 31, 1890, Liber 122/193; L.C.A. 1450, R.P. 2839, Hamohamo, Waikiki, Oahu;

35. Deed of Kahae Aea (releasing dower), April 29, 1890, Liber 108/23; land described in and conveyed by deed of J. Aea, dated July 17, 1886, L. 108/23;

36. Deed of Trustees of Estate R.W. Holt, June 16, 1890, Liber 125/215; R.P. 136, Manoa, Oahu;

37. Deed of Kalela et al., August 8, 1891, Liber 133/164; L.C.A. 1433, R.P. 1272, Hamohamo, Waikiki, Oahu;

38. Deed of Oahu Railway & Land Co., October 21, 1891, Liber 154/262; Lots 1, 2, and 3 in Block 25, Pearl City Lots, Ewa, Oahu;

39. Deed of W.R. Castle, December 3, 1891, Liber 133/445; L.C.A. 1923, R.P. 6867, Manoa, Oahu;

40. Deed of Estate of Kalakaua, February 18, 1892, Liber 136/29; R.P. 3424, Kamanaiki, Kalihi, Oahu;

41. Deed of Kealoalii, October 8, 1894, Liber 148/384; 1 share in Hui Land of Holualoa 1 and 2, North Kona, Hawaii;

42. Deed of Lau Chong, April 16, 1894, Liber 167/121; L.C.A. 10295, R.P. 6637, Hookena, South Kona, Hawaii;

43. Deed of Kaoaopa, June 28, 1895, Liber 155/151; L.C.A. 735, R.P. 5722, Honolulu;

44. Deed of Helen Boyd, Trustee, January 7, 1896, Liber 159/33; Apana 1 of L.C.A. 1454, R.P. 2558, Waikiki, Oahu;

45. Deed of Kahakuakoi et al., September 3, 1898, Liber 178/267; Interest in Estates of Charles Kanaina, W.C. Lunalilo, Bernice P. Bishop, and Queen Hokaleleponi;

46. Deed of Kaehuahanui Kuihelani, October 8, 1898, Liber 186/259; Lots 190 and 203, Kulaokahua Plains;

47. Deed of Kapiolani Estate, Ltd., January 31, 1901, Liber 219/163; part of Waikiki residence;

48. The Ahupua'a of Keohuole, at Kailua, Hawaii, L.C.A. 8452, R.P. 6851;

49. Leasehold interest, under lease from Keelikolani, July 1, 1882, Liber 74/383; 40 years from July 1, 1882, R.P. 2057, Pawaa, Honolulu.[80]

Schedule B listed Lili'uokalani's lands held by Royal Patents that were to be conveyed to the trust:

1. R.P. 3550, June 29, 1891, Book 18 of Grants. Lot 11 at Honuakaha, Honolulu, 5000 square feet; and

2. R.P. 3575, December 22, 1891, Book 18 of Grants. Lots B and C at Kaauwailoa, Palolo, Oahu.[81]

Schedule C listed the land that Lili'uokalani held by descent or devise. These 'Āina included all of the lands and interests devised to Lili'uokalani by her late husband John Owen Dominis, by the *Will of Bernice Pauahi Bishop,* and by the *Will of Miriam Likelike.* The lands and interests in lands devised by Dominis included the following:

1. Deed of Wahinelii, May 18, 1864, Liber 18/434; 1/2 of R.P. 2822;

2. Deed of Kanui, December 2, 1864, Liber 18/435; 1/2 of R.P. 2822;

3. Deed of Estate of L. Haalelea, May 6, 1865, Liber 19/319; Ahupua'a of Naiwa, Molokai;

80. *Trust Deed of Liliuokalani,* December 2, 1909.
81. *Id.*

4. Deed of Makini, June 6, 1865, Liber 19/366; land of "Lanilua," Hilo, Hawaii;

5. Deed of J.W. Keawehunahala, June 11, 1867, Liber 23/378; Apana 4 of L.C.A 2699, R.P. 876, at Lokoea, Waialua, Oahu;

6. Deed of Ki and James Robinson, October 7, 1868, Liber 26/293; Apana 3 of L.C.A. 3373, R.P. 2895, at Lokoea, Kawailoa, Wailua, Oahu;

7. Deed of Charles Pouzat, February 17, 1874, Liber 39/127; Interest in land at Waiakea, Hilo, Hawaii, conveyed to him by deed of Kamakina, May 12, 1866;

8. Deed of Naunauna, Liber 39/499; Apana 2 of R.P. 909 at Alapii, Waialua, Oahu;

9. Deed of R. Keelikolani, August 26, 1874, Liber 40/207; Lot No. 1 on Diagram of Ahupuaʻa of Kawailoa, Waialua, Oahu;

10. Deed of Herman Kockemann, March 26, 1883, Liber 77/404; land at Hamohamo, Waikiki, Oahu;

11. Deed of Trustees of Estate of Bernice P. Bishop, September 4, 1889, Liber 116, 386; land at Paalaa, Waialua, Oahu; and

12. Royal Patent No. 3462 to John O. Dominis January 22, 1890, Book 17 of Grants; "Washington Place," on Beretania Street, Honolulu.[82]

Liliʻuokalani originally selected Archibald S. Cleghorn, Curtis P. Iaukea, and William O. Smith[83] as Trustees and empowered them with ample authority and discretion to manage the trust corpus, which in 1909 was valued at approximately $125,000.[84] The Trustees were empowered to "sell, lease, exchange, partition, mortgage, pledge and/or otherwise deal with and dispose of any of the lands and/or other property and interest of the trust estate, and to purchase . . . and or take leases . . . for the benefit of the estate."[85] Paragraph 3 of Section VIII provided that "No trustee shall be answerable or liable for any loss occasioned to the trust estate except as may arise from his own willful misconduct or gross negligence; neither shall any trustee be personally liable for any obligation contracted or incurred in his capacity as a trustee."

The Trustees were restricted by guidelines requiring them to report annually to a court of competent jurisdiction, as well as to Liliʻuokalani during her lifetime, regarding the administration, investments, expenditures, and condition of the trust.[86] A requirement that at least two Trustees be in agreement to take any trust actions served as a check on power.[87] Section VIII instructed that, prior to appointment by a judge or court of competent jurisdiction, the remaining Trustees had priority to nominate vacancy replacements. If they failed to so do, then it was up to the court to appoint the replacement.

82. *Id.*
83. The *Trust Deed of Liliuokalani,* December 2, 1909, named these individuals. An Amendment on October 22, 1911, substituted Samuel M. Damon for the deceased Archibald S. Cleghorn.
84. *Queen Liliʻuokalani Children's Center Manual,* 5 (February 1991).
85. *Trust Deed of Liliuokalani,* December 2, 1909.
86. October 22, 1911, Amendment.
87. *Trust Deed of Liliuokalani,* December 2, 1909.

Section I instructed the Trustees that during Lili'uokalani's life, the trust's income was to be prioritized as follows: (1) to maintain and improve the trust property and the administration of the trust; (2) to discharge interest due on Lili'uokalani's mortgage debts; (3) to pay Lili'uokalani any moneys necessary for personal expenses during her lifetime; (4) to pay down the principal of debts owed by Lili'uokalani; and (5) to assist orphans as provided.

Upon her death, the generous Mō'ī provided for her hānai children, her dear friends, and her relatives. Section II through Section V instructed the Trustees to provide for those closest to her. Section II conveyed outright to Curtis P. Iaukea, her business agent and personal friend,[88] the fee simple ownership of the Lele of Hamohamo at Waikīkī, consisting of about 8 acres of land and improvements.

Section III instructed the Trustees to set aside portions of the trust property for the use and occupation of twelve individuals during their lifetime, with these properties reverting to the trust upon the deaths of these individuals.[89] Section IV instructed the Trustees to make $100 payments to five female individuals, and Section V instructed them to pay eleven individuals annual annuities ranging from $180 to $6,000 during their lives. The last of these payments was made in 1941, and since then the entire trust net income has been devoted to charitable purposes.[90]

Lili'uokalani was aware that her gift to her people would not be fully realized until it was no longer necessary to provide for those closest to her. Section VII instructed the Trustees that the building of an orphanage be started as soon as financially practical. Section VII also provided that whether or not the institution was completed, the Trustees had discretion "in caring for or educating or otherwise providing for any child or children, . . . whether such child or children [resided] within or without any such institution."

By 1933, the value of the estate had increased to $835,330.[91] But by this time, foster homes were viewed as better environments than orphanages for those children the Queen sought to assist.[92] The Trustees sought permission from the Equity Court to emphasize coordination and administration of services for the beneficiaries instead of building an institution, and on October 3, 1934, the court responded favorably to the Trustee's petition, ruling that Section VII authorized them to exercise discretion to use trust income to place beneficiaries in foster homes, boarding

---

88. *Kalanianaole v. Liliuokalani,* 23 Hawai'i 457, 474 (1916).

89. The Amendment of October 22, 1911, added a thirteenth individual to this list. An Amendment of September 2, 1915, deleted Joseph Kaiponohea Aea, the Queen's recently deceased hānai son, as future heir to a life estate interest in "Kealohilani" at Waikīkī, substituting therefore Prince Jonah Kūhiō Kalaniana'ole and his wife. On November 30, 1915, Kalaniana'ole filed a suit charging Curtis P. Iaukea (the Mō'ī's business agent and personal friend) and John Aimoku Dominis (Lili'uokalani's hānai son) with conspiracy and undue influence resulting in the December 2, 1909 *Trust Deed. See Kalanianaole v. Liliuokalani,* 23 Hawai'i 457 (1916). This challenge was unsuccessful, because the Court found that Kalaniana'ole's interest was a mere expectancy in a future inheritance and, therefore, insufficient to maintain the suit.

90. *Queen Lili'uokalani Children's Center Manual,* 25 (February 1991).

91. *Id.* at 6.

92. *Id.*

schools, or other appropriate settings.[93] Although the court further stated that establishment of an institution should not be permanently tabled, the Trustees' discretion includes determination of when conditions and circumstances are favorable.[94]

The Mō'ī's trust has evolved into the Queen Lili'uokalani Children's Center, a member of the Child Welfare League of America, which has served more than 215,000 eligible children to date,[95] with an operating budget of $14 million in 1996.[96] Since that time, the annual operating budget has ranged from $11 to 14 million a year. In 2003 alone, the center serviced more than 9,000 children directly and more than 30,000 indirectly by providing programs in their communities.[97] The center has recognized that its primary commitment is to the "immediate needs of the child," but it has also recognized the traditional and "vital connection" between a child, the family, the community, and the nation.[98] The center has therefore served such diverse needs as education, culture, health, housing, social services, recreation, crime, and sovereignty.[99]

In the final pages of *Hawaii's Story by Hawaii's Queen,* Lili'uokalani spoke of her devotion to her native race.[100] She pledged her final drop of blood and everything she owned to restore the Hawaiian Nation.[101] The Mō'ī asked, however, "Would it be in vain?"[102] The many programs funded by Lili'uokalani's Trust have been and continue to be a source of strength for the Hawaiian Community. Recent collaborative efforts on the part of the Lili'uokalani Children's Center, Queen Emma's Trust, and the Kamehameha Schools[103] have provided additional opportunities to strengthen the people. This Ali'i was able to ensure that lands distributed to Ali'i during the Mahele have continued to serve the Native Hawaiian People. Her vision of a restored Hawaiian Nation continues to gain in strength, and the Mō'ī's efforts were not in vain.

---

93. *Id.* at 7.

94. *Id.*

95. *Annual Report, Queen Lili'uokalani Children's Center* (1995). Eligible children include "orphans," "a minor who has lost both parents through death," "half-orphan's," "minor who has lost one parent through death or a child born to a single, unmarried parent," a "destitute," "any other minor of Hawaiian ancestry who, by reason of divorce, desertion, illness or neglect on the part of parents, is lacking in adequate parental care financially or emotionally." *Queen Lili'uokalani Children's Center Manual,* 24 (February 1991). "Hawaiian or Part-Hawaiian" is defined as "a child whose Hawaiian ancestry, no matter how slight, can be verified by birth records or other reliable evidence; also, any child legally adopted by a family of Hawaiian ancestry." *Id.*

96. Telephone Interview with Harriet Rechnitz, Librarian with Queen Lili'uokalani Children's Center (March 10, 1997).

97. *Annual Report, Queen Lili'uokalani Children's Center* (2003), available at http://www.qlcc.org/annual_rpts.htm (visited November 19, 2006).

98. *Id.*

99. *Id.*

100. Liliuokalani, *Hawaii's Story By Hawaii's Queen,* 373–74 (1898, reprinted 1997).

101. *Id.* at 374.

102. *Id.*

103. *1995 Annual Report, Queen Lili'uokalani Children's Center* (1995).

Conclusion

The Aliʻi Nui demonstrated concern and aloha for their people by making them the beneficiaries of their trusts. The act of giving ʻĀina back to the people demonstrated that the Aliʻi understood their Kuleana to mālama their people, recognizing the responsibilities of Aliʻi as they had existed before the Mahele. The Aliʻi were acutely aware of the ailments consuming their people and they wanted to provide relief. Lunalilo demonstrated his concern for the kupuna, Emma showed her concern for the sick, and Pauahi and Liliʻuokalani for orphans and the indigent. Both Emma and Pauahi wanted to create more educational opportunities for their people. Today, all of these trusts have provided relief for and are still contributing to the well-being of Native Hawaiians. The trusts that have been able to prevent the alienation of their lands—specifically the trusts of Pauahi and Liliʻuokalani—have been the most successful in sustaining and healing the people and will continue to do so in perpetuity. Those that have sold or lost their ʻĀina, such as the Lunalilo Trust, have battled just to stay alive. Even with the considerable resources of the remaining Aliʻi trusts, they are sufficient to benefit only a fraction of the Native Hawaiian population today. When the Native Hawaiian Nation is reestablished to support, sustain, and benefit all Native Hawaiian people, it will require much more land than is now held by the Aliʻi trusts.

27

The British Crown Lands

The Hawaiian Monarchs looked to the royalty of Great Britain for inspiration and ideas, and so it may be helpful to examine the relationship between the British Monarchs and their Crown Lands to understand how the Crown Lands of Hawai'i should be perceived. Such an examination reveals that the relationship between the British Crown Lands and the British Monarchs changed dramatically over time, but the British Crown Lands have always been part of the trust relationship between the British royalty and their people, which is similar to the trust relationship that connected the Hawaiian Monarchs and the Native Hawaiian People.

The lands in the British Crown Estate are not the property of the Government of the United Kingdom of Great Britain and Northern Ireland. Nor are these lands considered to be the Sovereign's private estate. Rather, they are part of the hereditary possessions of the Sovereign "in the right of the Crown." The history of the lands that now make up the Crown Estate is a dynamic and complex one, following the evolution of a feudal kingdom into a modern nation, the development of a fiscal system of national taxation, and the power struggles between Monarchs and Parliaments. The Crown Estate Lands are now managed by appointed Commissioners, with the Monarchs receiving annual payments from the revenues they generate.

The origin of the Crown Estates is rooted in the development of feudalism and the concept that "[a]ll land ultimately was held 'of' the king." [1] The understanding of the early British regarding the King's control over these lands is similar to the view held by the precontact Hawaiians—namely that each new Monarch controlled the lands and could distribute them as appropriate to reward allies and maintain order. The origins of the British Crown Estate can be traced to the beginning of the modern era of governance of the British Isles and to the lands that were won by William the Conqueror after he crossed the English Channel from Normandy in 1066. To consolidate his control, William commissioned the preparation of the *Domesday Book,* which was completed in 1086, to document England's landholdings, build-

---

1. Robert S. Hoyt, *The Royal Demesne in English Constitutional History: 1066–1272,* at 6 (1950).

ings, people, and livestock. After William's victory, all land in Britain was essentially "Crown Lands," because the King had dominion and power everywhere.[2] King William immediately began distributing plots of land and manors to his vassals, using the Crown Lands for patronage in a way that continues to the present day.

For generations of kings in Britain (as in Hawai'i), the Crown Lands were valued not as a source of revenue but primarily as a way to gain political power and to reward loyal subjects.[3] One British historian has reported that the extent and value of the Crown Lands in those early years "approach[ed] one-fourth of the total value of the landed wealth of England." [4] In this early feudal era, "annual and regular revenues" from these Crown Lands provided the income from which William and future Kings lived. The extent of these lands and the revenue they generated fluctuated, however, and depended greatly on the Monarch's ability to retain tight control over war expenditures and the management of the lands.

The management of these Crown Lands was controlled by the exchequers and later by the receivers. With the transition from an Absolute Monarchy to a Constitutional Monarchy, Parliament increased its power over the King's finances. Although the King continued to exercise direct control over the lands for several hundred years, an expectation arose that the King would "live of his own" and use these landed revenues to finance his household expenses. Increasing royal expenditures and years of weak management by spendthrift monarchs resulted in these land revenues becoming woefully insufficient for the royal budget. In one such financial crisis, King George III signed the Crown Estates Act, agreeing to surrender most of the Crown Lands to Parliament in return for a yearly fixed sum. The British Monarchy today continues to be supported by this fixed sum, but they have also cultivated the remaining Crown Lands, which are now managed under a successful corporation. Estate revenues support the various investments in the Crown Lands and benefit the taxpayers of Great Britain.

Background

When William the Conqueror became King of England in 1066, he seized lands that became the basis of his royal power and the source of his revenue.[5] These lands were distributed to the leading men who helped him win the land or supported his rule.[6] Lands were also distributed to members of the royal family, but the King retained the

---

2. *See* B. P. Wolffe, *The Royal Demesne in English History: The Crown Estate in the Governance of the Realm from Conquest to 1509,* 34 (1971). Wolffe distinguished King William's Crown Lands from those of France, where the Crown's control over its property was clearly defined and more limited, both in the scope of property held and the power over people on the land. In England, in contrast, the Crown's power was such that it "rendered superfluous a royal demesne set apart or preserved as an entity." *Id.* at 34, 38–40.

3. *See generally id.,* providing a history of the Crown Lands from 1066 to the 1400s.

4. Hoyt, *supra* note 1, at 231.

5. *Id.* at 7.

6. *Id.*

largest royal estate.[7] Over time, many of these lands became the seats of local government and were associated with the Crown rather than with the person of the King.[8] The "annual and regular revenues"[9] derived from these lands provided the income from which William and future Kings lived. From 1087 to 1154, some of the Crown Lands were alienated under the reigns of William Rufus, Henry I, and Stephen.[10]

The formal distinction between the King's personal lands and the Crown Lands belonging to the Monarchy was a gradual process, carved out of practical administrative convenience rather than from a royal fiat.[11] Under the reign of King Henry II (1154–89), "administrative and legal reforms . . . resulted in the growth of a royal demesne which was both distinct from the rest of the realm and [was] also beginning to be treated as one whole, an entity from which the monarchy drew strength clearly separate from the power it possessed by virtue of the feudal rights of the king as overlord."[12] These reforms included more centralized administration under the Exchequer and the development of a "nonfeudal" tax, which increased Crown revenues.

To promote the efficient collection of revenues, the responsibility for collecting these revenues shifted from the sheriffs to special commissioners called exchequers.[13] These officials appointed subordinates who became directly accountable for the payments owed to the King.[14] Other such administrative and legal reforms led to greater centralized control that not only brought in more revenue[15] but also established the King's right to receive revenue on lands that he owned as King.[16]

At the same time, the King's ownership of the land and his collection of revenues from them quickly led to the notion that the King must "live of his own." The British historian B. P. Wolffe noted that this phrase was coined in response to Edward II's arbitrary takings of property, including cattle and horses for the maintenance of his household.[17] This young King was implored to begin living on what was legally his so that the burden of taxation could be lightened.[18]

---

7. *Id.*

8. *Id.*

9. *Id.* at 65.

10. *Id.* at 85.

11. Historians who dispute the extent, value, and development of the original British Crown Estates, such as B. P. Wolffe, argue that the term "royal demesne" was a vague phrase that was never used in official or important records of the time. Rather, the common *Domesday Book* use of *in dominio* occurred mainly in reference to designated land that belonged to the King, as opposed to other lands held by his tenants-in-chief. Wolffe, *Royal Demesne, supra* note 2, at 17–18. Although this transition is difficult to trace because of the scarcity of historic royal documents, the *Domesday Book,* commissioned by William the Conqueror to account for England's landholdings, buildings, people, and livestock, hints at the evolving relationship between the King as landlord and his Crown Lands. Hoyt, *supra* note 1, at 64.

12. Hoyt, *supra* note 1, at 232.

13. *Id.* at 94.

14. *Id.* at 97.

15. *Id.* at 97–98.

16. *Id.* at 123–24.

17. B. P. Wolffe, *The Crown Lands 1461 to 1536: An Aspect of Yorkist and Early Tudor Government,* 17 (1970); Wolffe, *Royal Demesne, supra* note 2, at 46.

18. Wolffe, *Crown Lands, supra* note 17, at 17.

But the phrase "live of his own" took on a new meaning when King Henry IV usurped the throne from Edward III in 1399, ushering in the Lancastrian period (1399–1461), amidst great economic and political turmoil.[19] The Monarchs in the previous decades and centuries had distributed land to allies and relatives, but these distributions were usually thought of as lasting only for the reign of that particular Monarch (just as in precontact Hawai'i). In 1404, Parliament passed the Act of Resumption, reclaiming for the Crown Lands all the property that had been distributed by the Plantagenets since 1366. This reclamation of land made Henry IV land-rich, and in response to the King's request for more money, Parliament noted the King's unusual landed wealth and asked that the King "live of his own."[20] King Henry IV nonetheless continued to request financial assistance to support his unstable reign, which fueled tensions between the Monarch and Parliament.[21] According to Wolffe, "parliamentary critics" likely believed that "properly used, the crown lands ought to be able to make a substantial and reliable contribution to the vexatious expenses of an extravagant and unbridled royal Household."[22]

Although King Henry IV's son was able to ward off Parliament's demands for reforms, his grandson was unable to do so.[23] Henry VI distributed his lands with a lack of prudence and eventually brought his Government to complete financial and political bankruptcy.[24] He gave freely (and rashly) of the Crown Lands, seeking to curry favor with those who would fight for him in the Hundred Years' War.[25] Parliament responded with another series of resumptions, taking back much of the land Henry had squandered.[26] In 1450, after the murder of the Treasurer of England and the Chief Minister, the King agreed to sign Parliament's Act of Resumptions and revoke all his previous grants of lands.[27] The Acts of Resumption passed from 1450 to 1456 eliminated sinecure offices, removed perquisites attached to those offices, annulled annuities that had been granted, reversed unreasonable alienations of royal lands and rights, and introduced greater supervision of royal grants.[28] Parliament approved a budget of 11,000 pounds, mostly secured from the revenues generated by royal lands, in order to alleviate the burden on the public.[29] When these land rev-

---

19. *Id.* at 24.

20. *Id.* at 24–25.

21. *Id.* at 25.

22. B. P. Wolffe, *Royal Demesne, supra* note 2, at 227. "The only financial innovations in his reign were further experiments designed to spread the incidence and increase the yield of direct taxation." *Id.*

23. Wolffe, *Crown Lands, supra* note 17, at 25.

24. *Id.; see also id.* at 36.

25. See Wolffe, *Royal Demesne, supra note* 2, at 110–15.

26. There were three Resumption Acts passed, in 1450, 1451, and 1455–56. Although the King initially resisted them, making exemptions so that his supporters could keep their land, eventually he faced the fact that no other solution was available to address the Kingdom's financial crisis. *See id.* at 124–40.

27. Wolffe, *Crown Lands, supra note* 17, at 25.

28. Wolffe, *Royal Demesne, supra* note 2, at 227.

29. Wolffe, *Crown Lands, supra* note 17, at 27.

enues proved to be insufficient to support the Royal Household, Parliament eventually gave the King a larger grant of revenues from direct and indirect taxation.[30]

When Edward IV seized power in 1461, the resumptions began anew. Seeking to right the wrongs of the Lancasters, King Edward seized voluminous amounts of land for the Crown, some of which had not been controlled by the throne for a long time. In 1467, Edward IV formally addressed Parliament and declared his purpose to "live upon mine own, and not to charge my subjects but in great and urgent causes."[31] Edward IV owned about one-fifth of England's land area, as well as properties in Wales, and he continued the practice of living off the income from these estates. He reduced household expenses somewhat but still "managed to keep a splendid and impressive court."[32] Because the revenues from the lands remained insufficient to support the royal household, Edward IV ordered reforms that increased the efficiency of the management of the lands. The first major reform was to remove profitable and fee farms from the jurisdiction of the sheriffs and reserve their revenues for household expenses.[33] Edward IV also placed trusted agents throughout his Kingdom to ensure that he was well served.[34] These agents, also known as receivers, had duties "'to ride, survey, receive and remember on every behalf that might be most for the king's profit and thereof yearly to make report.'"[35] Because these receivers handled the King's money, they appeared before the exchequers.[36] Although the exchequers could demand a summary of account, they lacked the power to control the assigned revenues that were being paid directly into the King's coffers.[37] Edward IV also departed from royal tradition by keeping his Lancaster Estates separate from other royal estates under private management.[38] These efficiencies and administrative reforms allowed Edward IV to "live of his own,"[39] and he died a rich man.

When the Tudor dynasty succeeded to the throne, Parliament again passed Acts of Resumption granting Henry VII the power to "'resume' into his hands all lands and possession legally belonging to Henry VI."[40] The Tudor dynasty patterned its financial administration after that of the House of York and utilized methods of control such as the collection of revenues that went directly to the King's coffers and the utilization of the Treasury Department instead of the exchequers to manage the King's finances.[41] Even after the practice became established that the King would live

---

30. *Id.*

31. *Id.* at 27, 102.

32. *Id.* at 53.

33. *Id.*

34. *Id.*

35. Wolffe, *Royal Demesne, supra* note 2, at 167.

36. Wolffe, *Crown Lands, supra* note 17, at 56. Despite such required appearances, the royal receivers received a "royal acquittance in the form of a prohibition sent to the Exchequer." *Id.* at 58.

37. *Id.* at 59.

38. *Id.* at 53.

39. Wolffe, *Royal Demesne, supra* note 2, at 180.

40. Wolffe, *Crown Lands, supra* note 17, at 67–68.

41. *Id.* at 69–70.

off the income derived from the Crown Estates, the stability of the Monarchy remained precarious as a succession of spendthrift Tudor and Stuart Monarchs whittled away at the Crown's landholdings. Henry VIII, son of Henry VII, began with revenues greater than any of his predecessors because of his father's careful administration of finances,[42] but his father also reigned during the start of Sir Walter Raleigh's "foreign adventures" and the military campaign to bring Ireland under English control, both of which required much royal expenditure.[43] Henry VII was successful in introducing careful practices of management and living off the Crown Lands, but his efforts were squandered by Henry VIII, whose interests lay elsewhere.

By the end of the reign of Elizabeth I (Tudor), the need to conserve the Crown Lands became recognized.[44] One strategy was to annex selected estates to the Crown to "restrain the King from making further gifts."[45] This attempt failed because the annexation law contained a major loophole that allowed the alienation of lands "in case of wars, increase of issue or such like considerations of state,"[46] "with the written approval of eight privy councilors."[47] Thus, despite indenture, land sales continued, with commissioners selling off land in 1603, 1609, 1610, and 1613.[48] Many of these sales took place in times of crisis or war, in a buyer's market, and the Crown frequently received less for the lands than they were worth. After it had transferred major components of its land base, the Crown lost its financial independence and Parliament was able to gain substantially in power. In 1626, the first Bishop's War between England and Scotland marked the first time during this period that the Monarch lacked enough assets to sell or secure loans for the war and was forced to ask Parliament for funding.[49] These developments led to the decline in the Crown's dominant role and to the evolution of Britain into a Constitutional Monarchy.

Decreasing revenues made it necessary for the kings to continue requesting funds from Parliament for the running of civil government. By the time William III reigned between 1689 and 1702, the net revenue had fallen to a mere £6,000 a year.[50] Because of these decreasing revenues, kings continued to request funds from and Parliament continued to grant funds for the running of civil government. In 1698, during the reign of William III, the British Parliament ruled that the annual sum of £600,000 would be used for civil government. In 1727, George II persuaded Parliament that he would need £800,000. In 1760, King George II died and left behind a collection of debts for his grandson, George III. The first Parliament that met under

---

42. *Id.* at 76.

43. *See id.* at 87.

44. R. W. Hoyle, "Introduction: Aspects of the Crown's Estate," in *The Estates of the English Crown, 1558–1640,* at 21 (R. W. Hoyle, ed., 1992).

45. *Id.*

46. *Id.* at 22.

47. *Id.*

48. *Id.* at 23.

49. *Id.* at 27–28.

50. Peter Lane, *Prince Charles: A Study in Development,* 152 (1988).

the new King wanted to rescue him from the relative poverty of the earlier kings and from the debts incurred by George II and others, so it enacted the Crown Estate Act,[51] whereby George III surrendered most of the Crown Lands to Parliament in return for a fixed allowance that is now known as the Civil List. Under this arrangement, similar in some respects to the Act of January 3, 1865, enacted by Hawai'i's Legislature,[52] the British Parliament took over the entire cost of running the administration of the country. Within a few years, George III was arguing that his List was too small, and in 1777 it was increased to £900,000 a year.[53] The Crown Lands ceded by George III remained, in theory, the property of the Crown, and each new Monarch would regain the lands and then surrender most of them to Parliament in exchange for a negotiated agreement regarding financial support for the royal household.

Each Monarch would retain control of some of the lands and adjust the amount received under the Civil List accordingly. George III, for instance, kept control over the major estates of the Duchies of Lancaster and Cornwell, and this selection proved popular with other Monarchs as well, with the effect that the estates of Lancaster and Cornwall have been separately administered during most of the past millennium.[54] These lands have special protection, and during the period of Elizabethan land sales the commissioners responsible for the sale of land were guided by articles of instruction that "forbad the sale of lands belonging to the 'ancient inheritance of the Crown,' the Duchies of Lancaster and Cornwall and the earldom of Chester and properties lying near the Queen's houses. Lands in strategically sensitive areas were also withheld; by the end of the century they included Portsmouth, the Isles of Wight, Scilly, Sheppey and the Anglo-Scottish marches."[55]

The independent administration of the Duchy of Cornwall was reasserted by Charles I upon ascending the throne in 1625, when he "departed from previous constitutional practice by not merging the Duchy with the Exchequer."[56] Instead, Charles I issued a new council commission, giving these new commissioners full authority to enter agreements, make leases, audit accounts, and supervise the administration of the Duchy.[57]

In 1837, when Victoria came to the throne, she surrendered the rest of the Crown Estates and had her Civil List fixed at only £385,000 a year, less than half of what it had been for George III. With financial guidance from Prince Albert, Queen Victoria was nonetheless able to save £200,000 to buy Osborne House on the Isle of Wight and pay for the Sandringham and Balmoral Estates.[58]

---

51. *Id.* at 152–53.

52. *See supra* chapter 9.

53. Lane, *Prince Charles, supra* note 50, at 153.

54. David Thomas, "The Elizabethan Crown Lands: Their Purposes and Problems," in *The Estates of the English Crown, 1558–1640*, at 61 (R. W. Hoyle, ed., 1992).

55. Hoyle, "Introduction," *supra* note 44, at 17.

56. Graham Haslam, "Jacobean Phoenix: the Duchy of Cornwall in the Principates of Henry, Frederick and Charles," in *The Estates of the English Crown, 1558–1640*, at 284 (R. W. Hoyle, ed., 1992).

57. *Id.*

58. Lane, *Prince Charles, supra* note 50, at 154–55.

The Crown Estates today are run by the Crown Estate Commissioners (CEC). They encompass 177,000 acres of agricultural land in England, another 88,000 acres in Scotland, and many valuable sites in London including Trafalgar Square, Regent Street, Jermyn Street, and Carlton House Terrace.[59] The Crown Estate Commissioners now handle an annual income of about £40 million (1987 valuation).[60] In 1980 the commissioners transferred some £20 million to the Treasury, and in 1986 they transferred some £30 million.[61] In 1987, the net income from those estates was about £30 million, while the amount returned to the Royal Household pursuant to the Civil List for its expenses was £5.6 million.[62]

The List is only a fraction of the real cost of the Monarchy and is meant to cover only immediate "operational costs," such as office expenses and the salaries of the palace staff. It does not include the costs of the royal yacht *Britannia,* the Queen's Flight, the royal train, the upkeep of Windsor Castle, Buckingham Palace, and Holyroodhouse or various other items of expenditure. The actual annual cost of the Monarchy is about £40 million (1987 figures),[63] but this sum does not appear on the Civil List. It is tucked away in the budgets of the various Government departments such as Defense, Environment, and so on.

In 1962, when Prince Charles became Duke of Cornwall, the income from the Duchy was about £112,000 a year.[64] In the Civil List Act of 1952, it was agreed that he should retain one-ninth of this revenue for his education and other expenses.[65] By 1966, the remaining eight-ninths of the Duchy's revenue had provided the Treasury with about £1.7 million.[66]

In 1969, Charles followed the precedent set by Edward VIII when he had been Prince of Wales, and he announced that, since he was now twenty-one, he would pay back half of the Duchy's revenue to the Government while retaining the other half in lieu of any contribution from the annual Civil List.

In 1979, Prince Charles' last year as a bachelor, the income was £550,445. In 1981 it was £771,480, and in 1982 it was £795,126. In 1986 it was almost £1.5 million. (Since 1977 the Duchy has reinvested £9 million into the property and has invested £14 million in the stock market.)

The Queen's Four Sources of Funding

The term "Crown Estate" now refers to property owned by the United Kingdom "in right of the Crown." In 1998, this property generated more than £113 million profit

---

59. *Id.* at 153.
60. *Id.*
61. *Id.*
62. *Id.*
63. *Id.*
64. *Id.* at 158.
65. *Id.*
66. *Id.*

for the British taxpayer. The Queen today has four sources of funding: the Civil List, Grants-in-Aid, the Privy Purse, and the Queen's personal wealth and income. The Queen pays tax on her personal income and capital gains. The Civil List and the Grants-in-Aid are not taxed because they cover official expenditures.

The Civil List

The Civil List is the sum provided by Parliament to meet the official expenses of the Queen's Household in order for the Queen to fulfill her role as Head of State and Head of the Commonwealth. The Civil List dates back to the Restoration of the Monarchy in 1660, but the current system was created when George III acceded to the throne in 1760, as explained above, when it was decided that the whole cost of civil government should be provided by Parliament in return for the surrender of the hereditary revenues (principally the net surplus of the Crown Estate) by the King for the duration of the reign. In 1997–98, revenue from the Crown Estate amounted to £113.2 million, which was paid to the Treasury.[67] The Civil List was set by Parliament as a fixed annual amount of £7.9 million for the ten-year period from 2000 to 2010.[68] The budget for each year's projected net Civil List is reviewed by the Treasury, which audits the accounts and verifies that the Household's financial management is in line with best practices.

Grants-in-Aid

The Occupied Royal Palaces in Britain are held by the Queen in her capacity as Monarch and are used to support her responsibilities as Head of State. The Queen invites approximately 50,000 guests annually to the palaces, and approximately 1.7 million paying visitors also come.[69] Her palaces include Buckingham Palace, St. James' Palace and Clarence House, Marlborough House Mews, the residential and office areas of Kensington Palace, Windsor Castle and related buildings, and the Hampton Court Mews and Paddocks.[70] In addition, the Queen's Gallery at Buckingham Palace contains some 285 properties available for residential use on a rental basis and nine properties used as communal residential accommodation for staff.[71]

Parliament, through the Department for Culture, Media and Sport, provides a Property Maintenance Grant-in-Aid annually to the Royal Household to meet the cost of maintenance and of certain utilities and related services. The Royal Household annually submits a rolling five-year plan to the department for its approval, as well as detailed quarterly reports and a detailed budget at the start of each financial

---

67. *The 2003 Crown Estate Annual Report and Accounts,* 3.

68. "Civil List, Sources of Funding, Royal Finances," The Official Website of the British Monarchy, http://www.royal.gov.uk/output/page361.asp (visited November 16, 2006).

69. "Property Services Grant-In-Aid, Sources of Funding, Royal Finances," The Official Website of the British Monarchy, <http://royal.gov.uk/output/page393.asp>.

70. *Id.*

71. *Id.*

year. The Grant-in-Aid for 1996–97 was £19,609,000, in 1997–98 it was £16,409,000, and for 2003–04 it was reduced to £15.3 million.[72]

The costs of maintaining the Palace of Holyroodhouse are met directly by the Scottish Office, and this palace is administered by Historic Scotland. Costs of Historic Royal Palaces or Unoccupied Palaces are not the responsibility of the Royal Household. The Historic Royal Palaces Trust looks after the Unoccupied Palaces, which include the Tower of London, the Hampton Court, and the State Apartments at Kensington Palace. The Unoccupied Palaces receive no Government funding. These buildings are maintained using visitor admissions and related sources of income. The Royal Household also receives annual funding to meet the costs of official travel in the form of a Royal Travel Grant-in-Aid from Parliament.

Privy Purse

The principal responsibility of the Privy Purse Office is to manage the Monarch's private income from the Duchy of Lancaster, which amounted to £7.9 million before tax for the year ending March 31, 2003.[73] The Duchy is a landed estate that has been held in trust for the Monarch since 1399. Although the income is "private," the Queen uses the larger part of it to meet official expenses incurred by other members of the Royal Family. Only the Queen, the Queen Mother, and the Duke of Edinburgh receive payments from Parliament for expenses that are not reimbursed by the Queen. The Duchy of Lancaster survived "suggestions made in the 1550s and again in 1917 that it should be merged into the Exchequer as a cost cutting measure, [thus preserving its] institutional continuity . . . through to the present day."[74]

The Queen's Personal Wealth and Income

The Queen's personal income, derived from her personal investment portfolio, is used to meet private expenditures. These private funds remain a private matter, but the Lord Chamberlain said in 1993 that estimates of £100 million and upward were grossly overstated.[75]

The Queen owns Balmoral and Sandringham, both inherited from her father. She also owns the stud at Sandringham (with a small amount of land in Hampshire), West Illsely Stables, and Sunninghill Park (home of the Duke of York). Income derived from public access to Balmoral and Sandringham is used to meet the costs of managing these properties, with surplus amounts contributed to charity. Her Majesty owns no property outside the United Kingdom.

Estimates of the Queen's wealth have often been greatly exaggerated because

72. *Id.*
73. "Privy Purse, Sources of Funding, Royal Finances," The Official Website of the British Monarchy, <http://www.royal.gov.uk/output/page395.asp>.
74. Hoyle, "Introduction," *supra* note 44, at 7.
75. "The Queen's Personal Wealth and Income, Sources of Funding, Royal Finances," The Official Website of the British Monarchy, <http://www.royal.gov.uk/output/page396.asp>.

they frequently mistakenly include items that are held by the Queen as Monarch of the Kingdom, which are not her private property. These properties include the Royal Palaces, most of the art treasures from the Royal Collection, heirlooms in the Queen's jewelry collection, and the Crown jewels. These "inalienable" items held by Her Majesty as Monarch, rather than as an individual, cannot be disposed of and must be passed on to the next Monarch.

The Future of the Monarchy: Prince Charles

The Prince of Wales does not receive any money from Parliament. Instead, he receives the annual net revenues of the Duchy of Cornwall and uses them to meet the costs of all aspects of his public and private commitments and those of his children.

The Duchy's name is derived from the Earldom of Cornwall (developed from a compilation of lands spread throughout England), which Edward III elevated to a duchy in 1337. The Duchy's founding charter stated that it should be in the stewardship of the Heir Apparent, to provide the Heir with an income independent of the Sovereign or the State. After 660 years, the Duchy's landholdings have altered slightly, but they are still largely agricultural. Today these lands consist of about 51,885 hectares, mostly in the south of England, which are managed on a commercial basis as prescribed by parliamentary legislation.[76]

Prince Charles became the twenty-fourth Duke of Cornwall on Queen Elizabeth's accession to the throne in 1952. He is in effect a trustee of the Duchy's lands and is not entitled to dispose of its assets. The Prince must pass on the estate intact so that it will continue to provide an income for future dukes.

The Duchy's net surplus for the year ending March 31, 2002, was £7,827,000.[77] Because it is part of the Crown's assets, the Duchy is tax exempt, but the Prince of Wales voluntarily pays income tax (currently 40 percent) on his income from it. In time, Charles is expected to inherit his mother's tax-free position, along with Sandringham, Balmoral, the other private estates, and the Queen's vast investment portfolio, part of which she inherited and part of which she accumulated through the judicious use of her private income as Duke of Lancaster—some £500,000 a year, tax free.

Crown Estate Management

The Crown Estate Commissioners publish their annual *Commissioners' Report* online,[78] which includes a description of their financial objectives, financial highlights, and a business review of the Crown Estate Portfolio. The *Report* begins by explain-

---

76. "Financial Arrangements of the Prince of Wales, Royal Finances," The Official Website of the British Monarchy, <http://www.royal.gov.uk/output/page316.asp>.

77. *Id.*

78. *See, e.g., 2003 Report, supra* note 67.

ing that the Crown Estate consists of lands that belong to the Sovereign "in right of the Crown"; they are not the Queen's personal lands, nor are they the property of the Government. The Crown Estate is managed by a Board of Commissioners, with trustee duties that are outlined in the Crown Estate Act of 1961, such as the duty to "maintain and enhance its capital value and the income obtained from it." The eight commissioners are appointed by the Queen based on recommendations of the Prime Minister and are selected based on their skills and experience to provide an appropriate balance for management of the Crown Estates.[79] The board meets seven times during the year and carries out a number of estate visits. A number of firms are appointed to carry out the direct management of the estates and to provide professional advice.

The Crown Estate contains a diverse portfolio of assets, which have evolved from the lands that belonged to King William the Conquerer. These properties are managed by commercial mandates and are guided by principles of social responsibility. Wise management has increased their overall value to £4.06 billion in 2003. The net profits for 2003 were £170.8 million.[80] Although the Crown Estate is part of the hereditary possessions of the Sovereign, the profit is paid to the Exchequer for the benefit of the taxpayers.[81]

The Crown Estate's portfolio is divided into five sections: Urban, Marine, Agriculture, Scotland, and Windsor. The Urban Estate includes more than 600 commercial properties in London and other major cities throughout the United Kingdom and also includes 2,500 residential properties in London, ranging from low-cost flats to elite residences in Kensington and Regent's Park. The Urban Estate accounts for about 75 percent of the Crown Estate's capital value.[82] The Marine section is the second largest business group of the Crown Estate. It includes holdings of half of the foreshore around the United Kingdom, 55 percent of the beds of tidal rivers, and almost all of the seabed out to the 12-mile territorial limit. The Crown Estate manages activities including marine aggregate extraction, pipelines, cables, outfalls, fish farms, ports, jetties and boating facilities, as well as a large number of conservation leases.[83] A major ongoing project of the Marine group is the establishment of an offshore wind-farm industry.[84]

The Agriculture Estate includes 84,000 hectares of agricultural lands and forests. This group also manages mineral resources and quarries producing limestone,

79. *Id.*

80. *2003 Report, supra* note 67, at 10. *See also* Guardian Unlimited Special Reports, "Crown Estate Profits Rise 10.6%," July 10, 2002.

81. *2003 Report, supra* note 67, at 11.

82. *Id.* at 36.

83. *Id.* at 37. The *2002 Report* emphasized that more than 500 leases for fish and shellfish farms have been granted. In addition, the Crown Estate also provided a £600,000 research and development grant to the Fish Farming Research Committee. This committee is represented by experts ranging from the Scottish Environment Protection Agency to the Association of Salmon Fishery Board, who determine which research proposal should be funded. *See id., The 2002 Crown Estate Annual Report and Accounts.*

84. *2002 Report, supra* note 83.

Queen Elizabeth, Prince Charles, and Prince William

sand, gravel, clay, granite, slate, gold, and silver. The commissioners recently helped tenants who suffered because their cattle had been destroyed to deal with foot-and-mouth disease recovery. The Forestry Estate covers some 6,000 hectares, much of which is leased to the Forestry Commission.[85] The Scotland Estate includes urban commercial property, agricultural land, and forests, as well as much of the ocean and shoreline resources around Scotland, comprising about 5 percent of the total value of the Crown Estate.[86] The Windsor Estate includes forest land, Windsor Great Park, the Savill and Valley Gardens, some rental property, and farmlands.[87]

Today, the Crown Estate is pursuing investments such as the further development and branding of Regent Street, which is an exclusive shopping street in London; establishment of winter storage water reservoirs for a number of farms in the Norfolk area; reinvestment in the St. James Estate, including new hotels and refurbishment of the streets in the area; and renovating the Ascot Racecourse on the Windsor Estate.

In 2005, the British Royalty reported that its annual expenses were $67,100,000, costing each British taxpayer $1.12.[88] The *Sunday Times* "Rich List" of 2004 had reported Queen Elizabeth's personal wealth to be $457,000,000, which included her residences at Balmoral and Sandringham, her stamp collection, her private jewelry, and her private investments, but it did not include the castles, palaces, art collections, or crown jewels, which are held in trust to be passed on to her successors.[89]

---

85. *2003 Report, supra* note 67, at 37.

86. *Id.* at 38.

87. *Id.*

88. Associated Press, "British Royals Cost Each Taxpayer $1.12 a Year," *Honolulu Star-Bulletin,* June 23, 2005, at C-8, col. 1.

89. *Id.,* at C-8, col. 3.

Conclusion

During the past millennium, the lands in the British Crown Estates evolved from being owned absolutely by the King to a form of ownership in trust for the benefit of all the people of the United Kingdom, as well as the Crown, with the lands managed by the Crown Estate Commissioners. The early Kings were able to use these lands to gain alliances among vassals and to raise money for war. In later centuries, the Monarchs, with the help of additional revenues from Parliament, continued to rely on these lands as a source of support for their royal responsibilities. Today, with its successful financial portfolio, the Crown Estate is able to support the Monarchy and provide benefits for the people as well.

This evolution was not unlike the evolution of the Crown Lands in Hawai'i. In both situations, as the Kingdoms evolved into Constitutional Monarchies, the Monarchs formalized the recognition that they "owned" the Crown Lands as Trustees for the people. In both cases, the lands came to be managed by commissioners with skill and experience in using assets productively. In both cases, the lands came to be viewed as inalienable. Although some of the revenues supported the activities of the Monarchs, their activities as heads of state were designed primarily to provide leadership and guidance for their people. In both cases, although the Monarchs might be said to own the lands during their reign, or at least to own a life-estate interest in the lands, the beneficial ownership of the lands rested in the people.

28

Claims of Aliʻi Descendants

Because the focus of this volume is the status of the Crown Lands—the lands specifically selected by Kauikeaouli (Kamehameha III) at the time of the Mahele to be under his own personal control in order to support his Monarchy—the book concentrates on the unique role of the Monarchs and the other high Aliʻi. As explained in the beginning chapters, the Aliʻi had important responsibilities, as well as rights, and they understood their duty to mālama (care for) their people and the ʻĀina of the Islands. Even though the Kingdom was eventually lost and much of the land passed into non-Hawaiian control, the Aliʻi tried to avoid this result and protect the ʻĀina for their people, and most Native Hawaiians remember the nineteenth-century Aliʻi with respect and admiration.

With the Native Hawaiian renaissance now in full swing and Native Hawaiians working to build upon their cultural heritage, recover their ʻĀina, and restore their Nation, should the descendants of the nineteenth-century Aliʻi continue to play a special role, with some or all of the rights and responsibilities of the earlier Aliʻi? In particular, do they have some special claim to the Crown Lands? Some serious claims have been put forward by descendants of the nineteenth-century Aliʻi, and the Hawaiʻi State Legislature gave some credibility to these claims in 1977 when it passed a resolution stating that

> the Congress of the United States of America be respectfully requested to enact legislation to compensate the family or families who would be considered to be the highest among the chiefs and would have been considered the presumptive heirs to the throne and the Hawaiian Kingdom for the Crown Lands so taken and damages suffered, and the aborigine or Native Hawaiians for damages suffered by them at the time of the Annexation of the Hawaiian Islands to the United States of America.[1]

---

1. "Senate Resolution 393 Requesting the U.S. Congress to Include Crown Lands Claims as Subject Matter for the Study Commission," proposed by S.J. Res. 4, 95th Cong., 1st Sess., adopted by the Hawaiʻi State Legislature April 14, 1977.

Kamehameha I, sketched by
Louis Choris, published in
1843

Before examining the specific claims, it is useful to review the sequence of leadership during the nineteenth century in order to provide the framework for evaluating the current claimants. Although some of the material that follows is also included in earlier chapters, it is consolidated here in order to provide a capsule summary of the foundation for today's claims by Aliʻi descendants.

Prior to the sustained arrival of westerners that began in 1778, the Hawaiians were divided into many separate communities and political units. Although kingdoms occasionally consisted of small groupings of islands, management of them was difficult because of the challenges of communicating and traveling quickly from one Mokupuni to the next. The islands were finally unified into a single political unit under Kamehameha I in 1810 because of his political leadership, his military skill, and his quick mastery of Western weaponry.[2]

Kamehameha was the poʻolua (shared, two-headed) son of fathers Keouakupuapaikalani and Kahekili by his mother Kekuʻiapoiwa.[3] The date of his birth is disputed, with estimates ranging from 1736 to 1753.[4] Born into the Keawe line of Hawaiʻi

2. Samuel M. Kamakau, *Ruling Chiefs of Hawaii*, 146 (1961, revised ed. 1992). Kamehameha retained Issac Davis and John Young as his advisors so that they could familiarize him with muskets and other weaponry and aid him in warfare. *Id.* at 146–47. "It was through the aid of muskets and of foreigners to instruct in their use that Kamehameha was able in so short a time to bring all of the islands under his rule." *Id.* at 146.

Although Kamehameha controlled Hawaiʻi, Maui, Molokaʻi, Lānaʻi, and Oʻahu after defeating Kalanikupule at the battle of Nuʻuanu in 1795, his attempts to reach Kauaʻi in order to wage war were unsuccessful. In 1810, however, Kaumualiʻi, Mōʻī of Kauaʻi, ceded his kingdom of Kauaʻi and Niʻihau to Kamehameha in order to avoid bloodshed. John Papa Ii, *Fragments of Hawaiian History*, 15–16 (1959, revised ed. 1983).

3. Hawaiian Studies Institute, "Genealogy of the Chiefs of Na Lani Kamehameha" (June 1994) (on file at the Kamehameha Schools Bishop Estate Archives, Midkiff Learning Center).

4. Kamakau, *supra* note 2, at 66. It is generally agreed that Kamehameha's place of birth was Kapaʻakai, Kokoiki, Kohala, on the Island of Hawaiʻi. *Id.* at 210.

Ali'i, Kamehameha was carried away immediately following his birth, and until the age of five was raised in the Kohala region of Hawai'i by Nae'ole, the Ali'i of Kohala.[5] Kamehameha was then returned to his great uncle Alapa'i (ruler of Hawai'i), whose wife Keaka was appointed his guardian.[6] Shortly after the death of Keouakupuapai-kalani, Kamehameha's uncle Kalaniopu'u defeated Alapa'i and became Ali'i Nui of Hawai'i.[7] Kamehameha then went to live with his mother until her death, where-upon he fulfilled the wish of Keouakupuapaikalani by joining the court of his uncle Kalaniopu'u.[8]

Kamehameha thrived in the court of Kalaniopu'u, excelling in the various martial arts and sports.[9] He was noted for his skill as a warrior and became a favorite of his uncle.[10] Although Kalaniopu'u's son, Kalanikauikeaoulikiwala'o, was desig-nated heir to the kingdom, Kalaniopu'u left his war god, Kuka'ilimoku, to Kameha-meha.[11] This bestowal facilitated Kamehameha's rise to power, because he used the art of war to gain mana and 'Āina.

In order to increase his own linkage to the highest Ali'i ranks, Kamehameha carefully selected Keopuolani as one of his wives.[12] Keopuolani was an Akua by vir-tue of the fact that she was a Nī'aupi'o Ali'i.[13] Keopuolani was also Kamehameha's niece, because her mother was his half sister (their father was Kalanikupuapaikala-nikeoua).[14] Kamehameha and Keopuolani's marriage was thus a Nī'aupi'o (intra-family) union, and their children (Liholiho, Kauikeaouli, and Nahienaena), were Akua of sufficient rank to be considered possible candidates to become Mō'ī.

After Kamehameha died in 1819, his son Liholiho became Mō'ī as Kamehameha II.[15] The direct heirs of Kamehameha continued to rule as Monarchs until the death of Lot Kapuāiwa (Kamehameha V) in 1872. Because Lot died without direct heirs and failed to appoint a successor, a public election was held among all the male sub-jects of the Kingdom to select a new Mō'ī.[16] Several candidates were suggested, but

---

5. *Id.* at 69.

6. Ii, *supra* note 2, at 3.

7. *Id.* at 4. Kalaniopu'u was the older brother of Keouakupuapaikalani and thus Kamehameha's uncle. *Id.* at 3.

8. *Id.* at 6.

9. *Id.* at 7.

10. Kamakau, *supra* note 2, at 84.

11. *Id.* at 107.

12. The exact number of Kamehameha's wives is debated because historical records providing docu-mentation of this history were destroyed. Bingham compiled a list of twenty-one wives, but earlier studies done by Kawena Pukui showed twenty-six. Because the genealogy records collected by Pukui are missing, it is now difficult to trace more than twenty-one wives. Telephone interview with Rubellite K. K. Johnson (August 26, 1996).

13. Lilikala Kame'eleihiwa, *Native Land and Foreign Desires: Pehea La E Pono Ai?* 42 (1992). Keopuo-lani's mother (Kuku'iapoiwa Liliha) and father (Kiwala'o) were half brother and half sister; thus she was an Akua. *Id.*

14. *Id.*

15. Kamakau, *supra* note 2, at 219.

16. 2 Ralph S. Kuykendall, *The Hawaiian Kingdom 1854–1874: Twenty Critical Years,* 243 (1953, reprinted 1982). The Legislature confirmed the election results and recognized Lunalilo as Mō'ī. *Id.* at 244. *See* discussion *supra* in chapter 10.

King David Kalākaua

the race narrowed to William Charles Lunalilo and David Kalākaua.[17] Lunalilo won the election but died after holding office for only a little more than a year.[18]

Like his predecessor Lot Kapuāiwa, Lunalilo failed to name a successor, and a legislative election had to be held upon his death. In this second election, in 1874, Kalākaua competed with Queen Emma for the throne.[19] Although Kalākaua was selected by the legislators, many questioned the appropriateness of his ascending to the throne (because he was not of the Kamehameha line, and also because some viewed him as being too pro-United States), and a riot by Queen Emma's followers broke out after the election.[20] Nonetheless, Kalākaua reigned for seventeen years, and he was succeeded by his sister Lili'uokalani after he died in San Francisco in 1891.[21] Lili'uokalani ruled for two years until the overthrow of the Kingdom in 1893 by westerners, who received crucial support from the United States.[22]

---

17. 2 Kuykendall, *supra* note 16, at 243.

18. Kame'eleihiwa, *supra* note 13, at 313. David Kalākaua was born on November 16, 1836, to Kapa'akea and Keohokalole. Although Kalākaua was an Ali'i who—like Kamehameha—traced his lineage to Keaweikekahiali'iikamoku (generally referred to as Keawe), he was actually a cousin to the Kamehamehas, descending from another of Keawe's wives named Lonoma'aikanaka. What is considered to be the Kamehameha line descends from Keawe and his wife (and sister) Kalanikauleleiaiwi.

19. 3 Ralph S. Kuykendall, *The Hawaiian Kingdom 1874–1893: The Kalakaua Dynasty,* 8–9 (1967, reprinted 1987); *see* discussion *supra* in chapter 11, text at notes 1–9.

20. Kame'eleihiwa, *supra* note 13, at 313; *see supra* chapter 11, text at note 10.

21. Kame'eleihiwa, *supra* note 13, at 315–16.

22. *See* "Joint Resolution to Acknowledge the 100th Anniversary of the January 17, 1893 Overthrow of the Kingdom of Hawaii," whereas para. 9, Pub. L. No. 103-150, 107 Stat. 1510 (1993); and *see supra* chapter 16.

The customs observed in Kamehameha's time changed dramatically during the years immediately following his death. Warfare and the use of the god Ku to gain status and power became less popular among the Ali'i. The breaking of the 'Aikapu by Ka'ahumanu and Liholiho in 1819 and the subsequent renunciation of the kapu system by a large portion of the people brought precontact practices and beliefs into question.[23] The sacred Nī'aupi'o unions were denounced as "incest" by the missionaries, so Ali'i were challenged to establish their qualification and ability to rule in other ways. The staggering decline in population and virtual collapse of the precontact social system threatened both the Ali'i and the maka'āinana who looked to them for leadership to find a new state of pono (goodness, balance), and to do so quickly.

These and other forces convinced the Mō'ī to identify contemporary methods of evaluating status and aptitude to rule. With the promulgation of the Constitution of 1840, the Kingdom slowly evolved into a Constitutional Monarchy and formalized the rights and responsibilities of the Mō'ī. Kauikeaouli's later introduction of the more detailed Constitution of 1852 simplified the qualifications for the position of Mō'ī to a matter of appointment and proclamation.[24] Despite these "new" methods of ranking Mō'ī and other Ali'i, many individuals continued to embrace precontact standards and expectations. The indeterminate and ambiguous degree to which precontact standards were applied and intermingled with newer criteria and selection mechanisms has complicated the process of assessing current claims based on Ali'i status and genealogy.

Individual Ali'i other than the Mō'ī began asserting rights to the Crown Lands as early as 1864.[25] These claims have varied in theory and character, but all are based on some genealogical link to the Kamehameha line, their relation to William Charles Lunalilo, or their connection to the Kalākaua Dynasty.

Kamehameha Crown Lands Corporation

The descendants of Elizabeth Keka'ani'au Pratt, who was the great-great-granddaughter of Kalokuokamaile (the older half brother of Kamehameha I), have maintained that title to all of the Crown Lands as well as compensation for use of these lands by the Federal Government since 1893 belongs to their 'ohana.[26] Elizabeth

---

23. Kame'eleihiwa, *supra* note 13, at 67–68.

24. Article 25 of the 1852 Constitution restricted the Crown to "His Majesty Kamehameha III during his life and to his successor. *The successor shall be the person whom the King and the House of Nobles shall appoint and publicly proclaim as such, during the King's life;* but should there be no such appointment and proclamation, then the successor shall be chosen by the House of Nobles and the House of Representatives in joint ballot." (Emphasis added.) Hawaiian Kingdom Constitutions are available online at http:www.hawaii-nation.org/constitution-1852.html and at http:www.pixi.com/kingdom.

25. In 1864, during the probate of his late Majesty Alexander Liholiho, Queen Emma asserted her right of dower to the Crown Lands. For additional information see *In the Matter of the Estate of His Majesty Kamehameha IV,* 2 Hawai'i 715 (1864), and chapter 8 *supra.*

26. Telephone interview with Monica Wilcox-Hatori, President of the Kamehameha Crown Land Corporation, July 24, 1996. Interview with members of the Kamehameha Crown Land Corporation, August 5,

Kekaʻaniʻau was born in 1834 to Princess Theresa Owana Kaheiheimalie and Gideon Laʻanui.[27] She was raised in her father's home in Haleʻiwa but boarded at the Royal School while she was being educated there.[28] Throughout her life and travels in the Islands, Elizabeth Kekaʻaniʻau recognized her role as an Aliʻi and cared for her people.[29] Because she was the last survivor of the Aliʻi who attended the Royal School, many assert that she should have ascended the throne after Queen Liliʻuokalani.[30] The individuals making this claim do not claim direct lineage from Elizabeth Kekaʻaniʻau, because she was childless, but rather from her brother, Gideon Kailipalaki Laʻanui.[31] They state that they "are the descendants of Princess Theresa Owana Kaohelelani Wilcox, and directly related to the High Chieftess Elizabeth Kekaʻaniʻau Pratt."[32] Princess Theresa Owana was the daughter of Gideon Laʻanui and was adopted by Elizabeth Kekaʻaniʻau after her father died. She had four husbands, producing four children from her first two, Alexander Cartwright III and Robert William Kalanihiapo Wilcox.[33]

In 1977, five individuals in this ʻohana filed a 111-page petition with the U.S. Congress "for reparation relative to the taking by the United States Government of certain lands known as the Crown Lands."[34] They argued that when Kauikeaouli (Kamehameha III) designated certain parcels of ʻĀina as Crown Lands in the Mahele of 1848, he reserved those pieces as "his own private property" to be retained for

---

1996. Kalokuokamaile was the son of Keoua and Kahikikala, and Kamehameha I was the son of Keoua and Kekuiapoiwa. Membership in the Kamehameha Crown Land Corporation is open to the general public for those interested in seeking the return of title to the Crown Lands to KCLC.

27. George S. Kanahele, *Emma: Hawaiʻi's Remarkable Queen,* 26 (1999);

28. Telephone interview with Myrtle Kinau Schumann, KCLC, January 20, 1997.

29. *Id.*

30. *Id.*

31. Elizabeth Kekaʻaniʻau did not have any direct heirs. Members of the KCLC, however, make their claim through Kekaʻaniʻau (as opposed to Laʻanui) because she was the last surviving member of the Royal School and thus the last individual from this group eligible to assume the throne. *Id.*

32. "Crown Land Compensation Claim," presented to 95th Cong., 1st Sess. (1977), at i.

33. Cartwright was the grandson of the father of baseball and Wilcox was an active military and political leader described *supra* in chapters 14–17. Daisy Emmalani Cartwright and Eva Kuwailanimamao Cartwright were born from the first marriage and Robert Kalanikupuapaikaininui Wilcox and Virginia Kahoa Kaahumanu Kaihikapumahana Wilcox were born from the second.

34. *Id.* The five named petitioners were Helen Kalokuokamaile Wilcox Salazar, 1363 N. King Street, Honolulu, Hawaiʻi 96817; Viola Marguerite Kapiolani Waltjen, 1362 Wanaka, Honolulu, Hawaiʻi 96818; Myrtle Kinau Schumann, 98-851 "D" Iho Place, ʻAiea, Hawaiʻi 96701; Robert K. Keoua Wilcox, Jr., 3154 Waiʻalae Avenue, Box 204, Honolulu, Hawaiʻi 96816; and George Montague Anthanasius Keeaumoku Wilcox, 436 171st Place N.E., Bellevue, Washington 98008. This petition was filed by Attorney Dennis M. Hindman of Bellingham, Washington.

A separate petition was filed by former Hawaiʻi Supreme Court Justice Kazuhisa Abe of Honolulu on June 27, 1977, on behalf of Gordon Lunalilo Wilcox, Gertrude Kapiolani Toledo, and others who were also related to Elizabeth Kekaʻaniʻau and Theresa Owana Wilcox. "Petition in the Matter of Senate Joint Resolution No. 4," Senate, 95th Cong.

See generally Leonard Lueras, "Alii Heirs, Too, Want Reparations," *Honolulu Advertiser,* April 5, 1976, at A-3, listing potential claimants at A-6; Milton Rubincam, "America's Only Royal Family: Genealogy of the Former Hawaiian Ruling House," *National Genealogical Society Quarterly* (1962, reprinted 1968) (on file in the Hawaiian-Pacific Collection, University of Hawaiʻi Library).

himself and "his heirs, and successors forever." [35] Further, they pointed out that the Mō'ī established the Royal School to "create a pool of eligibles" of individuals of royal lineage qualified to ascend to the throne.[36] In the event that a Mō'ī died without issue, the new Monarch would be chosen from this pool of eligibles.[37]

The Royal School (also called the Chiefs' Children's School) clearly played a central and defining role in the life of the young Ali'i.[38] This school was established in June 1839 by missionary teacher Amos Starr Cooke and his wife Juliette Montague Cooke, first in their home and after April 1840 in a school building complete with boarding facilities.[39] The Royal School was in operation from June 1839 to 1850, and during this period the Cookes educated sixteen young Ali'i.[40] The object of the school was to educate these future chiefs in Western practices and religion in order to "qualify them for their future stations and duties in life." [41]

Because Elizabeth Keka'ani'au was among the sixteen children selected to attend the Royal School and was the last living survivor, those related to her have asserted that her heirs are entitled to the Crown Lands. Elizabeth Keka'ani'au was also included in a list of fifteen "Princes and Chiefs Eligible to Be Rulers" published in 1844.[42] Members of this 'ohana have argued further that the Republic of Hawaii

---

35. Interview with members of the Kamehameha Crown Land Corporation, August 5, 1996.

36. *Id.*

37. *Id.* The list of Ali'i children who attended the Royal School is found *supra* in chapter 3, note 64, and is reprinted here because of its importance to the present discussion:

Complete list of children in the school from report furnished to Mr. Wyllie by Mr. Cooke, 1844. Chiefs' Children's School . . . 3. Names, Ages, Rank, Parentage, etc.:

1. Moses Kekuaiwa . . . 2. Lot Kamehameha [also called Lot Kapuaiwa, who became Kamehameha V] . . . 3. Alexander Liholiho [who became Kamehameha IV] . . . 4. Victoria Kamamalu . . . 5. William Charles Lunalilo . . . 6. Bernice Pauahi . . . 7. Abigail Maheha . . . 8. Jane Loeau . . . 9. *Elizabeth Kekaniau, daughter of La'anui and Oana Ana (daughter of John Rives), born Jan. 2, 1836.* 10. Emma Rooke . . . 11. Peter Young Kaeo . . . 12. James Kaliokaani . . . 13. David Kalākaua . . . 14. Lydia Makaeha [Lili'uokalani] . . . 15. Polly Paaina. [A sixteenth pupil, John Pitt Kinau, entered after 1844.]

Mary Atherton Richards, *The Hawaiian Chiefs' Children's School,* v (1970) (emphasis added). Five of these children (Alexander Liholiho, Lot, William Charles Lunalilo, David Kalākaua, and Lili'uokalani) eventually became Mō'ī.

38. *See generally* Kanahele, *supra* note 27, at 23–40 (1999); Helena G. Allen, *The Betrayal of Liliuokalani: Last Queen of Hawaii 1838–1917,* at 47–65 (1982); Elizabeth Kekaaniauokalani Kalaninuiohilaukapu Pratt, *History of Keoua Kalanikupuapa-i-kalani-nui, Father of Hawaii Kings, and His Descendants, with Notes on Kamehameha I, First King of All Hawaii,* 52–55 (1920).

39. "Family School for the Children of the Chiefs," *The Polynesian,* July 4, 1840.

40. *Id.;* Merze Tate, "The Sandwich Island Missionaries Lay the Foundation for a System of Public Instruction in Hawaii," 30:4 *Journal of Negro Education,* 396, 402–03 (fall 1961). After the Cookes retired, "children of white residents began attending as day pupils, [and] the Royal School became a select academy housed in a new and commodious structure erected in pleasing surroundings in the suburbs of Honolulu. . . . By 1853 the young chiefs were in a minority, for 95 of the Royal School's 121 pupils were white, 8 were Hawaiian, and 18 part-Hawaiian." *Id.,* citing *Report of the Minister of Public Instruction,* 1854, at 9.

41. "Family School for the Children of the Chiefs," *The Polynesian,* July 4, 1840.

42. "Princes and Chiefs Eligible to Be Rulers," *The Polynesian,* July 20, 1844, at 1, col. 3. The others included in this list were Alexander Liholiho ("Heir Apparent to the Crown"), Moses Kekuaiwa ("Expectant Gov. of Kauai"), Lot Kamehameha ("Expectant Gov. of Maui"), William Lunalilo, Victoria Kamamalu ("Expectant Premier"), Belinda Pauahi, David Kalākaua, Polly Paaina, Jane Loeau, James Kali, Peter Young Kaeo, Emma Rooke, Abigail Maheha, and Lydia Kamakaeha. *Id.* These are the same individuals listed *supra*

in 1894 and the United States in 1898 illicitly combined the private property of the Kamehamehas (the Crown Lands) with the Government Lands to create what is now the Public Lands Trust.

Franklin S. Pratt—a U.S. citizen from New England who was the husband of Elizabeth Kekaʻaniʻau and was serving in San Francisco as the Consul-General of the Hawaiian Government—wrote to the Vice President of the United States (and President of the Senate) Levi P. Morgan in February 1893, right after the overthrow, protesting the merging of the Crown Lands with the Government Lands and explaining that it would be a "an act of injustice" for the United States to "confiscat[e] a large amount of property, without investigation or compensation." [43] He emphasized that the Crown Lands had been held in trust and that the revenues they generated "have never been treated as public revenue, available for appropriation, by the Hawaiian Legislature, but has gone to sustain the state and dignity of Hawaiian sovereigns up to the date of the late revolution." [44] He also wrote a letter to the *San Francisco Chronicle* at the same time arguing that the Provisional Government "has no more right to cede the private lands of the Kamehamehas [referring to the Crown Lands], now that the crown has been suppressed, than it has to transfer the Bishop or Lunalilo estates, or any other lands owned or held in trust under bequests from members of the Kamehameha line." [45] He asserted that "[t]he ex-Queen and her heirs have no claim whatever to the reversion of these lands," but, because they were part of the "private lands" of Kamehameha III, they "should revert to his heirs" according to his will. [46] On March 28, 1893, shortly after these protests, which Pratt had signed as "Hawaiian Consul-General" in San Francisco, Pratt was relieved of his post by Sanford Ballard Dole and the Executory and Advisory Council of the Provisional Government. [47]

Because the Crown Lands were the private property of the Aliʻi for the maintenance of the Crown, the Aliʻi descendants now argue, the United States and later the State of Hawaiʻi acted improperly in claiming title. Their 1977 Petition to Congress asserted that although the Hawaiian commoners "were able to acquire fishing, wood gathering and occupation rights in the Crown Lands, such rights were subject to spe-

---

note 36 as those attending the Royal School, although a few names are different (i.e., "Belinda Pauahi" referred to "Bernice Pauahi" and "Lydia Kamekaeha" referred to "Liliʻuokalani").

43. F. S. Pratt, "Telegram of Protest," sent to Vice President Levi P. Morgan, February 16, 1893, attached to letter from Pratt to Sanford B. Dole, Minister of Foreign Affairs, Provisional Government, February 23, 1893, Hawaiʻi State Archives; "Crown Land Compensation Claim," *supra* note 32, at 42.

44. *Id.*

45. F. S. Pratt, "Are They Private: The Crown Lands of the Hawaiian Kingdom," Letter to the Editor, *San Francisco Chronicle,* February 1893, attached to letter from Pratt to Sanford B. Dole, Minister of Foreign Affairs, Provisional Government, February 23, 1893, Hawaiʻi State Archives.

46. *Id.*

47. Letter from F. S. Pratt to Sanford B. Dole, Minister of Foreign Affairs, Provisional Government, April 11, 1893. In this letter, Pratt acknowledged that he registered his protest on behalf of his wife's claim using his official title but said he did not know how he could have acted on this personal matter without identifying himself in this fashion. He also noted that he had not opposed annexation "in any way" and stated that "reporters in this city have seen fit to publish an interview with me that never took place." *Id.*

cific permission of the Commissioners" of the Crown Lands,[48] and thus that their "use was not a vested right and that the only vested right was in the King, and, at the present time, in the Claimants herein."[49]

In 1989, individuals in this 'ohana organized the Kamehameha Crown Lands Corporation (KCLC) to pursue a claim to the Crown Lands by virtue of their Ali'i lineage. The basis of KCLC's claim is Elizabeth Keka'ani'au's right to the throne. Its members have encouraged other individuals of Ali'i descent to present their genealogies, and they have said that they believe that the Crown Lands should go to the highest ranking descendants of the Kamehameha line. KCLC members have taken the position that King Kalākaua and Queen Lili'uokalani were entitled to only a possessory interest to the Crown Lands (by virtue of their ascending the throne) but not fee simple title, because they were not of the Kamehameha line and because Kauikeaouli (Kamehameha III) specifically reserved the Crown Lands as his "personal private property for his heirs and successors forever."

If the Crown Lands were returned to these descendants, the members of KCLC believe that title should be vested in their family-based corporation, with management decisions made by a majority of its members.[50] Although KCLC's position is that the Crown Lands are now the private property of the heirs of the Kamehameha line, they favor working with as many individuals as possible in the interests of the majority of the Native Hawaiian People. In fact, the KCLC members view the return of the Crown Lands as enabling them to "fulfill their role as Ali'i" and to "be of service to the land, and the people."[51] Monica Wilcox-Hatori, President of KCLC, has explained that the Crown Lands were "originally to sustain the Crown . . . but now their purpose is to sustain the people, and the dignity of the race."[52] Members have discussed using revenues generated by the lands to finance education and provide universal health coverage for Native Hawaiians. Others have described homesteading programs and providing land for all those needing a place to live. KCLC members have expressed their desire to gain actual control of the Crown Lands, as opposed to mere revenue or other compensation, but they understand that as Ali'i they have responsibilities to provide for the people with the revenues generated by these lands.

For a time, the sovereignty organization Ka Lāhui[53] emphasized the importance of establishing an Ali'i Council as a "fourth branch" of the Native Hawaiian Government and had identified Noa Salazar, the son of Owana Ka'ohelelani Salazar, as the Ali'i Nui of Ka Lāhui Hawai'i.[54] In 1998, the two Salazars withdrew from

---

48. *Id.* at 33.

49. *Id.* at ii.

50. Interview with members of the Kamehameha Crown Land Corporation, August 5, 1996.

51. *Id.*

52. Interview with Monica Wilcox-Hatori, August 5, 1996.

53. Ka Lāhui was active in the 1980s and 1990s, seeking to form a government for Native Hawaiians and to pursue the return of land and resources.

54. *See, e.g.,* Lee McDonald, "Hawaiian Royals Visit Cherokee Emperor at Royal Gala," *Cherokee Observer,* October 1994, at 17. Owana Salazar, an accomplished musical entertainer, is the direct descendant of Princess Theresa Owana Ka'ohelelani La'anui and Robert K. Wilcox.

their exclusive relationship with Ka Lāhui but continued to claim the Crown Lands.[55] Owana Salazar explained at that time that

> My family holds the legitimate claim to all the crown lands of Hawaii. It has always been my family's desire to claim the lands for our people. We hoped back in '86 that our claims could come forward with Ka Lāhui, but they were not interested. They thought they should claim the land, but they cannot. The only ones who can claim the crown lands are people of the crown, and that's my family.[56]

She also explained at that time why her claim was superior to that of the Kawananakoas (discussed below):

> I don't see any Kawananakoa in the 1844 list [of students at the Royal School]. David Kawananakoa and Jonah Kūhiō were the nephews of Queen Kapiolani from her sister. To say that they would enter the line of succession would be like saying in England that Prince Consort Philip's nephews would become king before William.[57]

Rubellite Kawena Kinney Johnson

Another Kamehameha descendant asserting a claim to the Crown Lands as a matter of birthright is Rubellite Kawena Kinney Johnson,[58] a retired professor of Hawaiian language and literature at the University of Hawai'i at Mānoa,[59] who has said she is the great-granddaughter of Kamehameha I and High Chiefess Ka'akaupalahalaha of Moloka'i.[60] Professor Johnson has made numerous contributions in the areas of Hawaiian history, culture, and arts.

Professor Johnson filed a complaint on November 21, 1991, in the United States Claims Court to establish that living descendants of the Kamehameha line are the true owners of the Crown Lands and should be awarded title and monetary compensation.[61] On November 22, 1991 (the very next day), Judge Christine Cook

---

55. Dan Boylan, "Battle Royal," *Midweek Magazine,* August 7–13, 1998, available at http://www.hawaii-nation.org/midweek-owana.html.

56. *Id.*

57. *Id. See also* Dan Nakano, "Another Royal Scion Presses Claim: Hearing Urged on Annexation," *Honolulu Advertiser,* July 24, 1998.

58. "Answer for Appellant," at A-34 to A-38, *Johnson v. United States,* No. 92-5058, 976 F.2d 747 (Fed. Cir. 1992).

59. *Id.* at A-46 to A-56.

60. Letter from Rubellite K. K. Johnson to Lee MacDonald, Chief Genealogist, Society of American Royalty, November 19, 1997 (on file with the author). The Society of American Royalty in Dallas, Texas, has not accepted this claim but has said that Professor Johnson is the descendant of Kamehamehanui-Ai'Luau, who ruled Maui and Moloka'i a generation before Kamehameha I united the Islands. This lineage, according to the Society, would give Professor Johnson "a very high and notable pedigree" but not royalty. Letter from Lee MacDonald, Chief Genealogist, Society of American Royalty, Dallas, Texas to Whom It May Concern, November 29, 1997 (on file with the author).

61. "Brief and Appendix for the United States as Appellee," at 5, *Johnson v. United States,* No. 92-5058, 976 F.2d 747 (Fed. Cir. 1992).

Nettesheim dismissed Johnson's complaint for lack of subject-matter jurisdiction and because the six-year statute of limitations governing most claims brought to the Claims Court had expired long ago.[62] Johnson appealed, but the judgment of the lower court was affirmed by the Federal Circuit on August 10, 1992.[63] On November 19, 1991, Johnson had filed a similar action in United States District Court for the District of Hawai'i, which was also dismissed,[64] and she filed another such claim in 1995.[65]

Professor Johnson is the president and founder of the Princess Nahoa 'Ōlelo O Kamehameha Society. This association was established and committed, in part, to "preserving and expanding the moral and social integrity of Hawaiian Culture, [and] the integrity of individual property rights set forth in the Great Mahele."[66] The society's position has been similar to that advocated by Professor Johnson in court—that Lot Kapuāiwa (Kamehameha V) ascended to the throne unconstitutionally because the Legislature never confirmed his ascension to the throne, as was required by Article 25 of the 1852 Constitution.[67] According to the society's views, when the Republic of Hawaii was declared following the overthrow of Lili'uokalani, the Crown Lands were appropriated "without deference to constitutional due process as required by law wherein the Kamehameha heirs could have exercised their reversionary rights."[68] Thus, Professor Johnson and the Princess Nahoa 'Ōlelo O Kamehameha Society have sought to exercise what they have believed is their constitutionally protected right of due process. The organization has publicly proclaimed that it would bring suit against any action "leading to or affecting transfer of title and/or administration of the Crown Lands portion of the Ceded Lands Trust to any entity, party or designee other than to ALL the legitimate and verifiable living lineal heirs of Kamehameha IV (according to and respecting long established Hawaiian Laws of Succession)."[69]

This claim is grounded on the absence of a legislative election confirming Lot's ascent to the throne in 1863,[70] but its primary weakness is that the allocation of the throne to Kamehameha V was accepted at the time even though the constitutional requirement of a confirming election did not take place.[71] Many contemporary historical accounts recognized the rule of Lot Kapuāiwa as legitimate, and this accep-

---

62. The decision of the Claims Court is published at *Johnson v. United States,* 976 F.2d, 747 (Table), 1992 WL 188872 (Text) (Fed. Cir. 1992). The time for filing suit is in 28 U.S.C. sec. 2501.

63. *Johnson v. United States,* 976 F.2d 747 (Table), 1992 WL 188872 (Text) (Fed. Cir. 1992).

64. *Johnson v. United States,* No. 91-662 (D. Hawai'i, complaint filed November 19, 1991).

65. *Johnson v. United States,* Civ. No. 95-00148 HG (D. Hawai'i, 1995).

66. *Declaration of the Princess Nahoa Olelo O Kamehameha Society,* 1 (February 12, 1993) (on file with author).

67. *See, e.g.,* "Memorandum in Support of Motion for Summary Judgment," filed June 16, 1995, at 8, in *Johnson v. United States,* Civ. No. 95-00148 HG (D. Hawai'i, 1995); *see supra* chapter 7, text at notes 8–13.

68. *Declaration of the Princess Nahoa Olelo O Kamehameha Society,* 3 (February 12, 1993) (on file with author).

69. *Id.* at 5.

70. *See supra* chapter 7, text at notes 8–10.

71. For additional information, see chapter 7 *supra.*

tance of his rule as Kamehameha V complicates Professor Johnson's claim to the Crown Lands.

The Kalākaua Heirs

Not all Ali'i descendants have asserted a claim to the Crown Lands. The living heirs of David Kalākaua, for example, have not expressed any claim to these lands, even though they have worked to perpetuate the traditions and artistic creations of the Hawaiian royalty. King Kalākaua and his sister Queen Lili'uokalani traced their royal lineage through their father Kapa'akea, who was the great-grandson of Keawe and Lonoma'aikanaka.[72] Kalākaua and his wife Kapi'olani did not have any children of their own. Kalākaua's sister Lili'uokalani (who married John O. Dominis) was also childless, and his brother William Pitt Leliohoku died of rheumatic fever when he was twenty-two.[73] Kalākaua's other sister, Princess Miriam Likelike, had one child in 1875, Princess Victoria Kai'ulani, but she died tragically, also of rheumatism, in 1899 when she was twenty-three.[74]

Shortly after his election as Mō'ī, Kalākaua ordered the issuance of Letters Patent granting Queen Kapi'olani's sister Esther Kinoiki Kekaulike (and her children) honorary title on February 10, 1883. King Kalākaua later named the sons of Princess Kinoiki Kekaulike and her husband David Kahalepouli Pi'ikoi—Prince David Laamea Kahalepouli Kawananakoa and Prince Jonah Kūhiō Kalaniana'ole[75]—as his heirs to the throne.[76] Queen Lili'uokalani also later confirmed that these nephews of hers should be considered heirs to the throne after Princess Kai'ulani.[77]

Because the Kalākaua Dynasty was in control of the Monarchy at the time of the 1893 overthrow, it is plausible that their designated heirs might assert a claim to the Crown and to the Crown Lands. In 1910, Queen Lili'uokalani brought suit in the United States Court of Claims for the return of her portion of the revenues generated by the Crown Lands after the properties were seized by the Provisional Government and later ceded to the United States.[78] Although the Court denied Queen Lili'uokalani's request, some individuals believe that current heirs could seek some form of reparation.

Prince David Kawananakoa married Abigail Wahiikaahuula Campbell, the eldest daughter of industrialist James Campbell. Three children were born during

---

72. *See supra* chapter 11, note 11.

73. Kristin Zambucka, *Princess Kaiulani: The Last Hope of Hawaii's Monarchy*, 4 (1984).

74. *Id.* at 128–29.

75. Prince Kūhiō was elected to be the nonvoting delegate from the Territory of Hawai'i to the U.S. House of Representatives and played a major role in the enactment of the Hawaiian Homes Commission Act, as described *supra* in chapter 22. He married Elizabeth Kahanu, but they had no children.

76. Interview with Quentin Kawananakoa, July 31, 1996. The third son of Princess Kinoiki Kekaulike and her husband David Kahalepouli Pi'ikoi—Edward Keli'iahonui—died when he was eighteen. A. Grove Day, *History Makers of Hawaii*, 73 (1984).

77. Interview with Quentin Kawananakoa, July 31, 1996.

78. *Liliuokalani v. United States,* 45 Ct. Cl. 418 (1910); *see generally supra* chapter 21.

Princess Abigail Kinoiki Kekaulike Kawananakoa *(back row, with lei)* with the members of the Hawai'i State Senate, April 2006

this marriage: Abigail Kapi'olani[79] (who had three children), Edward David Kalākaua Kawananakoa (who had no children), and Lydia Kamakaeha Liliuokalani Kawananakoa (who married William Ellerbrock and had one child, Abigail Kinoiki Kekaulike Kawananakoa). This young princess was adopted as a hānai child by her grandmother Abigail Wahiikaahuula Campbell Kawananakoa in order to recognize her priority as royal heir (and as heiress to the Campbell Estate).[80]

Descendants of Prince David Kawananakoa have, however, declined to assert any individual claims to the Crown Lands. Princess Abigail Kinoiki Kekaulike Kawananakoa, who celebrated her eightieth birthday in April 2006 and who was described by U.S. Senator Daniel Inouye as "a member of the family with the closest blood ties to the Kalākaua dynasty,"[81] has devoted much of her life to restoring 'Iolani Palace in Honolulu and preserving the important creations of the Native Hawaiians. Just as

---

79. Prince David issued a declaration that Abigail Kapi'olani was not his daughter, but the significance of this declaration has been disputed. *See* "Abigail Kapiolani Kawananakoa," *Wikipedia,* http://en.wikipedia.org/wiki/Abigail_Kapiolani_Kawananakoa.

80. Abigail Kinoike Kekaulike Kawananakoa has played an active role in the restoration of Iolani Palace, and in 2005–06 she was active through the foundation Na Lei Alii Kawananakoa in litigation to recover eighty-three valuable Hawaiian artifacts that were found in 1905 on the Big Island but were taken from the Bishop Museum and reburied in 2000 by the group Hui Malama I Na Kupuna 'O Hawai'i Nei.

81. Senator Daniel Inouye, "Anniversary of Coronation of King Kalākaua," 129 *Congressional Record,* 10,098 (April 27, 1983).

King David Kalākaua worked during his reign to "restor[e] so many of the ancient customs, symbols, and rites of his own people and of the age-old line of kings and princes from whom he descended and whose living successor he was,"[82] Princess Abigail Kinoiki Kekaulike Kawananakoa has sought also to carry forward these traditions into the coming generations:

> We are the future of the Hawaiian nation. In our desire to enjoy and preserve our heritage we are not so very different from Kalākaua's people of 1883. Like our forebearers who came to these grounds a century ago we may, if we chose, draw strength and pride and hope from the works of David Kalākaua. The past, the present, and the future are one in the calculus of the ages, but one century ago a spark of brilliance lit the Pacific, a moment of glory was ours, and it is that spark, that moment that we remember today.[83]

One of Abigail Kapiʻolani's grandsons, Quentin Kawananakoa, who served in the Hawaiʻi House of Representatives from 1994 to 1998,[84] has explained that he views the Crown Lands as "part and parcel"[85] of the Public Land Trust for the purpose of "bettering the nation."[86] Quentin Kawananakoa entered the race for a seat in the U.S. House of Representatives in 1998 but dropped out of that race because of health problems. He subsequently served as a commissioner on the Hawaiian Homes Commission and in 2006 once again entered the campaign for a seat in the U.S. House of Representatives.[87]

Representative Kawananakoa has expressed his belief that although the Public Trust Lands must be governed in light of their history and purpose, the notion of the Crown Lands as private property is not the same as it was in the time of the Kingdom.[88] Although he agrees that the Crown Lands were the private property of Kauikeaouli (Kamehameha III), he has explained that this status ended with the legislative Act of January 3, 1865,[89] which confirmed the Supreme Court's 1864 decision—*In Re Estate of His Majesty Kamehameha IV*[90]—and deemed the Crown Lands to be the

---

82. Abigail Kinoiki Kekaulike Kawananakoa, "The Importance of the Coronation to Hawaii" (speech given at ʻIolani Palace marking the 100th anniversary of the 1883 coronation of King David Kalākaua), 129 *Congressional Record,* 10,099 (April 27, 1983).

83. *Id.*

84. Quentin is one of the five children (and three other stepchildren) of Edward Abnel Keliiahonui Kawananakoa, who was one of the three children of Abigail Kapiʻolani Kawananakoa. As explained *supra* note 79, Abigail Kapiʻolani Kawananakoa was the eldest daughter of Abigail Wahiikaahuula Campbell Kawananakoa, the wife of Prince David Kawananakoa, and was born during their marriage. *See* "Abigail Kapiolani Kawananakoa," *Wikipedia,* http://en.wikipedia.org/wiki/Abigail_Kapiolani_Kawananakoa.

85. Interview with Quentin Kawananakoa, July 31, 1996.

86. *Id.*

87. Derrick DePledge, "U.S. House Race Draws Kawananakoa Back into Politics," *Honolulu Advertiser,* April 23, 2006, at A-33, col. 1.

88. Interview with Quentin Kawananakoa, July 31, 1996.

89. "An Act to Relieve the Royal Domain from Encumbrances and to Render the Same Inalienable," January 3, 1865, 1 *Sess. Laws of Hawaiʻi,* 69 (1851–70); *see supra* chapter 9.

90. *In Re Estate of His Majesty Kamehameha IV,* 2 Hawaiʻi 715 (1864); *see supra* chapter 8.

property of the Crown as opposed to that of any individual ruler and not subject to sale or transfer. Representative Kawananakoa has recognized a possible role for an Ali'i Council, and he has explained that genealogy should be taken note of and that the ultimate use of the Crown Lands must be pono.

Conclusion

The different views held by the living Ali'i descendants reflect the complexity of the issues underlying the status of the Crown Lands, as earlier chapters of this book have explained. Kamehameha I brought the Islands under his control and asserted a right to all of the 'Āina within his new Kingdom, but this unification was unprecedented in Hawaiian history and was realized largely through the aid of Western arms. Some individuals therefore question whether the 'Āina of all of the islands were actually the private property of Kamehameha and subsequently that of his heirs. Assuming that Kauikeaouli (Kamehameha III) had the authority to divide the 'Āina at the time of the Mahele among himself, the Government, the other Ali'i, and the people, should title to the Crown Lands reserved as Kauikeaouli's personal property in the Mahele of 1848 have passed to descendants of the Ali'i—and, if so, to which ones?

These issues raise a host of complex questions concerning how a person attained Ali'i status and how claims and genealogy should be evaluated. Did an individual become an Ali'i solely by birth, or were merit and an ability to act in a pono manner also essential elements? Should one look to precontact criteria or to the evolving society in the nineteenth century for guidance? The intricate hierarchy and kapu of precontact society evolved rapidly when faced with foreign invasion and influence, and so it is difficult to establish a universal standard for Ali'i descendants. The genealogy of any individual is also complicated by the fact that in precontact society and for some time thereafter, many Hawaiians had more than one husband or wife, and they sometimes paired with one individual for the purpose of procreation and others for companionship. In light of the fact that the precontact tradition of Hawai'i was oral rather than written and that much of the genealogy was recited as opposed to being recorded in texts, should credence be given to precontact or Western standards of documentation—or both?

The answers to these questions are not simple, and current Native Hawaiian leaders have different perspectives and mana'o (thoughts, ideas) on the claims of Ali'i descendants. Nation of Hawai'i Alaka'i Dennis "Bumpy" Kanahele (whose lineage is linked to that of Professor Rubellite Johnson) has expressed the belief that the majority of the Hawaiians must decide how Ali'i claims should be evaluated and what, if any, compensation should be provided.[91] He has said that the 1852 Constitu-

---

91. Interview with Dennis "Bumpy" Kanahele, Nation of Hawai'i and Ohana Council, August 7, 1996. *See generally* Tomas Alex Tizon, "Rebuilding a Hawaiian Kingdom," *Los Angeles Times,* July 21, 2005, at http://www.hawaii-nation.org/rebuilding-kingdom.html.

tion of Kauikeaouli (Kamehameha III) should be honored and that Aliʻi descendants and heirs should receive some type of retribution.[92] But if the majority of Native Hawaiians are opposed to reparations, he has said that he would side with the people.[93] Kanahele has acknowledged that many individuals have "legitimate ties to the Crown Lands," [94] but he favors education as the means to emancipate the Hawaiian People.

Ka Pakaukau Alakaʻi Dr. Kekuni Blaisdell has said that he favors precontact views and practices of land tenure and rejects Western notions of private ownership, commercial exploitation, and degradation of the ʻĀina.[95] Consequently, Dr. Blaisdell believes that communities must structure and organize themselves by considering the views and needs of all of their members through consensus and thereby address issues like Aliʻi claims.[96] In doing so, identification as Kanaka Maoli[97] and education about the history of ka poʻe Hawaiʻi is essential.[98] Dr. Blaisdell has emphasized that the allegiance of Kanaka Maoli should be to their ancestors and has cautioned against being seduced by Western law and values.[99]

Professor Lilikala Kameʻeleihiwa of the University of Hawaiʻi's Center for Hawaiian Studies has highlighted the difficulty of evaluating what role Aliʻi will have in a contemporary context.[100] She has distinguished between chiefly lineage and function by explaining that the role of the Aliʻi was "not a hierarchy that stays forever." [101] Although Native Hawaiians have great respect for their Aliʻi, she has explained, current descendants must exhibit interests and behavior that are pono. For Aliʻi to assert that they are the sole owners of ʻĀina as opposed to being responsible for caring for it would make their claim subject to scrutiny.[102] Ultimately, Dr. Kameʻeleihiwa has said, Aliʻi claims must be evaluated and decided by the people.[103]

This process of community involvement will require raising questions and promoting dialogue to address not merely the Crown Lands but also other issues related to history, culture, and sovereignty. Because the process of becoming Mōʻī was complex at each time of transition during the nineteenth century, it is difficult to say with any confidence that any particular individual was inevitably entitled to or destined

---

92. Interview with Dennis "Bumpy" Kanahele, Nation of Hawaiʻi and Ohana Council, August 7, 1996.

93. *Id.*

94. *Id.*

95. Interview with Dr. Kekuni Blaisdell, Ka Pakaukau, July 30, 1996.

96. *Id.*

97. The term "Kanaka Maoli" was apparently not used in precontact times but was "seen frequently in the nineteenth-century Hawaiian-language newspapers. ʻKanaka' means ʻperson,' and ʻmaoli' means ʻreal; true; original; indigenous.'" Noenoe K. Silva, *Aloha Betrayed: Native Hawaiian Resistance to American Colonialism,* 12 (2004, reprinted 2005). This term is increasingly being used by modern Native Hawaiians to refer to themselves.

98. *Id.* Interview with Dr. Kekuni Blaisdell, Ka Pakaukau, July 30, 1996.

99. *Id.*

100. Interview with Professor Lilikala Kameʻeleihiwa, September 5, 1996.

101. *Id.*

102. *Id.*

103. *Id.*

to become Mō'ī. And each of those who did rise to this position understood with humility their trust responsibilities to the 'Āina and the Hawaiian People. Because of this cultural heritage, it is awkward now for any limited or exclusive group of Hawaiians to make a specific property claim to the Crown Lands. The Hawaiian tradition was to respect the 'Āina and to share it with each other.

However these disputes are ultimately resolved, it is clear that the Crown Lands held a special status in the Kingdom of Hawai'i and that their incorporation into the Public Lands Trust after the 1893 overthrow was inconsistent with this special status. These lands are still covered by trust obligations, the Native Hawaiian People as a collective group continue to have a strong claim to these lands, and it would appear to be appropriate for these lands to form the nucleus of the lands of the sovereign Native Hawaiian Nation that is now emerging.

29

Summary and Conclusions

 This book has been written to serve as a resource for those concerned about how to bring about a fair resolution of some of the disputes haunting Hawai'i. It has been written in the hope that a review and reexamination of the rich historical tapestry that has led to the present conundrum might help to promote the "reconciliation" called for by the U.S. Congress in the 1993 "Apology Resolution."[1] This concluding chapter attempts to tie together some of the loose ends from the previous chapters and provide an overview that may help to promote a solution.

To understand the current legal status of the Crown Lands, it is necessary to unravel a complex set of issues from both our modern standpoint and from the perspective of those living in Hawai'i more than a century ago. This process can be aided by breaking this problem down into its several subcomponents.

Traditional Roles and Responsibilities of the Ali'i

What were the traditional roles and responsibilities of the Ali'i in relation to the 'Āina and to the maka'āinana? In precontact Hawai'i, the Ali'i played a dominant role in the community and supervised management of the 'Āina. But their relationship with the 'Āina was not one of "ownership," as modern westerners would use that term, because 'Āina was not a commodity subject to ownership. In the traditional Hawaiian culture, 'Āina is itself a life force. It is not something that can be traded for profit, but it can be utilized respectfully to provide physical and mental sustenance. Individuals lived in reciprocity with the 'Āina, which would sustain them if properly respected and cared for. The maka'āinana cultivated the 'Āina under the oversight of the Ali'i, who in turn received guidance from Akua. The Hawaiians practiced Mālama 'Āina—the nurturing of the land—to produce the food and spiritual values necessary for subsistence and prosperity. Ali'i only rarely displaced maka'āinana

---

1. "Joint Resolution to Acknowledge the 100th Anniversary of the January 17, 1893 Overthrow of the Kingdom of Hawaii," Pub.L. 103-1 50, 107 Stat. 1510 (1993) (hereafter cited as "Apology Resolution").

from lands they were occupying and utilizing, because all benefited if the lands were being farmed productively. Maka'āinana who were being abused had the right to move to another Ahupua'a and would occasionally rise up against an abusive Ali'i and proclaim a new ruler. The relationship between chiefs and commoners was thus one of interdependence and cooperation for the benefit of all.[2]

An understanding of these traditional relationships is critical, because they help explain why attempts to apply modern legal principles to the events of the nineteenth century are challenging and fraught with complexities. The Monarchs of that period did not make decisions based on Western legal concepts, and their actions cannot be easily compartmentalized using such terminology. They understood their responsibilities as Ali'i to facilitate the utilization of 'Āina for the benefit of all Hawaiians.

Intentions of Kauikeaouli

What did Kauikeaouli (Kamehameha III) intend with regard to the lands that he assigned to himself and that became the Crown Lands? The takeover of Hawai'i by Lord George Paulet on behalf of Great Britain for five months in 1843 convinced Kauikeaouli to take steps to ensure that the 'Āina remained in the hands of Hawaiians even if a foreign power should once again claim sovereignty over Hawai'i. If all the 'Āina were "owned" by the Government, then ownership of the land would pass to the new sovereign. But if the land were to be owned by private citizens, the Mō'ī came to believe, a new sovereign would have to respect such private ownership and leave it in place. The Mahele that occurred during the remainder of the decade thus was designed, in significant part, to prevent the wholesale seizure of 'Āina and ensure that the bulk of the land remained in the hands of Native Hawaiians. Unfortunately, this goal was not achieved.

Kauikeaouli retained the largest collection of 'Āina for himself. He managed these lands as a private landowner would, leasing and transferring some and mortgaging others. But he also used them to carry forth his responsibility as an Ali'i and as the Mō'ī, to Mālama 'Āina and care for the maka'āinana. It is thus impossible to identify an exact legal terminology to describe the status of these 'Āina. The Mō'ī viewed them as an Ali'i in earlier generations would have viewed them: He understood that the 'Āina was his to control but also that he had a duty to care for the 'Āina and the larger responsibility as Mō'ī to provide for the well-being of his people, to manage the 'Āina for their benefit.

Views of Alexander Liholiho

What were the views of Alexander Liholiho (Kamehameha IV) regarding the Crown Lands? Again, it is difficult to impose modern legal terminology to answer this ques-

---

2. "Originally, all Hawaiian land was owned collectively by the people of Hawaii and held in trust for their benefit by the King." *Napehai v. Paty,* 921 F.2d 897, 899 (9th Cir. 1990).

tion. Alexander Liholiho managed the Crown Lands as his own, and like his predecessor Kauikeaouli he asked his wife to waive her dower right to the ʻĀina when land
transfers occurred. But this Mōʻī and his beloved wife Queen Emma had a strong
sense of their social obligations as Aliʻi, and she set up a trust in her will that was
intended to ensure that her personal lands would provide continued health and
social benefits for Native Hawaiians. It would therefore be unfair and unrealistic to
say that Alexander Liholiho believed he had the power to exploit the Crown Lands
for personal profit. In fact, all evidence supports the view that he acted with a strong
sense of his responsibilities as Mōʻī and as Aliʻi to care for the ʻĀina and to use it to
promote the dignity of the Monarchy and the well-being of the Hawaiian People.

The Hawaiʻi Supreme Court's 1864 Ruling

Was the Hawaiʻi Supreme Court correct in its 1864 ruling that the Crown Lands
should pass to the successor to the throne rather than to the heirs of the late Monarch? The Hawaiʻi Supreme Court's 1864 decision in *Estate of His Majesty Kamehameha IV*[3] is the crucial event in defining the legal status of the Crown Lands. The
decision appears to be a compromise between the competing positions and reaches
the somewhat inconsistent results that (1) the ʻĀina should pass to the successor
to the Crown but (2) the Queen of the deceased Monarch should receive a dower
share. These results are inconsistent because the passage of the ʻĀina to the new Mōʻī
(Kamehameha V) was based on the view that the lands were public in nature—that
is, "owned" by the Crown as an institution rather than by the individual who happens to be Monarch, but, on the other hand, the awarding of a dower share to Queen
Emma would be appropriate only if the lands were privately owned by Alexander
Liholiho as an individual. Justice Robertson, who knew the competing parties well,
was probably looking for a Solomonic ruling in which each party would gain a partial victory. He also realized that it would be difficult for a Mōʻī to govern effectively
without a land base and thus ruled that Lot (Kamehameha V) should receive the
Crown Lands as successor to the Crown, rather than awarding these lands to Alexander Liholiho's heirs—his wife and father.

The 1864 opinion is "incorrect" in the sense that it does not reach a decision
that is based on clear, consistent, and understandable principles of law. But the decision can nonetheless be defended as "equitable," because it provides each party with
a partial victory and was designed to provide support for the Monarchy at a time
of economic difficulties. The unfortunate result of the decision is that it provided
the precondition for the loss of control of the Crown Lands by the Native Hawaiian
People three decades later, at the time of the overthrow and annexation, when the
ʻĀina moved into foreign control—exactly the result that Kauikeaouli had feared
and had tried to prevent.

---

3. *Estate of His Majesty Kamehameha IV*, 2 Hawaiʻi 715 (1864), discussed in detail *supra* in chapter 8.

The Legislature's 1865 Enactment

Was the Legislature's 1865 enactment rendering the Crown Lands inalienable appropriate and fair? On January 3, 1865, the Hawai'i Legislature passed "An Act to Relieve the Royal Domain from Encumbrances and to Render the Same Inalienable," which was designed (1) to address and eliminate the considerable debt that the previous Monarchs had accumulated and (2) to protect the Crown Lands from further depletion.[4] This enactment thus formalized the result that the Supreme Court's 1864 decision had pointed toward—that the lands were not the "private" lands of the individual who happened to be Monarch but instead belonged to the Monarchy as an institution. The Court's 1864 decision had not gone quite this far; it would have permitted the new Mō'ī to continue to manage the lands as his own during his term in office, with the power to sell, lease, or mortgage, even if that action reduced the 'Āina that would be passed on to the next Mō'ī. But the 1865 enactment took away the power of alienation and required that the Crown Lands be managed exclusively for the benefit of the Monarchy and the people.

This enactment was designed to protect and promote the Monarchy by ensuring that its wealth remained intact.[5] Especially when combined with a public commitment to pay off the debts accumulated by previous Monarchs, the statute appears designed to assist the Kingdom and to address its challenges in a pragmatic and fair manner. But, like the 1864 Court decision, the practical result of this legislation was to facilitate, three decades later, the passing of the Crown Lands into foreign hands, the result Kauikeaouli had feared and had sought to prevent.

Lot's Agreement

Why did Lot (Kamehameha V) agree to the 1865 enactment? The method by which Lot ascended to the throne was not consistent with Article 25 of the 1852 Constitution, because no vote by joint ballot was conducted by the House of Nobles and House of Representatives. Even though his coronation as Mō'ī was widely accepted by the people, some commentators have questioned its legitimacy.[6]

Lot's personal claim to the Crown Lands was even more tenuous, because he was not one of the main heirs of Alexander Liholiho (Kamehameha IV). The heirs were the deceased King's wife Queen Emma and his father Mataio Kekūanaō'a. Lot received control over these lands only in his capacity as the new Mō'ī and thus may well have been sympathetic to the idea that the lands should pass with the Crown to the next Mō'ī. He certainly had no particular standing to argue that the lands should be viewed as entirely private, with no link to the Monarchy. He may also have been

---

4. This statute is discussed in detail *supra* in chapter 9.

5. *See supra* discussion in chapter 9.

6. *See supra* discussion in chapters 7, text at notes 1–13, and in chapter 28, text following notes 68.

concerned about the debt that his predecessors had accumulated and may have real-ized that the lands needed statutory protections to ensure that they would remain unimpaired for future Monarchs. In any event, he acquiesced in the 1865 enact-ment that prevented future alienation of the lands, and his stamp of approval on this statute has given it a legitimacy that makes it hard for subsequent commentators to challenge.

Rioting Following King Kalākaua's Election

Why did rioting occur when Kalākaua was elected King in 1874 (and the lands left the Kamehameha line)? The contest for Mōʻī in 1874 was hotly disputed between David Kalākaua and Queen Emma, the widow of Alexander Liholiho (Kamehameha IV). The Legislature's selection of Kalākaua by a vote of 39 to 6 meant that the line of leadership linked directly to Kamehameha I had ended.[7] The contest was in part between those who favored stronger ties with Britain, the position favored by Queen Emma, and those who favored stronger ties with the United States, the position asso-ciated with Kalākaua. In part, it was simply a contest of personalities. But the fact that the selection of Kalākaua meant that the Crown Lands were truly moving out of the Kamehameha ʻohana no doubt also played a part in the high tension of this moment. The resulting riot continued until armed forces from U.S. and British warships came ashore to reestablish the peace.

Trust Status of the Crown Lands before the Overthrow

What was the trust status of the Crown Lands before the overthrow? Because the makaʻāinana did not receive anything near the one-third share that they were sup-posed to receive during and after the Mahele,[8] they continued to look to the Crown Lands as lands that were held for their benefit:

> While the fee simple ownership system instituted by the Mahele and the laws that followed drastically changed Hawaiian land tenure, the Government and, sub-sequently, the Crown Lands were held for the benefit for the people of Hawaiʻi. For Hawaiians, the Government and Crown lands marked a continuation of the concept that lands were held by the aliʻi on behalf of the gods and for the benefit of all.[9]

The Aliʻi certainly recognized this trust status throughout this period, as demon-strated by the trusts created by the key Aliʻi when they died without issue[10] and by

---

7. *See supra* discussion in chapter 11.

8. *See supra* chapter 4, text at notes 84, 104–12, 120–41.

9. Melody K. MacKenzie, "The Ceded Lands Trust," *Hawaii Bar Journal,* June 2000, at 6.

10. *See supra* chapters 25 and 26.

the arguments presented by the Hawaiian leaders during the hearing leading to the enactment of the Hawaiian Homes Commission Act.[11]

Significance of the Takeover of Lands

What is the significance of the takeover of the lands by the Provisional Government (1893), the Republic of Hawaii (1894), and then the United States Government (1898), without the consent of or compensation to the Native Hawaiian People? The foreign takeover that Kauikeaouli (Kamehameha III) had feared finally occurred in the 1890s, and his concern that the Native Hawaiians would lose their 'Āina to foreign interests came to pass in 1898 with annexation and the accompanying reclassification of the Government and Crown Lands as Public Lands of the United States. Even though the 1898 Newlands Resolution[12] and the 1900 Organic Act[13] both clearly stated that these lands must be held in trust for the benefit of the people of Hawai'i (meaning the Native Hawaiian People),[14] the Native Hawaiians lost actual control of these lands. In the 1993 "Apology Resolution,"[15] the U.S. Congress characterized these events by saying that "the Republic of Hawaii also ceded 1,800,000 acres of crown, government and public lands of the Kingdom of Hawaii, without the consent of or compensation to the Native Hawaiian people of Hawaii or their sovereign government." Although the United States assumed the public debt of Hawai'i at the time of annexation, that action was not in any sense "compensation" for the takeover of lands, because the public assets of Hawai'i were worth substantially more than the public debt,[16] and the Crown Lands were not truly "public" but were an entitlement of the Native Hawaiian People as the beneficiaries of a trust maintained by their Monarch.

The Trust Established at Annexation

What was the nature of the trust established at the time of annexation (1898)? Because of its understanding that lands had been taken and transferred without consent or compensation, Congress made it clear in both the 1898 Newlands Resolution[17] and the 1900 Organic Act[18] that these lands must be held in trust for the inhabitants of Hawai'i, referring to the Native Hawaiians.[19] That generous phrasing remained

---

11. *See supra* chapter 22, text at notes 7–21, 28–32.

12. "Joint Resolution to Provide for Annexing the Hawaiian Islands to the United States," July 7, 1898, ch. 55, 30 Stat. 750 (1898).

13. "An Act to Provide a Government for the Territory of Hawaii," sec. 73(e), 31 Stat. 141 (1900).

14. *See supra* chapter 19, note 89, and chapter 20, text at note 18.

15. "Apology Resolution," *supra* note 1.

16. *See supra* discussion in chapter 19, text at notes 94–96.

17. "Joint Resolution to Provide for Annexing the Hawaiian Islands to the United States," July 7, 1898, 30 Stat. 750 (1898).

18. "An Act to Provide a Government for the Territory of Hawaii," ch. 339, 31 Stat. 141 (1900).

19. *See supra* chapter 19, note 89, and chapter 20, text at note 18.

largely meaningless during the territorial period, when the socioeconomic position of Native Hawaiians declined and their culture and language were suppressed. In 1921, the Hawaiian Home Lands Program was established for persons with at least 50 percent Hawaiian blood,[20] but the lands provided for this program were marginal, with little agricultural potential, and the program has never been adequately funded to build the infrastructure needed to allow all the Hawaiians seeking homesteads to have meaningful access to them. Nonetheless, the hearings and reports that preceded the passage of the Hawaiian Homes Commission Act made it clear that the United States recognized it had a trust relationship with the Native Hawaiian People and that Native Hawaiians had a continuing legitimate claim to the Crown Lands.[21]

Trust Established at Statehood

What was the nature of the trust confirmed in the Admission Act at the time of statehood (1959)? Section 5(f) of the 1959 Admission Act is explicit in stating that the revenues of the Government and Crown Lands then transferred to the State of Hawai'i (which were four-fifths of the amount that had been "ceded" to the United States in 1898) were to be used for the betterment of the conditions of the Native Hawaiian people (and for four other named purposes). The State ignored this responsibility until 1978, when amendments were added to the State Constitution reaffirming this responsibility and establishing the Office of Hawaiian Affairs (OHA) to receive revenues from these lands. Although substantial debates continue regarding the amount of revenue it should collect, OHA is receiving a revenue stream now and is developing and administering programs designed to benefit the Native Hawaiian People.

Significance of the "Apology Resolution" and State Enactments

What is the significance of the 1993 "Apology Resolution" and comparable enactments of the Hawai'i State Legislature? The 1993 "Apology Resolution" of the United States Congress[22] and Act 359 (1993)[23] of the Hawai'i State Legislature characterize the overthrow of the Kingdom of Hawai'i as "in violation of . . . international law" and acknowledge that the taking of lands was without consent or compensation. The federal bill calls for a reconciliation, and the state bill was designed to facilitate a process whereby Native Hawaiians could reestablish a sovereign nation. These statutes are significant not only because of their findings, but also because they confirm that a process is underway to reexamine the status of the Public Lands in light of their uncompensated illegal transfers and their historical purposes.

---

20. "Hawaiian Homes Commission Act," 1920, Pub.L. No. 67-34, 42 Stat. 108 (1921), reprinted in 15 *Hawai'i Revised Statutes Ann.*, 331 (Michie 1997)

21. *See supra* chapter 22, text at notes 5–32.

22. "Apology Resolution," *supra* note 1.

23. "An Act Relating to Hawaiian Sovereignty," ch. 359, 1993 Hawai'i Sess. Laws, 1009.

Claims of Kamehameha Descendants

How should the claims of some of the Kamehameha descendants be evaluated? A number of sincere and well-intentioned Kamehameha descendants have developed claims to Crown Lands based on their genealogical links to the nineteenth-century Monarchs. These individuals have well-documented genealogies, but their claims to the lands would have to overcome a number of significant obstacles before they could be taken seriously. Some argue that the 1864 Supreme Court decision and 1865 legislative enactment were incorrect or wrongful, and others contend that the ascension to the throne by Lot in 1863 was illegitimate, even though these events were largely accepted as appropriate at the time.[24] It is even more difficult for them to establish that any specific person would be in line to be Mō'ī, because Monarchs in the Kingdom were chosen not through primogeniture or any other fixed system but rather by designation of the previous Mō'ī or by election by joint ballot of the House of Nobles and House of Representatives. Those who claim through Elizabeth Keka'ani'au, for instance, are certainly of Ali'i lineage, but how can they prove that she would ever have been chosen Mō'ī—or, even if she had been so chosen, that someone in the present generation would have succeeded her as Monarch? Because it is impossible to link the Crown Lands to any specific individual or group of individuals today, it seems more appropriate to view these lands as the heritage and entitlement of Native Hawaiians as a whole.

The Crown Lands:
The Core of the Land Base for the Native Hawaiian Nation?

Should the Crown Lands become the core of the land base for the emerging Native Hawaiian Nation? The Crown Lands do appear to be appropriate to serve as the core land base for the restored Native Hawaiian Nation, along with the Hawaiian Home Lands, Kaho'olawe, and perhaps other lands as well, including possibly some now held in the Ali'i Trusts. The Crown Lands were separated from the Government Lands by Kauikeaouli (Kamehameha III) at the time of the Mahele, and they served different purposes during the remainder of the Kingdom. The Government Lands were utilized as general Public Lands to support the Government and the general population, so it can be argued that these lands should continue to be used by successor governments for the same purpose of serving the entire population. But the Crown Lands were kept by Kauikeaouli as his own, and then in 1865 became attached to the Monarchy itself to promote the dignity of the Crown and to allow succeeding Monarchs to fulfill their obligations to their people. It was always understood and accepted that only Native Hawaiians could serve as Mō'ī, and so the Hawaiians have a particular linkage to the Crown Lands. It was also understood that these lands were held in trust for the maka'āinana, who did not receive their fair share of the lands distributed during the

24. *See supra* chapter 28.

Mahele, and the U.S. Congress accepted that position at the time the Hawaiian Homes Commission Act was passed.[25] Although their ultimate destiny must be decided by the Native Hawaiian People, these lands have a unique linkage to the history, culture, and spiritual values of Native Hawaiians and would be a logical choice to form the core of the land base needed by the sovereign Native Hawaiian Nation.[26]

The Private Aliʻi Trusts

What about the lands in the private Aliʻi trusts? The origin and general purposes of these lands are similar to those of the Crown Lands, and the establishment of these trusts demonstrates that the Aliʻi understood that they held these lands in trust for the Native Hawaiians. In a democratic society, it is logical that beneficiaries should have input with regard to resources designed to serve them. The Native Hawaiian People may thus decide in the long run that the Aliʻi ʻĀina now controlled by the private Aliʻi trusts should be linked to the land base of the Native Hawaiian Nation.

Conclusion

Native Hawaiians are on the verge of a new era in which they will once again control land and resources and govern their own affairs. With the process now underway to reorganize the Native Hawaiian Government and then negotiate for the return of lands, Hawaiians will be able to resume the development of their distinct culture. They cannot turn back the hands of time and will have to cope with the rest of the modern world. But they will be able to do so on their own terms and will thereby contribute to efforts of all the world's peoples to preserve the planet's resources while promoting sustainable development for all.

Native Hawaiians need and deserve to have a land base today. This book has explained the historical twists and turns that the Crown Lands have taken and has demonstrated that the best way to view these lands now is as a shared resource of the Native Hawaiian People. These varied and wonderful lands would provide a substantial core to help launch the reorganized Native Hawaiian Nation and to enable Native Hawaiians to prosper once again.

---

25. *See supra* discussion in chapter 22, text at notes 5–32.

26. U.S. District Judge Samuel P. King endorsed this view in 1994:

> The Supreme Court decision of 1864 and the Act of Jan. 3, 1865, and the actions of the revolutionists in 1893 resulted in a land grab at the expense of the Kamehameha line of 971,463 acres.
>
> In the course of rewriting history and correcting past wrongs, as a start it would not be unjust for the state of Hawaii to transfer whatever is left of the crown lands, one half to the trustees of the Bernice Pauahi Bishop Estate for the education of the children of Hawaii, and one-half to the Queen's Hospital for its health programs. Settlement for the rest of the crown lands could follow in due course.
>
> *Or better yet, all of these lands could be transferred to the Office of Hawaiian Affairs to form the beginnings of a land base for the benefit of all Hawaiians.*

Samuel P. King, "History of Crown Lands May Determine Their Future," *Honolulu Star-Bulletin,* December 23, 1994, at A-13 (emphasis added).

Appendix 1

Principles Adopted by the Land Commission, 1846–47

PRINCIPLES ADOPTED BY THE BOARD OF COMMISSIONERS TO QUIET LAND TITLES IN THEIR ADJUDICATION OF CLAIMS PRESENTED TO THEM (ADOPTED BY THE LAND COMMISSION AUGUST 20, 1846, APPROVED BY THE LEGISLATURE OCTOBER 26, 1846, PUBLISHED IN THE LAWS OF 1847).

When the islands were conquered by Kamehameha I., he followed the example of his predecessors, and divided out the lands among his principal warrior chiefs, retaining however, a portion in his hands, to be cultivated or managed by his own immediate servants or attendants. Each principal chief divided his lands anew, and gave them out to an inferior order of chiefs, or persons of rank, by whom they were subdivided again and again; after passing through the hands of four, five or six persons, from the King down to the lowest class of tenants. All these persons were considered to have rights in the lands, or the productions of them. The proportions of these rights were not very clearly defined, but were nevertheless universally acknowledged.

The tenures were in one sense feudal, but they were not military, for the claims of the superior on the inferior were mainly either for produce of the land or for labor, military service being rarely or never required of the lower orders. All persons possessing landed property, whether superior landlords, tenants or sub-tenants, owed and paid to the King not only a land tax, which he assessed at pleasure, but also, service which was called for at discretion, on all the grades from the highest down. They also owed and paid some portion of the productions of the land, in addition to the yearly taxes. They owed obedience at all times. All these were rendered not only by natives, but also by foreigners who received lands from Kamehameha I. and Kamehameha II., and by multitudes still alive; of this there are multitudes of living witnesses, and a failure to render any of these has always been considered a just cause for which to forfeit the lands.

It is therefore certain that the tenure was far from being allodial, either in principle or practice; but even if living testimony were wanting at the present time, the treaty established in 1836, between this government and Lord Edward Russell on behalf of the British government, would show the views then entertained on the subject by the contracting parties. It is there declared, "The land on which the houses are built is the property of the King." The same rights which the King possessed over the superior landlords and all under them, the several grades of landlords possessed over their inferiors, so that there was a joint ownership of the land; the King really owning the allodium, and the person in whose hands he placed the land, holding it in trust. But when he put it in the hands of a third person, that third person bore a similar relation to him that he did to the King. The superior always had the power at pleasure to dispossess his inferior, but it was not considered just and right to do it without cause, and dispossession did not often take place, except on the decease of one of the landlords, when changes were often numerous, and the rights of heirs and tenants comparatively disregarded, for the purpose of favoring a new class of persons.

Such was the nature of the tenures, and such the titles by which the lands were held, when in 1839 protection was declared both for person and property, in the following words: "Protection is hereby secured to the persons of all the people; together with their lands, their building lots, and all their property." (See Declaration of Rights, p. 10 of translation.) In section 6 of the same act, p. 33, the nature of the protection given to landed property is in some degree defined. It is there declared that the landlord cannot "causelessly dispossess his tenant," and it is also stated what shall be considered a sufficient cause. The same law confirms what has been already stated in relation to the rights of His Majesty the King in all lands. Section 3 requires that every tenant of land, by whomsoever owned, shall work 36 days in the year for the King or government, showing clearly that there is no individual who has an allodial title to the soil, the title remaining with the King.

It seems natural then, and obviously just, that the King, in disposing of the allodium, should offer it first to the superior lord, that is to the person who originally received the land in trust from the King; since by doing so, no injury is inflicted on any of the inferior lords or tenants, they being protected by law in their rights as before; and most obviously the King could not dispose of the allodium to any other person without infringing on the rights of the superior lord. But even when such lord shall have received an allodial title from the King by purchase or otherwise, the rights of the tenants and sub-tenants must still remain unaffected, for no purchase, even from the sovereign himself, can vitiate the rights of third parties. The lord, therefore, who purchases the allodium, can no more seize upon the rights of the tenants and dispossess them, than the King can now seize upon the rights of the lords, and dispossess them. This appears clear, not only from the first principles of justice, but also from the act of 1839, declaring protection for tenants as well as for landlords. That act particularly recognizes but three classes of persons as having rights in the sale, viz: The King or government, the landlords and the tenants. Indeed, section 9, chapter 3 of that statute positively forbids the lord who receives land in trust from the King to place another lord under himself, over the tenants. If then any landlord violate this law, he only divides his own rights; he cannot thereby diminish the rights of the King or government, nor the rights of the tenants.

It being therefore fully established, that there are but three classes of persons having vested rights in the land—1st, the government, 2nd, the landlord, and 3rd, the tenant—it next becomes necessary to ascertain the proportional rights of each. Happily, evidence on this point is not wanting, though it may be the most difficult one to settle satisfactorily of any connected with land claims. The testimony elicited is of the best and highest kind. It has been given immediately by a large number of persons, of a great variety of character, many of them old men, perfectly acquainted with the ancient usages of the country; some were landlords, and some were tenants. There has been no contradictory testimony, but all have agreed on all essential points. Several foreign landholders under Kamehameha I., Kamehameha II. and Kamehameha III., have been full in their testimony as to the rights of the King. Ancient practice, according to testimony, seems to have awarded to the tenant less than justice and equity would demand, and to have given to the King more than the permanent good of his subjects would allow. If the King be disposed voluntarily to yield to the tenant a portion of what practice has given to himself, he most assuredly has a right to do it; and should the King allow to the landlord one third, to the tenant one third, and retain one third himself, he, according to the uniform opinion of the witnesses, would injure no one unless himself; and in giving this opinion, the witnesses uniformly gave it against their own interests. According to this principle, a tract of land now in the hands of a landlord and occupied by tenants, if all parts of it were equally valuable, might be divided into three equal parts, and an allodial title to one then be given to the lord, and the same title be given to the tenants of one third, and the other one third would remain in the hands of the King, as his proportional right. It is altogether probable that since the act of 1839, a few individuals may have acquired allodial ownership of landed property, either by purchase or by voluntary grant on the part of the King. Such ownership must be proved or it cannot be acknowledged; for the King, representing the government; having formerly been the sole owner of all the soil, he must be considered to be so still, unless proof be rendered to the contrary; and even possession of ever so long standing cannot be proof, any thing more than that which is specified above as belonging to the landlord, or to the landlord and tenant, as the case may be.

All the above principles and remarks apply most particularly and clearly to districts, plantations and farms, and to their owners. But between the ownership of lands for cultivation, and mere building lots, there are often broad lines of distinction. Mere building lots were never bestowed by the King or lords for the purpose of being given out to tenants, as was uniformly the case with lands suitable for cultivation. It follows therefore, that (with some exceptions, which in all cases must be proved) in relation to building lots, there is no third class of persons having the rights of lords over tenants. The exceptions would be in those cases where individuals having received building lots from the King for their own particular use, those individuals have themselves for some considerations, expressed or implied, transferred such lots to third parties. Another exception exists in relation to building lots, especially if large, which were formerly within the defined boundaries of plantations and farms, and have since been occupied by persons owning no rights in the farms other than the building lots. Such lots must still be considered a part of the plantation or farm, in such a sense that the tenant must pay rent to the lord. This appears clear, not only from ancient usage, but also from the last clause of section 7, of chapter 3, old laws: "But possessions [possessors] of house lots that are large like farm gardens, must aid the owners of the farms from which they are taken, in payment of the yearly tax."

Although the above facts and principles are most perfectly clear and unquestionable, yet great evils have existed down to the present moment, owing mainly to the circumstance that several different classes of persons had undivided rights in the same lands, and each class was very liable to claim more than the due proportions. In such cases, lords, or persons of superior power or rank have generally been the oppressors, and perhaps there are none of those classes, from the throne down, who have not sometimes taken advantage of the powerless in this respect. Neither the laws of 1839 nor of 1840 were found adequate to protect the inferior lords and tenants, for although the violators of law, of every rank, were liable to its penalty, yet it was so contrary to ancient usage, to execute the law on the powerful for the protection of the weak, that the latter often suffered, and it was found necessary to adopt a new system for ascertaining rights, and new measures for protecting those rights when ascertained, and to accomplish this object the Land Commission was formed.

The decisions of an executive board would be so far surrenders of the Chief Executive Magistrate, who has approved the powers conferred upon that Board, as to be an authorization from him to adjust all the past tenures in the manner most equitable, and if abstractly just, power to alienate for him any rights, which he as King could surrender in regard to these lands. The whole power of the King to confer and convey lands to which private, equitable claim now attaches, is reposed in the Commission. What is the nature and extent of that power which the King has bestowed upon this board? It can be no other than his private or feudatory right as an individual participant in the ownership, not his sovereign prerogatives as head of the nation. Among these prerogatives which affect lands, are the following:

1st. To punish for high treason by forfeiture, if so the law decrees.

2nd. To levy taxes upon every tax yielding basis, and among other lands, if so the law decrees.

3rd. To encourage and even to enforce the usufruct of lands for the common good.

4th. To provide public thoroughfares and easements, by means of roads, bridges, streets, etc., for the common good.

5th. To resume certain lands upon just compensation assessed, if for any cause the public good or the social safety requires it.

These prerogatives, powers and duties, His Majesty ought not, and ergo, he cannot surrender. Hence the following confirmations of the board, and the titles consequent upon them must be understood subject to these conditions.

But the King's private or feudatory rights, understood by the natives, differ greatly from the above enumerated corporate rights, understood in civilized and refined nations, and in which the commonwealth is rather represented by the person of the monarch than the monarch himself. By the ancient usage, the taxes went not to the body corporate, in trust for political uses, but to the King, as his private income or revenue, and this gave him a private proprietorship in all lands. This autocracy was, however, diminished by the King's liberal and voluntary surrender to his people in the Constitution, 8th October, 1840, in which the government or body politic and the King are for the first time contradistinguished as follows: "He (the King) also shall have the direction of the government property, the poll tax, the land tax, the three days monthly labor, though in conformity to the laws. He also shall retain his own private lands, and lands forfeited for the nonpayment of taxes shall revert to him," in which clause is perceivable the line of distinction above adverted to. All that is essential to the common good in regard to lands, taxes on lands, and revenue from lands, is reposed in the King, as the head of a corporation aggregate; or in himself as a corporation sole, and from these is contradistinguished his own private lands.

In the spirit of this constitutional distinction, on the 7th of June, 1839, the Nobles, with the sanction of the King, passed some ordinances or rules respecting applications for farms, forsaking of farms, disposing of farms, and the management of farms, having in view the encouragement of industry. In these the landlords are recognized as a distinct and independent class of local proprietors over such portions of their lands as are actually in cultivation, subject to the claims of their tenantry; and as to those lands not in actual use, it gives a community of ownership between the government and landlords, by saying, "Those men who have no land, not even a garden, nor any place to cultivate, and yet wish to labor for the purpose of obtaining the object of their desires, may apply to the land agent, or the governor, or the King, for any piece of land which is not already cultivated by another person, and such piece shall be given him."

This appropriation was to be with co-operation of the King and the landlords. In like manner the corporate right is recognized in what the same law declares respecting the "residuum lands," and "respecting landlords."

Yet the principle of suzerainship seems to have followed the King in those lands which are otherwise declared to be the proper possession of the landlords: for the "advice to the governors and landlords" commences with, "It shall be the duty of those to whom the King gives lands to see that they do not establish other landlords under themselves, over the people;" and in the 18th section, landlords are cautioned lest they "be dispossessed, according to the principles of the eleventh section," which makes the landlords' right of possession dependent upon industry and intelligence.

It would thus seem inferable, that as late as the 7th of June, 1839, and before the Constitution was given, the chiefs considered themselves tenants at special will of the

King as the head of the nation, or in his corporate right. Also that that corporate right to dispossess them was only to be exercised for causes of a public nature, inconsistent with the public well being. To suppose that the landlords could be lawfully dispossessed by the King at will, for causes of private pique, or because of personal disfavor, would be to make the King the real or intrinsic owner of the land in his individual capacity, a doctrine neither sustained by the current or past legislation, nor the testimony which has already been elicited by the board. But to recognize his right of forfeiting the lands of the landlords for misuser or nonuser, or for crime, is itself a recognition beneficial to the mass of the people, for whose happiness the corporation is instituted.

The Hawaiian rulers have learned by experience, that regard must be had to the immutable law of property, in things real, as lands, and in things personal, as chattels; that the well being of their country must essentially depend upon the proper development of their internal resources, of which land is the principal; and that in order to [insure] its proper cultivation and improvement, the holder must have some stake in it more solid than the bare permission to evolve his daily bread from an article, to which he and his children can lay no intrinsic claim. They perceive by contact with foreign nations, that such is their uniform practice, and that the rules of right under that practice are contended for, understood and likely to be applied, in regard to the lands otherwise held at their hands by a tenancy incomprehensible to the foreigner. They are desirous to conform themselves in the main to such a civilized state of things, now that they have come to be a nation in the understanding of older and more enlightened governments.

Such we the commissioners understand to have been the reason of the distinction in the Constitution of 1840, between government lands and private lands of the King, and such we now understand to be the spirit of article 4th, chapter 7th, of the first part of the Act to organize the executive departments of the Hawaiian Islands, founded upon the Law Report of May 21, 1845, in which it was recommended to prepare His Majesty's government to consort in some measure with the recognizing powers. In consequence, it was enacted that the King is to appoint five commissioners for quieting land titles, and thus confer upon them all his private and public power over the corporate property in lands claimed by private parties, which in the nature of things he can delegate.

The requisition to appoint such a board is found in the fourth article of the 7th chapter of the first part of an Act of the Legislature, passed on the 10th of December, 1845, which took effect on the 7th of February following. The statute of which said article is a part, is as a whole denominated "An Act to organize the Executive Departments," indicating that the decisions of the board are not purely judicial, but executive adjudications. The Act as a whole in five parts, passed its final reading and received the approbation of His Majesty, on the 27th of April, 1846, and was promulgated on the 20th June following.

The Board of Commissioners thus instituted, was organized in strict conformity with the law, which having taken effect on Saturday, the 7th of February, the Minister of the Interior, on Monday, the 9th, in Privy Council, with the approbation of His Majesty, appointed and commissioned the undersigned, who at the same time in the presence of the King and Council, took and subscribed the following oath of office:—

"We, and each of us, do solemnly swear, that we will carefully and impartially investigate all claims to land submitted to us by private parties against the government of the Hawaiian Islands; and that we will equitably adjudge upon the title, tenure, duration and quantity thereof, according to the terms of article 4th of the 7th chapter of the first part of an Act entitled 'An Act to organize the Executive Departments of the Hawaiian Islands,' passed at Honolulu, the 10th day of December, 1845.

"(Signed)   WILLIAM RICHARDS,

"   JOHN RICORD,

"   J. Y. KANEHOA,

"   JOHN II,

"   Z. KAAUWAI.

"Subscribed and sworn to this 9th day of February, 1846, before me.

JOHN YOUNG. Minister of Interior."

On the 11th day of February, the day following their appointment, the Commissioners organized as follows:

"NOTICE.

"At a meeting of the Board of Commissioners appointed to quiet land titles, having in view the proper organization required and allowed by article 4th of chapter 7th of the first part of an Act entitled 'An Act to organize the Executive Departments of the Hawaiian Islands.'

"The members of said board having convened, it was

"Resolved, 1st. That William Richards, Esq., be, and he is hereby chosen President.

"2nd. That Joseph Henry Smith, Esq., be employed as one of our stated secretaries, at a compensation to be hereafter determined, derivable solely from the fees and perquisites resulting to the government from the labors of the Board.

"3rd. That said secretary be duly sworn to fidelity in the discharge of his duties as such. That he be, and is hereby authorized to receive claims and evidences for our after consideration, from and after the first publication hereof. That he be required to endorse upon each claim the day and hour of its receipt by him. That he keep an office in Hale Kauwila, in Honolulu, for the transaction of his duties, and for the facility of claimants. And that he be charged with keeping the minutes of this board, and of its proceedings upon claims.

"4th. That claims submitted for settlement be taken up and acted upon according to the order of their presentation, and be settled according to order taken in each case by a majority in number of the board.

"5th. That the stated meetings of this board be held on Wednesday of each week, commencing at 9 o'clock, A. M., at the said office at Hale Kauwila, in Honolulu, for the transaction of business. The first meeting to be held on the 4th day of March next.

"6th. That these resolutions be published in the Polynesian newspaper, concurrently with the notice to claimants required by law, to the end that they may be apprised of these by-laws established by the board.

"Done at Honolulu, this 11th day of February, A. D. 1846.

"(Signed)   WILLIAM RICHARDS,

"   JOHN RICORD,

"   J. Y. KANEHOA,

"   JOHN II,

"   Z. KAAUWAI."

Which resolutions were published in the Polynesian of the 14th February, 1846, together with the following notice, required by law:

"TO ALL CLAIMANTS OF LANDS IN THE HAWAIIAN ISLANDS.

"The undersigned have been appointed by His Majesty the King, a Board of Commissioners to investigate and confirm or reject all claims to land arising previously to the 10th day of December, A. D. 1845.

"Patents in fee simple, or leases for terms of years, will be issued to those entitled to the same, upon the report which we are authorized to make by the testimony to be presented to us.

"The Board holds its stated meetings weekly, at the Hale Kauwila, in Honolulu, on the Island of Oahu, to hear the parties or their counsel in defense of their claims, and is prepared every day to receive in writing the claims and evidences of title which parties may have to offer, at the office of Joseph Henry Smith, Esq., Secretary of said board, at Hale Kauwila, in Honolulu, between the hours of 9 A. M., and 3 P. M.

"All persons are required to file with the Board by depositing with its Secretary specifications of their claims to land, and to adduce the evidence upon which they claim title to any land in the Hawaiian Islands, before the expiration of two years from this date; or in default of so doing, they will after that time be forever barred of all right to recover the same in the courts of justice.

"Dated 11th day of February, 1846.

"(Signed)   WILLIAM RICHARDS,

"   JOHN RICORD,

"   J. Y. KANEHOA,

"   JOHN II,

"   Z. KAAUWAI."

lst. The field of the Commissioners is "the investigation and final ascertainment or rejection of all claims of private individuals, whether natives or foreigners, to any landed property acquired anterior to the passage of the Act" of which Article 4th is an integral portion, to wit, 27th April, 1846.

2nd. The more minute powers of the Board for organization, and to carry out these objects, are specified and conferred; as the power to meet and adjourn, to appoint clerks, to summon parties and enforce mandates, to administer oaths, and to issue commissions for taking testimony. These are auxiliary to the powers and objects of the Board respecting land titles, which it is created to confirm or reject definitely.

3rd. The principles by which the Board are to be governed in deciding certain questions, (i. e.) "Prescription occupancy, fixtures, native usages in regard to landed tenures, water privileges and rights of piscary, the rights of women, the rights of absentees, tenancy and subtenancy, primogeniture, and the rights of adoption," are to be those "Established by the civil code of the kingdom," which the general provisions of the Act to organize the Executive departments, section 3rd, defines as follows: "Until the passage of the civil code, the principles of the foregoing Act, and the prescriptions of all the civil statutes now existing, not at conflict therewith, shall serve and be binding as a civil code for this kingdom, of which the courts of justice shall take notice, in administering the rights to which they are applicable."

A wide latitude is thus left to the Commissioners, who must, in passing upon the merits of each claim, first elicit from creditable witnesses, the fact or history of each; and thus assort or reconcile those facts to the provisions of the civil code, whenever there is a principle in past legislation applicable to the point under consideration; but when no such principle exists, they may judicially declare one, in accordance with ancient usage and not at conflict with any existing law, nor at variance with the facts, and altogether equitable and liberal.

4th. From the fact that His Majesty, the intrinsic proprietor, has reposed in this Board, such power of confirming or rejecting, the Commissioners must infer that he intended the utmost liberality to prevail towards the claimants, rather against the pecuniary interests of the body politic than against those of the claimants. But,

5th. The Commissioners do not understand that in virtue of such latitude, they are at liberty to disregard certain restrictions contained in the same Act, by the 4th Article of the 7th chapter of the first part of which they are created. For the same legislature by whose authority they exist, has elsewhere limited them as follows:

1st. Aliens are not allowed to acquire any allodial or fee-simple estate in lands.

2nd. No leasehold estate shall be considered validly acquired by any alien "until he shall have obtained a certificate of nationality, as in this" the first article of chapter 5th required.

6th. The Commissioners are only authorized by the Act to ascertain the claimant's kind and amount of title, and to award for or against that title, "wholly or in part."—They are not authorized to grant leases or patents, or to receive the commutation allowed by section 10th. Yet since the government share in the land confirmed has intimate connection with the amount of the claimant's title, the Commissioners must ascertain and report upon that share, for the guidance and information of the Minister of the Interior.

7th. Connected with each claim for land, is its configuration and superficial contents, without the ascertainment and demarkation of which, it were impossible to make an award, or to quiet the title as between neighboring proprietors. The Board is therefore under the necessity of causing each piece of land to be surveyed at the claimant's expense, before awarding upon it. This is clearly contemplated by the 12th section of the law, among the "expenses incidental to the proposed investigation."

The following benefits will result from these investigations and awards:

1st. They will separate the rights of the King, and Government, hitherto blended, and leave the owner, whether in fee, or for life, or for years, to the free agency and independent proprietorship of his lands as confirmed. So long as the King or Government continue to have an undivided proprietory [sic] share in the domain, the King's and Premier's consent is necessary, by the old law, to real sales, or transfers from party to party, and, by parity of reasoning, to real mortgages also. This is because of the share which Government or the body politic has in the lands of the kingdom uniformly. To separate these rights, and disembarass the owner or temporary possessor from this clog upon his free agency, is beneficial to that proprietor in the highest degree, and also to the body politic; for it not only sets apart definitely what belongs to the claimant, but untying his hands, enables him to use his property more freely, by mortgaging it for commercial objects, and by building upon it, with the definite prospect that it will descend to his heirs. This will tend more rapidly to an export, and to a permanency of commercial relations, without which, there can never be such a revenue as to enable the Government to foster its internal improvements.

2nd. The patents or leases given to claimants, are for certain fixed and ascertained extents or dimensions of land. This must prevent after litigation in regard to boundaries. All parties having been cited before awarding, there can be no counter claims to the same piece of land after award, except on appeal, and such appeal cannot be taken, except by a party who has presented his claims to the Board.

The patents and leases are recorded in duplicate, in the Department of the Interior. This will enable the foundation of every one's right to be known to the Government, and inquiring parties. No pretended ownerships can exist without the means of undeceiving the public in regard to them. Subsequent purchasers and mortgagees need not be in ignorance of prior defects in the title, or of prior incumbrances.

The undersigned deem the foregoing prefatory remarks and explanations necessary to a clear understanding of the awards upon which they are about to enter, and indispensable to which awards, it is necessary to lay down the following general principles, to which they have arrived by critical study of the civil code, and careful examination of numerous witnesses; among whom are some of the oldest chiefs, possessing large tracts of land, which, equally with other lands, come under the adjudication of the Board, and under the principles here laid down.

The chiefs so situated, cannot have a personal interest in testifying to the facts leading to these principles, since they thereby clog their own rights, and become liable to pay the commutation to which the King and Government are entitled. Native proprietors and foreign residents are thus put upon the same footing in regard to their titles, in consistency with Article 2nd of the treaties concluded with Great Britain and France, 26th March, 1846.

1st. For the purposes of this Board in all cases where the land has been obtained from the King or his authorized agent without a written voucher, anterior to the 7th of June, 1839, the Board will inquire simply into the history of the derivation; and if the land claimed has been continuously occupied, built upon, or otherwise improved since that time, without molestation, the Board will, in case no contests exist between private claimants, infer a freehold less than allodial.

2nd. In all such cases as above specified, when there are counter claims to the same piece of land, the Board will confine their inquiry to which of the claimants has the freehold, less than allodial.

3rd. In all cases where the land has been obtained from the King or his authorized agent, or from any governor, chief, or pretended proprietor, subsequent to the 7th of June, 1839, the Board will strictly inquire into the right of the King, or chief, or landlord, to make such disposition of the land; and will confirm or reject, according to the right of such donor, grantor, or lessor, regardless of consideration, occupancy or after improvements.

4th. In all cases where the land has been legally and validly obtained from the lawful proprietor, by written grant, deed, or lease, the Board will construe the claimant's rights by the wording of the instrument.

5th. When rights were originally acquired either in writing or verbally, in a lawful manner, and from the bona fide owner, for a valid consideration or otherwise, and yet were never occupied, or have not been occupied by such claimant since the 7th of June, 1839, the Board will infer an absence of title. Especially in view of section 6, chapter 3, old law.

6th. The share of government, or the body politic, to be commuted for with the Minister of the Interior, by any confirmed claimant wishing to obtain a fee simple title under chapter 7 of part first of the Act to organize the Executive Departments, this Board understands, from the evidence adduced before them, to be one third part of the value of the land, without improvements, which third part of unimproved value, being paid by the confirmed claimant, should extinguish the private rights of the King in the land, and leave such claimant an allodium, subject only to the corporate rights of the body politic, to be exerted by the King under authorization of the laws, and through the agency of his officers created by the laws. The Board, in asserting this principle, do not mean however to restrict the power of His Majesty in Privy Council, to fix upon a less commutation, under section 10th of the article creating this Board, and subject to the private rights of tenants, if there be any on the land; for the King has no power to convey away the rights of individuals without their consent. They deem it their duty to state the maximum value of the interest retained in all lands of the kingdom at this date, which was never relinquished, and which the government to this day has never received any valuable consideration for, even from the private chiefs from whom the claimants derive. Claimants cannot derive more than the original proprietor had, neither could the original proprietors grant more than they had to the present claimants. They had a possessory right under the crown, equal to two thirds undivided of the value of the land, provided there were no tenants; and in consideration of the undivided third of the King, they paid an annual rent, in produce of the soil, and in service. The foreign claimants, deriving from these, have not, in all cases, paid the rent which was due from their grantors, and have lost sight of the corporate rights in their lands, pertaining originally to the government. That rent can be sold by the Minister of the Interior, for not exceeding one third of the unimproved value of the land as aforesaid, which would divest the land so commuted for of all interference, save that of the community, for the causes and in the way aforesaid.

7th. The titles of all lands, whether rightfully or wrongfully claimed, either by natives or foreigners, in the entire kingdom, which shall not have been presented to this Board for adjudication, confirmation or rejection, on or before the 14th day of February, 1848, are declared to belong to this government, by section 8th of the article creating this Board. Parties who thus neglect to present their claims, do so in defiance of the law, and cannot complain of the effect of their own disobedience.

Upon these principles, the undersigned proceed to take up the claims now before them in the order of their presentation.

"(Signed) WILLIAM RICHARDS,
" JOHN RICORD,
" J. Y. KANEHOA,
" JOHN II,
" Z. KAAUWAI."

Hale Kauwila, August 20, 1846.
Ratification of Principles: L. 1847, p. 94.
RESOLUTION OF THE LEGISLATIVE COUNCIL.
The principles adopted by the Board of Commissioners to quiet Land Titles, under date of August 20th, 1846, having been read before the Nobles and Representatives of the people, in Legislative Council assembled, and having been carefully considered, it was,

Resolved, That the same are hereby approved; and it is enacted that from the date hereof, all claims for landed property in this kingdom shall be tested by those principles, and according to them be confirmed or rejected.
KAMEHAMEHA.
KEONI ANA.
Council House, Honolulu, Oct. 26, 1846.

Appendix 2

An Act Relating to the Crown, Government, and Fort Lands, June 7, 1848

AN ACT RELATING TO THE LANDS OF HIS MAJESTY THE KING AND OF THE GOVERNMENT.

Whereas, It hath pleased His Most Gracious Majesty Kamehameha III., the King, after reserving certain lands to himself as his own private property, to surrender and forever make over unto his Chiefs and People, the greater portion of his Royal Domain:

And Whereas, It hath pleased our Sovereign Lord the King, to place the lands so made over to his Chiefs and People, in the keeping of the House of Nobles and Representatives, or such person or persons, as they may from time to time appoint, to be disposed of in such manner as the House of Nobles and Representatives may direct, and as may best promote the prosperity of this kingdom and the dignity of the Hawaiian Crown: Therefore,

Be it Enacted by the House of Nobles and Representatives of the Hawaiian Islands, in Legislative Council assembled:

That, expressing our deepest thanks to His Majesty for this noble and truly royal gift, we do hereby solemnly confirm this great act of our good King, and declare the following named lands, viz:

NAMES OF LANDS	AHUPUAʻA	DISTRICTS	ISLANDS
Puuwaawaa,	Ahupuaʻa,	Kona,	Hawaii.
Haleohiu,	Ahupuaʻa,	Kona,	Hawaii.
Puaa,	Ahupuaʻa,	Kona,	Hawaii.
Onouli,	Ahupuaʻa,	Kona,	Hawaii.
Honomalino,	Ahupuaʻa,	Kona,	Hawaii.
Waiohinu,	Ahupuaʻa,	Kau,	Hawaii.
Kapapala,	Ahupuaʻa,	Kau,	Hawaii.
Olaa,	Ahupuaʻa,	Kau,	Hawaii.
Apua,	Ahupuaʻa,	Kau,	Hawaii.

NAMES OF LANDS	AHUPUA'A	DISTRICTS	ISLANDS
Waiakolea,	Ili no Kalapana,	Puna,	Hawaii.
Kaimu,	Ahupua'a,	Puna,	Hawaii.
Waiakea,	Ahupua'a,	Hilo,	Hawaii.
Ponahawai,	Ahupua'a,	Hilo,	Hawaii.
Piihonua,	Ahupua'a,	Hilo,	Hawaii.
Humuula,	Ahupua'a,	Hilo,	Hawaii.
Kalopa,	Ahupua'a,	Hamakua,	Hawaii.
Honokaia,	Ahupua'a,	Hamakua,	Hawaii.
Waipio,	Ahupua'a,	Hamakua,	Hawaii.
Lalakea,	Ili no Waipio,	Hamakua,	Hawaii.
Kaohia,	Ili no Waipio,	Hamakua,	Hawaii.
Pohakumauluulu,	Ili no Waipio,	Hamakua,	Hawaii.
Muliwai,	Ili no Waipio,	Hamakua,	Hawaii.
Waimanu,	Ahupua'a,	Hamakua,	Hawaii.
Pololu,	Ahupua'a,	Kohala,	Hawaii.
Aamakao,	Ahupua'a,	Kohala,	Hawaii.
Iole,	Ahupua'a,	Kohala,	Hawaii.
Kaauhuhu,	Ahupua'a,	Kohala,	Hawaii.
Kawaihae,	Ahupua'a,	Kohala,	Hawaii.
Waimea,	Ahupua'a,	Kohala,	Hawaii.
Puukapu,	Waimea,	Kohala,	Hawaii.
Mala,	Ahupua'a,	Lahaina,	Maui.
Alamihi,	Ahupua'a,	Lahaina,	Maui.
Kuholilea Hikina,	Ahupua'a,	Lahaina,	Maui.
Kuhua 1,	Ahupua'a,	Lahaina,	Maui.
Kuhua 2,	Ahupua'a,	Lahaina,	Maui.
Lapakea,	Ahupua'a,	Lahaina,	Maui.
Ilikahi,	Ahupua'a,	Lahaina,	Maui.
Opaeula,	Ahupua'a,	Lahaina,	Maui.
Polapola,	Ahupua'a,	Lahaina,	Maui.
Waianae,	Ahupua'a,	Lahaina,	Maui.
Wainee 1,	Ahupua'a,	Lahaina,	Maui.
Wainee 2,	Ahupua'a,	Lahaina,	Maui.
Puehuehu 1,	Ahupua'a,	Lahaina,	Maui.
Puehuehu 2,	Ahupua'a,	Lahaina,	Maui.
Kauaula,	Ahupua'a,	Lahaina,	Maui.
Olowalu,	Ahupua'a,	Olowalu,	Maui.
Ukumehame,	Ahupua'a,	Ukumehame,	Maui.
Aweoweo,	Ili i Ukumehame,	Ukumehame,	Maui.
Keokea,	Ahupua'a,	Kula,	Maui.
Kealahou 1,	Ahupua'a,	Kula,	Maui.

NAMES OF LANDS	AHUPUA'A	DISTRICTS	ISLANDS
Kealahou 2,	Ahupua'a,	Kula,	Maui.
Waiohonu,	Ahupua'a,	Hana,	Maui.
Wailua,	Ahupua'a,	Hana,	Maui.
Wailua 1,	Ahupua'a,	Koolau,	Maui.
Wailua 2,	Ahupua'a,	Koolau,	Maui.
Keanae,	Ahupua'a,	Koolau,	Maui.
Honomanu,	Ahupua'a,	Koolau,	Maui.
Wailuku,	koe na Ili na Konohiki,	Napoko,	Maui.
Polipoli,	Ahupua'a,	Napoko,	Maui.
Kahakuloa,	Ahupua'a,	Kahakuloa,	Maui.
Waiokila,	Ili i Kahakuloa,	Kahakuloa,	Maui.
Napili,	Ahupua'a,	Kaanapali,	Maui.
Polua,	Ahupua'a,	Kaanapali,	Maui.
Honokowai,	Ahupua'a,	Kaanapali,	Maui.
Ahoa,	Ahupua'a,	Kaanapali,	Maui.
Ualapue,	Ahupua'a,	Kona,	Molokai.
Kalamaula,	Ahupua'a,	Kona,	Molokai.
Palaau,	Ahupua'a,	Kona,	Molokai.
Kahauiki,	Ahupua'a,	Kona,	Oahu.
1/2 Kamookahi,	Ili i Kapalama,	Kona,	Oahu.
1/2 Kaukahoku,	Ili i Kapalama,	Kona,	Oahu.
1/2 Nauwala,	Ili i Kapalama,	Kona,	Oahu.
1/2 Paepaealii,	Ili i Kapalama,	Kona,	Oahu.
Kumupali,	Ili i Kapalama,	Kona,	Oahu.
1/2 Kawaiiki,	Ili i Honolulu,	Kona,	Oahu.
Kawaiiki,	Ili i Honolulu,	Kona,	Oahu.
Hauhaukoi,	Ili i Honolulu,	Kona,	Oahu.
Kahookane,	Ili i Honolulu,	Kona,	Oahu.
Luakaha,	Iii i Honolulu,	Kona,	Oahu.
1/2 Kawananakoa,	Ili i Honolulu,	Kona,	Oahu.
Kukanaka,	Ili i Honolulu,	Kona,	Oahu.
Kapaloa,	Ili i Honolulu,	Kona,	Oahu.
Kahehuna,	Ili i Honolulu,	Kona,	Oahu.
Auwaiolimu,	Ili i Honolulu,	Kona,	Oahu.
1/2 Pawaa,	Loi Ili o Waikiki,	Kona,	Oahu.
Pukele,	Ili o Waikiki,	Kona,	Oahu.
1/2 Kahaumakaawe 1,	Ili o Waikiki,	Kona,	Oahu.
1/2 Kahaumakaawe 2,	Ili o Waikiki,	Kona,	Oahu.
Halelena,	Ili o Waikiki,	Kona,	Oahu.
Mookahi 1,	Ili o Waikiki,	Kona,	Oahu.
Kaloiiki,	Ili o Waikiki,	Kona,	Oahu.

Appendix

NAMES OF LANDS	AHUPUA'A	DISTRICTS	ISLANDS
Mookahi 2,	Ili o Waikiki,	Kona,	Oahu.
Puahia,	Ili o Waikiki,	Kona,	Oahu.
Piliamoo,	Ili o Waikiki,	Kona,	Oahu.
Kaalawai,	Loi Ili o Waikiki,	Kona,	Oahu.
Kaluaolohe,	Ili o Waikiki,	Kona,	Oahu.
Hamama,	Ili o Waikiki,	Kona,	Oahu.
1/2 Poloke,	Ili o Waikiki,	Kona,	Oahu.
Kahalauluahine,	Ili o Waikiki,	Kona,	Oahu.
Waiomao,	Ili o Waikiki,	Kona,	Oahu.
Kaneloa,	Ili o Waikiki,	Kona,	Oahu.
1/2 Wailupe,	Ili o Waikiki,	Kona,	Oahu.
Waimanalo,	Ahupua'a,	Koolau Poko,	Oahu.
Kawailoa,	Ili i Kailua,	Koolau Poko,	Oahu.
Kaluapuhi,	Ili i Kaneohe,	Koolau Poko,	Oahu.
Halekou,	Ili i Kaneohe,	Koolau Poko,	Oahu.
Kuou,	Ili i Kaneohe,	Koolau Poko,	Oahu.
Waikalua,	Ili i Kaneohe,	Koolau Poko,	Oahu.
Keaahala,	Ili i Kaneohe,	Koolau Poko,	Oahu.
Kahalekauwila,	Ili i Kaneohe,	Koolau Poko,	Oahu.
Kanohouluiwi,	Ili i Kaneohe,	Koolau Poko,	Oahu.
Kahaluu,	Ahupua'a,	Koolau Poko,	Oahu.
Maluaka,	Ili o Waihee,	Koolau Poko,	Oahu.
Makawai,	Ili o Waiahole,	Koolau Poko,	Oahu.
Hopekea,	Ili o Waiahole,	Koolau Poko,	Oahu.
Kualoa 1,	Ahupua'a,	Koolau Poko,	Oahu.
Kualoa 2,	Ahupua'a,	Koolau Poko,	Oahu.
Hauula,	Ahupua'a,	Koolau Loa,	Oahu.
Kahuku,	Ahupua'a,	Koolau Loa,	Oahu.
Kawela,	Ahupua'a,	Koolau Loa,	Oahu.
Waialee,	Ahupua'a,	Koolau Loa,	Oahu.
Paumalu,	Ahupua'a,	Koolau Loa,	Oahu.
Pupukea,	Ahupua'a,	Koolau Loa,	Oahu.
Waianae,	Ahupua'a,	Waianae,	Oahu.
Ohua Waikakalaua,	Ili Waikele	Ewa,	Oahu.
Papaa,	Ili Waikele,	Ewa,	Oahu.
1/2 Pouhala,	Ili Waikele,	Ewa,	Oahu.
Weloka,	Ili Waimano,	Ewa,	Oahu.
Honokawailani,	Ili Waiau,	Ewa,	Oahu.
Kauhihau,	Ili Waiau,	Ewa,	Oahu.
Aiea,	Ahupua'a,	Ewa,	Oahu.
Kalaheo,	Ahupua'a,	Kona,	Kauai.

An Act Relating to the Crown, Government, and Fort Lands, 1848

NAMES OF LANDS	AHUPUA'A	DISTRICTS	ISLANDS
Hanapepe,	Ahupua'a,	Kona,	Kauai.
Waimea,	Ahupua'a,	Kona,	Kauai.
Hanalei,	Ahupua'a,	Halelea,	Kauai.
Anahola,	Ahupua'a,	Koolau,	Kauai.
Kapaa,	Ahupua'a,	Puna,	Kauai.
Wailua,	Ahupua'a,	Puna,	Kauai.

To be the private lands of His Majesty Kamehameha III, to have and to hold to himself, his heirs, and successors, forever; and said lands shall be regulated and disposed of according to his royal will and pleasure subject only to the rights of tenants.

And be it further enacted, That we do hereby in the name of the Chiefs and People of the Hawaiian Islands, accept of the following lands, viz:

NAMES OF LANDS	AHUPUA'A	DISTRICTS	ISLANDS
Puuanahulu,	Ahupua'a,	Kona,	Hawaii.
Kukio 1,	Ahupua'a,	Kona,	Hawaii.
Kukio 2,	Ahupua'a,	Kona,	Hawaii.
Maniniowali,	Ahupua'a,	Kona,	Hawaii.
Manaiula,	Ahupua'a,	Kona,	Hawaii.
1/2 Kaulana,	Ahupua'a,	Kona,	Hawaii.
Awalua,	Ahupua'a,	Kona,	Hawaii.
Ohiki,	Ahupua'a,	Kona,	Hawaii.
Makaula,	Ahupua'a,	Kona,	Hawaii.
Kalaoa 1,	Ahupua'a,	Kona,	Hawaii.
Kalaoa 2,	Ahupua'a,	Kona,	Hawaii.
Kalaoa 3,	Ahupua'a,	Kona,	Hawaii.
Kalaoa 4,	Ahupua'a	Kona,	Hawaii.
Ooma 1,	Ahupua'a,	Kona,	Hawaii.
Ooma 2,	Ahupua'a,	Kona,	Hawaii.
Kohanaiki,	Ahupua'a,	Kona,	Hawaii.
Elepaio,	Ili no Honokohau,	Kona,	Hawaii.
Kalakehe,	Ahupua'a,	Kona,	Hawaii.
Lanihau 2,	Ahupua'a,	Kona,	Hawaii.
Honuaala,	Ahupua'a,	Kona,	Hawaii.
Hianaloli 1,	Ahupua'a,	Kona,	Hawaii.
Hianaloli 2,	Ahupua'a,	Kona,	Hawaii.
Auhaukeae,	Ahupua'a,	Kona,	Hawaii.
Puaa 3,	Ahupua'a,	Kona,	Hawaii.
Puaa 2,	Ahupua'a,	Kona,	Hawaii.
Kahului,	Ahupua'a,	Kona,	Hawaii.
Laula,	Ili i Holualoa 2,	Kona,	Hawaii.

Appendix

NAMES OF LANDS	AHUPUA'A	DISTRICTS	ISLANDS
Kooai,	oia o Holualoa 3,	Kona,	Hawaii.
Kaulehua,	Ili,	Kona,	Hawaii.
Kamakaolohe,	Ili i Pahoehoe,	Kona,	Hawaii.
Pahoehoe,	Ahupua'a,	Kona,	Hawaii.
Pahoehoe,	Ahupua'a,	Kona,	Hawaii.
Laaloa,	Ahupua'a,	Kona,	Hawaii.
Kapalaalaea 2,	Ahupua'a,	Kona,	Hawaii.
Honalo,	Ahupua'a,	Kona,	Hawaii.
Maihi,	Ahupua'a,	Kona,	Hawaii.
Kuamoo,	Ahupua'a,	Kona,	Hawaii.
Lehuulaiki 2,	Ahupua'a,	Kona,	Hawaii.
Honuaino,	Ahupua'a.	Kona,	Hawaii.
Papalele,	Ili i Honuaino,	Kona,	Hawaii.
Hokukano 1,	Ahupua'a,	Kona,	Hawaii.
Hokukano 2,	Ahupua'a,	Kona,	Hawaii.
Kanaueue 1,	Ahupua'a,	Kona,	Hawaii.
Kanaueue 2,	Ahupua'a,	Kona,	Hawaii.
Keekee 1,	Ahupua'a,	Kona,	Hawaii.
Keekee 2,	Ahupua'a,	Kona,	Hawaii.
Kanakau,	Ahupua'a,	Kona,	Hawaii.
Kalukalu 1,	Ahupua'a,	Kona,	Hawaii.
Kalukalu 2,	Ahupua'a,	Kona,	Hawaii.
Keopuka 1,	Ahupua'a,	Kona,	Hawaii.
Keopuka 2,	Ahupua'a,	Kona,	Hawaii.
Kaawaloa,	Awa a me kahihonua i kai,	Kona,	Hawaii.
Kealakekua,	Awa a me kahihonua i kai,	Kona,	Hawaii.
Kiloa nui 1,	Ahupua'a,	Kona,	Hawaii.
Kiloa iki 2,	Ahupua'a,	Kona,	Hawaii.
Kauahia,	Ili i Kiloaiki,	Kona,	Hawaii.
Waipunaula 1,	Ahupua'a,	Kona,	Hawaii.
Waipunaula iki 2,	Ahupua'a,	Kona,	Hawaii.
Kalama 2,	Ahupua'a,	Kona,	Hawaii.
Kalama 5,	Ahupua'a,	Kona,	Hawaii.
Kipu,	Ili i Keei,	Kona,	Hawaii.
Kaiko,	Ili i Kealia	Kona,	Hawaii.
Kauhako,	Ahupua'a,	Kona,	Hawaii.
Kapuai,	Ili i Kalahiki	Kona,	Hawaii.
Waiea,	Ahupua'a,	Kona,	Hawaii.
Pahoehoe 1,	Ahupua'a,	Kona,	Hawaii.
Pahoehoe 2,	Ahupua'a,	Kona,	Hawaii.
Pahoehoe 3,	Ahupua'a,	Kona,	Hawaii.

An Act Relating to the Crown, Government, and Fort Lands, 1848

NAMES OF LANDS	AHUPUA'A	DISTRICTS	ISLANDS
Pahoehoe 4,	Ahupua'a,	Kona,	Hawaii.
Maunaoui 1,	Ahupua'a,	Kona,	Hawaii.
Maunaoui 2,	Ahupua'a,	Kona,	Hawaii.
Maunaoui 3,	Ahupua'a,	Kona,	Hawaii.
Maunaoui 4,	Ahupua'a,	Kona,	Hawaii.
Maunaoui 5,	Ahupua'a,	Kona,	Hawaii.
Maunaoui 6,	Ahupua'a,	Kona,	Hawaii.
Makuu 1,	Ahupua'a,	Kona,	Hawaii.
Makuu 2,	Ahupua'a,	Kona,	Hawaii.
Haleili,	Ahupua'a,	Kona,	Hawaii.
Haukalua,	Ahupua'a,	Kona,	Hawaii.
Alae,	Ahupua'a,	Kona,	Hawaii.
Pahoehoe 1,	Ahupua'a,	Kona,	Hawaii.
Pahoehoe 2,	Ahupua'a,	Kona,	Hawaii.
Kaohe 1,	Ahupua'a,	Kona,	Hawaii.
Kaohe 2,	Ahupua'a,	Kona,	Hawaii.
Kukuiopae,	Ahupua'a,	Kona,	Hawaii.
Kolo,	Ahupua'a,	Kona,	Hawaii.
Opihihali,	Ahupua'a,	Kona,	Hawaii.
Opihihali 2,	Ahupua'a,	Kona,	Hawaii.
Kipahoehoe,	Ahupua'a,	Kona,	Hawaii.
Alika,	Ahupua'a,	Kona,	Hawaii.
Papa 1,	Ahupua'a,	Kona,	Hawaii.
Anapuka,	Ahupua'a,	Kona,	Hawaii.
Hoopuloa,	Ahupua'a,	Kona,	Hawaii.
Milolii,	Ahupua'a,	Kona,	Hawaii.
Omokaa,	Ahupua'a,	Kona,	Hawaii.
Okoe 1,	Ahupua'a,	Kona,	Hawaii.
Okoe 2,	Ahupua'a,	Kona,	Hawaii.
Kaulanamauna,	Ahupua'a,	Kona,	Hawaii.
Manuka,	Ahupua'a,	Kau,	Hawaii.
Kiao,	Ahupua'a,	Kau,	Hawaii.
Manienie,	Ahupua'a,	Kau,	Hawaii.
Puulena,	Ahupua'a,	Kau,	Hawaii.
Keaa 1,	Ahupua'a,	Kau,	Hawaii.
Keaa 2,	Ahupua'a,	Kau,	Hawaii.
Kamaoa,	Ahupua'a,	Kau,	Hawaii.
Waiopua,	Ahupua'a,	Kau,	Hawaii.
Mohowae,	Ahupua'a,	Kau,	Hawaii.
1/2 Puueo,	Ahupua'a,	Kau,	Hawaii.
Kau,	Ahupua'a,	Kau,	Hawaii.

Appendix

NAMES OF LANDS	AHUPUA'A	DISTRICTS	ISLANDS
Nukakaia,	Ahupua'a,	Kau,	Hawaii.
Papohaku 1,	Ahupua'a,	Kau,	Hawaii.
Papohaku 2,	Ahupua'a,	Kau,	Hawaii.
Puuoehu,	Ahupua'a,	Kau,	Hawaii.
Kiolakaa,	Ahupua'a,	Kau,	Hawaii.
Kahaea,	Ahupua'a,	Kau,	Hawaii.
Kahilipali,	Ahupua'a,	Kau,	Hawaii.
Kawala,	Ahupua'a,	Kau,	Hawaii.
Aemalo,	Ahupua'a,	Kau,	Hawaii.
Poupouwela,	Ahupua'a,	Kau,	Hawaii.
Kaunamano,	Ahupua'a,	Kau,	Hawaii.
Papaikou 1,	Ahupua'a,	Kau,	Hawaii.
Papaikou 2,	Ahupua'a,	Kau,	Hawaii.
Papaikou 3,	Ahupua'a,	Kau,	Hawaii.
Hionaa,	Ahupua'a,	Kau,	Hawaii.
Hokukano,	Ahupua'a,	Kau,	Hawaii.
Kaalaiki,	Ahupua'a,	Kau,	Hawaii.
Ninole,	Ahupua'a,	Kau,	Hawaii.
Wailau,	Ahupua'a,	Kau,	Hawaii.
Moaula,	Ahupua'a,	Kau,	Hawaii.
Kopu,	Ahupua'a,	Kau,	Hawaii.
Makaka	Ahupua'a,	Kau,	Hawaii.
Makaka,	Ahupua'a,	Kau,	Hawaii.
Iliokoloa	Ahupua'a,	Kau,	Hawaii.
Wailoa,	Ahupua'a,	Kau,	Hawaii.
Kaalaala,	Ahupua'a,	Kau,	Hawaii.
Waimuku	Ahupua'a,	Kau,	Hawaii.
Waimuku,	Ahupua'a,	Kau,	Hawaii.
Kealakomo me Kilauea,		Puna,	Hawaii.
Panauiki,	Ahupua'a,	Puna,	Hawaii.
Poupou 1,	Ahupua'a,	Puna,	Hawaii.
Poupou 2,	Ahupua'a,	Puna,	Hawaii.
Kapaahu,	Ahupua'a,	Puna,	Hawaii.
Ki,	Ahupua'a,	Puna,	Hawaii.
Kupahua,	Ahupua'a,	Puna,	Hawaii.
3 Ili i Kupahua,	Ahupua'a,	Puna,	Hawaii.
Lonokaeho,	Ili i Kupahua,	Puna,	Hawaii.
Hapaiki,	Ili i Kupahua,	Puna,	Hawaii.
Makena,	Ahupua'a,	Puna,	Hawaii.
Kikala,	Ahupua'a,	Puna,	Hawaii.
Kikala,	Ahupua'a,	Puna,	Hawaii.

NAMES OF LANDS	AHUPUAʻA	DISTRICTS	ISLANDS
Keokea,	Ahupuaʻa,	Puna,	Hawaii.
Keauohana,	Ahupuaʻa,	Puna,	Hawaii.
Kamaili,	Ahupuaʻa,	Puna,	Hawaii.
Kaualea,	Ahupuaʻa,	Puna,	Hawaii.
Pohoiki,	Ahupuaʻa,	Puna,	Hawaii.
Opihikao,	Ahupuaʻa,	Puna,	Hawaii.
Malama,	Ahupuaʻa,	Puna,	Hawaii.
Kaukulau,	Ahupuaʻa,	Puna,	Hawaii.
Oneloa,	Ahupuaʻa,	Puna,	Hawaii.
Aahalanui,	Ahupuaʻa,	Puna,	Hawaii.
Kaniahiku,	Ili i Kapoho,	Puna,	Hawaii.
Kanekiki,	Ahupuaʻa,	Puna,	Hawaii.
Halepuaa,	Ahupuaʻa,	Puna,	Hawaii.
Waawaa,	Ahupuaʻa,	Puna,	Hawaii.
Nanawale,	Ahupuaʻa,	Puna,	Hawaii.
Kaikowowo,	Ili i Nanawale,	Puna,	Hawaii.
Honolulu,	Ahupuaʻa,	Puna,	Hawaii.
Kaohe,	Ahupuaʻa,	Puna,	Hawaii.
Keonepoko,	Ahupuaʻa,	Puna,	Hawaii.
Popoki,	Ahupuaʻa,	Puna,	Hawaii.
Halona,	Ahupuaʻa,	Puna,	Hawaii.
Makuu,	Ahupuaʻa,	Puna,	Hawaii.
Makaoku,	Ili i Waiakea,	Hilo,	Hawaii.
Wainaku,	Ahupuaʻa,	Hilo,	Hawaii.
Waialua,	Ahupuaʻa,	Hilo,	Hawaii.
Mokuhonua,	Ahupuaʻa,	Hilo,	Hawaii.
Papaa,	Ahupuaʻa,	Hilo,	Hawaii.
1/2 Kauhiula 1,	Ahupuaʻa,	Hilo,	Hawaii.
Kauhiula 2,	Ahupuaʻa,	Hilo,	Hawaii.
Kaiwiki 1,	Ahupuaʻa,	Hilo,	Hawaii.
Kaiwikinui 2,	Ahupuaʻa,	Hilo,	Hawaii.
Maumau,	Ahupuaʻa,	Hilo,	Hawaii.
Kikala,	Ahupuaʻa,	Hilo,	Hawaii.
1/2 Pueopaku 1,	Ahupuaʻa,	Hilo,	Hawaii.
1/2 Paihaaloa,	Ahupuaʻa,	Hilo,	Hawaii.
Aleamai,	Ahupuaʻa,	Hilo,	Hawaii.
Mokuhooniki,	Ahupuaʻa,	Hilo,	Hawaii.
Alakahi,	Ahupuaʻa,	Hilo,	Hawaii.
Kahalii,	Ahupuaʻa,	Hilo,	Hawaii.
Kawainui 1,	Ahupuaʻa,	Hilo,	Hawaii.
Kawainui 2,	Ahupuaʻa,	Hilo,	Hawaii.

NAMES OF LANDS	AHUPUA‘A	DISTRICTS	ISLANDS
Kulaimano,	Ahupua‘a,	Hilo,	Hawaii.
Kahua,	Ahupua‘a,	Hilo,	Hawaii.
Makea,	Ahupua‘a,	Hilo,	Hawaii.
Kaupakuea,	Ahupua‘a,	Hilo,	Hawaii.
Kaoma,	Ahupua‘a,	Hilo,	Hawaii.
1/2 Kaoma,	Ahupua‘a,	Hilo,	Hawaii.
Kiapu,	Ahupua‘a,	Hilo,	Hawaii.
Haukalua 1,	Ahupua‘a,	Hilo,	Hawaii.
Haukalua 2,	Ahupua‘a,	Hilo,	Hawaii.
Nene,	Ahupua‘a,	Hilo,	Hawaii.
Kapehu,	Ahupua‘a,	Hilo,	Hawaii.
Malamaiki,	Ahupua‘a,	Hilo,	Hawaii.
Honomu,	Ahupua‘a,	Hilo,	Hawaii.
Kuhua,	Ahupua‘a,	Hilo,	Hawaii.
1/2 Kaiwiki,	Ahupua‘a,	Hilo,	Hawaii.
Wailea,	Ahupua‘a,	Hilo,	Hawaii.
Kamaee 1,	Ahupua‘a,	Hilo,	Hawaii.
Kamaee 2,	Ahupua‘a,	Hilo,	Hawaii.
Kamaee 3,	Ahupua‘a,	Hilo,	Hawaii.
Kamaee 4,	Ahupua‘a,	Hilo,	Hawaii.
Umauma,	Ahupua‘a,	Hilo,	Hawaii.
Awapuhi,	Ahupua‘a,	Hilo,	Hawaii.
Paleau,	Ahupua‘a,	Hilo,	Hawaii.
Opea,	Ahupua‘a,	Hilo,	Hawaii.
Puaakuloa,	Ahupua‘a,	Hilo,	Hawaii.
Puuhune,	Ahupua‘a,	Hilo,	Hawaii.
Ninole,	Ahupua‘a,	Hilo,	Hawaii.
Puuohua,	Ahupua‘a,	Hilo,	Hawaii.
Puuohua,	Ahupua‘a,	Hilo,	Hawaii.
Kahinalo,	Ahupua‘a,	Hilo,	Hawaii.
Kulanakii,	Ahupua‘a,	Hilo,	Hawaii.
Pohakupuka,	Ahupua‘a,	Hilo,	Hawaii.
Puuohai,	Ahupua‘a,	Hilo,	Hawaii.
Paeohi,	Ahupua‘a,	Hilo,	Hawaii.
Kaalau 1,	Ahupua‘a,	Hilo,	Hawaii.
Kaalau 2,	Ahupua‘a,	Hilo,	Hawaii.
Kaalau 3,	Ahupua‘a,	Hilo,	Hawaii.
Kaalau 4,	Ahupua‘a,	Hilo,	Hawaii.
Kaiwilahilahi,	Ahupua‘a,	Hilo,	Hawaii.
Paapaaloa 1,	Ahupua‘a,	Hilo,	Hawaii.
Paapaaloa 2,	Ahupua‘a,	Hilo,	Hawaii.

An Act Relating to the Crown, Government, and Fort Lands, 1848

NAMES OF LANDS	AHUPUA'A	DISTRICTS	ISLANDS
Kihalani 1,	Ahupua'a,	Hilo,	Hawaii.
Kihalani 2,	Ahupua'a,	Hilo,	Hawaii.
Pualaea,	Ahupua'a,	Hilo,	Hawaii.
Kilau,	Ahupua'a,	Hilo,	Hawaii.
Laupahoehoe,	Ahupua'a,	Hilo,	Hawaii.
Laupahoehoe,	Ahupua'a,	Hilo,	Hawaii.
Haakoa,	Ahupua'a,	Hilo,	Hawaii.
Kuaai,	Ahupua'a,	Hilo,	Hawaii.
Kaohaoha 1,	Ahupua'a,	Hilo,	Hawaii.
Kaohaoha 2,	Ahupua'a,	Hilo,	Hawaii.
Ulukanu,	Ahupua'a,	Hilo,	Hawaii.
Ookala,	Ahupua'a,	Hilo,	Hawaii.
Manowaialee 1,	Ahupua'a,	Hamakua,	Hawaii.
Manowaialee 2,	Ahupua'a,	Hamakua,	Hawaii.
Manowaialee 3,	Ahupua'a,	Hamakua,	Hawaii.
Kaholo 1,	Ahupua'a,	Hamakua,	Hawaii.
Kaholo 2,	Ahupua'a,	Hamakua,	Hawaii.
Kaapahu,	Ahupua'a,	Hamakua,	Hawaii.
Maonakomalie,	Ahupua'a,	Hamakua,	Hawaii.
Kuhia,	Ahupua'a,	Hamakua,	Hawaii.
Kealakaha,	Ahupua'a,	Hamakua,	Hawaii.
Hoea,	Ahupua'a,	Hamakua,	Hawaii.
Manowaikohao,	Ahupua'a,	Hamakua,	Hawaii.
Manowaikohao,	Ahupua'a,	Hamakua,	Hawaii.
Kaawikiwiki,	Ahupua'a,	Hamakua,	Hawaii.
Kekualele,	Ahupua'a,	Hamakua,	Hawaii.
Kekualele,	Ahupua'a,	Hamakua,	Hawaii.
Kaao 1,	Ahupua'a,	Hamakua,	Hawaii.
Kaao 2,	Ahupua'a,	Hamakua,	Hawaii.
Kainehe,	Ahupua'a,	Hamakua,	Hawaii.
Kaohe,	Ahupua'a,	Hamakua,	Hawaii.
Aaamanu,	Ahupua'a,	Hamakua,	Hawaii.
Paauilo,	Ahupua'a,	Hamakua,	Hawaii.
Kakaalaea,	Ahupua'a,	Hamakua,	Hawaii.
Kamokala,	Ahupua'a,	Hamakua,	Hawaii.
Hauola 1,	Ahupua'a,	Hamakua,	Hawaii.
Hauola 2,	Ahupua'a,	Hamakua,	Hawaii.
Opihilala 1,	Ahupua'a,	Hamakua,	Hawaii.
Opihilala 2,	Ahupua'a,	Hamakua,	Hawaii.
Opihilala 3,	Ahupua'a,	Hamakua,	Hawaii.
Manienie,	Ahupua'a,	Hamakua,	Hawaii.

Appendix

NAMES OF LANDS	AHUPUA'A	DISTRICTS	ISLANDS
Kamauli,	Ahupua'a,	Hamakua,	Hawaii.
Kaulekohao,	Ahupua'a,	Hamakua,	Hawaii.
Pahakuhaku,	Ahupua'a,	Hamakua,	Hawaii.
Kemau,	Ahupua'a,	Hamakua,	Hawaii.
Kaumoali,	Ahupua'a,	Hamakua,	Hawaii.
1/2 Kaunamano,	Ahupua'a,	Hamakua,	Hawaii.
Heneheneula 2,	Ahupua'a,	Hamakua,	Hawaii.
Kalua 1,	Ahupua'a,	Hamakua,	Hawaii.
Kalua 2,	Ahupua'a,	Hamakua,	Hawaii.
1/2 Kaapahu,	Ahupua'a,	Hamakua,	Hawaii.
Waikaalulu 1,	Ahupua'a,	Hamakua,	Hawaii.
Waikaalulu 2,	Ahupua'a,	Hamakua,	Hawaii.
Kalua,	Ahupua'a,	Hamakua,	Hawaii.
Keahua,	Ahupua'a,	Hamakua,	Hawaii.
Kaao 1,	Ahupua'a,	Hamakua,	Hawaii.
Kaao 2,	Ahupua'a,	Hamakua,	Hawaii.
Ouhi,	Ahupua'a,	Hamakua,	Hawaii.
Pakiloa,	Ahupua'a,	Hamakua,	Hawaii.
Papaanui,	Ahupua'a,	Hamakua,	Hawaii.
Haina,	Ahupua'a,	Hamakua,	Hawaii.
Lauka,	Ahupua'a,	Hamakua,	Hawaii.
Ahualoa,	Ahupua'a,	Hamakua,	Hawaii.
Au,	Ahupua'a,	Hamakua,	Hawaii.
Kuilei,	Ahupua'a,	Hamakua,	Hawaii.
1/2 Malanahae,	Ahupua'a,	Hamakua,	Hawaii.
Haukoi,	Ahupua'a,	Hamakua,	Hawaii.
Kaauhuhu,	Ahupua'a,	Hamakua,	Hawaii.
Waialeale,	Ahupua'a,	Hamakua,	Hawaii.
Waikoloa,	Ahupua'a,	Hamakua,	Hawaii.
Puanui,	Ahupua'a,	Hamakua,	Hawaii.
Puopaha,	Ahupua'a,	Hamakua,	Hawaii.
Keaa 1,	Ahupua'a,	Hamakua,	Hawaii.
Keaa 2,	Ahupua'a,	Hamakua,	Hawaii.
Keaa 3,	Ahupua'a,	Hamakua,	Hawaii.
Pueo, Ili no Waipio,	Ahupua'a,	Hamakua,	Hawaii.
Laupahoehoe,	Ahupua'a,	Hamakua,	Hawaii.
Nakooka,	Ahupua'a,	Hamakua,	Hawaii.
Apua,	Ahupua'a,	Hamakua,	Hawaii.
Waikapu,	Ahupua'a,	Hamakua,	Hawaii.
Honopue,	Ahupua'a,	Hamakua,	Hawaii.
Awini,	Ahupua'a,	Kohala,	Hawaii.

NAMES OF LANDS	AHUPUA'A	DISTRICTS	ISLANDS
Makanikahio,	Ahupua'a,	Kohala,	Hawaii.
Hinaweo,	Ili i Niulii,	Kohala,	Hawaii.
2 Ili i Niulii,	Ahupua'a,	Kohala,	Hawaii.
Kaha, Ili i Niulii,	Ahupua'a,	Kohala,	Hawaii.
1/2 Halawa,	Ahupua'a,	Kohala,	Hawaii.
Pualoalo, Ili i Halawa,	Ahupua'a,	Kohala,	Hawaii.
Hopeolaa, Ili i Halawa,	Ahupua'a,	Kohala,	Hawaii.
Apuakohau,	Ahupua'a,	Kohala,	Hawaii.
Kekikiki,	Ili i Apuakohau,	Kohala,	Hawaii.
1/2 Pueke,	Ahupua'a,	Kohala,	Hawaii.
Maulili,	Ahupua'a,	Kohala,	Hawaii.
Halaula,	Ahupua'a,	Kohala,	Hawaii.
Ainakeanui,	Ahupua'a,	Kohala,	Hawaii.
Papiha,	Ili no Ainakeanui,	Kohala,	Hawaii.
Ainakeaiki,	Ahupua'a,	Kohala,	Hawaii.
Laaumama 1,	Ahupua'a,	Kohala,	Hawaii.
Laaumama 2,	Ahupua'a,	Kohala,	Hawaii.
Puehuehu,	Ahupua'a,	Kohala,	Hawaii.
Kapua,	Ahupua'a,	Kohala,	Hawaii.
Honomakau,	Ahupua'a,	Kohala,	Hawaii.
Lanikele,	Ili i Honomakau,	Kohala,	Hawaii.
Hawi,	Ahupua'a,	Kohala,	Hawaii.
Kahei 1,	Ahupua'a,	Kohala,	Hawaii.
Kahei 2,	Ahupua'a,	Kohala,	Hawaii.
Kahei 3,	Ahupua'a,	Kohala,	Hawaii.
Kahei 4,	Ahupua'a,	Kohala,	Hawaii.
Hualua,	Ahupua'a,	Kohala,	Hawaii.
Opihipau,	Ahupua'a,	Kohala,	Hawaii.
Hukiaa 2,	Ahupua'a,	Kohala,	Hawaii.
Puuepa, ma Mookini,	Ahupua'a,	Kohala,	Hawaii.
Kokoiki 1,	Ahupua'a,	Kohala,	Hawaii.
Kokoiki 2,	Ahupua'a,	Kohala,	Hawaii.
Upolu 1,	Ahupua'a,	Kohala,	Hawaii.
1/2 Upolu 2,	Ahupua'a,	Kohala,	Hawaii.
Honoipu,	Ahupua'a,	Kohala,	Hawaii.
Puakea 1,	Ahupua'a,	Kohala,	Hawaii.
Puakea 2,	Ahupua'a,	Kohala,	Hawaii.
Lahuiki,	Ili i Kukuipahu,	Kohala,	Hawaii.
Awalua,	Ahupua'a,	Kohala,	Hawaii.
Haina,	Ahupua'a,	Kohala,	Hawaii.
Kapunapuna,	Ahupua'a,	Kohala,	Hawaii.

NAMES OF LANDS	AHUPUA'A	DISTRICTS	ISLANDS
Kou,	Ahupua'a,	Kohala,	Hawaii.
Paopao,	Ahupua'a,	Kohala,	Hawaii.
Mahukona,	Awa a me kahihonua i kai,	Kohala,	Hawaii.
Mahukonapulehu,	Ahupua'a,	Kohala,	Hawaii.
Mahukonakaluapaa,	Ahupua'a,	Kohala,	Hawaii.
Hihiu 1,	Ahupua'a,	Kohala,	Hawaii.
Hihiu 2,	Ahupua'a,	Kohala,	Hawaii
Lapakahi,	Ahupua'a,	Kohala,	Hawaii.
Lamaloloa,	Ahupua'a,	Kohala,	Hawaii.
1/2 Paoo 1,	Ahupua'a,	Kohala,	Hawaii.
Paoo 2,	Ahupua'a,	Kohala,	Hawaii.
Paoo 3,	Ahupua'a,	Kohala,	Hawaii.
Paoo 4,	Ahupua'a,	Kohala,	Hawaii.
Paoo 5,	Ahupua'a,	Kohala,	Hawaii.
Paoo 6,	Ahupua'a,	Kohala,	Hawaii.
Makeanehu 1,	Ahupua'a,	Kohala,	Hawaii.
Makeanehu 2,	Ahupua'a,	Kohala,	Hawaii.
Makeanehu 3,	Ahupua'a,	Kohala,	Hawaii.
Makeanehu 4,	Ahupua'a,	Kohala,	Hawaii.
Kipi,	Ahupua'a,	Kohala,	Hawaii.
Kehena 1,	Ahupua'a,	Kohala,	Hawaii.
Pohakulua,	Ahupua'a,	Kohala,	Hawaii.
Puaiki,	Ahupua'a,	Kohala,	Hawaii.
Kiiokalani,	Ahupua'a,	Kohala,	Hawaii.
Kaihoa 1,	Ahupua'a,	Kohala,	Hawaii.
Kaihoa 2,	Ahupua'a,	Kohala,	Hawaii.
Kokio,	Ahupua'a,	Kohala,	Hawaii.
Kalala,	Ahupua'a,	Kohala,	Hawaii
Kalala,	Ahupua'a,	Kohala,	Hawaii.
Pauahi 1,	Ahupua'a,	Kohala,	Hawaii.
Pauahi 2,	Ahupua'a,	Kohala,	Hawaii.
Lanikepue,	Ahupua'a,	Kohala,	Hawaii.
Waawaa,	Ahupua'a,	Kohala,	Hawaii.
1/2 Kapunakea,	Ahupua'a,	Lahaina,	Maui.
1/2 Puuki,	Ahupua'a,	Lahaina,	Maui.
Moanui,	Ahupua'a,	Lahaina,	Maui.
1/2 Kuholilea,	Ahupua'a,	Lahaina,	Maui.
1/2 Uhao,	Ahupua'a,	Lahaina,	Maui.
1/2 Puahoowale,	Ahupua'a,	Lahaina,	Maui.
1/2 Kooka,	Ahupua'a,	Lahaina,	Maui.

An Act Relating to the Crown, Government, and Fort Lands, 1848

NAMES OF LANDS	AHUPUA'A	DISTRICTS	ISLANDS
1/2 Puunauiki,	Ahupuaʻa,	Lahaina,	Maui.
Kamaole,	Ahupuaʻa,	Kula,	Maui.
Naalae,	Ahupuaʻa,	Kula,	Maui.
Waiokoa,	Ahupuaʻa,	Kula,	Maui.
Kamehame 1,	Ahupuaʻa,	Kula,	Maui.
Kamehame 2,	Ahupuaʻa,	Kula,	Maui.
Pulehu,	Ahupuaʻa,	Kula,	Maui.
Omaopio 6,	Ahupuaʻa,	Kula,	Maui.
Omaopio 7,	Ahupuaʻa,	Kula,	Maui.
Omaopio 8,	Ahupuaʻa,	Kula,	Maui.
Omaopio 9,	Ahupuaʻa,	Kula,	Maui.
Omaopio 10,	Ahupuaʻa,	Kula,	Maui.
Omaopio 11,	Ahupuaʻa,	Kula,	Maui.
Aapueo 3,	Ahupuaʻa,	Kula,	Maui.
Aapueo,	Ahupuaʻa,	Kula,	Maui.
Kukuiaio,	Ahupuaʻa,	Kula,	Maui.
Kauau 1,	Ahupuaʻa,	Kula,	Maui.
Kauau 2,	Ahupuaʻa,	Kula,	Maui.
Koheilo 1,	Ahupuaʻa,	Kula,	Maui.
Koheilo 2,	Ahupuaʻa,	Kula,	Maui.
Keahua,	Ahupuaʻa,	Kula,	Maui.
Hokuula,	Ahupuaʻa,	Kula,	Maui.
Ahupau,	Ahupuaʻa,	Kula,	Maui.
Paeahu 1,	Ahupuaʻa,	Honuaula,	Maui.
Paeahu 2,	Ahupuaʻa,	Honuaula,	Maui.
Kalihi 1,	Ahupuaʻa,	Honuaula,	Maui
Kalihi 2,	Ahupuaʻa,	Honuaula,	Maui
Waipao,	Ahupuaʻa,	Honuaula,	Maui.
Papaa,	Ahupuaʻa,	Honuaula,	Maui.
1/2 Kaeo,	Ahupuaʻa,	Honuaula,	Maui.
Maluaka,	Ahupuaʻa,	Honuaula,	Maui.
Mohopilo 1,	Ahupuaʻa,	Honuaula,	Maui.
Mohopilo 2,	Ahupuaʻa,	Honuaula,	Maui.
Mooiki,	Ahupuaʻa,	Honuaula,	Maui.
Mooloa,	Ahupuaʻa,	Honuaula,	Maui.
Moomuku,	Ahupuaʻa,	Honuaula,	Maui.
Onau,	Ahupuaʻa,	Honuaula,	Maui.
Kualapa,	Ahupuaʻa,	Honuaula,	Maui.
Papaka,	Ahupuaʻa,	Honuaula,	Maui
Kaunuahane,	Ahupuaʻa,	Honuaula,	Maui.

Appendix

NAMES OF LANDS	AHUPUA'A	DISTRICTS	ISLANDS
Kaloi,	Ahupua'a,	Honuaula,	Maui.
Kanaio,	Ahupua'a,	Honuaula,	Maui.
Kahikinui,	he Moku,	Kahikinui,	Maui.
Kaupo,	66 Ahupua'a,	Kaupo,	Maui.
Kaupo, koe na ku ikeia mahele,		Kaupo,	Maui.
Kukuiulaiki,	Ahupua'a,	Kipahulu,	Maui.
Popoloa,	Ahupua'a,	Kipahulu,	Maui.
Popoloa,	Ahupua'a,	Kipahulu,	Maui.
Kapuaikini,	Ahupua'a,	Kipahulu,	Maui.
Kapuaikini,	Ahupua'a,	Kipahulu,	Maui.
Kaehoeho,	Ahupua'a,	Kipahulu,	Maui.
Poponui,	Ahupua'a,	Kipahulu,	Maui.
Kakanoni,	Ahupua'a,	Kipahulu,	Maui.
Maulili,	Ahupua'a,	Kipahulu,	Maui.
Kikoo,	Ahupua'a,	Kipahulu,	Maui.
Kalena,	Ahupua'a,	Kipahulu,	Maui.
Kalenaiki,	Ahupua'a,	Kipahulu,	Maui.
Halemano,	Ahupua'a,	Kipahulu,	Maui.
Nailiilipoko 1,	Ahupua'a,	Kipahulu,	Maui.
Nailiilipoko 2,	Ahupua'a,	Kipahulu,	Maui.
Wailamoa, aoao ma Hana,		Kipahulu,	Maui.
Wailamoa, aoao ma Kaupo,		Kipahulu,	Maui.
Kakalahale 1,	Ahupua'a,	Kipahulu,	Maui
Kakalahale 2,	Ahupua'a,	Kipahulu,	Maui
Alae,	Ahupua'a,	Kipahulu,	Maui
Kaumakani,	Ahupua'a,	Kipahulu,	Maui
Koanawai,	Ahupua'a,	Kipahulu,	Maui
Koali,	Ahupua'a,	Hana,	Maui.
Maakaalae,	Ahupua'a,	Hana,	Maui.
Wananalua 1,	Ahupua'a,	Hana,	Maui
Wananalua 2,	Ahupua'a,	Hana,	Maui.
Waikiu,	Ahupua'a,	Hana,	Maui.
1/2 Honomaele,	Ahupua'a,	Hana,	Maui.
Koolau,	he Moku,	Koolau,	Maui.
Keaa,	Ahupua'a,	Koolau,	Maui.
Hanawana,	Ahupua'a,	Hamakualoa,	Maui.
Hoalua,	Ahupua'a,	Hamakualoa,	Maui.
Hanehoi 1,	Ahupua'a,	Hamakualoa,	Maui.

NAMES OF LANDS	AHUPUA'A	DISTRICTS	ISLANDS
Hanehoi 2,	Ahupua'a,	Hamakualoa,	Maui.
Poulua 1, Poulua 2	Ahupua'a,	Hamakualoa,	Maui.
Honokala, Papaaea, Holowa, Kuiaha,	Ahupua'a,	Hamakualoa,	Maui.
Honopou,	Ahupua'a,	Hamakualoa,	Maui.
Pauwela,	Ahupua'a,	Hamakualoa,	Maui.
Ouaoa,	Ahupua'a,	Hamakualoa,	Maui.
Peahi 1,	Ahupua'a,	Hamakualoa,	Maui.
Peahi 2,	Ahupua'a,	Hamakualoa,	Maui.
1/2 Hamakuapoko,	1/2 Hikina,	Hamakuapoko,	Maui.
Paniau,	Ahupua'a,	Hamakuapoko,	Maui.
Makawao,	Ahupua'a,	Kula,	Maui.
Kealakekua,	Ahupua'a,	Kula,	Maui.
Kapalaia,	Ahupua'a,	Kula,	Maui.
Kealia,	Ahupua'a,	Kula,	Maui.
Honokohau,	Ahupua'a,	Kaanapali,	Maui.
Kahana 1,	Ahupua'a,	Kaanapali,	Maui.
Kahana 2,	Ahupua'a,	Kaanapali,	Maui.
Mahinahina 1,	Ahupua'a,	Kaanapali,	Maui.
Mahinahina 2,	Ahupua'a,	Kaanapali,	Maui.
Mahinahina 3,	Ahupua'a,	Kaanapali,	Maui.
Lupehu,	Ahupua'a,	Kona,	Molokai.
Onoulimaloo,	Ahupua'a,	Kona,	Molokai.
Onouliwai,	Ahupua'a,	Kona,	Molokai.
Moanui,	Ahupua'a,	Kona,	Molokai.
Poniuohua,	Ahupua'a,	Kona.	Molokai.
1/2 Poniuohua,	Ahupua'a,	Kona,	Molokai.
Kawaikapu,	Ahupua'a,	Kona,	Molokai.
1/2 Kamanoni,	Ahupua'a,	Kona,	Molokai.
1/2 Ahaino,	Ahupua'a,	Kona,	Molokai.
Pukoa 2,	Ahupua'a,	Kona,	Molokai.
Pukoa 1,	Ahupua'a,	Kona.	Molokai.
Kaluaaha,	Ahupua'a,	Kona,	Molokai.
1/2 Kahananui,	Ahupua'a,	Kona.	Molokai.
Ohia 1, Hikina,	Ahupua'a,	Kona,	Molokai.
Kaamola 1,	Ahupua'a,	Kona.	Molokai.
Kaamola 2,	Ahupua'a,	Kona.	Molokai.
Kuamola 3,	Ahupua'a,	Kona,	Molokai.
Kaamola 4,	Ahupua'a,	Kona.	Molokai.
1/2 Kaamola 5,	Ahupua'a,	Kona,	Molokai.
1/2 Kaamola 6,	Ahupua'a,	Kona,	Molokai.

Appendix

NAMES OF LANDS	AHUPUA'A	DISTRICTS	ISLANDS
Heanaokuino,	Ahupua'a,	Kona,	Molokai.
Makakupaianui,	Ahupua'a,	Kona,	Molokai.
1/2 Kamiloloa,	Ahupua'a,	Kona,	Molokai.
1/2 Kahanui,	Ahupua'a,	Kona,	Molokai.
Hoolehua,	Ahupua'a,	Kona,	Molokai.
Kaluakoi 1,	Ahupua'a,	Kaluakoi,	Molokai.
Kaluakoi 2,	Ahupua'a,	Kaluakoi,	Molokai.
Manowainui,	Ahupua'a,	Kalae	Molokai.
Hipu,	Ahupua'a,	Kalae	Molokai.
Mahulile,	Ahupua'a,	Koolau,	Molokai.
Pohakuloa,	Ahupua'a,	Koolau,	Molokai.
Hawaluna,	Ahupua'a,	Koolau,	Molokai.
Halawao,	Ahupua'a,	Koolau,	Molokai.
Manienie, Ili oWaikolu,	Ahupua'a,	Koolau,	Molokai.
Haulei,	Ahupua'a,	Koolau,	Molokai.
Hainalu,	Ahupua'a,	Koolau,	Molokai.
Kahoolawe,	Mokupuni Okoa,	Koolau,	Kahoolawe.
Puunui 1,	Ili no Honolulu,	Kona,	Oahu.
Puunui 2,	Ili no Honolulu,	Kona,	Oahu.
Puunui 3,	Ili no Honolulu,	Kona,	Oahu.
Alewa,	Ili no Honolulu,	Kona,	Oahu.
Hahapaakai,	Ili no Honolulu,	Kona,	Oahu.
Huwili,	Ili no Honolulu,	Kona,	Oahu.
Lapiwai 1,	Ili no Honolulu,	Kona,	Oahu.
Lapiwai 2,	Ili no Honolulu,	Kona,	Oahu.
Luhimana,	Ili no Honolulu,	Kona,	Oahu.
Hauhaukoi,	Ili no Honolulu,	Kona,	Oahu.
Aala,	Ili no Honolulu,	Kona,	Oahu.
Huaiula,	Ili no Honolulu,	Kona,	Oahu.
Laukalo,	Ili no Honolulu,	Kona,	Oahu.
Hunawai,	Ili no Honolulu,	Kona,	Oahu.
Huaipaako,	Ili no Honolulu,	Kona,	Oahu.
Apowale,	Ili no Honolulu,	Kona,	Oahu.
Oluku,	Ili no Honolulu,	Kona,	Oahu.
Palikea,	Ili no Honolulu,	Kona,	Oahu.
Niupaipai,	Ili no Honolulu,	Kona,	Oahu.
KawananakoaKaolu,	Ili no Honolulu,	Kona,	Oahu.
Kahui,	Ili no Honolulu,	Kona,	Oahu.
Pouhuluhulu,	Ili no Honolulu,	Kona,	Oahu.
Kaukahoku,	Ili no Honolulu,	Kona,	Oahu.
Punaanana,	Ili no Honolulu,	Kona,	Oahu.

An Act Relating to the Crown, Government, and Fort Lands, 1848

NAMES OF LANDS	AHUPUA'A	DISTRICTS	ISLANDS
Puiwa,	Ili no Honolulu,	Kona,	Oahu.
Kapalepo,	Ili no Honolulu,	Kona,	Oahu.
Olomana,	Ili no Honolulu,	Kona,	Oahu.
Kalokohonu,	Ili no Honolulu,	Kona,	Oahu.
Kaikahi,	Ili no Honolulu,	Kona,	Oahu.
Kaalaalalo,	Ili no Honolulu,	Kona,	Oahu.
Kaaleo,	Ili no Honolulu,	Kona,	Oahu.
Keonepanee,	Ili no Kalihi,	Kona,	Oahu.
Kaluaauau,	Ili no Kalihi,	Kona,	Oahu.
Kalia,	Ili no Waikiki,	Kona,	Oahu.
Kaluaolohe,	Ili no Waikiki,	Kona,	Oahu.
Haole,	Ili no Waikiki,	Kona,	Oahu.
Halelena,	Ili no Waikiki,	Kona,	Oahu.
Wahinalo,	Ili no Waikiki,	Kona,	Oahu.
Kumuulu,	Ili no Waikiki,	Kona,	Oahu.
Kahoiwai,	Ili no Waikiki,	Kona,	Oahu.
Kaluaalaea,	Ili no Waikiki,	Kona,	Oahu.
Waihi,	Ili no Waikiki,	Kona,	Oahu.
Hapuna,	Ili no Waikiki,	Kona,	Oahu.
Kaaumoa,	Ili no Waikiki,	Kona,	Oahu.
Waiaka,	Ili no Waikiki,	Kona,	Oahu.
Pahupahuapuaa,	Ili no Waikiki,	Kona,	Oahu.
Nukunukuaula,	Ili no Waikiki,	Kona,	Oahu.
Auaukai,	Ili no Waikiki,	Kona,	Oahu,
Mookahi,	Ili no Waikiki,	Kona,	Oahu.
Pawaa, o Maalo,	Ili no Waikiki,	Kona,	Oahu.
Kaluahole,	Ili no Waikiki,	Kona,	Oahu.
Mahani,	Ili no Kalihi,	Kona,	Oahu.
Niau 1,	Ili no Kalihi,	Kona,	Oahu.
Niau 2,	Ili no Kalihi,	Kona,	Oahu
Pohakea,	Ili no Kailua,	Koolaupoko,	Oahu.
Waipakiki,	Ili no Kailua,	Koolaupoko,	Oahu.
Kamakalepo,	Ili no Kailua,	Koolaupoko,	Oahu.
Kohanaiki,	Ili no Kailua,	Koolaupoko,	Oahu.
Pookea,	Ili no Kailua,	Koolaupoko,	Oahu.
Malamalama,	Ili no Kailua,	Koolaupoko,	Oahu.
Kuailima,	Ili no Kailua,	Koolaupoko,	Oahu.
Kaioa,	Ili no Kailua,	Koolaupoko,	Oahu.
Waimaauau,	Ili no Kailua,	Koolaupoko,	Oahu.
Maunawili,	Ili no Kailua,	Koolaupoko,	Oahu.
Puanea,	Ili no Kailua,	Koolaupoko,	Oahu.

Appendix

NAMES OF LANDS	AHUPUA'A	DISTRICTS	ISLANDS
Pohakea,	Ili no Kailua,	Koolaupoko,	Oahu.
Kalaheo,	Ili no Kailua,	Koolaupoko,	Oahu.
Kapaeli,	Ili no Kailua,	Koolaupoko,	Oahu.
Waiopihi,	Ili no Kailua,	Koolaupoko,	Oahu.
Kahoa,	Ili no Kailua,	Koolaupoko,	Oahu.
1/2 Kapakapa,	Ili no Kailua,	Koolaupoko,	Oahu.
1/2 Kaluaihakoko,	Ili no Kailua,	Koolaupoko,	Oahu.
1/2 Manulele,	Ili no Kailua,	Koolaupoko,	Oahu.
1/2 Kaohia,	Ili no Kailua,	Koolaupoko,	Oahu.
1/2 Kaeleuli,	Ili no Kailua,	Koolaupoko,	Oahu.
1/2 Kaaihee,	Ili no Kailua,	Koolaupoko,	Oahu.
1/2 Kaulu,	Ili no Kailua,	Koolaupoko,	Oahu.
1/2 Kaimi,	Ili no Kailua,	Koolaupoko,	Oahu.
1/2 Kapalai,	Ili no Kailua,	Koolaupoko,	Oahu.
1/2 Kaanokama,	Ili no Kailua,	Koolaupoko,	Oahu.
1/2 Kukanono,	Ili no Kailua,	Koolaupoko,	Oahu.
1/2 Kapaloa,	Ili no Kailua,	Koolaupoko,	Oahu.
1/2 Kulapuaa,	Ili no Kailua,	Koolaupoko,	Oahu.
1/2 Kalelekamani,	Ili no Kailua,	Koolaupoko,	Oahu.
1/2 Paalae,	Ili no Kailua,	Koolaupoko,	Oahu.
1/2 Manu,	Ili no Kailua,	Koolaupoko,	Oahu.
1/2 Kionaole,	Ili no Kailua,	Koolaupoko,	Oahu.
1/2 Pohakupu 1,	Ili no Kailua,	Koolaupoko,	Oahu.
1/2 Pohakupu 2,	Ili no Kailua,	Koolaupoko,	Oahu.
1/2 Kapia,	Ili no Kailua,	Koolaupoko,	Oahu.
1/2 Kalaepaa,	Ili no Kailua,	Koolaupoko,	Oahu.
1/2 Puukaeo,	Ili no Kailua,	Koolaupoko,	Oahu.
Waiohaka,	Ili no Kaneohe,	Koolaupoko,	Oahu.
Waikapoki,	Ili no Kaneohe,	Koolaupoko,	Oahu.
Puiwa,	Ili no Kaneohe,	Koolaupoko,	Oahu.
Lilipuna,	Ili no Kaneohe,	Koolaupoko,	Oahu.
1/2 Kahuauli,	Ili no Kaneohe,	Koolaupoko,	Oahu.
1/2 Wailele,	Ili no Kaneohe,	Koolaupoko,	Oahu.
1/2 Punaluu,	Ili no Kaneohe,	Koolaupoko,	Oahu.
1/2 Puawahakea,	Ili no Kaneohe,	Koolaupoko,	Oahu.
1/2 Pakui,	Ili no Kaneohe,	Koolaupoko,	Oahu.
1/2 Hooleinaiwa,	Ili no Kaneohe,	Koolaupoko,	Oahu.
Iolekaa,	Ili no Heeia,	Koolaupoko,	Oahu.
Luukoi,	Ili no Kahaluu,	Koolaupoko,	Oahu.
Waihee,	Ahupua'a, i Waihee,	Koolaupoko,	Oahu.
Kapuna,	Ili no Waihee,	Koolaupoko,	Oahu.

An Act Relating to the Crown, Government, and Fort Lands, 1848

NAMES OF LANDS	AHUPUA'A	DISTRICTS	ISLANDS
Kihewa,	Ili no Waihee,	Koolaupoko,	Oahu.
Kaniaia,	Ili no Waihee,	Koolaupoko,	Oahu.
Keahupuolo,	Ili no Waihee,	Koolaupoko,	Oahu.
Mauinoni,	Ili no Waihee,	Koolaupoko,	Oahu.
Ainoni,	Ili no Waihee,	Koolaupoko,	Oahu.
1/2 Kaululoa,	Ili no Waihee,	Koolaupoko,	Oahu.
Kaieie,	Ili no Kaalaea,	Koolaupoko,	Oahu.
1/2 Apuakuikui,	Ili no Kaalaea,	Koolaupoko,	Oahu.
Makanilua,	Ili no Waiahole,	Koolaupoko,	Oahu.
Apua,	Ili no Waiahole,	Koolaupoko,	Oahu.
Kuaiomuku,	Ili no Waiahole,	Koolaupoko,	Oahu.
Kaaniu,	Ili no Waiahole,	Koolaupoko,	Oahu.
Kupapaulau,	Ili no Waiahole,	Koolaupoko,	Oahu.
Poea,	Ili no Waiahole,	Koolaupoko,	Oahu.
Kumupali,	Ili no Waiahole,	Koolaupoko,	Oahu.
Ii,	Ili no Waiahole,	Koolaupoko,	Oahu.
Poahamai,	Ili no Waiahole,	Koolaupoko,	Oahu.
Kapuakea,	Ili no Waiahole,	Koolaupoko,	Oahu.
Uwau,	Ili no Waiahole,	Koolaupoko,	Oahu.
Waikane,	Ahupua'a i Waikane,	Koolaupoko,	Oahu.
Kahalaa,	Ili no Waikane,	Koolaupoko,	Oahu.
Kaiiki,	Ili no Waikane,	Koolaupoko,	Oahu.
Pahalona,	Ili no Hakipuu,	Koolaupoko,	Oahu.
Puukaluha,	Ili no Hakipuu,	Koolaupoko,	Oahu.
Lupehu,	Ili no Hakipuu,	Koolaupoko,	Oahu.
1/2 Kanahoanahopu,	Ili no Hakipuu,	Koolaupoko,	Oahu.
Kaaawa,	Ahupua'a,	Koolauloa,	Oahu.
Makaua,	Ahupua'a,	Koolauloa,	Oahu.
Waiono,	Ahupua'a,	Koolauloa,	Oahu.
Puheemiki,	Ahupua'a,	Koolauloa,	Oahu.
Kapano,	Ahupua'a,	Koolauloa,	Oahu.
Kaipapau,	Ahupua'a,	Koolauloa,	Oahu.
1/2 Keana,	Ahupua'a,	Koolauloa,	Oahu.
Ulupehupehu,	Ahupua'a.	Koolauloa,	Oahu.
Oio 1,	Ahupua'a,	Koolauloa,	Oahu.
Oio 2,	Ahupua'a,	Koolauloa,	Oahu.
Hanakaoe,	Ahupua'a,	Koolauloa,	Oahu.
Opana 1,	Ahupua'a,	Koolauloa,	Oahu.
Opana 2,	Ahupua'a,	Koolauloa,	Oahu.
1/2 Waimea,	Ahupua'a,	Koolauloa,	Oahu.
Kamananui,	Ahupua'a,	Waialua,	Oahu.

Appendix

NAMES OF LANDS	AHUPUA'A	DISTRICTS	ISLANDS
Mokuleia 1,	Ahupua'a,	Waialua,	Oahu.
Mokuleia 2,	Ahupua'a,	Waialua,	Oahu.
Kawaihapai,	Ahupua'a,	Waialua,	Oahu.
Kealia,	Ahupua'a,	Waialua,	Oahu.
Kaena,	Ahupua'a,	Waialua,	Oahu.
1/2 Keawaula,	Ahupua'a,	Waianae,	Oahu.
1/2 Kahanahaiki,	Ahupua'a,	Waianae,	Oahu.
Makua,	Ahupua'a,	Waianae,	Oahu.
1/2 Kalena,	Ili no Waianae,	Waianae,	Oahu.
Ulemoku,	Ili no Waikele,	Ewa,	Oahu.
Kaohai,	Ili no Waikele,	Ewa,	Oahu.
Onio,	Ili no Waikele,	Ewa,	Oahu.
Kahakuohia,	Ili no Waikele,	Ewa,	Oahu.
Waikele,	Ili no Waikele,	Ewa,	Oahu.
Paiwa,	Ili no Waikele,	Ewa,	Oahu.
Kahaupuupuu,	Ili no Waikele,	Ewa,	Oahu.
Waipahu,	Ili no Waikele,	Ewa,	Oahu.
Ulumalu,	Ili no Waikele,	Ewa,	Oahu.
1/2 Auiole,	Ili no Waikele,	Ewa,	Oahu.
1/2 Kanupoo,	Ili no Waikele,	Ewa,	Oahu.
1/2 Honopue,	Ili no Waipio,	Ewa,	Oahu.
1/2 Ulu,	Ili no Waipio,	Ewa,	Oahu.
Mananauka,	Ili no Mananaiki,	Ewa,	Oahu.
Kalanihale,	Ili no Mananaiki,	Ewa,	Oahu.
Kai,	Ili no Mananaiki,	Ewa,	Oahu.
Lihue,	Ili o Manananui	Ewa,	Oahu.
Kaihuokapuaa,	Ili no Waimano	Ewa,	Oahu.
Kahapapa,	Ili no Waimano,	Ewa,	Oahu.
Pualehua,	Ili no Waimano,	Ewa,	Oahu.
Puukapu 1,	Ili no Waimano,	Ewa,	Oahu.
Puukapu 2,	Ili no Waimano,	Ewa,	Oahu.
1/2 Lopa,	Ili no Waimano,	Ewa,	Oahu.
Nalima,	Ili no Waiau,	Ewa,	Oahu.
Naono,	Ili no Waiau,	Ewa,	Oahu.
1/2 Kaluaolohe,	Ili no Waiau,	Ewa,	Oahu.
Kahalaa,	Ili no Waimalu,	Ewa,	Oahu.
Kaumiumi,	Ili no Waimalu,	Ewa,	Oahu.
1/2 Pohakupu,	Ili no Waimalu,	Ewa,	Oahu.
1/2 Anana,	Ili no Waimalu,	Ewa,	Oahu.
1/2 Kahikiea,	Ili no Waimalu,	Ewa,	Oahu.
1/2 Kapaeli,	Ili no Kalauao,	Ewa,	Oahu.

An Act Relating to the Crown, Government, and Fort Lands, 1848

NAMES OF LANDS	AHUPUA'A	DISTRICTS	ISLANDS
1/2 Kauapoolei,	Ili no Kalauao,	Ewa,	Oahu.
1/2 Kauaopai,	Ili no Kalauao,	Ewa,	Oahu.
1/2 Kahawai,	Ili no Kalauao,	Ewa,	Oahu.
1/2 Kapuai,	Ili no Kalauao,	Ewa,	Oahu.
Maona,	Ili no Kalauao,	Ewa,	Oahu.
1/2 Kionawawana,	Ili no Kalihi,	Kona,	Oahu.
1/2 Kupehau,	Ili no Kalihi,	Kona,	Oahu.
1/2 Kalaepaa,	Ili no Kalihi,	Kona,	Oahu.
Kaluaopalena,	Ili no Kalihi,	Kona,	Oahu.
Keauhou,	Ili no Kalihi,	Kona,	Oahu.
1/2 Pawaa,	Ili no Waikiki,	Kona,	Oahu.
Kukuluaeo,	Ili no Waikiki,	Kona,	Oahu.
1/2 Kaalawai, *he kula wale no,*	Ili no Waikiki,	Kona,	Oahu.
Weliweli,	Ahupua'a,	Kona,	Kauai.
Koloa Hikina,	Ahupua'a,	Kona,	Kauai.
Koloa Komohana,	Ahupua'a,	Kona,	Kauai.
Wahiawa,	Ahupua'a,	Kona,	Kauai.
1/2 Punalau,	Ili no Hanapepe,	Kona,	Kauai.
1/2 Koula,	Ili no Hanapepe,	Kona,	Kauai.
Makaweli,	Ahupua'a, Eia naili a me na Moo, ame na Loi, no koa,	Kona,	Kauai.
Honopu,	Ahupua'a,	Napali,	Kauai.
Kalalau,	Ahupua'a,	Napali,	Kauai.
Pohakuao,	Ahupua'a,	Napali,	Kauai.
1/2 Honokoa,	Ahupua'a,	Napali,	Kauai.
Hanakapiai,	Ahupua'a,	Napali,	Kauai.
Waioli,	Ahupua'a,	Halelea,	Kauai.
Kilauea,	Ahupua'a,	Koolau,	Kauai.
Waiakalua Hikina,	Ahupua'a,	Koolau,	Kauai.
Pilaa, Kekahi aoao,	Ahupua'a,	Koolau,	Kauai.
Moloaa,	Ahupua'a,	Koolau,	Kauai.
Papaa,	Ahupua'a,	Koolau,	Kauai.
Aliomanu,	Ahupua'a,	Koolau,	Kauai.
Homaikawaa,	Ahupua'a,	Koolau,	Kauai.
Halaula,	Ahupua'a,	Koolau,	Kauai.
Ulakiu, Ili no Kapaa,	Ahupua'a,	Puna,	Kauai.
Paikahawai, Ili no Kapaa,	Ahupua'a,	Puna,	Kauai.
1/2 Olohena,	Ahupua'a,	Puna,	Kauai.
Kikiaola,	Ili no Waimea,	Kona,	Kauai.

419

NAMES OF LANDS	AHUPUA'A	DISTRICTS	ISLANDS
Niihau,	Ka Mokupuni,	Kona,	Niihau.
Pohueloa,	Ahupua'a,		Niihau.
Kaluahonu,	Ahupua'a,		Niihau.
Pauahula,	Ahupua'a,		Niihau.

Made over to the Chiefs and People, by our Sovereign Lord the King, and we do hereby declare those lands to be set apart *as the lands of the Hawaiian Government, subject always to the rights of tenants.* And we do hereby appoint the Minister of the Interior and his successors in office to direct, superintend, and dispose of said lands, as provided in the Act to organize the Executive Departments, done and passed at the Council House in Honolulu, the 27th day of April, A. D., 1845: Provided, however, that the Minister of the Interior and his successors in office shall have the power, upon the approval of the King in Privy Council, to dispose of the government lands to Hawaiian subjects, upon such other terms and conditions as to him and the King in Privy Council, may Seem best for the promotion of agriculture, and the best interests of the Hawaiian Kingdom:

    And Be It Further Enacted, That, in accordance with ancient custom, the following land, viz.:

NAMES OF LANDS	AHUPUA'A	DISTRICTS	ISLANDS
Kuwili,	Ili no Honolulu,	Kona,	Oahu.
Kuhimana,	Ili no Honolulu,	Kona,	Oahu.
Hauhaukoi,	Ili no Honolulu,	Kona,	Oahu.
Aala,	Ili no Honolulu,	Kona,	Oahu.
Kuaiaula,	Ili no Honolulu,	Kona,	Oahu.
Laukalo,	Ili no Honolulu,	Kona,	Oahu.
Kunawai,	Ili no Honolulu,	Kona,	Oahu.
Kuaipaako,	Ili no Honolulu,	Kona,	Oahu.
Apowale,	Ili no Honolulu,	Kona,	Oahu.
Oloku,	Ili no Honolulu,	Kona,	Oahu.
Alewa,	Ili no Honolulu,	Kona,	Oahu.
Puunui 1,	Ili no Honolulu,	Kona,	Oahu.
Puunui 2,	Ili no Honolulu,	Kona,	Oahu.
Puunui 3,	Ili no Honolulu,	Kona,	Oahu.
Palikea,	Ili no Honolulu,	Kona,	Oahu.
Niupaipai,	Ili no Honolulu,	Kona,	Oahu.
Kaolu Kawananakoa,	Ili no Honolulu,	Kona,	Oahu.
Kahui,	Ili no Honolulu,	Kona,	Oahu.
Pouhuluhulu,	Ili no Honolulu,	Kona,	Oahu.
Kaukahoku,	Ili no Honolulu,	Kona,	Oahu.
Punanaakaa,	Ili no Honolulu,	Kona,	Oahu.

NAMES OF LANDS	AHUPUA‘A	DISTRICTS	ISLANDS
Puiwa,	Ili no Honolulu,	Kona,	Oahu.
Kahapaakai,	Ili no Honolulu,	Kona,	Oahu.
Kapalepo,	Ili no Honolulu,	Kona,	Oahu.
Olomana,	Ili no Honolulu,	Kona,	Oahu.
Kalokohonu,	Ili no Honolulu,	Kona,	Oahu.
Kaikahi,	Ili no Honolulu,	Kona,	Oahu.
Kapiwai 1,	Ili no Honolulu,	Kona,	Oahu.
Kapiwai 2,	Ili no Honolulu,	Kona,	Oahu.
Kaalaalalo,	Ili no Honolulu,	Kona,	Oahu.
Kaaleo,	Ili no Honolulu,	Kona,	Oahu.
Keonepanee,	Ili no Kalihi,	Kona,	Oahu.
Kaluaauau,	Ili no Kalihi,	Kona,	Oahu.
Kalia,	Ili no Waikiki,	Kona,	Oahu.
Kaluaolohe,	Ili no Waikiki,	Kona,	Oahu.

Shall be the same are hereby set apart for the use of the Fort in Honolulu, to be cultivated by soldiers and other tenants under the direction of the Governor of O‘ahu, and his successors in office, native born Chiefs of the Hawaiian Islands, according to the instructions of the Minister of the Interior and his successors in office, approved by the King in Privy Council.

Done and Passed at the Council House, in Honolulu, this 7th day of June, A.D., 1848.

KAMEHAMEHA

KEONI ANA

Appendix 3

The Kuleana Act (Enactment of Further Principles), August 6, 1850

BE IT ENACTED *by the House of Nobles and Representatives of the Hawaiian Islands, in Legislative Council assembled:*

That the following sections which were passed by the King in privy council on the 21st of December, A.D. 1849, when the legislature was not in session, be and are hereby confirmed, and that certain other provisions be inserted, as follows:

1. That fee-simple titles, free of commutation, be and are hereby granted to all native tenants, who occupy and improve any portion of government land, for the lands they so occupy and improve, and whose claims to said lands shall be recognized as genuine by the land commission: Provided, however, that this resolution shall not extend to konohikis or other persons having the care of government lands, or to the house lots and other lands in which the government have an interest in the districts of Honolulu, Lahaina and Hilo.

2. By and with the consent of the King and chiefs in privy council assembled, it is hereby resolved, that fee-simple titles, free of commutation, be and are hereby granted to all native tenants who occupy and improve any lands other than those mentioned in the preceding resolution, held by the King or any chief or konohiki for the land they so occupy and improve: Provided, however, that this resolution shall not extend to house lots or other lands situated in the districts of Honolulu, Lahaina and Hilo.

3. That the board of commissioners to quiet land title be, and is hereby empowered to award fee-simple titles in accordance with the foregoing resolutions; to define and separate the portions of lands belonging to different individuals; and to provide for an equitable exchange of such different portions, where it can be done, so that each man's land may be by itself.

4. That a certain portion of the government lands in each island shall be set apart, and placed in the hands of special agents, to be disposed of in lots of from one to fifty acres, in fee-simple, to such natives as may not be otherwise furnished with sufficient land, at a minimum price of fifty cents per acre.

5. In granting to the people, their house lots in fee-simple, such as are separate and distinct from their cultivated lands, the amount of land in each of said house lots shall not exceed one quarter of an acre.

6. In granting to the people their cultivated grounds, or kalo lands, they shall only be entitled to what they have really cultivated, and which lie in the form of cultivated lands; and not such as the people may have cultivated in different spots, with the seeming intention of enlarging their lots; nor shall they be entitled to the waste lands.

7. When the landlords have taken allodial titles to their lands, the people on each of their lands, shall not be deprived of the right to take firewood, house timber, aho cord, thatch, or ti leaf, from the lands on which they live, for their own private use, should they need them, but they shall not have a right to take such articles to sell for profit. They shall also inform the landlord or his agent, and proceed with his consent. The people also shall have a right to drinking water, and running water, and the right of way. The springs of water, and running water, and roads shall be free to all, should they need them on all lands granted in fee-simple: Provided that this shall not be applicable in wells and water courses which individuals have made for their own use.

Done and passed at the council house in Honolulu, this 6th day of August, A.D. 1850.
KAMEHAMEHA.
KEONI ANA.

Appendix 4

In the Matter of the Estate of His Majesty Kamehameha IV, 2 Hawai'i 715, 1864 WL 2485 (1864)

SUPREME COURT OF THE KINGDOM OF HAWAII.

IN THE MATTER OF THE ESTATE OF HIS MAJESTY KAMEHAMEHA IV., LATE DECEASED.

APRIL TERM—1864.

May 27, 1864.

Syllabus by the Court

HISTORY of the nature of land tenures in this Kingdom, and construction of the Act of 7th June, 1848, as affecting the rights of dower and inheritance in the lands set apart to the Crown by the instrument of reservation, executed by Kamehameha III. on the 8th March, 1848.

By the said Act, which is entitled "An Act relating to the lands of his Majesty the King and of the Government," the lands reserved to the then reigning sovereign, descend in fee, the inheritance being limited to the successors to the throne, each successive possessor having the right to dispose of the same as private property, subject however to her Majesty's right of dower, there being nothing in the said Act, taking away the Queen's right to dower in the reserved lands, therein named: Nor is there any law of the Kingdom, making the matrimonial rights of the wife of the King, any less or different from those of the wife of any private gentleman.

The descent of that part of his late Majesty's estate, other than the lands, reserved to the Crown by the Act of 1848, must be governed by the general law of inheritance and distribution, and her Majesty Queen Emma is entitled as statutory heir to one-half of that property, instead of dower, the latter right being merged in the superior right of heir, after payment of such debts as are not specifically charged upon the reserved lands.

Attorney-General Harris, for his Majesty the King.

Messrs. Bates and Montgomery, for her Majesty Queen Emma.

Justice ROBERTSON delivered the judgment of the Court as follows:

A difference of opinion having arisen touching the descent of the property held and possessed by his late Majesty Kamehameha IV., a case has been submitted to the Court, upon an agreed statement of facts, in order that the rights of the several high personages interested may be solemnly adjudicated upon and amicably settled.

It is claimed on behalf of his Majesty Kamehameha V., that he, as hereditary successor to the throne, shall inherit the entire estate, both real and personal derived from his Majesty Kamehameha III., at his decease, and held by Kamehameha IV., the King lately deceased.

On the part of Queen Emma, lately the consort of his Majesty Kamehameha IV., it is claimed that all the property possessed by her late royal husband was his private property, and must descend in accordance with the general law of the Kingdom, and that she is therefore entitled to inherit one-half of his real and personal estate, after payment of his debts, and to take dower in the other half.

We deem it unnecessary to recapitulate here the statement of facts submitted on behalf of the parties, as these facts will be referred to in the course of our decision, as such reference may be necessary to elucidate the grounds upon which our judgment rests.

In order to simplify the case we will first dispose of the claim for dower in one-half of the estate, in addition to an absolute right in the other half, as heir under the statute, set up on behalf of Queen Emma. In our opinion, if she is entitled to dower at all, she must take dower in the entire estate which came to her late royal husband with the Crown, at the demise of his predecessor Kamehameha III. If, as is claimed on her behalf, she is entitled as a statutory heir to take one-half of her late husband's estate absolutely by way of inheritance, she cannot take dower also in the other half. In that case her right to dower, as widow, would be lost in her superior right to inherit as an heir. She cannot take in both those rights in the same estate.

The claim to the entire estate, as an appanage of the Crown, put forward by the Attorney-General on behalf of his Majesty the present King, is made to rest chiefly on the construction which it is contended should be given to the statute passed on the 7th day of June, A. D. 1848, entitled "An Act relating to the lands of his Majesty the King, and of the Government." The preamble to that Act, and the portions of it which bear upon the case, read as follows:

"*Whereas,* It hath pleased his most gracious Majesty Kamehameha III. the King, after reserving certain lands to himself as his own private property, to surrender and forever make over unto his chiefs and people the greater portion of his royal domain;

"*And whereas,* It hath pleased our Sovereign Lord the King, to place the lands so made over to his chiefs and people in the keeping of the House of Nobles and Representatives, or such person or persons as they may from time to time appoint, to be disposed of in such manner as the House of Nobles and Representatives may direct, and as may best promote the prosperity of this Kingdom and the dignity of the Hawaiian Crown; therefore,

"Be it enacted by the House of Nobles and Representatives of the Hawaiian Islands in Legislative Council assembled,

"That, expressing our deepest thanks to his Majesty for this noble and truly royal gift, we do hereby solemnly confirm this great act of our good King, and declare the following named lands, viz: (Here follow the names of the several lands.) To be the private lands of his Majesty Kamehameha III., to have and to hold to himself, his heirs and successors forever; and said lands shall be regulated and disposed of according to his royal will and pleasure, subject only to the rights of tenants."

After the foregoing follows the acceptance by the Legislature of the lands made over by the King to the Hawaiian Government, the lands being mentioned by name.

It is contended by the Attorney-General that by the true construction of this act it must be understood as declaring that the lands reserved to himself by Kamehameha III., in the grand division of 1848, were to descend forever to his heirs and successors on the throne, as a Royal Domain annexed to the Hawaiian Crown, and that they are not subject even to the right of dower.

On the other hand it is argued that by a fair construction of the act taken in connection with the instrument of reservation signed and sealed by Kamehameha III. on the 8th day of March, 1848, of which the act of the Legislative Council was simply a confirmation, the lands in question were declared to be the private property of Kamehameha III., his heirs and assigns, that as such, they are not only subject to the right of dower, but distributable under the statute regulating the descent of property generally like other private estates of persons dying intestate, and that therefore her Majesty Queen Emma, in the absence of any lineal heir of her husband, the late King, is entitled to one-half of the estate under the peculiar provisions of Hawaiian law, which would pass the other half to his Royal Highness M. Kekuanaoa, the surviving father of the late as of the present King.

The view which the Court takes of this matter, after the most careful examination and reflection, agrees in some respects with the views so ably propounded by the learned counsel for both the royal claimants, and yet as will be seen, differs materially from either.

It is conceded that the Court, in order to enable it to give a just construction to the act of the 7th of June, 1848, is at liberty to refer not only to the two instruments executed by his Majesty Kamehameha III., on the 8th of March, 1848, which were unquestionably the foundation of the Legislative enactment, but also to Hawaiian history, custom, legislation and polity, as well as to the records of the Privy Council, and the acts of the parties immediately interested subsequent to the great division.

The nature of land tenures in this Kingdom, prior to the great changes effected during the reign of Kamehameha III., will be found very clearly explained in the "Principles adopted by the Board of Commissioners to quiet Land Titles," (vol. 2 Statute Laws, page 81,) which were drawn up with much care upon the most valuable testimony that could be obtained. It is therein declared that "When the islands were conquered by Kamehameha I., he followed the example of his predecessors, and divided out the lands among his principal warrior chiefs, retaining, however, a portion in his own hands to be cultivated or managed by his own immediate servants or attendants. Each principal chief divided his lands anew and gave them out to an inferior order of chiefs or persons of rank, by whom they were subdivided again and again after (often) passing through the hands of four, five or six persons from the King down to the lowest class of tenants. All these persons were considered to have rights in the lands, or the productions of them, the proportions of which rights were not clearly defined, although universally acknowledged. All persons possessing landed property, whether superior landlords, tenants or sub-tenants, owed and paid to the King not only a land tax, which he assessed at pleasure, but also service which was called for at discretion, on all the grades from the highest down. They also owed and paid some portion of the productions of the land in addition to the yearly taxes. A failure to render any of these was always considered a just cause for which to forfeit the lands. The same rights which the King possessed over the superior landlords and all under them, the several grades of landlords possessed over their inferiors, so that there was a joint ownership of the land, the King really owning the allodium, and the person in whose hands he placed the land, holding it in trust." Such was the nature of the tenures, and such the titles by which the lands were held, when in 1839 protection was declared both for person and property in the following words: "Protection is hereby secured to the persons of all the people, together with their lands, their building lots and all their property." (See old Laws, page 10.) "The same law confirms what has been already stated in relation to the rights of his Majesty the King in all lands. Section 3d requires that every tenant of land shall work thirty-six days in the year for the King or Government, showing clearly that there is no individual who has an allodial title to the soil, that title remaining with the King." (Principles, vol. 2, Stat. Laws, p. 82.) The Commissioners proceed to say that the King could not dispose of the allodium to any other person without infringing on the rights of the superior lord, nor could the lord, if he purchased the allodium, seize upon the rights of the tenants and dispossess them. "It being therefore fully established, that there are but three classes of persons having vested rights in the lands: 1st, the Government, (i.e. the King); 2d, the landlord; and 3d, the tenant—it next becomes necessary to ascertain the proportional rights of each." (Ibid, p. 83.) The Commissioners, in view of the evidence given, arrived at the conclusion that, should the King allow to the landlord one-third, to the tenant one-third, and retain one-third himself, he, according to the uniform opinion of the witnesses, would injure no one unless himself. (Ibid, p. 83.) It was the imperative necessity of separating and defining the rights of the several parties interested in the lands, which led to the institution of the Board of Land Commissioners, and to the division made by the King himself, with the assistance of his Privy Council.

At the death of Kamehameha I., his son Liholiho, Kamehameha II., was recognized as King in accordance with his father's express will. Along with the Crown, Kamehameha II, inherited all his father's rights as an absolute sovereign and as suzerain or lord paramount of all the lands in the Kingdom, which rights, unimpaired, descended with the Crown to Kamehameha III. upon the death of his brother and predecessor.

In the year 1839 began that peaceful but complete revolution in the entire polity of the Kingdom which was finally consummated by the adoption of the present Constitution in the year 1852. His Majesty Kamehameha III. began by declaring protection for the persons and private rights of all his people from the highest to the lowest. In 1840 he granted the first Constitution by which he declared and established the equality before the law of all his subjects, chiefs and people alike. By that Constitution, he voluntarily divested himself of some of his powers and attributes as an absolute Ruler, and conferred certain political rights upon his subjects, admitting them to a share with himself in legislation and government. This was the beginning of a government as contradistinguished from the person of the King, who was thenceforth to be regarded rather as the executive chief and political head of the nation than its absolute governor. Certain kinds of public property began to be recognized as Government property, and not as the King's. Taxes which were previously applied to the King's own use were collected and set apart as a public revenue for Government purposes, and in 1841 his Majesty appointed a Treasury Board to manage and control the property and income of the Government. But the political changes introduced at that period did not affect in the least the King's rights as a great feudal Chief or Suzerain of the Kingdom. He had not as yet yielded any of those rights. It was expressly declared that he should still retain his own lands, and lands forfeited for the non-payment of taxes should revert to him. (Old Laws, p. 12.) Under the first law relating to the descent of lands to heirs, a portion of the lands held by any landlord were at his death to be restored to the King; and in case the landlord died leaving no heir, his lands and other property belonged to the King, by escheat. (Old Laws, p. 47.) Kamehameha III. gave a striking proof of his power as suzerain of the Kingdom, when he resumed the possession of all the fishing grounds within his dominions, for the purpose of making a new distribution of them, with the consent of his chiefs in Council. (Old Laws, p. 36; Haalelea vs. Montgomery, vol. 2, Haw. Rep., p. 62.)

The laws organizing the executive departments of the Government were enacted in the year 1846. Those laws provided among other things for the establishment of the Board of Land Commissioners, for the purpose of effecting a division of rights in land and of quieting the titles throughout the Kingdom. The subject of rights in land was one of daily increasing importance to the newly formed Government, for it was obvious that the internal resources of the country could not be developed until the system of undivided and undefined ownership in land should be abolished. Several expedients were resorted to with a view to obviate in some measure the existing difficulties, in advance of the action of the Land Commission. With that view the Legislative Council on the 7th November, 1846, passed a series of joint resolutions on the subject of rights in lands, and the leasing, purchasing and dividing the same. (Statute Laws, vol. 2, page 70; see Oni vs. Meek, Haw. Rep., vol. 2, p. 87.) But it was evident that such expedients could be of but little real benefit, while it must also have been foreseen that the operations of the Land Commission would occupy a long series of years, and that the Commission would encounter much difficulty in settling the rights of the chiefs and konohikis. In the month of December, 1847, the subject was discussed at length in the Privy Council. The record of that discussion is of the highest interest and has been carefully examined by the Court. It was finally resolved by the King in Council to effect through the assistance of a Committee, a division of lands between the King, as suzerain, and the high chiefs and konohikis, his feudatories. That division appears to have been effected with dispatch, for by the end of February, 1848, it was completed.

The King had resumed the possession of the larger part of the lands previously in the possession of the chiefs and landlords, and the remainder had been granted to the several holders by freehold title certified to the Land Commission for its formal award, and capable of being converted into an allodial title, by payment to the Government of a commutation to be fixed in Privy Council.

His Majesty's suzerainty over the lands held by his chiefs and other individuals was then at an end. He stood possessed of the lands which were in his own hands previous to the division, and of those resumed in the division, constituting together a large part of the landed property of the kingdom—a truly royal domain. But it is evident from the minutes of the Privy Council, that the lands comprised in that domain were not regarded as the King's private property strictly speaking. Even before his division with the landholders, a second division between himself and the government or state was clearly contemplated, and he appears to have admitted that the lands he then held might have been subjected to a commutation in favor of the government, in like manner with the lands of the chiefs. The records of the discussion in Council show plainly his Majesty's anxious desire to free his lands from the burden of being considered public domain, and as such, subjected to the danger of confiscation in the event of his islands being seized by any foreign power, and also his wish to enjoy complete control over his own property. Moved by these considerations and by a desire to promote the interest of his Kingdom, he proceeded with an exalted liberality to set apart for the use of the government the larger portion of his royal domain, reserving to himself what he deemed a reasonable amount of land as his own estate. To effect that object he signed and sealed on the 8th of March, 1848, two instruments contained in the Mahele Book, the first of which reads as follows:

"E ike auanei na kanaka a pau ma keia palapala, owau o Kamehameha III., no ka lokomaikai o ke Akua, ke ʻLii o ko Hawaii nei Pae Aina, ua haawi au i keia la no koʻu makemake maoli no, a ua hoolilo a me ka hookaawale mau loa aku i na ʻLii a me na kanaka, ka nui o koʻu aina alii e pono ai a e pomaikai ai ke Aupuni Hawaii, nolaila, ma keia palapala ke hookoe nei au noʻu iho a no koʻu poe hooilina a no koʻu poe hope a mau loa aku, na aina aʻu i kakauia ma na aoao 178, 182, 184, 186, 190,

194, 200, 204, 206, 210, 212, 214, 216, 218, 220, 222, o keia buke, ua hookaawaleia ua poe aina la no'u a no ko'u poe hooilina a me na hope o'u a mau loa, he waiwai ponoi no'u aole mea e ae."

The instrument we translate into English thus:

"Know all men by these presents, that I, Kamehameha III., by the grace of God, King of these Hawaiian Islands, have given this day of my own free will and have made over and set apart forever to the chiefs and people the larger part of my royal land, for the use and benefit of the Hawaiian Government, therefore by this instrument I hereby retain (or reserve) for myself and for my heirs and successors forever, my lands inscribed at pages 178, 182, 184, 186, 190, 194, 200, 204, 206, 210, 212, 214, 216, 218, 220, 222, of this book, these lands are set apart for me and for my heirs and successors forever, as my own property exclusively."

The other instrument which was also executed in the Hawaiian language, we translate into English thus: Know all men by these presents, that I, Kamehameha III., by the grace of God, King of these Hawaiian Islands, do hereby give, make over and set apart forever to the chiefs and people of my Kingdom, and convey all my right, title and interest in the lands situated here in the Hawaiian Islands, inscribed on pages 179 to 225, both inclusive, of this book, to have and to hold to my chiefs and people forever.

These lands are to be in the perpetual keeping of the Legislative Council (Nobles and Representatives) or in that of the superintendents of said lands, appointed by them from time to time, and shall be regulated, leased, or sold, in accordance with the will of said Nobles and Representatives, for the good of the Hawaiian Government, and to promote the dignity of the Hawaiian Crown.

By referring now to the confirmatory Act of the 7th June, 1848, it must be apparent to every one, from the close similarity of the language used in said Act with that of the instruments just recited, that the Legislative Council simply intended by that Act to ratify what had been already done by the King in Privy Council, and thereby bind the nation to its faithful observance forever. We think the Attorney-General was mistaken when he said the Act of 7th June, 1848, appeared to have been drafted hastily or inadvertently. It is within the knowledge of the Court that the Act in question was prepared in the English language by the late Chief Justice Lee, who had taken a prominent part in the discussion of the subject in the Privy Council, and who in common with other councillors appears to have been fully alive to the nature and importance of the business, and knew well the legal import of the language introduced into the Act.

His Majesty King Kamehameha III. had no surviving child of his own, but had adopted his nephew, Prince Alexander Liholiho. In the month of April, 1853, his Majesty, with the consent of the House of Nobles, and in accordance with the 25th Article of the Constitution, publicly proclaimed Prince Liholiho as his successor on the Throne. At the same time he made and executed his last will and testament, declaring his will both in regard to the descent of the Crown and the disposition of his estate. By the first clause of that instrument he declared his will that, Prince Liholiho, his adopted child should be his heir and successor to the Crown. By the second clause he declared that if Prince Liholiho should not survive him or should become incapacitated under the Constitution, his will was that Prince Lot Kamehameha should be heir to the Throne, and failing him, the Princess Victoria Kamamalu. By the third clause he directed that all his just debts should be paid out of his estate by his executors as soon as convenient after his decease. By the forth clause he devised to his consort Queen Kalama, certain lands in lieu of dower provided she should accept the same. By the fifth clause he devised all his remaining estate to his adopted son Prince Liholiho. His Majesty died on the 15th December, 1854, and was succeeded by Prince Liholiho as Kamehameha IV. The will of Kamehameha III. was duly proved before the Hon. Lorrin Andrews, Judge of Probate, on the 27th day of January, 1855, and the provision thereof, touching the King's estate, were carried out by the executors.

It is admitted that from the time when Kamehameha III. separated his own property from that of the Government, in 1848, up till his death, he dealt with his reserved lands, as his own private estate, leasing, mortgaging or selling the same at his pleasure. Ever since the division, those lands, except such as have been sold, have always been known as the King's lands, and have been managed by an agent or land steward appointed by the King. After the death of Kamehameha III., Queen Kalama declined to accept the lands devised to her by the King's will, in lieu of dower, on the ground that she had received these lands from him in the division of 1848. Her right to dower was acknowledged by King Kamehameha IV, who made an amicable arrangement touching the same, by setting upon her a fixed annuity for life, in consideration of which she relinquished her claim for dower by deed. In the year 1856 the late King married his still surviving consort Queen Emma. No ante-nuptial agreement was made as to their property, nor any provision in the nature of a jointure for the Queen. During his Majesty's reign, a period of nearly nine years, he constantly dealt with the lands in question as his private property in like manner as his predecessor had done, and her Majesty Queen Emma was always in the habit of joining with him in deeds to individuals, whenever it was necessary that she should do so in order to bar her dower. On the 30th day of November last, his Majesty died intestate.

Having stated fully all the facts and circumstances which seem to us calculated to throw light on the subject, and to guide the Court in ascertaining the intention of Kamehameha III. as declared in the instrument of reservation of the 8th March, 1848, and in giving a sound construction to the confirmatory act of the Legislative Council, it only remains for us now to announce the conclusions at which we have arrived.

In our opinion, while it was clearly the intention of Kamehameha III. to protect the lands which he reserved to himself out of the domain which had been acquired by his family through the prowess and skill of his father, the conqueror, from the danger of being treated as public domain or Government property, it was also his intention to provide that those lands should descend to his heirs and successors, the future wearers of the crown which the conqueror had won; and we understand the act of 7th June, 1848, as having secured both those objects. Under that act the lands descend in fee, the inheritance being limited however to the successors to the throne, and each successive possessor may regulate and dispose of the same according to his will and pleasure, as private property, in like manner as was done by Kamehameha III.

In our opinion the fifth clause of the will of Kamehameha III. was not necessary to pass the reserved lands to Kamehameha IV., any more than the first clause was necessary to pass to him the crown. He was entitled to inherit those lands by force of the act of 7th June, 1848, when he succeeded to the crown, in virtue of the public proclamation made by his predecessor with the consent of the House of Nobles, and he was entitled as the adopted son of Kamehameha III., to inherit the remainder of his estate not devised to any one else, subject to dower.

We are clearly of opinion also that her Majesty Queen Emma is lawfully entitled to dower in the reserved lands, except so far as she may have barred her right therein by her own act and deed. There is nothing in the Act of 7th June, 1848, which can be understood as taking away the Queen's right of dower in the lands therein named; nor is there any law of this Kingdom which renders the matrimonial rights of the wife of the King any less than or any different from those of the wife of any private gentleman. Such was unquestionably the understanding of both Kamehameha III, and his successor as to dower in those lands, which are to be dealt with in all respects as private inheritable property, subject only to the special legislative restriction on the manner of their descent.

But his Majesty Kamehameha IV. was possessed of other property, both real and personal, at the time of his death, not affected with the special character attached to the reserved lands. The descent of that part of his estate must be governed by the general law of inheritance and distribution, and her Majesty Queen Emma is therefore entitled as statutory heir to one-half of that property, after the payment there out of such portion of the late King's debts as are not specifically charged by mortgage or otherwise upon the reserved lands. Debts of the latter class ought clearly to be paid out of the estate encumbered therewith.

Let judgment be entered accordingly in favor of both the claimants.

N. B.—Since the above decision the Legislature, by the law of January 3d, 1865, have decreed the lands reserved to the Crown, by the Act of 1848, to be henceforth inalienable and not lawful to lease the same for any term of years to exceed thirty.

Appendix 5

Act Rendering the Crown Lands Inalienable,
January 3, 1865

An Act to Relieve the Royal Domain from Encumbrances, and to Render the Same Inalienable.

WHEREAS, by the Act entitled "An Act relating to the lands of His Majesty the King, and of the Government," passed on the 7th day of June, A. D. 1848 it appears by the Preamble, that His Most Gracious Majesty Kamehameha III, the King, after reserving certain lands to himself as his own private property, to surrender and make over unto his chiefs and people, the greater portion of his Royal Domain. *And whereas,* by the same Act it was declared that certain lands therein named, shall be the private lands of Kamehameha III., to have and to hold to himself, his heirs and successors forever; and that the said lands shall be regulated and disposed of according to his royal will and pleasure, subject only to the rights of tenants. *And whereas,* by the proper construction of the said statute the words "Heirs and Successors," mean the heirs and successors to the Royal Office. *And whereas,* the history of said lands shows that they were vested in the King for the purpose of maintaining the Royal State and Dignity; and it is therefore disadvantageous to the public interest, that the said lands should be alienated, or the said Royal Domain diminished. *And whereas, further,* during the two late reigns, the said Royal Domain has been greatly diminished, and is now charged with mortgages to secure considerable sums of money; now, therefore,

Be It Enacted, by the King and the Legislative Assembly of the Hawaiian Islands, in the Legislature of the Kingdom assembled:

Section 1. The Minister of Finance is hereby authorized to issue Exchequer Bonds, with coupons attached, to the amount of not more than thirty thousand dollars, said bond to bear interest, at not more than twelve per cent. per annum, payable half yearly, and to be redeemable at such times within the next twenty years, as the said Minister of Finance shall deem expedient, which said bond shall be issued whensoever necessary to the Commissioners of Crown Lands, hereinafter provided for, to be used to extinguish those mortgages which may remain unsatisfied after the

433

Administrator of his late Majesty's Estate has exhausted all the Estate belonging to his late Majesty, in a private capacity, which the said Administrator may be legally entitled to use for the payment of the debts of the Estate.

SECTION 2. Full authority is hereby given to such Commissioners, jointly with the Minister of Finance, to negotiate for the redemption of the mortgages in the preceding section referred to, and dispose of the said Exchequer Bonds for that purpose, in such manner as may be most advantageous to the public interest.

SECTION 3. It is further enacted, that so many of the lands which by the Statute enacted on the 7th of June, 1848, are declared to be the private lands of His Majesty Kamehameha III., to have and to hold to himself, his heirs and successors forever, as may be at this time unalienated, and have descended to His Majesty Kamehameha V., shall be henceforth inalienable, and shall descend to the heirs and successors of the Hawaiaan Crown forever; and it is further enacted, that it shall not be lawful hereafter to execute any lease or leases of the said lands, for any term of years to exceed thirty.

SECTION 4. The Commissioners of the Crown Lands shall have full power and authority to make good and valid leases of the said lands for any number of years not exceeding thirty; but in no case shall it be lawful to collect the rents on the same for more than one year in advance, or to receive anything in the nature of a bonus for signing the said lease, and all the rents, profits and emoluments derived from the said lands, after deducting the necessary and proper expenses of managing the same, shall be for the use and benefit of the Reigning Sovereign, and payable by the said Commissioners to the order of the King, except when the King shall be a minor, and then they shall be invested for the benefit of the said minor King, as the Legislature may direct, until the said minor shall have arrived at the age of majority, and excepting further as in the succeeding section set forth.

SECTION 5. There shall be set apart by the said Commissioners, one-fourth part of the annual revenue of the said Estate, which shall be paid into the Public Treasury, and be devoted first to the payment of the interest on the Exchequer Bonds herein above provided for, and so much of the said fourth part of the said income as may be in excess of the said interest on the said bonds, shall be applied to the payment of the principal of the said bonds, until the entire sum by this Act authorized to be issued shall be fully paid.

SECTION 6. The Board of Commissioners of Crown Lands shall consist of three persons, to be appointed by His Majesty the King, two of whom shall be appointed from among the members of his Cabinet Council, and serve without any remuneration, and the other shall act as Land Agent, and shall be paid out of the revenues of the said land, such sum as may be agreed by His Majesty the King.

Approved this 3rd day of January, A. D. 1865.
KAMEHAMEHA R.

Appendix 6

Joint Resolution of Annexation, July 7, 1898

JOINT RESOLUTION TO PROVIDE FOR ANNEXING THE HAWAIIAN ISLANDS TO THE UNITED STATES, 30 STAT. 750 (1898).

Whereas the Government of the Republic of Hawaii having, in due form, signified its consent, in the manner provided by its constitution, to cede absolutely and without reserve to the United States of America all rights of sovereignty of whatsoever kind in and over the Hawaiian Islands and their dependencies, and also to cede and transfer to the United States the absolute fee and ownership of all public, Government, or Crown lands, public buildings or edifices, ports, harbors, military equipment, and all other public property of every kind and description belonging to the Government of the Hawaiian Islands, together with every right and appurtenance thereunto appertaining; Therefore

Resolved by the Senate and House of Representatives of the United States of America in Congress Assembled, That said cession is accepted, ratified, and confirmed, and that the said Hawaiian Islands and their dependencies be, and they are hereby, annexed as a part of the territory of the United States and are subject to the sovereign dominion thereof, and that all and singular the property and rights hereinbefore mentioned are vested in the United States of America.

The existing laws of the United States relative to public lands shall not apply to such lands in the Hawaiian Islands; but the Congress of the United States shall enact special laws for their management and disposition: *Provided,* That all revenue from or proceeds of the same, except as regards such part thereof as may be used or occupied for the civil, military, or naval purposes of the United States, or may be assigned for the use of the local government, shall be used solely for the benefit of the inhabitants of the Hawaiian Islands for educational and other public purposes.

Until Congress shall provide for the government of such islands all the civil, judicial, and military powers exercised by the officers of the existing government in said islands shall be vested in such person or persons and shall be exercised in such manner as the President of the United States shall direct; and the President shall have the power to remove said officers and fill the vacancies so occasioned.

The existing treaties of the Hawaiian Islands with foreign nations shall forthwith cease and determine, being replaced by such treaties as may exist, or as may be hereafter concluded, between the United States and such foreign nations. The municipal legislation of the Hawaiian Islands, not enacted for the fulfillment of the treaties so extinguished, and not inconsistent with this joint resolution nor contrary to the Constitution of the United States nor to any existing treaty of the United States, shall remain in force until the Congress of the United States shall otherwise determine.

Until legislation shall be enacted extending the United States customs laws and regulations to the Hawaiian Islands the existing customs relations of the Hawaiian Islands with the United States and other countries shall remain unchanged.

The public debt of the Republic of Hawaii, lawfully existing at the date of the passage of this joint resolution, including the amounts due to depositors in the Hawaiian Postal Savings Bank, is hereby assumed by the Government of the United States; but the liability of the United States in this regard shall in no case exceed four million dollars. So long, however, as the existing Government and the present commercial relations of the Hawaiian Islands are continued as hereinbefore provided said Government shall continue to pay the interest on said debt.

There shall be no further immigration of Chinese into the Hawaiian Islands, except upon such conditions as are now or may hereafter be allowed by the laws of the United States; no Chinese, by reason of anything herein contained, shall be allowed to enter the United States from the Hawaiian Islands.

The President shall appoint five commissioners, at least two of whom shall be residents of the Hawaiian Islands, who shall, as soon as reasonably practicable, recommend to Congress such legislation concerning the Hawaiian Islands as they shall deem necessary or proper.

SEC. 2. That the commissioners hereinbefore provided for shall be appointed by the President, by and with the advice and consent of the Senate.

SEC. 3. That the sum of one hundred thousand dollars, or so much thereof as may be necessary; is hereby appropriated, out of any money in the Treasury not otherwise appropriated, and to be immediately available, to be expended at the discretion of the President of the United States of America, for the purpose of carrying this joint resolution into effect.

SEREXO E. PAYNE, Speaker of the House of Representatives Pro Tempore.
GARRETT A. HOBART, Vice-President of the United States and President of the Senate.
Approved July 7th, 1898.
WILLIAM McKINLEY.

Appendix 7

Excerpts from the Organic Act,
April 30, 1900

AN ACT TO PROVIDE A GOVERNMENT FOR THE TERRITORY OF HAWAII
(ACT OF APRIL 30, 1900, C 339, 31 STAT 141) (as amended)

73. COMMISSIONER OF PUBLIC LANDS.

(a) That when used in this section—

(1) The term "commissioner" means the commissioner of public lands of the Territory of Hawaii;

(2) The term "land board" means the board of public lands, as provided in subdivision (1) of this section;

(3) The term "public lands" includes all lands in the Territory of Hawaii classed as government or crown lands previous to August 15, 1895, or acquired by the government upon or subsequent to such date by purchase, exchange, escheat, or the exercise of the right of eminent domain, or in any other manner; except (1) lands designated in section 203 of the Hawaiian Homes Commission Act, 1920, (2) lands set apart or reserved by Executive order by the President, (3) lands set aside or withdrawn by the governor under the provisions of subdivision (q) of this section, (4) sites of public buildings, lands used for roads, streets, landings, nurseries, parks, tracts reserved for forest growth or conservation of water supply, or other public purposes, and (5) lands to which the United States has relinquished the absolute fee and ownership, unless subsequently placed under the control of the commissioner and given the status of public lands in accordance with the provisions of this Act, the Hawaiian Homes Commission Act, 1920, or the Revised Laws of Hawaii of 1915; and

(4) The term "person" includes individual, partnership, corporation, and association.

(b) Any term defined or described in section 347 or 351 of the Revised Laws of Hawaii of 1915, except a term defined in subdivision (a) of this section, shall, whenever used in this section, if not inconsistent with the context or any provision of this section, have the same meaning as given it by such definition or description.

(c) The laws of Hawaii relating to public lands, the settlement of boundaries, and the issuance of patents on land commission awards, except as changed by this Act, shall continue in force until Congress shall otherwise provide. Subject to the approval of the President, all sales, grants, leases, and other dispositions of the public domain, and agreements concerning the same, and all franchises granted by the Hawaiian government in conformity with the laws of Hawaii, between the 7th day of July, 1898, and the 28th day of September, 1899, are hereby ratified and confirmed. In said laws "land patent" shall be substituted for "royal patent"; "commissioner of public lands," for "minister of the interior," "agent of public lands," and "commissioners of public lands," or their equivalents; and the words "that I am a citizen of the United States," or "that I have declared my intention to become a citizen of the United States, as required by law," for the words "that I am a citizen by birth (or naturalization) of the Republic of Hawaii," or "that I have received letters of denization under the Republic of Hawaii," or "that I have received a certificate of special right of citizenship from the Republic of Hawaii."

(d) No lease of the surface of agriculture lands or of undeveloped and public land which is capable of being converted into agricultural land by the development, for irrigation purposes, of either the underlying or adjacent waters, or both, shall be granted, sold, or renewed by the government of the Territory of Hawaii for a longer period than sixty-five years. Each such lease shall be sold at public auction to the highest bidder after due notice as provided in subdivision (i) of this section and the laws of the Territory of Hawaii. Each such notice shall state all the terms and conditions of the sale. The land, or any part thereof so leased, may at any time during the term of the lease be withdrawn from the operation thereof for homestead or public purposes,upon the payment of just compensation for such withdrawal. Every such lease shall contain a provision to that effect: Provided, That the commissioner may, with the approval of the governor and at least two-thirds of the members of the land board, omit such withdrawal provision from, or limit the same in, the lease of any lands whenever he deems it advantageous to the Territory of Hawaii, and land so leased shall not be subject to such right of withdrawal, or shall be subject only to a right of withdrawal as limited in the lease.

(e) All funds arising from the sale or lease or other disposal of public land shall be appropriated by the laws of the government of the Territory of Hawaii and applied to such uses and purposes for the benefit of the inhabitants of the Territory of Hawaii as are consistent with the joint resolution of annexation, approved July 7, 1898.

(f) No person shall be entitled to receive any certificate of occupation, right of purchase lease, cash freehold agreement, or special homestead agreement who, or whose husband or wife, has previously taken or held more than ten acres of land under any such certificate, lease, or agreement made or issued after May 27, 1910, or under any homestead lease or patent based thereon; or who, or whose husband or wife, or both of them, owns other land in the Territory, the combined area of which and the land in question exceeds eighty acres; or who is an alien, unless he has declared his intention to become a citizen of the United States as provided by law. No person who has so declared his intention and taken or held under any such certificate, lease, or agreement shall continue so to hold or become entitled to a homestead lease or patent of the land, unless he becomes a citizen within five years after so taking.

(g) No public land for which any such certificate, lease, or agreement is issued after May 27, 1910, or any part thereof, or interest therein or control thereof, shall, without the written consent of the commissioner and governor, thereafter, whether before or after a homestead lease or patent has been issued thereon, be or be contracted to be in any way, directly or indirectly, by process of law or otherwise, conveyed, mortgaged, leased, or otherwise transferred to, or acquired or held by or for the benefit of, any alien or corporation; or before or after the issuance of a homestead lease or before the issuance of a patent to or by or for the benefit of any other person; or, after the issuance of a patent, to or by or for the benefit of any person who owns, or holds, or controls, directly or indirectly, other land or the use thereof, the combined area of which and the land in question exceeds eighty acres. The prohibitions of this paragraph shall not apply to transfers or acquisitions by inheritance or between tenants in common.

(h) Any land in respect of which any of the foregoing provisions shall be violated shall forthwith be forfeited and resume the status of public land and may be recovered by the Territory or its successors in an action of ejectment or other appropriate proceedings. And noncompliance with the terms of any such certificate, lease, or agreement, or of the law applicable thereto, shall entitle the commissioner, with the approval of the governor before patent has been issued, with or without legal process, notice, demand, or previous entry, to retake possession and thereby determine the estate: Provided, That the times limited for compliance with any such approval upon its appearing that an effort has been made in good faith to comply therewith.

(i) The persons entitled to take under any such certificate, lease, or agreement shall be determined by drawing or lot, after public notice as hereinafter provided; and any lot not taken or taken and forfeited, or any lot or part thereof surrendered with the consent of the commissioner, which is hereby authorized, may be disposed of upon application at not less than the advertised price by any such certificate, lease, or agreement without further notice. The notice of any sale, drawing, or allotment of public land shall be by publication for a period of not less than sixty days in one or more newspapers of general circulation published in the Territory: *Provided however,* That (1) lots may be sold for cash or on an extended time basis, as the Commissioner may determine, without recourse to drawing or lot and forthwith patented to any citizen of the United States applying therefor, possessing the qualifications of a homesteader as now provided by law, and who has qualified for and received a loan under the provisions of the Bankhead-Jones Farm Tenant Act, as amended or as may hereafter be amended, for the acquisition of a farm, and (2) with or without recourse to drawing or lot, as the commissioner may determine, lots may be leased with or without a right of purchase, or may be sold for cash or on an extended time basis and forthwith patented, to any citizen of the United States applying therefor if such citizen has not less than two years' experience as a farm owner, farm tenant, or farm laborer: And provided further, That any patent issued upon any such sale shall contain the same restrictive provisions as are now contained in a patent issued after compliance with a right of purchase lease, cash freehold agreement, or special homestead agreement.

The Commissioner may include in any patent, agreement, or lease a condition requiring the inclusion of the land in any irrigation project formed or to be formed by the Territorial agency responsible therefor and making the land subject to assessments made or to be made for such irrigation project, which assessment shall be a first charge against the land. For failure to pay the assessments or other breach of the condition the land may be forfeited and sold pursuant to the provisions of this Act, and, when sold, so much of the proceeds of sale as are necessary therefor may be used to pay any unpaid assessments.

(j) The commissioner, with the approval of the governor, may give to any person (1) who is a citizen of the United States or who has legally declared his intention to become a citizen of the United States and hereafter becomes such, and (2) who has, or whose predecessors in interest have, improved any parcel of public lands and resided thereon continuously for the ten years next preceding the application to purchase, a preference right to purchase so much of such parcel and such adjoining land as may reasonably be required for a home, at a fair price to be determined by three disinterested citizens to be appointed by the governor. In the determination of such purchase price the commissioner may, if he deems it just and reasonable, disregard the value of the improvements on such parcel and adjoining land. If such parcel of public lands is reserved for public purposes, either for the use of the United States or the Territory of Hawaii, the commissioner may with the approval of the governor grant to such person a preference right to purchase public lands which are of similar character, value, and area, and which are situated in the same land district. The privilege granted by this paragraph shall not extend to any original lessee or to an assignee of an entire lease of public lands.

(k) The commissioner may also, with such approval, issue, for a nominal consideration, to any church or religious organization, or person or persons or corporation representing it, a patent for any parcel of public land occupied continuously for not less than five years heretofore and still occupied by it as a church site under the laws of Hawaii.

(l) No sale of lands for other than homestead purposes, except as herein provided, and no exchange by which the Territory shall convey lands exceeding either forty acres in area or $15,000 in value shall be made. Leases may be made by the commissioner of public lands, with the approval of two-thirds of the members of the board of public lands, for the occupation of lands for general purposes, or for limited specified purposes (but not including leases of minerals or leases providing for the mining of minerals), for terms up to but not in excess of sixty-five years. There shall be a board of public lands, the members of which are to be appointed by the governor as provided in section 80 of this Act, and until the legislature shall otherwise provide said board shall consist of six members, and its members be appointed for a term of four years: Provided, however, That the commissioner shall, with the approval of said board, sell to any citizen of the United States, or to any person who has legally declared his intention to become a citizen, for residence purposes lots not exceeding three acres in area; but any lot not sold after public auction, or sold and forfeited, or any lot or part thereof surrendered with the consent of the commissioner, which consent is authorized, may upon application be sold without further public notice or auction within the period of two years immediately subsequent to the day of the public auction, at the advertised price if the sale is within the period of six months immediately subsequent to the day of the public auction, and at the advertised price or the price fixed by a reappraisal of the land, whichever is greater, if the sale is within the period subsequent to the said six months but prior to the expiration of the said two years: and that sales of Government lands or any interest therein may be made upon the approval of said board for business uses or other undertakings or uses, except those which are primarily agricultural in character, whenever such sale is deemed to be in the interest of the development of the community or area in which said lands are located, and all such sales shall be limited to the amount actually necessary for the economical conduct of such business use or other undertaking or use: Provided further, That no exchange of Government lands shall hereafter be made without the approval of two-thirds of the members of said board, and no such exchange shall be made except to acquire lands directly for public uses: Provided further, That in case any lands have been or shall be sold pursuant to the provisions of this paragraph for any purpose above set forth and/or subject to any conditions with respect to the improvement thereof or otherwise, and in case any said lands have been or shall be used by the United States of America, including any department or agency thereof, whether under lease or license from the owner thereof or otherwise, for any purpose relating to war or the national defense and such use has been or shall be for a purpose other than that for which said lands were sold and/or has prevented or shall prevent the performance of any conditions of the sale of said lands with respect to the improvement thereof or otherwise, then, notwithstanding the provisions of this paragraph or of any agreement, patent, grant, or deed issued upon the sale of said lands, such use of said lands by the United States of America, including any department or agency thereof, shall not result in the forfeiture of said lands and shall result in the extension of the period during which any conditions of the sale of said lands may be complied with for an additional period equal to the period of the use of said lands by the United States of America, including any department or agency thereof.

(m) Whenever twenty-five or more persons, having the qualifications of homesteaders who have not therefore made application under this Act shall make written application to the commissioner of public lands for the opening of agricultural lands for settlement in any locality or district, it shall be the duty of said commissioner to proceed expeditiously to survey and open for entry agricultural lands, whether unoccupied or under lease with the right of withdrawal, sufficient in area to provide homesteads for all such persons, together with all persons of like qualifications who shall have filed with such commissioner prior to the survey of such lands written applications for homesteads in the district designated in said applications. The lands to be so opened for settlement by said commissioner shall be either the specific tract or tracts applied for or other suitable and available agricultural lands in the same geographical district and, as far as possible, in the immediate locality of and as nearly equal to that applied for as may be available: Provided, however, That no leased land, under cultivation, shall be taken for homesteading until any crops growing thereon shall have been harvested.

(n) It shall be the duty of the commissioner to cause to be surveyed and opened for homestead entry a reasonable amount of desirable agricultural lands and also of pastoral lands in the various parts of the Territory for homestead purposes on or before January 1, 1911, and he shall annually thereafter cause to be surveyed for homestead purposes such amount of agricultural lands and pastoral lands in various parts of the Territory as there may be demand for by persons having the qualifications of homesteaders. In laying out any homestead the commissioner shall include in the homestead lands sufficient to support thereon an ordinary family, but not exceeding eighty acres of agricultural lands and two hundred and fifty acres of first-class pastoral lands or five hundred acres of second-class pastoral lands; or in case of a homestead, including pastoral lands only, not exceeding five hundred acres of first-class pastoral lands or one thousand acres of second-class pastoral lands. All necessary expenses for surveying and opening any such lands for homesteads shall be paid for out of any funds of the territorial treasury derived from the sale or lease of public lands, which funds are hereby made available for such purposes.

(o) The commissioner, with the approval of the governor, may by contract or agreement authorize any person who has the right of possession, under a general lease from the Territory, of agricultural or pastoral lands included in any homestead, to continue in possession of such lands after the expiration of the lease until such time as the homesteader takes actual possession thereof under any form of homestead agreement. The commissioner may fix in the contract or agreement such other terms and conditions as he deems advisable.

(p) Nothing herein contained shall be construed to prevent said commissioner from surveying and opening for homestead purposes and as a single homestead entry public lands suitable for both agricultural and pastoral purposes, whether such lands be situated in one body or detached tracts, to the end that homesteaders may be provided with both agricultural and pastoral lands wherever there is demand therefor; nor shall the ownership of a residence lot or tract, not exceeding three acres in area, hereafter disqualify any citizen from applying for and receiving any form of homestead entry, including a homestead lease.

(q) All lands in the possession, use, and control of the Territory shall hereafter be managed by the commissioner, except such as shall be set aside for public purposes as hereinafter provided; all sales and other dispositions of such land shall, except as otherwise provided by the Congress, be made by the commissioner or under his direction, for which purpose, if necessary, the land may be transferred to his department from any other department by direction of the governor, and all patents and deeds of such land shall issue from the office of the commissioner, who shall countersign the same and keep a record thereof. Lands conveyed to the Territory in exchange for other lands that are subject to the land laws of Hawaii, as amended by this Act, shall, except, as otherwise provided, have the same status and be subject to such laws as if they had previously been public lands of Hawaii. All orders setting aside lands for forest or other public purposes, or withdrawing the same, shall be made by the governor, and lands while so set aside for such purposes may be managed as may be provided by the laws of the Territory; the provisions of this paragraph may also be applied where the "public purposes" are the uses and purposes of the United States, and lands while so set aside may be managed as may be provided by the laws of the United States. The commissioner is hereby authorized to perform any and all acts, prescribe forms of oaths, and, with the approval of the governor and said board, make such rules and regulations as may be necessary and proper for the purpose of carrying the provisions of this section and the land laws of Hawaii into full force and effect.

All officers and employees under the jurisdiction of the commissioner shall be appointed by him, subject to the Territorial laws of Hawaii relating to the civil service of Hawaii, and all such officers and employees shall be subject to such civil service laws.

Within the meaning of this section, the management of lands set aside for public purposes may, if within the scope of authority conferred by the legislature, include the making of leases by the Hawaii aeronautics commission with respect to land set aside to it, on reasonable terms, for carrying out the purposes for which such land was set aside to it, such as for occupancy of land at an airport for facilities for carriers or to serve the traveling public. No such lease shall continue in effect for a longer term than fifty-five years. If, at the time of the execution of any such lease, the governor shall have approved the same, then and in that event the governor shall have no further authority under this or any other Act to set aside any or all of the lands subject to such lease for any other public purpose during the term of such lease.

(r) Whenever any remnant of public land shall be disposed of, the commissioner of public lands shall first offer it to the abutting landowner for a period of three months at a reasonable price in no event to be less than the fair market value of the land to be sold, to be determined by a disinterested appraiser or appraisers, but not more than three, to be appointed by the governor; and, if such owner fails to take the same, then such remnant may be sold at public auction at no less than the amount of the appraisal: *Provided,* That if the remnant abuts more than one separate parcel of land and more than one of the owners of these separate parcels are interested in purchasing said remnant, the remnant shall be sold to the owner making the highest offer above the appraised value. The term "remnant" shall mean a parcel of land landlocked or without access to any public highway, and, in the case of an urban area, no larger than five thousand square feet in size, or, in the case of a suburban or rural area, no larger than one and one-half acres in size.

Any person or persons holding an unpatented homestead under a special homestead agreement, entered into prior to the effective date of this paragraph, excluding those homesteads under the control of the Hawaiian Homes Commission as provided in section 203 of the Hawaiian Homes Commission Act, 1920, shall be entitled to a reamortization of the indebtedness due the Territory of Hawaii on account of such special homestead agreement upon filing an application for the reamortization of said indebtedness with the commissioner within six months after the effective date of this paragraph. Upon the filing of any such application, the commissioner shall determine the balance due the Territory in the following manner: The amount of the principal which would have been paid during the full period of payment provided for in the special homestead agreement had the agreement been duly performed according to its terms and the amount of the interest which would have been paid under the special homestead agreement prior to the effective date of this paragraph had the agreement been duly performed according to its terms shall be computed and added together; from the sum of these amounts there shall be deducted all moneys that have been actually paid to the Territory on account of the special homestead agreement, whether as principal or as interest. The balance thus determined shall be the total amount remaining due and payable for the homestead covered by such special homestead agreement, any other terms, conditions, or provisions in any of said agreements, or any provisions of law to the contrary notwithstanding: Provided, however, That nothing herein contained shall be deemed to excuse the payment of taxes and other charges and assessments upon unpatented homestead lands as provided in said agreements, nor to excuse or modify any term, condition, or provision of said agreements other than such as relate to the principal and interest payable to the Territory. The total amount remaining due, determined as hereinabove provided, shall be payable in fifteen equal biennial installments. Simple interest at the rate of three per centum per annum shall be charged upon the unpaid balance of such installments, whether matured or unmatured, said interest to be computed from the effective date of this paragraph and to be payable semi-annually. The first payment on account of principal shall be due two years subsequent to the effective date of this paragraph, and thereafter the due dates of principal payments shall be at regular two-year periods; the first payment on account of interest shall be due six months subsequent to the effective date of this paragraph, and thereafter the due dates of interest payments shall be at regular six-month periods. In case of default in payments of principal or interest on the due dates as hereby fixed the commissioner may, with the approval of the governor, with or without legal process, notice, demand, or previous entry, take possession of the land covered by any such special homestead agreement and thereby determine the estate created by such agreement as hereby modified, whereupon liability for payment of any balance then due under such special homestead agreement shall terminate. When the aforesaid payments have been made to the Territory of Hawaii, and all taxes, charges, and assessments upon the land have been paid as provided by said agreements, and all other conditions therein stipulated have been complied with, except as herein excused or modified, the said special homestead agreements shall be deemed to have been performed by the holders thereof, and land-patent grants covering the land described in such agreements shall be issued to the parties mentioned therein, or their heirs or assigns, as the case may be.

Neither the Territory of Hawaii nor any of its officers, agents or representatives shall be liable to any holder of any special homestead agreement, past or present, whether or not a patent shall have issued thereon, or to any other person, for any refund or reimbursement on account of any payment to the Territory in excess of the amount determined as provided by the preceding paragraph, and the legislature shall not recognize any obligation, legal or moral, on account of such excess payments. . . .

91.

That, except as otherwise provided, the public property ceded and transferred to the United States by the Republic of Hawaii under the joint resolution of annexation, approved July seventh, eighteen hundred and ninety-eight, shall be and remain in the possession, use, and control of the government of the Territory of Hawaii, and shall be maintained, managed, and cared for by it, at its own expense, until otherwise provided for by Congress, or taken for the uses and purposes of the United States by direction of the President or of the Governor of Hawaii. And any such public property so taken for the uses and purposes of the United States may be restored to its previous status by direction of the President; and the title to any such public property in the possession and use of the Territory for the purposes of water, sewer, electric, and other public works, penal, charitable, scientific, and educational institutions, cemeteries, hospitals, parks, highways, wharves, landings, harbor improvements, public buildings, or other public purposes, or required for any such purposes, may be transferred to the Territory by direction of the President, and the title to any property so transferred to the Territory may thereafter be transferred to any city, county, or other political subdivision thereof, or the University of Hawaii by direction of the governor when thereunto authorized by the legislature; Provided, That when any such public property so taken for the uses and purposes of the United States, if instead of being used for public purpose, is thereafter by the United States leased, rented, or granted upon revocable permits to private parties, the rentals or consideration shall be covered into the treasury of the Territory of Hawaii for the use and benefit of the purposes named in this section.

Appendix 8

Liliuokalani v. United States, 45 Ct.Cl. 481, 1909 WL 905
(U.S. Court of Claims 1910)

UNITED STATES COURT OF CLAIMS
LILIUOKALANI V. THE UNITED STATES
No. 30577

Decided May 16, 1910

Mr. S. S. Ashbaugh (with whom was Mr. Assistant Attorney-General John Q. Thompson) for the demurrer.

Mr. Sidney M. Ballou opposed. Kinney, Ballou, Prosser, and Anderson were on the brief.

BOOTH, J., delivered the opinion of the court:

This is a demurrer to claimant's petition. The claimant, Liliuokalani, was formerly Queen of the Hawaiian Islands. Her cause of action is predicated upon an alleged "vested equitable life interest" to certain lands described in the petition, known as "crown lands," of which interest she was divested by the defendants. It is conceded that the absence of such an interest rendered the crown lands subject to the usual transmission of title appurtenant to a change of sovereignty. The solution of the question involves a detailed examination of the various acts of the Hawaiian legislative body and reference to various sections of the Hawaiian constitutions, which for convenience will be set forth as an appendix to this opinion.

The origin of the crown lands and history connected therewith is epitomized by Justice Robertson in an exhaustive opinion in 2 Haw., 715. Previous to the reign of Kamehameha III a system of land tenure akin to the ancient feudal system prevailed in the islands. In 1839 the dissatisfaction and disputes engendered by the payment of rents, the rendition of personal service, etc., imposed upon landholders, encouraged the King to bring about a settled policy with reference to land titles. In 1840 Kamehameha III granted the first constitution, in which it is recited that: "Kamehameha I was the founder of the Kingdom, and to him belonged all the land from one end of the islands to the other, though it was not his own private property. It belonged to the chiefs and people in common, of whom Kamehameha I was the head and had the management of the landed property." In another clause it is provided that all lands forfeited for nonpayment of taxes shall revert to the King. (Fundamental Laws of Hawaii.) In 1846 a board of land commissioners was appointed by law, charged with the duty of dividing the rights of the various individuals in lands, and quieting titles thereto, and finally, in March, 1848, the King "signed and sealed two instruments contained in the Mahele Book," by which he demised specified lands described therein to the chiefs and people and reserved unto himself the lands now in suit, then and ever afterwards known as the crown lands. On June 7, 1848, the legislature for the islands confirmed the action of the King, and thereafter all portions of the royal domain except the reserved crown lands were treated as public domain and managed and disposed of by appropriate legislation. The title to the crown lands was vested in the Sovereign; he leased and alienated the same at his pleasure; the income and profits therefrom were his without interference or control. In January, 1865, the unlimited latitude allowed the King in the control of the crown lands found them charged with mortgages to secure sums of money which threatened their extinguishment, and the legislature, by the act of January 3, 1865, relieved the lands from the oppression of the mortgages, by the issuance of bonds, provided against their alienation, and put their management and control in the hands of commissioners as provided in the act. Subsequently, on July 6, 1866, the legislature relieved the crown lands from the liquidation of the bonds previously provided for, and the Government assumed and paid the mortgage debt.

The claimant became Queen of the islands on January 20, 1891, succeeding her brother, King Kalakaua. On January 17, 1893, she yielded her authority over the islands by an instrument in writing, abdicated her throne, and was succeeded in authority by a provisional government. On July 4, 1894, said provisional government was succeeded by a government known as the Republic of Hawaii, and thereafter the Hawaiian Islands were peaceably, upon request, on August 12, 1898, annexed to and became a part of the United States of America.

The history of the Hawaiian Islands from the earliest time to the ascension of Kamehameha I is the usual story of conquest. Kamehameha I established a monarchy; his title and sovereignty was the usual one of conquest, and while the attendant civilization was much advanced the King retained his sovereign authority and prerogatives. The act of Kamehameha III in 1848 was, as before observed, the culmination of numerous dissensions as to land tenures, and the King divided the public domain as hereinbefore set forth. Since 1848 the crown lands have descended to the reigning sovereign. At the April term of the Supreme Court of Hawaii in 1864 the nature and extent of the King's title in the crown lands was squarely before the court, and the court in an exceedingly able opinion held that under said act "the lands descended in fee, the inheritance being limited, however, to the successors to the throne, and each successive power may regulate and dispose of the same according to his will and pleasure, as private property, in like manner as was done by Kamehameha III."

Taking the language of the court we find an estate in lands presumably vested in fee simple in so far as the Crown is concerned, as distinguished from the personality of the Sovereign, and yet limited as to possession and descent by conditions abhorrent to a fee-simple estate absolute. The act of 1865 further curtails the title vested in the King. The preamble of the act recites expressly the nature and extent of the King's tenure, "for the purpose of maintaining the royal state and dignity," followed by appropriate legislation to thereafter prevent their alienation or incumbrance.

The act of 1865 to become effective under the Hawaiian constitution required the approval of the King. (Fundamental Laws of Hawaii, p. 172.) On January 3, 1865. Kamehameha V approved the statute which expressly divested the King of whatever legal title or possession he theretofore had in or to the Crown lands. (6 Haw., 195-208.) The Hawaiian Government in 1865 by its own legislation determined what the court is now asked to determine.

The decision of the court in 2 Haw., *supra,* was some time previous to the passage of the act of 1865, and although the court sustained the right of dower in the widow of the King, it is clear from the opinion that the crown lands were treated not as the King's private property in the strict sense of the term. While possessing certain attributes pertaining to fee simple estates, such as unrestricted power of alienation and incumbrance, there were likewise enough conditions surrounding the tenure to clearly characterize it as one pertaining to the support and maintenance of the Crown, as distinct from the person of the Sovereign. They belonged to the office and not to the individual. Significant in this connection is the transaction with Claus Spreckels in July, 1882. Her Highness Ruth Keelikolani, sister and heir of Kamehameha V, though never succeeding to the throne, conveyed to Spreckels all her interest in the crown lands. The sovereign authorities hastened to dispute the transaction, and subsequent legislation by way of compromise restored the attempted conveyance to the general body of the crown lands. (Appendix, p. 8.) Since 1865, so far as the record before us discloses, the character of the crown lands has not been changed; they have passed to the succeeding monarch. The income, less expense of management, has been used to support the royal office and treated as belonging to the Crown. All other property of the King has uniformly passed to his *heirs* regardless of his royal successor.

The court in 2 Haw., 722, in commenting upon the motives of the King in executing the conveyances of March 8, 1848, attributes the establishment of the crown land estate to a desire to prevent the impoverishment of the Sovereign in the event of a successful foreign invasion. This statement has been seized upon and assiduously emphasized by the claimant. It is not in harmony with the detailed history given by the court in its opinion. On page 719 the court says: "It was the imperative necessity of separating and defining the rights of the several parties interested in the lands which led to the institution of the board of land commissioners, and to the division made by the King himself, with the assistance of his privy council." It was in fact the usual contest between the monarch and his people. Certainly under a monarchy it would be unusual for the reigning sovereign to divest himself of all landed property; always jealous of the dignity attached to the Crown they were likewise alert in securing sufficient revenue to support its royal pretensions.

Kamehameha III reorganized the Government, granted a constitution, organized executive departments, established courts, and otherwise extended the liberties of his people and protected their rights of property. Suppose that during the progress of his reign a pretender for the throne had successfully established his claim and deposed the monarch without changing the existing governmental conditions. Is it possible that Kamehameha III could have recovered the rents and profits from the crown lands during the remainder of his life? *(Fundamental Laws of Hawaii.)*

It seems to the court that the crown lands acquired their unusual status through a desire of the King to firmly establish his Government by commendable concessions to his chiefs and people out of the public domain. The reservations made were to the Crown and not the King as an individual. The crown lands were the resourceful methods of income to sustain, in part at least, the dignity of the office to which they were inseparably attached. When the office ceased to exist they became as other lands of the Sovereignty and passed to the defendants as part and parcel of the public domain. (*O'Reilly de Camara v. Brooke,* 209 U. S., 45; *Hijo v. United States,* 194; *Sanchez v. United States,* 216 U. S., 167.)

The constitution of the Republic of Hawaii, as respects the crown lands, provided as follows:

"That portion of the public domain heretofore known as crown land is hereby declared to have been heretofore, and now to be, the property of the Hawaiian Government, and to be now free and clear from any trust of or concerning the same, and from all claim of any nature whatsoever upon the rents, issues, and profits thereof. It shall be subject to alienation and other uses as may be provided by law. All valid leases thereof now in existence are hereby confirmed."

Section 99 of the organic act of 1900 (31 Stat. L., 161) adopts substantially the same language. We have not entered into a discussion of the defenses predicated upon the above provisions of law, believing the case disposed of before we reached them. It is, however, worthy of note that the organic act of 1900 puts an end to any trust—if the same possibly existed—and the petition herein was not filed until January 20, 1910, more than six years thereafter.

Demurrer sustained, with leave to the claimant to amend her petition within ninety days.

Appendix 9

"Apology Resolution," November 23, 1993

100TH ANNIVERSARY OF THE OVERTHROW OF THE HAWAIIAN KINGDOM
JOINT RESOLUTION
To acknowledge the 100th anniversary of the January 17, 1893 overthrow of the King-dom of Hawaii, and to offer an apology to Native Hawaiians on behalf of the United States for the overthrow of the Kingdom of Hawaii. Public Law 103-150, November 23, 1993, 107 Stat 1510.

Whereas, prior to the arrival of the first Europeans in 1778, the Native Hawaiian people lived in a highly organized, self-sufficient, subsistent social system based on communal land tenure with a sophisticated language, culture, and religion;

Whereas a unified monarchical government of the Hawaiian Islands was estab-lished in 1810 under Kamehameha I, the first King of Hawaii;

Whereas, from 1826 until 1893, the United States recognized the independence of the Kingdom of Hawaii, extended full and complete diplomatic recognition to the Hawaiian Government, and entered into treaties and conventions with the Hawaiian monarchs to govern commerce and navigation in 1826, 1842, 1849, 1875, and 1887;

Whereas the Congregational Church (now known as the United Church of Christ), through its American Board of Commissioners for Foreign Missions, spon-sored and sent more than 100 missionaries to the Kingdom of Hawaii between 1820 and 1850;

Whereas, on January 14, 1893, John L. Stevens (hereafter referred to in this Resolution as the "United States Minister"), the United States Minister assigned to the sovereign and independent Kingdom of Hawaii conspired with a small group of non-Hawaiian residents of the Kingdom of Hawaii, including citizens of the United States, to overthrow the indigenous and lawful Government of Hawaii;

Whereas, in pursuance of the conspiracy to overthrow the Government of Hawaii, the United States Minister and the naval representatives of the United States caused armed naval forces of the United States to invade the sovereign Hawaiian nation on January 16, 1893, and to position themselves near the Hawaiian Government buildings and the Iolani Palace to intimidate Queen Liliuokalani and her Government;

Whereas, on the afternoon of January 17, 1893, a Committee of Safety that represented the American and European sugar planters, descendents of missionaries, and financiers deposed the Hawaiian monarchy and proclaimed the establishment of a Provisional Government;

Whereas the United States Minister thereupon extended diplomatic recognition to the Provisional Government that was formed by the conspirators without the consent of the Native Hawaiian people or the lawful Government of Hawaii and in violation of treaties between the two nations and of international law;

Whereas, soon thereafter, when informed of the risk of bloodshed with resistance, Queen Liliuokalani issued the following statement yielding her authority to the United States Government rather than to the Provisional Government:

"I Liliuokalani, by the Grace of God and under the Constitution of the Hawaiian Kingdom, Queen, do hereby solemnly protest against any and all acts done against myself and the Constitutional Government of the Hawaiian Kingdom by certain persons claiming to have established a Provisional Government of and for this Kingdom.

"That I yield to the superior force of the United States of America whose Minister Plenipotentiary, His Excellency John L. Stevens, has caused United States troops to be landed at Honolulu and declared that he would support the Provisional Government.

"Now to avoid any collision of armed forces, and perhaps the loss of life, I do this under protest and impelled by said force yield my authority until such time as the Government of the United States shall, upon facts being presented to it, undo the action of its representatives and reinstate me in the authority which I claim as the Constitutional Sovereign of the Hawaiian Islands.".

Done at Honolulu this 17th day of January, A.D. 1893.;

Whereas, without the active support and intervention by the United States diplomatic and military representatives, the insurrection against the Government of Queen Liliuokalani would have failed for lack of popular support and insufficient arms;

Whereas, on February 1, 1893, the United States Minister raised the American flag and proclaimed Hawaii to be a protectorate of the United States;

Whereas the report of a Presidentially established investigation conducted by former Congressman James Blount into the events surrounding the insurrection and overthrow of January 17, 1893, concluded that the United States diplomatic and military representatives had abused their authority and were responsible for the change in government;

Whereas, as a result of this investigation, the United States Minister to Hawaii was recalled from his diplomatic post and the military commander of the United States armed forces stationed in Hawaii was disciplined and forced to resign his commission;

Whereas, in a message to Congress on December 18, 1893, President Grover Cleveland reported fully and accurately on the illegal acts of the conspirators, described such acts as an "act of war, committed with the participation of a diplomatic representative of the United States and without authority of Congress", and acknowledged that by such acts the government of a peaceful and friendly people was overthrown;

Whereas President Cleveland further concluded that a "substantial wrong has thus been done which a due regard for our national character as well as the rights of the injured people requires we should endeavor to repair" and called for the restoration of the Hawaiian monarchy;

Whereas the Provisional Government protested President Cleveland's call for the restoration of the monarchy and continued to hold state power and pursue annexation to the United States;

Whereas the Provisional Government successfully lobbied the Committee on Foreign Relations of the Senate (hereafter referred to in this Resolution as the "Committee") to conduct a new investigation into the events surrounding the overthrow of the monarchy;

Whereas the Committee and its chairman, Senator John Morgan, conducted hearings in Washington, D.C., from December 27, 1893, through February 26, 1894, in which members of the Provisional Government justified and condoned the actions of the United States Minister and recommended annexation of Hawaii;

Whereas, although the Provisional Government was able to obscure the role of the United States in the illegal overthrow of the Hawaiian monarchy, it was unable to rally the support from two-thirds of the Senate needed to ratify a treaty of annexation;

Whereas, on July 4, 1894, the Provisional Government declared itself to be the Republic of Hawaii;

Whereas, on January 24, 1895, while imprisoned in Iolani Palace, Queen Liliuokalani was forced by representatives of the Republic of Hawaii to officially abdicate her throne;

Whereas, in the 1896 United States Presidential election, William McKinley replaced Grover Cleveland;

Whereas, on July 7, 1898, as a consequence of the Spanish-American War, President McKinley signed the Newlands Joint Resolution that provided for the annexation of Hawaii;

Whereas, through the Newlands Resolution, the self-declared Republic of Hawaii ceded sovereignty over the Hawaiian Islands to the United States;

Whereas the Republic of Hawaii also ceded 1,800,000 acres of crown, government and public lands of the Kingdom of Hawaii, without the consent of or compensation to the Native Hawaiian people of Hawaii or their sovereign government;

Whereas the Congress, through the Newlands Resolution, ratified the cession, annexed Hawaii as part of the United States, and vested title to the lands in Hawaii in the United States;

Whereas the Newlands Resolution also specified that treaties existing between Hawaii and foreign nations were to immediately cease and be replaced by United States treaties with such nations;

Whereas the Newlands Resolution effected the transaction between the Republic of Hawaii and the United States Government;

Whereas the indigenous Hawaiian people never directly relinquished their claims to their inherent sovereignty as a people or over their national lands to the United States, either through their monarchy or through a plebiscite or referendum;

Whereas, on April 30, 1900, President McKinley signed the Organic Act that provided a government for the territory of Hawaii and defined the political structure and powers of the newly established Territorial Government and its relationship to the United States;

Whereas, on August 21, 1959, Hawaii became the 50th State of the United States;

Whereas the health and well-being of the Native Hawaiian people is intrinsically tied to their deep feelings and attachment to the land;

Whereas the long-range economic and social changes in Hawaii over the nineteenth and early twentieth centuries have been devastating to the population and to the health and well-being of the Hawaiian people;

Whereas the Native Hawaiian people are determined to preserve, develop and transmit to future generations their ancestral territory, and their cultural identity in accordance with their own spiritual and traditional beliefs, customs, practices, language, and social institutions;

Whereas, in order to promote racial harmony and cultural understanding, the Legislature of the State of Hawaii has determined that the year 1993 should serve Hawaii as a year of special reflection on the rights and dignities of the Native Hawaiians in the Hawaiian and the American societies;

Whereas the Eighteenth General Synod of the United Church of Christ in recognition of the denomination's historical complicity in the illegal overthrow of the Kingdom of Hawaii in 1893 directed the Office of the President of the United Church of Christ to offer a public apology to the Native Hawaiian people and to initiate the process of reconciliation between the United Church of Christ and the Native Hawaiians; and

Whereas it is proper and timely for the Congress on the occasion of the impending one hundredth anniversary of the event, to acknowledge the historic significance of the illegal overthrow of the Kingdom of Hawaii, to express its deep regret to the Native Hawaiian people, and to support the reconciliation efforts of the State of

Hawaii and the United Church of Christ with Native Hawaiians: Now, therefore, be it *Resolved by the Senate and House of Representatives of the United States of America in Congress assembled,*

SECTION 1. ACKNOWLEDGMENT AND APOLOGY.
The Congress—

(1) on the occasion of the 100th anniversary of the illegal overthrow of the Kingdom of Hawaii on January 17, 1893, acknowledges the historical significance of this event which resulted in the suppression of the inherent sovereignty of the Native Hawaiian people;

(2) recognizes and commends efforts of reconciliation initiated by the State of Hawaii and the United Church of Christ with Native Hawaiians;

(3) apologizes to Native Hawaiians on behalf of the people of the United States for the overthrow of the Kingdom of Hawaii on January 17, 1893 with the participation of agents and citizens of the United States, and the deprivation of the rights of Native Hawaiians to self-determination;

(4) expresses its commitment to acknowledge the ramifications of the overthrow of the Kingdom of Hawaii, in order to provide a proper foundation for reconciliation between the United States and the Native Hawaiian people; and(5) urges the President of the United States to also acknowledge the ramifications of the overthrow of the Kingdom of Hawaii and to support reconciliation efforts between the United States and the Native Hawaiian people.

SEC. 2. DEFINITIONS.
As used in this Joint Resolution, the term "Native Hawaiian" means any individual who is a descendent of the aboriginal people who, prior to 1778, occupied and exercised sovereignty in the area that now constitutes the State of Hawaii.

SEC. 3. DISCLAIMER.
Nothing in this Joint Resolution is intended to serve as a settlement of any claims against the United States.
Approved November 23, 1993.

Glossary

Ahupua'a:	Political land district varying in size, usually stretching from the mountains to the sea.
'Aikapu:	Regulated eating rituals comprised of specific gender roles and restricted food items.
'Āina:	Land, earth, that which feeds.
Akua:	God, goddess, spirit, ghost, devil, image, idol, corpse, super-natural and divine ancestors.
Ali'i:	Chief, chiefess, officer, ruler, monarch, peer, hereditary leader, noble, aristocrat.
Ali'i 'ai Ahupua'a:	Managing Ali'i of an Ahupua'a.
Ali'i 'ai Moku:	Managing Ali'i of a Moku.
Ali'i 'ai Mokupuni:	Managing Ali'i of a Mokupuni.
Ali'i Nui:	Leader outranking other Ali'i; great chief; sometimes used to refer to the Mō'ī.
Hānai:	Adopted child; adoption.
Haole:	Foreign, foreigner; currently used to refer to Caucasians.
Ho'i:	Form of sacred mating between an uncle and niece or aunt and nephew. The child of a ho'i union was considered Akua.
Honua:	Land, earth, world.
'Ili:	Land section, next in importance to the Ahupua'a and usually a subdivision of an Ahupua'a. 'Ili were usually used to cultivate crops for maka'āinana or Ali'i.
'Iliahi:	Sandalwood.
Ka po'e Hawai'i:	The people of Hawai'i.

Kālana:	District of land smaller than a Moku, sometimes referred to as 'Okana.
Kālai'Āina:	The procedure whereby a new Mō'ī would distribute 'Āina to Ali'i.
Kalo:	Taro.
Kanaka Maoli:	Collective term describing the indigenous people inhabiting the Hawaiian islands prior to 1778 and their descendants.
Kapu:	Taboo or tabu, a set of rules dictating proper actions and forbidding certain conduct based on religious doctrine.
Kaua:	War, battle.
Kaukau Ali'i:	An Ali'i who was subservient to another and usually of lower rank.
Kauoha:	Oral will, order, decree.
Kauwā:	Outcast, pariah, slave, untouchable, menial, a caste that lived apart and was drawn upon for human sacrifices.
Ke Ali'i Pauahi:	Bernice Pauahi Bishop (referring to her title as Ali'i).
Kia 'Āina:	Governor, usually responsible for managing an island.
Konohiki:	Managing Ali'i of an Ahupua'a responsible to and appointed by the Ali'i Nui.
Kuleana:	Responsibility; individual plot of land assigned to maka'āinana in the Kuleana Act of 1850.
Lo'i:	Irrigated terrace, especially for kalo (taro).
Lo'i 'ai:	Kalo (taro) patch.
Mahele:	Division; share; also refers to the division of 1848 creating fee simple landownership in Hawai'i.
Maka'āinana:	Commoner, populace, people in general; citizen, subject, class of individuals usually of lesser rank than Ali'i.
Makai:	Toward the sea.
Mālama:	To care for.
Mālama 'Āina:	Caring for the land; the governing concept of land stewardship used in precontact Hawai'i.
Mana:	Spiritual power.
Mana'o:	Thought, idea, belief.
Mauka:	Inland, toward the mountains.
Mō'ī:	Supreme ruler, highest ranking Ali'i.

Glossary

Moku:	Political land district made up of several Ahupuaʻa.
Mokupuni:	Island.
Moʻolelo:	History; story.
Naha:	Union of an Aliʻi with a half sibling considered Akua.
Nīʻaupiʻo:	Offspring of closely related Aliʻi such as half siblings, uncle and niece; types of niʻaupiʻo matings include hoʻi, piʻo, and naha.
ʻOhana:	Family, extended family.
ʻOkana:	District or subdistrict usually comprising several Ahupuaʻa.
Palapala:	Document, paper.
Piʻo:	Sacred; pairing between siblings.
Pono:	Goodness; proper, just, balanced.
Poʻolua:	Child with two or more fathers or mothers and able to claim the genealogies of each.
Tabu:	Kapu.

Selected Bibliography

Adler, Jacob. *Claus Spreckels: The Sugar King in Hawaii.* Honolulu: University of Hawai'i Press, 1966.

Adler, Jacob, and Robert M. Kamins. *The Fantastic Life of Walter Murray Gibson: Hawaii's Minister of Everything.* Honolulu: University of Hawai'i Press, 1986.

Aina, Charleen. "John Ricord: Hawaii's First Attorney General." *Hawaii Bar Journal,* October 1999: 104.

Akinaka, Arthur Y., and James M. Dunn. *A Land Inventory and Land Use Study for the Department of Hawaiian Home Lands.* Honolulu: Arthur Y. Akinaka, Ltd., December 18, 1972.

Alexander, W. D. *A Brief History of the Hawaiian People.* New York: American Book Co., 1899 (reprint Honolulu: University Press of the Pacific, 2001).

———. "A Brief History of Land Titles in the Hawaiian Kingdom." *Hawaiian Almanac & Annual,* 1891 (Thomas G. Thrum compiler and publisher): 105.

Allen, Helena G. *The Betrayal of Liliuokalani: Last Queen of Hawaii 1838–1917.* Honolulu: Mutual Publishing, 1982.

———. *Sanford Ballard Dole: Hawaii's Only President.* Glendale, CA: A. H. Clark Co., 1988.

Anaya, S. James. "The Native Hawaiian People and International Human Rights Law: Toward a Remedy for Past and Continuing Wrongs." *Georgia Law Review* 28 (1994): 309.

Andrade, Ernest, Jr. *Unconquerable Rebel: Robert W. Wilcox and Hawaiian Politics, 1880–1903.* Niwot: University Press of Colorado, 1996.

Ballou, Sidney M. *Appeals and Exceptions in Hawaiian Courts.* Honolulu: Hawaiian Gazette Co., 1900.

———. *Civil Laws of the Hawaiian Islands.* Honolulu: Hawaiian Gazette Print, 1897.

———. *Penal Laws of the Hawaiian Islands.* Honolulu: Hawaiian Gazette Print, 1897.

Barrère, Dorothy B. *The King's Mahele: The Awardees and Their Lands.* Hawaii: D. B. Barrère, 1994.

Beckwith, Martha W., ed. *Kepelino's Traditions of Hawaii.* Bernice P. Bishop Museum Bulletin 95. Honolulu: Bishop Museum Press, 1932.

Benjamin, Stuart Minor. "Equal Protection and the Special Relationship: The Case of Native Hawaiians." *Yale Law Journal* 106 (1996): 537.

Bennett, Marion T. *The United States Court of Claims: A History.* Vol. 1. Washington, DC: Committee on the Bicentennial of Independence and the Constitution of the Judicial Conference of the United States, 1976.

Benton, Russell E. *Emma Naea Rooke: Beloved Queen of Hawaii.* Lewiston, NY: Edwin Mellen Press, 1988.

Bernice P. Bishop Estate. *Wills and Deeds of Trust.* Honolulu: Bernice P. Bishop Estate, Bernice P. Bishop Museum, Charles R. Bishop Estate. 3rd ed., 1957.

Bevans, Charles I. *Treaties and Other International Agreements of the United States of America, 1776–1949.* Vol. 8. Washington, DC: Department of State, 1968.

Black, Cobey, and Kathleen Dickenson Mellen. *Princess Pauahi and Her Legacy.* Honolulu: Kamehameha Schools Press, 1965.

Blackman, William Fremont. *The Making of Hawaii: A Study in Social Evolution.* New York: Macmillan, 1906 (reprinted New York: AMS Press, 1977).

Blondin, Karen. "A Case for Reparations for Native Hawaiians." *Hawaii Bar Journal* 16 (winter 1981): 13.

Bradley, Harold W. "Thomas ap Catesby Jones and the Hawaiian Islands, 1826–1827." In *Thirty-Ninth Annual Report of the Hawaiian Historical Society* (1931): 17.

Brock, Ralph H. "'The Republic of Texas Is No More': An Answer to the Claim that Texas Was Unconstitutionally Annexed to the United States." *Texas Tech Law Review* 28 (1997): 679, 724–34.

Budnick, Rich. *Stolen Kingdom: An American Conspiracy.* Honolulu: Aloha Press, 1992.

Bushnell, O. A. *The Gifts of Civilization: Germs and Genocide in Hawai'i.* Honolulu: University of Hawai'i Press, 1993.

Cachola, Jean Iwata. *Kamehameha III: Kauikeaouli.* Honolulu: Kamehameha Schools Press, 1995.

Cannelora, Louis. *Summary of the Hawaii Law of Dower, Curtesy and Community Property.* Honolulu: Security Title Corp., 1971.

Chinen, Jon J. *The Great Mahele: Hawaii's Land Division of 1848.* Honolulu: University of Hawai'i Press, 1958.

———. *Original Land Titles in Hawaii.* Honolulu: University of Hawai'i Press, 1971.

———. *They Cried for Help.* Philadelphia: Xlibris Corp., 2002.

Chock, Jennifer M. L. "One Hundred Years of Illegitimacy: International Legal Analysis of the Illegal Overthrow of the Hawaiian Monarchy, Hawai'i's Annexation, and Possible Reparations," *University of Hawai'i Law Review* 17 (1995): 463.

Christensen, Carl C. "Native Hawaiians and the Constitution: Can the Indian Commerce Clause Cross the Pacific?" (Paper for Indian Law Seminar, Harvard Law School, spring 1997).

Clarkson, Gavin. "Not Because They Are Brown, But Because of Ea: Why the Good Guys

Lost in Rice v. Cayetano, Why They Didn't Have to Lose." *Michigan Journal of Race & Law* 7 (2002): 317.

Close Up Foundation. *Micronesia: A Guide through the Centuries.* Alexandria, VA: Close Up Foundation, 2000.

Coffman, Tom. *The Island Edge of America: A Political History of Hawai'i.* Honolulu: University of Hawai'i Press, 2003.

————. *Nation Within: The Story of America's Annexation of the Nation of Hawai'i.* Kaneohe, HI: Tom Coffman/EPICenter, 1998.

Cohen, Felix. *Felix Cohen's Handbook of Federal Indian Law.* Rennard Strickland et al., eds. Charlottesville, VA: Michie Co., 1982.

Concise Encyclopedia of Australia and New Zealand. St. Leonards, Australia: Horowitz Publications, 1995.

Cooke, Lydia (Pat) Schaefer. *The Family of George Morison Robertson and Sarah Symonds Humphreys Robertson after 122 Years, 1851–1973.* 2d ed. Honolulu: Hawaiian Printing Co., Ltd., 1973.

Cooley, Thomas M. "Grave Obstacles to Hawaiian Annexation." *The Forum* 15 (1893): 389.

Crocombe, Ron. *The South Pacific.* Suva: University of the South Pacific, 2001.

Damon, Ethel M. *Sanford Ballard Dole and His Hawaii.* Palo Alto, CA: Pacific Books, Hawaiian Historical Society, 1957.

Davies, Jack. *Legislative Law and Process in a Nutshell.* 2d ed. St. Paul, MN: West, 1986.

Daws, Gavan. *Shoal of Time: A History of the Hawaiian Islands.* Honolulu: University of Hawai'i Press, 1968 (reprinted 1974).

Day, A. Grove. *History Makers of Hawaii.* Honolulu: Mutual Publishing, 1984.

Department of Business, Economic Development and Transportation. *State of Hawaii Data Book: A Statistical Abstract.* Honolulu: Department of Business, Economic Development and Transportation, State of Hawaii, 2000.

Department of Planning and Economic Development. *State of Hawaii Data Book: A Statistical Abstract.* Honolulu: Department of Planning and Economic Development, State of Hawaii, 1987.

Diechert, Robert J. "The Fifteenth Amendment at a Crossroads: Rice v. Cayetano." *Connecticut Law Review* 32 (2000): 1,075.

Douglas, Norman, and Ngaire Douglas, eds. *Pacific Islands Yearbook.* 17th ed. Suva: University of the South Pacific, 1994.

Dutton, Meiric K. *The Succession of King Kamehameha V to Hawaii's Throne.* Honolulu: Loomis House Press, 1957.

Expressing the Policy of the United States Regarding the United States Relationship with Native Hawaiians and to Provide a Process for the Recognition by the United States of the Native Hawaiian Governing Entity, and for Other Purposes. Report 107-66 of the Senate Committee on Indian Affairs, 107th Cong, 1st Sess., at 14 (September 21, 2001).

Feher, Joseph. *Hawaii: A Pictorial History.* Honolulu: Bishop Museum Press, 1969.

Fuchs, Lawrence H. *Hawaii Pono: A Social History.* New York: Harcourt, Brace & World, 1961 (reprinted San Diego: Harcourt Brace Jovanovich, 1983).

George Morison Robertson. Honolulu, 1917. (Pamphlet containing articles about Robertson.)

Getches, David. "Alternative Approaches to Land Claims: Alaska and Hawaii." In *Irredeemable America: The Indians' Estate and Land Claims,* Imre Sutton, ed., 1985: 301.

Goehlert, Robert U., and Fenton S. Martin. *Congress and Law-Making: Researching the Legislative Process.* Santa Barbara: Clio Books, 1979 (2d ed., 1989).

Handy, E. S. Craighill, and Elizabeth Green Handy. *Native Planters in Old Hawaii.* Honolulu: Bishop Museum Press, 1972.

Hanifin, Patrick W. "To Dwell on the Earth in Unity: Rice, Arakaki, and the Growth of Citizenship and Voting Rights in Hawaii." *Hawaii Bar Journal* 5 (2002): 15.

———. "Hawaiian Reparations: Nothing Lost, Nothing Owed." *Hawaii Bar Journal* 17 (1982): 107.

Hart, John W. *History of Samoa.* Apia: Church Schools of Western Samoa, Church of Jesus Christ of Latter-day Saints, 1971.

Hawaii Advisory Committee to the United States Commission on Civil Rights. *A Broken Trust: The Hawaiian Homelands Program: Seventy Years of Failure of the Federal and State Governments to Protect the Civil Rights of Native Hawaiians* (December 1991).

Hobbs, Jean. *Hawaii: A Pageant of the Soil.* Palo Alto, CA: Stanford University Press, 1935.

Hom, Sharon, and Eric K. Yamamoto. "Collective Memory, History, and Social Justice." *UCLA Law Review* 47 (2000): 1747.

Horwitz, Robert H., Judith B. Finn, Louis A. Vargha, and James W. Ceaser. *Public Land Policy in Hawaii: An Historical Analysis.* State of Hawaii Legislative Reference Bureau, Report No. 5, 1969.

Hoyle, R. W. "Introduction: Aspects of the Crown's Estate." In *The Estates of the English Crown, 1558–1640,* R. W. Hoyle, ed. (Oxford: Cambridge University Press, 1992): 21.

Hoyt, Robert S. *The Royal Demesne in English Constitutional History: 1066–1272.* Ithaca, NY: Cornell University Press, American Historical Association, 1950.

Hutchins, Wells A. *The Hawaiian System of Water Rights.* U.S. Department of Agriculture and the Board of Water Supply, City and County of Honolulu, 1946.

Iaukea, C. P. *Biennial Report of the Commissioners of Crown Lands.* Honolulu: Hawaiian Gazette Co., 1894.

Ii, John Papa. *Fragments of Hawaiian History.* Honolulu: Bishop Museum Press, 1959 (revised ed., 1983).

Inciong, Mark A. "The Lost Trust: Native Hawaiian Beneficiaries under the Hawaiian Homes Commission Act." *Arizona Journal of International & Comparative Law* 8 (1991): 171.

Judd, A. F. "Constitution of the Republic of Hawaii." *Yale Law Journal* 4 (1893): 53.

Judd, Walter F. *Hawaiʻi Joins the World*. Honolulu: Mutual Publishing, 1999.

Kahanu, Noelle M., and Jon M. Van Dyke. "Native Hawaiian Entitlement to Sovereignty: An Overview." *University of Hawaiʻi Law Review* 17 (1995): 427.

Kalakaua, King David. *The Legends and Myths of Hawaii*. Honolulu: Mutual Publishing, 1983.

Kalanianaole, Prince J. K. "The Story of the Hawaiians." *Mid-Pacific Magazine* 21 (February 1921): 117.

Kamakau, Samuel M. *Ruling Chiefs of Hawaiʻi*. Honolulu: Kamehameha Schools Press, 1961 (revised ed., 1992).

Kameʻeleihiwa, Lilikala. *Native Land and Foreign Desires: Pehea La E Pono Ai?* Honolulu: Bishop Museum Press, 1992.

Kamehameha Schools Bernice Pauahi Bishop Estate. *The Land of KSBE*. Honolulu: Kamehameha Schools Press, 1983.

Kanahele, George S. *Emma: Hawaiʻi's Remarkable Queen*. Honolulu: Queen Emma Foundation, 1999.

———. *Pauahi: The Kamehameha Legacy*. Honolulu: Kamehameha Schools Press, 1986.

Kelly, Marion. "Changes in Land Tenure in Hawaii, 1778–1850." Master's Thesis, 1956, University of Hawaiʻi Library.

———. "Land Tenure in Hawaiʻi." *Amerasia Journal* 7:2 (fall-winter 1980): 65.

King, Samuel P. "The Federal Courts and the Annexation of Hawaii." *Western Legal History* 2 (1989): 1.

King, Samuel P., and Randall W. Roth. *Broken Trust: Greed, Mismanagement and Political Manipulation at America's Largest Charitable Trust*. Honolulu: University of Hawaiʻi Press, 2006.

Kinzer, Stephen. *Overthrow: America's Century of Regime Change from Hawaii to Iraq*. New York: Times Books, 2006.

Kirch, Patrick. *Feathered Gods and Fishhooks: An Introduction to Hawaiian Archeology and Prehistory*. Honolulu: University of Hawaiʻi Press, 1985.

Kmiec, Douglas W. "Legal Issues Raised by Proposed Presidential Proclamation to Extend the Territorial Sea." *Territorial Sea Journal* 1 (1990): 1.

Krout, Mary H. *The Memoirs of Hon. Bernice Pauahi Bishop*. New York: Knickerbocker Press, 1908.

Kuykendall, Ralph S. *Constitutions of the Hawaiian Kingdom: A Brief History and Analysis*. Hawaiian Historical Society Paper No. 21, 1940 (reprinted 1978).

———. *The Hawaiian Kingdom 1778–1854: Foundation and Transformation*. Vol. 1. Honolulu: University of Hawaiʻi Press, 1938 (7th printing, 1989).

———. *The Hawaiian Kingdom 1854–1874: Twenty Critical Years*. Vol. 2. Honolulu: University of Hawaiʻi Press, 1953 (reprinted 1982).

———. *The Hawaiian Kingdom 1874–1893: The Kalakaua Dynasty*. Vol. 3. Honolulu: University of Hawaiʻi Press, 1967 (reprinted 1987).

Kuykendall, Ralph S., and A. Grove Day. *Hawaii: A History from Polynesian Kingdom to American State.* New York: Prentice-Hall, 1948 (reprinted, 1961).

Lane, Peter. *Prince Charles: A Study in Development.* London: Hale, 1988.

Lapilio, Lani Maʻa. "The 19th Century Hawaiian Judicial System." *Hawaii Bar Journal* (October 1999): 86.

Levinson, L. Harold. "Balancing Acts: Bowsher v. Synar, Gramm-Rudman-Hollings, and Beyond." *Cornell Law Review* 72 (1987): 527, 545.

Levy, Neil M. *Micronesia Handbook.* 6th ed. Chico, CA: Moon Publications, 2003.

———. "Native Hawaiian Land Rights." *California Law Review* 63 (1975): 848.

Liermann, Annmarie M. *Comment:* "Seeking Sovereignty: The Akaka Bill and the Case for the Inclusion of Hawaiians in Federal Native American Policy." *Santa Clara Law Review* 41 (2001): 509.

Liliuokalani. *Hawaii's Story by Hawaii's Queen.* Boston: Lothrop, Lee & Shepard Co., 1898 (reprinted 1997).

Lind, Andrew W. *Hawaii's People.* 4th ed. Honolulu: University of Hawaiʻi Press, 1990.

Linde, Hans, George Bunn, Fredericka Paff, and W. Lawrence Church. 2d ed. *Legislative and Administrative Processes.* Mineola, NY: Foundation Press, 1981.

Linnekin, Jocelyn. *Sacred Queens and Women of Consequence.* Ann Arbor: University of Michigan Press, 1990.

Lucas, Paul F. Nahoa, ed. *A Dictionary of Hawaiian Legal Land-Terms.* Honolulu: Native Hawaiian Legal Corp and University of Hawaiʻi Committee for the Preservation and Study of Hawaiian Language, Art, and Culture, 1995.

Lydgate, J. M. "The Vanishing Kuleana." In *Hawaiian Almanac and Annual,* Thomas G. Thrum, compiler and publisher, 1915.

Lyons, C. J. "Land Matters in Hawaii: Nos. 2, 3, 5, 6, 7, 8." *The Islander,* July 9, 1875, at 111; July 16, 1875, at 118–19; July 30, 1875, at 135; August 6, 1875, at 143; August 13, 1875, at 151: August 20, 1875, at 159.

MacKenzie, Melody K. "The Ceded Lands Trust." *Hawaii Bar Journal* 4:6 (June 2000): 6.

———, ed. *Native Hawaiian Rights Handbook.* Honolulu: Native Hawaiian Legal Corporation and Office of Hawaiian Affairs (distributed by University of Hawaiʻi Press), 1991.

MacLellan, Nic, and Jean Chesneaux. *After Moruroa: France in the South Pacific.* Melbourne and New York: Ocean Press, 1998.

Malo, David. *Hawaiian Antiquities.* National B. Emerson, trans., 1898 (republished by Bishop Museum, 1951).

McGregor, Davianna Pomaikaʻi. "The Cultural and Political History of Hawaiian Native People." In *Our History, Our Way: An Ethnic Studies Anthology,* Gregory Yee Mark, Davianna Pomaikaʻi McGregor, and Linda A. Revilla, eds., 1996: 336.

———. "An Introduction to the Hoaʻaina and Their Rights." *Hawaiian Journal of History* 30 (1996): 1.

———. "Kupaʻa I Ka ʻĀina: Persistence on the Land." University of Hawaii Ph.D. dissertation, December 1989.

McGregor-Alegado, Davianna. "Voices of Today Echo Voices of the Past." *Malama: Hawaiian Land and Water,* special issue of *Bamboo Ridge: The Hawaiian Writers Quarterly* 29 (Dana Naone Hall, ed., 1985): 44.

McPherson, Michael M. "Trustees of Hawaiian Affairs v. Yamasaki and the Native Hawaiian Claim: Too Much of Nothing." *Environmental Law* 21 (1991): 427.

Meleisea, Malama. *The Making of Modern Samoa.* Suva: Institute of Pacific Studies of the University of the South Pacific, 1987.

Melendy, H. Brent. "The Controversial Appointment of Lucius Eugene Pinkham, Hawaii's First Democratic Governor." *Hawaiian Journal of History* 17 (1983): 185.

Merry, Sally Engle. *Colonizing Hawai'i: The Cultural Power of Law.* Princeton, NJ: Princeton University Press, 2000.

Miyahira, Sheryl L. "Hawaii's Ceded Lands." *University of Hawai'i Law Review* 3 (1981) 101.

Moore, John Bassett. *A Digest of International Law.* Washington, DC: U.S. Government Printing Office, 1906.

Must We Wait in Despair: The 1867 Report of the 'Ahahui La'au of Wailuku, Maui on Native Hawaiian Health. Malcom Naea Chun, trans./ed. Honolulu: First Peoples' Productions, 1994.

Mutu, Margaret. "Political Reviews of Maori Issues in 1993–94." *Contemporary Pacific* 7 (1995): 152–55.

Native Hawaiians Study Commission. *Report on the Culture, Needs and Concerns of Native Hawaiians.* Vols. 1 and 2. Report issued pursuant to Pub. L. 96-565, Title III, 1983.

O'Connell, D. P. "Mid-Ocean Archipelagos in International Law." In *British Year Book of International Law 1971,* Sir Humphrey Waldock and R. Y. Jennings, eds. (London: Oxford University Press): 1.

Office of Hawaiian Affairs. *Native Hawaiian Data Book.* Mark Eshima ed. Honolulu: Office of Hawaiian Affairs, Planning and Research office, 1998.

O'Malley, Eric Steven. "Irreconcilable Rights and the Question of Hawaiian Statehood." *Georgetown Law Review* 89 (2001): 501.

Osborne, Thomas J. *Annexation Hawaii: Fighting American Imperialism.* Waimanalo, HI: Island Style Press, 1998. (Originally published as *Empire Can Wait,* Kent, Ohio: Kent State University Press, 1981.)

Oshiro, Lisa Cami. "Recognizing Na Kanaka Maoli's Right to Self-Determination." *New Mexico Law Review* 25 (1995): 65.

Osorio, Jonathan Kay Kamakawiwo'ole. *Dismembering Lāhui: A History of the Hawaiian Nation to 1887.* Honolulu: University of Hawai'i Press, 2002.

Parker, Linda S. *Native American Estate: The Struggle over Indian and Hawaiian Lands.* Honolulu: University of Hawai'i Press, 1989.

Parsonson, Ann. "The Fate of Maori Land Rights in Early Colonial New Zealand: The Limits of the Treaty of Waitangi and the Doctrine of Aboriginal Title." In *Law, History, Colonialism: The Reach of Empire,* Diane Kirby and Catherine Coleborne, eds., 2001: 173–86.

Perry, Antonio. "Hawaiian Water Rights." In *Hawaiian Almanac & Annual* (Thomas G. Thrum, compiler and publisher, 1912): 90.

Pratt, Elizabeth Kekaaniauokalani Kalaninuiohilaukapu. *History of Keoua Kalanikupuapa-i-kalani-nui, Father of Hawaii Kings, and His Descendants, with Notes on Kamehameha I, First King of All Hawaii.* Honolulu: Honolulu Star-Bulletin, Ltd., 1920.

Pratt, Julius W. *Expansionists of 1898: The Acquisition of Hawaii and the Spanish Islands.* Chicago: Quadrangle Books, 1936.

Proceedings of the Constitutional Convention of 1950. Honolulu: Attorney General, 1960.

Proceedings of the Constitutional Convention of Hawaii of 1978. Honolulu: State of Hawaii, 1980.

Pukui, Mary Kawena, and Samuel H. Elbert. *Hawaiian Dictionary.* Honolulu: University of Hawaiʻi Press, 1986.

Quinn, William F. "Native Hawaiian Claims: The Issue of the 80s." Essay delivered to the Social Science Association, May 7, 1984.

Rappolt, Miriam E. *Queen Emma: A Woman of Vision.* Kailua, HI: Press Pacifica, 1991.

Read, Horace E., John W. MacDonald, Jefferson B. Fordham, and William J. Pierce. *Materials on Legislation.* 4th ed. Mineola, NY: Foundation Press, 1982.

"Report of Commissioner to the Hawaiian Islands." In *Executive Documents of the House of Representatives for the Second Session of the Fifty-third Congress, 1893–94* 27 (1895): 640. (Originally in Executive Document No. 47, 53rd Cong., 2d Sess., 1893 ["Blount Report"]).

Richards, Mary Atherton. "Foreword." In *The Hawaiian Chiefs' Children's School 1839–1850,* Mary Atherton Richards (Rutland, VT: Charles E. Tuttle Co., 1970): xiii. (Originally published by Honolulu Star-Bulletin, 1937.)

Richardson, James D. *A Compilation of the Messages and Papers of the Presidents.* Washington, DC: Government Printing Office, 1896–99.

Richardson, Lynn, ed. *New Zealand Encyclopedia.* 5th ed. Auckland: Bateman, 2000.

Rubincam, Milton. "America's Only Royal Family: Genealogy of the Former Hawaiian Ruling House." *National Geneological Society Quarterly* (June 1962, reprinted 1968).

Russ, William A. *The Hawaiian Revolution: 1893–94.* Selinsgrove, PA: Susquehanna University Press, 1959.

Sahlins, Marshall. *Historical Metaphors and Mythical Realities: Structure in the Early History of the Sandwich Islands Kingdom.* Ann Arbor: University of Michigan Press, 1981.

Sai, David Keanu. "American Occupation of the Hawaiian State: A Century Unchecked." *Hawaiian Journal of Law and Politics* 1 (2004): 46, 53–56 (available at http://www2.hawaii.edu/~hslp/journal_vol1.html).

Samson, Jane. *Imperial Benevolence: Making British Authority in the Pacific Islands.* Honolulu: University of Hawaiʻi Press, 1998.

Schmitt, Robert C. *Historical Statistics of Hawaii.* Honolulu: University Press of Hawai'i, 1977.

Silva, Noenoe K. *Aloha Betrayed: Native Hawaiian Resistance to American Colonialism.* Durham, NC: Duke University Press, 2004 (reprinted 2005).

Slade, David C. *Putting the Public Trust Doctrine to Work.* Washington, DC: Coastal States Organization, 1990.

Spaulding, Thomas Marshall. *The Crown Lands of Hawaii.* University of Hawaii Occasional Papers No. 1, October 10, 1923.

Stannard, David E. *Before the Horror.* Honolulu: Social Science Research Institute, University of Hawai'i, 1989.

Stauffer, Robert H. "The Hawai'i–United States Treaty of 1826." *Hawaiian Journal of History* 17 (1983): 40.

———. *Kahana: How the Land Was Lost.* Honolulu: University of Hawai'i Press, 2004.

Stevens, Sylvester K. *American Expansion in Hawaii 1842–1898.* Harrisburg: Archives Publishing Co. of Pennsylvania Inc., 1945; reissued 1968.

Tansill, Charles Callan. *Diplomatic Relations between the United States and Hawaii 1885–1889.* Fordham University Historical Series No. 1, 1940.

Tate, Merze. "Great Britain and the Sovereignty of Hawaii." *Pacific Historical Review* 31 (1962): 327.

———. *Hawaii: Reciprocity or Annexation.* East Lansing: Michigan State University Press, 1968.

———. "The Sandwich Island Missionaries Lay the Foundation for a System of Public Instruction in Hawaii." *Journal of Negro Education* 30:4 (fall 1961): 396, 402–03.

———. "Slavery and Racism as Deterrents to the Annexation of Hawaii, 1854–1855." *Journal of Negro History* 47 (1962): 1.

Thomas, David. "The Elizabethan Crown Lands: Their Purposes and Problems." In *The Estates of the English Crown, 1558–1640,* R. W. Hoyle, ed. (Oxford: Cambridge University Press, 1992): 61.

Thrum, Thomas, G., compiler and publisher. *Hawaiian Almanac and Annual.* Honolulu: Black & Auld, Printers, 1899.

Thurston, Lorrin. *A Handbook of the Annexation of Hawaii.* St. Joseph, MI: A. B. Morse, n.d. (ca. 1897).

———. *Memoirs of the Hawaiian Revolution.* Honolulu: Advertiser Publishing Co., Ltd., 1936.

Trial of a Queen: 1895 Military Tribunal. Honolulu: Hawai'i Judicial History Center, 1995.

Trifonovitch, Kelli Abe. "Bring the Locals Back: The Queen Emma Foundation's Mike Hastert Says the Redevelopment of the International Marketplace is a Part of Reinventing Waikiki." *Hawaii Business,* April 2004 (available at http://www.hawaiibusiness.cc/ hb42004/default.cfm?articleid=15).

Twain, Mark. *Roughing It.* New York: Signet Classics, 1987 (originally published in 1871).

Twigg-Smith, Thurston. *Hawaiian Sovereignty: Do the Facts Matter?* Honolulu: Goodale Publishing, 1998.

U.S. Dept. of the Interior and U.S. Dept. of Justice. *From Mauka to Makai: The River of Justice Must Flow Freely.* Report on the Reconciliation Process between the Federal Government and Native Hawaiians, October 23, 2000.

U.S. Dept. of State. *Papers Related to the Foreign Relations of the United States for the Year 1887.* Washington, DC: Government Printing Office, 1888.

U.S. Dept. of State. *Papers Relating to the Foreign Relations of the United States for the Year 1888.* Washington, DC: Government Printing Office, 1889.

U.S. Hawaiian Commission. *The Report of the Hawaiian Commission.* Washington, DC: Government Printing Office, 1898.

VanBrackle, Joseph D. "Pearl Harbor from the First Mention of 'Pearl Lochs' to Its Present Day Usage." Undated manuscript on file in Hawaiian-Pacific Collection, Hamilton Library, University of Hawai'i at Mānoa.

Van Dyke, Jon M. "The Constitutionality of the Office of Hawaiian Affairs." *University of Hawai'i Law Review* 7 (1985): 63.

———. "The Kamehameha Schools/Bishop Estate and the Constitution." *University of Hawai'i Law Review* 17 (1995): 413.

———. "The Political Status of the Native Hawaiian People." *Yale Law & Policy Review* 17 (1998): 95.

Van Dyke, Jon M., Carmen Di Amore-Siah, and Gerald W. Berkley-Coats. "Self-Determination for Nonself-Governing Peoples and for Indigenous Peoples: The Cases of Guam and Hawai'i." *University of Hawai'i Law Review* 18 (1996): 623.

Van Dyke, Jon M., Joseph R. Morgan, and Jonathan Gurish. "The Exclusive Economic Zone of the Northwestern Hawaiian Islands: When Do Uninhabited Islands Generate an EEZ?" *San Diego Law Review* 25 (1988): 425.

Vause, Marylyn M. "The Hawaiian Homes Commission Act, 1920: History and Analysis." University of Hawai'i Masters' Thesis, June 1962, University of Hawai'i Library.

Willoughby, W. *The Constitutional Law of the United States.* 2d ed. New York: Baker, Voorhis, 1929.

Wise, John H. "The History of Land Ownership in Hawaii." In *Ancient Hawaiian Civilization,* Frank Midkiff, ed. (Rutland, VT: Charles E. Tuttle Co., 1965). (Series of lectures delivered at the Kamehameha Schools in the 1930s.)

Wolffe, B. P. *The Royal Demesne in English History: The Crown Estate in the Governance of the Realm from Conquest to 1509.* Athens: Ohio University Press, 1971.

Work, Shannon D. "Comment: The Alaska Native Claims Settlement Act: An Illusion in the Quest for Native Self-Determination." *Oregon Law Review* 66 (1987): 195.

Yamamoto, Eric K., and Chris Iijima. "The Colonizer's Story: The Supreme Court Violates Native Hawaiian Sovereignty—Again." *ColorLines* (summer 2000) (available at http://www.arc.org/C_Lines/CLArchive/story3_2_01.html).

Young, Lucien. *Real Hawaii: Its History and Present Conditions Including the True Story of the Revolution (American Imperialism)*. Manchester, NH: Ayer Co. Publishers, 1970. (A revised and enlarged edition of *The* Boston *at Hawaii,* 1898).

———. *The* Boston *at Hawaii.* Washington, DC: Gibson Bros., 1898.

Zambucka, Kristin. *The High Chiefess, Ruth Keʻelikolani.* Honolulu: Green Glass Productions, 1992.

———. *Kalakaua: Hawaiʻi's Last King.* Honolulu: Mana Publishing Co., Marvin/Richard Enterprises, Inc., 1983.

General Index

209–11, 227; supporters, 130, 157–62, 168–69, 172, 205–8; treaty, 208–9. *See also* Hawai‘i, Territory of

Aotearoa (New Zealand). *See* Maoris

Apoliona, Samuel K., Jr., 256

"Apology Resolution": acknowledgment of illegality of overthrow, 170, 235, 263, 266–67, 381; acknowledgment of lands taken without consent or compensation, 267, 380; adoption, 266; cited in *Rice v. Cayetano* majority opinion, 274, 276, 277–78; definition of Native Hawaiian, 1n1; recognition of Hawaiian sovereignty, 297; as relevant to Queen Lili‘uokalani's claim, 235; signed by Clinton, 266n91, **268;** significance, 381; text, 266–67, 450–54

Armstrong, Richard, 83

Ashford, Clarence W., 122–23, **241**

Asian immigrants: Chinese, 134, 135, 136, 137–38, 147, 224; excluded from political community, 133, 138, 147, 150, 183, 184, 224; Japanese, 133, 135, 136–37, 147, 186, 207, 211. *See also* contract labor system; immigrant workers

Bacon, Augustus O., 211, 212

Ballou, Sidney M., 229–31, 229n18, 234

Barrett, Patrick, 286

Bates, Asher B., 73–75, 79

Bayard, Thomas F., 126, 146, 155

Bayonet Constitution. *See* Constitution of 1887

Bingham, Hiram, 23

Bishop, Bernice Pauahi, Princess. *See* Pauahi Bishop, Bernice, Princess

Bishop, Charles Reed, **309;** administration of Bishop Estate, 307; on admissions policies of Kamehameha Schools, 310–11; arrival in Hawai‘i, 36–37; Lee and, 36–37, 39; marriage, 312; as Minister of Foreign Affairs, 94, 95; sugar plantation, 39; support of King Kalākaua, 97

Bishop Estate: administration, 307; ‘Āina held by, 53, 116, 311–15; criticism of, 315–16; land sales, 221; trustees, 116, 310, 315–16, 316n54; "unassigned" lands, 114–16. *See also* Kamehameha Schools

Blackman, William Fremont, 57, 65, 196

Blaine, James G., 202n8, 205, 206

Blaisdell, Kekuni, 373

Blount, James H., 136, 137, 138, 148, 164–65, 166–68, **166,** 187, 207

"Blount Report," 48, 136, 137, 138, 166, 167

Board of Commissioners of Crown Lands. *See* Commission of Crown Lands

Board of Commissioners of Public Lands, 196, 219

Board of Commissioners to Quiet Land Titles. *See* Land Commission

Bolte, C., **161**

Booth, Fenton W., 231–35, 231n34

Boston, USS, **159,** 160, 162, 165

Boyd, Robert, 128–29, 156

Brandt, Gladys, 315n53

Breyer, Stephen G., 132, 281–83, **282,** 295n121, **299**

Britain. *See* Great Britain

"Broken Trust," 315–16

Brown, Andrew, **161**

Brown, George, 154

Brown, Godfrey, 122–23

Brown, J. F., 198

Buke Mahele. See Mahele Book

Bush, John E., 205

Bush Administration (1989-93), 265–66, 269

Bybee, Jay, 289, 318–19, 321–22

Carroll, John, 286

Carter, George R., 222

Carter, Henry A. P., 126, 127, 129–30, 205

Carter, Jimmy, 265

Carter-Blaine Treaty, 205–6

Cartwright, Alexander, 332–33

Cartwright, Alexander, III, 363

Cartwright, Bruce, 334

Cash Freehold program, 193, 194, 195, 198

Castle, William R., 103, 121, **161**

Cayetano, Benjamin J., 252, 262

CEC. *See* Crown Estate Commissioners

Ceded Lands, 198. *See also* Public Lands

Charles, Prince of Wales, 351, 354, **356**

Charlton, Richard, 28

chiefs. *See* Ali‘i

Chiefs' Children's School. *See* Royal School

Chinese immigrants, 134, 135, 136, 137–38, 147, 224. *See also* Asian immigrants; immigrant workers

Christian missionaries. *See* missionaries

citizenship: definition of subjects, 138–39; in Kingdom of Hawai‘i, 132, 138–42; naturalization, 139–40, 147; in Republic of Hawaii, 183; rights of denizens, 139, 140, 141; in territorial period, 224–25. *See also* voting rights

Civil Rights Act of 1866, 318, 320, 321, 322

claims to Crown Lands. *See* Crown Lands, claims to; Native Hawaiians, land claims

Cleghorn, Archibald S., 340

Cleveland, Grover, **167;** defeat by McKinley, 200; disavowal of protectorate of Hawai‘i, 164; election as president, 165–66, 206–7; opposition to overthrow of Hawaiian monarchy, 168, 169–70, 186; ratification of Supplemental Convention of Reciprocity Treaty, 127; withdrawal of annexation treaty, 172, 206. *See also* "Blount Report"

Clinton, Bill, 266n91, **268**

Clinton Administration, 266

Cockett, J. Pia, 256

Coffman, Tom, 186

Commission of Crown Lands, 90, 110, 111, 116–17

Committee of Safety, **161,** 162–63, 162n62

commoners. *See* maka‘āinana

Congress, U.S.: "Akaka Bill," 270–72, 288; debates

Index

Hawai'i, Island of: Crown Lands listing, 176–77; Hawaiian Home Lands, 249; map of Crown Lands and Government Lands, **color insert;** military bases, 270

Hawai'i, Kingdom of: citizenship, 132, 138–42; demographics, 21, 131, 133–38; political dominance of Native Hawaiians, 92, 131–32, 133, 148, 149, 150; social change, 32, 362; unification, 17, 359; voting rights, 132, 140, 142–49. *See also* Hawaiian Monarchy; overthrow of 1893; precontact Hawai'i; United States, relations with Kingdom of Hawai'i

Hawaii, Republic of: appropriation of Crown Lands, 9, 174–75, 221, 230, 240, 365, 380; citizenship, 183; Constitution of 1894, 172–73, 174, 183–86, 230; debt, 214; Dole as president, 45, 173, 189, 190, 191–92; elections, 185; establishment, 9, 173–74; homestead programs, 190, 192, 193–98; immigration, 186; Land Act of 1895, 192–97, 198–99, 221, 222; legislature, 184; presidential government, 184–85; Public Lands, 175, 183, 380; sales of Government Lands, 58; treatment of Crown Lands, 190–97; voting rights, 172, 183–84

Hawai'i, State of: acknowledgment of Native Hawaiian land claims, 262–63; Department of Hawaiian Home Lands, 259, 286, 288, 294–95; governors, 251, 252, 260, 262–63; Hawaiian Home Lands Program administration, 248, 257, 302, 303–4; legislature, 252, 259–60, 263, 302, 358, 381; sales of Ceded Lands, 58; trust obligation toward Native Hawaiians, 258, 260–61, 286–87, 300–302; trust responsibility for Public Lands, 257–58, 295–97, 305. *See also* Constitution of 1950; Office of Hawaiian Affairs; statehood, Hawai'i

Hawai'i, Territory of: administration of Public Lands, 9, 214–15, 216–26; citizenship, 224–25; Delegates to U.S. Congress, 239–41, 246–47, 255; Dole as governor, 190, 199, 222, 229; government, 214; homestead programs, 196, 221–23, 226; immigration laws, 224–25; legislature, 229, 236, 238, 246–47, 254–55, 257; Public Land sales, 58; suppression of Hawaiian culture, 225–26. *See also* annexation of Hawai'i by United States; Organic Act of 1900

Hawaiian Commission, 228

Hawaiian culture: genealogies, 15–16, 372; impact of missionaries, 21–23, 24; kapu, 15, 22, 32, 362; language, 225–26, 259; marriage customs, 15–16, 362; preservation efforts of Mō'ī, 24, 32, 99, 118, 121; religion, 15, 21–23; significance of Crown Lands, 10, 273; suppression of, 225–26. *See also* Native Hawaiians; precontact Hawai'i

Hawaiian Homelands Homeownership Act of 2000, 284–85, 300

Hawaiian Home Lands Program: acreage, 251; administrative issues, 250–51; claims, 252–53; as compensation for lands not granted in

Mahele, 239–43, 245–46; eligibility criteria, 237n2, 246–47, 280–81, 282, 381; funding, 251; lands available, 246, 247–48, 249–50, 381; leases, 251; as state responsibility, 248, 257, 302, 303–4

Hawaiian Home Lands Recovery Act (HHLRA) of 1995, 252

Hawaiian Home Lands Trust Individual Claims Review Panel, 252

Hawaiian Homes Commission Act (HHCA) of 1921, 223, 237–38, 246–48, 251, 280–81, 282, 300, 381

Hawaiian language, 225–26, 259

Hawaiian League, 121–23

Hawaiian Monarchy: as constitutional monarchy, 27, 32–33, 69–70, 88, 362; evolution, 65, 88; sequence, 359–61. *See also* Crown Lands; Mō'ī; overthrow of 1893

Hawaiian Patriotic League (Hui Hawaiian Aloha 'Āina), 152, 209–10

Hawaiian Protective Association (Aha Hui Pu'uhonua O Na Hawai'i), 239, 242

Hawaiian Sovereignty Advisory Commission, 263

Hawaiian Sovereignty Elections Council, 263

Hawaiian Sugar Planters' Association, 39

Hawai'i Civil Code of 1859, 74, 83, 87

Hawai'i Supreme Court: appointments of trustees of Ali'i trusts, 316, 328; chief justices, 38, 39, 70, 73, 84, 244; citizenship cases, 140; Crown Lands claims cases, 221; on landownership rights of Hawaiian people, 26–27; opinion summarizing history of Mahele, 44–45; Public Land Trust cases, 260–61; unassigned lands case, 114–15; voting rights cases, 147

Hawai'i Supreme Court, *Estate of Kamehameha IV* case, 8; importance in defining status of Crown Lands, 52, 89–90, 232, 233–34, 377; inconsistency, 85, 86, 87–88, 89–90, 235; opinion, 84–88, 89–90, 235

Hawkins, Allen, 335

Hayes, Flora K., 246, 256

HCDCH. *See* Housing and Community Development Corporation of Hawai'i

Heen, Walter, 315n53

Heen, William H., 256

Henry II, King of England, 346

Henry IV, King of England, 347

Henry VI, King of England, 347–48

Henry VII, King of England, 348

Henry VIII, King of England, 349

HFDC. *See* Housing Financing Development Corporation

HHCA. *See* Hawaiian Homes Commission Act

HHLRA. *See* Hawaiian Home Lands Recovery Act

Hite, Charles M., 334

Holt, John Dominis, II, **241**

Home Rula Ku'oko'a (Independent Home Rule Party), 229, 254

Homestead Act of 1884, 113, 188–89

Index

Case Index

Page numbers followed by "n" refer to notes. Those followed by "nn" indicate multiple notes on the same page.

11.2 Acres of Land, More or Less, in Ferry County, Washington, United States v., 301n
78.61 Acres of Land in Dawes and Sioux Counties, Nebraska, United States v., 301n

Adarand Constructors v. Pena, 286n, 291, 298
Ahlo v. Smith, 147
Ahuna v. Department of Hawaiian Home Lands, 237nn, 295n
Alamo Land & Cattle Co. v. Arizona, 301n
Alaska Pacific Fisheries Co. v. United States, 297n
Alaska v. Udall, 261n
Aliens and Denizens, 140n, 141
American Federation of Government Employees (AFL-CIO) v. United States, 279n
Ann Arbor R. Co. v. United States, 266n
Antoine v. Washington, 297n
Arakaki v. Cayetano, 170, 288n, 301n
Arakaki v. Lingle, 279n, 288–90
Arakaki v. State of Hawaiʻi, 285–86

Bishop v. Mahiko, 217n
Branson School District RE-82 v. Romer, 301n
Branson v. Romer, 301n
Bush v. Watson, 251n

Carroll v. Nakatani, 286, 288
Chippewa Indians v. United States, 295n
City of Mesquite v. Malouf, 296n
City of Richmond v. J. A. Croson Co., 291
County of Hawaii v. Sotomura, 217n
County of Skamania v. State, 301n
Creek Nation, United States v., 295n

DaimlerChrysler v. Cuno, 289–90
De Lima v. Bidwell, 212n
Doe v. Kamehameha Schools/Bernice Pauahi Bishop Estate, 170, 225n, 292n, 317–23

Dowsett v. Maukeala, 183n
Duro v. Reina, 290n

Emma Kaleleonalani and Ruth Keelikolani v. Commissioners of Crown Lands, 109n
Ervien v. United States, 301n
Estate of His Late Majesty Lunalilo, In the Matter of the, 328–30
Estate of His Majesty Kamehameha IV, In the Matter of the, 8, 49n, 52, 54n, 63n, 64nn, 71, 73–79, 84–88, 89–90, 102n, 232, 233–34, 235, 244n, 371, 377, 424–32

Fort Berthold Reservation v. United States, 296n

Galt v. Waianuhea, 90n, 113n
Gladden Farms v. State, 301n
Glover, Estate of, 75n
Grutter v. Bollinger, 291n

Harris v. Carter, 45, 90n, 113, 115n, 232n
Hijo v. United States, 233n
Hite v. Queen's Hospital et al., 332n, 334, 335n
Hoohuli v. Ariyoshi, 289
Hunter v. Regents of the Univ. of California, 291n

Johnson, State v., 141n
Johnson v. United States, 367nn, 368nn
Jones, State v., 141

Kadish v. Arizona State Land Department, 301n
Kahawaiolaa v. Norton, 271n, 287–88, 290n
Kalanianaole v. Liliuokalani, 341n
Kalima v. State of Hawaii, 252–53
Kalipi v. Hawaiian Trust Co., Ltd., 49n, 50n, 83n
Ka Paʻakai o Ka ʻĀina v. Land Use Commission, 297n
Kapiolani Estate, Territory v., 221
Kapiolani Estate v. Cleghorn, 59, 87n, 113
Keanu v. Kaohi, 75n
Kekiekie v. Dennis, 45n
Kohala Corporation v. State, 110

Index

Credits for Photographs

Bernice Pauahi Bishop Museum: 80, SP 202141, photo by unknown photographer, ca. 1860; 157, CP 58388–SP 58388, photo by unknown photographer, ca. 1890; 166, CP 39757–SP 39757, photo by Severin-Bolster, n.d.; 241, CP 111666–SCP111666, photo by Bushnell, 1904

Clinton Library: 268

Francis Benjamin Johnson: 201

Hawai'i Judiciary History Center: 33, 37, 73, 244

Hawai'i State Archives: 8, photo by H. L. Chase

Supreme Court Historical Society: 275, 282, 284, 299

Unless otherwise stated above, photos are courtesy of the Hawai'i State Archives

About the Author

Jon M. Van Dyke has been professor of law at the William S. Richardson School of Law, University of Hawai'i at Mānoa, since 1976, where he teaches constitutional law, international law, international ocean law, and international human rights. Previously he taught at the Hastings College of the Law (University of California) in San Francisco (1971–76) and Catholic University Law School (1967–69) in Washington, D.C. He has served as an associate dean at the University of Hawai'i's Law School (1980–82) and as director of the University's Spark M. Matsunaga Institute of Peace (1988–90). He earned his J.D. degree at Harvard (1967) and his B.A. degree at Yale (1964), both cum laude. He was a law clerk for Roger L. Traynor, chief justice of the California Supreme Court, in 1969–70. Professor Van Dyke has written or edited ten books and has authored many articles on constitutional law and international law topics. He has served as legal counsel for the Office of Hawaiian Affairs in federal and state court litigation involving the resources and status of the Native Hawaiian People. He has served as a consultant for the State Council of Hawaiian Homestead Associations and served on the board of the Native Hawaiian Legal Corporation from 1978 to 1985.